Wissenschaftliche Untersuchungen
zum Neuen Testament · 2. Reihe

Herausgeber / Editor
Jörg Frey (München)

Mitherausgeber / Associate Editors
Friedrich Avemarie (Marburg)
Judith Gundry-Volf (New Haven, CT)
Hans-Josef Klauck (Chicago, IL)

224

Benjamin Schließer

Abraham's Faith in Romans 4

Paul's Concept of Faith
in Light of the History
of Reception of Genesis 15:6

Mohr Siebeck

BENJAMIN SCHLIESSER, born 1977; studied theology at the Universities of Tübingen, Glasgow (M. Th. 2001), and Pasadena (USA, Ph. D. 2006); currently Vikar (assistant pastor) in Lichtenstein (Württembergische Landeskirche).

ISBN 978-3-16-149197-9
ISSN 0340-9570 (Wissenschaftliche Untersuchungen zum Neuen Testament, 2. Reihe)

Die Deutsche Nationalbibliothek lists this publication in the Deutsche Nationalbibliographie; detailed bibliographic data is available in the Internet at *http://dnb.d-nb.de*.

The book was printed by Laupp & Göbel in Nehren on non-aging paper and bound by Buchbinderei Nädele in Nehren.

Printed in Germany.

To Christine
and Naemi Joy

Preface

The seeds for this study have been laid during my third semester at the University of Tübingen. At a book sale I acquired A. Schlatter's large-scale study on faith in the New Testament, *Der Glaube im Neuen Testament*, which sought to investigate historically how the concept of faith attained its powerful position in the intellectual history of humankind. This goal – together with P. Stuhlmacher's contention that with the exception of R. Bultmann no scholar's description of faith has arrived at a comparable systematic unity and historical precision – caught my interest and kindled my vision for revisiting some aspects of the New Testament concept of faith.

The first fruit of this fascination was my Master of Theology thesis on "Faith in the Synoptics" handed in at Glasgow University, on which Professors J.M.G. Barclay and J.K. Riches have made valuable comments. The debate between Tübingen and Durham on the question of "justification by faith" and in particular the vigorous defence of the "Lutheran" position by Professor P. Stuhlmacher made my attention grow towards Paul's understanding and use of πίστις in his letter to the Romans. Evidently, a "Biblical Theology" suggested itself as proper methodology and framework for working out Paul's specific concern.

The present study was written at Fuller Theological Seminary in Pasadena (USA) under the proficient and caring supervision of my *Doktorvater* Professor R.P. Martin; it was submitted beginning this year. Professors D.A. Hagner and K. Haacker have read the work as second and external readers and have made many incisive criticisms and corrections, not least with regards to my English.

I am very grateful to all these teachers for their erudition and encouragement. Also, I express my sincere thanks to the editor of *WUNT*, Professor J. Frey, who extended to me the invitation to contribute to the series. My friends and family have been a constant source of support and have always reminded me not to lose sight of the needs of the community. Most of all, I wish to express my loving appreciation to my wife Christine and my daughter Naemi Joy, who have always been for me a pledge of the joy in Christ. To them I dedicate this book.

Lichtenstein, November 2006   Benjamin Schließer

Table of Contents

Chapter I

Introduction and Methods

A. Schlatter, who was the first to write an in depth historical treatment on the New Testament concept of faith, stated: A theology and a Christendom that no longer know what the New Testament calls "faith," is dead.[1] From the perspective of a systematic theologian, P. Tillich contended that at first the word "faith" has to be healed, before the human being can be healed.[2] However, despite the urgency to develop an adequate understanding of faith, and furthermore despite the overwhelming flood of books in biblical studies, the brook that helps to quench this urgency remains remarkably slim. This is true for both the Old Testament[3] and New Testament concept of faith in general, but also for that New Testament writer who, according to R. Bultmann, put the concept of "faith" at the very center of theology[4]: the apostle Paul. Together with "a tendency of New Testament theologians to minimize the Pauline doctrine of faith,"[5] there is also a pre-formed understanding of faith that appears resistant to further analysis.[6]

---

[1] A. Schlatter 1977, 100. – Even from the perspective of statistics, which certainly is without theological value *per se*, πίστις and πιστεύειν play a central role in the New Testament language, as both terms occur 243 times each (cf. K. Aland 1978).

[2] P. Tillich 1961, 7. Tillich worked significantly on the concept of Christian faith. – On this, see W. Hertel, 1971; M. Korthaus 1999.

[3] The monumental Old Testament theology of W. Brueggemann dedicates a mere three lines to the fundamental verses Gen 15:6 and Isa 7:9 (1997, 467).

[4] R. Bultmann 1959, 218. On the central significance of faith for Paul, see also, e.g., H. Binder 1968, 79; G. Barth 1992, 220; B.S. Childs 1992, 606; M. Theobald 1999, 283.

[5] G.R. Beasley-Murray 1973, 304. The recent annotated bibliography on the Pauline writings by M.A. Seifrid and R.K.J. Tan, which contains a total of 846 entries, lists only very few monographic treatments on "faith in Paul," some of which dealing with "faith" only secondarily (2002, 180-183). – A similar diagnosis applies to the concept of faith in systematic theology (cf. M. Seils 1996, 15, who also quotes W. Härle and R. Preul: "[D]er Begriff des Glaubens [ist] noch nicht zu derjenigen Klarheit ausgearbeitet..., die angesichts seiner schlechterdings fundierenden Stellung und Funktion erforderlich ist.").

[6] Cf. P. Stuhlmacher 1966, 81. Conventionally, one argues for instance that "faith ... is the openness to the *gospel*" (C.E.B. Cranfield 1975, 90), that "Glaube ist die Realisierung der *Gnade* Gottes im Menschen" (G. Friedrich 1982, 112), that "faith is the only appropriate human correlate to God's gracious *righteousness*" (J.D.G. Dunn 1998, 384n.205) or that "[f]aith ... appropriates for the believer the benefits of what *Christ* has

The focus of the present study is the history of reception[7] of Gen 15:6.[8] It takes this momentous verse from the Abraham-cycle and attempts to detect and describe trajectories of the faith-theme from the Old Testament through Second Temple Judaism to Paul. This *modus operandi* will allow a picture of Paul's concept of faith in its distinctiveness compared to the theological background of his time and in its dialogue with text and tradition.[9]

That our task cannot exhaust itself exclusively in the historical-exegetical work is self-evident. The attained results need to be connected systematically[10] in order to receive a harmonious whole and to create the framework in which the various ancient authors' specific understanding of faith comes into view – not in terms of an enumeration of manifold different meanings of πίστις, but in terms of its theological peak(s).[11]

With regard to the exegetical chapters, a few methodological remarks are in place. Just as the history of scholarship will require a contextual, objective, and sympathetic description of the respective authors' positions, one cannot analyze the relevant terms in the texts to be expounded without giving due consideration to the context. Only then terms like faith/believing, count/consider, righteousness, law, works, boasting, sin, salvation-history, soteriology, eschatology, etc. can be filled with meaning, and only then structural equivalents between the texts can be identified.[12] Both in the case of ancient writings and modern works, this method seeks to pay respect to the authorial intention and to allow for a relatively precise account of a term's intended meaning in a respective context[13]; it prevents

---

done" (S. Westerholm 2004, 91) (italics added). These descriptions are not incorrect, but incomplete.

[7] See, for instance, the deliberations in H. Räisänen 1992.

[8] The biblical quotations are normally taken from the NRSV, though occasionally altered for the sake of clarity. Other ancient sources are dealt with correspondingly.

[9] Cf. U. Luz 1998, 333: "Die Wirkungsgeschichte biblischer Texte ist ... eine Dokumentation der Lebendigkeit der Traditionen und Texte und damit auch der Pluralität."

[10] See on the relation of the exegetical and systematic work, A. Schlatter 1927, xvi-xvii; R. Gyllenberg 1936, 614; D. Lührmann 1976, 16 ("die beiden Versuchungen des Exegeten – der Rückzug in die rein historische Arbeit und die Flucht in die Systematik").

[11] Cf., with respect to Paul, F. Neugebauer 1961, 150; also M.-E. Boismard 1955, 65.

[12] Cf. J.D.G. Dunn 2002, 275 and his reference to F.D.E. Schleiermacher (275n.8). This principle that makes the context the criterion of meaning has certainly been formulated and employed prior to Schleiermacher. See only Cicero, *De Inventione* 2,40,117: "[E]x superiore et ex inferiore scriptura docendum id, quod quaeratur, fieri perspicuum."

[13] Even though the notion of "the author's intention" sounds like the old, never-realized historical-critical dogma, our approach requires this method. The current emphasis on reception history is still reflected in this study – obviously, it even constitutes its core, insofar as all is concentrated on the history of interpretation of one Old Testament verse (Gen 15:6).

avoidable misunderstandings and unnecessary, one-sided polarizations, or "illegitimate totality transfer[s]."[14] In short, one has to strive to understand the Genesis text, the writings quoting or alluding to it, including Paul, but also their interpreters "on their own terms"[15] and thereby treat the authors *in optimam partem.* Only then comparisons and criticism are justified and valid.

A. History of Scholarship on "Faith"

A history of interpretation constitutes the first main part of this study. The survey of works dealing with the Pauline concept of faith concentrates on the major monographs and essays published on this topic.[16] The stress of this presentation lies on the results of the exegetical process. Consequently the authors' direct references to passages in Paul remain unmentioned for the most part. For the sake of objectivity, no extensive external critique of their viewpoints will be provided in the course of the presentation of their views, but rather some concluding evaluative remarks. Most sections, on the other hand, will be introduced by a brief theological-historical classification, in order to make visible the dependences, trajectories, or demarcations of the views portrayed.

B. Genesis 15:6

It is justified and important to provide a rather extensive discussion of the problems of Genesis 15, since the theological significance of this chapter as a whole can hardly be overestimated and since, furthermore, its central verse, Gen 15:6, has a history of reception, with which only very few individual texts can compete.[17] Already within the Old Testament,[18] this verse was attributed great theological weight, but also in later Jewish theology it enjoyed a wide influence and import. Paul and James used it in a way that

---

[14] J.E. Botha 1987, 233. Especially J. Barr (1961) pointed to the problem that certain dictionaries tend to load the totality of meanings of a term on each of its occurrences. See also D.A. Campbell 1992a, 91-93 (referring to F. de Saussure); J.-N. Aletti 1989, 238.

[15] E.P. Sanders 1977, 18f.

[16] Those viewpoints expressed in works larger in scope, like New Testament theologies, theologies of Paul or commentaries receive little attention here, but will be noted in the exegetical chapters. (The exception are those older works that appear in the introductory chapter II.A.) – Some essays that do not specifically aim at offering new scholarly results, but rather gather and assess results and theses of previous scholarship, will not figure in the history of interpretation (such as F. Knoke 1922; H.H. Wernecke 1934; W.G. Kümmel 1937; M.-E. Boismard 1955; O. Kuss 1956; H.-W. Bartsch 1960; 1968; R. Schnackenburg 1962; K. Haacker 1970; 1993; G.R. Beasley-Murray 1982; J.-N. Aletti 1989; E. Schnabel 1991; H.-J. Eckstein 2000).

[17] Cf. R.W.L. Moberly 1990, 103.

[18] On the qualified use of the traditional phrase "Old Testament" in contrast to "clumsy neologisms," see, e.g., W. Brueggemann 1997, 1n.1.

was foundational for Christian theology, though they referred to it with different accentuations and implications.

Diachronic questions should not be deemed superfluous,[19] even if the main concentration of our study lies on Paul and his ("synchronic") reading of Gen 15:6, which presupposes the present final text-form as canonical. The temporal background and formal structure of Israel's literary heritage bears upon theology.[20] Accordingly, subsequent to a literary, source-critical, tradition-historical, and structural analysis of the chapter as a whole, we will engage in a study of the fundamental terms "consider," "righteousness," and "believe," clarifying their place in the Old Testament as a whole, but also in the syntactical structure of the verse itself.[21]

C. Genesis 15:6 in Jewish Theology

The reception history of Gen 15:6 presents itself at first as an inner-biblical development and materializes in the historical Psalm 106 and the penitential prayer Nehemiah 9. Then, throughout the intertestamental period, in the most diverse geographical, historical, and theological conditions, a multifaceted and nuanced reception history could develop and comes into sight in the Septuagint, Sirach 44, *Jubilees* 14, 4QPseudo-Jubilees, 4QMMT, 1Maccabees, and Philo. Though the differences between the single interpretations of Gen 15:6 might partly appear of negligible nature, they own considerable weight and expressiveness: First, from a reception-hermeneutical perspective, they illuminate the practice of the *relecture* of a biblical text by means of its textual variations, its orientation towards a specific intention, its response to certain historical or theological situations, its combination with other scriptural or traditional ideas, etc. Second, they afford an insight into a theological process, in which one seeks to answer the question of nature, implication, and consequence of faith always anew, in discussion with the existing text, which acquired increasingly a canonized status. We become witnesses of the hermeneutical effort to adapt this text to the present time and its needs.[22]

---

[19] Against, e.g., M. Oeming 1983, 183n.9; M. Neubrand 1997, 199 with n.6; cf. A. Behrens 1997, 334n.43.

[20] See the foundational deliberations in G. von Rad 1962, 7f.

[21] Especially the latter has been neglected in scholarship (cf. J.A. Soggin 1997, 252).

[22] See the deliberations in M. Oeming 1998, 90. – There is still great reluctance in New Testament scholarship to use rabbinic evidence to illuminate the Jewish religion of Paul's time, even though there are currently great efforts to accomplish the challenging task of trying to make available material from the Mishnah, Tosefta, Tannaitic Midrashim, and the Talmuds to gain a clearer picture of pre-70 B.C. Judaism (cf. the monograph of F. Avemarie 1996, but also the new multivolume project *Traditions of the Rabbis from the Era of the New Testament* [TRENT]). For the sake of objectivity and

D. Genesis 15:6 in Paul

One modern systematic theologian who like P. Tillich has written extensively on the essence of the Christian faith is G. Ebeling.[23] He claimed that
the statement: "Faith is entirely a work of God" is in no way contradictory
to the other contention that faith is a wholly personal act of the human subject.[24] It will be argued that this claim can be corroborated through an
analysis of Paul's interpretation of Gen 15:6 and its context.

Our starting point is the formulation ἐκ πίστεως εἰς πίστιν (Rom 1:17),
a formulation which is the better understood – to cite A. Schlatter – the
deeper the causal dimension of ἐκ and the teleological dimension of εἰς is
grasped.[25] Schlatter himself pointed out that God is the single causal power
of faith.[26] Yet, as will be argued here, only if this power is perceived as his
manifesting the salvation-historical reality of faith in the Christ-event (ἐκ)
and as his disclosing the salvation-historical possibility for the individual
to participate in that reality as part of the community of believers (εἰς), we
can comprehend the whole breadth of Paul's notion of πίστις. It shall be
shown that these two basic dimensions are reflected in the argument of
Rom 3:21-26(.27-31) and Romans 4.

The exegesis of the first text unit, Rom 3:21-31, oftentimes called the
locus classicus of the Pauline doctrine of justification,[27] seeks to establish
that Paul has in mind the salvation-historical, trans-subjective element of
πίστις, an eschatologically qualified *activitas dei*. This paves the way to
the subjective perspective of faith elaborated in chapter 4, in which Paul
portrays Abraham, Israel's figure of identification, as one who in an anticipatory way participated in that faith in order to become the father of the
community of all believers, according to God's plan of salvation; in the
corporate figure of Abraham, Paul can include the intersubjective or ecclesiological dimension of faith, which is inseparable from both the trans-
subjective and subjective. This conception of the Pauline faith could contribute to bridging the dichotomy in modern Pauline scholarship between
"the 'Lutheran Paul' and his critics,"[28] i.e., between the two positions

---

clarity, however, we will limit ourselves to texts that are unambiguously older than or
contemporaneous to Paul.

[23] See G. Ebeling 1959, where he presents in distilled form the quintessence of his
studies on the nature of faith.

[24] Cf. G. Ebeling 1959, 104-107.

[25] A. Schlatter 1935, 42.

[26] A. Schlatter 1910, 267; 1927, xvii; cf. G. Friedrich 1982, 109.

[27] Cf. W. Mundle 1932, 86. See also K. Berger 1966, 64n.24 ("das eigentliche Kern-
stück"); O. Kuss 1963, 110 ("theologische und architektonische Mitte des Römerbriefs").

[28] Thus the title of S. Westerholm 2004.

commonly labeled with catchwords such as "justification and inclusion," or, with regard to Abraham, "faith and fatherhood."

Chapter II

Paul's Concept of Faith: History of Interpretation

A. Setting the Stage: Some Landmark Works[1]

According to F.C. Baur, faith originates formally and primarily from the proclamation and denotes therefore accepting its content and considering it true.[2] In a more specific sense, faith is the conviction of something transcendent, religious belief, trust in God, and finally Christian faith. The principle,[3] on which the Christian faith rests, is Christ; and therefore, when Paul mentions πίστις in the context of justification, it implies faith in God's grace, in Christ's death and resurrection.[4] Faith becomes the subjective prerequisite of justification that individually actualizes and realizes the unity with Christ and confers δικαιοσύνη τοῦ θεοῦ to the believer. Adapting Hegelian ideas, Baur makes clear that the believer's identity with Christ can only be thought of in terms of an inner relationship between the human-subjective spiritual consciousness and the divine-objective spirit.[5] Eventually, the function of faith coincides, or rather competes, with the principle of the spirit, as the bond of community and identity with Christ is either granted by πίστις or by πνεῦμα.[6]

Based on his discovery of two anthropological foundations in Paul, characteristically reflected by different concepts of σάρξ, H. Lüdemann affirms the existence of two unrelated and unconnected circles of thought: the religious or subjective-ideal ("subjektiv-ideel"), which derives from Jewish-religious categories, and the ethical or objective-real ("objektiv-real"), which is based on Hellenistic-dualistic motifs.[7] The two poles of those circles in the Pauline thinking are signified by πίστις on the one side,

---

[1] On the history of older scholarship, see especially E. Wißmann 1926, 1-29 and F. Neugebauer 1961, 9-17, 150-156.

[2] F.C. Baur 1867, 161; cf. 1864, 154.

[3] Baur is the first to use the term "principle" in the meaning of "event of salvation," which in a modified way will be taken over by E. Lohmeyer (see Baur's heading "Das Prinzip christlichen Bewußtseins," 1867, 133; cf. F. Neugebauer 1961, 156n.35).

[4] F.C. Baur 1864, 154f.; 1867, 161f.

[5] F.C. Baur 1867, 170-178.

[6] F.C. Baur 1864, 143, 176; 1867, 177. E. Wißmann comments on this competition: "[S]o wird die πίστις für Baurs Logik schier zu einer überflüssigen Größe" (1926, 2).

[7] H. Lüdemann 1872, 171-173.

and by πνεῦμα on the other.[8] Against the common view that regards Christ's vicarious suffering and death and justification by faith as primary objects of Paul's theology, Lüdemann argues that those elements were successively pushed out of the center, so that in the most mature form of Paul's thinking they merely symbolize the preparation and premise of the access to the pneumatical gifts.[9] Hence, the juridical-forensic line of thought appears in clear separation from the ethical-physical; and πίστις and πνεῦμα are no longer two focal points of an ellipse (thus F.C. Baur, R.A. Lipsius), but the centers of two essentially different, autonomous circles.[10]

In his prominent work on the Christian doctrine of justification and reconciliation, A. Ritschl carries out a distinction of those concepts with reference to their effects: Justification merely means a "synthetic" judgment, as it does not carry within itself the sign of an effective moral change of the individual,[11] while the effect of the καταλλαγή drives the sinners towards God.[12] On the basis of this partition, Ritschl develops his definition(s) of πίστις, arguing for the existence of two entirely different concepts of faith in Paul with equal rights, yet without relationship: In the framework of justification, faith surrenders to God's decree of grace, which is effective through Christ and warranted through his resurrection,[13] and with regard to reconciliation, faith denotes the exertion of love, active righteousness, and interest in God's kingdom.[14] Both ways, faith relates to the rational-intellectual realm of the person and does not imply a personal relationship to the exalted Christ.

Like H. Lüdemann, also O. Pfleiderer – almost simultaneously – recognized diverse, intertwined lines of thought in Paul: Paul shaped his own experiences into different forms of ideas, which the exegete has to relate to the unity of Paul's complex personality.[15] As for Paul's concept of faith, Pfleiderer distinguishes between a common conviction or feeling of the truth of the divine revelation[16] and a particular, affectionate relationship to Christ that creates the feeling of a moral unity between the loving savior

---

[8] The first circle is marked by the ideal δικαιοσύνη ἐκ πίστεως, and the second by the real δικαιοσύνη ἐκ πνεύματος ἁγίου (H. Lüdemann 1872, 164, 166).

[9] H. Lüdemann 1872, 165, 215f.

[10] Cf. E. Wißmann 1926, 5.

[11] A. Ritschl 1889, 330f., 356; 1888, 77-79.

[12] A. Ritschl 1889, 231.

[13] A. Ritschl 1889, 325. Ritschl, like later R. Bultmann (see below pages 39-41), identifies faith and obedience: "Es ist also der Gehorsam gemeint, welcher in specie der religiöse Glaube an Christus und an Gott ist, so wie Gott durch Christus sich offenbart."

[14] A. Ritschl 1889, 343.

[15] O. Pfleiderer 1902, 69.

[16] O. Pfleiderer 1902, 245f. ("Gefühlsweise oder Gemütsstimmung").

and the believer, a mystical Christ-communion.[17] The personal and at the same time mystical-ethical relationship with Christ is the *proprium* of the Pauline faith, which overcomes a merely forensic imputation and provides an ethical foundation for justification.[18] Pfleiderer's conception is obviously based on a certain view of the person, in which the human being is regarded primarily in terms of feeling; and this understanding is transferred to Christ, the loving savior, as well.[19] Hence, from a formal point of view, Pfleiderer's approach can be compared to A. Ritschl's because of its bipartition of πίστις, yet on the other hand it opposes to the more rational understanding of Ritschl and introduces an experiential-emotional view.

Confronting the misunderstanding of πίστις as achievement, A. Deißmann carries out a psychologizing of the Pauline faith (even to a greater degree than Pfleiderer) and regards it not as prerequisite of justification, but as the experience of justification, as the communion with Christ.[20] Accordingly, Paul is not a systematic theologian, but a "religious genius,"[21] as "classic of Christ-mysticism,"[22] in whom his experience before Damascus has produced inexhaustible religious energy. Two equivalent phrases express this: "Christ in Paul" and "Paul in Christ."[23] Paul himself gives to this energy *inter alia* the religious-technical term πίστις. Accordingly, for Paul faith is not directed *to* Christ ("Glaube *an* Christus"), but faith is *in* Christ ("Glaube *in* Christus")[24] and takes place in the life connection with the pneumatical Christ.[25] Deißmann labels the genitival formula πίστις Χριστοῦ with a new grammatical category: *genitivus communionis* or *genitivus mysticus*.[26] God, not Christ, is the object of such faith, since the be-

---

[17] O. Pfleiderer 1890, 174f.; 1902, 249, 247: "Diese mystische Christusgemeinschaft, dieses Sichidentifizieren mit Christo in Todes- und Lebensgenossenschaft ist das eigentümlich Neue und Bedeutsame in Paulus' Glaubensbegriff."

[18] O. Pfleiderer 1890, 181f., 185.

[19] Cf. F. Neugebauer 1961, 152.

[20] A. Deißmann 1925, 132. "[D]er Glaube ist bei ihm [*sc.* Paulus] nicht Aktion, sondern Reaktion, nicht menschliche Leistung vor Gott, sondern göttliche Wirkung auf den Menschen in Christus... Der Glaube ist nicht die Vorbedingung der Rechtfertigung, er ist das Erlebnis der Rechtfertigung."

[21] A. Deißmann 1925, 105; cf. already 1892, 93 (Paul as "religiös-ethischer Genius").

[22] A. Deißmann 1925a, 25.

[23] A. Deißmann 1925, 106. Both ideas are identical, as both express "die Gewißheit von Damaskus" (125).

[24] On Deißmann's interpretation of the "in Christ"-formula, see his groundbreaking work from 1892. The category of religious experience shapes his analysis of this phrase, which he considers as Pauline coinage used as *terminus technicus* (70).

[25] A. Deißmann 1925, 126.

[26] A. Deißmann 1925, 126f. N. Turner (1963, 212), but also K. Barth (1932, 240) basically accept Deißmann's terminology; but see against the introduction of this novel genitive category the reactions against the first edition of Deißmann's Paul book from

liever, mystically connected to Christ, trusts in God's grace, just as Abraham spoke his heroic "Dennoch!" through his unshakable trust.[27] In the end, faith and mysticism belong together.[28]

H.J. Holtzmann affirms the existence of two streams of ideas that flow individually side by side without forming one unified course. Both, however, are of equal value for the movement of the Pauline thinking and complement each other successfully.[29] By means of the mystical circle,[30] which derives from the Hellenistic mysticism of the syncretistic age, Paul expresses his own personal experience, while the juridical circle represents his elaboration of the theme of "faith in Christ" on the basis of ideas he inherited from his Jewish background.[31] Ultimately, though, the concept of faith integrates both circles: Faith is acceptance, acknowledgment, and affirmation of the content of the proclamation,[32] but at the same time faith is the entire pneumatically exalted emotion of the one who is reconciled.[33]

According to O. Schmitz, the tension between the two circles can be resolved by pointing to the general-human constitution in the face of infinity, which results in both a feeling of distance and a mystical perspective.[34] Consequently, faith is the person's affirmation of God's deed in Christ (feeling of distance), but at the same time it comprises the "Lebensgefühl" of the believer (mystical perspective); both, Paul's non-mystical and mystical statements describe therefore the inner disposition called "faith."[35] In line with J. Haußleiter and G. Kittel,[36] Schmitz rejects the understanding of πίστις Χριστοῦ as objective genitive, but equally discards the label "sub-

---

1911: W. Bousset 1911, 781; W.H.P. Hatch 1917, 46; O. Schmitz 1924, 237; also H. Lietzmann 1928, 48.

[27] A. Deißmann 1925, 128. "Der Glaube des Paulus ist also die in der Gemeinschaft mit Christus hergestellte Verbindung mit Gott, die ein unerschütterliches Abrahamsvertrauen auf die Gnade Gottes ist. Gott-Innigkeit in Christo Jesu, Gott-Innigkeit des Christ-Innigen, das ist der Glaube des Paulus." – Notably, in a speech on war and religion from 1915, Deißmann calls the religion of the New Testament a religion of polarities, a "Dennochsglaube" and continues: "[S]ie [*sc.* die Religion] verlangt ein Einsetzen der ganzen Persönlichkeit und die Bereitschaft, das eigene Leben hinzugeben, sie ist ein Kriegsdienst, sie ist Märtyrerreligion" (1915, 120).

[28] A. Deißmann 1925, 128.

[29] H.J. Holtzmann 1911, 130 ("wohltätige[.] Ergänzung").

[30] Appealing to W. Wrede, Holtzmann favors the designation "mystical" as being more appropriate than Lüdemann's "ethical" (H.J. Holtzmann 1911, 125).

[31] H.J. Holtzmann 1911, 125-127.

[32] H.J. Holtzmann 1911, 132f.: "[S]treng genommen [ist] der Glaube nur die erste Annahme des Evangeliums."

[33] H.J. Holtzmann 1911, 134.

[34] O. Schmitz 1924, 41.

[35] O. Schmitz 1922, 46f., 71; 1924, 249.

[36] See below chapters II.H.I and II.H.II.

jective genitive"; rather, the genitive belongs to the "common characterizing genitives" ("allgemein charakterisierende Genetive"), meaning simply
"Christ-faith."[37]

W. Bousset challenges Deißmann's purely mystical interpretation, because on the one hand it neglects the strongly juridical character of Paul's
theology and on the other deduces the mystical aspect merely from the
Damascus experience, without investigating the cult of the first Christians
and the wide history-of-religions background.[38] Generally speaking, for
Bousset, faith is the basic *datum* of all religions, the simple subordination
under God,[39] and the elevation of the heart to the godhead in love, fear,
and trust.[40] As for the specific Pauline conception of faith, Bousset regards
the cultic veneration of the κύριος Χριστός in the Gentile-Christian community as decisive. Paul's personal Christ-piety emerges from this foundation.[41] Moreover, the cultic mysticism represents the roots from which
Paul's Christ-mysticism, signified by the formula ἐν Χριστῷ, grew. In the
phrase πίστις κυρίου Ἰησοῦ Χριστοῦ, this mysticism culminates. It is
Paul, then, who places faith ("Christusglaube") into the center of religious
life[42] and who deepens and spiritualizes what has been handed down to
him[43]; one could talk therefore of a mystical twist in Paul's idea of faith.[44]
Eventually, faith and mysticism are intertwined and interconnected.[45]

Against that A. Schweitzer famously stated that all attempts to harmo-
nize the ideas of (the juridical) "faith in Christ" and (the mystical) "being
in Christ" have been and will be doomed to failure, for the mystical doctrine of redemption through the "being in Christ" outweighs everything

---

[37] O. Schmitz 1924, 108, 230. E. Wißmann criticizes Schmitz's methodology, as he
discusses the genitive-connections of πίστις prior to making clear what πίστις itself
means (1926, 70f.n.3)

[38] W. Bousset 1911, 780f.

[39] W. Bousset/H. Greßmann 1966, 388.

[40] W. Bousset/H. Greßmann 1966, 193.

[41] W. Bousset 1926, 102, 104.

[42] In fact, Bousset (1916, 52f.) maintains together with Wrede that the experience of
the communion with Christ is for Paul the most essential aspect of Paul's theology and
the separation from the law merely the result, which constitutes the rationale for the right
of mission among Gentiles. "Die Hauptfaktoren des paulinischen Christentums sind nicht
dieselben wie die des reformatorischen" (47).

[43] W. Bousset 1926, 145, 149.

[44] W. Bousset 1916, 47.

[45] P. Wernle (1915, 42) sharply criticizes Bousset's position and rejects both the derivation of Christ-mysticism from the cult of the congregation as well as the term "Christ-
mysticism" in general. Paul's "mysticism" is his faith: "An ihn glauben heißt: ihn haben,
in ihm sein" (cf. E. Sommerlath 1923, 84: "Der Gläubige ist als solcher in Christo"; see
in addition O. Schmitz 1924, 249, but also W. Mundle 1932, 133, 150; R. Bultmann
1958, 328-330; F. Neugebauer 1961, 171).

else.[46] The doctrine of justification by faith, so central for the Reformation, is merely a subsidiary crater.[47]

Also W. Wrede reduced the weight of the doctrine of justification: It is only a "Kampfeslehre" of Paul that arose from his dispute with Judaism,[48] while the doctrine of redemption forms the heart of Paul's theology. However, since Christ is the center of both circles of thought, they continually reach beyond their respective boundaries and exhibit a close affiliation.[49] In his book on Paul Wrede discusses "faith" – against the convention of his time – in the section on the doctrine of redemption, claiming that faith is simply the obedient acceptance and affirmation of the proclamation of redemption. But the conviction of its truth establishes immediately this mystical connection to Christ, through which his death and resurrection translate themselves into the believer.[50] Justification is in the same line as the mystical dying and rising with Christ.[51]

W. Heitmüller confirms Wrede's and Bousset's distinction of Reformation and Pauline theology and points to the prevalence of Christ-mysticism compared to the complex of justification.[52] Paul's Christ-mysticism broke forth in his Damascus experience and connected secondarily to the faith in Christ in the Hellenistic community.[53] Both aspects, though remain separate: The relationship of faith and mysticism is not that of identity or interconnection, but of coexistence, for both types of religiosity came into being successively and side by side.[54] Yet even though (biographically) faith followed on Paul's vision before Damascus as intellectual consequence, he

---

[46] A. Schweitzer 1930, 117. – R.B. Hays, however, claims to have found the Pauline coherence of thought by means of his subjective reading of the phrase πίστις Χριστοῦ (1997, 287). See below chapter II.H.V.

[47] A. Schweitzer 1930, 220. As a consequence, in Schweitzer's work the concept of faith disappears (cf. the index, which lacks the term at all; cf. R. Gyllenberg 1936, 615).

[48] W. Wrede 1907, 72. Before Wrede, H. Lüdemann and C. Weizsäcker came to similar results, but only Wrede's exposition had such far-reaching consequences.

[49] W. Wrede 1907, 52.

[50] W. Wrede 1907, 67, 70. Therefore, trust and hope recede into the background as aspects of the Pauline faith. This thought recurs in R. Bultmann (see below page 42).

[51] W. Wrede 1907, 77. – A. Schweitzer, for instance, criticizes Wrede for not having clearly worked out the distinction and interconnection between the two circles (cf. 1911, 133: "Überhaupt wird der Zusammenhang zwischen der eigentlichen, in der Erlösungsmystik angelegten Theologie und der 'Kampfeslehre' nicht offenbar").

[52] Paul's doctrine of justification is "Verteidigungs- und Kampfeslehre," a product of a later development of Paul (W. Heitmüller 1917, 152).

[53] W. Heitmüller 1917, 150f.

[54] W. Heitmüller 1917, 152f. For Paul's consciousness however faith and mysticism do not fall apart.

has transformed it into the precondition of Christ-mysticism upon reflection in the context of his missionary practice.[55]

Amidst the modern symphathy for the mentioned critics of Reformation theology, one should also listen to a representative of contemporary counter-critique: P. Feine, for instance, seeks to re-establish the doctrine of justification into the center of Pauline theology and determines faith as subjective-human disposition that is required to receive justification.[56] Faith not only considers true the message of salvation, not only trusts in Christ, but also creates the inner connection of the believer with Christ, draws Christ into the heart, and transfers the believer ἐν Χριστῷ.[57] An ethical notion is always implied in this communion with Christ.

But before taking up the issue of two alleged circles in Paul's thought,[58] we will listen to a rather different voice, namely, that of A. Schlatter, who regarded the notion of repentance to be the central idea in Paul's concept of faith.

B. Faith and Repentance

I. A. Schlatter, Der Glaube im Neuen Testament *(1885, [4]1927)*

1. Introduction

A. Schlatter's groundbreaking book *Der Glaube im Neuen Testament* is the fruit of his participation in a contest organized in the year 1882 by the "Haager Gesellschaft zur Vertheidigung der christlichen Religion" on the topic "Glaube und Glauben im Neuen Testament."[59] To him implications of our understanding of faith extend not only to the exegetical-theological realm, but they also have existential consequences for the individual.[60] Compared to previous studies on this New Testament concept, Schlatter entered entirely new terrain in some respects, especially in his extensive philological studies of the Jewish sources.[61] The insights that grew from his exploration of rabbinic theology form his conviction that in the New

---

[55] W. Heitmüller 1917, 153.

[56] P. Feine 1919, 291.

[57] P. Feine 1919, 292-294. "Der Glaube im Zusammenhang der paulinischen Rechtfertigungslehre ist also Anerkennung des gestorbenen und auferstandenen Christus als des königlichen Herrn und unlösbarer Zusammenschluß mit diesem Herrn" (284). The term "mysticism" is to be rejected due to its magic, emotional, or mystical-natural connotation.

[58] See below chapter II.C.

[59] Cf. W. Neuer 1996, 186.

[60] Cf. A. Schlatter 1927, xxii.

[61] Cf. P. Stuhlmacher 1982, x.

Testament, person and work cannot be separated and are responsible that time and again the categories of deed, work, and act recur in his description of the Pauline faith.

It is the unity of Schlatter's presentation that makes the greatest impression on the reader; this unity is closely connected with his perception of the historical Jesus and his convictions regarding questions of New Testament introduction: Jesus Christ himself is the founder and giver of faith, through his pre-Easter and post-Easter work, and the apostles, who are called to be messengers of this Christ, spread the word of faith in an undistorted and faithful way. The line of tradition is continuous and unadulterated.[62] Differences in the various expressions of the concept of faith are no contradictions; there is unity in this diversity, as the one God created individual personalities.[63] The common root and content of faith in God connects all believers in the history of the church, even beyond Scripture; thus, the church still grows as the continuous, living revelation of Christ and God.[64]

In order to make possible the reader's undivided attention to the matter itself, Schlatter refused to discuss the opinion of his colleagues and include relevant literature[65] and to accommodate to any terminological conventions. This method, of course, complicates the theological-historical assessment and categorization of his works. But despite the lack of references to other authors and views, it is possible to determine some demarcations and differentiations that Schlatter carries out with respect to other approaches. The apostles did not reflect on the "how" of the formation of their faith, but were content with the "that."[66] This principle refutes the psychologizing method of the Schleiermacherian theology and of the History-of-Religions School, as it points out the character of faith not as "productive," but as "receptive."[67] Consequently, the theory that the contents of faith are produced by our own consciousness, which would factually make

---

[62] This is certainly the junction where the ways of R. Bultmann and Schlatter part. For Bultmann faith cannot be the work of revelation of the historical Jesus; the line from Jesus' proclamation to the proclamation of the apostles is not uninterrupted (cf. R. Bultmann 1929, 195; 1958, 598-600). It goes without saying that both approaches, Bultmann's and Schlatter's, testify to the circular structure of any historical-theological enterprises. Cf., in the case of Schlatter, A. Schlatter 1977, 103: "Daß ich die neutestamentliche Geschichte als eine fest verbundene Einheit vor mir sah, fand in der Einheitlichkeit des neutestamentlichen Glaubens die Bestätigung und Erläuterung."

[63] A. Schlatter 1927, xvii, xxi.

[64] A. Schlatter 1927, 536.

[65] Cf. A. Schlatter 1977, 119. See on Schlatter's method O. Kuss 1956, 187f.n.1.

[66] A. Schlatter 1927, 257: "Daher wird auch nirgends das Werden des Glaubens nach seinem psychologischen Hergang beschrieben ..." Cf. 349.

[67] R. Slenczka 1984, 349.

them changeable and situational and reduce them to mere reflections of self-fashioned expressions of faith, is refuted by Schlatter.[68] The faith of the apostles did not originate in their minds, but relates to historical realities that exist alongside faith (resurrection, eternity, eschatological hope, etc.). Paul, "the strongest dogmatic theologian" among them, clearly shows the awareness of this relationship between truths of history and truths of faith.[69] The receptive nature of faith, however, is not to be equated with quietism or tranquility, that would result in the inclination to withdraw from own thinking, willing, and doing. Here, Schlatter seeks to correct a misunderstanding of Reformation theology that originated – in Schlatter's perception – already in Luther's own faith[70]: the one-sided emphasis on the calming, salvation-giving function of faith, which does not release adequately its active component. On the other hand, Schlatter confirms a fundamental insight of the Reformers, suppressed by most Protestant theologians in the 19th century: As God justifies through faith, he also makes the unbeliever to the vessel of his wrath.[71] Positively speaking, Schlatter argues that the mediation of faith happens through the Spirit: the Spirit establishes the presence of Christ in the believer.[72]

2. The Motive for Faith: The Acceptance of Our Incapability

This leads us into the core of Schlatter's treatment of the Pauline understanding of faith.[73] Schlatter begins with a negative statement: Faith cannot happen without renunciation in its widest sense, comprising the entire life-content ("Lebensinhalt") of the person: One's works, rights, and justification are all reduced to nothing.[74] This initial, unlimited abandonment, however, is factually merely the act of repentance which comprehends that we may not ignore our evil: Who has done evil, has to confess guilty.[75] It is this "simple" rule that bears the entire weight of Paul's argument in the negative part of his letter to the Romans (Rom 1:18-3:20). The acknowl-

---

[68] A. Schlatter 1927, 319: "Diese Theorie entstellt aber die Geschichte." But he can still call faith "das entscheidende *Erlebnis*, das aus dem Menschen den Christen macht" (1935, 44; italics added).

[69] A. Schlatter 1927, 319; cf. 353.

[70] A. Schlatter 1977, 174. Cf. W. Neuer 1996, 191.

[71] A. Schlatter 1927, 364: "Auch die Kraft zu seinem Trotz hat er aus Gott ..." Cf. R. Slenczka 1984, 350.

[72] A. Schlatter 1927, 365.

[73] A. Schlatter 1927, 323-418.

[74] A. Schlatter 1927, 344, 373f., 324: "Somit beginnt das Glauben für Paulus mit einem von jeder Beschränkung befreiten Verzicht auf das eigene Recht und das eigene Leben." The reason for this fateful state lies in the fact that through the disobedience of Adam all have been positioned in sinfulness and mortality (cf. 355).

[75] Schlatter does not propose an abstract concept of guilt, but regards it as moral inability (cf., e.g., 1927, 356: "sittliche[s] Unvermögen").

edgment of one's guilt leads into total *aporia* due to the absolute judgment over guilt: Guilt destroys all life relationships and makes us enemies of the law and of God.[76]

Repentance leaves open but one possibility, which God has prepared as an "other way"[77] to overcome the separation from him: faith.[78] To be sure, the causal connection between *aporia* and faith is not a natural one, but only possible through a new knowledge ("Wissen") that regards the recognized emptiness as being filled by Christ. Thus, together with the *aporia*, this knowledge serves as motive for faith in the one, in whom one has righteousness and salvation.[79] Since, however, on the one side we permanently experience our sinfulness, but on the other want to honor God and accept his gift in Christ, faith has the character of a powerful deed, of a conscious decision and is therefore connected to the most inner movement of the will.[80] Faith grasps in an act of the will the actuality of our acquittal, ignoring the apparent gap between the visible circumstances and the divine judgment on them, by looking at Christ's destiny and by learning that, in truth, people are what they are before God. He then will fulfill his work, while we have to hope and wait with "still certainty."[81] The will cannot be excluded from the act of faith, because God's goodness has to be affirmed willingly in order to become a present reality.[82] God's relationship with humans is something personal and accordingly affects and requires the whole person.[83] Yet all this does not suggest that faith due to its own inherent value or its character as "collaborating cause" would activate God's giving; for Paul, the free divine will is regarded as initiative, creative causality that chooses to grant grace unconditionally – and faith affirms and

---

[76] A. Schlatter 1927, 331, 343f. While the first part of Romans is concerned with will and deed, the first part of 1Corinthians deals with the human failure in the realm of wisdom and knowledge and is therefore an "exact parallel" (388; cf. 393).

[77] A. Schlatter 1927, 331 ("anderer Weg").

[78] However, the relationship between repentance and faith consists in a firm "Wechselwirkung," in which the one transfers its power to the other (A. Schlatter 1927, 356).

[79] A. Schlatter 1927, 332f.: "Aus dieser Erkenntnis ... erwächst das Glauben."

[80] A. Schlatter 1927, 336n.1, 346f., 379. "Damit ist das Glauben mit der innersten Bewegung des Willens verknüpft und seine Unerlässlichkeit ist nachgewiesen" (346). Cf. 1935, 22: "Glaube ist das, was die Botschaft vom Hörer erwartet und was sie in ihm bewirkt, und dieser Glaube ist ... Hingabe des Willens an ihn [*sc.* Gott], Bereitschaft, sein Gebot zu tun. Die Annahme des Worts und den Entschluß zum Gehorsam hat Paulus nicht voneinander getrennt; beides ist eine und dieselbe Bewegung des Willens." The aim of the believer to honor God's glory makes faith an offering.

[81] A. Schlatter 1927, 349f. It is not ours and not part of our faith to reflect on *how* the good of salvation might become our possession.

[82] Hence, faith assumes the full significance of a "mitwirkende[.] Ursache" towards the possession of righteousness and life (A. Schlatter 1927, 362).

[83] A. Schlatter 1927, 361; cf. 346, 351.

awaits this grace. This divine cause is not derivable from anything else and only apparent in what it establishes, and hence it is defined as miracle.[84] In analogy to the faithful, willing assertion of God's kindness – which is the only appropriate and acceptable consequence of the divine gift, an act of obedience – unbelief is characterized as powerful activity, as sinful disobedience that cannot accept the truth due to a blind mind bound by satanical forces. Since, however, God himself keeps the unbeliever under sin, thus even the power for insolence comes from God.[85]

3. The Transformation through Faith

This transposition of one's attention away from oneself results in the total transformation of one's existence: Our nothingness is filled by God through the life-content of his Son.[86] Christ's cross makes discernible God's graceful righteousness and righteous grace.[87] His mission is to make effective God's grace, to fulfill the promise, to give righteousness and life and thus to pacify the consciousness of guilt.[88]

˒ The total human need and lack correlate exactly with the perfect gift and effect of Christ; in faith we receive help, because we are deficient.[89] To express the association of anthropological and christological perspective, Paul creates systematically two exactly parallel rows, whose components correspond to and cause each other: sin, law, flesh, wrath, death on the one side, and righteousness, Christ, Spirit, grace, life on the other.[90] Paul names the believer ὁ ἐκ πίστεως, because faith becomes the principle and root of and determines the whole existence.[91] Faith says: "God is righteous and justifies through his righteousness," knowing that in Christ

---

[84] A. Schlatter 1927, 357f., 360, 366, 382. "Der Glaubende erwartet die Gabe, weil sie ihm im Christus dargeboten ist; sie wird ihm nicht deswegen dargeboten, weil er sie erwartet hat" (358). Any boasting is therefore excluded.

[85] A. Schlatter 1927, 364.

[86] A. Schlatter 1927, 374.

[87] A. Schlatter 1927, 342; cf. 347, 362. The consequence is this: "Aus dem Kreuz läßt sich keine andere Folgerung ziehen als Glauben mit dem Verzicht auf Werk, Gesetz und Gerechtigkeit und mit seiner Bejahung jener Gerechtigkeit Gottes, die ... uns die Rechtfertigung gewährt" (344).

[88] A. Schlatter 1927, 334f. Against that, the law does not act for the sake of humans and does not forgive, rather, it calls for acts and punishes negligence and evil. Therefore, it cannot serve as motive and content of faith. Accordingly, law and works on the one hand, and Christ and faith on the other are each categories that belong together (ἔργα νόμου and πίστις Χριστοῦ).

[89] A. Schlatter 1927, 355f.: "Wir erhalten die Hilfe, weil sie uns fehlt."

[90] A. Schlatter 1927, 350.

[91] A. Schlatter 1927, 374.

this righteousness has been revealed; hence, it rejects any desire for own righteousness.[92]

The negative verdict about the human situation remains comprehensively and permanently valid, even for the believer, insofar as any (repeated) reliance on own ability and work would destroy the very foundation of faith. The focus and goal of faith is Christ,[93] *solus Christus*, and the believer once and for all has obtained the position of the receiver, not the worker, who seeks the good solely in Christ.[94] Without Christ, faith is nothing.[95] Consequently, faith carries within itself a double rejection, which is firmly linked: the rejection of the guilty person, i.e., the act of repentance, and the rejection of the earthly person, i.e., the affirmation that Christ's form of life has been given to us. The first leads into despair, the second into the acceptance of Christ and our new being, in which all consequences of our sinfulness are void.[96] From the manner how the gift of this new existence was received follows that faith remains the only means to maintain the righteous position before God, *sola fide*,[97] since any reliance on human ability would again call forth the radical judgment of the law and remove faith. The believer is a non-worker, and the worker is a non-believer.[98]

4. The Consequences of Faith

The new situation of the believer is marked by complete righteousness, which is not abstractly received, but actively lived, and reaches all life-dimensions: It is obedience towards Christ and love towards others.[99]

---

[92] A. Schlatter 1927, 341.

[93] In this context, some apparent inconsistencies in Schlatter's terminology need to be mentioned that concern his view of the πίστις Χριστοῦ formula (cf. already W. Mundle 1932, 76n.1): On the one hand he can state that faith belongs to Christ (A. Schlatter 1927, 265: "Jesus gehörender Glaube" – subjective genitive; cf. 607), and on the other hand he translates the same expression with faith that is given to Jesus (262: "...als Jesus erwiesen" – objective genitive). He seems to reconcile implicitly both perspectives by regarding Jesus as "Grund und Ursprung" (265) as well as the only "Ziel" (336). – J.G. Janzen (1993, 266) refers to S.T. Coleridge who utters a similar thought: "[O]ur faith is not ours in its origin: but it is the faith of the Son of God graciously communicated to us." On the πίστις Χριστοῦ-debate, see below chapter II.H.

[94] A. Schlatter 1927, 336; cf. 335: Christ "ist selbst der Wirkende an unserer Statt."

[95] A. Schlatter 1927, 376, 382; cf. 395f.: Christ is "Grund, Inhalt, Kraft des Glaubens."

[96] A. Schlatter 1927, 347; cf. 375.

[97] A. Schlatter 1927, 336, 377f., 381, 393.

[98] A. Schlatter 1927, 338; cf. 339: "Der Wirkende sucht die Kraft bei sich und den Mangel auf Gottes Seite, der Glaubende hat den Mangel in sich selbst und seinen Besitz in Gott."

[99] A. Schlatter 1927, 374.

Therefore, "work" is reintroduced into the life of the believer on a "higher level": The abandoned work returns as "work of faith" and the renounced law as "the law of the Spirit." Whereas before faith the person sought to obtain righteousness on the basis of works, now righteousness is the basis of works.[100]

The connection to Christ results in a total separation from sin: Since Christ is dead to sin, also the believer is dead to sin; grace and faith cannot produce any evil and every will that wants to sin cannot be rooted in faith, but is the opposite of faith. Together with grace we received the means to accomplish the moral task and a good will that is not capable of willing evil.[101] To be sure, this insight does not derive from self-perception, but from the perception that sees what God realizes in us through Christ. Thus, faith generates a double self-consciousness of which both parts are rooted in the same reality of the believer: Introspection causes repentance, renunciation, and fear; looking at Christ brings the triumphant victory over sinfulness.[102] Eventually, the task of the believer is to be what he became through faith.[103]

The good will obtains and maintains the supremacy and governs the believer's inner conditions – from the very beginning of the Christian life, since in baptism the radical severance from sin happened.[104] The will initiated by faith is love, because the attachment to Christ establishes Christ's love as the power which rules over the believer's will. Love relates to faith like the fruit to the root; it avoids the danger of only receiving and not giving and thus demonstrates the completion of God's love and the undivided acceptance of his grace in us.[105] The dimension of our acting in faith, i.e., the sphere where the Spirit prevails over our natural powerlessness, is not unchangeable. Rather, there are two opposing borderlines within which the movement of faith happens: On the one side it is the unconquerable human incapability and on the other the perfection of the awarded grace. All acting in faith therefore correlates to the measurement of faith, which every believer was granted.[106]

---

[100] A. Schlatter 1927, 374f.; cf. 381: Due to this order: righteousness by faith – works, faith remains the only saving power, and neither synthesis nor separation of faith and works, no synergism are possible.

[101] A. Schlatter 1927, 367-369.

[102] A. Schlatter 1927, 379f.: This is the "triumph" of the ethics of Paul: the correspondence between "Sein" and "Sollen," insofar as the imperative: "Be dead to sin!" is not merely a claim, but indicative in the life of the community.

[103] A. Schlatter 1927, 378; cf. 346, 384f.

[104] A. Schlatter 1927, 370; cf. 352.

[105] A. Schlatter 1927, 371.

[106] A. Schlatter 1927, 385-387. For instance, Paul's extraordinary faith gave him great freedom in dealing with the prescriptions of the law.

5. Salvation History

The event of faith has to be placed into the framework of God's history with humanity.[107] The principle that the will of God is undivided and directed towards one goal underlies the entire line of Paul's reasoning. Despite their antithetical tension, law and Christ are connected in a synthesis, insofar as both serve the one purpose of God.[108] This is why Paul unconditionally affirms the law in regard to content, right and effects (even if they are pernicious) and thus acknowledges and uses it according to the God-given essence and purpose.[109] Only God can put an end to its power, and only for the one who is in faith connected to Christ.[110] What God wants is work: Within the human life, work possesses decisive significance. God's demand for κατεργάζεσθαι is his basic statute and binds everybody, believer and non-believer.[111] But since the human will counters the divine will as expressed in the law and is thus exposed to its radical judgment,[112] God prepared righteousness for the guilty person through an act of "inestimable divine grace"[113]: Christ bears the condemnation of sin and is exalted as Lord, whereas the believer assumes the fall effected by the law and becomes capable of being connected to Christ. Thus, both Christ and the law are in the service of the same divine purpose.

For Schlatter, the oneness of God's will also manifests itself in the fact that Paul's theology is not only in conformity with the law, but also in an essential congruity both with the teaching of Jesus[114] and with the elements of Jewish belief.[115] Yet contrary to the latter, Paul takes the decisive and last step to the ultimate consequence and overcomes Judaism: He does affirm the basic Jewish doctrines of work, law, sin, etc., but emphatically rejects the "double truth" that evil is both convicting and pardonable,[116] that righteousness and grace can stand together in an unresolved way.[117] The radical conviction that anyone who does not observe everything writ-

---

[107] Cf. A. Schlatter 1927, 395f.

[108] A. Schlatter 1927, 357n.1.

[109] A. Schlatter 1927, 330: "Seine [*sc.* Paulus'] Stellung ist dem Gesetz konform." Cf. 329, 332, 404.

[110] A. Schlatter 1927, 357.

[111] A. Schlatter 1927, 326; cf. 327f., 332, 375, 382, 398. "Work" is certainly not defined as some outward success apart from will and consciousness, but as sincere obedience (328).

[112] A. Schlatter 1927, 361n.1.

[113] A. Schlatter 1927, 331; cf. 401.

[114] Cf. A. Schlatter 1927, 326, 336n.1, 341, 365n.1, 370n.1, 373, 375n.1, 381n.1, 384n.1, 391n.1, 395, 396n.1, 397.

[115] A. Schlatter 1927, 332.

[116] A. Schlatter 1927, 332.

[117] A. Schlatter 1927, 342.

ten in the law is cursed, produces an *aporia* which can only be eliminated through a change of one's view, away from oneself and one's work to Christ and his work. Thus Paul's interpretation of the law remains faithful to the Jewish view and is in fact more rigorous. His encounter with Christ[118] led him to the insight that due to the human sinfulness no work of the law, no combination of faith and work, no faith understood as virtue can lead to righteousness – for in all those instances the person remains self-centered. Only through faith in Christ the crucified, God's righteousness and grace become visible in a way that God makes our guilt vanish and justifies us in a juridical act with the result that we are made righteous and thus escape the condemnation of the law.[119]

Even the example of Abraham testifies to the unity of the divine government in and over history, as his fatherhood of all believers from all nations is foretold in the law and the prophets and was from the beginning part of God's plan.[120] The situation of Abraham also provides a vivid picture of faith as a conscious decision of the will, based on the indispensable necessity to bridge the human incapacity and weakness, by not neglecting God's gift.[121] Moreover, it demonstrates the universalism of God's plans, as neither moral integrity nor intellectual, social, or national distinctions are relevant: Sinfulness and mortality, human deficiency and need are the only requirements for God's gift.[122]

6. Reception

The immediate reactions to Schlatter's first book-length publication ranged from wholehearted agreement to skeptical distance, but mostly they included respect for its author's erudition and its breadth. Whereas E. Luthardt, for instance, praised that the great scope and wealth of the New

---

[118] Cf. A. Schlatter 1927, 399-404: The teaching that Paul develops is deeply rooted in his biography and evolved from his own spiritual life and is not dependent on the formal acquirement of a principle or on the speculative invention of an ideal. His encounter with Christ exposed his enmity against God precisely in his religiosity and piety and led to his full connection to Christ. "Der Glaube 'kam' ihm, als Christus zu ihm kam" (402; cf. 396). There exists a "Kongruenz seines Gedankens mit der Lebensgeschichte des Apostels" (404).

[119] A. Schlatter 1927, 329, 340, 342, 357n.1, 360, 402n.1.

[120] A. Schlatter 1927, 396. Paul's line of thought demonstrates the difference between his teaching from the Jewish doctrines. According to the latter, Abraham's faith has vicarious power that covers times of unbelief and thus serves the assurance of the election; on the contrary, Paul affirms that faith results in the kinship with Abraham – for Jews and for Gentiles, and therefore he speaks of a real faith that is in true analogy to Abraham's relationship to God. "Er [*sc.* Paul] ist Abraham nicht ferner, sondern näher gekommen als seine einstigen Genossen" (396n.2).

[121] A. Schlatter 1927, 336, 346-348.

[122] A. Schlatter 1927, 352, 355, 394-397; cf. 136.

Testament concept of faith had not been presented in such comprehensive manner before, H.J. Holtzmann charged the book for its overly broad and repetitive dialectic.[123] The strong interrelation between exegetical work and philosophical theory, as well as Schlatter's locating faith primarily in the human will ("repentance"[124]), impeded at first the full effect of his approach on subsequent scholarship,[125] which in the following decades was primarily occupied with the question how the Pauline doctrine of justification relates to his doctrine of redemption or Christ-mysticism and the role of πίστις in this framework. Only after this phase came to an end, Schlatter's presentation gained its deserved influence in the exegetical discussion. The fact that R. Bultmann continually refers and appeals to it, despite different theological accentuations, witnesses to the great impact and importance of Schlatter's insights.[126]

As could be seen, the framework of *Der Glaube im Neuen Testament* is rather broad, and one has to agree with the statement of Bultmann that the book almost amounts to a New Testament theology.[127] This breadth is due to Schlatter's methodological starting point: Empirical philological-

---

[123] Holtzmann criticized the book's "allzu breitspurige und in mannigfachen Wiederholungen sich ergehende Dialektik" (quoted in W. Neuer 1996, 191-193, where additional reviews are listed). As with all of Schlatter's books, its heavy and clumsy, sometimes "barbaric" style (H. Thielicke 1959, 8) is repeatedly reprimanded (cf. E. Grafe 1886, 371f.), which however may not conceal that Schlatter's language can produce formulations that are unsurpassed in their density and precision (cf. P. Stuhlmacher 1982, xi).

[124] "Repentance" is by no means an obvious key term in Paul.

[125] Cf. K. Haacker 1984, 289. Both, W. Mundle and R. Gyllenberg, criticize Schlatter's "modern" understanding of faith: Schlatter's study is "trotz vieler feiner und zutreffender Beobachtungen allzusehr von seinem modernen Glaubensverständnis geleitet und nicht selten konstruktiv; seine Reflexionen sind oft nicht derart, daß man sie bei den neutestamentlichen Schriftstellern voraussetzen darf" (W. Mundle 1932, 1), it is "allzu sehr von dem modernen Glaubensverständnis des Verfassers geleitet" (R. Gyllenberg 1936, 614). – Even according to his own testimony, Schlatter did not expect his work to play a significant role in New Testament scholarship (cf. A Schlatter 1977, 114).

[126] Cf. D. Lührmann 1976, 15: Bultmann's own expositions on the topic of faith "sind ihr [*sc.* Schlatters Darstellung] in auffälligem Maße verpflichtet." Even the dedication of the *Theologisches Wörterbuch zum Neuen Testament* to Schlatter signifies, in how far his method furthered the study of the New Testament and contributed to a novel historical-exegetical approach. With regard to the conception of his dictionary, the editor, G. Kittel, emphasizes that Schlatter's first work has been a model for the investigation of biblical-theological terms in general.

[127] R. Bultmann 1927, 195; 1958, 598: Schlatter's "Buch 'Der Glaube im NT' ... kann als eine neutest[amentliche] Theologie in nuce gelten." Cf. E. Grafe 1886, 371 ("Biblische[.] Theologie des N[euen] T[estament]s)"; P. Stuhlmacher 1982, viii; K. Haacker 1984, 289 ("das Wesen des [Ur-]Christentums"). One has to agree with those verdicts, even if Schlatter occasionally explicitly demarcates his study from a New Testament theology (cf. only 1927, 329n.1, 348n.1, 356n.1, 394n.1, etc.).

historical observations that examine the facts are supplemented and completed by a speculative element that penetrates the observed evidence theologically.[128] The presentation of the whole phenomenon "faith and believing" entails analysis, reconstruction, and interpretation; thus, the study receives systematic unity and historical precision, which is still unsurpassed, as P. Stuhlmacher maintains; only Bultmann's treatment of the topic is comparable in that respect.[129]

Not only the coherence and cogency of Schlatter's work, but also his independence with respect to the mainstream of New Testament scholarship warrants the actuality of his results. The following chapter, however, will engage in the already mentioned, most disputed issue of this time: the relationship between "mystical" and "juridical" thought patterns in Paul.

C. Faith and Mysticism

I. W.H.P. Hatch, The Pauline Idea of Faith in Its Relation to Jewish and Hellenistic Religion *(1917)*

The goal of W.H.P. Hatch's doctoral thesis is "to examine in detail the Pauline idea of faith, which was fundamental in the Apostle's conception of Christianity,"[130] in relation to the Old Testament and Jewish piety and the religious thought of the Greco-Roman world and oriental mystery cults.[131] Adopting to a great degree the ideas of the History-of-Religions School, he seeks to prove that in Paul (as in Philo) traces of mysticism are discernible,[132] while in Palestine – hence even in Jesus' teaching – such extraneous influences never existed and the object of trust was always God.[133] Paul created a novel concept of faith by commingling Jewish and Hellenistic elements. For his thinking, faith is of such primary and fundamental significance that it became to him "the basic principle of religion and the source of moral excellence."[134] Only through faith the gospel is

---

[128] A. Schlatter 1927, xvi.

[129] P. Stuhlmacher 1982, vii-viii.

[130] W.H.P. Hatch 1917, preface; cf. 33.

[131] Cf. W.H.P. Hatch 1917, 67-81. – In a later publication (1925), Hatch traced "the idea of faith in Christian literature from the death of St. Paul to the close of the second century" (title).

[132] While Philo derived his mysticism from the religious teaching of the Stoics (W.H.P. Hatch 1917, 47, 79-81), Paul was influenced by the religious atmosphere of the Greco-Roman world, which "was laden with mysticism" (47; cf. 66).

[133] Cf. W.H.P. Hatch 1917, 1-29, 37 on the Old Testament and Jewish concept of faith as trust in Yahweh. Out of this notion Paul developed his own idea of faith, though factually for him "πίστις is very different from trust" (65).

[134] W.H.P. Hatch 1917, 64f. (here, this definition appears three times), 74.

able to save and everything which is associated to the Christian life depends on it: "membership in the community of believers, mystical communion with Christ, and all the blessings comprised under the name of
salvation."[135]

Though faith and its individual measure is foreordained by God and of
divine origin,[136] it nevertheless begins with the missionary preaching and
the receptive hearing of the gospel, that is, with the active belief and trust
that Christ's death and resurrection bring about salvation.[137] Yet since for
Paul faith signifies the permanent principle of a mystical type of religion,
it is not restrained to the intellectual realm, but involves feelings, will, and
intellect.[138] To be a Christian is synonymous with being a believer, being
in faith, and likewise with being in Christ: In a realistic and mystical way,
Paul conceives Christ, identified with the divine Spirit, to be the "pneumatical" atmosphere in which the believer lives and works and under
whose influence becomes a new creature that is guided by the ethical principle of love.[139] Thus, religion is in Paul's view "not merely a relation to a
divine person, but possession by a divine power and divinization."[140] To
the subjective entering into the mystical communion with Christ in faith,
baptism correlates as the objective side of one and the same event.[141] There
is also a social dimension to faith, since by virtue of their common faith,
all Christians are incorporated into a distinct social group, in which all
natural or racial differences lose their significance and where "the principal product of faith," love, rules.[142]

---

[135] W.H.P. Hatch 1917, 37; cf. 46, 53-55, 64. Due to the fundamental character of
faith for the Christian life, Christians are called "believers," πιστεύειν denotes "being a
Christian" and πιστεῦσαι "becoming a Christian."

[136] W.H.P. Hatch 1917, 36.

[137] W.H.P. Hatch 1917, 33f. "If the hearers do not believe, ... the gospel ... is wholly
ineffective" (34).

[138] W.H.P. Hatch 1917, 35, 47f.

[139] W.H.P. Hatch 1917, 39-41, 46f. Faith not only inaugurates the mystical relationship with Christ, but is also necessary for its continuance (45). However, despite the
ensuing "striking resemblances" between Paul's conception of Christianity and the mystery type of religion, "the religious ideal involved and the means by which the mystical
state is brought about are different": The believer, who is in Christ, is thought of as being
under the control of Christ and as being pneumatic or divine, just as Christ is pneumatic
or divine; yet this does not imply an identification with Christ or to lose one's identity in
him (74; cf. 40, 63).

[140] W.H.P. Hatch 1917, 42.

[141] W.H.P. Hatch 1917, 42-44.

[142] W.H.P. Hatch 1917, 39, 47, 49-53, quote: 50. Love that springs from faith is "the
bond of perfection by which all believers are bound together" and which grants "social
morality" (53). Besides love, everything else connected to the Christian life is a product
of faith (cf. 54: Christian virtues, 55: hope, 56: joy).

In the context of his doctrine of justification by faith, Paul uses Abraham's faith as illustration and confirmation as to how righteousness and the sense of justification are attained – even though the "Christian has faith in a much deeper sense than Abraham had it."[143] Paul knows by experience that the law, which stands between Abraham and Christianity, is incapable of producing righteousness, and therefore he views it solely as preparation for "the higher and final dispensation of faith."[144] While the experience of justification and forgiveness is made in the present, salvation is conceived in an eschatological way: At Christ's Parousia, the believer's divinization will be completed and the Christian life will reach its consummation.[145]

In evaluation, one does not need to follow entirely W. Mundle's fairly harsh verdict that this work is a beginner's work which lacks the familiarity with the subject-matter and the awareness of exegetical problems,[146] but he is certainly right that Hatch's presentation and application of the history-of-religions data is oftentimes insufficient[147]; often the logical connection between Hatch's theses is obscure, which obviously must be attributed to the fact that his work is entirely dominated by its mystical outlook.[148]

II. E. Wißmann, Das Verhältnis von ΠΙΣΤΙΣ und Christusfrömmigkeit bei Paulus *(1926)*

Not content with the (in his opinion) mostly un-Pauline concept of faith of earlier works, in his *Licentiatenarbeit* E. Wißmann sets himself the goal to provide both a comprehensive investigation of the meaning of πίστις in Paul – considering the pre-Pauline-Christian, the non-Christian-Jewish, and the Hellenistic usage – and the answer to the question: What is the implication of πίστις for the relationship of the believer to the exalted Christ.[149] Though Wißmann claims that the results of both elements of his treatise stand in "sharp contrast" to the vast majority of scholarship, there is a certain affinity to H. Lüdemann and W. Heitmüller, who propagate a clear distinction of faith in Christ and Christ-mysticism and claim that the first was without significance for Paul's personal piety and Christ-experience.[150] Wißmann's extreme opposition against an understanding of the Pauline faith as personal relationship of trust reflects a tendency in

---

[143] W.H.P. Hatch 1917, 58.

[144] W.H.P. Hatch 1917, 59.

[145] W.H.P. Hatch 1917, 63f.

[146] W. Mundle 1932, 2. Contrast E.D. Burton 1921, 485 ("excellent discussion").

[147] W. Mundle 1932, 4.

[148] Cf. F. Neugebauer 1961, 160.

[149] E. Wißmann 1926, v. This fact creates the necessity for an extensive (and today still useful) discussion of the history of scholarship on the respective theme (1-29).

[150] Cf. E. Wißmann 1926, 29, 117.

scholarship of this period, which, after the psychologizing interpretation of, e.g., O. Pfleiderer and A. Deißmann, returns to the more rational understanding of πίστις, but does not want to lose the aspect of the mystical-affectionate relationship with Christ (ἐν Χριστῷ).[151] Wißmann mentions explicitly R. Reitzenstein[152] and W. Bousset as previous proponents of his view that the history-of-religions context of the term πίστις is the missionary propaganda.[153]

The first part of the monograph's main corpus consequently dissects the terms πίστις and πιστεύειν. It takes as its starting point Paul's allegedly contradictory and unclear doctrine of justification, which leaves unconnected the two entities πίστις and χάρις and represents a peculiar illogicality that compromises the character of justification as grace by slipping into the requirement of human faith.[154] Especially the "sphinx" of the πίστις Χριστοῦ-formula constitutes exegetical problems. According to Wißmann, to the addressees of Paul's letters this phrase must have been a well known entity.[155] He argues that the phrase πίστις Χριστοῦ, which appears only in polemical sections on the doctrine of justification,[156] is not about a personal faith-relationship to the exalted, but has "salvation-historical" meaning.[157] "Faith in the facts of salvation" that God accomplished in Christ, is abbreviated to "faith in Christ" and in this form used in the argumentation against the Jewish concept of grace.[158] And thus, on the basis of this struggle, the contradictions and inconsistencies, explain themselves: With grand nonchalance Paul places side by side both the handed down "vulgär-christliche" faith, emptying it of its quality as human merit, and the radical divine grace, the decisive character of the Christian religion. It is a "both ... and," not an "either ... or."[159]

In result, πίστις hears and gets acquainted with the Christian missionary message of salvation[160] (εὐαγγέλιον τοῦ Χριστοῦ), considers true its con-

---

[151] Cf. F. Neugebauer 1961, 152.

[152] Cf. R. Reitzenstein's influential description of πίστις as "Schlagwort Propaganda treibender Religionen" (1927, 234-236).

[153] E. Wißmann 1926, 46. To the proof texts of Reitzenstein, he adds passages from the Hermetic and Mandean literature.

[154] E. Wißmann 1926, 30-33 ("merkwürdige Verdoppelung und Unlogik" [33]).

[155] E. Wißmann 1926, 90.

[156] E. Wißmann 1926, 48, 69.

[157] E. Wißmann 1926, 69, 72, 74. The same is true for those prepositional expressions that connect πίστις with Χριστός (71-75).

[158] E. Wißmann 1926, 75, 88f.

[159] E. Wißmann 1926, 89-91.

[160] E. Wißmann 1926, 38, 65. Wißmann continually emphasizes the character of faith as "Missionsglaube" that reacts to the "Missionspropaganda" (38, 42, 46, 49, 55, 66f.).

tent,[161] accepts it,[162] and surrenders with unconditional obedience to God's radical grace contained therein,[163] in order to receive salvation.[164] Eventually, it characterizes therefore the affiliation and confession to one's own religion[165] and simply denotes as *terminus technicus* "being a Christian" or "Christianity."[166] Notably, πίστις never denotes trust in or any other personal relationship to Christ, but retains its intellectual-dogmatic character throughout,[167] since it remains confined to the missionary work.[168] It primarily refers to the past, as it is directed to God's act in the past, to his raising Christ from the dead.[169] It answers as salvific faith ("Heilsglaube") the question of the certainty of salvation and the righteousness before God.[170] Thus, the believer stands before God.[171] As regards history-of-religions patterns, the Pauline concept of faith is tied to the propaganda of salvation ("Heilspropaganda")[172] of the other religions and especially to the eschatological-juridical position of Second Temple Judaism.

Second, Wißmann examines the relationship between the believer and Christ, the Christ-piety ("Christusfrömmigkeit"), of which πίστις is the indispensable prerequisite.[173] In the center of the communion with Christ,

---

[161] E. Wißmann 1926, 38, 67f.: Πίστις as "Fürwahrhalten des christlichen Kerygmas" is therefore dogmatic faith, *fides quae creditur* (38) – hence the content of the kerygma and of faith eventually coincide (66); this dogmatic understanding is parallel to the Jewish and Pagan (40, 45, 78). The content of the specifically Christian kerygma and faith is constituted by three pillars: death, resurrection and Second Coming of Christ (56f.).

[162] E. Wißmann 1926, 38, 40, 65, 84. Thereby, in analogy to the converts to Judaism (50-54), for the Gentiles monotheism becomes the necessary prerequisite for their Christian faith (49, 57).

[163] E. Wißmann 1926, 83-85. In the notion of obedience to God's will and in the consequence of obedience, δικαιοσύνη, Paul again agrees with Judaism.

[164] E. Wißmann 1926, 68.

[165] E. Wißmann 1926, 37, 42, 66. In this regard, Paul's use and understanding of faith is in direct analogy to that of Second Temple Judaism, both Palestinian and Diaspora Judaism, where "faith" is used "als Inbegriff der jüdischen Religion und Frömmigkeit" (40), and that of the other contemporaneous religions, where faith is too "Bezeichnung der Zugehörigkeit zu der betreffenden Religion" (45).

[166] E. Wißmann 1926, 35, 37. Under the presupposition of its non-personal character, the formula πίστις Ἰησοῦ Χριστοῦ becomes in Paul "der knappste gemeinverständliche Ausdruck für die christliche Religion" (75).

[167] E. Wißmann 1926, 40, 67, 74, 81, 95. This is for the most part also true for Jewish religiosity (51, 54), yet there the element of trust confers to faith the "blood of life" (80).

[168] "Πίστις [ist] Zweck und Folge aller Verkündigung" (E. Wißmann 1926, 66).

[169] E. Wißmann 1926, 55, 112. Only secondarily faith turns as eschatologically disposed hope towards the future, to Christ's Parousia (55, 57).

[170] E. Wißmann 1926, 68, 82, 85.

[171] E. Wißmann 1926, 95.

[172] E. Wißmann 1926, 38.

[173] E. Wißmann 1926, 95, 111.

there is a mystical fusion with Christ in his pneumatical mode of existence,[174] a holy experience, a feeling of elation, the jubilant veneration of
the exalted,[175] all caused and carved by Paul's Damascus experience and
the enthusiasm of the Christian-Hellenistic cult.[176] Paul appears – in contrast to those contexts where he speaks as missionary – to have a strongly
visionary-ecstatic and mystical inclination and disposition.[177] Here he
stands before Christ.[178] For Wißmann, this pneumatic-mystical religiosity
of Paul shows his proximity to contemporary mystery religions.

An evaluation of those two circles of thought, πίστις and Christ-piety,
in view of their relationship, reveals that one deals with two entirely different attitudes to life, two kinds of piety, two different perspectives with
different interests and intentions, questions and answers.[179] Mostly, both
appear juxtaposed, not systematically connected, and without reciprocal
impact; they belong to two different spheres of life. Qualitatively, faith
appears on a lower lever than the lofty liaison with Christ.[180] However,
Paul's personality remains whole and unbroken despite this double orientation; in fact he can switch from one realm to the other without perceiving
the discrepancy.

It is obvious that Wißmann's wedge that he drove between the notions
of Christ-mysticism and faith has not much grounding in exegesis, but is
rather based on his own presuppositions and reflects unmistakenly the current theological atmosphere. Thus, his analysis of Christ-mysticism remains rather vague despite the intense language employed.[181] That Paul's

---

[174] E. Wißmann 1926, 99-101, 110. In baptism one enters into a new life-sphere and
breathes Christ's "geistig-reale-supranaturale Lebensluft" (101; cf. 104).

[175] Whereas in the first part of his work, Wißmann retains a rather technical language,
his style seems to adapt to the elated content in the subsequent parts. One finds in abundance terms and expressions like "innerlich ergriffen von Jesus Christus," "überwallende
Erfahrung," "mystische Verbundenheit mit Christus" (98), "erfahrungsfreudig," "Ergrif-
fensein," "Aufgehen in ihm [*sc.* Christus]" (102), "glutvoll-mystisches Verhältnis," "En-
thusiasmus," "magisch," "Brandungen religiöser Hochflut" (107), "das lebenssprühende
Hochgefühl des kraftvollen religiösen Genius" (108), "heiliges Erleben," "unaussprechli-
che[s] Hochgefühl" (115).

[176] E. Wißmann 1926, 96, 106f., 113f.

[177] E. Wißmann 1926, 106, 114.

[178] E. Wißmann 1926, 102-104. "Gott versinkt hier" (102; against that R. Bultmann
1959, 218).

[179] E. Wißmann 1926, 110, 112. "Πίστις und Christusfrömmigkeit sind ihrem Wesen
nach ganz verschiedene Motive" (117).

[180] E. Wißmann 1926, 112.

[181] This also seems to be the critique of E. Lohmeyer; he does not mention Wißmann's
name explicitly (though knowing his work; cf. 1929, 122n.3; 126n.1), but he is clearly
one of the targets of the following verdict: "[Die Formel ἐν Χριστῷ] ist nicht der Ausdruck einer mehr oder minder verschwommenen Christusmystik, sondern einer klaren
und in sich geschlossenen Christusmetaphysik" (145).

idea of faith omits the element of trust or personal relationship is clearly one-sided, though scholars appreciatively adopted some of Wißmann's insights – among them W. Mundle[182] and R. Bultmann.[183] As regards the comparative texts of Hermetic and Mandean literature, he clearly underrates their being influenced by Jewish, even Christian language.[184]

III. F. Neugebauer, In Christus. Eine Untersuchung zum Paulinischen Glaubensverständnis *(1961)*

A brief examination of the history of Pauline scholarship since H. Lüdemann's study on Pauline anthropology illustrates that one assumed since then the existence of two circles of thought within Paul's theology: The juridical circle is shaped by Jewish concepts and responsible for Paul's doctrine of justification, the mystical circle derives from Hellenistic ideas and formed Paul's mystical-real doctrine of salvation. Characteristically, the term πίστις is assigned to the first, and the formula ἐν Χριστῷ to the latter circle. In his monograph, F. Neugebauer attempts to scrutinize the attribution of those expressions to their alleged sphere and to decide on the principal legitimacy of splitting the Pauline thinking into two parts.[185]

Moreover, Neugebauer sees the need to analyze the concept of πίστις anew, above all in discussion with R. Bultmann, since despite Bultmann's "masterly" description some aspects of Paul's idea of πίστις remain unappreciated, especially those, in which πίστις seems to convey an objective-eschatological rather than a subjective-anthropological entity.[186] To accomplish his purpose, Neugebauer draws on the work of A. Schlatter and – more importantly – E. Lohmeyer; the latter brings to expression the ambivalence of eschatological event and human deed in the Pauline faith.

The content with which Paul fills the πίστις-idea is dependent on Old Testament motifs (the root אמן) mediated through the Septuagint and to a lesser extent on Second Temple Judaism; formally, Paul connects to those

---

[182] W. Mundle 1932, 35. Mundle also praises the amount of material that Wißmann collected, but apart from that his critique is less friendly: Like Hatch's work it that of a beginner, which shines through in his vague conception of Christ-mysticism (2, 121, 153) and the sharp contrast between faith and mysticism – both based on weak and superficial exegesis (33, 169) and own presuppositions (96).

[183] Bultmann mentored Wißmann's *Licentiatenarbeit* so that the influences are of course mutual. – See also below chapter VI.A.V.

[184] Cf. also G. Ebeling 1958, 81n.3.

[185] F. Neugebauer 1961, 9f., 16. – See on this question also M. Dibelius 1931; 1941; cf. 1937, 89.

[186] Nevertheless Bultmann's presentation of the Pauline concept of faith continues to be the guideline, according to which Neugebauer develops his own position (cf. 1961, 156, 160), especially regarding the characterization of faith as hope and fear (168) and confession (170), and regarding the placing of faith into the historical life of the individual (170).

contemporaneous religions that used the term πίστις as technical term in their propaganda.[187] Yet those presuppositions merely constitute the sub-structure, as for Paul the interpretation of the eschatological Christ-event stands in the center of the term πίστις: Faith is about Christology.[188] The correlation of deed ("Tun") and event ("Geschehen") plays a significant role both in Jewish and Pauline theology, yet with a decisive difference of order: According to Neugebauer, Paul views the Christ-event as basis for the human deed, whereas Judaism considered the individual deed as consti-tutive for the ensuing event. The Pauline πίστις can describe both, the sal-vation that happens *with* the ecclesia (event) and the salvation that happens *in* the ecclesia (deed).[189]

The eschatological event of πίστις terminates the reign of the νόμος; and since Christ himself is the end of the νόμος it entails that faith (and with it righteousness and life) came with the Christ-event and became the only possibility of salvation. Thus, faith is primarily God's decision (indicative) and the human decision is only relevant in the context of the imperative that is dependent on the reality created by the divine decision: Paul does not say πιστεύετε, but στήκετε ἐν τῇ πίστει.[190] Paul's proclamation of πίστις indicates that he comprehends the eschatological event πίστις as present and effective reality.

To the revealed and also proclaimed event of πίστις the ecclesiological πίστις and also πιστεύειν correspond. Since, however, faith believes what it will see one day (righteousness and life), it is understood in strictly es-chatological terms.[191] Yet it is clear, too, that even though the ecclesia is already removed from this world, it still lives in and is part of it; and there-fore, faith requires obedient deeds (ὑπακοὴ πίστεως): Faith works through

---

[187] F. Neugebauer 1961, 160f. Moreover, he agrees with Bultmann that compared to the Old Testament idea of faith, decisive shifts took place in Second Temple Judaism: The relation to history and to God's acting in history degenerated and the notion of merit became dominant (161f.).

[188] F. Neugebauer 1961, 162f.

[189] F. Neugebauer 1961, 164.

[190] Obviously, this is said against Bultmann's stress on the importance of the human decision (cf. F. Neugebauer 1961, 165, 167, 169f.). Also, Neugebauer states against con-ventional language: "Paulus ... sagt gerade nicht, daß der Mensch zum Glauben kommt, sondern er sagt, daß der Glaube zum Menschen kommt" (164f.).

[191] When Paul composed the pieces on Abraham, he did not speak of Abraham as ex-ample of faith (this is how Second Temple Judaism understood Abraham), but sought to demonstrate that Abraham's faith contained δικαιοσύνη, and even more: "Abraham [ist] der Typus des neuen Gottesvolkes ... gewissermaßen das präexistente Glied der Ekklesia, er ist eine ekklesiologische Gestalt" (168f.).

love and in that it finds perseverance;[192] it strives for the deed which seeks to implement now what once will be.

Neugebauer now defines the relationship between πίστις and ἐν Χριστῷ[193] as follows: Πίστις articulates what ἐν Χριστῷ determines,[194] and for that reason ἐν Χριστῷ embraces and incorporates πίστις. This explains their parallel structure: For instance, ἐν Χριστῷ *determines* the indicative, πίστις *is* wholly indicative; both have the tendency to yield the imperative; both appear in connection with the provisional nature and imperfectness of the ecclesia and hence bear the eschatological character of the "not yet" and "already"; both are spoken of in ecclesiological, not individualistic terms. Consequently, the alleged double structure of Paul's thinking was not confirmed, and the "ghost" of the two circles should disappear.[195]

Neugebauer's work is very helpful in describing the relationship between πίστις and ἐν Χριστῷ and in eliminating the wedge that has been driven between two intrinsically connected elements within Paul's theology. He has shown that in this regard there is no contradiction in Paul. Even though his description proper of Paul's concept of faith is largely dependent on Bultmann's, his insights in the eschatological nature of πίστις prove to be very valuable. Unfortunately, many of his statements remain rather programmatic and thetical which hinders their verification in the Pauline texts.

Also the following study to be presented, written by W. Mundle, seeks to overcome the dichotomy between faith in and communion with Christ, but does so in a specific sacramental framework: He portrays Paul's concept of faith by way of a clarification of the relationship between faith and baptism.

---

[192] F. Neugebauer 1961, 169. One term that expresses both, believing and doing, is ὁμολογία, because it is the human response to faith ("Bekennen"), but contains nothing else than precisely this faith ("Bekenntnis"). "In der Zusammengehörigkeit von Bekenntnis und Bekennen aber ist der Glaube Akt und Inhalt zugleich" (170).

[193] On the ἐν Χριστῷ-formula, see the summary in F. Neugebauer 1961, 148f.

[194] F. Neugebauer 1961, 171: "Was 'in Christo' also bestimmen möchte, das ist in der πίστις ausgesprochen." Cf. 173f.

[195] F. Neugebauer 1961, 173.

D. Faith and Baptism

I. W. Mundle, Der Glaubensbegriff des Paulus (1932)[196]

Despite the existence of numerous monographs on single Pauline problems, there is still, in W. Mundle's view, the scientific need of an unbiased, exegetical-historical exposition of Paul's idea of faith, which will
place essential questions of Pauline theology into the right perspective.
The reason why all previous scholarship failed to explain fully the subject
matter lies in the insufficient recognition of the connection between the
Pauline concept of faith and baptism.[197] As regards his methodology,
Mundle maintains that the historical "Distanzbetrachtung" may not be dis-
turbed by theological presuppositions; in fact, ideally, the subjectivity of
the exegete is to be extinguished. Mundle demarcates himself from the
"primitive kind" of history-of-religions scholarship and also from the
"new" theological perspective, namely, "dialectical theology."[198]

Mundle's reflections on the nature of the act of faith seek to prove that
since the content of the Christian proclamation is identical with the content
of faith, the Pauline faith means to consider the kerygma true, to be convinced of facts.[199] Yet more significantly, Paul essentially equates faith and
knowledge ("Wissen"), πιστεύειν and εἰδέναι; in the realm of πίστις no
doubt and uncertainty exist.[200] Even the content of γνῶσις ("Erkenntnis"),
i.e., the way to knowledge, is not different from faith as regards its nature.[201] Besides and despite the significance of γνῶσις, faith is, like hope,
distinguished by the paradox that lies in the provisional character of the
"not yet" of its fulfillment.[202] This irrational, even anti-rational, aspect of

---

[196] See also W. Mundle's work on the Pauline triad "faith, love, hope" (1949).

[197] W. Mundle 1932, 170. W.H.P. Hatch, for instance, states – following R.A. Lipsius
– that baptism and faith "constitute a single act of which faith is the subjective and baptism the objective" (W.H.P. Hatch 1917, 43), but his following remarks show "daß er die
Tragweite seiner Beobachtung von der Einheit von Glauben und Taufe nicht erkannt hat"
(W. Mundle 1932, 85n.1; cf. 153n.2). Even A. Schweitzer, who shares with Mundle the
emphasis on baptism, "[hat d]en Zusammenhang von Glauben und Taufe ... nicht gesehen" (W. Mundle 1932, 153n.1), because he considered any attempt to connect "being in
Christ" with "believing in Christ" to be in vain (cf. A. Schweitzer 1930, 117, 254).

[198] W. Mundle 1932, 5-8.

[199] W. Mundle 1932, 16, 29, 35, 38f. "Jede moderne Antipathie gegen den Glauben als
Fürwahrhalten ist ihm [sc. Paulus] fremd" (18).

[200] W. Mundle 1932, 17f.

[201] Πίστις and γνῶσις may not be identified (W. Mundle 1932, 20), but their structure
is comparable, as there is different measure of faith and understanding, growth and in-
crease (23, 25; cf. 45).

[202] W. Mundle 1932, 26-28. "Als hoffender Glaube steht er ... im Gegensatz zum
Schauen" (27).

faith is illustrated even more clearly by Paul's description of faith as obedience, which is based on the authoritative character of the kerygma as
word of truth.[203] Though not as decisive factor, also trust arises as nuance
of the Pauline faith.[204]

The content of πίστις or the *fides quae creditur*, is constituted by the
Pauline gospel, the message of God and Christ.[205] The existential character
of this message of salvation requires a decision of faith or unbelief, obedience or disobedience.[206] Moreover, due to its truth-character it serves as
critical canon of all revelation, both previous and future,[207] and has unconditional authority.[208] Notably, however, Paul's gospel is not confined to the
few sentences of the situational kerygma,[209] but comprises the whole of his
proclamation,[210] even that of Jesus and the other apostles,[211] but also Scripture[212] and (new) pneumatical revelations[213] – for their message is in full
congruence to his own. Paul only knows of *one* gospel, the one that originates from divine revelation.[214]

Faith as act of obedience is not only directed to the gospel, but in its ultimate intention towards God or Christ, the final originator(s) of the gospel. Those passages in which πίστις or πιστεύειν are connected with

---

[203] W. Mundle 1932, 29-34, 35; cf. 43. The authority that characterizes the gospel and
that does not tolerate doubt or criticism, rests on the manner how Paul received it: as
ἀποκάλυψις Ἰησοῦ Χριστοῦ, i.e., equipped with God's and Christ's authority (31f.; cf.
47, 57), and marked by truth. Thus, the demand of obedience and the sense for truth are
not incompatible for Paul (33).

[204] W. Mundle 1932, 35-39. Cf. however 92: Πιστεύειν ἐπί does not mean "ver-
trauende[s] Glauben."

[205] W. Mundle 1932, 50. Christ and the facts of salvation ("Heilstatsachen") – death,
resurrection, Second Coming – and God, the father of Jesus Christ, build the gospel's
consistent center, and direct faith comprehensively to past, present, and future (41-43).

[206] W. Mundle 1932, 44. "Es gibt dem Evangelium gegenüber keine Neutralität" (43).

[207] This canon factually evaluates the apostolic proclamation, words of Jesus, and the
Old Testament; it discerns and distinguishes the spirits (W. Mundle 1932, 68, 71).

[208] W. Mundle 1932, 47, 58, 62, 65f.

[209] W. Mundle 1932, 44f.

[210] W. Mundle 1932, 49.

[211] W. Mundle 1932, 50f., 54f. "Für das Urteil des Paulus ist das paulinische Evangelium mit dem apostolischen schlechthin identisch" (54), and even the words of the historical Jesus, which are congruent with the revelation of the exalted, are "Bestandteil des
Evangeliums" (61). The canonization of the Pauline letters (which happened in agreement with Paul's intentions, 48) and of the apostolic and evangelic tradition alike, is a
consequence of the fact that the *one* gospel is both uniform and normative (W. Mundle
1932, 47-49, 62, 70, 72).

[212] W. Mundle 1932, 64.

[213] W. Mundle 1932, 64-71.

[214] W. Mundle 1932, 50, 53f.

Christ,[215] demonstrate that faith in Christ not only means to accept the message of the gospel, but also includes to be baptized[216] and to become member of the Christian community,[217] so that eventually it is identical with becoming or being a Christian or even with Christianity.[218] On the basis of the identity of faith and Christianity, for Paul faith in God is only present where it is linked to faith in Christ, i.e., to the acceptance of God's revelation in Christ.[219] As Paul's doctrine of justification makes plain, the attitude of the believer towards the law and its commands cannot be decisive, but since there is no faith without baptism, the believer receives justification in baptism.[220] The Pauline antithesis against the works of the law is not directed against any kind of human achievement and work, but specifically against the Mosaic law; therefore, no discrepancy between grace and faith can arise, even if faith always includes a certain amount of own human activity ("Selbsttätigkeit"). For the apostle, grace became like faith the epitome of Christianity.[221] Even Judaism is a religion of faith – faith that is directed to God and to the divine revelation, i.e., the law, but that has to be accompanied and complemented by the obedient fulfillment of the single commandments of the Torah.[222] For Paul, the law is overshadowed by the new, immediate, and greater divine revelation, and therefore faith is detached from the law and bound to this other object, to Christ.[223]

---

[215] For instance, πιστεύειν εἰς Χριστόν, πίστις Ἰησοῦ Χριστοῦ etc. (W. Mundle 1932, 73). Even the term πιστεύειν ἐπί and the absolute use of πίστις and πιστεύειν turn out to be identical in meaning (92f.).

[216] W. Mundle 1932, 81. Baptism is "[das] selbstverständliche Kennzeichen des Christseins" (89).

[217] W. Mundle 1932, 79, 81-86, 90, 110. Faith is a decision that is followed by the "schwerwiegendsten praktischen Folgerungen" (30). Disregard or rejection of this fact leads to a modern, individualistic concept of faith (84). Since faith does not exist apart from the affiliation to the church, the Pauline "by faith alone" also contains the *extra ecclesiam nulla salus* (103; cf. 111).

[218] W. Mundle 1932, 79f.n.1, 83, 89, 92, 94, 97; cf. 30; 1923, 69: "[D]er Glaube [ist] für Paulus zur umfassendsten Bezeichnung für das Christentum überhaupt geworden."

[219] W. Mundle 1932, 94f. As a consequence, one can speak of a "Christianisierung der Gottesauffassung" in Paul (98). Even Abraham's faith serves as an example for the Christian faith, and one should not neglect *a priori* that for Paul Abraham possessed faith in Christ (97).

[220] W. Mundle 1932, 83, 86, 100.

[221] W. Mundle 1932, 100-102. Grace and righteousness are offered to the individual χωρὶς ἔργων, i.e., without fulfilling the law; that faith includes "immer ein gewisses Maß menschlicher Selbsttätigkeit" (101) is no contradiction to this Pauline maxim.

[222] W. Mundle 1932, 104-111. Faith is "ein Werk des Menschen neben andern" (108).

[223] The law and its correlate, works, are entirely excluded from the sphere of salvation (W. Mundle 1932, 110). This new faith, that divests Judaism from its character as religion of faith (139) and is based on the "'Faktum Jesus Christus'" cannot be explained, but merely stated as a fact (114).

Both religions tie salvation to the membership in the respective community.[224]

The correlation of faith, baptism, and membership in the community implies that all effects of baptism are considered consequences of faith, and especially that becoming a believer concurs with the entry into the communion with Christ ("Christusgemeinschaft") and with the receipt of the Spirit.[225] In baptism, the permanent state of "being in Christ" and the mediation of the Spirit are inaugurated constitutively and effectively, for all Christians.[226] Notably, Paul is not concerned about the empirical circumstances and subjective experiences that accompany the transformation of the believer into the καινὴ κτίσις, but to him the objectivity of the sacramental event and the reality of the dying and rising with Christ are decisive.[227] With the new creation, justification coincides – it is one single act.

---

[224] In Hellenistic religiosity, faith attained only smaller significance so that it contributes much less to the understanding of the Pauline concept of faith than Judaism (W. Mundle 1932, 111).

[225] This observation prevents the separation of justification by faith and sacramental community with Christ as two juxtaposed and unconnected circles of Paul's thought, the one juridical-objective, the other ethical-mystical. Faith that only accepts the kerygma and is not followed by the entrance into the sphere of salvation ἐν Χριστῷ through baptism is not justifying faith (W. Mundle 1932, 133). – Those utterances seem to modify what Mundle said in his earlier work. There he did not suggest the interchangeability of "being a believer" and "being in Christ," but considered faith and mysticism as two poles that stand side by side and that complete and condition each other (1923, 80): Faith is the foundation and Christ-mysticism "Höhepunkt und Ziel der paulinischen Frömmigkeit" (71).

[226] W. Mundle 1932, 114f., 123f., 127, 129f., 134. The assumption that for Paul baptism has only minor importance, since for him the beginning of his communion with Christ originated with his Damascus experience is exegetically not verifiable (118). For, according to Paul, the entire life of every Christian takes place "in Christ" – the communion with Christ is not limited to some ecstatic moments in the life of a few people with extraordinary pneumatical gifts (120f.). Paul regards his encounter with Christ before Damascus as exception and bases on it his authority as apostle; yet without exception all Christians are "in Christ" and possess the Spirit since baptism. Pneumatical experiences and charismata are not condition, but consequence of the receipt of the Spirit (123, cf. 152, 155); the subjective side of the communion with Christ is nothing else than a reflex that originates from an objective fact (154).

[227] W. Mundle 1932, 126f., 131f.; cf. 155, 159f. A separation between objective-historical (death and resurrection) and subjective-mystical (faith and communion with Christ) statements misses Paul's point (132; cf. 154). Consequently, Christians are not merely declared righteous, but factually made righteous and sacramentally created as new creation that is dead to sin (135). By that, the eschatological character of justification is not void, but God's acquittal will reveal what is already given to the Christians in baptism (136f.). Likewise, eschatology will bestow to the Christian the full realization of what is already granted through the sacramental communion with Christ and the gift of the Spirit (168f.).

From all this follows that baptism moves into the center of the Pauline "Rechtfertigungsglauben," of his entire religiosity.[228]

Whereas faith in its aorist function (πιστεῦσαι) signifies becoming a Christian, the present (πιστεύειν) denotes and implies the following, all identical, aspects: persevering and remaining in the sacramental state that began with baptism, being a Christian, a believer, standing and acting ἐν Χριστῷ ('Ιησοῦ), ἐν κυρίῳ, in the sphere of Christ, i.e., in the Christian community, living in the Spirit.[229] Only in this comprehensive sense, Paul understands faith as *fides iustificans*[230]; and since in the Pauline conception of faith, a sociological element resonates, love becomes its first and most prominent expression, love towards the other members of the σῶμα Χριστοῦ.[231]

Mundle's presuppositions are not free from influences of liberal theology and are dependent on a particular concept of anthropology,[232] which is dominated by a firm subject-object scheme: the believer and Christ, the believer and the community. Also, his results are partly due to rather idiosyncratic lines of thought – especially his connection of Paul with "Early Catholicism."[233] R. Bultmann especially took offense at Mundle's concession that faith includes a certain degree of human "Selbsttätigkeit."[234] As we will see in the subsequent chapter, Bultmann himself circumvented a like notion by distinguishing between "Tat" and "Werk," arguing that the central aspect of faith, obedience, is to be considered as act, not as work.

---

[228] W. Mundle 1932, 135, 137; cf. 156f. The central significance of baptism warrants that the religious existence ἐν Χριστῷ comprises community and individual alike (158).

[229] W. Mundle 1932, 149-151. Paul uses the expressions ἐν Χριστῷ ('Ιησοῦ), ἐν κυρίῳ due to the lack of a term for "Christian." "Gläubigsein und In-Christus-Sein [sind] Wechselbegriffe" (150); "Christsein und In-Christus-Sein [fallen] zusammen" (152).

[230] W. Mundle 1932, 156f.

[231] W. Mundle 1932, 152 with n.1, 162. "Die Liebe ist ... für den Apostel die Betätigung der sakramentalen Gottes-, Christus- und Glaubensgemeinschaft" (160).

[232] Cf. also F. Neugebauer 1961, 153.

[233] See especially W. Mundle 1932, 171-180; cf. 21, 22, 34n.1, 48f., 103, 110, 139. Cf. O. Merk 1977, ix-x.

[234] R. Bultmann 1958, 283f.; 1959, 221n.336.

E. Faith and Obedience

I. R. Bultmann, Theologie des Neuen Testamentes *(1953, ³1958);*
Art. "πιστεύω κτλ." (1959)²³⁵

1. Introduction

R. Bultmann's comments on the Pauline concept of faith can be compared
to A. Schlatter's in regard to their historical-philological accuracy, systematic consistency, and preciseness of formulation.[236] Structurally, Bultmann
places Paul's exposition of faith in the framework of the common Christian concept of faith (which includes the specifically Christian usage) and
demonstrates both his agreement and separation from Judaism (the accent
on the "no longer"), as well as his demarcation from Gnosticism (the emphasis on the "not yet").[237]

Whereas scholarship of the previous decades, especially around the turn
of the 20th century, emphasized that Paul's focus was the "community
with Christ," Bultmann replaces this by the term ὑπακοή.[238] Compared to
Schlatter, who made "repentance" the governing structural element of his
interpretation, Bultmann places the aspect "obedient decision" in the center; yet the structure of his approach remains closely related to Schlatter's,
despite the divergent terminology.[239] Bultmann's dependence on and connection to existential philosophy[240] in his interpretation of Paul shines
through in his arranging the concept πίστις into "the structure of πίστις"

---

[235] As regards their substance, the presentations in the dictionary entry and in
Bultmann's Theology correspond almost entirely. There are a few structural differences:
In the dictionary, most of the passages in which πίστις denotes an independent entity,
principle or norm are treated among the presuppositions for the Pauline concept of faith,
while in his Theology they appear within the framework of the Pauline concept of faith
under the heading "Die πίστις als eschatologisches Geschehen" (cf. F. Neugebauer 1961,
157f.). Moreover, in the dictionary Bultmann develops his understanding of πίστις as
"obedience" to a greater degree from the notion of confession (this is the structure that is
adapted in the following presentation of Bultmann's view).

[236] Cf. P. Stuhlmacher 1982, viii.

[237] R. Bultmann 1958, 323, 325; 1959, 217, 223f.

[238] Bultmann does not think of faith as a personal relationship to Christ (1958, 93; cf.
F. Neugebauer 1961, 157).

[239] Cf. D. Lührmann 1976, 55.

[240] E. Fuchs though points to the place where Bultmann's and Heidegger's ways part,
namely their specific conception of the nature of the Christian faith: "Auch Heidegger
sah, daß zur menschlichen Existenz Glaube gehört. Aber er wehrte sich gegen den christlichen Glauben, weil dieser als 'Überzeugung' konzipiert wurde, die er selber nicht teile.
Für Bultmann dagegen war der christliche Glaube jedenfalls bei Paulus so etwas wie
Entscheidung" (1977, 74).

(obedience, confession, hope, fear, trust) and "the life in πίστις"[241]: It equals a distinction between "das Existentiale" and "das Existentielle," or, between the ontological and the ontical.[242] This existential-philosophical approach also implies that Bultmann describes πίστις principally in anthropological terms.

Bultmann's history-of-religions classification of the term πίστις follows that of R. Reitzenstein: Πίστις became a catchword in religions engaged in propaganda.[243]

2. Becoming a Believer

Paul, who put the concept of πίστις in the center of theology,[244] conceived of faith both as the act of coming to believe and the state of believing, the receipt of the gift of the δικαιοσύνη θεοῦ and the actualization of the divine act of salvation in the individual.[245]

Firstly, πίστις is the acceptance of the Christian kerygma and consequently always "faith in ...,"[246] i.e., it is the confession (ὁμολογία) of the message that there is one God, and at the same time of the message of Jesus Christ. This usage explains itself from the fact that the employed terminology derives from the context of missions.[247] Through his death and resurrection, Christ became the κύριος, and so it is intrinsic to the Christian faith that Jesus is acknowledged as Lord and that the miracle of his resur-

---

[241] This arrangement is used only in his Theology.

[242] Cf. F. Neugebauer 1961, 159, referring to M. Heidegger 1927, 12-15. From a formal point of view, E. Lohmeyer's distinction of "principle" and "deed" of faith correlates to Bultmann's partition into the "structure of" and the "life in" faith, but as regards content, it is Bultmann's category of πίστις as "eschatological event" that equals Lohmeyer's idea of "principle."

[243] R. Bultmann 1959, 180. In classical Greek, the πιστ-stem had not acquired religious connotations, but nevertheless, there are first beginnings ("Ansätze") to such religious use (179). – D.R. Lindsay considers these "first beginnings" decisive for the development of the use of πιστεύειν as a theological term (1993, 106; see below chapter II.G.VII). Cf. also G. Schunack 1999, 296 (see below chapter II.G.VIII).

[244] R. Bultmann 1959, 218.

[245] R. Bultmann 1958, 315.

[246] R. Bultmann 1927a, 89; 1958, 318. The acceptance of the kerygma is the actual "Heilsglaube" (1959, 209).

[247] Cf. R. Bultmann 1958, 315; 1959, 200. In the language of mission, therefore, the usage πιστεύειν εἰς (and πίστις εἰς) corresponds with πιστεύειν ὅτι, because the preposition εἰς refers factually – as abbreviation (1958, 91-93) – to the content of the kerygma, which the corresponding expression πιστεύειν ὅτι gives more fully. Instead of the prepositional phrase, a *genitivus objectivus* can be connected with πίστις (πίστις Χριστοῦ). Even in the absolute usage of πίστις and πιστεύειν, the object of faith, the event of salvation accomplished in Christ through God, remains present, for Paul always has in view the totality (R. Bultmann 1959, 204, 210f.).

ism of ἐν πίστει, ἐν κυρίῳ, and ἐν χάριτι. With πίστις, the eschatological time has come,[281] which is, as possibility, the newly disclosed way of salvation.[282]

Yet the eschatological attitude may not be misapprehended as eschatological fulfillment, because the believer remains rooted in temporality, struggles continuously for perfection, and does not own salvation as disposable possession, but hopes with a sure hope, with the knowledge of the new existence that nobody who believes will be put to shame.[283] The presence of the δικαιοσύνη is an eschatological one, which is why it always stands before the believer, the righteous, as yet to come.[284] Notably, however, even in the eschatological fulfillment, in the state of εἶδος, πίστις will abide.

Faith is connected to the past – to what God has done in Christ, and to the future – to what God will do, and both, past and future, are united, as God's act in the past has eschatological character and determines the whole future. The radical committal to the grace of God, however, implies the renunciation of any control and will to possess, both of the old own being and of the new eschatological existence[285]: This is the "not yet" of the historical life from which the person cannot escape; yet there is an "already" from Christ's perspective, a καταλημφθῆναι ὑπὸ Χριστοῦ Ἰησοῦ.[286]

The individual decision of faith is itself an eschatological event. The decision remains the believer's decision, even if its possibility and thus the decision itself are a gift of grace. Paul's predestinational utterances therefore may not be taken in their literal sense: It would not be true obedience, if faith was produced by God outside of the person, but nonetheless faith is effected by God, as his prevenient grace opened the possibility for a decision. Those Pauline statements therefore (merely) express that the decision is not based on inner-worldly motives.[287]

---

[281] R. Bultmann 1959, 222. As an attitude that constitutes the eschatological existence of the Christian, πίστις governs the life totally. Hence, the absolute usage of πίστις becomes dominant and "faith" receives a wider definition: "Glaube [wird] zur schlechthinnigen Bezeichnung der Religion" (217).

[282] R. Bultmann 1958, 330. This salvation-historical notion does not take away from the character of πίστις as decision, for even though the believer experiences the possibility for a decision as grace and therefore the decision itself as gift of grace, it remains the believer's decision, and as such the individual decision of faith is an eschatological event.

[283] R. Bultmann 1958, 321; 1959, 217.

[284] R. Bultmann 1958, 320.

[285] Cf. R. Bultmann 1940, 43: "Wo der Mensch nichts ist, da ist die Gnade Gottes mächtig."

[286] R. Bultmann 1958, 323; 1959, 225.

[287] R. Bultmann 1958, 330f.

5. Critique

Bultmann's method that leads him to the definition of faith as first and foremost obedience has to be challenged for linguistic reasons, since he presupposes one aspect of faith to be determinative for the entire concept, making the notion of obedience the overall *scopos* of the Pauline faith without giving due respect to the respective context[288]; he has to proceed that way, because the Pauline proof texts for his thesis are rare. Especially, one has to ask, if Bultmann's decisive phrase ὑπακοὴ πίστεως supports his view – for, the connection of the terms πίστις and ὑπακοή could equally imply that Paul did not understand faith primarily as obedience.[289]

Bultmann's principally anthropological description of πίστις leads to the fact that the paragraph on the character of πίστις as eschatological event is attached like an "erratic block,"[290] in which Bultmann struggles with the contradicting correlation between "eschatological event" and "decision."[291] Rather than Pauline anthropology, the existential analysis of M. Heidegger[292] stands in the background of his assertion that faith, effected outside of the person, could not be true obedience. The classification "true obedience" is based on the question of the human self-understanding that governs Bultmann's argumentation and possibly produces wrong alternatives by determining God's deed and the human deed through a paradoxical identification.[293]

It is precisely the salvation-historical dimension of faith that has inspired other exegetes – partly openly criticizing Bultmann – to look at the Pauline πίστις from a different angle than the principally anthropological. Their studies will occupy us in the following.

---

[288] Approaches like this one have been criticized by J. Barr, E. Nida, or J.P. Louw (cf. J.E. Botha 1987, who also argues – curiously without referring to Bultmann – that for πιστεύειν the meaning "'to obey' could not be validated in the New Testament," 236).

[289] Cf. F. Neugebauer 1961, 158.

[290] F. Neugebauer 1961, 160. "Insofern ärgert sich der hermeneutische Ansatz Bultmanns de facto an den Texten, weil er sich de jure daran ärgern muß" (166n.55). Cf. W. Schenk 1972, 163.

[291] R. Bultmann 1958, 330f. Especially the problem of the relationship between the predestination statements of Paul and Bultmann's accent on faith as obedience remains unsolved at the end: Under the presupposition that faith is "true obedience," Bultmann has to interpret the pertinent Pauline assertions against their literal meaning with the help of the assumption that the prevenient grace merely enables human decision, but does not invalidate it. Thus, eventually, Bultmann's scheme cannot master all Pauline statements, and he has to suppose contradictions where Paul did not see any.

[292] Cf. the structural analogy between Bultmann's "Entscheidung" and Heidegger's "Entschlossenheit" (cf. M. Heidegger 1927, 297f.).

[293] Cf. F. Neugebauer 1961, 52f.n.45, 167.

F. Faith As Salvation-Historical Event

I. R. Gyllenberg, "Glaube bei Paulus" (1936)[294]

In this essay, R. Gyllenberg summarizes and develops some theses that he first expressed in his two-volume work *Pistis* from 1922 (in Swedish), in which he suggested in essential agreement with W. Wrede that the Pauline doctrine of justification is a special case of his doctrine of redemption and that faith is the pneumatical recognition of justification.[295]

Gyllenberg suggests that from a linguistic-historical perspective, πίστις and אֱמוּנָה represent as religious terms two entirely different spheres of language, the Hellenistic and the Old Testament. Though both Paul and Philo found πίστις in the Septuagint, Paul follows closely the Old Testament conception, governed by its dynamic-dramatic thinking and its focus on community, while Philo understands πίστις in Hellenistic terms, i.e., individualistic-mystical and static.[296] Logic and reflection rule Philo's philosophy, while Paul proclaims the kerygma within God's history and calls for a decision. Since Scripture is a testimony of divine revelation in history, Paul employs the proof from Scripture for any significant doctrine in order to demonstrate its place in the dynamic stream of historical life.[297] Therefore, Paul's doctrine of justification can be regarded as proof from Scripture of his doctrine of redemption; those two aspects of Pauline theology do not represent two unrelated, originally autonomous systems of thought, but two intrinsic parts of his total perception.[298]

Coming from the Old Testament world of thought, in which receptivity and activity, the subjective and objective, are coupled, Paul considers his proclamation a real event, not a declaration of facts, and the hearing of the kerygma a real hearing, not an intellectualistic recognition of facts; hence, faith is entering into the new community with God.[299] The human πίστις,

---

[294] See also R. Gyllenberg 1937.

[295] R. Gyllenberg 1936, 614f. "Christ sein heißt bei Paulus Pneumatiker sein und in Christusverbundenheit leben." Primarily, this pneumatical aspect distinguishes Gyllenberg's approach from W. Mundle's, who develops a more sober ("nüchtern") interpretation of the Pauline concept of faith.

[296] R. Gyllenberg 1936, 619, 623.

[297] "Der Schriftbeweis ist bei ihm [*sc.* Paulus] gar nicht nur totes rabbinisches Beiwerk, sondern ganz im Gegenteil das Lebendigste von allem, das Zeugnis seiner geschichtlich-dynamischen Auffassung der Wirklichkeit" (R. Gyllenberg 1936, 625).

[298] R. Gyllenberg 1936, 624. "Sie [*sc.* die Rechtfertigungslehre] ist, so könnte man beinahe sagen, die Geschichtsphilosophie des Apostels" (626). This terminology shows resemblances to E. Lohmeyer's philosophical interpretation of Paul's doctrine of faith and justification.

[299] R. Gyllenberg 1936, 624, 626f.

consisting in obedience and trust, corresponds to God's call (κλῆσις) into his community.[300]

II. E. Lohmeyer, *Grundlagen paulinischer Theologie (1929)*

In his analysis of the phenomenon of the Pauline faith, E. Lohmeyer developed an original, unique approach that lacks precursors for the most part. Only his point of departure, i.e., Judaism, and the consistency with which he describes Paul's concept of πίστις on the background of Judaism, joins him with A. Schlatter.[301]

Lohmeyer starts from a consideration, which in his opinion has not been reflected adequately in New Testament scholarship, namely, that despite, or rather amid, the unsystematic vigor of Paul's thinking there is one problem that confers direction and unity to his life and work: It is the problem of possibility and reality of religious revelation on the whole. Revelation is possible if it establishes metaphysically an absolute conflict between the truth of the divine work and the reality of human truth; it is constitutively eschatological in character.[302] The concept of revelation only knows the fundamental distance from the conditions of historical life; it is without "home." But it seeks and creates a new "home" in history. Paul's life and work correspond to this process: He becomes "homeless" and through his missionary work seeks a new "home," replacing the accustomed and irreversibly lost one. Consequently, Paul is concerned with the foundation of his own and everybody's existence, not so much with religious experience.[303] His theme, which is set to him due to the short "dark break" between Christ's resurrection and Parousia,[304] is the divine truth, the reli-

---

[300] Obedience cannot be separated from trust ("Vertrauen") or even intimacy ("Vertraulichkeit"), because in the holistic perception of the Old Testament real obedience cannot happen without inner association to the one who commands (R. Gyllenberg 1936, 628). The obedience and intimacy grow continually, since the communion with Christ is a personal ("personhaft") and mystical-natural ("naturhaft") communion. – By contrast, R. Bultmann's exposition on the Pauline faith presupposes a clear distinction of obedience and trust, whereby the notion of obedience possesses obvious prevalence.

[301] Lohmeyer frequently stresses "die Gebundenheit paulinischen Denkens an die unveräußerlichen Fundamente jüdischen Glaubens und jüdischen Volkes" (1929, 124; cf. 119, 128, 130, 133, 141, 151f., 231).

[302] E. Lohmeyer 1929, 228. "Möglich ist Offenbarung, wenn sie einen absoluten Gegensatz zwischen der Wahrheit göttlichen Wirkens und der Wirklichkeit menschlicher Wahrheit metaphysisch setzt..."

[303] E. Lohmeyer 1929, 229.

[304] This "dark space" between resurrection and Parousia is to be filled by a mediation, which for Paul can only consist "through Christ," though it is not yet Christ himself. Paul has an abundance of names for the divine forces that exist through Christ and possess this mediating function: gospel and word, Spirit and power, community and faith (E. Lohmeyer 1929, 65, 113, 122f., 125 [faith stands "zwischen den Zeiten"]). They all have in

gious objectivity, or the metaphysical determination[305] and less importantly
the religious subjectivity. Hence, the concept of faith expresses (primarily)
divine operation and (secondarily) human work; it has an eschatological
orientation to the Day of Christ.[306] As Lohmeyer contends, the distinction
of general possibility and reality of the divine revelation in history and the
concrete deed of the person, comes to expression in the Pauline phrase ἐκ
πίστεως εἰς πίστιν, whereby ἐκ πίστεως denotes the principle and εἰς
πίστιν the deed.[307] Elsewhere, Paul expressed the double character of faith
through a terminological distinction: The first he calls πίστις Χριστοῦ,[308]
the latter πιστεύειν εἰς Χριστόν.[309]

---

common that they are established by God. Their unique relationship to the law is marked
by the fact that they, like the law, have their possibility and reality only through Christ,
so that all stand on the same level and bear the same functions. Christ is the principle that
creates unity amidst all conflicts. "[E]r ist des Gesetzes Ende und des Glaubens Anfang,
weil er beider Erfüllung ist" (123; cf. 128f., 143). "Deshalb kann von Geist und Glaube,
Wort und Evangelium nur geredet werden, weil durch sie auch vom Gesetz geredet wird;
deshalb aber auch vom Gesetz nur, weil mit ihm jene anderen Mächte gegeben sind"
(114; cf. 123, 154f.). Describing the function of Christ in regard to the law, Lohmeyer
employs and plays with the double meaning of the word "aufheben": The law's final
realities are given and preserved through Christ, but at the same time eliminated, i.e.,
ripened to a new creation; the law is fulfilled as religious revelation, but terminated as
historical entity (64).

[305] Cf., e.g., E. Lohmeyer 1929, 116-118, 121f., 125, 127, 137f., 154.

[306] According to this structure, Lohmeyer develops the main aspects of his description
of Paul's concept of faith: "Glaube als Prinzip" (E. Lohmeyer 1929, 115-125), "Glaube
als Tat" (125-133), and "Doppelheit des Glaubensbegriffes" (146-153). – On the description of "faith" as "principle," see already F.C. Baur 1867, 133, but also A. Schlatter
1927, 374; H. Schlier 1965, 167: "Der Glaube ist das Mittel (als solche auch das Prinzip)
des Heils, Christus aber sein Grund"; R.B. Hays 1983, 155.

[307] E. Lohmeyer 1929, 119, 126.

[308] Πίστις Χριστοῦ "ist nicht nur der Glaube, den Christus *hat*, auch nicht nur der,
den er *gibt*, sondern vor allem der Glaube, der er selber *ist* ... Er ist also im gleichen
Sinne Offenbarung, wie Christus es ist" (E. Lohmeyer 1929, 121 [Lohmeyer's emphasis];
cf. 1929a, 74). Though faith is mediated through Christ, it is ultimately God's gift, since
both, faith and Christ, derive from God's revelatory act. Thus, faith is identical with
Christ, but simultaneously distinct or under him, since faith relates insolubly to the existence in time and world.

[309] The double orientation of faith reveals a historical parallelism to the religious origin of Paul: With his double concept of faith, Paul creates a contrast to the Jewish ideas
of work and law: Faith opposes as historical experience to work, and as metaphysical fact
to the law (E. Lohmeyer 1929, 119). The conceptual relationship to and contrast with the
law counter an understanding of faith in terms of mystical experience (122; cf. 142f.:
There is no Jewish "law-mysticism"). Also the formula ἐν Χριστῷ disproves a mystical
view of the believing existence; "so meint sie [*sc.* die Formel] niemals jene Einheit, in
die das gläubige Ich aus seinen empirischen Grenzen entrückt wäre" (140). Rather, like
faith, even this expression embraces both, closeness to Christ and historically determined
distance to him. Ἐν Χριστῷ is the transformation of the inherited Jewish formula ἐν

Therefore, on the one hand, faith appears as an objectively established and transcendent power that stands outside of the unstable circumstances of history in timeless imperturbability. In this objectivation, it becomes – in Aristotelian terms – the *forma substantialis*, which molds the matter, and the individual becomes the substrate, in whom the common essence of faith becomes visible.[310]

On the other hand, the metaphysics of faith seeks its "home" in history, and it is bound to the free deed of the individual.[311] The aspects of the believing experience include the knowledge and understanding of the religious-objective fact that has been established in Christ, which, in Paul's thinking, cannot be thought of outside of moral norms and the morally acting person.[312] Obedience characterizes the life of the believer as the only attitude a historically bound individual can assume in the face of a divine revelation. For this reason, the believer is forced to represent paradigmatically before the world what God intended for the world through his revelation. The believer thus stands between God and the world. From this fact, the motivation to missions and the desire to martyrdom arise.[313]

The impreciseness and double perspective of the Pauline concept of faith embrace different theological angles. Pelagian and Augustinian, Catholic and Protestant motives are placed side by side and intermingled in peaceful agreement.[314]

What has been criticized the most in Lohmeyer's exposition of faith is his (sometimes inadequate) use of modern-philosophical categories, especially the terms "principle" and "metaphysics," or the application of the Aristotelian idea *forma substantialis* to πίστις.[315] Indeed, one has to question if those categories are capable of elucidating the Pauline statements

---

νόμῳ and thus confirms the deep relationship that connects Christ and the law (see above note 304).

[310] E. Lohmeyer 1929, 117, 127. "Man könnte scharf sagen: nicht ich glaube, sondern es glaubt in mir" (118); "das Ich ist kaum mehr als ein Schauplatz, auf dem göttliche Mächte ihr Werk und Wesen treiben" (147; cf. 1930, 88: Humans are "Schauplatz" of the powers of sin and law).

[311] E. Lohmeyer 1929, 137. Analogically to the double direction of faith, Lohmeyer describes sin as deed, for which the individual is accountable, and at the same time as ontological effect of a metaphysical power. Through the metaphysical principle of faith, however, the metaphysical power of sin is principally broken.

[312] E. Lohmeyer 1929, 126f. "So wird denn aber auch Erkennen und Gehorchen zu einer unlöslichen Korrelativbeziehung" (127).

[313] Lohmeyer attributes an eminent meaning to martyrdom, because there the principle and deed of faith are united (cf. E. Lohmeyer 1927).

[314] E. Lohmeyer 1929, 139.

[315] Cf., e.g., W. Mundle 1932, 2; F. Neugebauer 1961, 156: "Man muß Lohmeyer hier besser verstehen, als er sich ausgedrückt hat." – Notably, H.-J. Schoeps calls Paul's theology "Christusmetaphysik" (1959, 108).

properly. Due to Lohmeyer's peculiar terminology, his line of thought appears opaque and obscure at times,[316] even thought it contains valuable insights.

III. H. Binder, Der Glaube bei Paulus (1968)[317]

Being convinced that the comprehensive understanding of the Pauline concept of faith would greatly advance theological studies in general, H. Binder attempts to determine – against the flow of current exegesis[318] – what Paul meant with πίστις, this most crucial term of Pauline theology.[319] In fact, since (according to Binder) our idea of faith is de-christianized, the attainment of a proper conception of faith from the New Testament is the foremost duty of theologians and has far-reaching consequences.[320]

Binder opposes primarily the anthropological-individualized description of faith of R. Bultmann,[321] which governs the current discussion. Yet he also observes a shift in some representatives of more recent theology, for instance in G. Ebeling who coins the term "Wortgeschehen" or in E. Käsemann[322] who works out the character of God's righteousness as powerful force. This change, away from anthropocentrism towards the objective event-character, is analogous to Binder's own new interpretation of πίστις, for word, righteousness, and faith are all correlates of the Christ-event.[323] O. Cullmann's emphasis on the salvation-historical dimension in Paul's theology[324] played a significant role in the development of Binder's

---

[316] Cf. W. Mundle 1932, 2.

[317] Binder had put forward his view in a summarized form in a study, which appeared in an unpublished Festschrift for F. Müller in 1954.

[318] In Binder's analysis, the prevailing position considers the Hellenistic understanding of πίστις to be decisive for Paul (cf. H. Binder 1968, 39, 46f., 51, 74, 78 – notably, Paul himself, has been shaped by Hellenistic influences, which shines through especially in Romans [cf. 47, 77]; the use of πίστις with personal pronoun in 1Thessalonians points to the co-authorship of Silvanus [cf. 47n.31, 69, 81]).

[319] H. Binder 1968, 5, 11. Even the numerous appearances of the term πίστις in Paul demonstrates "daß Paulus mit dem Wort *pistis* die für ihn wichtigste theologische Aussage hat machen wollen" (79).

[320] H. Binder 1968, 9, 78, 108.

[321] Cf. especially "Anhang: Die Interpretation des paulinischen Glaubensbegriffes bei Bultmann" (H. Binder 1968, 83-108).

[322] Cf. E. Käsemann 1961, 183 *et passim*. See also the important observation in W. Schenk 1972, 163: "Hier [*sc.* in Binders These] hat für das Gebiet des paulinischen Glaubensbegriffes dieselbe Phasenverschiebung stattgefunden wie hinsichtlich des Gerechtigkeitsbegriffs in der Käsemann-Schule." See however Käsemann's reproach against Binder's thesis: "absurde[.] Vereinseitigung" (1980, 103). – R.B. Hays wants to utilize this shift as support of his view of the πίστις Χριστοῦ question (1983, 147).

[323] H. Binder 1968, 5.

[324] See for instance O. Cullmann 1965.

view[325]; furthermore, he incorporates insights of A. Seeberg,[326] E. Loh-meyer,[327] and P. Stuhlmacher,[328] but gives his own thesis a remarkable peak.[329]

In modern times, the term "faith" is filled with an entirely different meaning than for Paul[330]: Contrary to Paul, the modern usage perceives faith not as a genuinely Christian, not even religious word ("Rela-tivierung")[331] and views faith as psychological phenomenon and thus ad-vocates an anthropocentric and individualistic perspective ("Psychologis-ierung"),[332] and consequently sets the person as subject and God or the divine as content, point of reference, or object of the human faith ("Objek-tivierung").[333]

The named three characteristics are eventually conditioned by the sub-ject-object-scheme that governs the Greek thinking; thus, one cannot draw lines of connection from the Greek speech tradition to Paul.[334] Against that, Paul's development of his concept of faith from the exegesis of Hab 2:4 proves his connection to and continuity with the Old Testament think-ing, its emphasis on covenant and the experience of historicity (– features

---

[325] Cf. F. Hahn/H. Klein 1982, 6.

[326] Cf. A. Seeberg 1966, 165: Πίστις is not a function of the individual, but "Tat-bestand der Heilsannahme."

[327] Binder himself does not recognize Lohmeyer as precursor of his thesis despite the close analogies (cf. H. Binder 1968, 12f.: Lohmeyer is classified among those theologi-ans that regard faith as common psychological disposition). This fact surprises, even if one assumes that Binder did not have Lohmeyer's work at his disposal (thus W. Schenk 1972, 163 with n.12): For, Binder is well aware of F. Neugebauer's book, which portrays Lohmeyer's basic points in due breadth. As for Neugebauer's interpretation, which also seeks to overcome Bultmann's anthropocentrism, Binder still finds there an individuali-zation and psychologization of πίστις (1968, 43n.19).

[328] On the basis of Käsemann's thesis that all theological concepts in Paul denote both power and gift, Stuhlmacher describes faith as "überindividuelle[s] Gesamtphänomen," as new salvation-historical reality (1966, 81f., quote: 81); yet Stuhlmacher's assertion that eventually it is the matter of the individual to enter this reality (83n.1), demonstrates to Binder his adherence to the individualized perspective (cf. H. Binder 1968, 57n.17)

[329] Cf. G. Friedrich 1982, 97f.

[330] According to Binder, Paul never uses πίστις in a verbal sense, which is also con-trary to the modern usage: "'Der Glaube' ist für uns gedanklich-abstrakte Zusammenfas-sung der Tätigkeit 'glauben'" (1968, 11; cf. 29, 63, 71; also D.A. Campbell 2005, 182).

[331] H. Binder 1968, 14f. As a result, Christianity is described merely as *one* possibility of faith beside others.

[332] H. Binder 1968, 15-20.

[333] H. Binder 1968, 20-28, 29f. 73, 80f. Reformation theology could not defeat the factual anthropocentrism, neither through its theocentric re-orientation nor through its reversal of the subject-object-scheme, not even through its designating the believing subject as *punctum mathematicum* (21).

[334] H. Binder 1968, 30.

that receded into the background in Second Temple Judaism).[335] Thus, Paul was the first to describe, on the basis of the Old Testament, the Christian God-relationship with the term πίστις, independent from Hellenism, Judaism, the Christian communities, and Jesus' proclamation.[336]

Paul determines faith not as dogmatic or cultic entity, nor as idea beyond historicity, but as event that involves both God and humans, as salvation-historical power, which has not always existed,[337] but breaks with the Christ-event into the course of God's history at a certain καιρός[338] and remains until the Eschaton. It is to be described as a trans-subjective, extra-personal reality,[339] a divine work,[340] a sphere with measurable extension,[341] a "geschichtlich-heilsgeschichtliche" entity,[342] which sets off a new epoch of salvation history: the New Covenant.[343] The category of Paul's thinking is temporal-dynamic-historical, not spatial-static-unhistorical.[344] Since the characteristics of the expression ἐν Χριστῷ basically coincide with the

---

[335] H. Binder 1968, 33f., 59.

[336] H. Binder 1968, 35-38. "Die Urgemeinde hat Jesus 'nachpaulinisch' vom Glauben reden lassen, weil sie selbst nachpaulinisch redete" (38). Also in John and James the Greek-Hellenistic thinking prevails (30f.).

[337] In Old Testament times, πίστις had not appeared yet, but had been announced and promised (H. Binder 1968, 39); this does not exclude, however, that πίστις can occur in advance, so that Abraham could encounter it and become, as it were, a pre-existent member of the ἐκκλησία (not an example of pre-Christian faith) (42, following F. Neugebauer 1961, 168f.).

[338] The event of the cross was constitutive for the coming of πίστις, as it brought the end to the salvation-historical era of the law. This implies, however, that πίστις existed before the resurrection and thus represents for Paul the "Realgrund wie der eschatologischen Güter im allgemeinen, so auch der Auferweckung Jesu" (H. Binder 1968, 46, cf. 82) – accordingly, against the *opinio communis*, Jesus' resurrection does not mediate faith and instigate the Christian proclamation, but is itself consequence of πίστις (47-49).

[339] H. Binder 1968, 40, 48f., 56, 68, 70, 82. "Sie [*sc.* πίστις] existiert ohne jegliche menschliche Bezogenheit zu ihr [cf. 71]. Sie ist eine göttliche Geschehenswirklichkeit, eine *transsubjektive* Größe [...] Bei der Interpretation des paulinischen Glaubensbegriffes liegt alles am Erfassen dieser Transsubjektivität oder Übersubjektivität" (53).

[340] H. Binder 1968, 55, 59, 64, 81f. God is the actual *auctor* or subject of πίστις, so that it is misleading to describe faith as directed to God – rather, faith originates and comes from God.

[341] H. Binder 1968, 56f., 72.

[342] H. Binder 1968, 53.

[343] H. Binder 1968, 49, 59, 79. Πίστις is "eine erfülltere Heilsgestalt," a better one than the one represented by the Old Testament (41f., 49, 52), though one day it will be replaced by the "erfüllteste[.] heilsgeschichtliche[.] Epoche" (52). The Pauline term καταλλαγή conveys this idea of a universal change of the reality of salvation, "ein Austausch von 'Heilsgestalten'" (79f.).

[344] H. Binder 1968, 21, 26, 30, 39, 60, 62, 69. Cf. already R. Gyllenberg 1936, 625 ("geschichtlich-dynamisch[.]"); F. Neugebauer 1961, 41 ("dynamisch-zeitlich-geschichtlich[.]").

notion of space of the πίστις-concept, it would appear that both phrases represent the same sphere: (Standing) ἐν πίστει and (standing) ἐν Χριστῷ are synonymous.[345] The sphere of πίστις, however, only becomes concrete, visible, historically tangible, if it is filled with people, the members of the ἐκκλησία, through their act of joining the realm of πίστις (which practically concurs with baptism).[346] This joining (cf. the aorist ἐπίστευσεν) is made possible by the self-declaration of πίστις in the proclamation of the preachers who are put into service by πίστις itself.[347] Therefore, Paul does not know of a temporal precedence of the word over faith; the word only precedes the continual human activity within the πίστις-sphere (cf. the present tense πιστεύειν).[348] There, the person stands under the authority and the driving force of πίστις and is not merely spectator, but actor, participating and being involved in the divine work of πίστις and its dynamic progression.[349] The individual is drawn into the process, not as "instrument" or "object," but as co-working "Untersubjekt" that is instituted into the "Übersubjekt."[350] With faith, God grants a new existence, which is accompanied by further (objective) gifts: First, the πνεῦμα that is neither received as a result of πίστις nor identical with it, but that coincides with πίστις and opens to the believer the blessings of the coming eon (ζωή, εἰρήνη, δόξα) and makes aware the fact of being in πίστις and its consequences (σωτηρία, ἐλπίς, δύναμις). Second, the divine action πίστις guarantees the anticipation and the eventual attribution of δικαιοσύνη, the positive verdict in the last judgment, which is conferred to the believers on the basis of their existential connection to Christ.[351]

Binder's justified criticism of an individualized, psychologized view of faith leads to the other extreme of an exclusively trans-individual, non-

---

[345] H. Binder 1968, 59f., 62. The genitive in the phrases πίστις τοῦ υἱοῦ τοῦ θεοῦ and πίστις Ἰησοῦ Χριστοῦ, therefore, is to be determined as *genitivus identificationis*, not as *genitivus objectivus* (61, 63).

[346] H. Binder 1968, 64f. For Paul, baptism is a "reales Hinzugetanwerden zum Gottesgeschehen (= *pistis*)" (82).

[347] H. Binder 1968, 65-67. Paul's own biographical example illustrates how he came into contact with and was appropriated by πίστις at the Damascus event (πεπίστευμαι) and how this effected his evangelistic activity among the Gentiles in the framework of the divine plan of salvation. "Der Mensch befindet sich im Verhältnis zur *pistis* gewissermaßen in einer Zwangslage" (68).

[348] H. Binder 1968, 68. This is obviously strikingly different to Reformation theology.

[349] H. Binder 1968, 68-74. "Glaube ist nicht der Griff Gottes nach dem Menschen, damit er diesen zu sich ziehe, sondern der Sturmwind Gottes, der den Menschen mitreißt an die von Gott gesetzte Aufgabe" (72). Pointedly speaking, for Paul there is no "faith in ...," but only participation in the divine event πίστις (73).

[350] H. Binder 1968, 73.

[351] H. Binder 1968, 75f. ("Existenzialzusammenhang"). "Die *pistis* ist das die *dikaiosyne* Verursachende," not the other way round (77).

subjective conception of faith. Neither view does justice to the comprehensive Pauline perspective, and both poles have their right in Paul's theology – not in terms of an antagonistic contrast, but of a harmonic interplay.

IV. W. Schenk, "Die Gerechtigkeit Gottes und der Glaube Christi" (1972)

Adapting and developing ideas of E. Lohmeyer, F. Neugebauer, and H. Binder, W. Schenk advances on the basis of the phrase ὑπακοὴ πίστεως an identification of πίστις and the message of faith, i.e., the gospel itself.[352] Consequently, πίστις can be interpreted as objective reality, which represents the early Christian proclamation.[353] Correspondingly, with regard to the expression πίστις Χριστοῦ, Schenk argues that it does not abstract the verbal understanding "to believe in...," but rather articulates in a more objective way the message of faith, whose content is Christ.[354] Insofar, figuratively speaking, the noun πίστις and the verb πιστεύειν relate to each other like the opening of a business and our entering it.[355] The interpretative presupposition that the verbal use provides the explanation for the substantival use is not adequate in Schenk's opinion,[356] because it disregards Paul's use of πίστις in the sense of an objective fact (like a Christ-event) and neglects that the noun is employed twice as much as the verb and is rarely accompanied by a personal pronoun. Thus, rather the verb should be interpreted through the noun.

In all the works portrayed until now, the question how the recipients of the Pauline letters would have understood Paul's talk of faith was implicitly or explicitly present, and at the same time the answer had been basically presupposed: Following R. Reitzenstein's thesis, supported through

---

[352] W. Schenk 1972, 165f., with reference to H. Lietzmann. This means that he analyzes the genitive construction in the sense of a *genitivus objectivus*: "obedience to the message of faith."

[353] This goes beyond the general description of πίστις as "transsubjektive, göttliche Geschehenswirklichkeit" (H. Binder) or as "metaphysisches Prinzip" (E. Lohmeyer).

[354] Schenk specifies Lohmeyer's distinctive interpretation of πίστις Χριστοῦ which says that first and foremost πίστις Χριστοῦ is the faith that Jesus *is* rather than the faith he *has* or *gives* (E. Lohmeyer 1929, 121; see above note 308): It is the gospel. "Πίστις Χριστοῦ ist das Evangelium Christi als die Anerkennung heischende Botschaft" (W. Schenk 1972, 168; cf. 170). In this case, the genitive Χριστοῦ is analyzed as *genitivus epexegeticus*. (Schenk rejects *a priori* an understanding of πίστις Χριστοῦ in terms of Christ's personal faith.) To him, the supposition that the construction πίστις Χριστοῦ represents a semantically pre-formed use is indeed probable (170). – Notably, C.H. Cosgrove arrives – though by different ways – at a similar conclusion when he understands πίστις Χριστοῦ as metonymy for Paul's gospel (1988, 57f., referred to in R.B. Hays 1997, 273f.n.4; see also D.M. Hay 1989, 473).

[355] W. Schenk 1972, 170, 171; cf. 165.

[356] Against F. Neugebauer 1961, 168n.69.

"some rashly collected examples,"[357] one regarded the term πίστις to be situated in the language of missions.[358] The intelligibility of these common assumptions is the center of interest in the studies to be presented now.

G. The Horizon of Understanding of Faith

I. D. Lührmann, "Pistis im Judentum" (1973); Glaube im frühen Christentum (1976); "Confesser sa foi à l'époque apostolique" (1985)[359]

Methodically, D. Lührmann does not – like A. Schlatter and R. Bultmann – presuppose a common Christian concept of faith that has been unfolded into various directions in the New Testament writings, but perceives the different expressions of faith as different solutions to the fundamental problem of the reconciliation between confession and experience.

As to his history-of-religions classification of πίστις, Lührmann (adopting remarks of G. Ebeling[360]), maintains in opposition to the proponents of the History-of-Religions School (R. Reitzenstein, W. Bousset) and against E. Wißmann and R. Bultmann that faith is not simply a common category in the phenomenology of religion, but belongs exclusively to the Jewish and Christian speech tradition.[361] By arguing that their proof texts either fail to mention "faith" at all or are dependent on Jewish-Christian tradition, he seeks to refute their widespread, "almost canonical" thesis of the significance of faith as technical term in those Hellenistic religions at the time of early Christianity that engaged in propaganda. The constant rendition of the stem אמן with πιστ- in the Septuagint is in Lührmann's opinion not due

---

[357] R. Reitzenstein 1927, 234 ("ein paar rasch zusammengeraffte Beispiele").

[358] G. Ebeling 1958, 82f.n.1 quotes the relevant passages of W. Bousset and R. Reitzenstein, who were followed by E. Wißmann and R. Bultmann. The following statement of Bousset is representative: "[E]rst bei der Trennung von Nation und Religion kommt das zu seinem Recht, was wir Glaube, die persönliche Überzeugung des einzelnen nennen" (1926, 145).

[359] In addition one should note Lührmann's other publications on the theme of faith (1981; 1990; 1992). Already in 1970, Lührmann contended that one has to pose the question anew: "Wie ist πίστις bei Paulus zu bestimmen?" He also indicated the direction, into which the discussion ought to proceed, namely, to identify (against P. Stuhlmacher 1970, 25f.) law and faith as the more adequate alternative to describe Pauline theology than law and gospel (D. Lührmann 1970, 440n.11, 438n.9). Cf. W. Schenk 1972, 163, 172.

[360] Cf. G. Ebeling 1958, 81-83. The exceptional significance of the term πίστις could have been *cause* rather than *consequence* of the missionary enthusiasm (82f.n.1).

[361] As to the absence of a religious usage of πιστ- in classical Greek, Lührmann claims Bultmann as witness for his opinion (cf. R. Bultmann 1959, 179), yet he neglects that even Bultmann finds "first beginnings" (1959, 179) of such use in classical Greek (cf. G. Barth 1982, 113).

to a common religious linguistic usage; rather πίστις and πιστεύειν must be conceived as semantic loan words ("Bedeutungslehnwörter"[362]), which received their content from a different, namely the Hebrew, language.[363] The religious usage of πιστ- in the New Testament was prepared decisively through the usage of Hellenistic Judaism (especially Sirach and Philo); thus, that the "central meaning [of faith] was gained … in Christianity"[364] goes back to this linguistic-historical development.

The problem that the non-religious pagan usage of πίστις and πιστεύειν would prevent their understanding in the Christian sense, Lührmann counters by his claim that in Christianity (as in Judaism) these terms were *not* located in the language of mission, but in the internal usage.[365] In its characteristic Jewish-Christian sense, faith describes the relationship to God in its entirety.[366]

Paul's interpretation of Abraham demonstrates most clearly both his incorporation and his breaking-up of the Jewish perception of Abraham and faith: For Paul, faith in the God who gives life to the dead and calls into being the non-existing belongs inseparably together with faith in the God who has raised Christ from the dead and who justifies the ungodly.[367] Lührmann sees faith to be described in a double, almost tautological way: The salvation of justification by faith alone is disclosed by the faith in the one that achieved salvation in Christ.[368]

With the title Χριστός, a fixed area of tradition and language is associated, containing terms of proclamation (κήρυγμα, εὐαγγέλιον, ἀπόστολος) and their implication, i.e., the salvific significance of Jesus' death and resurrection.[369] Even the continual connection of πίστις/πιστεύειν with

---

[362] This terms goes back to A. Debrunner (cf. D. Lührmann 1985, 95).

[363] D. Lührmann 1973, 24f.; 1981, 62; 1985, 104.

[364] D. Lührmann 1990, 750f.; cf. 1973, 21-23 *et passim*; 1976, 49, 50f.; 1981, 54. Lührmann proposes "daß allein in der jüd[isch]-christl[ichen] Sprachtradition G[laube] die das ganze Verhältnis des Menschen zu Gott u[nd] der Welt benennende Bedeutung gewonnen hat" (1981, 49).

[365] "*[P]istis/pisteuein* [fehlt] in der Sprache der Mission …, im Judentum wie im Christentum" (D. Lührmann 1973, 23; cf. 1976, 45). Both terms are Jewish-Christian "Begriffe des internen Sprachgebrauchs" (1973, 37).

[366] D. Lührmann 1976, 32. In response to the critics of his thesis, he later specified the difference of the religious use of the πιστ-group in the pagan and Jewish-Christian sense: "[N]ous ne trouvons pas, en grec, de textes attestant l'usage spécifique de πίστις/πιστεύειν pour désigner une relation avec les dieux ou d'autres réalités divines." Conviction of the gods' existence is νομίζειν θεοὺς εἶναι, while εὐσέβεια denotes the relationship with the gods (1985, 94).

[367] D. Lührmann 1976, 46f., 53; 1990, 754.

[368] D. Lührmann 1981, 70f.

[369] D. Lührmann 1981, 68. Χριστός "begegnet … in einem sehr genau eingrenzbaren Bereich von Aussagen über die Heilsbedeutung von Tod und Auferweckung Jesu … Man

Χριστός is not specifically Pauline, but traditional usage. Therefore, faith in Christ is not faith in Jesus in a personal sense, but faith in the one who died and was raised for our salvation[370]; since God is the logical subject of the statement about the resurrection of Christ, Christian faith is not directed towards a "new" God, different from that of Judaism, but towards the same God, whose act of salvation in Christ, however, is new and final.[371] Paul's use of πιστεύειν in the aorist tense denotes conversion to and acceptance of the proclamation of God who raised Jesus from the dead.[372] Thereby, the state before faith is not "previous" faith or "wrong" faith, but no faith, unbelief, so that conversion entails turning to *the* faith, not merely change of faith.[373] Likewise, faith in contrast to ἔργα νόμου is not "another" or a "new" way of salvation, but discloses salvation in the first place.[374]

Like Jewish theology, Paul seeks to answer the basic "question of faith," i.e., the question of how confession and experience can be reconciled.[375] Whereas in Judaism faith was associated with law, righteousness, creation, and eschatology, Paul conceived his alternative in absolute opposition to the law as πίστις Χριστοῦ.[376] The shift that Paul accomplishes consists in his emphasis on the content of faith, the resurrection of Jesus, as opposed to the subjective tendency in Judaism that is primarily concerned with the believer and seeks to mediate *in the law* the confessional

---

sollte daher durchgehend im griechischen Text *christos* mit kleinem Anfangsbuchstaben schreiben, nicht mit großem wie einen Eigennamen" (1976, 48f.).

[370] This is in obvious congruence with Bultmann's judgment (cf., e.g., R. Bultmann 1958, 93).

[371] D. Lührmann 1976, 48f.; 1981, 68. Paul does not fashion own formulations, but uses the language of his tradition which his addressees were immediately familiar with. The same can be said for the christological content that determines faith.

[372] D. Lührmann 1981, 68.

[373] D. Lührmann 1976, 48, 50.

[374] D. Lührmann 1981, 70.

[375] D. Lührmann 1976, 47, 51, 53, 59, 86f.; 1981, 69. The "Grundfrage" associated with the term faith, "das alte Thema des Glaubens" (1976, 60), is the question "nach der Vermittlung zwischen dem Bekenntnis zu Gott als dem Schöpfer u[nd] Erhalter der Welt u[nd] der Erfahrung des Menschen mit sich selbst, Gott u[nd] der Welt, die diesem Bekenntnis zu widersprechen scheint" (1981, 58f.; cf. the almost identical passage, 1976, 34). Faith accomplishes the impossible: "Bekenntnis und Erfahrung zu vermitteln" (1976, 35). Lührmann takes over a thesis of H. Wildberger, when he maintains that the background of this explanation of faith is the oracle of salvation (cf. H. Wildberger 1968, 157). There are times when confession and experience coincide – then faith is unproblematic; yet the problem arises as soon as new experience balks at the handed over interpretation of experience (= confession). Insofar, "Glaube ist ... ein Krisenphänomen" (D. Lührmann 1976, 35).

[376] "[I]n the connection *pistis Christou* the genitive always designates the content of faith ..., not the faithfulness of Jesus" (D. Lührmann 1990, 753; cf. 1981, 69).

statements about creation and eschatology with the worldly experience ("Welterfahrung") of sin, suffering, and death. Pauline Christology does not (like the law) deny experience for the sake of confession, but links the two poles by means of the cross: The cross answers the eschatological expectation of the new creation, as it reveals God's righteousness, but it also implies for the believer taking over Christ's destiny, his suffering. Paul assumes the experience of suffering into his confession, for both relate intrinsically to Christology[377] – this is his answer to the principal "question of faith."

Paul removes the law entirely from the context of blessing and righteousness and replaces it with the event of salvation designated by Χριστός. Christology (and no longer the law) governs faith exclusively and includes as consequence justification, for faith is according to Paul bound to and God's righteousness found in the christologically determined εὐαγγέλιον.[378] Here, πίστις means relying ("Sich-Verlassen") on the salvation in Christ.[379] Paul can describe the replacement of the law through faith in terms of the apocalyptic scheme of the two eons: The appearance of faith as the new divine revelation terminates the time of the law.[380]

As regards the subjective side of faith, Paul never reflects on the coming to faith other than with reference to the proclamation of salvation, which conditions and makes possible faith. Due to the nature of faith as gift, ὑπακοὴ πίστεως is simply the realization of the superiority of grace.[381] Thus for Paul, there are no stages of faith, no qualitative classifications, but only the contrast faith and unbelief. The taking over of Christ's destiny constitutes the anthropological part of faith, so that the content of faith and not the believer's psychology determines the structure of the Christian existence as hope, freedom, and love.[382]

Lührmann's challenge of the hypothesis of the History-of-Religions School was commonly acknowledged in subsequent scholarship.[383] Even his antithesis that πίστις and πιστεύειν should be understood as "Bedeutungslehnwörter" received at first acclamation (E. Lohse, W. Schenk), yet

---

[377] D. Lührmann 1976, 53, 59.

[378] D. Lührmann 1976, 52.

[379] D. Lührmann 1981, 70.

[380] Even if occasionally faith is used absolutely, without specification of its content, it still implies "faith in God, who in the death and resurrection of Christ has achieved salvation, outside of the Law" (D. Lührmann 1990, 754). It is inappropriate therefore to translate πίστις simply with "Christianity," as this would neglect the christological focus of faith and the opposition to the νόμος (1976, 52).

[381] D. Lührmann 1981, 71 ("Verwirklichung der Übermacht der Gnade").

[382] D. Lührmann 1976, 54; 1981, 71.

[383] Cf. K. Haacker 1984, 290; A. von Dobbeler 1987, 295, 298; E. Brandenburger 1988, 166; G. Barth 1992, 217; G. Schunack 1999, 297.

was later contested and modified (G. Barth). His attempt to tie together all occurrences of "faith" in the "question of faith" that seeks to reconcile confession and concrete experience is in danger of becoming a total perspective in which distinct aspects are artificially unified and forced together.[384] The sole derivation of the concept of faith from the context of the oracle of salvation is likewise problematic, particularly since interpretation and historical classification of the relevant Old Testament passages are still debated.[385] In addition, the undistorted trajectory of the semantics of faith from the Old Testament to Paul, as Lührmann wants to see it, omits *inter alia* the aspect of coming to faith (conversion),[386] but also underrates the liberty and uniqueness of Paul's exegesis.[387]

II. E. Lohse, "Emuna und Pistis" (1977); "Glauben im Neuen Testament" (1978)

Apart from W. Schenk,[388] also E. Lohse accepts D. Lührmann's suggestion that regarding its understanding of faith early Christianity did not implement Hellenistic ideas and terminology, but adopted the usage of the Old Testament and Judaism.[389] He utilizes this insight in his argumentation against M. Buber, who asserted a dichotomy and difference in nature between the Jewish concept of faith and the Christian[390]: Whereas the Christian πίστις (epitomized by Paul), in Buber's view, is psychologized and intellectualized, being influenced by Greek premises, the Hebrew אֱמוּנָה (represented by Jesus) implies trust in God in the context of the historical

---

[384] Cf. W. Schenk 1982, 74n.20; E. Brandenburger 1988, 173f. Another issue is Lührmann's use of such multifaceted and hardly determinable expressions – confession and experience – in the definition of faith. On the one hand, Lührmann circumscribes confession as always new interpretation of experience (articulated in worship), on the other hand, faith is perceived as reflection on experience; yet both, confession and faith, are to be distinguished, as confession assumes "unproblematic" aspects of experience, while faith seeks to include "problematic" elements into the confession (D. Lührmann 1976, 35, 59, 87). One has to question if these are appropriate conceptions of confession and faith.

[385] Cf. E. Brandenburger 1988, 171.

[386] In the Old Testament only Jonah 3:5 contains this facet (cf. K. Haacker 1993, 131).

[387] See below chapter V.B.I.2 on Paul's interpretation of Hab 2:4.

[388] Cf. W. Schenk 1982, 72f. The *Sitz im Leben* of the πιστ-group is not in the context of mission: "Wissenssoziologisch handelt es sich also um eine ingroup-Terminologie" (73n.16).

[389] E. Lohse 1977, 150-153. "[D]ie Annahme, in der Missionspropaganda der verschiedenen Religionen, die sie [*lege:* sich] in der synkretistischen Welt der Spätantike entfalteten, sei die Forderung des Glaubens an die Heilsbotschaft in den Mittelpunkt der Predigt gerückt worden, trifft nicht zu ... Das frühe Christentum hat in seinem Verständnis des Glaubens ... die durch das Alte Testament und das Judentum vorgegebene Redeweise aufgenommen." (150f.). Cf. 1978, 87, 88 with n.54.

[390] M. Buber 1950; cf. E. Lohse 1977; 1978, 8, 89.

experiences of a people.[391] Lohse therefore maintains that for Paul Abraham's faith does not differ qualitatively from the faith of the Christian, since both trust exclusively in God's promised word (against all appearances), open up to the word's power, and hence position themselves in the only right relationship to God.[392] Thus, Abraham's faith is the *Urbild* of faith, and he is the father of all believers.[393] Faith is not sufficiently described as new self-understanding, because (in the Old Testament as in Paul) it continues to be based on and connected to the promise and to the awarded grace; it relies on what is recognized as valid and unfailing.[394] Yet while Israel's faith is directed to God's deed in history, Christian faith asserts the eschatological event of Christ's resurrection, knowing that God reveals himself exclusively in the crucified and risen Christ.[395] The unique and universal way, in which God offered his promise in Christ, leads to Paul's conviction that even Israel cannot receive salvation other than through the *iustificatio impiorum*.[396]

The event that won the persecutor of the Christian faith for this very faith in the crucified Christ determined his conception as to how salvation is received: through trust in the gospel and its acceptance in faith.[397] The attainment of the conviction that Christ died and has been raised for me, that he is my Lord, can only be the response of the individual, and therefore faith can only be confessed according to one's own responsibility.[398] This initial act adds the individual to the confessing community and coincides with baptism.[399] The assenting listening to the gospel can be described by Paul as obedience, which has the necessary consequence that

---

[391] Lohse refutes Buber's statement that Paul essentially molded the Christian concept of faith; rather Paul appealed to the early Christian confession and proclamation (1978, 107; 1977, 151f., 155).

[392] E. Lohse 1977, 157f.; 1978, 109-111. Abraham's trust is described with the verb אמן *hiphil*, which denotes in its original meaning "Sich-Festmachen," "Sich-Anklammern." "So klammerte sich Abraham an die ihm zugesagte Verheißung seines Gottes, das heißt: Er glaubte" (1977, 158).

[393] E. Lohse 1978, 110.

[394] E. Lohse 1977, 154, 156f., 159; 1978, 117.

[395] E. Lohse 1977, 154f.

[396] E. Lohse 1977, 159.

[397] E. Lohse 1978, 105, 113.

[398] E. Lohse 1977, 152, 154.

[399] E. Lohse 1978, 113 (following R.A. Lipsius). "Die in der Taufe zugeeignete Christuszugehörigkeit wird also von seiten des Täuflings im bekennenden Glauben angeeignet" (114). On the theme of faith and baptism see also above chapter II.D.

henceforth the gospel governs life and deed of the believer; faith considers the gospel to be true, and through love it becomes effective.[400]

As faith relates to the divine promise, it is also directed to the final fulfillment of the given promise, and thus characterized as hope.[401]

III. G. Barth, "Pistis in hellenistischer Religiosität" (1982)[402]

In critical dialogue with D. Lührmann's correction of the older history-of-religions perspective and its initially positive reception (E. Lohse, W. Schenk), G. Barth puts forward a new, more differentiated view. He bases his thesis on the evaluation of passages that have already been assembled by W. Bauer and R. Bultmann and that derive from his own reading of the Greek sources.[403] Contrary to the general verdict of Lührmann, these texts show that religious usage of πιστ- was widespread in pagan Hellenism.[404] Consequently, Lührmann's prominent thesis that due to the lack of such religious usage in pagan Hellenism, "faith" was not employed in the context of missions but is rather located in the internal usage, becomes void.[405] Together with the familiarity and currency of the religious usage of πιστ- in pagan Hellenism, also the "Verstehenshorizont" for the Christian proclamation and call for faith is demonstrated: The pagan hearer knows and understands this terminology.[406]

Moreover, it even seems that the New Testament follows in two instances at least a common Hellenistic usage rather than the specifically Jewish: first, when πίστις denotes the *fides quae creditur*, and second,

---

[400] "Die fides quae creditur und die fides qua creditur bilden eine Einheit im Hören auf die Christusbotschaft, so daß Glaubensinhalt und Glaubensvollzug unlöslich zusammenfallen" (E. Lohse, 1977, 152; cf. 156; 1978, 114f.).

[401] E. Lohse 1978, 115. In other words: "[D]er Glaubende [streckt sich] dem entgegen, was vor ihm liegt, um es ergreifen, nachdem er von Christus Jesus ergriffen worden ist" (1977, 159). – This and other statements demonstrate Lohse's proximity to and dependence on Bultmann.

[402] See also G. Barth 1992.

[403] Apart from some texts of classical Greek literature, Barth mentions passages from Polybios, Dio Chrysostom, Plutarch, and Lucian of Samosata (1982, 112-120).

[404] G. Barth 1982, 123.

[405] G. Barth 1982, 124f. – If one does not presuppose that the reports of the concrete missionary proclamation in Acts and elsewhere imported the term πιστεύειν secondarily, but reflect actual linguistic practice, then those New Testament texts, too, serve the refutation of Lührmann's point (cf. also K. Haacker 1984, 290, 297). Against this point, E. Brandenburger (1988, 167f.) remarks that it is necessary to reflect on the intention and interests of the author, before accepting the account as historically accurate. But he admits that it is still possible, "daß die Aufforderung zum Glauben nicht nur interner Missionstheologie ... zugehörte, sondern auch der Missionspraxis selbst."

[406] G. Barth 1982, 126.

when it appears in connection with the objective genitive.[407] Yet still, the fact that the Jewish usage of πιστ- predominantly influenced the New Testament remains unaffected by these modifications.

IV. A. von Dobbeler, Glaube als Teilhabe (1987)

According to A. von Dobbeler, a new treatment of the Pauline understanding of faith is desirable, since previous scholarship did not consider adequately the significance of πίστις for the reality of life ("Lebenswirklichkeit") of the early Christian communities. Therefore, the task consists in reflecting on the concrete associations that πίστις is connected to and in elucidating the historical-sociological situation of the author and the recipients of the Pauline letters.[408] Methodologically, the procedure does not aim at presenting the history of the *concept* πίστις, but at investigating the history of its *effect*.[409]

With regard to the question of the origin of the Pauline-Christian concept of πίστις, von Dobbeler supports Lührmann's criticism of the History-of-Religions School and their followers, but raises methodological and factual objections. Most importantly, Lührmann's premise itself, the lack of a religious usage of πίστις and πιστεύειν in pagan-Greek language tradition, can be disproved both by already presented and new material.[410] This common religious language tradition emerges as basis for the Jewish-Christian usage of πίστις.[411]

---

[407] G. Barth 1982, 122, 126 (with references to pagan Greek texts and the New Testament). In the first case, there are no comparable passages in the Septuagint, Philo, or Josephus; in the second case, only Josephus provides occasional parallels.

[408] A. von Dobbeler 1987, 1. Both aspects, the linguistic conventions and the sociological conditions form the "Verstehenshorizont" of the Pauline congregations (5).

[409] A. von Dobbeler 1987, 5 ("keine rein begriffsgeschichtliche Vorgehensweise," but rather "die 'wirkungsgeschichtliche Hermeneutik'").

[410] A. von Dobbeler 1987, 285-287. In a way, von Dobbeler complies with G. Barth's demand (1982, 112, 120) for an investigation of the whole breadth of Hellenistic literature for the religious usage of πιστ-, and he expands the material offered by W. Bauer, R. Bultmann, and G. Barth considerably. The results of the evaluation of the passages are: (1) Πίστις as faith in God constituted the basis of the Septuagint-translation of אמן with πιστ- (against Lührmann); (2) one cannot classify πίστις as theological keyword of all religions engaged in propaganda (against G.P. Wetter, R. Reitzenstein, R. Bultmann); (3) the "Verstehenshorizont" of the Pauline usage of πίστις must be primarily located in the framework of the pagan-Greek belief in oracles and revelations, as well as in miracles; (4) Paul's use of πίστις in the context of conversion and proclamation has parallels in Greek tradition (against Lührmann); (5) the widespread profane usage of πίστις is constitutive for the "Verstehenshorizont" of the pagan-Greek recipients of the Pauline letters (this point von Dobbeler deems as his original contribution to the discussion) (A. von Dobbeler 1987, 298).

[411] A. von Dobbeler 1987, 295. "Πίστις war zwar nicht *der* theologische Zentralbegriff zur Bezeichnung des rechten Gottesverhältnisses wie im frühen Christentum, wohl

Faith appears to be an entity creating participation in a double dimension, both in view of God's acting and in view of the community of the saved. Thus, πίστις may not be understood in an intellectualistic-abstract way as "considering true" or as "new self-understanding," but implies a personal relationship ("personale Beziehung"): first, access to God and participation in his immanence, and, second, entry into the community of believers and sharing in its social communication.[412] The foundation of faith happens as participation in a pneumatical-charismatic communication process that possesses divine authority and thus revelatory character. By means of the apostolic proclamation, the personal mediation of this divine revelation is realized; the ensuing faith places the individual on God's side and acquires the reconciliation which has been accomplished in Christ's death. Thus, faith is a "Schwellenphänomen," i.e., the individual's transition from one situation to another, which enables participation in revelation, Spirit and reconciliation.[413]

Faith is the only factual possibility to participate in the community characterized by δικαιοσύνη, since the common human sinfulness prevents the efficacy of the old order of salvation (νόμος). A lack of righteousness made the marks of Israel's election (law and circumcision) irrelevant, and opened up the prospect of sharing in the holiness of Israel indiscriminately for all, Jews and Gentiles. The sociological peak of the Pauline doctrine of justification emerges in the resulting constitution of unity between two traditionally hostile groups within the Christian community. Thus, the transition at the beginning of faith remains significant: At first it results in a radical transformation of ethical standards, and then it leads into the continual attempt to eliminate social differences and to establish equality and unity of the believers through love.

The power that enables the believer to stand before God and against satanic powers, does not derive from spontaneous psychological experiences, but has been established from the initiation of faith in the act of conversion. Consequently, there is a permanent and general attempt to remain connected to the beginning. Moreover, while through conversion both participation in the reconciliation and forgiveness of sin come to pass, solely faith guarantees life outside the power of sin so that the community of be-

---

aber kann in einer gemeinsamen religiösen Verwendung die Grundlage für den jüdisch-christlichen Gebrauch von πίστις gesehen werden."

[412] A. von Dobbeler 1987, 5f. Cf. von Dobbeler's explicit opposition of new self-understanding and new community-understanding; only the second is denoted by the Pauline πίστις (276).

[413] A. von Dobbeler 1987, 95f.

lievers views itself as "sinless enclave" amidst the universal dominion of sin.[414]

V. E. Brandenburger, "Pistis und Soteria" (1988)

Taking a position between the two poles represented by D. Lührmann and A. von Dobbeler, E. Brandenburger holds that, even though, viewed as a whole, religious usage of πιστ- is limited in pagan Greek and Hellenistic language regarding both content and currency, Christian mission could reckon with certain points of contact.[415] He is also critical of Lührmann's covering and explaining all occurrences of faith by means of his faith-definition: In order to maintain his thesis, Lührmann has to explain Paul's idea of faith from a late stage, i.e., from the dispute about the law, as there the problem of the mediation between confession and experience emerges. The early stage, i.e., the missionary practice, is ruled out as context by this definition.[416]

After assessing relevant Jewish texts, Brandenburger claims that one has to distinguish four types for the usage of faith,[417] one of which he discusses in some detail: coming to faith and turning away from the sinful life to God.[418] He develops his ideas under the aspect of a complex of ideas, which previous studies on the topic "faith" neglected in his opinion[419]: the use of faith in connection with the concepts ὀργὴ θεοῦ and σωτηρία, which relates to it. From the perspective of Paul and Hellenistic Jewish-Christianity, these elements constitute the basic paradigm of conversion:

---

[414] A. von Dobbeler 1987, 275-277.

[415] E. Brandenburger 1988, 168-170. On the one hand, the pointed usage of πίστις in early Christianity, which characterizes the relationship to God/Christ as exclusive way of salvation, has no parallels either in classical Greek or in contemporaneous Hellenistic usage (cf. D. Lührmann 1985, 93-96); but on the other hand, there were "gewisse[.] Verstehensvoraussetzungen im religiösen Sprachbereich" that the Jewish propaganda or Christian mission could refer to (modification of Lührmann). The existing linguistic convention of Hellenism regarding the religious πίστις may however not be considered as foundation ("Grundlage") for the Christian talk of faith (against von Dobbeler).

[416] E. Brandenburger 1987, 176.

[417] E. Brandenburger 1988, 173f. The four "Verwendungstypen" of faith are: "interne Prophetenfunktion," "Treue bzw. Gehorsam gegenüber dem Gesetz," "Bekehrung bzw. Mission," "Bewährung in der Anfechtung."

[418] This is the so-called "Verwendungstyp Bekehrung" (E. Brandenburger 1988, 185). The pertinent Jewish passages are Jdt 14,10; Wis 12,2; Jonah 3:5 (cf. 1988, 181-183). Within this type, three individual types can be distinguished according to different motives for conversion: divine revelation, miraculous event, or prophetic announcement of the divine judgment of wrath.

[419] E. Brandenburger 1988, 165, 186.

the eschatological horizon of a judgment of annihilation, coming to faith, and the prospect of protection from wrath and final salvation.[420]

VI. D.M. Hay "Pistis as 'Ground for Faith' in Hellenized Judaism and Paul" (1989)

D.M. Hay notes that in the New Testament discussion of πίστις one failed to acknowledge the tendency in ancient Greek literature to use this term in the sense of "pledge" or "evidence."[421] After briefly reviewing such occurrences in secular Greek writings, he explores Philo's use of πίστις and comes to the conclusion that it does denote "human faith in God," though "in only a minority of Philonic passages employing the term"[422]; the bulk of passages – almost sixty percent – uses it to mean something like "objective ground for subjective faith."[423] A similar result can be obtained through a reading of Josephus.

Applying his findings from this investigation of pagan and Jewish writings, Hay contends that Paul's use of πίστις in the absolute – which stimulated especially H. Binder's explanation – should be understood in an "objective salvation-historical" sense[424]: Jesus is the "decisive evidence ... given to humankind by God which makes faith possible."[425] Paul's treatment of Abraham as "prototype of faith," therefore, is subordinated to this salvation-historical event that God brought about in Jesus.[426]

From a theological perspective, this reading is attractive since it emphasizes the *extra nos* of faith in relation to the believer and removes it from the meaning as human capacity; it illuminates the relationship between "divine and human dimensions of Christian faith," between objective ground and subjective response.[427] Hay's proposal avoids the pitfall of Binder's approach in that he does allow for the individual-subjective com-

---

[420] In the letter to the Romans, this basic threefold pattern forms the foundation of Paul's theological position (E. Brandenburger 1988, 189). Compared to its Jewish tradition-historical roots, the early Christian idea of faith shows some distinctive features: It has christological orientation; the prophetic (apostolic) kerygma is primarily message of salvation, though the horizon of judgment is still constitutive; the threat of divine wrath is not limited to time and space, but has eschatological and universal nature (cf. the proclamation of John the Baptist).

[421] D.M. Hay 1989, 461.

[422] D.M. Hay 1989, 463f.

[423] D.M. Hay 1989, 465.

[424] D.M. Hay 1989, 472.

[425] D.M. Hay 1989, 471.

[426] D.M. Hay 1989, 472. In Hay's view, the idea that Jesus is proof and ground for faith is prominent in Paul, even in passages that do not explicitly use the term πίστις: Jesus confirms the divine promises, assures future salvation and resurrection, represents an ethical model, etc.

[427] D.M. Hay 1989, 475.

ponent in Paul's idea of πίστις. Since Paul proves more than once his capability of carrying out unique scriptural interpretations, one should be careful to counter Hay's results by pointing to "the importance of the LXX in constituting Paul's theological vocabulary,"[428] where "the 'evidence' sense is generally absent," as even Hay himself maintains.[429]

VII. D.R. Lindsay, "The Roots and Developments of the πιστ- Word Group as Faith Terminology" (1993)[430]

Based on the discussion between G. Barth and D. Lührmann, D.R. Lindsay seeks to explore "the roots and developments of the religious use of the πιστ- word group in Classical and Hellenistic Greek."[431] Conceding that the religious use of πίστις is a later development, Lindsay appeals to a few instances in Classical Greek literature before the fourth century B.C. that display the use of the verb πιστεύειν within a religious context and have the connotation of trust and personal commitment, i.e., not simply intellectual assent.[432]

The Septuagint stands in the line of this concept and even makes it the predominant use, as it understands πιστεύειν *primarily* as "action-modifying trust in God."[433] Further instances from the Hellenistic period, particularly from Sirach and Philo, demonstrate the use of the πιστ- word group as technical terminology. As his distinct contribution to the discussion, Lindsay points out *"two basic trends"* in the Hellenistic use of πιστεύειν,[434] which are associated to the classical usage: first, the notion of trust in a deity or a divine oracle, and, second, the idea of intellectual assent, which correlates to the sense of νομίζειν. In sum, therefore, already Classical Greek had the potential of being understood in both ways, and it

---

[428] R.B. Hays 1997, 283n.24. Especially D. Lührmann sought to prove that there is a straight line from the Hebrew "faith" to the Septuagint and finally to Paul.

[429] D.M. Hay 1989, 462.

[430] See also the Lindsay's monograph on faith in Josephus (1993a).

[431] D.R. Lindsay 1993, 105.

[432] D.R. Lindsay 1993, 108f., 116. He assumes that, therefore, a Greek audience would be capable of understanding this terminology. However, as for the notion of πιστεύειν as trust and commitment, Lindsay contends that Greek religion could not place such a relationship to the god(s) in the center of their belief, since it was primarily concerned with νομίζειν θεοὺς (εἶναι), i.e., with the belief in the existence of the god(s). It would require "another theological system" in which πιστεύειν could develop into a central concept (110).

[433] D.R. Lindsay 1993, 111.

[434] D.R. Lindsay 1993, 115 (italics original).

was the Septuagint that particularly accentuated the first, based on the semantics of אמן *hiphil*.[435]

VIII. G. Schunack, "Glaube in griechischer Religiosität" (1999)

G. Schunack follows G. Barth in arguing that in classical Greek, the πιστ-stem did not represent the main feature and totality of the human relationship with the deity or the divine, but that religious usage is nonetheless present.[436] The question whether the πιστ-group has become the decisive terminology for the human relationship to God in Hellenistic times[437] has to be illuminated by enquiring the horizon of understanding in the pagan Hellenistic world and the place of faith in its culture, but also by examining the factors responsible for the fact that in contrast to the early Jewish tradition, Greek religiosity was largely able to dispense with the terminology of faith.[438] Mostly, faith has its *Sitz im Leben* in critical situations of threat and distress and is situated in the framework of oracles. The recipient of the oracle trusts in the divine and reckons with the gods' epiphany and their intervention through a miracle.[439] The character of faith as "oracle faith" was one reason why later more enlightened generations with a more rational worldview took a critical stance towards religious faith,[440] while on a more popular-religious level, such a relativizing of the phe-

---

[435] Accordingly, Lindsay's approach is a modification of the "Bedeutungslehnwort"-theory of D. Lührmann, as he recognizes roots of the Septuagintal use of πιστεύειν already in Classical Greek.

[436] G. Schunack 1999, 296f. The term denoting the religious relationship to the deity was εὐσεβής/εὐσέβεια.

[437] Schunack again agrees with G. Barth's double critique of the opposing views of R. Bultmann (πίστις as catchword of religions engaged in propaganda) and D. Lührmann (πίστις as internal language of early Judaism).

[438] G. Schunack 1999, 298.

[439] G. Schunack 1999, 312. Especially in Hellenistic times "miracle faith" shaped the religious faith crucially. Schunack argues meticulously that faith is not a factor of the miraculous event itself, but "das Stichwort 'Glaube' thematisiert ... die Bedeutung der narrativen Kommunikation mirakulöser Ereignisse," i.e., faith belongs to the interpretation of extraordinary events and consequently to the religious public (322f.; quote: 322). The meaning of faith lies in the persuasive, apologetic intention of the one narrating the event and in the rejection of scepticism, doubt and unbelief. Hence, "miracle faith" confirms religious faith (324f.). Insofar as "oracle faith" like "miracle faith" is dependent on interpretation – for it is not prophecy or promise, but insinuation (301) – both "faiths" are connected through a structural homology (326).

[440] G. Schunack 1999, 300. For Euripides, for instance, oracles are worthless and cannot reveal the will of the gods (307), and Thucydides deems them vain hope (308). Also, the ἀσέβεια-trials, most prominently the one against Socrates, are illuminating (308-311). Aristotle, then, reduced the phenomenon of faith to the realm of public communication, to rhetorics (316).

nomenon of faith did not gain a foothold: For Plutarch, faith becomes the center and mark of religious self-understanding.[441]

Schunack shows that Aristotle, for instance, located faith in the area of rhetorics, i.e., he withdraws it from the religious realm. Therefore, one might call for "an exploration of how this notion functioned in ancient Greco-Roman rhetoric."[442] Within this current trend to exploit rhetorical criticism for the study of the New Testament, J.L. Kinneavy's book on the Greek rhetorical origins of Christian faith is most pertinent.[443] He seeks to establish that the Christian idea of πίστις shares the notion of "persuasion" as used in Greek rhetoric, not only implicitly, but also explicitly, meaning that the New Testament writers were conscious of the Greek rhetoric of persuasion and the function of πίστις therein.[444]

On the other hand, an expressly theological or christological notion is inherent in the last point of the history of scholarship of faith that we have to focus our attention to: the problem of the phrase πίστις Χριστοῦ, or more precisely, the problem of the kind of genitive of Χριστοῦ.

H. The Faith of Christ

In Anglo-Saxon exegesis dealing with Paul's concept of faith, "scholarship has focused especially on the interpretation of the expression 'the faith of Christ' in its various forms."[445] While some deem this problem a "life or death"-issue for the interpreter of Paul, others think that "its importance is easily exaggerated."[446] In any case, it is impossible to neglect it, given the amount of literature produced on this topic. Besides, some aspects that emerge in this discussion are reminiscent of the salvation-historical view of faith, while on the other hand insights on the horizon of understanding of πίστις become valuable.[447]

---

[441] G. Schunack 1999, 317-322.

[442] E.M. Heen 2003, 179.

[443] J.L. Kinneavy 1987.

[444] The rhetorical use of πίστις does not entail a lower kind of truth (J.L. Kinneavy 1987, 34-44). – On Plato's use of πίστις as persuasion, see M. Pohlenz (quoted in G. Ebeling 1958, 80n.2); also A. Taglia 1998.

[445] M.A. Seifrid and R.K.J. Tan 2002, 180 (in their bibliographical guide to the Pauline writings). The relatively little impact of this view on Continental scholarship can be seen exemplarily in E. Lohse's recent commentary on Romans, who dedicates a footnote to the whole problem (2003, 131n.6). – A "brief history of the question" reaching until about 1980 can be found in R.B. Hays 1983, 142-148; see also K. Kertelge 1971, 162-166.

[446] S. Westerholm 2004, 305n.18.

[447] See above chapters II.F and II.G.

I. J. Haußleiter "Was versteht Paulus unter christlichem Glauben?"
(1895)[448]

Against A. Ritschl's definition that faith is essentially a trustful relationship to Christ's historical work of reconciliation, J. Haußleiter seeks to re-
establish R.A. Lipsius's view that faith is a mystical bond with Christ.[449]
This mystical unity is objectively tied to baptism and subjectively to faith,
so that βαπτίζειν εἰς and πιστεύειν εἰς represent one single event.[450] According to this intimacy the phrases πίστις ἐν Χριστῷ and πίστις Χριστοῦ
cannot mean faith that is directed to Christ (*genitivus objectivus*), but only
faith that rests in Christ (*genitivus subjectivus*), that is effected by Christ,
and in which Christ is present.[451] This comes close to what A. Deißmann
called *genitivus mysticus*.[452] Haußleiter's novel approach introduced into
modern New Testament scholarship what became a significant exegetical
issue which is still unsolved.[453]

II. G. Kittel, "Πίστις Ἰησοῦ Χριστοῦ bei Paulus" (1906)

On the basis of Haußleiter's findings, Kittel proposed that Paul in fact
never regarded Christ as the object of religious faith.[454] To the unbiased

---

[448] Cf. also J. Haußleiter 1891.

[449] J. Haußleiter 1895, 162, following R.A. Lipsius, 1892, 32 (cf. E. Lohse 1978, 113).

[450] J. Haußleiter 1895, 168.

[451] J. Haußleiter 1895, 170, 178. In an earlier essay from 1891 Haußleiter placed much
emphasis on the (Pauline) distinction between Ἰησοῦς (the historical Jesus) and Χριστός
(Christ, the Lord), claiming that the phrase πίστις Ἰησοῦ Χριστοῦ (Rom 3:22) denotes
the "faith of Jesus Christ," while the (hypothetical) phrase πίστις Χριστοῦ Ἰησοῦ would
regard Christ as object of faith. Not only M. Kählers general rebuttal of such an anachronistic distinction that carries into Paul a differentiation between the historical Jesus and
the glorified Lord (1896, first published 1892), but also O. Schmitz's direct critique of
Haußleiter's schematizing approach (1924, 117) demonstrated the questionable method
underlying this thesis. Schmitz himself, should be noted, seeks to prove in his work that
the two categories "subjective genitive" and "objective genitive" are insufficient for the
description of πίστις Χριστοῦ. Rather, the genitive – belonging to the class of the "allgemein charakterisierenden Genetive" (230) – signifies a mystical, pneumatical union
with Christ (213), and hence πίστις Χριστοῦ "[ist] der auf oder in Christus hinein
gerichtete Glaube oder Glaube 'in Christo Jesu', der diese Vereinigung herbeiführt"
(108). With this psychological (107) description, Schmitz is again in agreement with
Haußleiter and also with Kittel.

[452] See above page 9. Even A. Schlatter's exposition is generally open to this direction
of interpretation (cf. the already noted passage 1927, 265).

[453] Cf. R.B. Hays 1983, 142. G. Howard mentions some earlier advocates of this view
(1974). F. Neugebauer (1961, 168n.69) refers to E.W. Mayer (1899).

[454] Even the formulation πιστεύειν εἰς is in his opinion equivalent to πιστεύειν κατά
(G. Kittel 1906, 428f.). Cf. S.K. Williams 1987, 434f., 442f. with a similar conclusion.

reader, the formula πίστις Χριστοῦ must have made the impression of a subjective genitive.[455]

One might question the statement that the studies by Haußleiter and Kittel (and Deißmann) "precipitated a flurry of answering studies,"[456] for a closer reading of those studies shows that these scholar's positions regarding the πίστις Χριστοῦ question are for the most part mentioned and rebutted *en passant*.[457] The primary concern of the subsequent investigations on the Pauline πίστις was its relationship to mysticism, i.e., the relationship between juridical and mystical concepts in Paul.[458] Actually, even Haußleiter, Kittel, and Deißmann remain in their studies within this basic question of mysticism in Paul, and it would be a mistake to place into the center the issue of πίστις Χριστοῦ. In the history of scholarship it has been and generally remained a marginal issue for the next decades.[459]

III. A.G. Hebert, "'Faithfulness' and 'Faith'" (1955);
T.F. Torrance, "One Aspect of the Biblical Conception of Faith";
"The Biblical Conception of 'Faith'" (1956/1957)

From a different angle and presumably without being aware of the research done on the topic, Hebert and Torrance again voted for a subjective understanding of the genitive Χριστοῦ – with considerable impact on English speaking scholarship. The inspiration for this exegesis derives – at least in Torrance's case – from Barth's commentary on Romans.[460] They sought to

---

[455] Cf. G. Kittel 1906, 424, 431. Already E. Wißmann observed that this argument is undermined as soon as one takes into account that this formula has already been known in the congregations the apostle addresses (1926, 69n.1). See also below note 325 in chapter V.

[456] R.B. Hays 1983, 144, referring to W.H.P. Hatch 1917; O. Schmitz 1924; E. Wißmann 1926; W. Mundle 1932. Cf. J.D.G. Dunn 1997, 249, for a similarly misleading assessment.

[457] Kittel does not appear at all in the index of Hatch's work, and Deißmann's and Haußleiter's results are briefly refuted in the small print (cf. W.H.P. Hatch 1917, 46). E. Wißmann considers Kittel's argument plainly unfounded (1926, 69n.1). Similarly, W. Mundle mentions the alternate position only in footnotes and labels it "künstliche Exegese" (1932, 76n.1). Thus, one cannot characterize those studies mentioned as "answering studies" that "emphatically rejected the arguments against an 'objective genitive' interpretation" (R.B. Hays 1983, 144).

[458] See especially above chapter II.C.III (on F. Neugebauer).

[459] The studies presented thus far do not consider this issue to be worth of a separate in depth treatment; some do not even mention it.

[460] See K. Barth 1922, 72, 77-79. Barth translates the phrase διὰ πίστεως Ἰησοῦ Χριστοῦ with "durch seine [*sc.* Gottes] Treue in Jesus Christus" (72). He does not justify the peculiarity of his translation on grammatical-exegetical grounds, but simply refers to the "Schillern des Begriffs" πίστις, which he sought to give adequate expression by means of this interpretation; as the "spiritual father" of his thought he names R.

determine the semantics of πίστις primarily from the meaning of the Hebrew root אמן and its derivates אֱמוּנָה and אֱמֶת and consequently to distinguish a Greek from a Hebrew category of meaning.[461] Rather than "believing in Christ," πίστις Χριστοῦ stands for "the faithfulness of God manifested in Christ's human faithfulness."[462] The influence of Barth's Christology is evident in the following statement by Torrance where he attempts
to ascertain an inherent relationship between Christ's faithfulness and human faith in Christ: "Jesus Christ is not only the incarnation of the divine
pistis, but he is the embodiment and actualization of man's *pistis* in covenant with God."[463] Consequently, the phrase πίστις Χριστοῦ has a bipolar
orientation, denoting both divine fidelity to humanity and human fidelity to
God – and Christ embodies both.

The renewed advocacy for the subjective genitive received several dis-
approving responses by C.F.D. Moule and others,[464] but only J. Barr subjected the methodology of Hebert and Torrance to a comprehensive,
"squelching" critique[465]: After scrutinizing the linguistic grounds on which
they build their case – the distinction between a Hebrew and a Greek
meaning – he concluded that these portions "contain practically no facts
which are not used or presented in extremely misleading ways."[466] Barr's
critique however was not generally directed against the theological peak of
the "subjective genitive"-solution, and consequently the following years
saw numerous efforts to sustain it by new arguments.[467] Among these interpretations, G.M. Taylor introduced a new thought into the discussion by
his understanding πίστις Χριστοῦ in terms of the juridical *fidei commis-
sum*, which refers to the reliability of Christ as a kind of trustee.[468]

Liechtenhahn (xxiv). However, compared to the first edition of his commentary (1919),
he reduces the number of passages in which he refers πίστις to God's faithfulness.

[461] Cf. A.G. Hebert 1955, 373.

[462] A.G. Hebert 1955, 376.

[463] T.F. Torrance 1956/1957, 113. The incarnation-language that Torrance employs
here is reminiscent of H. Binder, but see also H. Ljungman 1964, 39: "Christ [is] ... the
manifestation of God's ... 'faithfulness'."

[464] C.F.D. Moule 1956/1957, 157; J. Murray 1959, 363-374.

[465] Cf. J.D.G. Dunn 1997, 250. J. Barr devotes a large amount of his book to the issue
of "faith" (and "truth") (1961, 161-205).

[466] J. Barr 1961, 205.

[467] Cf. the following scholars mentioned in R.B. Hays 1983, 147n.105: P. Vallotton
1960; H. Ljungman 1964, 38-40; H.W. Schmidt 1966, 64-66, 71f.; G.M. Taylor 1966;
E.R. Goodenough 1968; R.N. Longenecker 1964, 149-151; 1974; G. Howard 1967; 1970;
1974; J. Bligh 1968; M. Barth 1969; D.W.B. Robinson 1970; S.K. Williams 1980; L.
Gaston 1980, 54f.; L.T. Johnson 1982. One could add, e.g., W. Grundmann 1964, 18.

[468] G.M. Taylor 1966, 72. Taylor's view is adopted, e.g., in L. Gaston 1980, 54, but
for the most part dismissed: cf. H.D. Betz 1979, 118n.45; K. Haacker 1983, 291; R.B.
Hays 1983, 184-188. A similar position is taken by D. Georgi, who argues for a "more

IV. H. Ljungman, Pistis. A Study of Its Presuppositions and Meaning in Pauline Use *(1964)*

H. Ljungman approaches the topic with the conviction that the "true significance of πίστις in Paul" can only be grasped by "using the Biblical and Rabbinic background appropriately."[469] From Paul's presuppositions, one can determine his usage of the term πίστις, namely, "to characterize man's relation in 'justification'."[470]

Ljungman takes his starting point in an examination of Paul's notion of God's πίστις and his being ἀληθής and their relation to the human "believing." He maintains that Paul wants to focus on both, God's faithfulness and his reliability and truth; the person's "believing in God" corresponds to the first and "to believe him" corresponds to the latter.[471] Israel's attitude, however, is opposed to God's πίστις (and thus labeled ἀπιστία),[472] since instead of affirming and witnessing to God's ἀλήθεια, it litigates with God by claiming its advantage over the peoples through ἔργα νόμου, it protests against God's action and direction, and therefore deserts its mission.[473] Paul now argues that this and all other human unrighteousness existed in order that God's truth and righteousness should become evident: Whereas all are liars, he is reliable, truthful, righteous, and faithful; he wins the case in the lawsuit, so that all protests die and God is accepted in his righteousness.[474] Πίστις therefore acknowledges and assents to the δικαιοσύνη θεοῦ, which implies both, God's faithfulness in his action and his truth, which his action bears witness to;[475] faith belongs to Christ "in the sense that 'the

---

objective sense" of the word πίστις as "faithfulness" and "reliability." Just as "Caesar represented the *fides* of Rome," also God owns πίστις in terms of "reliability" (1991, 84).

[469] H. Ljungman 1964, 106. The groundwork for his monograph was prepared in his dissertation (*Guds barmhärtighet och dom. Fariséernas lära om de två 'måtten'* [1950]) on the rabbinic doctrine of the two "measures," God's mercy and judgment (cf. 11f.).

[470] H. Ljungman 1964, 9.

[471] H. Ljungman 1964, 14, 36, 37; cf. 17-21 on Old Testament and rabbinic parallels to the idea of God's אֱמֶת (the equivalent to ἀληθής) and his being נֶאֱמָן (πιστός).

[472] H. Ljungman 1964, 19, 35, 39.

[473] H. Ljungman 1964, 22f., 25f., 33f., 39, 50-52, 83, 104, 106. The witnessing function and task of Israel is based on the fact that Israel has heard God speak and "can confirm the correspondence between what has come to pass and what the Lord has said" (24; cf. 97).

[474] H. Ljungman 1964, 26, 31, 33f., 36, 42, 45, 52, 105. To Paul, Israel's protest against God culminated in the crucifixion of the Messiah, yet even that cannot jeopardize God's unwavering faithfulness (34, cf. 82).

[475] H. Ljungman 1964, 37-40, 55.

redemption *in* Christ Jesus' is God's 'justifying' act, through which God 'has right' as the faithful one over against man's lie."[476]

When Paul argues that our faith is in vain if Christ had not been raised, his intention is not to insist simply on an affirmation of the factuality of Christ's resurrection,[477] but to point, on the one hand, to the correspondence between God's words and what has occurred, and, on the other, to the correlation between God's raising Christ from the dead and the victorious deliverance of the people from the sphere of death to the sphere of life.[478] Both elements are constitutive for the kerygma and demonstrate God's faithfulness, past and future,[479] to which faith on the part of humans is associated.[480] God maintains justice and carries out what he has said, by intervening on behalf of the accused and delivering them from death.[481]

In line with his emphasis on the reliability of God's word, Ljungman pays particular attention to the connection between believing and hearing. For Paul, God who *has* spoken is heard in Christ's word (ῥῆμα Χριστοῦ), in the present word of the Apostles,[482] so that the word is near, and with it Christ and righteousness and salvation.[483] Thus, any contradiction against the gospel amounts to an attitude that does not acknowledge the Lord who has spoken and therefore does not believe him and trust in him. Ultimately, it is a lack of understanding that disregards the continuity in God's word and act (although experienced time and again)[484] and ends in the fatal establishment of one's own righteousness against God's righteousness[485] and even in the opposition to the law.[486] The only right and appropriate attitude

---

[476] H. Ljungman 1964, 40, cf. 44, 47, 55. Christ represents Israel and realizes its mission, as his πίστις stands in contrast to Israel's ἀπιστία, but – more significantly – he himself also manifests God's righteousness, truth and faithfulness.

[477] H. Ljungman 1964, 65, 78.

[478] H. Ljungman 1964, 65.

[479] Faith relates to both the certitude of God's promised help, through which death *will* be destroyed, and to the conquering of death, which *has* already come to pass through Christ's resurrection; both is about God's faithfulness and the acceding human faith, linked to the past and to the final victory (H. Ljungman 1964, 75f.).

[480] H. Ljungman 1964, 55, 65f., 78f., 102.

[481] Against the Jewish view that assumes resurrection "to imply the restoration of the Adamic man in perfect form" (H. Ljungman 1964, 68) and to be associated with the Torah, Paul erases the "connection between the world of Adam and the life of the resurrection" (70). "Christ's resurrection is that of the 'second Adam'" (71, cf. 72), since the verdict of the human guilt brings about the death of the first.

[482] H. Ljungman 1964, 80; cf. 95f., 101.

[483] H. Ljungman 1964, 86f.

[484] Paul's numerous citations and allusions to Scripture passages serve precisely the proof of the continuity of word and occurrence and the confirmation of the truth of what God has said (H. Ljungman 1964, 84f.).

[485] H. Ljungman 1964, 81, 94, 105.

[486] H. Ljungman 1964, 104.

to the near and heard word of salvation in Christ and to God's faithfulness is therefore πιστεύειν, which in Paul "primarily means 'to trust in' and 'to give credence' ('to believe')."[487] "'Trust in' Christ is man's 'believing' God,"[488] since the truth of the divine word is certified by the salvation obtained through Christ's resurrection.

V. R.B. Hays, The Faith of Jesus Christ (1983)

In recent times, it is above all Hays's dissertation on the "narrative substructure of Galatians 3:1-4:11"[489] whose thesis of a subjective genitive has been shown by "much of subsequent scholarship ... to be correct in the directions it proposes."[490] Hays has in common with several of the already presented exegetes that his "great adversary" is R. Bultmann.[491] His positive argumentation draws on the precursors of the subjective understanding of πίστις Χριστοῦ and contributes further elements by an analysis of the narrative elements that undergird Paul's thought.[492] He reaffirms Kittel's assertion that an unprejudiced reading of the phrase suggests the meaning "faith of Christ";[493] he also draws attention to Howard's analysis of the occurrences of πίστις followed by a genitival name or pronoun (apart from Χριστοῦ and its equivalents), which concludes that all genitives are subjective genitives[494]; finally, together with Haußleiter and Kittel, he sees a parallel between the phrase ἐκ πίστεως Ἰησοῦ (Χριστοῦ) and ἐκ πίστεως Ἀβραάμ.[495] From a theological perspective, Hays argues for a "representa-

---

[487] H. Ljungman 1964, 89; cf. 87, 101. "[I]t should be emphasized that for Paul the two meanings of πιστεύειν presuppose each other so completely that one meaning is more or less implied in the other" (92).

[488] H. Ljungman 1964, 90; cf. 92, 100.

[489] Thus the subtitle of R.B. Hays 1983. The central thesis of Hays's book, therefore, is not a discussion of "the faith of Jesus Christ," but that Paul's argument in Galatians presupposes *"a story about Jesus Christ"* and that *"his theological reflection attempts to articulate the meaning of that story"* (xxiv; italics original). Hays contends that presently Paul's theological use of narrative is more and more acknowledged (cf. the scholars mentioned in xxviii note 16). Furthermore, he refers to J. Marcus who seems to support his thesis that "Paul's gospel story presages the development of the gospel genre" (R.B. Hays 2002, xliv, appealing to J. Marcus 2000). – Hays's work has been republished in 2002, with a new introduction by Hays, a foreword by L.T. Johnson, and a substantial dialogue between Hays (1997) and J.D.G. Dunn (1997).

[490] L.T. Johnson 2002, xv. – In some ways, Hays's work is the more forceful counterpart to the treatment of Rom 3:21-26 of L.T. Johnson (1982).

[491] R.B. Hays 2002, xxv.

[492] Cf. especially R.B. Hays 1983, 73-117.

[493] R.B. Hays 1983, 148; cf. G. Kittel 1906, 431.

[494] R.B. Hays 1983, 148; cf. G. Howard 1967, 459. In a later essay Howard adds evidence from the Septuagint and Hellenistic literature (1970).

[495] R.B. Hays 1983, 149; cf. J. Haußleiter 1891, 110f.; G. Kittel 1906, 424. See also E.R. Goodenough 1968, 45.

tive christology," which presupposes that in Paul's view "Jesus Christ, like Abraham, is justified [!] ἐκ πίστεως and that we, as a consequence, are justified *in* him ..., as a result of his faithfulness."[496] "Our participation in Christ, which does also yield a new self-understanding, is both posited within and engendered by the story itself."[497] Through this view, Hays wants to overcome an alleged weakness of the post-Reformation understanding of "faith" and "justification" in Paul, which already G. Ebeling had observed,[498] "that it offers no coherent account of the relation between the doctrine of justification and *christology*."[499]

An apparent weakness of Hays's work as regards methods is its failure to give attention to the semantic and cultural background of the term πίστις[500]; with respect to the disputed πίστις plus objective genitive, some corrective evidence has been brought to light.[501] It does not seem impossible to assume that Paul could presuppose that the recipients of his letter in Rome would have understood the phrase as well-known, pre-formulated abbreviation. With respect to Hays's hypothesized underlying narrative, one gets the impression that he sets narrative over against argument, the presupposed narrative sequence over against the actually used argumenta-

---

[496] R.B. Hays 1983, 151 (italics original); cf. 160; 1997, 293: "[W]e are saved by Jesus' faithfulness." For an articulation of representative Christology, Hays refers to Paul's mention of Jesus' obedience, which is presented by Paul as representative action having soteriological consequences (152).

[497] R.B. Hays 1983, 215. Hays concurs with Sanders and others (213n.8) in arguing that "participation in Christ [is] ... the central theme of Pauline soteriology" (xxvi note 12; cf. xxxii; 1997, 287). – Notably, while A. von Dobbeler puts the theme "participation" in a sociological framework, Hays is interested in the phenomenon of participation in narrative: "[W]e are caught up into the story of Jesus Christ" (xxix).

[498] Hays (1983, 119) quotes G. Ebeling 1958, 66n.1. Ebeling's essay "Jesus und Glaube" seeks to rediscover the Reformation conception of a coherent inner connection of justification and Christology.

[499] R.B. Hays 2002, xxix (italics original); cf. 1983, 119, 150; 1997, 293; L.E. Keck 1989, 454: A subjective reading clarifies "the role of Jesus in salvation." – In our exegesis (see below chapter V) we will find that πίστις is both an act of God and christologically defined; there is a profound coherence between justification and Christology.

[500] Hays himself concedes this problem in later publications (cf. R.B. Hays 1997, 275; 2002, xliv). One should not underrate it; for, if Paul could presuppose a certain understanding of the phrase πίστις Χριστοῦ, a large part of Hays's argumentation would miss its point. Above, we noted that already E. Wißmann (1926, 69n.1) criticized G. Kittel's failure to ask for the possibility of understanding of πίστις. Unfortunately, Hays did not enter the discussion with those scholars who had treated these problems (see above chapter II.G). He considered the discussion to be concluded by the essays of G. Howard (1967; 1974) and others.

[501] Cf. R.B. Matlock 2000, 19n.59, who finds several passages from Polybios, Strabo and Plutarch "with relative ease." See also the careful observations on the objective genitive in A. Schlatter 1927, 572f. (on Polybios), 581 (on Philo), and 584 (on Josephus).

tive logic.[502] As for Romans and Galatians, it appears that they are first and foremost argument and not narrative.[503] Hays's appreciative appeal to Barth for his narrative reading of Paul[504] should be confronted with Barth's own "interest" in the story of Jesus: Barth puts all emphasis on Jesus Christ's resurrection, so that all aspects of the personal life of the historical Jesus become ultimately irrelevant.[505] Likewise, an anthropological-existential reading of Paul, strongly opposed by Hays, enters again through the backdoor when it is claimed that "*both* Abraham and Jesus are paradigms for Christian faith"[506]: For both Bultmann and Hays faith is (characterized by) ὑπακοή.

In any case, the broad scope of Hays's work constituted a new basis, which was strengthened and substantiated by numerous other studies that concentrated on some of the single issues raised. A radical position (similar to that of G. Kittel) is taken by S.K. Williams who claims that Paul *never* really sees Christ as the object of faith.[507] He argues for a strong participatory sense of πιστεύειν εἰς Χριστόν, comparing it to βαπτίζειν εἰς Χριστόν: "to believe into Jesus Christ."[508] In like manner, M.D. Hooker contends in line with A. Schweitzer, E.P. Sanders and many others: "Justification is a matter of participation," and says on this basis: "[S]o, too, is believing." The person's participation in the life of Christ, i.e., also in his faithfulness "includes, necessarily, the answering faith of believers, who claim that faith as their own."[509] The result of this process is what could be called "interchange soteriology."[510] According to Hooker, therefore, the

---

[502] Cf. against the opposition of narrative and argument J. Moltmann 1999, 15: Both belong intrinsically together: "die *Erzählung* der Gottesgeschichte und das *Argument* für Gottes Gegenwart, die lebensgeschichtliche *Subjektivität* und die selbstvergessene *Objektivität*" (italics original). This is true also for Paul, though in his letters the argumentative structure naturally prevails over the narrative.

[503] Cf. J.D.G. Dunn 1997, 270.

[504] R.B. Hays 2002, xxiv.

[505] K. Barth 1920, 9-11.

[506] R.B. Hays 1997, 290.

[507] S.K. Williams 1987, 434f., 442f. See also H. Binder 1968, 63.

[508] S.K. Williams 1987, 442f. (cf. J. Haußleiter 1895, 168). One has to question the alleged correlation between βαπτίζειν εἰς and πιστεύειν εἰς: Does βαπτίζειν εἰς Χριστόν really has an exclusively "local," participatory meaning or does it not rather give the goal and direction of baptism? Passages that obviously oppose this interpretation are 1Cor 10:12: βαπτίζειν εἰς τὸν Μωϋσῆν and above all Mk 1:4: βάπτισμα μετανοίας εἰς ἄφεσιν ἁμαρτιῶν.

[509] M.D. Hooker 1989, 185. There is "a logical link between Christ's faith and ours" (167).

[510] Cf. M.D. Hooker 1989, 167 (both Christ and Christians are "righteous, obedient and faithful"), 176, 182; see also 1971.

neutral formulation "Christ-faith" of A. Deißmann might be most adequate, since it combines the subjective and objective understanding.[511]

While most participants in the debate seem to struggle earnestly with the issues at stake, one perceives in some instances a certain (false?) sense of security slipping into the debate. L. Gaston for instance thinks that the subjective interpretation "has been too well established to need any further support."[512] Such security can also lead to polarizing, polemizing, and perhaps simplifying lines of reasoning, as in D.A. Campbell recent œuvre[513]: His "grand strategy" is to set the misguided "Justification by Faith (JF)"-model against the appropriate "Pneumatologically Participatory Martyrological Eschatology (PPME)"-model, a wrong "anthropocentric" reading[514] against a correct christological, christocentric, trinitarian, or participatory reading.[515] In his analysis, the JF model operates with "contradictory principles and assumptions"[516] and therefore struggles with many (all?) aspects of Paul's theology like "revelation, giftedness, election, pneumatology, resurrection, and human depravity,"[517] soteriology and anthropology[518]; and since in this model "unconvincing caveats are piled on top of unsupported ellipses,"[519] it "begin[s] to collapse,"[520] so that Campbell decided to break *"decisively with the JF model"*[521] for the sake of the "far more cogent and comprehensive" PPME model, which does "no violence to Paul grammatically, lexically, argumentatively, or soteriologically"[522] and "provides (easily) the smoothest reading of Paul"[523]; there are

---

[511] Cf. M.D. Hooker 2000, 952; see also 2003, 104-106.

[512] Referred to in M.D. Hooker 1989, 165.

[513] D.A. Campbell 2005, 90-93, 178-207, 208-232; cf. 1992; 1992a; 1994; 1997

[514] Notably, R. Bultmann figures as "the classic representative" (228n.24). Likewise notable is the fact that others in Campbell's faction have called the *traditional* understanding of faith "christocentric," setting it against their own theocentric one (cf. R.B. Hays 1983, 151; but see 1997, 277).

[515] Cf., e.g., D.A. Campbell 2005, 92, 190, 200, 203, 206f., 218f., 225f., 230-232.

[516] D.A. Campbell 2005, 232.

[517] D.A. Campbell 2005, 198f.

[518] D.A. Campbell 2005, 201.

[519] D.A. Campbell 2005, 224.

[520] D.A. Campbell 2005, 206. Campbell's simplistic and misleading representation of the "Lutheran" "nonsense" reading comes into view in statements such as: "Faith is merely latent in human capacity" (229); "[i]t is merely a mental disposition"; it does "not seem possible for the enslaved, infantile prisoners of the pre-Christian condition" and "presupposes directly the *continuation* of the individual who has passed from unbelief to belief" (231; italics original). A reading of Luther's *Von der Freiheit eines Christenmenschen* (1520) with its thoughts on the nature of faith, justification and soteriological interchange would have prevented such one-sided statements.

[521] D.A. Campbell 2005, 199n.45 (italics original).

[522] D.A. Campbell 2005, 219.

[523] D.A. Campbell 2005, 207.

"no *cogent* objections"[524] against this model and it would only require a monograph to accomplish the "definite proof" of its overall accuracy.[525]

Apart from Hays, Williams, Hooker, Gaston, and Campbell and the earlier proponents mentioned, there are many who support the understanding "faith of Christ," such as S.K. Stowers, L.E. Keck, C.B. Cousar, G.N. Davies, B.W. Longenecker, N.T. Wright, I.G. Wallis, D.B. Wallace, M. Neubrand, J.L. Martyn, A. Vanhoye, A.K. Grieb, P. Eisenbaum and many more.[526]

However, from the time it was introduced into Pauline scholarship, exegetes have put forward counter arguments against the subjective understanding. With a wide array of reasons and intentions they seek to reestablish the "faith in Christ"-translation in the respective contexts and within Paul's theology as a whole. Among these scholars are, for instance, E. Wißmann, F. Neugebauer, D. Lührmann, W. Schenk, H.D. Betz, J.M.G. Barclay, G.W. Hansen, O. Hofius, V. Koperski, J.D.G. Dunn, C.E.B. Cranfield, R.B. Matlock, M.A. Seifrid, P. Stuhlmacher, S. Westerholm, etc.[527]

Others seek to settle the debate by exploring the interpretation of πίστις Χριστοῦ in patristic theology, but even this approach does not offer unanimous conclusions. On the one hand, I.G. Wallis states that the subjective understanding played a significant role up until the struggle against Arianism,[528] while on the other hand R.A. Harrisville contends that in patristic times the "faith in Christ" position prevailed.[529]

---

[524] D.A. Campbell 2005, 203 (italics original).

[525] D.A. Campbell 2005, 206.

[526] S.K. Stowers 1989; 1994, 194-226; L.E. Keck 1989; 2005, 104f., 110; C.B. Cousar 1990, 39f.; G.N. Davies 1990, 106-112; B.W. Longenecker 1993; 1996, 79-89; N.T. Wright 1995, 37f.; I.G. Wallis 1995; D.B. Wallace 1996, 125f.; M. Neubrand 1997, 118; J.L. Martyn 1997, 252, 276, 314; A. Vanhoye 1999; A.K. Grieb 2002, 37; P. Eisenbaum 2004, 695n.79. – See in addition the works mentioned in R.B. Hays 1997, 273n.3. – It should be noted, too, that the *Anchor Bible Dictionary* offers an article on "Faith of Christ" (G. Howard 1990a) and that the NRSV gives the subjective reading a place in the footnotes. Also, the dictionary *Religion in Geschichte und Gegenwart* in its fourth edition features M.D. Hooker on "Glaube III. Neues Testament" (2000).

[527] E. Wißmann 1926, 69; F. Neugebauer, 1961, 168; D. Lührmann 1990, 753; W. Schenk 1972, 168; H.D. Betz 1979, 118f. with n.45; J.M.G. Barclay 1988, 78n.8; G.W. Hansen, 1989, 102f., 113; O. Hofius 1990, 154f.n.51; V. Koperski 1993; J.D.G. Dunn 1997; 1998, 379-385; C.E.B. Cranfield 1998; R.B. Matlock 2000; 2002; 2003; M.A. Seifrid 2000, 142-145; P. Stuhlmacher 2001, 355; S. Westerholm 2004, 305f. B. Dodd takes a mediating position (1994). – See also the references in R.B. Hays 1997, 273f.n.4.

[528] I.G. Wallis 1995. See the critique in C.E.B. Cranfield 1998.

[529] R.A. Harrisville 1994. Compared to Wallis, who searched for and explored passages containing the idea of Christ's faithfulness, Harrisville carried out a narrower search on the phrase πίστις Χριστοῦ with the help of the *Thesaurus Linguae Graecae*. Much is dependent on the definition of the relationship between the Christ's πίστις and his ὑπακοή.

With this overview of the history of interpretation of Paul's concept of faith we should have gained a general idea of what interpreters of the New Testament deem the quintessence of πίστις in the writings of the apostle. On the other hand, the way how Paul himself describes the character of faith derives from his interpretation of the Old Testament, particularly of one specific passage: Gen 15:6. The origin, context, and *Sitz im Leben* of this verse will be the focus in the subsequent section.

Chapter III

Genesis 15:6

A. Genesis 15 in Historical Criticism

There is general agreement in modern Pentateuchal scholarship that Genesis 15 can be described as "one of the most interesting and complex chapters among the patriarchal narratives,"[1] which unfolds all basic themes of the Abraham cycle.[2] This assessment is commonly acknowledged despite the controversial literary-critical and tradition-historical classifications of the text.[3] However, before entering the theological exposition of Genesis 15 and especially of 15:6 within the framework of the Abraham cycle, the Pentateuch, and the Old Testament in general, one ought to trace in broad outline the complex history of interpretation since the critical era in Old Testament scholarship.[4] It will demonstrate the shifts that occurred in exploring the text, such as the fact that the main concentration changed from a diachronic, literary analysis to a synchronic and structural inquiry, a reaction against the tendency to give a privileged status to the earliest phases of the textual development.[5]

Since the beginning of the historical-critical investigation of Genesis 15, countless analyses to this most complex text have been advanced.[6] One has always perceived the resistance of the text against its categorization among the classical documents.[7] Though at first, scholars in the second

---

[1] M. Anbar 1982, 39. – For convenience, in the following we will use the more familiar form "Abraham," even though within the entire chapter 15 the form "Abram" appears.

[2] Cf. R. Rendtorff 1977, 37.

[3] Cf. among many others E. Blum 1984, 370; M. Oeming 1998, 77.

[4] Cf. for instance O. Kaiser 1958, 108n.4; H. Cazelles 1962, 321-325; A. Caquot 1962, 51-56; N. Lohfink 1967, 24-30; J. Van Seters 1975, 249-253; C. Westermann 1981, 253-255; H. Mölle 1988, 14-43; M. Köckert 1988, 326f. (table); J. Ha 1989, 30-36 (cf. the chart between 30 and 31); M. Oeming 1998, 77; T.C. Römer 2001, 198-211; A. Graupner 2002, 182-187.

[5] Cf., e.g., J. Blenkinsopp 1992, viii.

[6] N. Lohfink, already in 1967, mentions 39 different attempts since Wellhausen (1967, 24n.1).

[7] Cf. for example the summarizing statements of P. Heinisch 1930, 233: "Also versagt in diesem Kapitel die Charakteristik der Quellen," and M. Noth 1948, 6 (cf. 29n.85): "Es gibt Stücke," among which is Genesis 15, "deren überlieferter Zustand so ist, daß wohl

half of the 19th century generally assigned Genesis 15 to those texts that were regarded as Yahwistic (especially Genesis 12; 13; 18).[8] Only some decades later one divided the chapter into different sources, after one thought that the integrity of the text could no longer be maintained.[9] Several problematic methodological issues however emerge as soon as one engages in such literary analyses[10]: Historical criticism of the Old Testament indeed succeeded in establishing the compositional character of the Pentateuch, but not all elements of the multiple source theory proved to be equally efficient and persuasive. Already more than seventy years ago one started to question the existence of the Elohist source or at least cast doubt on the existence of clear criteria to demarcate it from the Yahwist and to define its distinct character.[11] Even the scholarly survival of the Yahwist is no longer guaranteed.[12]

I. Literary Features of Genesis 15

A literary-critical division seems to suggest itself due to a number of clues[13]: Some features are said to indicate a horizontal cut between Gen 15:1-6 and 15:7-21, such as the disagreement in the time of day (15:5 and 15:12.17)[14] and in the underlying theme,[15] the doublets regarding Yah-

---

niemals irgendeine literarkritische Analyse ihr literarisches Zustandekommen wirklich enträtseln wird."

[8] Cf. H. Mölle 1988, 14f. with the relevant representatives.

[9] The two Genesis commentaries by F. Delitzsch reflect this shift: At first he affirmed that all difficulties in the text of Genesis 15 can be removed through interpretation, conceding only that Gen 15:2 might have been taken from another source (1860, 367). Later, however, he admitted: "Die Erz[ählung] zerfällt in zwei Hälften" (1887, 272). J. Wellhausen's first edition of his study on the composition of the Hexateuch in 1885 paved the way for this new approach. Despite the modifications in subsequent scholarship, his presuppositions and questions remained decisive: The tensions in the text have to be explained by the distinction of different text pieces that themselves are part of the literary sources known from other Pentateuchal texts.

[10] Cf. N. Lohfink 1967, 24f.

[11] Cf. the general refutation of an own Elohist source in P. Volz/W. Rudolph 1933; A. Jepsen 1953/1954, 153. See also Y.T. Radday/H. Shore/M.A. Pollatschek/D. Wickmann 1982 and the replies by S.L. Portnoy/D.L. Peterson 1984 and R.E. Friedman 1996; see additionally A. Graupner 2002, 182-187.

[12] Cf. the recent volumes edited by J.C. Gertz et al. (2002; but see also the review by C. Levin 2004) and T.B. Dozeman/K. Schmid (2006).

[13] Cf. the enumeration of the problematic literary issues in Genesis 15 for instance in J. Wellhausen 1898, 21; H. Gunkel 1910, 177; J. Van Seters 1975, 249f.; H. Mölle 1988, 44f.; J. Ha 1989, 27-29, 39-42; P.R. Williamson 2000, 125-127; A. Graupner 2002, 184-186.

[14] Gen 15:5 presupposes a night scene, 15:12 points to the evening time, and in 15:17 once again it is night.

weh's self-introduction (15:1 and 15:7) and Abraham's response (15:2.3 and 15:8), as well as the contrasting juxtaposition of Abraham's faith and doubt[16] (15:6 and 15:8). Other aspects however would suggest a vertical division, i.e., a distinction of sources within those two sections, such as the two word advent formulas (15:1 and 15:4), the double response of Abraham containing the same theme, i.e., his childlessness (15:2 and 15:3), the distinctiveness between the promise of a single heir and numerous offspring (15:4 and 15:5), two promises of land donation (15:7 and 15:18), the almost identical temporal specification (15:12 and 15:17), the naming of the recipients of the land (15:7 and 15:18),[17] the time of the exodus of Abraham's descendants from the land of oppression (15:13 and 15:16),[18] the outcome of the enslavement of Abraham's descendants (15:13 and 15:14),[19] the interruption of the covenant rite by birds of prey and the prophecy (15:9-17) and the two speeches of Yahweh (15:13-16 and 15:18-21), the first of which occurring before the theophany. In sum, the composite nature of Genesis 15 seems to be betrayed by repetitions, discrepancies, antitheses, and discontinuity. Presupposing different sources, one has to further decide on the question whether the text consists of a basic core that was secondarily extended, or whether one deals with the secondary combination of two originally independent sources.

From a contextual-formal point of view, at first glance, one has to state an apparent lack of thematic coherence in Genesis 15, since diverse and unrelated themes seem to be accumulated.[20] Also, upon first reading one gets the impression that a "great number and complexity of genres ... have been combined in this chapter."[21] Moreover, as regards the overall genre, the chapter appears to have narrative character due to the large number of *waw*-imperfect forms, but both, the fact that only two personages participate in the story (Yahweh and Abraham) and the amount of verses containing direct speech, give the chapter the character of an imitated dialogic

---

[15] Abraham's heir and offspring are the topic of Gen 15:1-6, whereas the promise of land and the covenant shape 15:7-21.

[16] On Abraham's "doubt" see below page 97.

[17] The land is said to be given to Abraham (Gen 15:7) and to his descendants (15:18).

[18] Gen 15:13 mentions "four hundred years," while 15:16 speaks of "four generations."

[19] On the one hand, they are oppressed in the foreign land (Gen 15:13), but on the other they will come out with great possessions (15:14).

[20] Among these are Yahweh's promise of reward (Gen 15:1), Abraham's complaint (15:2), Yahweh's promise of one heir (15:4) and of countless offspring (15:5), Abraham's faith (15:6), Yahweh's promise of land (15:7.18), an animal rite (15:9-10.17), birds of prey (15:11), prophetic speech (15:13-16), and the covenant (15:18).

[21] J. Van Seters 1975, 260; cf. H. Mölle 1988, 335n.232. For instance a divine word advent together with an "oracle of salvation" (Gen 15:1.4), a form of lament (15:2-3), the request of a sign (15:8), or a prophetic discourse (15:13-16) etc.

narrative. Another problem appears to be the coexistence of archaic elements, like the name Eliezer (15:2) or the rite of animals cut in two (15:9-
10.17) and presumably late, Deuteronomic-Deuteronomistic features like
the introduction of the episode as a vision report (15:1), the verb ירשׁ
(15:3.4.7.8), the stars metaphor (15:5), the promise of land and offspring,
the gentilic list (15:19-21), or the fixation of the boundaries of the land
(15:18).

II. Literary and Source Criticism

All these observations led to the assumption of several layers in the chapter that could be traced back to the Yahwist, the Elohist, and a redactor. In
literary-critical scholarship since J. Wellhausen, those sources have been
discriminated and extracted by means of basically three different models:
(1) The first, advocated by Wellhausen himself, carries out a horizontal cut
between Gen 15:1-6 and 15:7-21, assigning the first half to the Elohist and
the second the Yahwist.[22] (2) The second regards the present text as consisting of two interlocked main text pieces, of which the first is basically
Elohistic and the second Yahwistic, but which also incorporate overlaps
and elements from the respective other source.[23] (3) In the third view, one
performs vertical cuts, perceiving the text as being formed by two strands
that are intertwined in a complex manner.[24] Those models dominated the
discussion until the middle of the last century.

Other literary-critical hypotheses separated themselves from the governing Yahwist-Elohist-redactor schema and suggested that one part of the
chapter is to be attributed to one of the two old Pentateuchal sources,
which then experienced later additions and supplements. Even here, schol-

---

[22] J. Wellhausen attributed Gen 15:1-6* to the Elohist and 15:7-21* to the Yahwist,
and all elements that do not fit the presupposed pattern to a redactor. Being aware of the
shortcomings of his theory, he formulated with caution that "möglicherweise ein gewisses Ineinander von E und J zu constatieren ist" (1898, 21). – Parenthetically, one should
not that if it is the Elohist who, *inter alia*, speaks in Genesis 15 we would have here the
"programmatischen Auftakt der elohistischen Geschichtsdarstellung" (R. Kilian 1966a,
380; cf. P. Weimar 1989, 391-399; against that A. Graupner 2002, 186f.).

[23] Cf. R. Smend 1912, 43-45; O. Eißfeldt 1964, 265f.; O. Procksch 1924, 107-112; A.
Alt 1929, 71f.; J. Skinner 1930, 277; G. von Rad 1951, 133; 1967, 153f. (but see 1972,
140f.); H. Seebass 1963 (differently 1983); E.A. Speiser 1964, 110-115; R. Kilian 1966,
36-73; H. Wildberger 1968, 142, 146f.

[24] Cf. H. Cazelles 1962. The two sources he discerns "répondent fort bien aux deux
couches appelées jahviste et élohiste par la critique" (347); in his analysis, the present
text switches about 20 times from the Yahwist to the Elohist. See also L. Ruppert 2000,
309.

ars put forward numerous disparate solutions, arguing either for the Elo-hist[25] or for the Yahwist[26] as source of the primary portion.

In the following years redaction-criticism changed to a certain degree the literary-critical *modus operandi*. For, the idea that a compiler gathered disparate pre-formed material and old traditions would account for contextual tensions and incoherencies. The accent therefore does not lie exclusively on the identification and chronological ordering of sources in order to find the earliest, but on the growth of the text into the present shape and on the determination of the nature and theological thematic invention that governs the text as a whole, in its canonical form. The "first" context is more and more emphasized, i.e., not the historically oldest, but the first regarding one's perception.[27] However, some deny the literary growth of the chapter and conceive it as a unity formed according to distinct organizing principles.[28]

But what theological-ideological background does our chapter presuppose and what historical circumstances are reflected? The answers to these questions exhibit a great variety and breadth: They range from pre-Yahwistic,[29] Yahwistic,[30] Jehovistic,[31] monarchical,[32] Deuteronomic-

---

[25] Cf. G. Hölscher 1952, 278-280; H. Mölle 1988, 377f.; L. Perlitt 1969, 68-77; P. Weimar 1989 (Weimar "a poussé les opérations de critique littéraire à l'extrême," according to T.C. Römer 2001, 200).

[26] C.A. Simpson 1948, 73f.; O. Kaiser (1958) assigns the old original kernel of Gen 15:7-21 to the Yahwist, who reworked even older traditions; a Deuteronomisticly influenced hand edited this portion, which is also responsible for the content the rest of the chapter (15:1-6) and the connection of those two parts (others followed this theory, such as R. Smend 1967, 286, 290; M. Oeming 1983, 183n.9). Cf. also E. Sellin/L. Rost 1949, 48, 54; H. Wildberger 1968, 146; H. Seebass 1983 (differently 1963).

[27] Cf. G. Steins 2001, 518.

[28] Especially J. Ha advocates this position by pointing to "progressive doublets," "progressive antitheses" and an "unbroken thread," which ties up all verses and themes. The author of Genesis 15 produced "a coherent and closely knit whole, whose unity has been remarkably worked out" (1989, 39-62, quote: 58). H. Mölle on the other hand denies categorically the possibility of the text's unity in view of the history of scholarship (1988, 43; cf. equally general O. Kaiser 1958, 109).

[29] P. Volz/W. Rudolph 1933, 25-34 (two self-contained texts combined in pre-Yahwistic times); A. Jepsen 1953/1954 (pre-Yahwistic basic core), 152f.; N. Lohfink 1967, 37, 114-116 (*Grundtext*, i.e., 15:1-2.4-12.17-21, "zur Zeit des Jahwisten in allen seinen wesentlichen Teilen denkbar," 37). – Quite wrongly, P.R. Williamson places J. Van Seters in this category of scholars who allegedly followed Lohfink (2000, 80 with n.12).

[30] M. Noth 1948, 29 (coherent Yahwistic text with remainders of E-variants); R.E. Clements 1967, 21; G.W. Coats 1983, 123; J.D. Levenson 1987, 60.

[31] H. Gese 1991, 43-46 (his Jehovist, though, is associated with the Deuteronomistic movement); E. Haag 1989.

Deuteronomistic[33] to post-Deuteronomistic and post-Priestly.[34] However, there is a clearly discernible trend to regard Genesis 15 as some kind of unity[35] that originated in the Deuteronomic-Deuteronomistic milieu in the late exilic period.[36]

The numerous solutions offered regarding the literary-critical problem lead to the question of the possibility to obtain a sound methodology and to gain relatively reliable results.[37] In particular Gen 15:1-6, including 15:6,

---

[32] J. Hoftijzer 1956 (late monarchy or exile); A. Caquot 1962, 66; C. Westermann 1981, 274 (late monarchy).

[33] J. Van Seters 1975, 249-278; H.H. Schmid 1976, 119-143; R. Rendtorff 1977, 165; 1980, 75, 79; J.A. Emerton 1982, 17; M. Anbar 1982, 40 ("conflation of two deutero-nomic narratives"); E. Blum 1984, 366-383 ([early] post-exilic context, 367); J. Blenkinsopp 1992, 123; H. Hagelia 1994, 206, 210, 219; E. Noort 1995, 143 ("early post-exilic time"). Already J. Skinner recognized affinities of this "J narrative" with the Deuteronomistic School (1930, 277). E. Blum (1984, 366n.37) refers to the even earlier commentary by J.W. Colenso (1865), who on the basis of a linguistic comparison considers the entire chapter "Deuteronomistic." See also C.A. Simpson 1948, 73f.; O. Kaiser 1958; R. Smend 1967, 286f.

[34] J. Ha argues: "Given the equally dominant Deuteronomistic, Priestly as well as prophetic traits in Gen 15, it is impossible to identify its author with any of these schools" (1989, 216). "Gen 15 makes a clean break from ... Deuteronomistic theology of history as it emphasizes the unilateral בְּרִית" (195f.; cf. 93 _et passim_). Cf. K. Schmid 1999, 172-186 (a summary of Genesis to 2Kings, 179); T.C. Römer 2001, 206 ("un résumé du Pentateuque"; cf. 1990); J.L. Ska 2001, 172. But see against these proposals H. Gese 1991, 30n.9; D.M. Carr 2001, 277 with n.13. – The later one dates Genesis 15 the more difficult it gets to explain the relationship between Gen 15:6 and Ps 106:31 (see below chapter IV.A).

[35] Cf. E. Blum 1984, 377; E. Noort 1995, 141. Among those who defend the basic unity of the chapter are the already mentioned P. Heinisch, J. Hoftijzer, M. Noth, A. Caquot, N. Lohfink, R.E. Clements, J. Van Seters, H.H. Schmid, R. Rendtorff, C. Westermann, M. Anbar, E. Blum, J. Ha, and T.C. Römer; in addition L.A. Snijders 1958; B. Vawter 1977, 203f.; A. Abela 1986, 14; M. Köckert 1988, 210-227; G. Wenham 1988, 326; K. Schmid 1999, 175f.; P.R. Williamson 2000, 124-133; J.C. Gertz 2002, 69. See, however, against that L. Ruppert 2000, 299. – Gertz offers the most recent treatment of Genesis 15: He argues for a substantial unity of the chapter (69) with a few traces of minor redactional work (70). While its _Grundbestand_ is non-Priestly/pre-Priestly and represents the youngest stage of an independent patriarchal history, the significant additions Gen 15:11.13-16 constitute a dogmatic correction by a post-Priestly redaction; this correction unfolds "die Gestalt und Geschichte Abrahams als Prolepse der heilsgeschichtlichen Daten der Exoduserzählung" (79; cf. 73f.). Primarily, Gertz seeks to prove that the patriarchal history and the exodus tradition are two competing conceptions of Israel's origins (76), which have only been combined by the Priestly Document (see against Gertz, C. Levin 2004, 333f.).

[36] Cf. S. Talmon 1990, 13; T.C. Römer 2001, 198: "Cette datation [_sc._ exilique] semble de plus en plus constituer la nouvelle _opinio communis._"

[37] For J. Van Seters, the countless suggestions show that source criticism has usually been pursued "on a largely arbitrary basis" (1975, 250; cf. P.R. Williamson 2000, 84).

brings to light the difficulties inherent in this method, as any verse or verse piece has been attributed to different sources or redactions. This element of insecurity is the main reason why several scholars deliberately disconnect their exegetical work from literary-critical analyses.[38] Yet not only the literary-critical investigation of Genesis 15 generated a great dissent among scholars, but also the determination of the tradition-historical setting of this text. Both methodical steps, to be sure, are interconnected.

III. The Tradition-Historical Environment of Genesis 15

Since A. Alt's suggestion that Gen 15:7-21 consists of the Yahwistic implementation of a most ancient, pre-Israelite covenant tradition of Abraham's God (possibly known as מָגֵן אַבְרָהָם),[39] several studies have sought to uncover this oldest patriarchal tradition.[40] Some took up and developed Alt's thesis, maintaining the ancient character and origin of the covenant tradition,[41] but it was O. Kaiser's analysis of Genesis 15 that advanced the study of this chapter to a new level – though not establishing a new consensus. In his view, which he substantiated by means of both tradition-historical analysis and comparative form-critical study, an author influenced by Deuteronomistic theology composed Gen 15:1-6 in analogy to 15:7-21 and edited 15:7-21, an old, possibly genuine Abrahamic tradition that came down to him in the Yahwistic form. The context of this composition and edition is the time of the exile when the existence of Israel as a people and the land as its possession had to be reassured and when Israel needed comfort in the hour of oppression.[42] After Kaiser, there have been efforts, among others by H. Cazelles, N. Lohfink, or R.E. Clement to refute his basic theses and to retain a relatively early date of the covenant

---

[38] Cf. already C. Westermann 1964, 21-24 (but see his commentary 1981, 250-275); recently P. Auffret 2002, 342.

[39] A. Alt 1929, 72f. Alt recognizes "eine alte Kultstiftungssage" (72) behind the Yahwistic strand of Genesis 15. This classification goes against scholars like H. Gunkel and W. Staerk, who deem the text to be a "spätere Neubildung" (H. Gunkel 1910, 183) or even as reaction to the fall of Samaria (W. Staerk 1924). Alt's suggestion that מָגֵן אַבְרָהָם denotes the archaic name of a God of the fathers was invalidated, following the insight that מָגֵן has its place in the "oracle of salvation."

[40] See the overview of suggestions in J. Ha 1989, 31-33.

[41] Cf. W.F. Albright 1968, 93 ("strikingly archaic"); A. Jepsen 1953/1954; G. von Rad 1962, 182 (Gen 15:7-21 as "höchst altertümliche[.] Erzählung").

[42] The three levels in the tradition-historical process are according to O. Kaiser (1958, 124f.): 1. oral tradition about the covenant of "Abraham's God" with the Abraham people, connected with Hebron/Mamre; 2. oral tradition linking the Abraham tradition with the Shechemite covenant of the tribal federation; Yahwistic editing towards a legitimization of the Davidic kingdom; 3. addition of Gen 15:1-6 and edition of the latter part according to Deuteronomistic theology with the aim to actualize the old story (cf. H.-J. Hermisson 1978, 25).

tradition,[43] while others, like J. Van Seters, sought to transcend literary and tradition-historical questions by means of form-critical and structural analyses, denying that "an ancient legend has been reworked or modified by a later author."[44]

B. Genre, Form, and Structure of Genesis 15

While there is still a "historical and theological necessity of a diachronic approach" to the Old Testament texts,[45] notably of Genesis 15, there can be much gained from exploring the "skilful literary artistry and theological understanding,"[46] the compositional design and movement that is reflected in the text's final form. Therefore, in the following, some elements of genre, form, language, and style will be highlighted in order to shed light on the working method of the narrator/author and to give some clues as to when those elements were essentially compiled.[47] Subsequently, a struc-

---

[43] H. Cazelles concludes that the Elohistic part of Genesis 15 is related to 2nd millennium Hittite and Semitic treaties and the Yahwistic part is in line with familial and dynastic expectations of the Phoenician texts of Ras Shamra. "Mais l'un comme l'autre ont de très bons répondants dans le vocabulaire, les institutions et les mouvements de peuples du second millénaire"; the redactor then combined the two strands with the goal to reinforce the union of Israel's tribes, all of whom are heirs of the covenant between God and Abraham. The sanctuary where the promise of offspring in the oldest tradition (J) occurs, is probably Mamre (1962, 348f.). – N. Lohfink counters Kaiser's "traditionsgeschichtliche Untersuchung," saying that "eigentlich kein Vers in Gn 15 aus traditionsgeschichtlichen Überlegungen später als ins 10. Jahrhundert angesetzt werden *muß*" (N. Lohfink 1967, 37, emphasis original; T.C. Römer quotes wrongly: "... *kann*" [2001, 195]). The oldest tradition, to be located at Shechem, contains the divine affirmation of the promise of land that Abraham sought for when he proceeded to the tree of oracles (the Oak of Moreh). The present text is a secondary compilation of oracles, created for the Jerusalem cult or school with the intention to reformulate and reinforce the old, but declining tradition of Yahweh's oath to Abraham, at a time when the traditions of the promise to David emerged (1967, 100, 113, 116f.). – A similar purpose of Genesis 15, namely, to lend support to the Davidic dynasty, is suggested by R.E. Clements, but he places the oldest tradition at Mamre where the El-deity made an oath to Abraham, promising that he and his offspring may inhabit the land (1967, 28, 60, 80; cf. also R. Kilian 1966).

[44] Cf. J. Van Seters 1975, 249-278, quote: 263. Building on Kaiser's work on Gen 15:7-21, but going beyond its results, he seeks to refute the "two dogmas" of previous scholarship, first that the basic literary source dates back to the 10th century, and second that the *Grundtext* is interpreted in terms of "the context of the Davidic-Solomonic 'empire'" (252). Cf. H.H. Schmid 1980, 398. See vigorously against this methodology, H. Mölle 1988, 43n.186.

[45] Thus the title of E. Noort 1995.

[46] P.R. Williamson 2000, 7.

[47] Cf. on the literary allusions and reflections in Genesis 15, e.g., M. Anbar 1982; J. Ha 1989; K. Schmid 1999, 182-186.

tural analysis will be presented, followed by an appraisal of the theological significance of these pericopes within the final compilation of Genesis, so far it is pertinent for the understanding of Gen 15:6 in the context of its reception history.

I. Genre, Forms – Date and Purpose

The literary connective "after these things..." (Gen 15:1) appears three times in the Abraham-story,[48] always having the function to insert a single episode into a larger context of events.[49] This phrase has counterparts in later biblical writings[50] and is stylistically characteristic for written prose.[51] It is followed by the statement that the opening "word of Yahweh came to Abraham in a vision" (15:1). Both expressions, הָיָה דְבַר־יְהוָה and מַחֲזֶה,[52] equally describe the prophetic reception of a divine revelation. Notably, the first represents, from Jeremiah onwards, a technical way to express the advent of divine speech coming to a prophet[53] – it would appear therefore that Gen 15:1-6 presupposes prophetism.[54]

Yahweh's speech follows in the form of a stylized[55] "oracle of salvation,"[56] adhering to a certain degree to the structure of a priestly "oracle of salvation." Generally, its *Sitz im Leben* are situations threatening the king's domestic political and foreign political subsistence, fights regarding the succession to the throne, and larger military campaigns. The constitutive

---

[48] Besides Gen 15:1 also in 22:1.20. Other occurrences are in the Joseph-story (Gen 39:7; 40:1; 48:1) and in Josh 24:29, 1Kgs 17:17, and 21:1.

[49] Cf. C. Westermann 1981, 435.

[50] Esth 2:1; 3:1; Ezra 7:1; cf. M. Anbar 1982, 40.

[51] Cf. J. Van Seters 1975, 253.

[52] Cf. Isa 1:1; Obad 1; Nah 1:1). The related term חָזוֹן implies – being derived from the *terminus technicus* חזה – the revelation to a נָבִיא, but due to the scarce occurrences of מחזה, precise facts about content and date cannot be discerned (cf. H. Seebass 1997, 68).

[53] Cf. O. Kaiser 1958, 110n.12. Apart from Jeremiah (1:2; 14:1; 20:8; 25:3; 32:6; 39:15; 46:1; 47:1; 49:34), it is above all Ezekiel who uses the expression (1:3; 26:1; 29:1.17; 30:20; 31:1; 32:1.17), but then also the late prophets Haggai (1:1; 2:1.10) and Zechariah (1:1.7; 7:1). In older prophecy it is not yet a technical term (cf. Isa 28:13). See also H.W. Wolff 1961, 1f.

[54] C. Westermann, among others, comes to this conclusion, considering Gen 15:1 and 15:4 (1981, 257f.). Cf. J. Ha 1989, 63-90.

[55] Cf. C. Westermann 1964, 21-24; 1981, 258, and, with certain modifications the majority of interpreters.

[56] Cf. O. Kaiser 1958, 111-115; H. Cazelles 1962, 326-334; N. Lohfink 1967, 49; H.M. Dion 1967; R.E. Clements 1967, 19; H. Wildberger 1968, 135f., 142f.; J. Körner 1979, 715; H.H. Schmid 1980, 398f.; L. Gaston 1980, 45f. See also the foundational study of J. Begrich (1934). R.W.L. Moberly, though, is critical of the heuristic value of this classification; he argues that it is "of only limited assistance in interpreting the passage as it stands in its present narrative context" (1990, 104n.5).

elements of this genre are (1) the appellative formula "Fear not!,"[57] (2) the assurance of salvation or victory, and (3) the motif of trust or faith. Particularly the latter is of interest to us.

Numerous comparable oracles following this schema can be found in the texts from the Ancient Near East, especially of Neo-Assyrian provenance.[58] The oracle of Ištar to Esarhaddon by an "unknown prophet"[59] is particularly instructive in the context of Genesis 15, since besides those three elements, additional analogies are present: the promise of long life (cf. 15:15), the motifs "shield" (15:1), "smoke" and "fire" (15:17), "prosperity for progeny" (15:18) and the deity's giving safe conduct on a dangerous journey (15:16), as well as the definition of the boundaries of the land to be possessed (15:19-21). The most illuminating passages of the oracle read[60]: "I am Ištar of [Arbela]. Esarhaddon, king of A[ssyria]! In the Inner City, Nineveh, Calah and Arbela I will give long days and everlasting years to Esarhaddon, my king ... For long days and everlasting years I have established your throne under the great heavens ... I let the lamp of amber shine before Esarhaddon ... and I watch him like the crown of my head. Have no fear, my king! ... I have given you faith, I will not let you come to shame. I will take you safely across the River ... O Esarhaddon, I will be your good shield in Arbela ... I keep you in the great heavens by your *curl*. I make smoke rise up on your right side, I kindle fire on your left."

In the Assyrian context, the oracles are institutionally bound to the royal court and stand in the framework of the cult. This connection, however, is successively weakened in central Old Testament texts that employ this genre[61]: Isaiah 7 presents an "oracle of salvation" situated in a non-cultic context, but still addressed to the king,[62] while in Exodus 14, in the account of the Crossing of the Red Sea, both links, to king and cult, are dissolved.[63] In an even more abstract way, now, the narrator of Genesis 15

---

[57] This appellation is also found in other narratives about theophanies to patriarchs: Gen 21:17; 26:24; 46:3. Moreover, the divine self-introduction אֲנִי יְהוָה is also typical of "salvation oracles" (cf. W. Zimmerli 1953, 24-27).

[58] As to Assyrian oracles, S. Parpola provides a chart demonstrating that the "demand for faith" is a significant structural element of an "oracle of salvation" (1997, lxv).

[59] According to Parpola, it dates to the year of the Assyrian civil war 681 B.C., "after the [decisive] battle but before Esarhaddon's arrival in Nineveh." "[T]he final victory had not yet been achieved" (S. Parpola 1997, lxviii-lxix).

[60] See S. Parpola 1997, 7f.

[61] Cf. H.H. Schmid 1980, 399.

[62] (1) "Fear not!" (Isa 7:4), (2) the plans of the enemies will not succeed (7:7), (3) "If you do not stand firm in faith, you shall not stand at all" (7:9).

[63] (1) "Fear not!" (Ex 14:13), (2) Yahweh will accomplish deliverance (14:13), (3) "the people feared Yahweh and believed in him and in his servant Moses" (14:31). H.H. Schmid argues that this account of the Crossing of the Red Sea is stylized as a "Holy

chose[64] to dissociate the formal pattern from both the military realm and the cult and to create an "ideal" scene,[65] whose elements are elevated to a metaphorical level: Abraham, the "king," whose "succession to the throne" is in jeopardy, receives a spontaneous "oracle" that calls him to relinquish his "fear,"[66] and gives him assurance of "victory"[67] – and in all that Abraham has faith.[68]

If the formal modifications, which are observable in this comparison between the Isaiah, Exodus, and Genesis passages, reflect a chronological process, the "oracle" in Gen 15:1-6 appears to derive from a relatively late literary-historical level.[69] The attempt to determine the historical horizon of the "oracle's" conclusion (15:6), leads most plausibly to exilic times, since an element, initially bound to cult and court, has been extracted from its original context and applied to a different situation in which the temple cult and the monarchical context were no longer given, but in which, instead, hope and faith in the divine promises became indispensable and existential.[70]

The image of innumerable stars in the promise to Abraham (Gen 15:5) appears in various other places: Yahweh repeats his promise towards both Abraham (Gen 22:17) and Isaac (Gen 26:4), and Moses reminds Yahweh of it (Ex 32:13); it is mentioned in Deuteronomy after the Israelites' so-

---

War" narrative (1976, 55f.; cf. H. Wildberger 1967, 380; several Deuteronomistic war addresses also allude to the oracle form [cf. Deut 1:20-21.29-32; 20:3-4; 31:6; Josh 10:25]). On "faith" in Exodus (4 and) 14, see H. Groß 1970. H.-C. Schmitt remarks, "daß hier [*sc.* in Gen 15:6] nicht nur eine zufällige terminologische Übereinstimmung mit dem Zentralbegriff der Exodusdarstellung vorliegt, sondern ein entsprechendes ... Glaubensverständnis zum Ausdruck kommt" (1982, 178; see also J.C. Gertz 2002, 79).

[64] J. Van Seters speaks of a "deliberate and conscious choice" (1975, 255).

[65] H.H. Schmid 1980, 399.

[66] Fear is not the expected reaction to childlessness.

[67] Associations with the theme of war emerge only secondarily and retrospectively: "Shield" refers to protection in war (cf. O. Kaiser 1958, 113-115), and "reward" recalls the pay of the soldier (cf. Ezek 29:19, but also Isa 40:10; 62:11; cf. H. Cazelles 1962, 328; see also H. Wildberger 1968, 143). Notably, the metaphorical use of שׂכר occurs predominantly in late passages, for instance in Isa 40:10; 62:11; Jer 31:16; 2Chr 15:7 (cf. M. Anbar 1982, 41).

[68] The most critical objection against the presupposed genre is based on the fact that Abraham's questioning response to God's assurance (Gen 15:1) has the form of a lament (15:2-3); the expected order would be the reversed. This surprising sequence, however, can be attributed to the passage's stylized character in general (cf. C. Westermann 1981, 257) and to the structural parallelism between 15:2-3 and 15:8 in particular (see the table below pages 100f.). – See in addition the enumeration of possible objections against the form-critical classification of Gen 15:1-6 as "oracle of salvation" in H. Mölle 1988, 273n.15.

[69] Cf. already C.A. Simpson 1948, 73; H.M. Dion 1967, 205.

[70] Cf. J. Van Seters 1975, 269; see also, with reservations, C. Westermann 1981, 264f.

journ in Egypt, before they enter the promised land.[71] Other passages refer
to the star metaphor in connection with David's kingship and progeny[72] –
at the time of David's and Solomon's kingship, the promise was fulfilled.[73]
As for the theological stance and provenance of these passages, it would
appear that the image used in Gen 15:5 draws on a Deuteronomic-
Deuteronomistic idea[74] and has the intention to recall themes of the exodus
and the Davidic kingdom for those still in the exile.

A new theme begins with 15:7, indicated by another self-introduction
formula, which strongly resembles the one in the Holiness Code (Lev
25:38)[75] and its adaptation in the exilic prophets.[76] There, i.e., in these
prophets, the theme of the exodus experience is taken up to emphasize in
confessional tone the possibility of being set free from bondage by God.[77]
It is not unlikely, therefore, that Gen 15:7 has the same purpose in the present context.[78] This connection is further strengthened by the occurrence of
the verbs נתן and ירש, which frequently appear in Deuteronomic land donation formulas[79] and in comparable passages in Jeremiah, Ezekiel, and Deutero-Isaiah.[80] In 15:8, the statement of knowledge ("Erkenntnisaussage"),
which is primarily known from Ezekiel, is formed as a question.[81] The specific formulation and content of this question reflects the concrete situation
of the addressees of the exile period, who desire an assurance of the land

---

[71] Deut 1:10; 10:22; 28:62; Neh 9:23.

[72] 1Chr 27:23; Jer 33:22.

[73] 1Kgs 3:8; 4:20. R.E. Clements reasons on the basis of these passages that the star
metaphor originated at the time of Solomon (1967, 19).

[74] On the Deuteronomistic character of Gen 22:17, see, e.g., R. Rendtorff 1977, 43f.;
Gen 26:4 sounds, already to F. Delitzsch, Deuteronomistic (1887, 361; cf. E. Blum 1984,
362); the same can be said for Ex 32:13 (cf. B.S. Childs 1974, 558f.). On Gen 15:5, see
for instance J. Skinner 1930, 279f.

[75] Cf. Ex 20:2; 29:46; Lev 11:45; 22:32-33; 26:45; Num 15:41; Deut 4:37-38; 5:6;
6:23; Jdg 6:8-9; Ps 81:11. Lev 25:38, though, is the closest parallel; yet it goes too far to
deduce from this fact that Gen 15:7 must be post-exilic, because it "is dependent on P,"
from which in turn Lev 25:38 is taken (J. Ha 1989, 102). Rather, Lev 25:38 belongs to
the Holiness Code, which for instance J. Milgrom considers "[w]ith the exception of a
few verses ... preexilic" (2000, 1361). Date and origin of the Holiness Code and its relationship to the Priestly Document are of course a matter of much debate (cf. succinctly E.
Zenger 1995, 159-161)

[76] Cf. Isa 43:16-19; Jer 16:14-15; Mic 7:15.

[77] Cf. Ex 6:6; 7:4-5; 12:17.51; 16:6; 18:1; 20:2; Lev 19:36; 25:38.42.55; Num 15:41.

[78] Cf. M. Anbar 1982, 45f. To him, the mention of the Chaldeans speaks for a "late
designation" as well (46).

[79] Cf. Deut 9:6; 12:1; 15:4; 19:2.14; 21:1; 25:19; Josh 1:11.

[80] Cf. Jer 30:3; 49:2; Ezek 33:24-26; 36:12; Isa 54:3; 57:13; 60:21; 61:7; 65:9. See R.
Rendtorff 1980.

[81] H. Seebass 1997, 73.

promise.[82] As for the instruction and preparation for the covenant rite in 15:9-10, there is hardly agreement among interpreters. Yet the account of a related ceremony in Jer 34:18 and other Ancient Near Eastern parallels could suggest – despite the modifications and differences – that the rite in Genesis 15 stands in relative proximity to the one described in Jeremiah.[83] The prediction in 15:13-16 is connected to 15:7-8 both terminologically and thematically: Abraham asks "How shall I know (אֵדַע)...?" (15:8) and Yahweh answers "Know this for certain (יָדֹעַ תֵּדַע)...." (15:13); and the theme inherent in both passages is the exodus.[84] Hence, God's confirming answer to Abraham's question and the following sign, emphasize the truth and faithfulness of his word – again a topic that became important in the Deuteronomy and in the later prophets.[85] In the passage 15:13-16, the hope and expectation are portrayed that build on the return of the people into the land of Abraham's grave[86] after a fixed duration of the oppression; even here, the congruence of the experiences in Babylon and Egypt are apparent.[87] Finally, the composition of the covenant scene, taken in comparison with other promise and oath texts, reveals its Deuteronomistic character as well as the centrality of Genesis 15 within the Pentateuch.[88] The author creates a significant theological climax, when he gives Yahweh's promise of the land in 15:18 the character of a legally binding document; this character is reinforced by means of the performative meaning of the verbal form,[89] as well as through the designation of the boundaries.[90]

---

[82] Cf. R. Rendtorff 1980, 78, 81.

[83] M. Anbar 1982, 46, 48.

[84] M. Anbar remarks that there is only one analogous passage to the expression בְּאֶרֶץ לֹא לָהֶם (Gen 15:13), namely, Jer 5:19, and only one parallel to בִּרְכֻשׁ גָּדוֹל (Gen 15:14), namely Dan 11:28 (1982, 47).

[85] Cf. J. Van Seters 1975, 259.

[86] Cf. H. Seebass 1997, 75.

[87] Cf. Jer 16:14-15.

[88] Cf. E. Blum 1984, 382 (approvingly cited by E. Noort 1995, 143, and many others): "[Die] Gestaltung der Landverheißung und vor allem die erzählerische Entfaltung der Verheißungen in V.5 und in der Szenerie des 'Bundesschlusses' erweisen *Gen 15* insgesamt als den *Basistext für die Mehrungs- und Landverheißung im Kontext der D-Überlieferungen*. Offenbar ist er auch für diese Funktion konzipiert worden" (italics original).

[89] Cf. C. Brockelmann 1956, §41d; W. Gesenius/E. Kautzsch 1962, §106m (see however the Septuagint: δώσω). The speech act coincides with the factual giving of the land. While the Masoretic Text – and also the Samaritan Pentateuch – use the performative perfect, the versions and, for instance, *Jub* 14,18, have imperfect or future forms (cf. J.C. VanderKam 1989, 86).

[90] Cf. E. Zenger 1995, 169. He uses the term "Urkundencharakter."

The mentioned features[91] of our text leave hardly any other option than to locate it in the wider milieu of the Deuteronomic-Deuteronomistic movement[92] and in the period of the prophets Jeremiah, Ezekiel, and above all Deutero-Isaiah.[93] One final aspect confirms this classification: Both in Genesis 15 and in Ezekiel 33 and Isaiah 51, Abraham functions as "corporate personality" and figure of identification[94] who represents the people of Israel and whose fate is analogous to Israel's. God's promise of land to Abraham is factually his promise to Israel, i.e., to his descendants.[95] According to Ezekiel, those who stayed in the land argue along those lines: "Abraham was only one man, yet he got possession of the land; but we are many; the land is surely given us to possess" (Ezek 33:24). In Deutero-Isaiah a similar point is made: "Look to Abraham your father and to Sarah who bore you; for he was but one when I called him, but I blessed him and made him many" (Isa 51:2). To be sure, due to the narrative genre of Genesis 15 the connecting lines between Abraham and Israel are not drawn as explicitly as in the two prophetic passages, but they are nevertheless clear and graspable.

II. Overall Genre – Narrative Technique

In an open, general sense, one can identify Genesis 15 as a narrative text that recounts the basic promises to Abraham. But one has to qualify this statement immediately, since the narrative features are somewhat modified and other features are conspicuously constructed. The narrative consists of two scenes, but in spite of that, the *dramatis personae* – Yahweh and Abraham – remain the same. This is at variance with the conventions of "proper" narratives with several scenes. Moreover, the whole account is governed by a "dialogic" structure[96] so that the actions and events happening outside of the conversation (15:5.10-11.12.17) appear to have only secondary character.[97] Thus, the words themselves form the "plot" of the

---

[91] See in addition L. Ruppert 2000, 296f.

[92] This specification does not exclude a distinctive theological outlook of Genesis 15 (see below chapter III.E and especially III.E.V).

[93] The demonstration of the proximity of Genesis 15 to Deutero-Isaiah is above all due to J. Van Seters (1975).

[94] Cf. B. Ego 1996, 35, referring to K. Koch 1991, 9; also T.C. Römer 2001, 192; J.L. Ska 2001, 175f. In contrast to David, Abraham is "Idenfikationsfigur nicht nur für Könige und herrschaftsgewohnte Kreise, sondern für jedermann in Israel" (W. Dietrich 2000, 53).

[95] Cf. L. Gaston 1980, 47-49; M. Köckert 1988, 243-247.

[96] Yahweh talks to Abraham eight times, and Abraham talks to Yahweh two times (Abraham's objection in Gen 15:2-3 belong together).

[97] Cf. G. von Rad 1951, 130: "Einem Minimum an Handlung steht ein Dialog zwischen Jahwe und Abraham gegenüber."

chapter, in this way that Yahweh's introductory statement: "Your reward will be very great" sets thetically the content of the subsequent dialogue. Abraham's questioning objections towards Yahweh's promise (15:2-3.8) mark the scenes' progression as they challenge God to develop, clarify, and assure what he initially said.[98] These questions, each introduced through the appellative אֲדֹנָי יהוה, are singular in the scope of the patriarchal narratives and point to the essential theme of Genesis 15: the issue of the validity of the promise,[99] or: "Who will receive the reward?"

From the perspective of the dramaturgy, the dialogic progression, however, does not steer towards a dramatic climax; rather, the development of the promise's content happens in a calm manner, finding its conclusion in the grave, legal formulation of the covenant, which answers the question of the beneficiaries of the divine promise posed in 15:1.[100] On the other hand, the statement about the covenant (15:18) indeed serves as "climax," though not regarding the outer plot, but rather regarding an inner dramatic movement, the covenant's background, content and consequence. Thus, the visionary and serene character of the narrative and its open horizon – the starry sky and the descendents yet to realize the promise – give to the chapter "a mood of timelessness."[101]

Another feature of Genesis 15 that deviates from the common characteristics of biblical narratives is the dissociation of the narrator from the events at the end of the two scenes. In both passages, he leaves the ground of the actual narrative and moves to a different level of communication by making an accentuated statement, in 15:6 on Abraham's faith and Yahweh's reckoning[102] and in 15:18 on the covenant between Yahweh and Abraham. The employed literary means that indicate the narrator's taking distance from the concrete account are the change from the narrative imperfect to a perfect form in an inversion, both in 15:6 (וְהֶאֱמִן)[103] and in

---

[98] Cf. N. Lohfink 1967, 32; J. Ha 1989, 58.

[99] Cf. R. Rendtorff 1980, 75.

[100] M. Köckert also notes the connection of Gen 15:1 and 15:18 (1988, 243).

[101] H. Hagelia 1994, 211. M. Oeming, too, deems Gen 15:1-6 as "eigentümlich schwebend formuliert" – "fast wie eine abstrakte Kerygma-Theologie" (1998, 77).

[102] On the particular character of 15:6, cf. H. Gunkel 1910, 180; N. Lohfink 1967, 32, 46; H. Seebass 1963, 135; G. von Rad 1972, 142; H. Groß 1981, 18; K. Seybold 1982, 258; C. Westermann 1981, 263; K. Haacker 1984, 283; R.W.L. Moberly 1990, 104, 128. A. Behrens compares with 15:6 the verses Ex 4:31 and 14:31, as they have similar "Fazitcharakter" and conclude each with אמן *hiphil*; he points to older rabbinic traditions that also identified a correlation between Gen 15:6, Ex 4:31 and 14:31 (1997, 332f., with reference to P. Billerbeck 1926, 198f.; D.U. Rottzoll 1994, 229f.).

[103] The type of perfect of וְהֶאֱמִן in Gen 15:6 will be examined in greater detail in chapter III.D.IV.1 below.

15:18 (כָּרַת); additionally, 15:6 has an unprepared change of subjects[104] and
15:18 the distancing prepositional construction בַּיּוֹם הַהוּא (15:18). On the
reader/hearer, this has an effect of surprise[105] and certainly increases the
attention. The disconnection from the otherwise dialogic structure, which
is tied to a third-person theological statement about Yahweh and his deal-
ings with Abraham in his act of reckoning righteousness and making a
covenant,[106] but also the use of central theological terms in these statements confirm both the exceptional nature and the correlation of those two
verses. But only in 15:6, the narrator – otherwise scarcely reporting about
the inward conditions of the acting persons – gives insight into the inmost
disposition and feeling of Abraham.[107] Likewise, the kind of comment
about Abraham and Yahweh in 15:6 is without parallel in the patriarchal
narratives, for only this verse purports "to give access to the mind and purposes of God," providing a theological judgment of great weight in the
third-person form.[108]

To sum up the evidence, one could classify the chapter as a narrative,
"carefully composed of two balanced parts,"[109] skillfully constructed in a
dialogic manner, including elements and connotations of prophetism,
court, and cult and displaying a high level of theological reflection.[110]

III. Literary Coherence, Unity, and Structure

Only the determination of the overall genre and, starting from there, a
structural analysis can provide criteria to evaluate the coherence and com-

---

[104] H. Cazelles, for instance, points to the fact that from 15:4 on Yahweh is the subject
of the verbs (1962, 332).

[105] Cf. K. Seybold 1982, 258.

[106] Otherwise in the Abraham cycle, Yahweh's making a covenant appears in first-
person statements by him, i.e., within a divine speech (cf. Gen 17:2.7.19.21).

[107] Cf. M. Oeming 1998, 78. There is but one passage in the Abraham cycle that
makes a direct comment on Abraham's attitude: In retrospective, Yahweh confirms towards Isaac that Abraham showed obedience (Gen 26:5).

[108] R.W.L. Moberly 1990, 104. Elsewhere (e.g., Gen 12:1-3; 18:17-19), theological
comments are given within divine speeches. Moberly though takes this observation as
reason to cut off 15:6 literary-critically from the rest of the text and to locate it in a different period than the main corpus (127-129; on a critique of this method see below note
190). In a comparable way, Isa 40:17 (cf. 40:15) portrays the thoughts of Yahweh.

[109] J. Van Seters 1975, 260.

[110] Many scholars pointed to the peculiar character of the chapter: Cf. H. Gunkel
1910, 183 ("kaum eine Geschichte"); G. von Rad 1951, 130; A. Caquot 1962, 63 ("une
fiction littéraire"); S. Mowinckel, 1964, 105; N. Lohfink 1967, 33, 114 ("nachgeahmte
Erzählung"; but contrast 116: "sekundäre Orakelzusammenstellung"); C. Westermann
1981, 254f. ("nachgeahmte Erzählung" [255]; see also C. Westermann 1976, 115); G.W.
Coats 1983, 123; E. Blum 1984, 389; J. Ha 1989, 27 ("character of a dialogue report").
Some commentators identify Genesis 15 as midrash (cf. A. Caquot 1962, 63; against that
H. Hagelia 1994, 212f.).

positional design of Genesis 15.[111] As the outward plot is superseded, almost superimposed, by the content and internal evolution of the dialogue, it would be inadequate to expect a uniformity of themes or ultimate narrative consequence regarding the story line[112] (even less if one considers that the narrator was inspired by and incorporated diverse themes and traditions handed down to him).[113]

Yahweh's promise of "great reward" for Abraham holds together the first part of the chapter (15:1-6). The "elastic," "general 'Heilswort'"[114] of 15:1, which Abraham received in a vision,[115] is specified and concretized by intermediate assurance of a genuine heir (15:4), reinforced by a cosmic sign (15:5), extended to "numerous descendants" (15:5), and finally related to Abraham's believing attitude (15:6). His double objection (15:2-3), each time introduced by וַיֹּאמֶר אַבְרָם, is no simple repetition, for 15:2 merely names the foreign heir, whereas 15:3 provides the reason *why* he would become Abraham's successor, namely his position as "Son of my house (בֶּן־בֵּיתִי)."[116] Structurally, the first four verses display a chiastic pattern of speech and response: Yahweh speaks (15:1) – Abraham responds (15:2), Abraham speaks (15:3) – Yahweh responds (15:4). It is not unlikely that Yahweh's response in the form of the son-promise and the following assurance of numerous descendants (15:5) combine two traditions with the

---

[111] Cf. N. Lohfink 1967, 29, 30n.19; J. Van Seters 1975, 252; but see also the critique of this methodological decision in W. Richter 1971, 45f.n48; H. Mölle 1988, 43n.186 (with reference to R. Rendtorff 1977, 149, 159).

[112] Cf. N. Lohfink 1967, 34. Especially the dissociation of the narrator in Gen 15:6 disrupts the narrative context.

[113] Cf. to the following primarily J. Ha 1989, 43-58. See also J. Van Seters 1975, 253-260; A. Abela 1986; P.R. Williamson 2000, 127-133. The methodical difficulty with Ha's approach, however, is that he seeks to prove the literary unity of Genesis 15 in its entirety by demonstrating the thematic and structural unity; to conclude the first from the latter, is not wholly consistent, as a skillful redactor could create such unity as well. D.M. Carr's review of Ha's work notes that in fact the overall thesis of his – Genesis 15 as "theological compendium" – does not necessarily depend on proving that one author wrote the chapter (1991, 507). The same objection can be raised against J. Van Seters, who claims that both the structuring of the chapter as a whole and the interconnections within it necessarily presuppose one author, one literary invention (1975, 261).

[114] J. Ha 1989, 43; cf. M. Oeming 1998, 77f.

[115] According to J. Ha, "there is no reason to take בַּמַּחֲזֶה as secondary," i.e., to regard it (with many scholars) as interrupting the word advent formula הָיָה דְבַר־יְהוָה. He refers to analogous passages in Jeremiah (1:13; 13:3; 28:12; 33:1; 36:27) (1989, 43). J. Van Seters sees a parallel to the Deuteronomistic account of 2Samuel 7 where the word advent formula (7:4) is also combined with a derivate of חזה (7:17) (1975, 253).

[116] Cf. A. Abela 1986, 28-31. B. Jacob suggests that Abraham speaks a second time, because he did not receive a response on his first speech (1934, 389).

intention of development and progression.[117] Both are connected through
the keyword יצא.

Within the narrative structure, 15:6 serves as an particularly accentuated, connecting link: The topic "faith" creates a retrospection to the two
promises given (son/descendants),[118] while the idea of "considering as
righteousness" anticipates the subsequent concretization of the promise of
great reward in the assurance of land and in the covenant. Yet the significance of 15:6 does not remain limited to the framework of the narrative by
such retrospection and anticipation; it also points to something universal
and makes a common theological-doctrinal statement, by means of which
the narrator leaves the concrete account in order to turn to the
reader/hearer, revealing a theological statement of great weight and suc-
cinctness.[119] It is useful to distinguish both aspects, though there is no methodical need to separate them, as the narrator's perspective[120] could have
embraced both sides: He wanted to present a reflection, a general statement, but a statement of that kind that is connected to the specific narrative
plot, looking backwards and forwards.[121]

The basic theme of "great reward," at first formulated vaguely and in-
definitely, receives further elaboration in the second section of the chapter
(15:7-21) and turns at the end into a specific promise (15:18-21). Though
clearly introducing a new theme, the narrative form ויאמר in 15:7 continues
the plot that began in 15:1 and points to a literary progress.[122] In fact, 15:7
refers back to the initial divine word of 15:1[123]: The appropriation of the

---

[117] Cf. N. Lohfink 1967, 46.

[118] Gen 15:1-5 necessitate a reaction of Abraham, according to C. Westermann (1981,
263); he counters thus an extraction of the verse from its context.

[119] The first standpoint is taken by Lohfink (cf. N. Lohfink 1967, 32 with n.2, 46),
which he formulates in critical demarcation of G. von Rad (cf. 1951, 130; 1972, 142).

[120] I. Willi-Plein notes that it is not necessary to point to the omniscient narrator (as
does von Rad), because he is the normal narrator of all ancient texts (2000, 397).

[121] Therefore, the relation of Gen 15:6 to both parts of the narrative has to be kept in
mind. Cf. H. Seebass 1963, 142f.; N. Lohfink 1967, 45-47; H. Groß 1981, 18; M. Kök-
kert 1988, 246; R. Mosis 1989, 78; M. Neubrand 1997, 201. Oftentimes, the bond of 15:6
to the second half of the chapter is acknowledged only insufficiently, and 15:6 merely
regarded as result of 15:1-5 (thus, e.g., H. Holzinger 1898, 149; G. von Rad 1951, 130;
L. Gaston 1980, 85f.; A. Behrens 1997, 332). K. Haacker reckons with the possibility of
a clear caesura between 15:6a and 15:6b (1984, 283), but both the suffix *ha* in וַיַּחְשְׁבֶהָ,
which refers back to a preceding element, and the connecting *we* of 15:6b point to a continuity between the two halves of the verse (cf. G.S. Oegema 1999, 67).

[122] Cf. I. Willi-Plein 2000, 396, against those who assert a cut between Gen 15:6 and
15:7.

[123] Yahweh's "self-introduction" in Gen 15:7 not only has the effect to introduce, but
also to affirm and assure continuing assistance (cf. numerous verses throughout Lev 22:
22:2.3.8.9.16.30.31.32-33). Therefore, a literary division is not in place (cf. N. Lohfink
1967, 38n.9).

land appeared in veiled form in the promise of "great reward," and Yahweh's self-identification as protecting "shield" became historically tangible through his leading (הוֹצֵאתִיךָ) Abraham from Ur to "this land." Moreover, the keyword יצא *hiphil* also appears in 15:5, and in both occurrences it expresses the liberation from old circumstances to a new future. Another literary connection is provided by the verbs נתן and ירשׁ, as they link Abraham's query: "What will you give me?" (15:2) with Yahweh's assurance "to give you this land" (15:7) and reiterate the promise of an heir (15:4). Abraham's question in 15:8, introduced like 15:2 with אֲדֹנָי יְהוִה, does not express open doubt nor creates a tension to 15:6[124]; rather, it requests a confirming sign – not in a doubting, but in a pleading way.[125] In fact, a request of a sign is a credit to God's name and can follow after having found favor in God's sight,[126] and it is therefore a proof of faith.[127]

Yahweh's instruction of the animal rite (15:9-10.17) is intended as answer to Abraham's request.[128] The birds of prey, coming down on the carcasses and jeopardizing the proper procedure of the rite (15:11), are set parallel to and symbolize other "foreign" threats to Abraham and to the fulfillment of the initial promise (15:1): first the presence of his steward (15:2),[129] then the oppression of his descendants (15:13).[130]

After the sign that answered Abraham's question regarding the land, one expects the confirmation of Yahweh's promise; in fact, both question and confirmation (15:13) are even tied together terminologically by the

---

[124] Against, e.g., J. Wellhausen 1898, 21; G. von Rad 1972, 144; also R. Davidson 1983, 42-44, who sees "behind ... [Abraham's] question hesitation and uncertainty" (44) and L.M. Barth 1992, 260, who detects in Gen 15:8 a "lack of faith.". – Gen 18:12 exhibits how doubt regarding God's promise looks like and how he reacts.

[125] Cf. H. Seebass 1997, 73: "[E]in Zweifel wird hier nicht ausgedrückt"; C. Westermann 1981, 266f., with reference to F. Delitzsch: "Es ist keine zweifelnde Frage, sondern eine bittende." G. Wenham 1988, 331, appealing to the analogous passages Jdg 6:36-40 and 2Kgs 20:8-11. J. Ha names the parallels in Gen 24:14; 42:33; Ex 33:16 (1989, 49n.19). Unbelief can reveal itself, if a sign is *not* requested despite divine promise (Isa 7:1-14). See, however, the interpretation of early Jewish exegetes, who admit doubt on Abraham's side, as listed in L.M. Barth 1992, 258-262. But again, see Philo, *Her* 101 and especially *Mut* 175-217: Relating Gen 15:6 to 17:17, he explains that Abraham's doubt remained in the mind: "[T]he swerving was short, instantaneous and infinitesimal, not belonging to sense but only to mind, and so to speak timeless."

[126] Cf. 2Kgs 20:8-11; Ex 33:12-13; see also H. Seebass 1963, 148.

[127] Even Gen 15:5 attests to the correlation of signs and faith; here, however, in the sense that signs give courage and power to believe (cf. H. Wildberger 1967, 383).

[128] Cf. J. Ha 1989, 55, referring to Jdg 6:11-24 as parallel.

[129] Cf. J. Ha 1989, 50f.; against that P.R. Williamson 2000, 131.

[130] Cf. G. Wenham 1982, 136. – A. Dillmann suggested an analogy between Gen 15:11 and Virgil, *Aeneid* 3,225-257, interpreting this incident as ill omen, which received its content in the following verses (15:13-16) (1892, 246; cf. P. Heinisch 1930, 231; J. Van Seters 1975, 258; M. Anbar 1982, 47). See also M. Jastrow 1912, 788-812.

verb ידע (15:8.13). Furthermore, the prophecy about Abraham's offspring
(זֶרַע) (15:13) has in view the promise of his offspring in 15:5. There is an
intentional antithetic structure between Abraham and his offspring, in
which Abraham's situation is set against that of this descendants: the exodus *into* versus *from* a foreign land (15:7.16), a peaceful death versus oppression (15:13.15). But this antithesis finds its solution in the assurance of
the land both for Abraham (15:7) and for his descendants (15:18), as well
as in the idea of blessing, both regarding Abraham – his old age (15:15) –
and his descendants – their great possessions (15:14). Through this prospect opened here, Abraham's objections (15:2-3) become void and the
great reward promised to Abraham (15:1) receives a concrete, double
counterpart: the reality of his offspring and its great possessions (15:14).

The repetitions discernible in 15:13-16[131] are no mere reiterations of the
same matter, but reflect different angles and connections[132]: The redundant
statement "Your descendants will be strangers in a land that is not their
own" (15:13) draws lines to and reaffirms the two main aspects that unite
the chapter as a whole: Abraham's seed (15:5) and the possession of the
land (15:18).

A comparison of 15:17 with the oracle to Esarhaddon marks the connection of this verse to the beginning of the chapter, demonstrating that fire
and smoke can accompany an oracle of salvation and are concomitants of a
theophany.[133] The reference to old age (15:15) recurs in the same Assyrian
oracle.

All these observations reinforce the structural coherence and the intentional character of Genesis 15. 15:18 recapitulates and combines the promises of seed and land. Structurally, 15:18a parallels 15:1a in order to form
an *inclusio*: Both verses give a temporal specification, identify Yahweh as
the speaker and Abraham as the addressee, name the particular circumstance (vision/covenant), and close with the introductory לֵאמֹר.[134] On the
other hand, 15:1b and 15:18b correlate, as far as the great extent of the
land specifies the promise of great reward. The mention of the covenant
introduces a new element, which drives the internal progression of the
promises to an ultimate climax.

As for the unity of Genesis 15, one should note also that the number
four plays a significant role in the entire text: It occurs in 15:13 and 15:16;
it unites two of the most eminent terms of Genesis 15: זֶרַע (15:3.5.13.18)

---

[131] Since J. Wellhausen many scholars consider Gen 15:13-16 as addition; he stated:
"V. 13-16 ist eine Art Incubation, die auf alle Fälle dem ursprünglichen Zusammenhang
fremd ist" (1898, 21). See, against that, already W. Staerk 1924, 74.

[132] Cf. J. Ha 1989, 52-55; A. Abela 1986, 39.

[133] See above page 88; cf. H. Wildberger 1968, 143.

[134] Cf. P. Auffret 2002, 343.

and יצא (15:4.5.7.14)[135]; Yahweh speaks to Abraham four times in each of
the two parts of the chapter, while Abraham's name occurs four times in
each half[136]; Yahweh's promise experiences a four-dimensional development: son (15:4) – numerous descendants (15:5) – land to Abraham (15:7)
– land to descendants (15:18).[137]

Two major chronological difficulties emerge regarding the time of day
(15:5 and 15:12) on the one hand and regarding the number of years or
generations related to the oppression (15:13 and 15:16) on the other. The
first can be solved by assuming two separate evenings,[138] by pointing to
the visionary character of Genesis 15,[139] or even by regarding the "if you
can"-phrase (15:5) as an ironical, impossible instruction, given in broad
daylight.[140] As for the second scholars suggested that different periods are
meant[141] or that דור (15:16) is to be rendered as "lifetime" so that both
temporal spans in question are in fact equal.[142] It seems, however, at least
equally likely, that the differing temporal specifications are due to the

---

[135] Cf. also the interjection הנה (Gen 15:3.4.12.17).

[136] Gen 15:1[*bis*].2.3.11.12.13.18. Yahweh's name, on the other hand, appears seven
(!) times (15:1.2.4.6.7.8.18).

[137] One could add the following: The animals prepared for the rite (15:9) are grouped
according to the schema 3 + 1: three large animals to be cut in two, and one pair of birds,
not to be cut in two (cf. Y. Zakovitch 1977, 150-154, as referred to in E. Blum 1984,
378).

[138] Cf. J. Ha 1989, 51f.

[139] Some argue that the initial statement about the vision (Gen 15:1), combined with
the puzzling allusions to time (15:5.12.17) and with the lack of local references and further persons, may indicate that the state of inner vision is retained throughout the chapter
(cf. B. Jacob 1934, 389; H. Hagelia 1994, 211n.46).

[140] S.B. Noegel 1998.

[141] Cf. A. Caquot 1962, 63-65 (approvingly cited in J. Ha 1989, 53f.): the "400 years"
refer to the stay in Egypt (cf. Ex 12:40: 430 years; rounded for the sake of congruence
with 15:16), and the "four generations" indicate the duration of the exodus. E. Blum
considers the "four generation" to represent the genealogical row Levi-Kohath-Amram-
Aaron/Moses (Ex 6:14-20) (1984, 379; cf. also J. Skinner 1930, 282; W. Zimmerli 1976,
58). See also the summary of the pertinent issues concerning the relationship between
Gen 15:13, 15:16, and Ex 12:40, including textual history and early Jewish interpretation,
in S. Kreuzer 2002, 213-218. – From the perspective of the narrator/author (situation at
the end of the exile), what could the time span of "four generations" signify? See for
example the following solutions: S. Kreuzer 1986: the 100 years between the expectation
of the end of the Northern Kingdom's exile (since 722 B.C.) and Josiah's reign (around
620 B.C.); T.C. Römer 2001, 202: "[O]n part de 597/587: avec la quatrième génération,
on arrive à l'époque d'Esdras-Néhémie, où commence un retour plus ou moins consé-
quent de la Golah mésopotamienne."

[142] Cf. V.P. Hamilton 1990, 436. A similar conclusion is reached, if one presupposes
the length of one "generation" to be Abraham's age when Isaac was born (thus S. Talmon
1990).

adopted traditions so that in both cases divergences explain themselves from there.[143]

A structural analysis will provide further criteria to judge the (kind of) unity of the whole chapter.[144] Gen 15:1-5 and 15:7-21 form two balanced parts, with 15:6 as connecting link between the two halves.[145] They each deal with one prominent theme: the first part with the promise of offspring, the second part with the promise of land to be fulfilled for these descendants.[146] In short, the symmetric structure can be presented as follows: After a divine self-introduction and promise there follows an objection of Abraham, which Yahweh answers by reinforcing his promise both verbally and through a sign; each half concludes with a word of Yahweh that fortifies, concretizes, but also extends the initial promise: The promise of an heir grows into the promise of numerous descendants, while the promise of land includes eventually the presence of offspring and the specification of the land's boundaries. Furthermore, both sections close with summarizing observations, in which the narrator leaves the primary level of communication and detaches himself – more (15:6) or less (15:18a) – from the narrated events. As has been set out above, the speeches of the two *dramatis personae* dominate the plot; in each half, there are four addresses of Yahweh to Abraham (15:1.4.5b.c and 15:7.9.13-16.18-21), and one response by Abraham (15:2-3 and 15:8)[147]:

	Gen 15:1-5: *promise of offspring*	*keyword connections*	Gen 15:7-21: *promise of land inheritance*
Yahweh's self-introduction	"I am your shield" (15:1)	אֲנִי – אנכי	"I am the Lord" (15:7)
Yahweh's promise	great reward (15:1)		land inheritance (15:7)
Abraham's invocation	"O Lord Yahweh" (15:2)	אֲדֹנָי יֱהוִה	"O Lord Yahweh" (15:8)

---

[143] Cf. N. Lohfink 1967, 36; M. Anbar 1982, 48f.; D.M. Carr 1991, 507.

[144] Cf. N. Lohfink 1967, 45-50; J. Van Seters 1975, 260-263; J. Ha 1989, 59-62; P.R. Williamson 2000, 122-124; P. Auffret 2002.

[145] To be sure, the evidence can either be interpreted in this way that one part was deliberately constructed in analogy to the other (cf. O. Kaiser 1958, 117f.; similarly, yet each with different consequences, M. Noth 1948, 29n.85; N. Lohfink 1967, 46n.4), or that through this structure the general unity is affirmed (cf. presently the majority of scholars; see above note 35).

[146] On the progressive dynamics from the first half to the second, see especially R. Rendtorff 1980.

[147] There are certainly some deviations from an "ideal" symmetric structure: For instance, as the table will show, the correspondence between Gen 15:4-5 and 15:9-16 is a chiastic one (cf. P. Auffret 2002, 344).

	Gen 15:1-5: promise of offspring	*keyword connections*	*Gen 15:7-21: promise of land inheritance*
Abraham's objection	lament of childlessness (15:2-3)	בְּמָה – מָה אִירָשֶׁנָּה – יוֹרֵשׁ	request of sign (15:8)
Yahweh's promise in reaction to objection	promise of genuine heir (15:4)	יָצְאוּ – יֵצֵא	assurance of land for descendants (15:13-16)
Yahweh's instruction	"Look... and number...!" (15:5)		"Bring me...!" (15:9)
sign, occurring outside at a specified time	stars, at night (15:5)		animal rite, late evening (15:9-11.17)
Yahweh's promise	promise of numerous descendants (15:5)	לְזַרְעֵךְ – זַרְעֶךָ	content of covenant: descendants and land (15:18-21)
narrator's accentuated statement	Abraham's faith (15:6)		Yahweh's covenant (15:18a)

C. Different Views of Genesis 15:6

In the preceding chapters, the central function and position of verse 6 has always been in view. When we will now present noteworthy interpretations of Gen 15:6, one interesting fact is worth highlighting: Almost all studies concentrate on the second half of the verse, on the understanding of "reckoning/considering" and "righteousness"; oftentimes, the meaning of "believing" is simply assumed to be evident. Nevertheless, we will take a look at all works that contributed significantly to the understanding of the verse as a whole or of its single parts, and based on that we will offer our own view of Gen 15:6, with special reference to the aspect of Abraham's faith.

I. The Impact of G. von Rad's Exegesis

In his groundbreaking essay on Gen 15:6, G. von Rad not only provided for several decades the normative interpretation of this momentous passage, but also impacted greatly the exegesis of those verses in the New Testament that quote it, i.e., Gal 3:6, Rom 4:3.9, and Jam 2:24. Due to its wide influence, it is worthwhile to portray von Rad's view and the responses to it in some detail. Von Rad sees in Genesis 15 more than a narrative tradition, but a concentrated theological reflection and consequently understands Gen 15:6 as a carefully balanced theological formula.[148] He

---

[148] G. von Rad 1951, 130.

builds his argument on the meaning of the verb חשב,[149] which in his understanding is an established technical term in the context of the institutional
cult. By means of the three passages Lev 7:18, 17:4, and Num 18:27, he
sustains this thesis: In each case חשב denotes a "declarative act" of the
priest who categorizes the condition of an offering "culticly," accepting or
refusing it, and thereby utters definitively the will of Yahweh.[150]

From a wider form-critical perspective, von Rad establishes that the
form of the priests' stating this result is reminiscent of the unique declaratory nominal clauses that oftentimes appear in the Priestly Document.[151] In
the name of Yahweh, the priest accepts the offering as performed *rite* and
thus "counts it."[152] The catechism-like moral declarations in Ezekiel 18,
the liturgies of entry in Psalms 15 and 24, as well as the prophetic liturgy
in Isaiah 33 contain similar declaratory expressions from different areas of
the Israelite religion,[153] which all correlate formally, insofar as they contain the announcements that are addressed to the participants in the cult. As
von Rad maintains, all those references mentioned are part of the tradition-
historical prehistory of the use of חשב in Gen 15:6.[154]

On this background, the statement of the Elohist seems to von Rad to be
revolutionary or even polemical, because it lacks entirely the idea of cultic
mediation, and the act of "counting" is transferred into the sphere of a free,
personal relationship between Yahweh and Abraham; there is no categoriz-
ing pronouncement of the priest to the one who sacrifices. The narrator is
merely stating that Yahweh "counted it to him as righteousness" – if and

---

[149] Von Rad is referring to H.-W. Heidland (1936, 4), who suggests to render חשב generally with "erdenken," "halten für," and "zurechnen." There is always involved an act of
thinking ("Denkakt"), whose result is a value judgment ("Werturteil"), which judges the
value of the object.

[150] G. von Rad 1951, 131. Lev 7:18 deals with ritual details under the heading "sacrifice of well-being" (זֶבַח הַשְּׁלָמִים, 7:11), while 17:4 portrays a statement from the altar law
of the Holiness Code. Num 18:27 (and 18:30) is about the offering for the Levites. –
Though without speaking of "cultic counting," J. Skinner had already pointed to the declarative nature of how Abraham was conferred righteousness: "צְדָקָה is here a right relation to God, conferred by a divine sentence of approval" (1930, 280).

[151] Cf. for instance in Leviticus 13 (on leprosy) the formulas צָרַעַת הוּא or טָהוֹר הוּא,
which the priest declares authoritatively towards the affected people (cf. Lev
13:17.25.28.37.44.46). Similarly, in Leviticus 1-5 (on the sacrifices) the priest states
about the sacrifice: עֹלָה הוּא or מִנְחָה הוּא or חַטָּאת הוּא or אָשָׁם הוּא.

[152] G. von Rad 1951, 132.

[153] Ezek 18:9; Ps 15:5; 24:5; Isa 33:16.

[154] G. von Rad 1951, 133. The difficulty that the tradition-historical precursors from
Leviticus 1-5, 13, Ezekiel 18, Psalms 15, 24, and Isaiah 33 do not have the term חשב, von
Rad explains by pointing out that those passages contain the wording of the statements to
the cult participants, while Lev 7:18, 17:4, and Num 18:27 are instructions to priests,
teaching them about the type of the categorizations to be performed.

how Abraham heard about it is not of interest. The most striking difference however is the following: Whereas the cultic counting happened on the basis of human achievements, here it is said that faith, i.e., fastening one-self to Yahweh and thus taking seriously his promise, establishes the right relationship with him.[155] Yahweh indicated his plan of history ("Geschichtsplan") in 15:5, and Abraham embraced it as something real.[156] Von Rad contends that even if Gen 15:6 is not to be taken as polemics, it expresses at least a generalizing, spiritualizing, and internalizing tendency. Faith is therefore a certain spiritual, subjective disposition.[157]

Despite the general approval that von Rad's tradition-historical and theological exposition of Gen 15:6 received[158] – not least because of its proximity to the Pauline reception of Gen 15:6 or more generally to the Protestant understanding of justification[159] – several arguments were raised against it, from different angles, but partly just because of the "Pauline-Lutheran interpretation."[160]

Two qualifications von Rad conceded himself: In his Old Testament Theology, he removed the sharpness of his argument and acknowledged that the words in Gen 15:6 may not be set absolute and exclusive as if they ruled out any other possible way for a person to exhibit righteousness; rather they are bound up with Abraham's particular situation – different situations might have asked for other expressions of faithfulness towards

---

[155] G. von Rad 1951, 134; cf. 1962, 185.

[156] G. von Rad 1951, 134: "Nur der Glaube, das Ernstnehmen der Verheißung Jahwes, bringt den Menschen ins rechte Verhältnis, ihn 'rechnet' Jahwe 'an'."

[157] G. von Rad 1951, 134 ("eine ganz bestimmte geistig-seelische Einstellung"). – R. Mosis (1989, 56n.6) remarks that before von Rad already H. Holzinger had maintained that Gen 15:6 displayed an overcoming of the cultic thinking: "Aber über die Kultreligi-on erhebt sich die Stelle allerdings: die Leistung ist keine kultische, sondern eine geisti-ge; Abraham erweist sich damit der Verheißung und Fürsorge Gottes würdig" (1922, 33n.e).

[158] See, e.g., O. Kaiser 1958, 118; E. Pfeiffer 1959, 158n.49; W. Eichrodt 1961, 192; H.-J. Hermisson 1965, 58f.; R. Smend 1967, 286; R.E. Clements 1967, 18n.16; H. Wild-berger 1968, 144f.; W. Schottroff 1971, 645; J. Van Seters 1975, 256f.; W. Zimmerli 1976, 51f.; R. Davidson 1979, 44; 1983, 42; H.H. Schmid 1980, 400, 408; C. Wester-mann 1981, 264; E. Blum 1984, 369; B. Johnson 1986/1987, 112; J.A. Soggin 1995, 260f. = 1997, 241f.; J.A. Fitzmyer 2003, 257. See also E. Käsemann 1980, 100; M. Dibe-lius/H. Greeven 1984, 203.

[159] E. Blum (1984, 369) clearly sees that tradition-historical background and intention of Gen 15:6 have to be distinguished. Thus, he accepts the first, i.e., the cultic counting as original setting of Gen 15:6 (together with von Rad), yet counters the allegedly po-lemical purpose, because this interpretation's systematical-theological interest is too obvious to him. Cf. L. Gaston 1980, 40; D.U. Rottzoll 1994, 23; R.W.L. Moberly 1990, 111: "[I]t is clearly the Protestant understanding of faith in the light of Paul and Luther that is the determining factor in the argument [of von Rad]."

[160] Cf. most forcefully J.D. Levenson 1987, 56-61, quote: 60.

Yahweh.[161] Moreover, following O. Kaiser's examination of the history of tradition in Genesis 15 and its classification "oracle of salvation," he no longer assigned 15:1-6 to the Elohistic tradition, but accepted a relatively late dating.[162]

While H. Cazelles in contrast to von Rad views the idea of "counting as righteousness" as being embedded in the framework of war, i.e., denoting political prosperity,[163] R. Smend's argument follows and furthers von Rad's and Kaiser's line of reasoning[164]: He examines all the appearances of אמן with God as the object of faith in regard to their place in the history of Israelite literature. He concludes that they are all younger than Isa 7:9 and 28:16, even those passages in the Pentateuch whose date is disputed in scholarship, namely, Gen 15:6, Ex 14:31, and Num 14:11. Only the first of them is of importance in the present context. The noun צְדָקָה is very unusual in the extra-Deuteronomic Pentateuch.[165] In Deuteronomy, צְדָקָה occurs in the passages Deut 4:4-6, 6:25, and 24:13, all of which according to Smend declare that the condition for being attributed the quality of צְדָקָה[166] is the observance of the commandments. In Gen 15:6, however, Torah observance is replaced by faith, which indicates that this verse presupposes the Deuteronomy passages and modifies their testimony[167] – in analogy to the modification of the priests' cultic counting; it cannot therefore be derived from one of the old Pentateuch sources. As a consequence of this temporal classification, it is not unlikely that Isa 7:9 marks the birth of the most important Old Testament term for the religious faith.[168]

H. Wildberger, too, takes over and develops von Rad's and Kaiser's findings. He emphasizes the distinction between acquired and attributed righteousness: The term שָׂכָר seems to presuppose the idea of merit, yet the military leader did not confer compensations to his mercenaries, but generous gifts; likewise, חשׁב denotes a sovereign priestly-juridical act, not the crediting of an achievement in the context of a commercial business. A comparison of Gen 15:6 with Ezekiel 18 and 33 reveals the tendency –

---

[161] Cf. G. von Rad 1962, 391.

[162] Cf. O. Kaiser 1958 with G. von Rad 1972, 140f. Notably, Kaiser does not see a discrepancy between his locating the "oracle of salvation" in the cult (111) and his accepting von Rad's cult-critical interpretation of Gen 15:6 (118).

[163] H. Cazelles 1962, 334 (referring to Isa 41:2 and Ps 72:1-11): "Cette justice" in Gen 15:6 "peut très bien être une prospérité politique, une victoire." Against that H. Wildberger 1968, 145f.

[164] R. Smend 1967, 286.

[165] Besides Gen 15:6 it only appears in Gen 18:19 and 30:33.

[166] On the problem of regarding צְדָקָה as "quality," see below chapter III.D.III.

[167] R. Smend 1967, 286f.

[168] R. Smend 1967, 288: "Jesaja hätte, vom Nif'al des Verbums אמן ausgehend … das im menschlichen Bereich geläufige Hifi'l [*sic*] erstmals religiös verwendet."

similar to Habakkuk 2 – to dissociate from the kind of piety that consists in cultic observation towards a piety that centers on faith, though without polemical traits against "works-righteousness."[169] Through his faith, Abraham proved that he found his appropriate place in the order of the world, and Yahweh acknowledges this right disposition of faith and attributes צְדָקָה to Abraham, which includes the valid expectation of great "reward."[170] Again, placing oneself appropriately in the structure of the world is not meritorious, but indeed salvific.

N. Lohfink expresses doubts that חשׁב in Gen 15:6 is used in a spiritual sense, even polemically against the cult. Lohfink, who against Kaiser firmly advocates an early date of Genesis 15 as a whole,[171] contends that the tradition-historical background of 15:6 is not formed by the declaratory acts in the context of the priestly categorization of a sacrifice or the liturgy of entry, but rather by the practice of the priestly "oracle of salvation."[172] Throughout Genesis 15, the "oracle of salvation" appears to be the area of experience ("Erfahrungsbereich") of the Israelites, and its world of imagination was employed there for the illumination of the old traditions about the Abraham promises.[173] Hence, Lohfink's view undermines von Rad's interpretation of the fact that any cultic mediation is missing, since the very setting of the passage is the cultic experience of the Israelites: Abraham's trustful acceptance of the promises is part of this cultic background, and through this he receives "rectitude" (15:7-21) and comes to his own "rectitude" (15:6b).[174]

An entirely different historical background is assumed by J. Van Seters, who locates Gen 15:6, together with the entire chapter, several centuries

---

[169] H. Wildberger 1968, 144f.

[170] H. Wildberger 1968, 146. Wildberger, therefore, understands צְדָקָה from the idea of order ("Ordnungsdenken") of the Ancient Near East. See below chapter III.D.III.

[171] Cf. N. Lohfink 1967, 37.

[172] Cf. N. Lohfink 1967, 57-59, with reference to Ex 14:31; Deut 1:32; Isa 7:9, as well as to extra-biblical salvation oracles announced to kings.

[173] N. Lohfink 1967, 59f.

[174] Lohfink supports his argument by means of a history-of-religions comparison with Mesopotamian texts. In assumed analogy to Ancient Israelite praxis, these texts describe complex ceremonies and rituals regarding the obtaining of oracles. Those rituals are concluded by a stereotyped prayer which expresses the concern about the proper performance and consequently the validity and truth of the obtained oracle, for everything needs to be in "rectitude." Supposedly, the oracle rite ended with a declaration of acceptance by the recipient of the oracle, which was followed, finally, by the priest's announcing the "rectitude" of the act. According to Lohfink, this (hypothetical) conclusion of obtaining an oracle could correlate to Gen 15:6: Abraham's faith equals the declaration of acceptance and the statement about his צְקְדָה is analogous to the priest's announcement. Consequently, Lohfink can maintain the cultic use of חשׁב (N. Lohfink 1967, 60). In this line he translates: "(In allem) glaubte er Jahwe. Das rechnete er ihm als Richtigkeit an" (118).

later in Israelite history: It was the period of the exile that saw a phase of great theological reflection on the figure of Abraham and elevated the patriarch to such prominence.[175] To Van Seters, only by taking into consideration these historical circumstances does the significance of Gen 15:6 become clear: Von Rad's argument that the priestly declaratory formula has been extracted from its usual cultic context and applied to faith, receives a different thrust when it is acknowledged that at that time "[c]ultic activity was at a minimum."[176]

On the other hand, K. Seybold notes the lack of חשב in the liturgies of entry and denies the view that חשב is *terminus technicus* in the context of the priestly accepting and counting; rather, the semantic field of חשב is located in the commercial language and denotes technical preciseness, the idea of calculating and reckoning[177] – it has "Fazit-Charakter."[178] Only secondarily, the ideas connected to this context entered the framework of priestly theory and praxis.[179] The concepts and reminiscences of the realm of business are in fact intentional in Gen 15:6, and insofar the counting of faith as צְדָקָה documents the satisfactory result of a negotiation.[180]

R.W.L. Moberly wants to understand the problematic issues of von Rad's interpretation, namely, the idea of the anti-cultic polemic and his temporal and literary-critical classification of Gen 15:1-6, from von Rad's "wider views about the history of Israel's religion."[181] Accordingly, von Rad's discussion of 15:6 is a "microcosm," which reflects his debatable general theory that in Israel's history theological traditions tend to move from inside the cult to outside the cult.[182] Moberly's contribution to this

---

[175] This is the principal point of Van Seters's thesis. Cf. such passages as Ezek 33:24; Isa 41:8; 51:1-2.

[176] J. Van Seters 1975, 269; cf. 256f. See also R.E. Clements 1967, 69; L. Gaston 1980, 49.

[177] K. Seybold 1982, 245, 253. "An חשב haftet die Vorstellung des technisch-rational kalkulierenden Rechnens" (247). – This rationalistic view stands against H.-W. Heidland's voluntaristic understanding (cf. 1936, 121: חשב as "freier Willensakt").

[178] K. Seybold 1982, 259.

[179] K. Seybold 1982, 257. He refutes von Rad's and Rendtorff's idea of a "Theologie der Anrechnung," because the חשב references in Leviticus and Numbers, which they appeal to, are rather incidental.

[180] K. Seybold 1982, 260. K. Haacker joins Seybold's interpretation of חשב: In Gen 15:6, this verb recalls the realm of business and is employed *ad hoc*; the themes of reward, possession, and heritage correlate to this usage (1984, 284; 1999, 102f.; cf. also D. Michel 1999, 107f.). See against Seybold, e.g., M. Oeming 1983, 186, referring to Prov 17:28; Neh 13:13.

[181] R.W.L. Moberly 1990, 112.

[182] Moberly refers to von Rad's thesis of a "Solomonic Enlightenment" during the early monarchical period, in which a shift from sacral to non-sacral took place and which is paradigmatic for the developments of later theological traditions.

discussion points out the distinction between the religion of the patriarchs and the Mosaic Yahwistic religion, which is carried out in the Old Testament itself, but not by von Rad and his followers, who combine all the premonarchical material under the general heading "patriarchal."[183] Therefore, one has to leave open the possibility for the consideration that Gen 15:6 "is not anti-cultic or even non-cultic but rather pre-cultic."[184]

Moberly's distinctive method starts from the heuristic assumption that the less significant, but terminologically similar passage in Ps 106:31 might provide the interpretive control for the meaning of Gen 15:6.[185] Against the *opinio communis* he refers the apposition "to all generations forever" in Ps 106:31 not to the fact that Phinehas's action was often recalled by Israel (which however was certainly also the case),[186] but to its continuous effects and value for Israel, because God reckoned it to Phinehas as צְדָקָה. From this thought it can be deduced that the original concern of Gen 15:6 is not – as in traditional Christian interpretation – Abraham's faith and his own standing before God, but rather – as in traditional Jewish interpretation – Abraham's faithfulness and its value for Israel.[187] After establishing the idiomatic nature of the expression "reckon righteousness to someone," Moberly proceeds to show that the meaning of צְדָקָה both in Gen 15:6 and Ps 106:31 takes on the two inseparable and difficult to distinguish aspects of right human behavior and divine blessing – and both affect positively and lastingly the quality of life both of individual and community.[188] Hence, the theological concern of Gen 15:6 is to show the dependence of Israel's existence as a people both on Yahweh and on Abraham and therefore converges with the intention of Gen 22:15-18.[189] Moberly, then, detaches Gen 15:6 from the rest of the narrative on contextual and form-critical reasons and labels it (like Gen 22:15-18) "a distinctive theological interpretation subsequent to the composition of the rest of the story."[190] Both passages, Gen 15:6 and Gen 22:15-18 have to be dated to

---

[183] The tradents' awareness of the distinction between patriarchal narratives and Mosaic Yahwism is the subject matter of a later work of R.W.L. Moberly (1992).

[184] R.W.L. Moberly 1990, 114.

[185] On Ps 106:31, see below chapter IV.A.

[186] Thus, e.g., L.C. Allen 1983, 46.

[187] R.W.L. Moberly 1990, 116-118, 120.

[188] R.W.L. Moberly 1990, 124f. Thus, צְדָקָה stands in close connection to בְּרָכָה. "The statement that Yahweh 'reckoned righteousness' indicates both the divine recognition of the true quality of the behaviour of Abraham and Phinehas and the affirmative response which brought lasting blessing" (126). In this case, human and divine action converges. – With somewhat different accentuation, this aspect of the correlation between righteousness and blessing is also highlighted by L. Gaston 1980, 47.

[189] Cf. R.W.L. Moberly 1988, 320f.

[190] R.W.L. Moberly 1990, 127. This literary-critical cut, which Moberly also carries out with 15:18, has to be criticized for several reasons, for it is not based on sufficient

the later phase of the exile (about 550-540 B.C.), a period when the meaning of the Abraham traditions was recognized and reflected on.[191]

In his new Genesis commentary, H. Seebass substantiates an older thesis of his, which he suggested as critique of von Rad's famous interpretation in a footnote. His alternative approach to Gen 15:6 contains the essential ideas that חשב does not have the meaning "to reckon/count," but, in analogy to Gen 50:20, denotes "to plan."[192] Consequently, the content of Yahweh's planning, his צְדָקָה, is a salvific act that relates to the future; in that way, the second half of 15:6 is organically connected to the following verses, as they present Yahweh's pronouncement and legal confirmation of this salvific act.[193]

In critical discussion with this proposal, D. Michel seeks to determine the meaning of Gen 15:6 primarily by evaluating two Deuteronomy passages that contain the term צְדָקָה: Deut 6:25 and 24:10-13.[194] Before presenting Michel's view, it needs to be noted that he has long been striving for a refined understanding of צְדָקָה in distinction to the related noun צֶדֶק: On grammatical and linguistic-historical grounds he argues that the first (feminine) is to be determined as *nomen actionis (agentis)* or *unitatis*, i.e., it denotes a single salvific deed, a right deed, while the second (masculine), as *nomen collectivum* is a common term, which represents a general disposition.[195] Deut 6:25 provides a conclusive answer to the question:

---

literary-critical, form-critical, or theological observations. The specific literary form of those two verses (third-person statement, dissociated from the context) speaks for the distinctiveness and significance of the statements and for their intentional contrast to the context, and not for two different authors, writing at different times; a removal of those verses would as well remove the theological center (15:6) and peak (15:18) of the chapter and therefore destroy the underlying structure and "the flow of the story" (128). Furthermore, the genre of "salvation oracle" in the first part of the chapter may not be disregarded, which is why the element "faith" (15:6a) is essential. Moberly's argument that concerning the oracle of salvation the precise sequence of Gen 15:1-6 is otherwise unparalleled (104n.5) ignores the constructed character of this passage; the elements that confirm the oracle pattern outweigh his counterargument.

[191] R.W.L. Moberly 1990, 128f. ("roughly contemporary with Second Isaiah," 128).

[192] Seebass's translation, thus, goes as follows: "Indem er (A[braham]) sich auf Jahwe verließ (sich in Jahwe beständig machte!), plante er (Jahwe) es ihm als Heilstat" (1997, 71; cf. 1983, 207n.48; see also H. Mölle 1988, 79, 381; G. Fischer 2001, 258n.63: "Gottes Tun an Abraham und an Josef weisen so einen gemeinsamen Zug auf").

[193] H. Seebass 1997, 72.

[194] Michel therefore, though without noting it, takes the same starting point as R. Smend. Yet it will become apparent that his approach diverts decisively from Smend's, especially regarding the question what kind of noun צְדָקָה represents.

[195] Initially, Michel presented this view in his (unpublished) *Habilitationsschrift* (D. Michel 1964), in which he argues that צֶדֶק denotes "nicht eine konkrete Handlung sondern eine Gesamthaltung" (108f.) while צְדָקָה on the other hand represents a "*nomen actionis/unitatis* zu der Wurzel sdq" (80; cf. D. Michel 1977, 65f.; 1999, 103f.). Conse-

What shall/will צְדָקָה be "for us (לָנוּ)" from now on? Namely, to "diligently observe this entire commandment before Yahweh our God, as he has commanded us." A declaration of that kind demarcates itself from other possible theological viewpoints, which Michel now seeks to determine. Deut 24:13 might point to the clearest demarcation; it reinterprets an older command from the Book of the Covenant (Ex 22:25-26): The Exodus passage threatens with divine sanctions the one who takes and keeps the neighbor's garment in pawn until after sunset. Against that, Deut 24:13 argues positively: Returning the neighbor's garment before sunset is regarded by Yahweh as צְדָקָה, as proof of the person's צֶדֶק.[196] Thus, the definition of Deut 6:25 is directed against the intention represented by Deut 24:13, namely, to regard as צְדָקָה a larger array of deeds than the commandments ordained by Yahweh, i.e., ethical deeds that are based on human insight.[197] As for the interpretation of Gen 15:6, Michel criticizes, in line with Seybold's perspective, von Rad's tradition-historical analysis and his accent on the cultic setting of חשׁב; rather, as in Deut 24:13, Abraham's faith is considered by Yahweh as צְדָקָה.[198]

II. Whose Righteousness, Abraham's or God's?

A separate quest is necessary concerning the consequential question that is caused by the semantic impreciseness of Gen 15:6: The wording leaves open the question of who counts righteousness to whom and therefore what is the theological implication, content and effect of faith. This ambiguity has both stimulated the discussion of the proper understanding of Gen 15:6 in its original context as well as created the necessity to consider afresh the reception history of this text in Second Temple Judaism as well as in Paul. The challenges that the traditional view encounters because of this novel approach have far-reaching significance.

---

quently, Gen 15:6 explains apodictically "daß (auch) das Vertrauen als Rechtschaffen-heits*tat* anzusehen sei" (1964, 31). Other exegetes, however, mostly in older works, assume the factual synonymity of those terms (cf., e.g., P. Stuhlmacher 1966, who writes "צדק(ה)," indicating synonymity; K. Kertelge 1971, 15n.1; K. Koch 1971, 508; M. Oeming 1983, 193 [see however 1998, 80]; J.A. Fitzmyer 2003, 257: both "righteous act" and "characteristic of a human being"; see also the dictionaries mentioned in R. Mosis 1989, 79n.65). It needs to be pointed out that Michel's interpretation has precursors in Old Testament exegesis (cf., e.g., E. Jacob 1962, 155, on the Hebrew understanding of justice: "[L]a justice ... est toujours un acte").

[196] D. Michel 1999, 106. Likewise, Ps 106:31 states that the deed of Phinehas is regarded as proof of his righteousness.

[197] D. Michel 1999, 110. This idea of human wisdom as the basis of ethical action (צְדָקָה) without reference Yahweh or his will, appears frequently in Proverbs (17 times). According to Michel it is this perspective that Deut 6:25 is disputing (111).

[198] D. Michel 1999, 108f.

1. God's Righteousness

M. Oeming insists that serious doubts have to be raised against von Rad's interpretation and finds one counterargument already implicitly put forward by von Rad himself: Granted that the process of "counting" takes place outside the cultic sphere, why should one presuppose at all a cultic categorization of offerings as background of Gen 15:6?[199] Through concordance research, Oeming maintains that von Rad can base his argument on merely three of 258[200] appearances of the verb חשׁב, and even more significantly, all three passages have the *niphal* of חשׁב, whereas Gen 15:6 uses the *qal*. Evaluating all *niphal* occurrences of חשׁב, he concludes that the act of being counted by a priest is a particular case of and derivative from the basic meaning "to be thought of," "regarded as."[201] Moreover, in the two instances in which חשׁב (*qal*) is to be rendered as "to count," only once Yahweh is the subject (Ps 32:2) and in the second instance David (2Sam 19:20) – and in both cases the cultic framework is missing.[202] In sum, it is very unlikely that the priestly cult practice forms the tradition-historical background of 15:6, let alone that an internalizing or polemical dissociation could be read into this passage.[203] As for his new interpretation of Gen 15:6, Oeming argues that to the unbiased eye the two halves of 15:6 appear as synthetic *parallelismus membrorum*; a change of subject within this short verse would seem abrupt, almost violent.[204] Hence, Abraham is the subject of both parts of this "uniquely floating" verse,[205] which consequently has to be translated: "Abraham believed[206] Yahweh / Abraham counted it[207] as righteousness to him (Yahweh)."[208]

---

[199] M. Oeming 1983, 185.

[200] Oeming also includes proper names of persons (25 times) and places (39 times) (cf. 1983, 185; D.U. Rottzoll writes erroneously 285 [1994, 23]).

[201] M. Oeming 1983, 186 ("gerechnet werden, geachtet werden, gelten"). Oeming argues further that the only passages in which חשׁב occurs in a meaning comparable to Gen 15:6 – however in the *niphal* – have a clearly non-cultic background (Ps 106:30-31; Prov 27:14).

[202] M. Oeming 1983, 187.

[203] M. Oeming 1983, 189.

[204] M. Oeming 1983, 191.

[205] M. Oeming 1998, 78 ("eigentümlich schwebend").

[206] On the meaning of the preposition *be*, cf. M. Oeming 1983, 190f.: "Jahwe ist Ort, Ziel, Grund und Objekt des Glaubens" (191).

[207] I.e., the promise of offspring: The suffix *ha* does not necessarily refer to וְהֶאֱמִן; rather, as Oeming points out, it is used also to refer back to a whole statement (1983, 192, appealing to W. Gesenius/E. Kautzsch 1909, §122q, even though there the traditional understanding is noted).

[208] M. Oeming 1983, 191; cf. 197: "Abraham glaubte in, an, durch Jahwe, und er (Abraham) achtete es (die Nachkommensverheißung) ihm (Jahwe) als Gerechtigkeit." In his other essay devoted to Gen 15:6, Oeming changes (without noting it) the translation

Yet is it conceivable from a theological perspective that Abraham counts the promise of descendants as righteousness to Yahweh? Oeming counters this main objection by pointing out that חשב can in fact denote an action of a person towards God. He refers to Mal 3:16 and *bBer* 14a.[209] Then, he defines the meaning of צְדָקָה in this context as the divine "iustitia salutiferra [*sic*]," i.e., the divine grace and help that grants the childless Abraham a son and great offspring and thus gives him justice[210] – this is the theological peak of the passage. Such new exegesis has to explain why in previous interpretation this understanding never surfaced: The reason for the continuing misapprehension of Gen 15:6 is the reinterpretation of the Septuagint, which translated the Hebrew perfect with the aorist, changed the *genus verbi* from active to passive and rendered חשב with λογίζεσθαι, thus decisively limiting the wide semantic field of the Hebrew term. According to Oeming, pure chance or ignorance cannot be the reason for this "simply wrong" translation of the Septuagint;[211] rather it is a change in the hermeneutical horizon: Faith became one part in the fulfillment of the law and thus lost its entirely unnomistic original meaning.

Three years before Oeming,[212] L. Gaston came to comparable results, but rather than concentrating predominantly on formal and semantic ques-

---

of the indirect object לֹו from "ihm (Jahwe)" (demonstrative: *ei*) to "für sich," i.e., for Abraham (reflexive: *sibi*) (M. Oeming 1998, 79; cf. R. Mosis 1989, 88f.). – It needs to be pointed out that (among Christian interpreters) H. Cazelles already in 1962 stated that חשב is generally about "plans humains" – therefore, "on peut se demander si le sujet, celui qui fait des plans, n'est pas le même qui a la foi, Abram." However, he prefers "l'interprétation traditionelle" (1962, 333). L. Gaston names another Christian author, who might see Abraham as the subject of Gen 15:6b (1980, 42n.11): G.A.F. Knight 1965, 208. He states, that "the words of Gen 15:6 ... mean literally, 'And he found himself firm upon Yahweh, and he counted it to him as saving activity'." R. Mosis however argues that Knight's wording is as ambiguous as the original Hebrew (1989, 62n.24). On some examples in Jewish interpretation which see Abraham as the subject of both parts of Gen 15:6 see below note 217.

[209] M. Oeming 1983, 191f. *bBer* 14a discusses the problem of greeting people during readings of prayer and criticizes a person greeting someone before the end of the prayer: במה חשבתו לזה ולא לאלוה. R. Mosis adds to these two passages CD 20,19-20, where Mal 3:16 is quoted (1989, 60n.20).

[210] M. Oeming 1983, 194. Oeming claims that with regard to the meaning of צְדָקָה in Gen 15:6, one has to take into account that in the Old Testament צְדָקָה is often paralleled with terms like חֶסֶד, חַנּוּן, and יֵשַׁע, all of which denote Yahweh's prevenient grace and are especially addressed to the poor, widows, orphans and strangers who imploringly turn to Yahweh for help.

[211] M. Oeming 1983, 196 ("schlicht falsch"). It should be noted that Oeming in his second essay withdraws the sharpness of his first argument to the degree that he acknowledges the ambiguous character of the passage and the difficulty to limit the wording to one meaning only (1998, 81).

[212] Oeming and Gaston did not influence each other (cf. M. Oeming 1998, 79).

tions, his starting point is the understanding of the "righteousness of God" on the background of Jewish exegesis and of the relationship between the two testaments. He too considers von Rad's interpretation of Gen 15:6 questionable, since it reads the verse through "modern Christian glasses."[213] Like Oeming, Gaston puts forward the exegetical argument of the Hebrew predilection for parallel structures. As "natural translation" he thus provides the following: "And he (Abraham) put his trust in YHWH / And he (Abraham) counted it to him (YHWH) righteousness."[214] An important proof text for Gaston's thesis is found in the "Rabbinic Bible," the *Mikraoth Gedoloth*: It is Ramban's exegesis of Gen 15:6.[215] Ramban questions the traditional view that God counted to Abraham "righteousness and merit because of the faith with which he had believed in him" – it is unintelligible that Abraham, who "is a prophet in himself," should not believe in the "faithful God."[216] "And he who believed to sacrifice his son, his only son, the beloved son, and [endured] the rest of the trials, how should he not believe in the good tidings? What would be correct in my judgment is that it is said: That he believed in the LORD and thought (חשב) that in the righteousness of the Holy One, blessed be He, he would give him seed in any case, not in the righteousness of Abram and as his reward, even though he said to him: 'your reward will be very great' [15:1]."[217] For a proof text Ramban refers to Isa 45:23, which is about God's unconditional righteousness. Consequently, while Oeming's main emphasis is the question of the subject of וַיַּחְשְׁבֶהָ, Gaston is concerned with the Deutero-Isaian understanding of צְדָקָה as "righteousness of God" and with the concept of

---

[213] L. Gaston 1980, 40.

[214] L. Gaston 1980, 41.

[215] Quoted in L. Gaston 1980, 42f. and J.D. Levenson 1987, 60; cf. D.U. Rottzoll 1994, 24; see also the translation in C.B. Chavel 1971, 197f. This exegesis of Ramban was generally unnoticed or ignored by modern Old Testament scholars.

[216] Cf. 2Chr 15:3 (אֱלֹהֵי אֱמֶת); Num 23:19.

[217] In his commentary, B. Jacob (1934, 394) names seven Jewish authors who assume that Abraham is also the subject of Gen 15:6b: besides Ramban (= Nachmanides, 1194-1268), Joseph Behor Shor of Orleans (1140-1210), Rabbi Levi ben Gerson of Perpignan (= Ralbag, 1288-1344), Isaac Arama (died ca. 1506), Isaac Abrabanel (1437-1508), Elieser Ashken (1513-1586), Samuel David Luzzato (1800-1865) (cf. B. Ego/A. Lange 2003, 172n.5 for the dates). D.U. Rottzoll (1994, 24n.16) refers also to S.R. Hirsch who writes: "Es dürfte zweifelhaft sein, ob Abraham oder Gott Subjekt im Satze ist"; cf. J.D. Levenson 1987, 59f.; R.W.L. Moberly 1990, 106n.12. J. Calvin apparently knew of Ramban's exegesis, yet rigorously rejected it as "corruption" of the text and stressed the unambiguity of the passage in the sense of the traditional meaning (cf. J. Calvin 1554, 157). Notably, M. Oeming and others do not seem to be aware of this line of tradition in Jewish theology (1983, 195: His own, "new" interpretation "[hat] die gesamte jüdische Auslegungstradition gegen sich"; cf. A. von Dobbeler 1987, 118).

"the righteousness of God as his present saving action."[218] In Gaston's view, this perception stands in the background of Gen 15:6, as well. In order to substantiate his thesis, he principally argues form-critically: Agreeing with O. Kaiser, he cautiously assumes that Gen 15:1-6 is based on the form of an "oracle of salvation," and consequently indirectly on the form of an "individual lament." If this classification however is correct, one element is compulsory, namely, the responding praise of God in the mouth of Abraham which is equivalent to the vow or praise of God in the individual laments. Thus, "in accordance with the postulated form, it would be very appropriate for Abraham to ascribe righteousness to God" as a form of his praise to God.[219] In search for passages within Deutero-Isaiah, in which the theme of God's righteousness is used in the context of salvation oracles, Gaston finds Isa 41:8-13 and 51:1-8 to be instructive: Both texts mirror the disastrous situation of Israel in the exile, which factually calls into question its existence as a people; they comfort Israel with reference to Abraham and to the presently exercised divine righteousness. There, the "blessing of Abraham now being fulfilled for Israel is called very impressively the 'righteousness of God'."[220]

In a brief essay on the problem of Gen 15:6b, D.U. Rottzoll carries on Oeming's thesis and claims that similar to Job 19:11 and 33:10, the prepositional expression לֹו needs to be reflexively connected to the subject of the verb חשׁב,[221] so that Gen 15:6b consequently implies: "...and he [Abraham] counted it [his believing] to himself as righteousness." Taking into account Michel's distinction of צְדָקָה (deed) and צֶדֶק (disposition), Rottzoll comes to the conclusion that Gen 15:6 is in fact a proof for "faith as righteousness by works"[222] as it was always and again seen in Jewish exege-

---

[218] L. Gaston 1980, 47, following Van Seters's argument of the temporal and theological proximity of Genesis 15 and Deutero-Isaiah (cf. J. Van Seters 1975, 249-278).

[219] L. Gaston 1980, 46, with reference to passages like Ps 7:17.

[220] L. Gaston 1980, 47. In Isa 51:4-6, the righteousness of God is even related to the Gentiles and therefore "provides an association for the later tradition of the understanding of Abraham" (48, with reference to Gen 22:16-18; 26:3-5; Jer 4:2; Ezek 33:24; Mic 7:18-20). Gaston concludes: "Israel's interest was never in the historical faith or righteousness of Abraham as a model to be imitated but in the righteousness of the God of Abraham who could be appealed to in the present" (49).

[221] D.U. Rottzoll 1994, 25. Against that one could mention instances with a non-reflexive use of חשׁב in connection with the preposition *le* (2Sam 19:20; Ps 32:2) (cf. A. Behrens 1997, 330). But more significantly, Rottzoll's appealing to the Job-passages is inadequate since in Job חשׁב takes on the meaning "he considers for himself," which cannot be utilized to support Rottzoll's translation of Gen 15:6 "he counts for himself."

[222] Thus the title of Rottzoll's essay. Even Oeming thinks that Rottzoll went too far with his proposal (1998, 80).

sis.[223] This means that the Septuagint-version of Gen 15:6 is an inappropriate translation and Paul does violence to the text by using this passage as
evidence for his thesis "faith without works."[224]

The two studies on Gen 15:6 by R. Mosis, written within a period of ten
years, aim at securing and specifying the main achievement of Gaston and
Oeming.[225] Mosis approaches the subject mainly from his analysis of the
Hebrew syntax on the one hand and on the other from investigations of the
history of the Hebrew text.[226] He agrees with many exegetes that Gen
15:6a is somewhat loosely connected to the previous sentences, yet constitutes the condition for 15:6b. Both halves form an "almost classical" syntactical unity.[227] The perfect וְהֶאֱמִן is to be explained as a static-durative
perfect with *waw-copulativum* and therefore denotes a permanently given
disposition in Abraham, not his reaction to the promise of 15:1-5.[228] In line
with Michel's semantic clarifications regarding צְדָקָה, he holds that in Gen
15:6 this term stands for a single act of righteousness, not for the characteristic of being righteous.[229] Hence it cannot qualify Abraham's "believing," since has been defined as a permanent attitude of Abraham; moreover, the suffix *ha* does not refer to Abraham's believing, but to Yahweh's
promise,[230] which makes improbable the assumption that Yahweh is the
subject of חשׁב. The meaning of חשׁב, as Mosis maintains, may not be narrowed down to "counting," but must be kept open by translating it generally as "assessing" or "evaluating." Therefore, Mosis claims that Abraham
carries out an "assessing evaluation," an "appraisal" of God's promise;
Abraham deems – for himself[231] – Yahweh's promise to be an act of his
righteousness and salvation. A major part of Mosis's contribution deals
with the question of how and why the "original" meaning of Gen 15:6, as
retrieved by him, was blurred and finally disappeared in the reception history. With reference to Jewish texts witnessing to the passive formulation,

---

[223] He refers to P. Billerbeck 1926, 186, who writes about the meaning of faith in Jewish theology: "...der Glaube [ist] genauso als ein verdienstliches Werk anzusehen wie
irgendeine andre Gebotserfüllung."

[224] D.U. Rottzoll 1994, 27.

[225] R. Mosis 1989, 63.

[226] He thus qualifies Oeming's obvious presupposition that the Hebrew text on which
the translation of the Septuagint is based is identical with the Masoretic.

[227] R. Mosis 1989, 77.

[228] See below chapter III.D.IV.2.

[229] R. Mosis 1989, 82f.

[230] R. Mosis 1989, 67.

[231] The preposition לוֹ is reflexive in meaning (R. Mosis 1989, 87, according to W. Ge-
senius/E. Kautzsch 1909, §135i; cf. P. Joüon/T. Muraoka 1991, §146k). Cf. D.U. Rottzoll
1994, 25. There is a great difference however, if one says "...Abraham counted his believing as righteous deed to himself" (Rottzoll) or "...Abraham evaluated for himself
Yahweh's promise as righteous deed" (Mosis).

he concludes that those texts represent a text form which in wide parts of Judaism at that time was better known than the version given by the Masoretic Text.[232] According to Mosis, the intention behind the transformation into the passive voice was clearly to counter the theologically questionable, "original" meaning of Gen 15:6.[233]

In the following, some critical arguments shall be raised against the "new perspective" on Gen 15:6 as represented by Oeming, Gaston, Rottzoll, and Mosis. Their views should not be passed over as if they were self-evidently mistaken[234] or theologically irrelevant for a Christian exegete.[235] A few scholars agree with this new interpretation,[236] while the majority still holds to the traditional view, with reasons and arguments of different weight and scope.[237] Some points in support of the latter perspective will be presented now, while others will be elaborated in connection with the subsequent detailed exegesis.

2. Some Arguments for the Traditional View

From the perspective of *Wirkungsgeschichte* and the history of interpretation, one has to assert: The fact that the main streams of Jewish as well as Christian exegesis followed naturally the accustomed understanding of Gen 15:6 signifies surely a strong argument in favor of the traditional view of Gen 15:6.[238] Thus, the point that the few Jewish exegetes countering this view are more likely to be right due to their original acquaintance with the "accustomed manner of speaking in the Scriptures"[239] is of course invalidated instantly as soon as one confronts this slim line of tradition with the vast majority of Jewish interpreters who go the traditional way. If one is not inclined to make the allegation that the scriptural and extra-scriptural allusions to Gen 15:6, as well as the Aramaic, Syriac, or Greek versions that regard Yahweh as logical subject of חשב fell prey to a theological shift,

---

[232] R. Mosis 1999, 118; cf. 1989, 92f.

[233] Cf. R. Mosis 1999, 116f.; 1989, 92f.

[234] Cf. E. Blum 1984, 369n.53: "[Es] gibt im Kontext keinen Sinn."

[235] Cf. M.W. Yeung 2002, 234.

[236] Cf. P. Weimar 1989, 364n.13, 381f., 410n.176; H.D. Preuß 1992, 172-174; A. Lindemann 1997, 48f.; M.A. Sweeney 1999, 73f.; M. Theobald 2001, 402n.20; J. Goldingay 2003, 266f. How J.A. Fitzmyer comes to name Mölle and Moberly among the supporters of this view, is unclear (2003, 258n.4; see following note).

[237] Cf. K. Haacker 1984, 283; E. Blum 1984, 369n.53; B. Johnson 1986/1987; H. Mölle 1988, 78f.; G.J. Wenham 1988, 330; M. Köckert 1988, 217n.260; E. Haag 1989, 101f.n.20; J. Ha 1989, 23; R.W.L. Moberly 1990, 107f.; A.H.J. Gunneweg 1993, 158; H. Hagelia 1994, 70-73; J.A. Soggin 1995, 260f. = 1997, 241f.; H. Seebass 1997, 71f.; A. Behrens 1997; D. Michel 1999, 107. Some scholars deliberately leave the question open (cf. J.C. Gertz 2002, 69n.28; P. Auffret 2002, 354).

[238] Cf. B. Ego/A. Lange 2003, 190.

[239] L. Gaston 1980, 61n.11; cf. R. Mosis 1989, 61n.21.

according to which the "original" meaning was intentionally changed, those texts too confirm the traditional perception.[240] Especially Ps 106:31, the only passage in the Old Testament besides Gen 15:6 in which חשׁב and צְדָקָה are combined and the object of חשׁב is clearly determined (Phinehas), represents a clear signpost as for the presupposed meaning of the Abraham passage.[241]

A few structural aspects may be highlighted, some of which have been discussed already above: (1) Against the assumed structure of a *parallelismus membrorum* in 15:6 it has to be pointed out that the sequence of the verb forms does not correspond to the normal syntax of a parallelism.[242] (2) Moreover, the seemingly abrupt change of subjects from 15:6a to 15:6b is by no means unparalleled in the Old Testament, as passages like Ex 14:8a prove: "Yahweh hardened the heart of Pharaoh king of Egypt, and he pursued the Israelites."[243] (3) The problem that God's ascribing righteousness to Abraham is in conflict with the typical structure of an "oracle of salvation" is eliminated, as soon as one views the structure of the chapter as a whole: As already mentioned,[244] the two halves of 15:6 show references and traces to the two halves of the chapter, i.e., the theme of faith concludes 15:1-5, while the mention of righteousness for Abraham looks ahead to the covenant being given. (4) The bond between 15:6b and the

---

[240] In fact, before the 12th century, there seems to be no evidence that showed any theological reflection about the differences between the simultaneously existing Masoretic Text of Gen 15:6 and passages derived from it, which have the passive form of חשׁב. Nor is there any reflection in the Old Testament or later Jewish theology of a conscious, theologically governed transformation from the active to the passive, as R. Mosis wants to see it (1999, 117) – all his arguments are *e silentio*. One example of an unproblematic coexistence of both (ambiguous) active voice (וחשׁבה) and (unambiguous) passive voice (ואתחשבת) are the two Aramaic paraphrases of Gen 15:6 of Targum *Onqelos* (see A. Sperber 1959, 20) and Targum *Neofiti* (see A. Dièz Macho 1968, 79). The first probably represents the traditional, later official, Jewish Targum of Babylonian Jewry and from around the ninth century onwards of Western Jewry as well (cf. M.J. McNamara 1992, 1); it is considered to preserve the earliest Aramaic rendering of Genesis and is dated to the third century A.D. (cf. B. Grossfeld 1988, 32). Regarding the Targum *Neofiti* there are grounds for presupposing continuity between this text with fourth-century Palestine or earlier (cf. M.J. McNamara 1992, 45). To assume a demarcation of the one from the other – whether conscious and deliberate or not – would be without any foundation.

[241] See below chapter IV.A.

[242] Cf. B. Johnson 1979, 84-91; K. Haacker 1984, 283; see even D.U. Rottzoll 1994, 25; R. Mosis 1989, 87: The parallelism is "keineswegs so eindrucksvoll und vollständig, wie Oeming dies darstellt."

[243] A. Behrens refers to this analogy (1997, 331f.). Cf. H. Cazelles 1962, 333 (with reference to C. Brockelmann 1956, §§48 and 139 – which however does not seem to support Cazelles's point): "[L]e changement implicite de sujet n'est pas inouï en hébreu."

[244] See above page 96.

second part of the narrative also links the verbs of 15:6b and 15:7a[245]; it seems likely therefore that the verb וַיֹּאמֶר (15:7a) with Yahweh as subject takes up the last-mentioned subject of the previous verse.[246] (5) Conversely, the divine name directly precedes the verb וַיַּחְשְׁבֶהָ so that Yahweh is quite naturally its subject.[247] (6) Also, the function of 15:6 both as central element of the entire chapter and as theological recapitulation, suggests that even and especially this verse follows the dialogic structure of the narrative and therefore provides insights into the heart of both parties, mentioning Abraham's faith and Yahweh's reaction.[248]

Other arguments dealing with the issues brought forth by the defenders of this new interpretation will appear in the following exegesis of Gen 15:6.[249]

D. Exegesis of Genesis 15:6

Our verse consists of three of the most critical (and therefore most disputed) terms in the Old Testament: the verb אמן *hiphil* with the preposition *be*, the noun צְדָקָה, and the verb חשׁב with an accusative suffix, with *le* of recipient and a second qualifying accusative. In fact, only in Gen 15:6, the two concepts "have faith" and "righteousness," which became so important in the New Testament and in the history of the church, appear together; they frame the verse as its starting point and final point. Furthermore, interestingly in 15:6 all three crucial terms make their first appearance in the Old Testament, which is a relevant point from the perspective of the Old Testament's final form: Abraham is the first recipient of the promises, the first who is said to have faith and who therefore found acceptance with God, and consequently the one who represents the paradigm for all future generations.[250]

---

[245] This does not mean that there is a break or caesura between Gen 15:6a and 15:6b (thus K. Haacker 1984, 283); 15:6 remains a coherent syntactical unity, as 15:7a begins something new with Yahweh's further self-introduction.

[246] Cf., e.g., A. Behrens 1997, 331; J.A. Fitzmyer 2003, 258n.4. To be sure, *within* a dialogue, the subject of וַיֹּאמֶר can take up the dialogue partner of the preceding subject (cf. e.g., Gen 15:8).

[247] Cf. B. Johnson 1986/1987, 113.

[248] Cf. B. Jacob 1934, 394: "Gottes וַיַּחְשְׁבֶהָ ist die Antwort auf Abrahams האמן. Für die zwischen ihnen ausgetauschten Worte werden sogleich die in ihnen ausgedrückten Gesinnungen gesetzt."

[249] G.J. Wenham points to the interesting fact that in the Pentateuch צְדָקָה applies to human rather than to divine activity (1988, 330).

[250] Cf. K. Haacker 1984, 283.

Depending on the grammatical and syntactical determination of those three keywords, considered individually and as compound, they take on different and distinguishable aspects of meaning, and those aspects combined constitute the meaning of the entire verse.[251] It seems appropriate to start with the second half of the verse and to disclose the meaning of אמן *hiphil* from there.[252]

I. Plan/Consider (חשׁב)

Since the occurrences of חשׁב do not seem to reflect the linguistic usage of certain theological groups or social layers, but rather belong to the general colloquial speech of Old Testament times,[253] its meaning is best determined by means of a broad examination of its occurrences under the criterion of both syntax and context. This will show that principally one has to distinguish between two basic categories of meaning, the first of which denotes a future oriented "planning," the second an evaluative "considering" of given facts.[254]

At the outset, however, the table of verses on the following page, arranged in canonical order according to their syntactical structure, provides an overview of those חשׁב-passages that appear most frequently in the discussion of Gen 15:6.[255]

1. Plan

Gen 50:20 is no exact parallel,[256] first because the "recipient" is missing, but more importantly because the construction חשׁב לְטֹבָה is formed in inten-

---

[251] J.A. Soggin rightly observes that H.-W. Heidland's and G. von Rad's important studies do not emphasize enough the syntactical connection of the three basic elements of Gen 15:6 (1997, 252).

[252] This is also the method of Heidland and von Rad, adapted by N. Lohfink 1967, 58.

[253] Cf. K. Seybold 1982, 252f.

[254] K. Seybold makes a similar distinction between two constitutive components of meaning of חשׁב: "rechnen" and "planen," but he wants to subsume both aspects under the narrow general idea of technical-rational calculation (1982, 246f.). – Besides the two categories, there are a few expressions of a separate syntactical and semantic class: חשׁב can be used in the absolute, determining one object and denoting "to respect, to regard highly." Among those instances is Mal 3:16, the only passage in the Old Testament in which חשׁב describes a human act in the direction of God. For the determination of the meaning of חשׁב in Gen 15:6, however, those passages are hardly valuable, because they lack a qualifying second accusative (against M. Oeming 1983, 191f.; cf. R. Mosis 1989, 84: Mal 3:16 is "keine vergleichbare Parallelaussage"). Passages comparable to Mal 3:16 are: Isa 2:22; 13:17; 33:8; 53:3; Ps 144:3.

[255] Some explanations regarding the decisions made in classifying the syntactical elements will follow in due course.

[256] Against, e.g., H. Seebass 1997, 71; G. Fischer 2001, 258n.63.

	the verb חשב	what is "planned/con-sidered"?	as what is it "planned/considered"?	to whom is it "planned/considered"?
Gen 15:6: וַיַּחְשְׁבֶהָ לּוֹ צְדָקָה	qal 3rd masc. sing.	accusative (verbal suffix)	accusative	לוֹ
Gen 50:20: אֱלֹהִים חֲשָׁבָהּ לְטֹבָה	qal 3rd masc. sing.	accusative (verbal suffix)	construed with *le*	/
Lev 7:18: לֹא יֵחָשֵׁב לוֹ	niphal 3rd masc. sing.	nominative	/	לוֹ
Lev 17:4: דָּם יֵחָשֵׁב לָאִישׁ	niphal 3rd masc. sing.	nominative	nominative	לָאִישׁ
Num 18:27: וְנֶחְשַׁב לָכֶם תְּרוּמַתְכֶם	niphal 3rd masc. sing.	nominative	construed with *ke*	לָכֶם
2Sam 19:20: אַל־יַחֲשָׁב־לִי אֲדֹנִי עָוֹן ... אֵת אֲשֶׁר	qal 3rd masc. sing.	accusative	accusative	לִי
Ps 32:2: לֹא יַחְשֹׁב יְהוָה לוֹ עָוֹן	qal 3rd masc. sing.	/	accusative	לוֹ
Ps 106:31: וַתֵּחָשֶׁב לוֹ לִצְדָקָה	niphal 3rd fem. sing.	nominative	construed with *le*	לוֹ
Prov 27:14: קְלָלָה תֵּחָשֶׁב לוֹ	niphal 3rd fem. sing.	nominative	nominative	לוֹ
Isa 53:4: וַאֲנַחְנוּ חֲשַׁבְנֻהוּ נָגוּעַ	qal 1st comm. pl.	accusative	accusative	/

tional opposition to the idiomatic expression חשב רָעָה, "to plan evil."[257] This expression denotes in most cases free rational calculation and planning, mostly with negative intention.[258] Obviously, this category of mean-

---

[257] The syntax of the second passage that Seebass appeals to, namely Ps 40:18, is unique: חשב is without object, but it mentions the recipient with the preposition *le* (*dativus commodi*). One might translate "Yahweh plans [good things] for me" as opposed to those who desire the psalmist's hurt (רָעָה) (40:15). Thus, as in Gen 50:20, "evil" is contrasted with "good." In Ps 41:8, חשב appears with the same preposition (*dativus incommodi*), though the object, רָעָה, is mentioned explicitly in this case.

[258] Cf. W. Schottroff 1971, 644. God has negative plans (רָעָה) with humans: Mic 2:3. Humans plan evil against God: Hos 7:15 (רַע); Nah 1:11 (רָעָה). Against each other, humans plan רָעָה (Gen 50:20; Ps 21:12; 35:4; 41:8; 140:3; Jer 48:2; Zec 7:10; 8:17) or אָוֶן (Ps 36:5; Ezek 11:2; Mic 2:1). Here, only those instances are mentioned that are syntactically related to Gen 50:20. This means, those passages (especially in Jeremiah), employing a *figura etymologica* or those using an infinitive to describe the content of the plan are left aside. Nevertheless, they align with the pattern described and denote the making

ing of חשב is oriented to the future, to a future act which is pictured and planned in the person's mind. It is about a creative-rational development of (predominantly negative) thoughts that arise and take shape on the basis of a particular motive or incident and are supposed to affect the other decisively (in a primarily negative way), once put into action. Hence, in this sense, the act of חשב marks the starting point of a future act, and the course of action points ahead. This is the syntactical rule for this pattern of the verb's usage: The verb is accompanied by but one object, which identifies the content of the plan (mostly רָעָה). Therefore, Gen 50:20 provides only little help in the search for the meaning of our verb in Gen 15:6, and we have to appeal to other passages that are closer to Gen 15:6 regarding syntax and context.

2. Consider

The other component of meaning that can be discerned is that of evaluating, classifying, or considering a person, an act or a thing according to certain criteria.[259] From the point of view of syntax, the instances that reflect this usage of חשב all have a double accusative (if חשב is *qal*), or double nominative (if חשב is *niphal*), or they are alternatively construed with a qualifying prepositional expression (*le* or *ke*) instead of the second qualifying accusative/nominative[260]; generally, they are to be translated with "to consider as," "to be considered as." In this second category, the direction of thought points to the past, and existing data – situations or actions – are gathered, considered and assessed. This act can happen in different types, which might be called: (1) objective-descriptive, (2) subjective, and (3) qualitative-authoritative or performative-creative.[261]

---

of evil plans. – A juxtaposition of "good" and "evil" similar to that of Gen 50:20 appears in the momentous passage Jer 29:11 where שָׁלוֹם and רָעָה are set side by side.

[259] Cf. W. Schottroff 1971, 643 ("wertende Zuordnung von Personen und Dingen zu bestimmten Kategorien").

[260] An analysis of the relevant passages seems to suggest that there is hardly any significant difference of meaning between instances that have a second accusative/nominative and those that use *ke* or *le* (against R. Mosis 1989, 83). A few examples each suffice: Compare Ps 106:31: וַתֵּחָשֶׁב לוֹ לִצְדָקָה with 4Q225 2 i 8: ותחשב לו צקדה, and compare Job 19:11: וַיַּחְשְׁבֵנִי לוֹ כְצָרָיו with 33:10: יַחְשְׁבֵנִי לְאוֹיֵב לוֹ, or Isa 29:16: כְּחֹמֶר הַיֹּצֵר יֵחָשֵׁב with 29:17: וְהַכַּרְמֶל לַיַּעַר יֵחָשֵׁב (cf. also W. Gesenius/E. Kautzsch 1909, §§117ii and 119t). Moreover, as regards the basic meaning it is irrelevant whether *qal* or *niphal* is used (cf. §121). Therefore, for the sake of lucidity, the following considerations are made without differentiating categorically between the conjugations *qal* and *niphal*. R.W.L. Moberly similarly concludes that the different syntactical patterns of חשב (*qal/niphal*; with *le*/with second accusative) do not have significant implications (1990, 116).

[261] The third group might also be called "religious" or "theological," but the fact that 2Sam 19:20 names David as the subject of חשב and that the setting is a court-setting, speaks for the wider nomenclature. R.W.L. Moberly insists on the label "religious"

(1) In the first, someone makes an objective judgment about a certain circumstance, a judgment which can be easily reenacted and affirmed by others, because it is rationally intelligible or follows the common sense, knowledge or experience. One example in point is Deut 2:20: "This land is [commonly] considered as a land of Rephaim."[262]

(2) In the second,[263] a person takes, according to a subjective, sometimes emotionally produced judgment, a second entity as standard of comparison and joins or parallels the object/person to be evaluated with this comparable category. This happens by means of an imaginative act of thinking. The subjectivity of the judgment implies at the same time that the subject of חשב is personally involved and affected by it.[264] One instance would be Rachel's and Leah's complaint about their father: "Are we not considered by him as foreigners?" (Gen 31:15).[265]

(3) In the third, a person or an act of a person is "classified" subjectively and willingly into a "category," over which the evaluating person possesses, or has received, the authoritative power of disposition. This act converges with a qualitative, essential change of the person, which can be caused only by the evaluator, or the one who transferred authority to the evaluator. For others, the formed judgment does not need to be understandable or plausible. There is a notable grammatical phenomenon con-

---

(1990, 121) and therefore notes that "2 Sam. xix 20 ... is less an exception than may initially appear, partly because of the obvious religious overtones of 'reckoning sin' and partly because of the king's position as God's vicegerent on earth" (108). Similarly to Moberly, J.-N. Aletti extracts a category of λογίζεσθαι-occurrences from the Septuagint, in which God is the subject: LXX Gen 15:6; Lev 7:18; 17:4; Num 18:27.30; Ps 31:2; 105:31; Job 31:28; 1Macc 2,52; he omits 2Sam 19:20, but adds Job 31:28 (it does read λογίζεσθαι, but does not go back to חשב) (2003, 311). "En ces passages, c'est l'agir humain, positif ... ou négatif ... qui a été ou sera pris en compte par Dieu. En contraste, Ps 31[32],1-2 semble être le seul où Dieu est décrit comme ne tenant pas compte des péchés, autrement dit de l'agir humain négatif" (312). Since Aletti's starting point is Paul's use of both LXX Gen 15:6 and Ps 31:2, his line of reasoning seeks to follow and explain Paul's logic. Here, the mere systematic collection and evaluation of the data are in the focus of attention.

[262] Cf. Gen 38:15 (second object construed with *le*); Deut 2:11; Josh 13:3 (with *le*); Isa 29:17 (with *le*); 32:15 (with *le*). See also 2Sam 4:2 (with *ʿal*).

[263] To be sure, there are some overlaps between the first two types, since the boundaries between objective criteria and subjective criteria are not always clearly defined.

[264] This aspect is especially highlighted by H.-W. Heidland 1936, 2-18; 1942, 287: "Der Denkakt nimmt subjektiven, gefühlsmäßigen, ja willensmäßigen Charakter an."

[265] Cf. 1Sam 1:13 (second object construed with *le*); 1Kgs 10:21; 2Chr 9:20; Neh 13:13; Job 18:3 (with *ke*); 19:15 (with *le*); 35:2 (with *le*); 41:19 (with *le*).21 (with *ke*).24 (with *le*); Ps 44:23 (with *ke*); Prov 17:28; Isa 5:28 (with *ke*); 29:16 (with *ke*); 40:15 (with *ke*).17; 53:4; Lam 4:2 (with *le*); Hos 8:12 (with *ke*). The subsequent arguments will show that Isa 53:4 belongs into this second category, not into that of Gen 15:6 (against, e.g., D. Michel 1999, 108). See also Ps 88:5 (with עם).

nected to the use of חשב in the verses that are listed in this particular group:
They all mention the person, who is affected by the assessment, by means
of the preposition *le*; it either refers reflexively to the one who considers
("for himself," *sibi*) or aims demonstratively at the recipient ("to him,"
ei).[266]

Generally, in all three categories mentioned, the initial idea in this process of assessment is to come to a conclusion, to a classification, which appears reasonable to the one who assesses. In contrast to the other meaning
of חשב, the future-oriented "planning," the emphasis lies here on the retrospective evaluation of existing facts or acts – in an objective, subjective, or
authoritative way. In spite of the backward orientation, certainly, it is not
excluded that especially in the third category the ensuing consequences of
the assessment might be all the more relevant. For reasons that will become apparent, it is the third type of the second category of meaning that
interests us, i.e., the qualitative-authoritative type.

In order to make the following thoughts more transparent, some examples for this use of חשב may be mentioned: Job, for instance, laments several times that God considers him "for himself" (*sibi*) as enemy, which is
equivalent to a fundamental change of his status before God and the world,
as it factually removes all attributes and goods from him that used to define him.[267] If, on the other hand, a person's act is classified, the condition
of the person, who performs the act, is altered: The act of slaughtering certain animals *non rite*, is considered as "bloodguilt" (דם) "to him" (*ei*), i.e.,
to the one who violates the prescriptions. He will be excluded and even cut
off from the people (Lev 17:4).[268] In consequence, the one who pronounces
the judgment, does so in an independent and authoritative manner, as a
performative utterance that constitutes a new situation for the one who, or
whose act, is assessed.[269] This line of reasoning paves the way for the
meaning and implication of חשב in Gen 15:6. Against the assertion of several scholars that this verse is a syntactical hapaxlegomenon without paral-

---

[266] Cf. W. Gesenius/E. Kautzsch 1909, §135i; P. Joüon/T. Muraoka 1991, §146k.

[267] Job 13:24 (with *le*); 19:11 (with *ke*); 33:10 (with *le*).

[268] In a like manner, the offering that the Levites set apart for Yahweh from the Israelites' tithe, is considered as their proper tithe (Num 18:27 [with *ke*].30 [with *ke*]). Only
Yahweh himself can pronounce authoritatively and effectively the judgment "it is considered as ... to him." 18:32 reflects the significance of this judgment for the life of the
Levites: If the offering is not performed *rite*, death will be the consequence. The correlating passage Lev 7:18 is formulated as ellipse: The sacrifice of well-being that is eaten on
the third day, shall not be "considered [as sacrifice of well-being]" to the one who offered it; rather, it is guilt to him (עון).

[269] It might be one step too far though when R.W.L. Moberly seeks to establish a distinctive, idiomatical category of "religious reckoning," which consistently implies a person's situation before God (1990, 107, 121f.).

lel in the Old Testament, one has to consider D. Michel's comments on 2Sam 19:20[270]: Both passages use חשב in the *qal*, both are factually construed with a double accusative, and both have the *le* of recipient.[271] Due to this unique syntactical analogy, this verse will provide the first controlling factor in discerning the most adequate meaning of Gen 15:6b. The significance of this parallel is even increased, as it reads חשב עָוֹן and therefore represents an interesting counter-expression to חשב צְדָקָה in Gen 15:6.[272] In 2Sam 19:20 Shimei says to David: "May my Lord not consider as guilt to me ... the fact that your servant did wrong..." Thus, Shimei pleads before the king to change his situation essentially and effectively and so to save him from being put to death. Only David has the power to avert the death penalty through an act of grace and mercy.

Ps 32:2 speaks of a similar situation, with similar intention, but on a distinctively theological level. It names the one "blessed" (אַשְׁרֵי) whom Yahweh forgives sin and for whom he renounces effectually the rights that he actually is entitled to. The syntax does not fit fully into the pattern discerned for the "qualitative-authoritative" usage, but the way how here חשב is connected to עָוֹן and to a recipient (לוֹ) situates this passage as theological parallel alongside 2Sam 19:20.[273]

The parallelism of syntax and the analogous circumstances, in which the judgment of 2Sam 19:20 (and Ps 32:2) is uttered, suggests that Gen 15:6 too possesses a performative character of speech, similar to that of 2Sam 19:20. In both cases, an authority – Yahweh or the king – decides about the act of a person by "considering it as...," a decision which means life or death. Shimei's disobedience would have to be considered as עָוֹן,

---

[270] D. Michel 1999, 108; cf. also H. Seebass 1997, 71). Against, e.g., M. Oeming 1983, 187, 191n.51 ("nur *ein* Akkusativ"); K. Seybold 1982, 250.

[271] Instead of the double accusative in Gen 15:6 (the verbal suffix *ha* and צְדָקָה), 2Sam 19:20 has the indeterminate object עָוֹן, followed by a determinate accusative (אֵת אֲשֶׁר הֶעֱוָה עַבְדְּךָ). In addition, Michel refers to passages, in which the indeterminate part is replaced by an object introduced with *le* (Gen 38:15; 1Sam 1:13; Hi 19:15; 35:2). Thus, with 2Sam 19:20 we have "sachlich ein genaues Gegenbeispiel zu Gen 15,6" (D. Michel 1999, 108; cf. already H. Cazelles 1962, 333: "[N]ous avons en II Sam., xix, 20 une phrase construite exactement comme la nôtre [*sc.* Gen 15:6]" – but see the qualification, 334n.57: "Mais le parallèle n'est pas parfait."). – Apparently, Michel does not distinguish between instances that name the "recipient" of the חשב-act and those that do not. This is the practice that R.W.L. Moberly argues against, when he says that חשב "used with accusative and *le* of recipient" consistently appears as a "religious term with reference to human standing before God" (1990, 121).

[272] Sometimes, עָוֹן and צְדָקָה are explicitly contrasted with each other (cf. Ps 18:24-25 = 2Sam 22:24-25; Ps 69:28).

[273] Possibly, the "missing" first object in Ps 32:2 has to be inferred from 32:1 so that the verse's meaning is: "Blessed is the one whom Yahweh does not consider as guilt," namely, his transgressions and sin (cf. 32:5).

from which his extinction follows; Abraham's faith is considered as צְדָקָה, which implies life, his right standing before Yahweh, old age and the subsistence of his descendants, to which Yahweh binds himself legally through the covenant. It is precisely the unexpected twist in the Samuel-narrative that proves the free, intentional[274] power of disposition of the person, who carries out the value judgment. Shimei's wrong deed was *not* followed by its expected consequence, because the king broke the fatal chain of action and consequence.

In result, all those passages that are subsumed in this last level of meaning: Lev 7:18, Num 18:27, 18:30, 2Sam 19:20, Job 13:24, 19:11, 33:10, Ps 32:2, but also Ps 106:31, which will be discussed in greater detail below,[275] resemble each other in syntax and context, relate to questions of guilt and righteousness, of death and life and therefore refer the judgment, which is given authoritatively by Yahweh, priest or king, to the person's very existence. The judgment transforms being and condition of the person and also of those who follow[276]; their "'being' is established in and through [Yahweh's] speech."[277] From this perspective, therefore, they carry a decisively soteriological connotation[278] and involve the notion of God's free salvation-giving grace.[279]

Those passages mentioned derive from different life settings, so that it is possible to maintain the thesis that חשׁב is situated in the general colloquial linguistic usage of the Old Testament[280] without narrowing it to the

---

[274] This is why H.-W. Heidland labels the act of חשׁב as "freier Willensakt" (1936, 121); K. Seybold's rationalistic understanding on the other hand reduces the breadth of meaning of חשׁב.

[275] See below chapter IV.A.

[276] Prov 27:14 is a verse that is difficult to categorize according to the suggested scheme. It deviates not as regards its syntax, but as regards the circumstance, into which this statement speaks: It does not mention the authority that utters the judgment (curse), but one could argue that it is the "effectual authority of wisdom" that pronounces the curse in an performative speech act – and a deserved curse is indeed effective and changes the condition of the cursed (cf. Prov 26:2). It is not instantly intelligible that Yahweh should be the implicit subject (thus H. Hagelia 1994, 69; Erroneously, Hagelia also states that Yahweh is the subject of 2Sam 19:20). More generally, "the language of blessing and curse … envisages the invoking of particular divine dispositions towards people" (R.W.L. Moberly 1990, 107n.17).

[277] W. Brueggemann 1997, 714n.21.

[278] The soteriological content emerges not only with the Septuagint-version of Gen 15:6 (against M. Oeming 1998, 82).

[279] See H.-W. Heidland's statements: "So entspringt auch Gn 15,6 das Urteil Jahves seinem freien Willen, und dieser Wille ist Gnade, da das Urteil ein Lob ist. In der Gnade also, nur in der Gnade empfängt der Glaube sein Gerechtigkeitsurteil. Wohl geht Jahve auf das Vertrauen Abrahams ein; daß er darauf eingeht, ist nicht Pflicht, sondern Gnade" (1936, 79; cf. 121). Cf. H. Wildberger 1968, 144f.

[280] Cf. K. Seybold 1982, 252f.

cult as its primary setting. It is not the *Sitz im Leben* that defines the authoritative nature of the pronouncement, but more generally the relationship of dependence between the one who judges and the one who receives the judgment, whose existence is dependent on and bound to the decision. Obviously, the king's not considering his inferior's transgression as guilt implies much more than just an intellectual act – it constitutes and restitutes a right relationship with the king to the effect: "You shall not die" (2Sam 19:24). Abstract-qualitative and concrete-existential aspects are not separated.

In the face of all these observations, the assumption that in Gen 15:6 Abraham might have been the one who considered Yahweh's promise as his צְדָקָה loses its foundation. Rather, in extension of von Rad's judgment, Yahweh not only makes a solemn, "konstatierend" statement,[281] but also makes a "constituting" statement that constitutes Abraham's relationship to Yahweh by considering his believing as "righteousness." This is what stands behind the phrase "and he considered it to him as righteousness."

II. The Suffix ha and the Preposition le

Even the little verbal suffix *ha* causes dissent among scholars, as it is not entirely clear to which preceding part of the narrative it refers. The proponents of the alternative interpretation who regard Abraham as the subject of חשׁב have to create a reference of the suffix to the activity of God reported in the previous verses, and not just to Gen 15:6a.[282] The prominent, somewhat autonomous character of 15:6 within the composition suggests however that it forms a self-referentially coherent entity.[283] Its elements should, if possible, at first be interpreted by looking for connections and references that offer themselves from the content of the sentence itself. There is no reason therefore to deny that the suffix of חשׁב makes the perfect clause (15:6a) to the object-clause and thus establishes a firm connec-

---

[281] Thus G. von Rad 1972, 143.

[282] Cf. M. Oeming 1983, 192. R. Mosis considers it not impossible, but very opaque if, as in the traditional interpretation, reason and condition for the act of חשׁב (Gen 15:6a) should at the same time be its object (1989, 67-69). This judgment seems overstated and not entirely intelligible on the background of his view of the syntactical relationship between 15:1-5 and 15:6 (69n.43, 77): He admits a caesura between 15:5 and 15:6, but simultaneously seeks to bind them closely together by referring the suffix to God's activity in 15:1-5. See also against this solution W. Gesenius/E. Kautzsch 1909, §135p (with explicit reference to 15:6): The suffix of the 3rd person singular feminine can refer in a general sense to the verbal idea of the preceding sentence, in our case, to 15:6a.

[283] Cf. R. Mosis 1989, 77.

tion between the two halves of the verse.[284] Thus, it is Abraham's faith that Yahweh considers as righteousness.[285]

Above, it has been established that Gen 15:6 belongs into the category of חשב-occurrences that mention the person in whose direction the act of חשב points – either in a reflexive (*sibi*) or in a demonstrative sense (*ei*). Both options need to be considered here, but with regard to the syntactical and contextual proximity to 2Sam 19:20, Ps 32:2, or Ps 106:31, it is only the demonstrative sense that comes seriously into question.[286]

III. Righteousness (צְדָקָה)

The expression צְדָקָה in the Old Testament was and is the topic of countless examinations, which all influence to some extent our understanding of Gen 15:6.[287] Here, only the most significant positions that pertain to this passage can be reflected. The first far-reaching decision takes place regarding the question, whether צְדָקָה denotes a quality or an act, a general, abstract disposition or a distinct, concrete conduct. Oftentimes, the following relationship between "act" and "quality" is established: צְדָקָה denotes primarily the quality of a person, which is the consequence of the person's conduct, expresses itself in the person's conduct, or is attributed due to the person's conduct.[288]

---

[284] Cf. K. Seybold 1982, 258. H. Cazelles rehearses all possibilities that the suffix *ha* could refer to (assuming that Yahweh is the subject of חשב): "soit l'acte de foi, soit la phrase d'Abram au v. 2, soit même la descendance" (1962, 334n.57). It could also refer to the "Gesamtvorgang des mehrfachen Gotteswortempfangs" (N. Lohfink 1967, 58). In the face of the narrative's structure and the position of 15:6 within it, the first option only – Abraham's faith – seems adequate. One should note in addition B. Johnson's point that the feminine suffix might be affected by the noun צְדָקָה (1986/1987, 113; 1989, 913, with reference to the grammar of H.S. Nyberg).

[285] Thus also the majority of scholars.

[286] It is of course the proponents of the thesis that Abraham is the subject of Gen 15:6b, who make a case for the second alternative (cf. R. Mosis 1989, 87, with reference to Job 13:24; 19:11; 33:10, where however *God* is the subject of חשב; M. Oeming 1998, 79 [see however 1983, 191, 197]; D.U. Rottzoll 1994, 25). L. Gaston, though retains the demonstrative sense (1980, 41).

[287] With reference to Gen 15:6, the questions concerning צְדָקָה are broadly discussed in R. Mosis 1989, 78-89 (including a brief history of scholarship); however, his conclusions diverge essentially from the ones reached here.

[288] Older exegesis especially argued along these lines; see symptomatically H. Gunkel 1910, 180: "צְדָקָה ist die Eigenschaft dessen, der צַדִּיק ist." Cf. R. Smend 1967, 286; H. Wildberger 1968, 146; also M.W. Yeung 2002, 235. This understanding is also unavoidable if one supposes (with G. von Rad) the pronouncement of declaratory formulas as background of Gen 15:6: A person is declared צַדִּיק, which means that צְדָקָה is assigned as qualifying characteristic. If צְדָקָה, apart from its use in the sense of "quality," denotes a person's concrete deed, the proponents of this widespread position maintain that such

More recently, however, this view has received substantial criticisms. On the one hand, there are exegetes, who maintain for linguistic-historical reasons a categorical distinction between צְדָקָה and צֶדֶק, according to which צְדָקָה throughout the Old Testament signifies not the quality of being right-eous, but a single righteous deed (as *nomen actionis/unitatis*).[289] On the other hand, others derive their distinction of צְדָקָה and צֶדֶק from the Ancient Near Eastern "concept of order" and distinguish between the objective idea (צֶדֶק) and the subjective attitude (צְדָקָה): According to this view צֶדֶק stands for the right order and צְדָקָה for the right conduct that aims at order.[290]

The following thoughts seek to integrate those views into the exegesis of Gen 15:6, but also to qualify aspects that seem one-sided. It seems doubtful, for instance, that the Hebrew thinking allows for such a dichot-omy between quality/being and act. In the anthropology of the Old Testa-ment, the borderline between what a person does and what a person is lacks a clear definition. Such an artificial-abstract differentiation would neglect the relational character of terms such as צְדָקָה (or עָוֹן)[291]: Deeds, right or wrong, always change the situation and relationship, positively or

---

instances that label a person's deed as צְדָקָה, do so in a derivative manner, i.e., they use an "Abstr[actum] p[ro] c[oncreto]" (E. König 1936, 382).

[289] Cf. D. Michel 1977, 65f. "צְדָקָה bezeichnet durchweg einen einzelnen Erweis der Gerechtigkeit, eine Gerechtigkeitstat." See also above pages 108 and in addition F. Crüsemann 1976; similarly R. Mosis 1989, 78-89; D.U. Rottzoll 1994, 26; H. Seebass 1997, 71; A. Behrens 1997, 331; K. Schmid 1999, 184f.n.90; M. Oeming 1998, 80; J.C. Gertz 2002, 69n.28. For the interpretation of Gen 15:6, it is above all Mosis who exploits Michel's insights: He notes an incongruence between the "stativisch-durativ" perfect וְהֶאֱמִן and the *nomen actionis* צְדָקָה (R. Mosis 1989, 83). The only feasible alternative, in his view, is to make Abraham the subject of חשב and to refer צְדָקָה to Yahweh's promise (15:1-5). – This suggestion however is not without problems: Besides the surprising fact that the assumed grammatical inconsistency was never noticed by a Jewish exegete (not even by those who favor the alternative understanding of Gen 15:6 like Ramban) this explanation cannot make plausible that and how Yahweh's spoken promise should be described as his deed of righteousness. See also the critique above note 282.

[290] Cf. O. Procksch 1950, 569, followed by, e.g, A. Jepsen 1965, 80 (צְדָקָה as "rechtes Verhalten, das auf Ordnung zielt"); cf. H. Wildberger 1968, 146; H.H. Schmid 1968; B. Johnson 1989, 916.

[291] Many exegetes emphasize the fact that all derivates of the stem צדק principally de-scribe a relational concept (cf., e.g., G. von Rad 1972, 143; K. Koch 1971; E. Jacob 1962, 155: "[L]a justice, étant dans la pensée hébraïque un concept de relation, est tou-jours un acte"; J.A. Fitzmyer 2003, 258: "'[R]ighteousness' is a relational concept and implies that one is acting in accord with one's social obligations." This insight goes back to H. Cremer, who talked of צְדָקָה as "Verhältnisbegriff" (1900, 34-40) and hence op-posed scholars like E. Kautzsch who distinguished between the following two aspects: "die einer objektiven Norm entsprechende Beschaffenheit" and "die durch eine bestim-mte Norm geregelte Art und Weise des Verhaltens" (1881, 28, 32; see below note 333 on the similarly formal analysis with regard to faith by A. Weiser).

negatively, to others and to God, and consequently re-constitute the doers own situation and being. For instance, it is a well-known point that "עָוֹן can signify both an evil act in itself and the result of that act, in such a way that it can sometimes be hard to distinguish between the different meanings."[292] A similar connection between the value of an act and its religious-moral consequence can be stated for the term צְדָקָה. Doing righteousness leads to a right relationship with God and therefore to life – but also conversely: A right relationship with God leads to doing righteousness.[293]

This means that the two anthropological categories "disposition" and "deed" remain intrinsically connected and both a "qualitative" and a "quantitative" perspective belongs to צְדָקָה.[294] Creating a diastase would oppose important foundations of Old Testament theologizing and is inadequate from an ontological perspective as well. The action of a person creates a sphere surrounding the person, which results in salvation (or in destruction)[295]; this tenet pervades the older wisdom tradition, the law and the cultic instructions of justice.[296] Furthermore, as Genesis 15 demonstrates sufficiently, צְדָקָה, both proof and consequence of one's righteousness,[297] has effects not only for the present, but also for future generations (Gen 15:18).[298] The structural parallel between 15:6 and 15:18 receives thus a material content, insofar as the terms "righteousness" and "covenant" interpret each other.[299] Hence, rather than limiting the range of meaning of צְדָקָה in Gen 15:6 by referring it to one single act of Abraham – even if this might be the primary focus of the term – one needs to think of the following: Abraham's "right" faith in Yahweh leads to a "right" standing before Yahweh, and this entails a lasting salvific impact not just for

---

[292] R.W.L. Moberly 1990, 123.

[293] Cf. similarly P. Stuhlmacher 1966, 218. "Rechts- und Seinsbegriffe" correlate and form no antithesis.

[294] This terminology applied by J. Lambrecht in the context of Paul's hamartiology, might as well be applied here (1986, 243f.; see below pages 253f.).

[295] Cf. G. von Rad 1962, 382-384; K. Koch 1971, 517: "Durch sein Tun 'schafft' der Mensch sich ein Sphäre, die ihn bleibend heil- und unheilwirkend umgibt. Diese Sphäre ... gehört zum Menschen in ähnlicher Weise wie sein Eigentum."

[296] Cf. Prov 11:19; 21:21. See H.H. Schmid 1980, 401.

[297] D. Michel 1999, 106.

[298] On this background, R.W.L. Moberly seeks to establish a "close connection between צְדָקָה and בְּרָכָה" (1990, 124 with n.57). Ps 106:31 provides another example, how something enduring can be related to צְדָקָה, for the temporal specification "to all generations, forever" should be related to צְדָקָה (117) (see below pages 155f.).

[299] Likewise, עָוֹן as evidence and manifestation of one's unrighteousness, impairs the life of "the third and the fourth generation" (Ex 20:5). – To be sure, the point to what extent a person's צְדָקָה or עָוֹן benefits or harms future generations, was difficult to resolve (cf. Ezek 14:12-20; Jer 31:29-30).

Abraham, but also for Israel. A person's action, a person's being and the consequence of it remain innately connected.

Though due to God's faithfulness one may trust that complying with his will results in a right relationship with him, a divine act establishing this status is always required. The analysis of the verb חשב has pointed to both the qualitative-authoritative and soteriological component of the verse Gen 15:6: If, and only if Yahweh evaluates a person's deed positively, it results in life. There is no "automatism," but dependency on the one who has the power of disposition.[300] Especially those cases, in which the sequence of deed and effect is interrupted, demonstrate the relative flexibility of this "system"; the one who carries out the value judgment of a deed can change the expected outcome in absolute freedom (2Sam 19:20; Ps 32:2). On the other hand, several passages affirm unreservedly that "Yahweh rewards everyone for his righteousness and his faithfulness (אֶת־צִדְקָתוֹ וְאֶת־אֱמֻנָתוֹ)" (1Sam 26:23). To diligently "observe this entire commandment before Yahweh, our God, as he has commanded us," is צְדָקָה and leads to life (Deut 6:24-25).[301] As Yahweh sees Abraham's faith, he recognizes that his conduct is "in order," and through his faith Abraham acquires the right place in the "Ordnungsgefüge."[302] Above, it has also been seen that Yahweh's considering Abraham's faith as צְדָקָה is both an evaluative and a creative act. God acts in righteousness for Abraham and his descendants.[303] His righteousness expresses itself in a helping and faithful act[304] that creates comprehensively the possibility of life ("Lebensmöglichkeit").[305] In a profound way, therefore, there is a "convergence between human and divine action."[306]

Whether or not the presented interpretation of צְדָקָה is valid, has to be shown *inter alia* in the analysis of the first verb of Gen 15:6, וְהֶאֱמִן, because those two terms interpret each other. But before proceeding Abraham's faith, we should have a brief glance at modern Jewish exegesis of Gen 15:6 and its understanding of צְדָקָה in the present context, as this offers an illu-

---

[300] Cf., e.g., A. von Dobbeler 1987, 119.

[301] This verse serves as another indication that in Gen 15:6b Yahweh is the syntactical subject: It is obvious that here Yahweh is the one who evaluates the person's righteous deed ("before Yahweh") (cf. D. Michel 1999, 109).

[302] H. Wildberger 1968, 146. Cf. M. Buber 1953, 682 ("Übereinstimmung einer Äußerung oder Handlung mit der Wirklichkeit").

[303] In this aspect, L. Gaston is right when he says: "Even if God rather than Abraham is the subject of the verb 'to count,' ... the righteousness is still God's and ... the sentence is a promise that God will exercise his righteousness in the future for Abraham's benefit" (1980, 50).

[304] Cf. P. Stuhlmacher 1966, 110.

[305] K. Kertelge 1971, 23.

[306] R.W.L. Moberly 1990, 126.

minating contrast. In line with the traditional notion of the so-called "merit
of the fathers" (זְכוּת אָבוֹת), Jewish interpreters regard Abraham's צְדָקָה as
claim to honor and merit, acquired through praiseworthy conduct.[307] God
rewards a life of obedience, and Abraham's life is a classic example of this
fact.[308] Abraham "put his trust in Jahweh, who accounted it to his
merit."[309] The difference between our interpretation offered above and the
just mentioned Jewish position is between a predominantly creative understanding – God's reaches his verdict apart from Abraham's claim or de-
serving attitude – and a predominantly descriptive or objective-necessary
understanding – God's judgment is an appropriate response to Abraham's
claim. We will be reminded of the distinction throughout the *Wirkungsgeschichte* of Gen 15:6, which is dealt with in the following chapters.

IV. Believe (אמן)

It is true that from a statistical perspective there are only few passages in
the Old Testament that have אמן *hiphil*, in the Old Testament so that reper-
cussions and interpretive traditions of this concept are indeed limited in
terms of quantity.[310] Nevertheless, there can be no doubt that concerning
the expression for a person's and Israel's relationship with God, אמן *hiphil*
clearly possesses a qualitative preeminence. This is due to linguistic, tradition-historical, and theological reasons,[311] but also – coming from the final

---

[307] B. Jacob 1934, 394, with reference to Deut 9:4-7; 6:25; 24:13; 2Sam 19:29; Neh
2:20; Ps 106:31: "צְדָקָה ist dasselbe wie das neuhebräische זְכוּת, der durch ein löbliches
Verhalten erworbene Anspruch auf Anerkennung und Lohn (לפני יי, vor Gott)." A.B.
Ehrlich 1908, 59: "Das verbum hat seine gewöhnliche Bedeutung, und צדקה ist = Verdienst (cf. Neh. 2,20 und siehe zu Deut. 24,13). JHVH rechnete Abraham den Glauben an
seine Verheissung, deren Erüllung unter den obwaltenden Umständen kaum wahrschein-
lich erscheinen musste, als Verdienst an." – On the disputed rabbinic term זְכוּת, see P.
Egger 2000. Egger discusses approaches of S. Schechter, A. Marmorstein, G.F. Moore, E.P.
Sanders, and J. Neusner, reaching the indeed vulnerable conclusion that זְכוּת generally denotes something like validity, effectiveness, force, realization, importance, or claim, but never
merit. Oftentimes the most adequate circumscription is, according to Egger, "*anerkennens-
werte antwortende Glaubenspraxis*" (297; italics original).
[308] Cf. R.W.L. Moberly 1990, 109.
[309] This is the translation of E.A. Speiser (1964, 110). See also the translation in M.
Buber/F. Rosenzweig 1930, 41: "Er aber vertraute IHM; das achtete er ihm als
Bewährung" (M. Fishbane points to the "*Leitwort 'Bewährung'*" in M. Buber's work
[1997, 221]; through this term Buber connects Gen 15:6 with Genesis 22 [225, 229f.]).
[310] Cf. F. Hahn 1971, 91.
[311] Cf. G. Ebeling 1958, 71; A. Weiser 1959, 197. The latter summarizes the three reasons for the fact of this verb's preeminence: (1) Linguistically, it is the most fluid one
that is capable of incorporating new elements without losing its basic sense; (2) historically, it has already at an early time depicted the relationship between Israel and Yahweh
in the context of the covenant tradition; (3) theologically, it describes, especially in
Isaiah, the ultimate depth of the relationship to God. – In critique, one should note the

form of the Old Testament – due to the fact that "faith" is first mentioned with regard to the first patriarch, thus receiving a great potential to crucial theological weight.

The following remarks on the term אמן will be arranged in two paragraphs, the first dealing with the syntax and the second with the semantics of the term. Obviously, in contrast to our treatment of the term חשב, we have to restrict ourselves first and foremost to the religious use of אמן and leave aside the occurrences in the profane sense. Within the framework of discerning the meaning of "faith," a consideration of the context of Genesis 15 as a whole is crucial, since the chapter has proven to be a carefully knit unit with numerous cross-references, literary progressions, antitheses, and a parallel structure.

1. Syntax

Instead of the perfect וְהֶאֱמִן one would rather expect the narrative form וַיַּאֲמֵן. Therefore, there have been some – eventually unsuccessful and text-critically unfounded[312] – attempts to emendate this indeed unexpected perfect form according to other text witnesses of this passage, which in fact place Abraham's believing directly into the narrative structure by using a respective narrative verb form.[313] A much more substantial problem, however, arises with the question what kind of perfect the form וְהֶאֱמִן represents[314]: Is it, as most exegetes and grammarians maintain, to be determined as *perfectum consecutivum*, even though possibly used in an anomalous manner,[315] or more plausibly as (regular) perfect with *waw-copulativum*? And linked to this syntactical question is the semantic issue, whether the verbal aspect expresses a single deed or the continuance of a

---

circular argumentation of Weiser who can achieve his results only on grounds of certain linguistic, historical, and theological presumptions.

[312] Cf. B. Jacob 1934, 394.

[313] On those attempts to emendate the text, cf. H. Holzinger 1898, xiv; O. Procksch 1924, 294 with note f; E. Pfeiffer 1959, 158; B. Johnson 1986/1987, 109; see also the *apparatus* of BHK: "l[ege] f[o]rt[asse] וַיַּאֲמֵן." – Another hardly noticed (and hardly feasible) possibility is proposed by J. Huesman, who thinks that "the simplest solution" would be to punctuate the form as infinitive: וְהַאֲמֵן (1956, 413; against that R. Mosis 1989, 65n.31; see on the general problem of the confusion of infinitive with perfect W. Gesenius/E. Kautzsch 1909, §112pp with n.1). The interesting paraphrase of Genesis 15 and 22 in 4QPseudo-Jubilees also reads ויאמן. See below chapter IV.F.

[314] A comprehensive discussion of the problems is found in R. Mosis 1989, 64-78.

[315] Cf. S.R. Driver 1892, 161: Gen 15:6 belongs to those instances, which "must simply be recorded as *isolated irregularities*, of which no entirely adequate explanation can be offered" (italics original; 161n.1: "[I]t is also an inelegancy"). On the peculiar character of וְהֶאֱמִן in the present context, see also W. Gesenius/E. Kautzsch 1909, §112pp and ss; B. Johnson 1979, 42f.; 1986/1987, 110f.; P. Joüon/T. Muraoka 1991, §119z ("abnormal w-qatálti ... form[.]"); and recently J.A. Fitzmyer 2003, 257n.1.

state,[316] a frequentative-iterative act[317] or a durative-stativic disposition.[318] Another, though rather unlikely option is to view the connotation of the perfect as inchoative, i.e., that due to Yahweh's promise, Abraham came to faith, and his permanent attitude towards God found its beginning.[319]

If וְהֶאֱמִן is *perfectum consecutivum*, one has to expect that it expresses actions, events or conditions, which refer as temporal or logical consequence to what precedes.[320] Abraham's faith would therefore be the consequence, which is dependent on the preceding event, i.e., Yahweh's promise, and this faith Yahweh considers as righteousness.[321] In spite of this temporal or logical association, the verb in such a syntactical construction seems to introduce "the mention of a fact not perhaps meant to be *immediately* connected with the previous narrative," or it confers to it "greater prominence and emphasis than it would otherwise have received"[322] – and maybe both.

There is a noticeable tendency, however, which challenges this traditional classification of the perfect as *perfectum consecutivum*, mainly on grounds of the syntactical relationships between 15:5, 15:6a and 15:6b: If one acknowledges that in 15:6 the narrator takes distance from the reported account and recapitulates, then the perfect form describes, as in many cases, a constant condition, a durative state. The note on Abraham's faith is then followed by the mention of a punctual event, which describes a

---

[316] On this alternative, cf. P. Joüon/T. Muraoka 1991, §§119u and v.

[317] The following scholars determine וְהֶאֱמִן as frequentative *perfectum consecutivum*: H. Gunkel 1910, 180; O. Procksch 1924, 296; N. Lohfink 1967, 32; B. Vawter 1977, 207; C. Westermann 1981, 252; R.W.L. Moberly 1990, 105; M. Oeming 1983, 190, 195. On the other hand, K. Seybold, considers the possibility of a frequentative perfect with *waw-copulativum* (1982, 258). *Inter alia* the following exegetes deny the possibility of a frequentative use here: H.L. Strack 1905, 58; H. Mölle 1988, 78, I. Willi-Plein 2000, 396.

[318] As *perfectum consecutivum* with durative connotation וְהֶאֱמִן is determined, for instance, by E. König 1919, 485; P. Heinisch 1930, 230; A. Caquot 1962, 59; R. Kilian 1966, 45, and factually also by W. Gesenius/E. Kautzsch 1909, §112ss (as variety of the frequentative perfect, denoting continuance in a past state). Against that R. Mosis opts for a durative perfect with *waw-copulativum* (1989, 67f., 75f.)

[319] Cf. K. Haacker 1984, 283; H. Mölle 1988, 78; see against that H. Wildberger 1968, 144, and R. Mosis 1989, 76f. with n.61. This solution is unlikely, because it presupposes factually that before this episode, Abraham's attitude to God was not marked by faith. (Mölle certainly bases his results on his literary-critical analysis, according to which 15:6a belongs to an early layer.)

[320] Cf. W. Gesenius/E. Kautzsch 1909, §112a; P. Joüon/T. Muraoka 1991, §119a; B. Johnson 1979, 42f. See also B.K. Waltke/M. O'Connor 1990, §32, on the current state of scholarship on the phenomenon "*perfectum consecutivum.*" They themselves translate: "Now he trusted..." (§16.4f).

[321] Cf. B. Johnson 1979, 42f.

[322] S.R. Driver 1892, 161 (italics original).

temporal succession and/or a logical necessity,[323] which results from the
fact stated in the perfect-expression. Hence, for the form וְהֶאֱמִן it implies
the assumption of a regular, classical perfect with simple *waw-
copulativum*, which creates a loose connection to what precedes.[324] Some
suggest translating this perfect most properly as pluperfect ("and he had
believed"),[325] others assume a durative connotation simultaneous to the
second verb.[326]

With regard to the type of perfect the latter position can claim the superior arguments. But as with the noun צְדָקָה one has to be cautious not to
create a diastase between those two aspects of faith that might be called act
and attitude, deed and disposition, act and being. Again, both a "quantitative" and a "qualitative" understanding have their right.[327] This is why for
some interpreters, the different verbal aspects are not alternatives excluding each other, but they overlap: Abraham's (repeated) believing in the
different promises correlates and oscillates with his permanent believing
state transcending the narrative. This results in an (indispensable) ambivalence of expression: Abraham's faith is both "repeated action" and "constant response,"[328] both "Tun und Sein,"[329] "Verhalten" and "Haltung."[330]
Faith in God as durative, constant characteristic cannot be separated from

---

[323] On the function of the imperfect with *waw-consecutivum* cf. W. Gesenius/E.
Kautzsch 1909, §111a; P. Joüon/T. Muraoka 1991, §118h.

[324] Cf. R. Mosis 1989, 68: "Das Perfekt וְהֶאֱמִן ist dann nicht ein Perfekt consecutivum,
das auf andere Verben folgt, sondern es steht am Anfang einer Satzfolge, die als ganze
durch Waw copulativum an das Vorausgehende angeschlossen ist." To determine the
perfect as *perfectum consecutivum* would be at most a "Not- und Verlegenheitslösung"
(77). For K. Seybold, too, *we* is no indication of *perfectum consecutivum*, but has the
function to create distance (1982, 258).

[325] Cf., e.g., K. Seybold 1982, 258 (alternative: frequentative); I. Willi-Plein 2000,
396f. Willi-Plein maintains that if וְהֶאֱמִן is composed of a (regular) perfect following on a
waw-copulativum, Gen 15:6 would be a retrospective parenthesis and therefore וְהֶאֱמִן
should be translated as pluperfect, Abraham being the subject (cf. also B. Jacob 1934,
394). If on the other hand וְהֶאֱמִן is understood as *perfectum consecutivum*, the subject of
15:6a would, according to the rule, be identical with the subject of the preceding non-
narrative verb form, i.e., in the present context יִהְיֶה (15:5). A change of subjects is almost
impossible, if regular grammatical circumstances are present; thus, זֶרַע would be the subject of the future וְהֶאֱמִן, and 15:6a would still belong to the direct speech.

[326] Cf. R. Mosis 1989, 88f.

[327] See above page 128.

[328] R.W.L. Moberly 1990, 105.

[329] M. Oeming 1983, 190.

[330] H.-J. Hermisson 1978, 10. See also R. Kilian 1966, 45; B. Vawter 1977, 207; H.
Groß 1981, 18; J.A. Soggin 1997, 242, 252. Against this potential double character, see
especially R. Mosis 1989, 75.

faith as an act that becomes concrete in the situations of life.[331] Faith is not
an abstract-metaphysical entity, but it is of relational nature and bound
God; it materializes in history,[332] in human experience.[333]

Only with this clarification, one can do justice to the grammatical phenomenon of the double accusative in Gen 15:6: The verb וְהֶאֱמִן, represented
in 15:6b through the suffix *ha*, has to correlate with the noun צְדָקָה, since
the double accusative means the equivalence of objects.[334] The two relational terms "righteousness" and "faith" – which correlate with each other
even formally, insofar as they frame 15:6[335] – also correspond regarding
contents: וְהֶאֱמִן, Abraham's fastening himself in Yahweh, denotes his constant attitude, which however expresses itself and has to become reality in
the concrete circumstance of the promise.[336] Yahweh considers this punctual believing as צְדָקָה and hence evaluates Abraham's faith in this situation; but its acceptance with God reaches to the future through the covenant and its blessing for Abraham's descendants (including the presence of
the reader/hearer).

This bipolar orientation of the two terms "believe" and "righteousness,"
on the one hand their direct reference to the narrated situation, on the other
hand their pointing beyond it, confirms another feature of Gen 15:6 that
has been pointed out above: The verse contains in itself the ambivalence of
being a kind of theological principle[337] as well as being directly bound to
the reported scene.[338]

An indirect, yet eloquent proof text supports the proposed view that
"righteousness," having deed-character, correlates to Abraham's durative
"faith" without constraint: The Aramaic paraphrase of Gen 15:6 in the
Targum *Pseudo-Jonathan* transforms the Masoretic finite-verbal expression "and he believed" into a nominal expression "and he had faith," thus
denoting the permanent character of Abraham's faith; and God considers
this disposition of Abraham as meritorious deed, as זְכוּ.[339] This means that

---

[331] Cf. E. Jacob 1962, 155: "[L]a foi est une marche qui s'exprime au-dehors d'une
manière très concrète."

[332] Cf. E. Pfeiffer 1959, 151.

[333] Cf. A. Weiser 1959, 184; 197n.148; see also G. Ebeling 1958, 71. However,
Weiser's methodical separation of "Begriff" and "Wirklichkeit" appears too formal a
scheme and underrates the relational character of faith.

[334] Cf. O. Procksch 1924, 296.

[335] Cf. A. Behrens 1997, 332.

[336] Cf. R.W.L. Moberly 1990, 105: "Gen xv 6 constitutes one particular example
which represents and summarizes a regular occurrence."

[337] This is emphasized by G. von Rad.

[338] This is emphasized by N. Lohfink.

[339] The paraphrase of Gen 15:6 in *Pseudo-Jonathan* reads: "And he had faith in the
Memra of the Lord (הימנותא במימרא דייי), and he reckoned it to him as a meritorious deed

the Aramaic translator did not sense an incompatibility of those terms, as some modern exegetes do.

2. Semantics

Having presented the syntactical difficulties and the scholarly disagreements regarding the verb וְהֶאֱמִן, we can proceed to some semantic issues, among which the question of the sense of the *hiphil* takes precedence.[340] In the course of scholarship of Hebrew linguistics, different solutions have been proposed, which can be distributed into two general categories[341]:

(1) According to the first option, "believe" denotes a declarative-estimative act and therefore necessarily presupposes an object, even if this is not explicitly mentioned: "consider something firm, trustworthy."[342]

(2) The other option deems those objects of reference to be semantically dispensable and votes for an intransitive or internal-transitive understanding of "believe": "gain firmness and stability."[343] – To be sure, some exegetes take an intermediate position.[344]

It is apparent that even from a systematic-theological view this question is of significance. A survey of the more than 50 occurrences of אמן *hiphil*[345] suggests that there is no certain passage in the Old Testament, in which an

---

(וחשבה ליה לזכו) because he did not argue against him with words." See E.G. Clarke 1984, 16; M. Maher 1992, 60.

[340] This endeavor is certainly marked by circularity: The sense of the *hiphil* can only be determined by examining the הֶאֱמִין passages, while on the other hand the meaning of those passages discloses itself only if one presupposes a certain sense of the *hiphil*. Thus it is difficult to decide which method one should give precedence, the one that starts from different categories of *hiphil* (cf. E. Pfeiffer 1959; H. Wildberger 1967), or to the one that examines the occurrences of the verb (cf. A. Jepsen 1973).

[341] The most important semantic issues are dealt with in E. Pfeiffer 1959; see also the summary in K. Haacker 1984, 280.

[342] Cf., e.g., J. Pederson 1926, 347 ("to consider a soul firm and thus to contribute to it firmness, that is to 'make true,' to believe in it"); E. Würthwein 1954, 142; G. Ebeling 1958, 72; E. Pfeiffer 1959, 152 ("für fest, sicher, zuverlässig erklären oder halten"); H.W. Wolff 1962, 23; G.S. Oegema 1999, 67.

[343] Cf., e.g., L. Bach 1900, 88 ("Festigkeit des Lebens"); A. Schlatter 1927, 557 ("Betätigung der innerlichen Festigkeit durch Zuversicht und Vertrauen"); O. Procksch 1950, 604; M. Buber 1953, 681 ("feste Beständigkeit"); J. Barr 1961, 183; H. Wildberger 1967, 375 ("Festigkeit haben oder gewinnen"); G. von Rad 1951, 134; 1962, 185; 1972, 143; A. Jepsen 1973, 333; W. Zimmerli 1976, 51; K. Haacker 1984, 280; H. Mölle 1988, 76; B.S. Childs 1992, 596.

[344] A. Weiser 1935, 90f. ("Fürwahrhalten des Berichteten ... ein dieser Sache entsprechendes Verhalten"); 1959, 186; W. Eichroth 1964, 190 ("für fest, zuverlässig halten, Zuverlässigkeit finden").

[345] Cf. the chart in L. Bach 1900, 30.

accusative follows on אמן *hiphil*[346] – rather, those instances that use the verb in the absolute, indicate that it is not dependent on an object.[347] This empirical fact opens up the further discussion, which will make lucid that it is only the intransitive understanding that can do justice to the texts, both on a contextual and on a theological basis.

There are three promises that God gave to Abraham in Gen 15:1-5: his assurance of reward (15:1), the promise of a genuine heir, a child of his own body (15:4), and the extension of this promise to numerous descendants (15:5). Which of the promise(s) does Abraham accept through his faith – if it is at all a reaction to the promise(s)? Is it those that stand closest to the statement on Abraham's faith (15:4-5),[348] or is it a second response to Yahweh's general word of salvation given at the beginning (15:1),[349] after the first reaction, his objections, have become invalid through the sign and the promise of descendants? Possibly also, Abraham reacts to the entirety of God's promises and assurances given in 15:1-5.[350]

These considerations, however, are interrupted through the remarkable formulation that describes Abraham's faith: The prepositional expression that belongs to וְהֶאֱמִן is בַּיהוָה. It does not say: Abraham believed Yahweh what he said (*credere deo*), but: Abraham believed *in* Yahweh (*credere in deum*).[351] Therefore, if read accurately and without limiting its meaning, וְהֶאֱמִן connotes: Abraham does not only consider or declare trustworthy the words of Yahweh and, furthermore, he does not only gain firmness and

---

[346] Cf. already A. Schlatter 1927, 557f.n.1. On the problematic passages that seem to have transitive use (Jdg 11:20; Hab 1:5), see H. Wildberger 1967, 374f.; A. Jepsen 1973, 325. – One extra-biblical passage that appears problematic is 4Q424 1,7-8, because here אמן *hiphil* could be read with an accusative (but see below note 204 in chapter IV).

[347] Those who prefer the declarative-estimative alternative have to assume an intentional omission of the object (cf. on Isa 7:9, E. Pfeiffer 1959, 159).

[348] Cf., e.g., A. Dillmann 1892, 46; E. Pfeiffer 1959, 158; R. Kilian 1966, 45; B. Johnson 1979, 42f.; L. Gaston 1980, 41; J.A. Fitzmyer 2003, 257.

[349] Cf., e.g., H. Mölle 1988, 78f., 335. C. Westermann is not entirely consistent and refers Abraham's faith once to 15:1, and then to 15:4-5 (1981, 263).

[350] Cf., e.g., G. Ebeling 1958, 72; A. Jepsen 1973, 328; M. Oeming 1983, 75; R. Mosis 1989, 71; R.W.L. Moberly 1990, 105; J.-N. Aletti 2003, 321. In a more intricate way, N. Lohfink wants to refer Abraham's faith as frequentative act to the three promises individually (1967, 32n.2: "bei allen drei Verheißungen glaubte er Jahwe"). If this idea, which divides up Abraham's faithful response into three acts of faith, was the intention of the author has to remain doubtful. On Gunkel's solution, which refers Abraham's (frequentative) acts of faith to situations beyond Gen 15:1-6, see below note 370.

[351] Cf., e.g., W.H.P. Hatch 1917, 3.

certainty in them,[352] but he gains firmness and fastens himself in the one, who gave these promises and assurances.[353]

The meaning of the preposition *be* gives a clue both to the question of the verbal aspect of וְהֶאֱמִן, posed above, and to the character of the relationship signified by "believe": Originally, *be* denotes the stillness at one place[354] and implies a firm ground and dependable security.[355] Hence, on the one hand, אמן *hiphil* in connection with *be* tends to place into the foreground the basic attitude of a person rather than the single act,[356] while on the other hand it stands for a relationship that implies trust and confidence in a person, even on a psychological level.[357]

Consequently, the declarative-estimative sense of אמן *hiphil* proves to be inadequate, and even the intransitive sense requires a closer description, as the focus is primarily directed to the person, to Yahweh, rather than to his utterances.[358] The words are the medium that both call for and create faith. Abraham, who is confronted with the words realizes the necessity to respond and does so by fastening himself to the one who speaks.[359] Thus, faith denotes a relationship between two persons, between Yahweh and Abraham, which is located in a "word-event."[360] This word-event is introduced by the word-advent formula (15:1) and constituted by Yahweh's self-assurance: "I am your shield. Your reward will be very great," anticipating the content of the ensuing story. Abraham's faith corresponds to the relationship that Yahweh promises and that already exists unconditionally from Yahweh's side on grounds of the promise.[361] Thus, faith is actually

---

[352] Against B. Jacob, who identifies Abraham's faith with firm conviction and unshakable certainty (1934, 394).

[353] Cf. the influential formulation of G. von Rad (1962, 185): "Glauben heißt im Hebräischen 'sich fest machen in Jahwe' (daher die Präposition בְּ nach הֶאֱמִין)." See also K. Haacker 1984, 283; H. Mölle 1988, 76f.

[354] Cf. C. Brockelmann 1956, §106a.

[355] F. Delitzsch 1887, 275.

[356] Cf. A. Weiser 1935, 91; 1959, 186. Apart from Gen 15:6, the religious use of אמן *hiphil* with the preposition *be* occurs in Ex 14:31; 19:9; Num 14:11; 20:12; Deut 1:32; 2Kgs 17:14; 2Chr 20:20; Ps 78:22; Jonah 3:5. Weiser distinguishes this use from אמן *hiphil* with the preposition *le*, which points to a single act; see Deut 9:23; Isa 43:10.

[357] Cf. H. Wildberger 1994, 188.

[358] Cf. already F. Delitzsch 1860, 368.

[359] Cf. H. Wildberger 1967, 377. In the religious use of אמן *hiphil*, facts and circumstances are never the object of faith.

[360] G. Ebeling 1958, 72.

[361] A few remarks are necessary concerning the use of the term "unconditional." W. Brueggeman argues that "it is futile and misleading to sort out unconditional and conditional aspects of Yahweh's covenant with Israel. The futility and misleading quality of such an enterprise can be stated on two quite different grounds. First, even in the covenant with the ancestors of Genesis, the covenant includes an imperative dimension (Gen 12:1; 17:1)..." (1997, 419; in n.14 reference to Genesis 15). However, since the final

something passive, a giving room to the *activitas dei.*[362] His objection
(15:2-3), on the other hand, does not touch upon this basic relationship, but
refers to the contents of the words, whose meaning is not yet intelligible to
Abraham.[363] Abraham's attitude, which is considered by Yahweh as righteousness, does not consist in his full understanding the ways of Yahweh –
even after he proved his faith, he fails to comprehend entirely (15:8) – but
in his full surrender to the assurance that came towards him on God's initiative.[364]

It is only God, who can demand such a thorough surrender, since in God
only, in fundamental contrast to humans, what he says cannot be disconnected from his person. God's word and his person belong together inseparably. Since God is the one whose word does not disappoint, only he can
be the ground and goal of faith. And hence it is in fact "natural" to put
faith in him,[365] because this reflects the appropriate human stance in the
divine "Ordnungsgefüge."[366] His word is always addressed to someone and
as such it can never remain unanswered, but requires a response,[367] which
has decisive consequences both for "object" and "subject."[368] The analysis
of the second verb in our verse, בשׁח, has shown, that the judgment, which
is expressed by it, involves the whole existence of the one who or whose
act is assessed. To this correlates that faith has to do with life and existence. In faith Abraham "throws" himself into the promise and fastens

---

form of Genesis presents the covenant reported in Gen 15:18 as the beginning of the
covenantal relationship between Yahweh and Abraham, such statements need to be scru-
tinized. Gen 15:18 is the climax and goal of the narrative's movement that started with
Yahweh's self-introduction and assurance. But precisely this assurance is in no way connected to a condition that Abraham would have to fulfill before Yahweh would grant the
covenant. Thus, it is justified and even necessary to speak here of the unconditional nature of the relationship between Abraham and God. As Genesis 22 however proves, the
covenant is nevertheless "at the same time utterly giving and utterly demanding" (419).

[362] Cf. G. von Rad 1972, 143; also B. Johnson 1979, 42f.

[363] Hence, there can be no talk of a contradictory opposition of Abraham's faith and
the objections he raised (– and neither should this be exploited in a literary-critical way).
For faith relates to the giver of the promise, to God himself whereas a questioning objection takes issue with the content of the words spoken, not with the speaker.

[364] Cf. W. Zimmerli 1976, 52. – It is another thing to say that without faith there is no
understanding, as does LXX Isa 7:9: ἐὰν μὴ πιστεύσητε οὐδὲ μὴ συνῆτε. Anselm of Can-
terbury speaks positively of *fides quaerens intellectum.*

[365] Cf. K. Kerényi 1952, 77f. (quoted in D.R. Lindsay 1993, 110): Faith is a
"Selbstverständlichkeit" in the Old Testament. "Es gab da die Verheißung Jahves und das
Vertrauen auf ihn."

[366] Cf. H. Wildberger 1968, 146 (see above page 129): "Den rechten Platz im Ordnungsgefüge einzunehmen ist nicht verdienstlich, sondern sollte selbstverständlich sein.
Aber es ist allerdings *heilvoll*" (italics original).

[367] Cf. G. Ebeling 1958, 72, 74.

[368] Cf. A. Weiser 1959, 186.

himself in Yahweh. The totality of his outer conduct and his inner life, his doing and being, is embraced by faith.[369]

In a next step we can approach questions of the function and meaning of וְהֶאֱמִן in the context of chapter 15 and within the Abraham cycle as a whole. It is remarkable that here for the first time and only here Abraham's faith (and God's reaction to it) is specifically mentioned, even though Abraham obviously believed consistently and his general trusting attitude can be presupposed. His stance towards God in Gen 15:6 does not appear to be more veritable than his response to the command in Gen 12:1-4, to leave home, family and country.[370] Also, Yahweh's promise of land and descendants – i.e., an ampler promise than in Gen 15:5 – and his subsequent command to "walk through" the land in Gen 13:14-17 obviously received Abraham's trusting and obedient response (13:18).[371] Already Ramban shows awareness of this issue, when he, in his abovementioned interpretation of Gen 15:6, anticipates the Aqedah-narrative (Genesis 22)[372] and asks his readers how Abraham "who believed to sacrifice his son, his only son, the beloved son, and [endured] the rest of the trials, ... should not believe in the good tidings."[373]

These observations urge us to solve the question: Why is it precisely in Genesis 15 that Abraham's faith and Yahweh's response are worth mentioning? Leaving questionable literary-critical methods aside,[374] we have to look at the context for an answer: The image of the stars and especially the strange, unprecedented covenant ritual point to a "highly pregnant context"[375] and an extraordinary "imaginative appeal of the scene"[376]; more

---

[369] Cf. A. Weiser 1959, 188. The whole existence anchors in God, which is more comprehensive than the Augustinian notion of "our heart resting in God."

[370] Cf. H. Gunkel 1910, 180. Therefore, Gunkel concludes that Abraham showed his faith for the first time when he left his country; now, in Gen 15:1-6, he confirms and proves it. To be sure, Gunkel's reasoning is fairly idiosyncratic: Through literary-critical artifice he places Gen 15:1-6 right after Gen 12:1-9, and his frequentative understanding of וְהֶאֱמִן he seeks to support by referring to W. Gesenius/E. Kautzsch 1909, §112g, dd, and ss (however, the last reference, §112ss, factually points to a durative rather than frequentative connotation; cf. the similarly problematic and contradicting reference to this paragraph in C. Westermann 1981, 252n.a).

[371] Cf. R.W.L. Moberly 1990, 118f. "The promise of [Gen] xiii 14-17 is in fact more amazing than that of xv 4-5" – but still: It "has received much less attention."

[372] Although the term Aqedah (עקדה; cf. Gen 22:9: אֶת־יִצְחָק בְּנוֹ [*sc.* אַבְרָהָם] וַיַּעֲקֹד) only "appears in the rabbinic tradition of the third-fourth century of the Christian era" (J.A. Fitzmyer 2002, 212) we will use in the context of earlier writings.

[373] See also M. Luther 1515/1516, 254.

[374] See above note 370.

[375] B.S. Childs 1992, 597.

[376] R.W.L. Moberly 1990, 119 ("a portrayal of unusual and imaginatively suggestive character").

importantly, only here the promises to Abraham are confirmed and interpreted in the sense of a covenant theology, which represents both a formal-
legal and symbolic commitment of Yahweh to Israel. Therefore, Genesis
15 appears to be "fullest and most formal portrayal of Yahweh's commitment to Israel ... in the whole Abraham cycle."[377] It might have been intentionally formulated as foundational text of the assurances of descendants and land to Abraham.[378] Hence, 15:6 as the core of Genesis 15 obtained the character as the proper center of the Abraham narratives and
"forms a climactic moment in the patriarch's sojourn of faith."[379]

All that has been said about the meaning and implication of faith is to
be transposed into the times of the intended audience, the exiled community of Israel. Despite their distress, or rather: amidst and because of their
distress, they are the ones who receive the promise, who do not yet see it
come true, but who still fasten themselves and stand firm in God. The employed genre of an oracle of salvation itself points to an extreme and ad-
verse political situation, in which Israel is helpless and without own re-
sources to escape the political menace, but can only believe and trust in
Yahweh.[380]

E. Genesis 15 and the Old Testament Abrahamic Tradition

One particular aspect in the Jewish picture of Abraham is the appearance
of ideas and motifs similar to Genesis 15[381]; they are already discernible in
the book of Genesis, though with decisively different accents: In Gen 12:1-
9 and 22:15-18, God appears to Abraham and gives or repeats his promises: uncountable descendants, possession of land, and universal blessing;
we encounter a similar scene in Gen 26:2-5, where God affirms his promises for Abraham towards Isaac. In this context, however, it is of interest to
us how Abraham's attitude or disposition is portrayed within the framework of the promises and if differences in emphasis are observable in this
regard when those narratives are compared.[382] The relationship of Genesis

---

[377] R.W.L. Moberly 1990, 119.

[378] Thus E. Blum 1984, 382.

[379] D.B. Garlington 1994, 50. Garlington however fails to provide an adequate reasoning for this statement.

[380] G. von Rad situated faith therefore in the context of the Holy War (cf. 1951a). This
Sitz im Leben is the starting point for D. Lührmann's "question of faith" (see above page
56).

[381] On the following see especially B. Ego 1996.

[382] The following table does not mention references to the promises to Abraham ap-
pearing outside of the Abraham cycle. However, one could add Gen 24:7 where Abraham
repeats God's promise of land and implicitly of descendants to his servant. Rendtorff

15 with Genesis 13 and 17 will not be discussed in greater detail here,[383] though one might note one aspect: According to the theology of the Priestly Document, Gen 17:7 gives account of a fuller unfolding of the covenant, i.e., of an "everlasting covenant (בְּרִית עוֹלָם)."

	Genesis 12	Genesis 13	Genesis 15	Genesis 17	Genesis 18	Genesis 22	Genesis 26[384]
Son			15:4	17:16.19	18:10		
Descendants	12:2	13:16	15:5	17:2.6	18:18	22:17	26:3.4
Blessing	12:3				18:18	22:18	26:4
Nations	12:2-3			17:4.5.6.16		22:18	26:4
Land	12:1.7	13:15.17	15:7.18	17:8	18:18	22:17	26:3.4
Covenant			15:18	17:2.4.7. (19.21)[385]			
Obedience	(12:4)[386]	(13:18)		(17:23)		(22:3) 22:18	26:5
Objection			15:2-3.8		18:12		
Faith			15:6				

---

arranges the content of the promise according to the following pattern, of which he considers the last category to be the final stage of the development of tradition (R. Rendtorff 1977, 42): (1) land to Abraham (Gen 13:17; 15:7); (2) land to Abraham and his descendants (Gen 13:15; 17:8; 26:3); (3) land to descendants (Gen 12:7; 15:18; 24:7; 26:4). On a discussion of Rendtorff's suggestions, see J.A. Emerton 1982.

[383] On the relationship between Genesis 15 and 17, see, e.g., T.C. Römer 1990; P.R. Williamson 2000.

[384] In Genesis 26, Yahweh not only repeats his assurance of descendants and land towards Isaac, but he also calls Abraham's conduct "obedience" (שמע), which is unique in the Old Testament.

[385] Those verses speak of a covenant with Isaac.

[386] The brackets indicate that Abraham's obedience is presupposed, but not explicitly mentioned.

I. Genesis 12:1-9

Gen 12:1-9 has generally been attributed to the Yahwist, but more recent
scholarship increasingly tends to dispense of the classic J-source of the
documentary hypothesis.[387] In any case, the text marks the beginning of the
significant motif of Abraham's obedience. The composition of this section
is highly artistic. God's command to Abraham displays a climactic structure: "Leave your country and your kindred and your father's house!,"
while the goal of Abraham's sojourn remains disclosed and vague: "...to
the land that I will show you." The way how Abraham responds to the divine command is striking: He obeys trustingly without any trace of doubt,
hesitation or skepticism. Yahweh says: "Go (לֶךְ-לְךָ)!" (12:1), and Abraham
"went (וַיֵּלֶךְ)" (12:4).[388] Therefore, as noted above, "Gen 15 is hardly the
beginning of God's dealing with Abraham, because a trusting relationship
between the two has been operative since Gen 12:1-9."[389] But in Genesis
12 the aspect of obedience is central.

Nevertheless, S. Kreuzer recently pointed to an interesting fact: Motivated through the divergences of the time spans in Gen 15:13 (400 years)
and Ex 12:40 (430 years) – rather than through the difficulty of the starting
point of Abraham's faith – Jewish exegetes arrived by means of artistic
numerical calculations at the conclusion that chronologically the covenant
described in Genesis 15 actually precedes Abraham's exodus from Haran
portrayed in Genesis 12.[390] One might argue about the circulation of this
exegetical tradition, but several texts from a wide array of authors or theological circles seem to suggest a fairly wide acceptance of this tradition.[391]

---

[387] Cf., e.g., K. Schmid 1999, 107-115.

[388] Cf. J. Ska 2001, 173. – A similar order appears in *Jub* 14,4-5 and 18,2-3 (see below chapter IV.E.I).

[389] D.B. Garlington 1994, 50.

[390] S. Kreuzer 2002, with reference to G. Stemberger 1976.

[391] Cf. S. Kreuzer 2002, 216 ("weit verbreitet"). Not all of Kreuzer's (and Stemberger's) references are equally persuasive, but nevertheless they should be mentioned (in
the order in which they appear in Kreuzer): (1) Acts 7:2: "The God of glory appeared to
our ancestor Abraham ... before he lived in Haran," i.e., before the events narrated in
Genesis 12; (2) *GenR* 39,8: According to R. Nehemya, Abraham migrated twice (Genesis
15 and Genesis 12), which is indicated by the phrase (לֶךְ לֶךְ, "Go! Go!" – not: "Go for
yourself!," Gen 12:1); (3) *Seder 'Olam Rabbah*: Abraham was 70 years old when the
covenant was made and therefore five years younger than at his exodus from Haran (Gen
12:4); (4) *GenR* 39,7; (5) *Jubilees* 11; (6) 4Q252 (= 4QcommGenA) ii 8-10: The figures
regarding Abraham's age presuppose the first call of Abraham in Ur; (7) Philo, *Abr* 15;
Migr 32-33; (8) Josephus, *Ant* 1,154-157; (9) *ApcAbr* 9-11.

II. *Genesis 22:1-14.19 and 22:15-18*

It is only with the birth of Isaac (Gen 21:1-7) that the promise of Gen 15:4 is fulfilled, after a long delay. He is the "only," the "beloved" son,[392] not Ishmael (16:15), whom Abraham abandoned and sent away to the wilderness of Beersheba together with his mother (21:8-21), nor his six other children by Keturah (25:2). But on God's command, this only son is to be sacrificed.[393] The text is a piece of narrated theology with little concrete details; hence, the theological intention and message comes to the fore even more.[394] Together with the complexity of the theological narrative, many layers of meaning are present[395]; and it is this character of the story which warranted that this pericope became a source of inspiration and opened up great theological dimensions in later Jewish theology, of which one central aspect is the praise of Abraham's obedience as meritorious deed.[396]

Generally, the basic story Gen 22:1-14.19 is ascribed to an earlier source than Gen 22:15-18 – predominantly to the Elohist,[397] sometimes to the Yahwist.[398] But the difficulty of attributing the text to one of the old Pentateuchal sources – see only the divine names used – prompted some to date it into post-exilic times,[399] which was in turn criticized as unnecessarily late by others.[400] Whichever theory one decides to follow, there is a significant analogy to what has been observed concerning Gen 12:1-9: Abraham's obedience is portrayed as unquestioning and unwavering. God says: "Take (קַח־נָא) your son...!" (Gen 22:2) and Abraham "took (וַיִּקַּח) ... his son" (22:3). Obedience becomes the main theme of the chapter, pushed

---

[392] The Masoretic Text reads יְחִיד, while the Septuagint has ἀγαπητός.

[393] Cf. among the abundant studies on Genesis 22: H. Graf Reventlow 1968; R. Kilian 1970; G. von Rad 1971; R.W.L. Moberly 1988; T. Veijola 1989; L. Kundert 1998; H.-D. Neef 1998; G. Steins 1999; 2001; R. Brandscheidt 2001; O. Boehm 2002; O. Kaiser 2003; see also B.S. Childs 2003. G. Steins (1999) offers an extensive bibliography to Genesis 22. Works that deal with the relationship between Abraham's faith and Genesis 22 are G.W. Coats 1973 and J.J. Collins 1999.

[394] Cf. J. Licht 1978, 118.

[395] Cf. G. von Rad 1972, 193. E. Blum names the following themes: testing, Abraham's trust, holy place, and child sacrifice (1984, 321). To Abraham's trust belong his obedience to and fear of God.

[396] Cf. T. Veijola 1988, 131. – On the history of interpretation in general, see the comprehensive study of D. Lerch 1950.

[397] H. Graf Reventlow 1968, 66-77. L. Schmidt calls Genesis 22 the culmination of the Elohistic presentation of Abraham (1996, 213; referred to in H.-D. Neef 1998, 77).

[398] Cf. H. Gese 1991, 40-42.

[399] Cf. T. Veijola 1988.

[400] Cf. H.-D. Neef 1998, 78-81, who dates the text to the end of the seventh century B.C. His criteria are the missing connection to the Priestly Document and the proximity both to the Jehovist and Deuteronomy (81).

to the very extreme as Abraham obeyed to sacrifice his son and thus proved steadfast in the greatest test. Faith in Yahweh was his attitude when he received the promise of a son (Gen 15:6), fear of God is what makes him obey (Gen 22:12). Hence, this story "is concerned with obedience and fear rather than faith or belief."[401] But it is likewise true that unconditional obedience to God is deeply related to unconditional trust and faith in God.[402] Both aspects, fear and faith, remain interconnected.[403]

The climax of the account in the present canonical shape is reached in the divine oath in Gen 22:15-18 pronounced by the angel in his second speech to Abraham. There, the "theological issue at stake is that God's command to slay the heir stands in direct conflict with his promise of salvation through this very child, and therefore Abraham's relation to God is under attack. The Old Testament bears witness that God was faithful to his promise and confirmed his word by providing his own sacrifice instead of the child."[404] Most exegetes consider these four verses as the product of a secondary redaction.[405] The supplement "serves to integrate the story into the Yahwistic theme of the promise, although these verses cannot be ascribed to the classic J source."[406] Apart from reflections of "Yahwistic" themes[407] there is a link to the Deuteronomistic star metaphor of Gen 15:5,[408] i.e., to the "faith-chapter." For our topic, this redactional addition provides an interesting clue as to how and when the interpretation emerged that Abraham's obedience led to the blessing for his descendants and that therefore his conduct is to be considered meritorious. For in this passage, we have *in nuce* what will become eminently important in later Jewish

---

[401] J.J. Collins 1999, 119.

[402] Cf. the summary of Genesis 22 in T. Veijola 1988, 162: "Kurzum: es geht hier um einen unbedingten Gehorsam gegen Gott, der sich auf ein unbedingtes Vertrauen auf Gott gründet." See in more general terms R. Bultmann 1948, 155 and also above chapter II.E.I.3).

[403] Cf. A. Weiser 1959, 182 with n.36, referring to Gen 22:12: "Gottesfurcht [ist] oft einfach der Ausdruck für Glaube."

[404] B.S. Childs 1992, 334.

[405] Cf., e.g., C. Westermann 1981, 445: "Es gibt nur wenige Texte in Gn 12-50, die sich so eindeutig als Nachtrag erkennen lassen." Among those who defend the unity of Genesis 22 are G.W. Coats 1973, 395: Gen 22:15-18 is "an integral part of the narrative arising from the test." J. Van Seters 1975, 239: "[I]t is only with the inclusion of the second speech [*sc*. Gen 22:15-18] ... that the ultimate aim of the testing becomes clear" (cf. 227-240). Against this position J.J. Collins argues that "[t]he original purpose was to establish whether Abraham feared God," and this purpose does not require the section under question (1999, 116n.4)

[406] J.J. Collins 1999, 116; cf. H. Seebass 1997, 200.

[407] The following "Yahwistic" texts are reflected in Gen 22:15-18: Gen 12.2-3; 13:16; 32:13.

[408] Cf. R. Rendtorff 1977, 43f. See also above pages 89f.

theology: an explicit causal connection between Abraham's obedience and the blessing of his descendants[409]: "Because you have done this..." (Gen 22:16); "because you have obeyed my voice" (22:18). Thus, the patriarch's obedience has salvific consequences for his offspring; the divine promise is *reactio* to Abraham's obedience, not *vice versa* as for instance in Genesis 12.[410] This gives indeed a different accent to the whole narrative.[411]

Several points support the assumption that Gen 15:6 and Gen 22:15-18 are approximately contemporaneous[412] and influenced by the Deuteronomic-Deuteronomistic world of thought. However, while on the one hand the theme of faith signifies the peculiarity of Genesis 15 compared to this world of thought, the just mentioned features of Gen 22:15-18 likewise point to significant theological nuances emerging out of a comparison between this redactional supplement with passages from Deuteronomy and Genesis 15.[413] Summarized, the differences concern the order of promise and obedience: Genesis 15 begins with God's self-introduction and promise and portrays his acceptance of Abraham's faith and the establishment of the covenant as free, unconditional divine decision; Deut 10:15 places love and election at the outset of God's relationship with the patriarchs, and Deut 9:5-6 mentions God's faithfulness to the promise as ground of the Israelites' taking the land. In Gen 22:15-18 on the other hand, Abraham's obedience constitutes the basis, on which both the promise to him and the salvific effects for his descendants ground.[414] However, what connects Gen 22:18 and, e.g., Deut 26:17 is the typical Deuteronomic-Deuteronomistic aspect of listening to the voice of Yahweh (שׁמע בְּקֹל יהוה), i.e., doing God's law and commandments, whereby in the Genesis passage it is concentrated on the specific command to Abraham and not used in a general sense. Nevertheless, the author of Gen 22:18 begins to regard Abraham as paradigm for the fulfillment of the law, even though his obedience to God's command does not appear yet as obedience to the law as trans-temporal entity (which will later be the case in Gen 26:3b-5).[415]

The interesting aspect for what follows lies in the temporal proximity of Gen 15:6 and Gen 22:15-18 on the one hand, but more importantly in the different theological emphases and accentuations that the two passages

---

[409] J. Van Seters 1975, 239 (on Gen 22:15-18): "Because of Abraham's obedience his children will be blessed."

[410] A similar causal connection between Abraham's obedience and the covenant appears in Sir 44,20-21 (see below chapter IV.D).

[411] Cf. B. Ego 1996, 29.

[412] Cf. R.W.L. Moberly 1990, 128f.

[413] Cf. B. Ego 1996, 29f.

[414] On the other hand, Deuteronomy points to the correlation between the people's fulfilling the law and life (Deut 4:1; 6:1-2; 8:1; cf. Neh 9:29).

[415] Cf. B. Ego 1996, 38.

received and in the effects they had on subsequent Jewish theologizing. The different theological shades could lead to diverse strands of tradition.

III. Genesis 26:3-5

The most direct reference to Abraham's obedience in the context of the promises can be discerned in Genesis 26, where it says explicitly, that they, the promises, will become true, because "Abraham obeyed my voice and kept my charge, my commandments, my statutes, and my laws (שָׁמַע אַבְרָהָם בְּקֹלִי וַיִּשְׁמֹר מִשְׁמַרְתִּי מִצְוֹתַי חֻקּוֹתַי וְתוֹרֹתָי)" (Gen 26:5). The connection to Gen 22:15-18 is close and manifests itself in conceptual bridges like the unique oath-motif and the expression "to obey God's voice." Other elements of the Abraham narratives are present as well: The promise of blessing recalls Gen 12:1-3, God's warning not to go down to Egypt is reminiscent of Gen 12:10-20, the promise of the land draws on Gen 12:7 (and/or Gen 13:15), and the promise of numerous descendants goes back to Gen 15:5. Thus, it is correct to say that Gen 26:3-5 is "a cumulative reading of at least Genesis 12, 15 and 22."[416] That Abraham's obedience has salvific effects for his offspring is expressed unambiguously in this context, even stronger than in Gen 22:16.18. The blessing for Isaac comes to pass only "... for the sake of my servant Abraham (בַּעֲבוּר אַבְרָהָם עַבְדִּי)" (Gen 26:24).[417] While in Gen 22:15-18, Abraham's listening and obeying to God's voice had a specific content and referred to God's concrete command, it receives here a characteristic widening and generalization. Synonymous terms describing God's will are enumerated in Deuteronomic-Deuteronomistic fashion, though presumably later elements are present as well.[418]

The intention of the author is to attribute to Abraham the quality of the one who fulfills the divine will comprehensively; and such obedience does not remain without consequences for his offspring. Abraham is disconnected from the concrete challenges of his life-history, and his obedience is detached from the concrete utterances of God calling for obedience. Thus, there is a tendency to make Abraham a trans-historical figure with model-character, and the "law" a trans-historical entity that provides the standard as to how this model is to be followed. As in Gen 22:18, the

---

[416] M.W. Yeung 2002, 237.

[417] Cf. Sir 44,22. Gen 26:24 also gives a notable parallel to Gen 15:1, God's appeal not to be fearful together with his self-assurance. Cf. H. Mölle 1988, 328, who also refers to Isa 41:10; 43:5; Jer 1:8, which display a similar combination.

[418] Possibly, the term תּוֹרֹת mirrors the influence of the Priestly Document (cf. Lev 26:46).

causal connection between Abraham's obedience and Israel's blessing points to the idea of the "merits of the fathers."[419]

IV. Genesis 18:19

An interesting nuance to the theme "Abraham and the law" is given within the framework of the narrative about God's judgment on Sodom and Gomorrah: In Gen 18:19 – which most commentators regard as late addition[420] –, Abraham appears as the teacher of the law who instructs his descendants to act in accordance with the divine decrees. It is his task to "charge his children and his household after him to keep the way of Yahweh by doing righteousness and justice." Then, in the following final clause it is stated what the promise is contingent on: "so that Yahweh may bring about for Abraham what he has promised him." Hence, in contrast to Gen 22:15-18 and Gen 26:3-5, the author does not point to Abraham's meritorious obedience regarding the law as condition for the realization of the blessing; but rather the obedient deeds of Abraham's seed bring about the fulfillment of the promise.[421] Notably, Abraham is placed at the side of Moses, the prophet who instructs the people in the divine will.

V. The Relationship to Genesis 15:6

How does now Gen 15:6 relate to these passages and how do both relate to the book of Deuteronomy? For Deuteronomy God's election, promise, and faithfulness form the precondition of the obedient answer of the people of Israel: "This will be our righteousness that we diligently observe this entire commandment before Yahweh our God, as he has commanded us" (Deut 6:25). Gen 15:6 offers a re-focusing and presents faith as the primary criterion according to which God bestows righteousness.[422] The passage portrays Abraham's faith as a permanently given disposition, as a constant "fastening oneself firmly" in Yahweh. Only secondarily, it is about Abraham's immediate faithful response to God's promise. The consequence of Abraham's faith is God's independent, positive judgment and the unconditional granting of the covenant for the benefit of Israel. The other Genesis passages just discussed connect rather to Deuteronomy than to Genesis 15 by their concentrating on the observance to the Torah: They broaden and generalize Abraham's attitude to God in terms of his Torah-obedience. Already Gen 22:15-18 shows a tendency into this direction, though Abra-

---

[419] Cf. L. Gaston 1980, 48.

[420] Cf., e.g., M. Köckert 1988, 180.

[421] Cf. B. Ego 1996, 38.

[422] It is not necessary though to argue that the author of Genesis 15 sought to replace "obedience" with "faith" with a polemical purpose (cf. in these lines R. Smend 1967, 286f.).

ham's obedience is still connected to the concrete event of the binding of
Isaac. The other passages advance this tradition: The statement in Gen 26:5
depicts Abraham's obedience as something permanent (on which concrete
acts like the sacrifice of Isaac and the exodus from Haran are dependent),
and Gen 18:19 presupposes Abraham's general observance of the Torah.
The stress of these passages lies on Abraham's obedient deed, his obedience to the Torah (not yet in Gen 22:15-18) and the ensuing, causally related consequences for his offspring.

According to the classification regarding the history of theology, all
passages belong into the greater framework of Deuteronomic-
Deuteronomistic theology. In line with this tradition, Abraham becomes
the representative, the figure of identification of the people of Israel and
functions as "corporate personality."[423] What characterizes Abraham, also
characterizes Israel. Both, Israel's attitude to the law as well as its faith are
projected into the story and figure of the patriarch. Therefore one can conclude that, as a whole, in the image of Abraham in Genesis those two dispositions, faith in God and obedience to his will, appear as a unity; both
are constitutive, distinguishable parts of Abraham's attitude towards God.
Nevertheless, this apparent unity may not blur the different accentuations
and the potential consequences of these accentuations in the history of interpretation. One can assert a fine, but pronounced nuance of the Abraham
image in Genesis 15 compared to those sections that affirm Abraham's
obedience to the Torah. Both traits of tradition emerged and existed (almost) simultaneously. The image of Abraham as Torah-obedient patriarch
became very prominent in early Jewish, extra-canonical writings, while the
"faith-theme" appears less prominent and represents no principal theme
within the Abraham cycle.

F. Summary

The narrator/author, shaped by Deuteronomic-Deuteronomistic ideas,
composed Genesis 15 as a well thought-out whole, as a "constructed narrative," in the context of the exile, with its end in sight. It seeks to encourage
the exiled community and opens up the perspective of a new future, re-
minding the people of the old covenant that Yahweh "cut" with Abraham.
This relatively late date does not exclude, however, that earlier and pre-

---

[423] B. Ego points to the tendency in this stage of Jewish theology that refers to Abraham such terms that in earlier literature related to Israel: Abraham is "redeemed" (פדה;
cf. Isa 29:22), "called" (קרא; Isa 51:2), and "chosen" (בחר; Neh 9:7; see below chapter
IV.B) (1996, 35f.). – On Abraham's function as father and example for Israel, see also L.
Ruppert 2002.

formed material and themes, of literary or non-literary nature, have been woven into the text. Distinct promises have been combined: the promise of a son, the promise of numerous descendants (15:1-5), and the promise to inherit the land (15:7-21).

Various forms found access into the text, deriving from the contexts of prophetism,[424] cult, and court. Nevertheless, there is evidence throughout the chapter, especially its thematic and structural coherence and its character of progression, that leads one to view it as much more than a redactional unity. On the other hand, however, one cannot prove conclusively the literary unity, meaning that one author composed the chapter as a whole. It is best to speak of a "compositional unity," as it takes into account the reworking of earlier traditions in the text, yet at the same time acknowledges the consistency that makes dispensable the presupposition of additions, doublets, and contradictions.

Though due to the integrity of the chapter one may not isolate single elements, the unique literary character of 15:6 and (to a lesser degree) of 15:18 opens the horizon of the whole chapter both temporally and geographically towards Abraham's children, to Israel in its generations at all times[425] – particularly in the present reality of the exile, in which the old promises seem to have become distant and unbelievable. The characterization of Abraham correlates to the characterization of Israel, his faith is model for Israel's faith. He is the first who is said to have faith in God,[426] and hence his trusting disposition marks the way for all future generations – especially for those whose foundation of faith seems to have been withdrawn. Even more, the connection of Abraham's faith with the covenant[427] for his descendants establishes a link of the patriarch with the existence of the people of Israel.

For these reasons, the difference between the narrated situation (i.e., the actual reported scene) and the narrative situation (i.e., the historical circumstances at the end of the exile) are relativized. What is said of Abraham is said of Israel: *Tua res agitur*.

---

[424] H.-C. Schmitt makes the case that even the faith-theme in Gen 15:6 reflects a prophetically influenced redaction at the end of the formation of the Pentateuch, which placed "faith" into the center of the Pentateuchal narratives (1982, 178-180). "[E]s [geht] hier darum ... mit dem aus der prophetischen Tradition entnommenen Begriff des 'Glaubens' eine Haltung herauszustellen, die später auch das Neue Testament als für das Gottesverhältnis zentral ansieht" (189).

[425] Cf. H. Seebass 1997, 67.

[426] This is also stressed by Philo (cf. *Virt* 216: Abraham "is the first person spoken of as believing in God..."; see below page 206)

[427] On this significant structural and theological correlation between Gen 15:6 and 15:18, between faith and the covenant, see H. Groß 1977.

Within the framework of the Abraham cycle, Genesis 15 is "distinct from the narrative context that surrounds it"[428] and different to all the other patriarchal narratives[429] in that it displays a remarkably high degree of theological reflection in dealing with the fundamental promises of son, descendants and land and in directing these promises to Israel's historical situation.[430] To the particularity of the chapter corresponds its centrality.

The extraordinary theological concentration of Genesis 15 is most clearly reflected in its pivotal verse Gen 15:6,[431] so that this verse can arguably be called the center of the Abraham narratives.[432] It is noticeably elevated from its context[433] and constitutes the decisive connecting link between the two parts of the chapter.[434] When the author solemnly states that God considered Abraham's faith as righteousness, he binds his declaration on the one hand to the concrete plot of the story – not only as "Schlußergebnis"[435] of 15:1-5, but also as opening remark for 15:7-21 –, yet at the same time makes a general, succinct theological *dictum* of fundamental importance, "a comment full of theological meaning."[436]

With the aid of comparative studies, the wide field of meaning of the term חשב could be concretized regarding its use in Gen 15:6: In his act of considering Abraham's faith as righteousness, God makes a performative,

---

[428] G.W. Coats 1983, 123.

[429] Cf. S. Mowinckel, 1964, 105 ("keine *Erzählung* derselben Art wie die anderen Patriarchenerzählungen").

[430] Cf. G. von Rad 1951, 130 ("eine konzentriert theologische Reflexion"); S. Mowinckel, 1964, 105 ("theologisch-reflektierend"); E. Blum 1984, 389 ("feierliche[.], theologische[.] 'Erzählung'").

[431] Cf. O. Kaiser 1958, 118; J. Blenkinsopp 1992, 123.

[432] Cf. J. Körner 1979, 716 ("Mitte der Abrahamerzählungen").

[433] As for the prominent character of Gen 15:6 due to the verb form וְהֶאֱמִן, R. Mosis points to part of the Greek and Latin text tradition, which instead of an introductive καί/*et* have a postpositive δέ/*autem*: cf., e.g., Rom 4:3; Jas 2:23; *1Clem* 10,6; Justin, *Dialogus cum Tryphone Judaeo* 92,3 (1989, 65); see the *apparatus* of the Septuagint in J.W. Wevers 1974, 168, and of the *Vetus Latina* in B. Fischer 1951-1954, 172f. (but compare the different explanation of the particle δέ in Rom 4:3 in D.-A. Koch 1986, 132f.; see below note 837 in chapter V). Moreover, the fact that many text witnesses add the subject "Abra(ha)m" indicates that the lack of coherence of the Masoretic Text of Gen 15:6 has always been perceived (cf. 4Q225 2 i 7: אברהם; LXX Gen 15:6: Αβραμ; and see especially the *apparatus* just mentioned).

[434] Cf. N. Lohfink 1967, 45f. Lohfink is followed by H. Groß 1977, 30; H.-C. Schmitt 1982, 178; M. Köckert 1988, 246 ("entscheidende Schaltstelle"); J.C. Gertz 2002, 69f.

[435] H. Holzinger 1898, 149.

[436] R. Davidson 1983, 43. Also according to G. von Rad, Gen 15:6 possesses "fast schon den Charakter eines allgemeinen theologischen Lehrsatzes" (1951, 130) and contains "theologische Urteile von großer theologischer Dichtigkeit" (1972, 142); see also H. Seebass 1963, 135 ("fast ein[.] allgemeine[r] theologische[r] Lehrsatz"); H.-J. Hermisson 1978, 25 ("theologisch-programmatischer Grundtext vom Glauben").

authoritative-qualitative judgment that he reaches freely and independently and according to subjective criteria. It is an act of grace and creation with "soteriological" implications, as it constitutes a new, righteous status of Abraham *coram deo*, impinging on his own and future generations' ground of life and existence. Yahweh's character and acting towards humans is defined by his "generative capacity of bringing to being what was not."[437]

These results concerning the verb חשׁב coincide with what has been said on the concept of צְדָקָה: It is a deeply relational concept and denotes Abraham's right standing before God, his new being, his new possibility of life, which is enabled through God's word to Abraham and through his acceptance of Abraham. These salvific implications of "righteousness" encompass both present and future and affect both the person who is ascribed righteousness and future generations. Hence, though linguistically צְדָקָה is to be classified as *nomen actionis/unitatis*, one may not split it off from the notion of the continuous status of rightness. On the other hand, God's judgment of righteousness at the same time causes, creates, and confirms the right relationship anew[438] so that eventually human and divine action converge.

The verb וְהֶאֱמִן is perfect tense with *waw-copulativum*, which indicates the loose connection to 15:1-5. In conjunction with other exegetical observations this fact corroborates the following insights: The verb does on the one hand describe Abraham's believing acceptance of the promises conveyed to him by Yahweh, but it primarily points to his continuous believing disposition and thus transcends the narrative; the two-sidedness of its meaning might be best expressed by word pairs such as "Verhalten" and "Haltung," deed and disposition, act and being. Just as with צְדָקָה a "quantitative" understanding is not opposed to a "qualitative" one. The shape of this disposition of Abraham consists in his constant fastening himself and gaining firmness in Yahweh; this requires, activates and involves the whole existence of the believer. But nevertheless, the prime activity comes from God, as he establishes this personal relationship through his promise. His turning to Abraham happened without condition on his own side and without prerequisites on Abraham's side. Though without preconditions, faith has fundamental consequences: Yahweh considered it as righteousness, which in turn marked the foundation for the covenant.

---

[437] W. Brueggemann 1997, 146n.2.
[438] K. Kertelge 1971, 305.

Chapter IV

Genesis 15:6 in Jewish Theology

In Second Temple Judaism, Abraham became one of the central figures in theology and self-understanding; there was the strong awareness that the story of the first patriarch had meaning and significance for Jewish identity.[1]

The theological importance of the statement about the connection between faith and righteousness resulted in a multifaceted and intricate reception history. Several ancient-Jewish versions, paraphrases or interpretations of Gen 15:6 are part of a broad tradition which displays both close commonalities and individual traits. Depending on the context and the situation in which the text was read, the recipients highlighted certain aspects, specified others, or drew new contextual or intertextual connections.[2] Nonetheless, despite the significance of Gen 15:6 and Abraham's faith, Abraham appears throughout the Jewish tradition, both of Palestinian and Hellenistic provenience, not primarily as "believer," but as truly pious and fully righteous on grounds of what he did.[3]

A. Psalm 106

The only other passage in the Old Testament besides Gen 15:6, in which the two theologically loaded terms חשב and צְדָקָה appear, is Ps 106:31. Psalm 106 (like Nehemiah 9[4]) retells Israel's past as a history of sin, or

---

[1] Our focus here is the interpretation (allusions, *relectures*) of Gen 15:6 in Old Testament and early Jewish texts. Many others have focused in a more general way on the figure of Abraham in early Judaism and the New Testament so that a detailed discussion of this theme seems superfluous (cf., apart from commentaries, dictionaries and essays, the following monographic treatments: C. Dietzfelbinger 1961; S. Sandmel 1971; F.E. Wieser 1987; G.W. Hansen 1989; R.A. Harrisville 1992; N. Calvert-Koyzis 2005).

[2] This high diversity of reception-historical processes and results is not due to the syntactical ambiguity of Gen 15:6 (against M. Oeming 1998, 78, 81), but rather the conciseness and theological substance of this verse became the driving force of a hermeneutical development. As for the dispute about the subject of Gen 15:6b – Abraham or God – these texts *all* insinuate that God is the subject of this half-verse.

[3] Cf. F. Hahn 1971, 94.

[4] See below chapter IV.B.

more precisely: as a history of judgment, always and again interrupted through acts of divine mercy.[5] As a whole, Psalm 106 is dependent on the completed Pentateuch narrative and follows with few alterations its canonical shape, even more than the structurally related Psalms 78, 105, and 136.[6] It reads like a *florilegium* of Pentateuchal themes. Though the Psalm is difficult to date,[7] it seems likely that the Babylonian exile lies in the immediate past, as the people is still scattered over the lands; it calls upon Yahweh to "gather us from among the nations" (106:47). There must also be temporal proximity of the Psalm to the final redaction of the Pentateuch, in view of the manner how it reworks Pentateuchal themes.[8]

Notably, commentators of both Genesis and Psalms oftentimes mention the parallel between Gen 15:6 and Ps 106:31, but do not discuss it[9]:

	Ps 106:30-31 (MT)	Ps 105:30-31 (LXX)
(30) Then Phinehas stood up and interceded, and the plague was stopped	(30) וַיַּעֲמֹד פִּינְחָס וַיְפַלֵּל וַתֵּעָצַר הַמַּגֵּפָה:	(30) καὶ ἔστη Φινεες καὶ ἐξιλάσατο καὶ ἐκόπασεν ἡ θραῦσις
(31) And it has been considered to him as righteousness from generation to generation forever.	(31) וַתֵּחָשֶׁב לוֹ לִצְדָקָה לְדֹר וָדֹר עַד־עוֹלָם	(31) καὶ ἐλογίσθη αὐτῷ εἰς δικαιοσύνην εἰς γενεὰν καὶ γενεὰν ἕως τοῦ αἰῶνος

The verses preceding our passage recapitulate and paraphrase Numbers 25, which recounts how Israel turned to the Baal of Peor,[10] and was therefore inflicted by a plague killing thousands. In the moment of greatest peril, Phinehas[11] spontaneously took the initiative to execute judgment, killing the Israelite Zimri and his Midianite wife amidst the Israelite community, and thus brought the plague to an end. Up until Ps 106:30, the Psalm follows its *Vorlage* from Numbers rather closely, but while according to Num 25:12 Yahweh rewards Phinehas's zeal (106:11: קִנְאָה/ζῆλος) with a priestly covenant of peace (בְּרִית שָׁלוֹם), Ps 106:31 portrays God's reaction by employing a phrase that clearly echoes and is dependent on Gen 15:6.[12]

---

[5] Cf. H.-J. Kraus 1978, 906.

[6] Cf. H.-J. Kraus 1978, 900.

[7] Cf. the caution of A. Weiser 1955, 467.

[8] Cf. H. Wildberger 1967, 380; B. Janowski 1983, 238f. with n.8.

[9] Cf. R.W.L. Moberly 1990, 114f.

[10] Josh 22:17 laments that the "sin at Peor" has still not been removed, and for Hos 9:10, Israel's turning to Baal-peor is decisive in its sedition against Yahweh.

[11] On the Phinehas tradition in Judaism, see M. Hengel 1976, 152-181 and most recently J. Thon 2006.

[12] Cf., e.g., B. Jacob 1934, 394; B. Janowski 1983, 243; K. Seybold 1996, 423. Apart from the allusion of Gen 15:6 in Ps 106:31, Abraham tradition might also resonate in

To be sure, the crucial terms of the formulation "consider as righteous-ness," are not identical in the Masoretic text of Ps 106:31 and Gen 15:6: The Psalm passage has *niphal*, while in Genesis *qal* is used, and Ps 106:31 adds the preposition *le* before the noun צְדָקָה, which excludes the possible understanding that צְדָקָה might be the subject, and hence makes entirely clear that the passive is to be understood as *passivum divinum*.[13] The femi-nine singular verb וַתֵּחָשֶׁב corresponds to the feminine suffix *ha* in וַיַּחְשְׁבֶהָ (Gen 15:6b). These syntactical observations seem to be of little signifi-cance as regards contents and theological implication; rather, one has to consider the context.

On the other hand, the Septuagint form of Ps 106:31a (= LXX Ps 105:31a) is identical with both LXX Gen 15:6b and 1Macc 2,52; they all read: καὶ ἐλογίσθη αὐτῷ εἰς δικαιοσύνην.

An analysis of how the psalmist utilizes the themes of the two passages, on which he draws (Genesis 15 and Numbers 25) suggests that in Ps 106:28-31 he combined their theologically significant components, but with one decisive shift. According to Genesis 15, Abraham's trusting faith is considered by God as righteousness, and a covenant is granted to him for generations to come.[14] On the other hand, Numbers 25 reports about Phi-nehas's zeal, which leads to a covenant[15] that guarantees to Phinehas and his descendants perpetual priesthood. Through the combination of those Pentateuchal narratives – which strikes the eye of any attentive reader – Psalm 106 attains a remarkable new theological peak: Here, Phinehas's zealous act is considered as proof of his righteousness for him, to all gen-erations, forever. A trusting relationship with God is virtually identified

---

106:45 and its covenant terminology (cf. N. Lohfink 1967, 12n.5), but according to H.-J. Kraus this second connection cannot be proved beyond doubt (1978, 905f., against J. Hoftijzer 1956, 72f.).

[13] On texts that translate, paraphrase, or allude to Gen 15:6, using the passive, see be-low the appendix chapter IV.K.I. – That the preposition *le* does not alter the meaning, can be presupposed, since for instance in 4Q225 2 i 8 the morphologically almost identi-cal statement is construed without the preposition (see below chapter IV.F; some inter-preters however have suggested to take צדקה in 4Q225 2 i 8 as subject; see below pages 187f.). The analysis of syntax and context of biblical חשׁב-occurrences (see above chapter III.D.I) has shown that the semantic difference between instances that have a second accusative/nominative or that use *ke* or *le* is negligible (cf. R.W.L. Moberly 1990, 116).

[14] There is no mention of an eternal covenant, but from the perspective of the psalmist it might be presupposed (cf. *Jub* 14,7, where under the influence of Gen 17:7 the aspect of "eternity" appears in the re-narration of Gen 15:7).

[15] Even though Psalm 106 does not mention the covenant explicitly, 106:31b appar-ently refers back to the covenant with Phinehas (cf. Num 25:12-13, but also Sir 45,24; see H.-J. Kraus 1978, 904).

with a fervent fight against idolatry. It needs to be conceded that the psalmist omits several details of the Numbers story and by doing so takes off its edge to a certain degree: He does not mention explicitly Zimri's transgression, but speaks generally of the provocative deeds of the Israelites in the desert; nor does he report Phinehas's act of judgment, but rather accentuates his act of intercession (פלל *piel*) and makes him – like Moses (106:23) – one of the great intercessors of the desert period.[16] Nevertheless, as clearly as the whole story of Numbers 25 stands in the background of the psalmist's allusion to Phinehas, as clearly his judging zeal is part of the story, even if not explicitly mentioned.[17] In the further Jewish history of reception of the Phinehas material, his radicalism is always present and emphasized.[18]

The syntax of Ps 106:31 is ambiguous regarding the point of reference of the phrase "to all generations, forever"; does it qualify the verb חשב or the noun צְדָקָה? The narrative form of the verb, which implies a completed single action, and the present reality of the priesthood, which is the perpetual result of this onetime act of "considering" (from the perspective of the psalmist), seem to speak in favor of the latter possibility.[19] Num 25:12-13 reports that the covenant granted to Phinehas entails eternal priesthood, and it is probable that the notion of this covenant is present in the Psalm text, though not explicitly mentioned.[20] Furthermore, the fact that God is the implied subject of the *passivum divinum* construction makes the first possibility unlikely, since in that case, it would be the community, which would always and again consider and remember Phinehas's deed as right-

---

[16] Cf. B. Janowski 1983. Janowski points out that while Numbers 25 combined the aspects of judgment and intercession, Psalm 106 stresses the latter, which in turn has been developed further in the *Vetus Latina*, the Targumic tradition, and the Peshitta when they reinterpret Phinehas's intercessory deed in terms of a prayer of intercession. Hence, one can state a spiritualizing tendency.

[17] Cf. H.-J. Kraus 1978, 899.

[18] Especially the Maccabean era emphasizes and demands the "zeal for the law," and in this and in the further tradition one places side by side Mattathias, Phinehas, Elijah, and Abraham. There, one can state a radicalizing tendency (see M. Hengel 1976, 151-234, especially 154-159: "In gleicher Weise wie der Eifer des Pinehas das spätere Hohepriestertum seines Geschlechts legitimierte, konnte der Eifer des Mattathias die späteren hohepriesterlichen Ansprüche der Hasmonäer rechtfertigen" [158]. 180: "Identifizierung von Pinehas und Elia ... im Laufe des 1. Jh. n. Chr.," 187n.1: "Gen. R. 42,8 erscheint ... Abraham ... als Eiferer.").

[19] Cf. R.W.L. Moberly 1990, 117. Against that L.C. Allen 1983, 46.

[20] Cf. L. Gaston 1980, 50: "It is more likely that the reference in vs 31b is to the 'covenant of peace' [Num 25:12-13] rather than to perpetual reputation for his righteous deed." Gaston refers to Ramban who states on Ps 106:31: "For forever God will keep his righteousness and steadfast love for him for the sake of it [*sc.* this deed]").

eousness.[21] It is another thing to say that the community joins God's judgment; if he considers Abraham's faith and Phinehas's deed as righteousness, so will Israel.

The relevance of this syntactical decision for Gen 15:6 and the meaning of צְדָקָה there, has been noted above[22]: Though being *nomen unitatis*, i.e., describing a deed, it connotes something lasting, just as the covenant established with Phinehas will endure.

Phinehas's zeal for the law, his killing the unfaithful Israelite and his Midianite wife "has been considered as righteousness for him" and has thus the same outcome as Abraham's faith.[23] A strict observance of the law that proceeds to action is thus paralleled and equated with a believing attitude, faithfulness with faith. There are other notable analogies regarding the viewpoint of the respective authors of Gen 15:6 and Ps 106:31. Both write from a situation and perspective that is dependent on a certain prehistory and on the conduct of a certain people: The psalmist who writes in the period of the priesthood of Phinehas's descendants owes his existence to Phinehas's faithful zeal and therefore relates it to those critical events in the desert period and to God's response, while the writer of Gen 15:6 looks back on Abraham's continual trust in Yahweh and Yahweh's reaction and bases thereupon his knowledge that Israel is God's people. Both, Phinehas's zeal and Abraham's faith led to covenants so that both, the priesthood and Israel owe their covenant status to Yahweh's response to Phinehas and Abraham.[24] The similarity and analogy of Abraham and Phinehas shows itself, furthermore, in Jewish tradition, as it regarded both of them as "great patriarchs" and mentioned the one along with the other.[25]

The noted shift of accentuation may not be attributed precipitately to the theological intention of the psalmist; rather, an envisaged similarity of meaning must be presupposed: In referring to Gen 15:6b, he understood Phinehas's deed as another way to "fasten oneself in Yahweh" and as an-

---

[21] Both the terminological and contextual overlap with Gen 15:6 and the syntactical analogy with passages like Lev 7:18 or Num 18:27 (חשב in the *niphal* and connected to *le* of recipient) suggests that God is the implied subject of the verb וַתֵּחָשֶׁב (D. Michel, though, leaves open the question, whether it is God or the community that "reckons righteousness" [1999, 106]).

[22] See above chapter III.D.III.

[23] H.-W. Heidland speaks here of a "Gleichwertigkeit von Glaube und 'Werk' hinsichtlich ihrer Verdienstlichkeit" (1936, 83).

[24] Cf. R.W.L. Moberly 1990, 119f. Moberly says that "it is always legitimate to seek to discern whether the perspective of Israel may not also be present in the text" (118).

[25] W.R. Farmer 1952, 27. On Phinehas's reputation in Jewish thought, see only Sir 45,23 (τρίτος εἰς δόξαν); 1Macc 2,54 (ὁ πατὴρ ἡμῶν; cf. 2,51; Sir 44,1); in these passages, Phinehas appears at the side of Abraham.

other means to exhibit of righteousness.[26] To him, Phinehas's faithful act is not a qualitatively different attitude towards God than Abraham's faith; both persons demonstrate correct behavior in a critical situation,[27] in which "trust" needs to be displayed.[28] Both passages, on the other hand, do not limit the scope of צְדָקָה to a one-time deed, but assign to it lasting consequences for both the individual, whose act is considered righteous, and for the community, who presently lives on grounds of the faithfulness of the ancestors.

The Septuagint version of Ps 106:30 highlights the latter aspect by using the heavily loaded term ἐξιλάσκεσθαι: In Phinehas's action, "there seems to be something essentially redemptive"[29] with respect to the people of Israel. Whatever the intention of the psalmist was when he quoted Gen 15:6b in his historical retrospective – the temporal gap between Gen 15:6 and Ps 106:31, should be noted, is not very large[30] – he opened up a new dimension of a possible understanding of what, how and why "God considers as righteousness." Moreover, the conception of the "merit of the fathers" does not represent an impossible extension of this view of the biblical text.[31]

B. Nehemiah 9

The place and function of the congregational prayer Nehemiah 9[32] in the book Nehemiah itself, as well as in the larger context of Chronicles-Ezra-Nehemiah or Ezra-Nehemiah is subject to a vigorous debate. From this confusing situation follows the difficulty to establish a temporal classifica-

---

[26] Cf. F. Hahn 1971, 92.

[27] Cf. C. Westermann 1982, 265.

[28] In a way, therefore, both Phinehas and Abraham are "outstanding example[s] of human faithfulness to Yahweh" (R.W.L. Moberly 1990, 126). Ramban, on the other hand, refers to the conduct of both, Abraham and Phinehas, as "trust" (quoted in L. Gaston 1980, 43). – As for the correlation of trust and obedience/fear in Genesis 22, see above notes 402 and 403 in chapter III.

[29] W.R. Farmer 1952, 29. The Septuagint translates the term פלל with ἐξιλάσκεσθαι, probably influenced by Num 25:13, which reads כפר *piel* (see also Sir 45,23).

[30] The relative proximity of Genesis 15 and Psalm 106 is also reflected in their common interest in the theme of faith – both have אמן *hiphil* + *be* – (cf. H.-C. Schmitt 1982, 185n.49), even if in Psalm 106 the primary orientation of faith is in Yahweh's words rather than in Yahweh himself (Ps 106:12: וַיַּאֲמִינוּ בִדְבָרָיו; cf. 106:24: לֹא־הֶאֱמִינוּ לִדְבָרוֹ). This divergence stands for a development from speaking of "faith in Yahweh" (Gen 15:6; Ex 14:31) to saying "faith in his words" (cf. H. Wildberger 1967, 380).

[31] Cf. H. Gunkel 1926, 467, who renders צְדָקָה with "Lohn," "Verdienst."

[32] An extensive discussion of this prayer is provided in J.H. Newman 1999, 63-116. See also M. Gilbert 1981.

tion of this chapter or an attribution to a certain "school" where it supposedly originated[33]; the number of suggestions can hardly be surveyed. Nevertheless, the character of the text "reflects a development of interpretive
tradition that takes it beyond Deuteronomistic bounds and gives the prayer
its own unique flavor."[34] Tentatively, one could assume together with the
majority of scholars a date around the turn from the fifth to the fourth century.

In the context of a large-scale historical retrospective on Israel's sinful
past[35] – comparable to Psalm 106 –, Neh 9:7-8 recounts *inter alia* the story
of Abraham[36] in the form of a penitential prayer[37]; among the patriarchs,
only Abraham is mentioned. The prayer itself is embraced on the one side
by the reading of the law (8:1-12.18) and on the other side by Israel's re-
commitment to observing "all the commandments of Yahweh, our Lord
and his ordinances and his statutes" (10:29-40). The primary interest and
intention of the prayer is not – as most exegetes argue[38] – to point to Abraham as the positive model in contrast to the unfaithful and insolent Israelites, his loyal obedience in contrast to their little faith; rather, first and
foremost Israel's unfaithfulness and rebellion is confronted with God's
faithfulness and righteousness in deed and word, from the creation (9:6)
until "today" (9:32): "You are righteous (צַדִּיק)" (9:8.33).[39] In the context of

---

[33] Cf., e.g., R. Klein 1976; M. Oeming 1990, 41-45.

[34] J.H. Newman 1999, 64f.

[35] The numerous allusions to biblical traditions in Nehemiah 9 are listed in J.M.
Myers 1965, 167-169.

[36] On the background of the Abraham-verses in this chapter, see M.J. Boda 1999, 102-
111 and J.H. Newman 1999, 70-76.

[37] The setting of the prayer is two days after the end of the Feast of Tabernacles, but
"[a]lthough the author wants the reader to relate the prayer to the feast, the setting does
not directly influence the content of the prayer" (R.A. Werline 1998, 56).

[38] Cf. only M. Oeming 1998, 84 (Abraham as "Modellisraelit").

[39] The proponents of the view that Abraham is the subject of Gen 15:6b (see above
chapter III.C.II.1) take this expression as argument against "the objection that Gen 15:6
cannot mean that Abraham ascribed righteousness to God because no later text so understands it" (L. Gaston 1980, 49; cf. M. Oeming 1998, 83; J.A. Fitzmyer 2003, 259: This
text "would give support to the alternate interpretation of Gen 15:6." R. Rendtorff 1999,
25: The alternative "findet eine Stütze in Nehemiah 9, wo es, wie ein Responsorium auf
den Satz, dass Gott das Herz Abrahams 'verläßlich' fand, heißt: 'denn du (Gott) bist
gerecht'." M. Theobald 2001, 402n.20). Yet the reference to God's righteousness in Neh
9:8 clearly goes beyond the re-narration of the Abraham-story and instead is connected to
the assertion that God fulfills his promise, but also to the repentance due to own disobedience to the one who promised (cf. O. Michel 1978, 138). Those who pray, the descendants of Abraham, they call upon and experience at the present time (cf. 9:32) God's
faithfulness, as they see the chance to return to the promised land. The difference of perspective – on the one hand the story of the patriarch and on the other hand the current
situation of his descendants – may not be blurred.

the penitential service, this opposition serves as impetus to question one's own behavior and to repent; it has been Israel's experience that the merciful God will hear their cry and send salvation,[40] and the author seeks to connect this past experience with the present situation (9:32.37). The post-exilic community of the fifth century still suffers under foreign domination and is governed by foreign kings (9:36-37; cf. Gen 15:13),[41] which means that the consequences of sin, God's punishment, are in effect to the present day. Within the framework of the effort to establish salvation-historical continuity, Abraham appears as the one in whom God's salvific action took shape in an exemplary way and who at the same time provides this needed continuity, because God made a covenant with him and assured him and his descendants of the land – the land that is still under foreign authorities.[42]

	Neh 9:7-8 (MT)	2Esdras 19:7-8 (LXX)
(7) You are Yahweh, the God who chose Abram and brought him out of Ur of the Chaldeans and gave him the name Abraham.	(7) אַתָּה־הוּא יְהוָה הָאֱלֹהִים אֲשֶׁר בָּחַרְתָּ בְּאַבְרָם וְהוֹצֵאתוֹ מֵאוּר כַּשְׂדִּים וְשַׂמְתָּ שְּׁמוֹ אַבְרָהָם:	(7) σὺ εἶ κύριος ὁ θεός σὺ ἐξελέξω ἐν ᾿Αβράμ καὶ ἐξήγαγες αὐτὸν ἐκ τῆς χώρας τῶν Χαλδαίων καὶ ἐπέθηκας αὐτῷ ὄνομα Αβρααμ
(8) You found his heart faithful before you, and made with him a covenant in order to give the land of the Canaanite, the Hittite, the Amorite, the Perizzite, the Jebusite, and the Girgashite (both to him and)[43] to his descendants;	(8) וּמָצָאתָ אֶת־לְבָבוֹ נֶאֱמָן לְפָנֶיךָ וְכָרוֹת עִמּוֹ הַבְּרִית לָתֵת אֶת־אֶרֶץ הַכְּנַעֲנִי הַחִתִּי הָאֱמֹרִי וְהַפְּרִזִּי וְהַיְבוּסִי וְהַגִּרְגָּשִׁי לָתֵת [44]לְזַרְעוֹ	(8) καὶ εὗρες τὴν καρδίαν αὐτοῦ πιστὴν ἐνώπιόν σου καὶ διέθου πρὸς αὐτὸν διαθήκην δοῦναι αὐτῷ τὴν γῆν τῶν Χαναναίων καὶ Χετταίων καὶ Αμορραίων καὶ Φερεζαίων καὶ Ιεβουσαίων καὶ Γεργεσαίων καὶ τῷ σπέρματι αὐτοῦ
and you have fulfilled your promise, for you are righteous.	וַתָּקֶם אֶת־דְּבָרֶיךָ כִּי צַדִּיק אָתָּה:	καὶ ἔστησας τοὺς λόγους σου ὅτι δίκαιος σύ

---

[40] The schema sin-punishment-repentance-salvation appears several times in the prayer (cf. R.A. Werline 1998, 57).

[41] Cf. H.G.M. Williamson 1985, 300-319.

[42] Also J.H. Newman states: "The 'punchline' of the Abraham traditions for the author lies in the promise of the land" (1999, 71). In the whole prayer the term "land" occurs thirteen times (75n.32).

[43] The words in parenthesis follow the Septuagint, which differs from the Masoretic Text (see following note).

[44] The double occurrence of לָתֵת in the Masoretic Text is regarded by some commentators as roughness, and they suggest to replace (in line with the Peshitta and the Septuagint [cf. the *apparatus* in BHS]) the second לָתֵת with לֹו plus *waw*, so that it would read: לֹו וּלְזַרְעוֹ (cf. W. Rudolph 1949, 154). Others however claim that the infinitive לָתֵת is re-

The verse introducing the Abraham passage reminds of two fundamental changes in Abraham's life that marked his relationship to Yahweh: change of place and of name. The mention of Ur in Chaldea and Abraham's leaving this native place on God's command allude to Gen 11:28-31 and 12:1, while the change of his name from Abram to Abraham refers to Gen 17:5.[45]

If and to what extent Neh 9:8 has in mind aspects from Genesis 15 is disputed in scholarship.[46] Though Abraham's exodus to Canaan recalls Genesis 12, the wording rather resembles Gen 15:7; through this reference the promise of the land to Abraham's descendants – not just to Abraham (as in Genesis 12) – is alluded to. The covenant theme also contains a terminological bridge between Gen 15:18 and Neh 9:8 due to the occurrence of the distinctive expression כרת בְּרִית[47]; this bridge is affirmed, if the Hebrew wording is accepted against the Septuagint version,[48] because both passages speak of the giving of the land to the descendants without directly mentioning Abraham.[49] The gentilic list in Nehemiah is not fully congruent with that in Gen 15:19-21, but both lists share one significant phenomenon: One the one hand they do not mention the people of the Hivites,[50] while on the other hand they name the Girgashites.[51] Compared to all other biblical gentilic lists, this phenomenon is unique and it is difficult to provide an indisputable explanation.[52] However, as for the relationship between the lists in Neh 9:8 and Gen 15:19-21, one could argue that the latter represents the model or the pre-text, and that Nehemiah adopts the exclusion of the Hivites and furthermore "omits the four peoples which do not appear in the classical lists: the Kenites, the Kenizzites, the Kadmonites

---

peated due to the long gentilic list that separated the first לְתֵת from its object (cf. H.G.M. Williamson 1985, 304).

[45] The Abraham cycle does not refer explicitly to Abraham's being elected by God (בחר); however, Deut 4:37 and 10:15 say that Yahweh chose the ancestors' descendants.

[46] Cf. on the different solutions M.J. Boda 1999, 103-110.

[47] Cf., e.g., J. Ha 1989, 57n.32. Ps 105:10-12 and 1Chr 16:16-18 contain a similar expression.

[48] See above note 44.

[49] Cf. R.W.L. Moberly 1992, 25.

[50] Some versions add the Hivites (LXX[L], Peshitta, Arabic; cf. *Jub* 14,18).

[51] In that regard, only Ezra 9:1 is comparable.

[52] On one suggestion, see M. Anbar 1982, 54n.111. See on the issue of gentilic lists W. Richter 1964, 41-43; T. Ishida 1979.

and the Rephaim."[53] Thus, the list of peoples in connection with the covenant clearly draws a line to Gen 15:18-21 on a literary level.[54]

Does this imply that the phrase "you found his heart faithful before you" functions as interpretation of Gen 15:6 and as quintessence of Gen 15:1-6[55]? At first this solution appears to be most plausible due to the mentioned correlation between Nehemiah 9 and Genesis 15.[56] Moreover, in both texts the covenant follows on a statement of Abraham's relationship to God and God's assessment of it; the correlation of "faith" and "covenant" that was emphasized in the structural analysis of Genesis 15 confirms this association.[57] The most obvious link however is given through the root אמן, which obviously binds together the two passages linguistically.

But others suggest – despite the lack of a terminological connection – that it is rather a second narrative of the Abraham cycle that is to be brought in relation to Nehemiah's note on Abraham's faithfulness, namely, Genesis 22.[58] They argue *inter alia* that Neh 9:7-8 does not display any chronological interest, according to which the covenant and the gentilic list would have to be preceded by a reference to Abraham's faith; the citation of Gen 17:5 in Neh 9:7 demonstrates the liberty that is applied in chronological matters. The strongest argument in favor for this interpretation

---

[53] M. Anbar 1982, 54. Cf. N. Lohfink 1967, 66; R.E. Clements 1967, 21n.25; M.J. Boda 1999, 109f.

[54] Against M. Oeming 1998, 83n.50, who regards the lists in Deut 7:1, Josh 3:10, and 24:8 as closer parallels than Gen 15:19-21 – those passages do not mention the establishment of a covenant.

[55] Cf., e.g., W. Rudolph 1949, 158f.; A. Weiser 1967, 185; L. Gaston 1980, 49 with n.34; A.H.J. Gunneweg 1987, 125; J. Becker 1990, 93; J.D. Levenson 1993, 175; B. Ego/A. Lange 2003, 182. In his comments on 4QPseudo-Jubilees, J.A. Fitzmyer also contends a relationship between the expression מצא נאמן and Gen 15:6 (2003, 268).

[56] When the focus lies on the faithful heart of Abraham, this does not imply a tendency towards inwardness as opposed to outward actions; the one who is said to have a faithful heart is one who obeys God's commands.

[57] See above pages 93f.

[58] Cf. e.g., J.C. VanderKam/J.T. Milik 1994, 153, 165; M. Oeming 1998, 83f.; J.H. Newman 1999, 70, 72. A third group deems it uncertain, if in Neh 9:8 "an den Glauben Abrahams, Gen 15,6, oder an sein Verhalten nach Gen 22 gedacht ist" (A. Jepsen 1974, 318). M.J. Boda suggests an alternate solution, arguing that the "fixation on the Genesis account of Abraham has limited the scope of research." He associates Neh 9:8 with the Deuteronomistic movement and concludes that it is "unlikely that the composer is thinking of Gen 15:6 as the event behind this verse" (1999, 104). Though he is able to draw terminological connecting lines to Deuteronomistic texts like Psalm 78, he fails to acknowledge the reference to and relevance of Abrahamic traditions. Later passages dealing with Abraham, his faith and his faithfulness (some of which are discussed in this chapter IV), demonstrate clearly that the mention of Abraham is never separated from the traditions surrounding the patriarch (most prominently Genesis 12; 15; 17; 22).

however is the phrase "to be found faithful," which appears years later in other *relectures* of the Abraham-story: Sirach 44, *Jubilees*, 4QPseudo-Jubilees, and 1Maccabees 2.[59] In those cases it seems clear that the situation, in which Abraham was found faithful, is God's testing him by commanding to offer his only son. It seems likely that even Neh 9:8 has in mind the Aqedah and that in effect all passages with the expression "to be found faithful" draw on a pre-formulated expression for the Aqedah.[60]

As a consequence, since the text does not provide a specific reason why God regards Abraham as faithful, the inherent logic of the text would equally allow for assigning both Genesis texts, Genesis 15 and 22, to Neh 9:8a. It is however not feasible to create a dichotomy between the two suggestions, so that the alternative interpretations would mutually exclude each other. Neither should one on the other hand assume a conglomerate of Abraham traditions that the writer of Neh 9:7-8 compiled, in which the single traditions are impossible to distinguish. Rather, the most plausible way to explain the traditions standing behind Neh 9:8 lies in drawing together both Gen 15:6 and Genesis 22, Abraham's faith in the context of the promise of a son and his faithfulness in his obedience to sacrifice his son. The theological relevance and to a certain degree astounding character of the passage then does not consist in the manner, how the various narratives of the forefather Abraham are summarized and recapitulated, but in the fact that the statement "Abraham believed in Yahweh, and he considered it to him as righteousness" is obviously regarded as equivalent to the phrase "Yahweh found his heart faithful before him." It seems that here we have in a still subtle manner the starting point to an understanding of Abraham's faith, which will shape Jewish theology and concept of faith deeply, both in Palestinian and Hellenistic tradition of Judaism. A shift is about to take place from regarding Abraham's faith as a kind of disposition, which makes itself entirely dependent on and firm in God, towards the idea of faithfulness and endurance in trial, of unquestioning obedience to God's command.[61] Reason for and at the same time result of this shift is the growing significance of the Aqedah in Jewish theology.[62] The intention of Genesis 15 is linked and fused with the purpose of Genesis 22, whereby – which is important – no essential theological difference is perceived. As in Ps 106:31, trust and faithfulness, faith and obedience are virtually equated.[63]

---

[59] See below chapters IV.D, IV.E, IV.F, and IV.H.

[60] Thus M. Oeming 1998, 83.

[61] Cf. F. Hahn 1971, 95f. Hahn thinks that this "new" concept of faith is "in dem Bußgebet Neh 9,8 wohl schon vorbereitet" (95); J.D.G. Dunn 1998, 225 with n.95.

[62] Cf., e.g., A. Schlatter 1927, 18n.2.

[63] See above note 28.

The outward indication of the factual synonymity of "faith" and "faithfulness" in the context of the Abrahamic tradition is the mode of the stem אמן: While Gen 15:6 uses the *hiphil*, Neh 9:8 employs the *niphal*. Below, we will see how for instance the book of *Jubilees* relates Abraham's faithfulness not only to the issue of the missing heir and the events of the Aqedah, but to other tests as well – ten in number.[64]

Another issue, which is related to the one just discussed, is the character of the relationship between Abraham's presupposed faithfulness and Yahweh's covenant, in other words: between Abraham's act and God's act. Is there a causal or conditional connection, or do both statements simply enumerate different actions of Yahweh without creating a logical tie? It is remarkable that in the context of the prayer which recounts the creation until the exodus, Yahweh continually appears as the protagonist, as the one who acts, and the various stages of his action are retold in the second person.[65] The intention of the prayer therefore is to demonstrate his righteousness in word and deed through which he governs all of Israel's history until the present (Neh 9:8.33) and which represents a counter-image to Israel's unfaithfulness. Under these conditions, the underlying objective of the reference to Abraham's faithful heart is the fact that it is Yahweh who came to this assessment. Abraham is "merely" one aspect of God's dealing with his people, though a very significant one, as only he is mentioned by name. The concern and *ductus* of the argumentation is not so much Abraham's conduct and God's reaction,[66] but, rather, the patriarch's faithful heart is presupposed; and God speaks a judgment on it and establishes the covenant that has a current implication for Abraham's descendants, for those who pray the penitential prayer. This is why the shift to the new understanding of faith is to be called "subtle": The chief interest does not center yet on Abraham's act or acts of faithfulness.[67]

C. The Septuagint

The Septuagint is of great importance for our quest how the Masoretic Text of Gen 15:6 has been understood in Jewish theology of pre-Christian

---

[64] See below page 180.

[65] Only from Israel's disobedience in the desert on (Neh 9:16), the perspective changes and the third person plural is used.

[66] Against B. Ego/A. Lange 2003, 182.

[67] Insofar as Abraham's faithful behavior did not cause God to grant the covenant, also the Israelites' disobedience does not entail the loss of the ownership of the land: "An important feature of this interpretation is that God's covenantal grant of the land is not described as contingent on behavior" (J.H. Newman 1999, 75).

times. It is the only version that can aid us in this endeavor, since the Samaritan Pentateuch is identical with the Masoretic Text[68] and since the manuscript of the Genesis Apocryphon ends abruptly in the middle of the paraphrase of Genesis 15.[69]

In this context it is impossible to enter the debates on the historical and text-historical relationship of the Masoretic Text and the Septuagint. It seems likely that the translation enterprise of the Septuagint began quite early, around 275 B.C., with the translation of the Pentateuch. The translators of the Pentateuch adopted a fairly literal approach toward the Hebrew text of that time. To be sure, "still earlier Hebrew manuscripts which could reflect vestiges of earlier editorial stages of the biblical books" served as *Vorlage* for the translation,[70] possibly also for Gen 15:6. This means that compared to the Masoretic Text and certainly to those other texts to be discussed below, the Septuagint version might witness to an earlier stage in the textual history of Gen 15:6.[71]

The contention of numerous exegetes that "the Greek of the LXX version of Gen. 15:6 is, though not exactly literal, a perfectly good and completely unambiguous translation of the Hebrew of the M.T.,"[72] has to be challenged. For, the variations between both texts are not limited to stylistic-formal matters,[73] but pertain to significant theological issues as well. The Septuagint reads:

LXX Gen 15:6[74]	
And Abraham believed God, and it was counted to him as righteousness.	καὶ ἐπίστευσεν 'Αβρὰμ τῷ θεῷ καὶ ἐλογίσθη αὐτῷ εἰς δικαιοσύνην.

This means that the following differences exist between the Septuagint and the Masoretic Text[75]:

(1) The remarkable change of tenses from the narrative form to the perfect וְהֶאֱמִן is not reflected in the Septuagint. The translator(s) lined up Abraham's "believing" with the other events by using the narrative aorist.

---

[68] See F.G. Uhlemann 1837, 22.

[69] See N. Avigad/Y. Yadin 1956.

[70] E. Tov 2003, 143.

[71] Cf. J.A. Fitzmyer 2003, 267.

[72] W.R. Farmer 1952, 27n.1; cf. also H.D. Betz 1979, 140n.14 (on Gal 3:6); J.D.G. Dunn 1988, 202.

[73] E. Pax assumes that the Hebrew active voice (וַיַּחְשְׁבֶהָ) was changed for the sake of a better Greek, i.e., to maintain a uniform syntactical subject (1961/1962, 100; referred to and criticized in R. Mosis 1999, 96n.5).

[74] See J.W. Wevers 1974, 168.

[75] See the detailed text-historical analysis in R. Mosis 1999, 96-100.

In the same way, as the word of Yahweh came to him,[76] he believed him; the narrative progression is not interrupted, and hence for the reader the reported events remain confined quite naturally to the concrete story without moving between different communicative levels.

(2) The intention to describe Abraham's faith as response to God's promise is supported by the expression πιστεύειν τῷ θεῷ as translation for הֶאֱמִן בַּיהוָה, because here the *immediate* direction of faith shifts from God to the content of the promise.

(3) Instead of the proper name יְהוָה, the Greek reads the appellative form θεός, as it also does in Gen 15:7.[77] This phenomenon is somewhat unusual, since the expected translation of the tetragrammaton would be κύριος. Nevertheless, elsewhere a similar translation practice can be observed,[78] and it is not imperative to presuppose אֱלֹהִים in the Septuagint-*Vorlage*, if further arguments do not suggest it.

(4) The remaining differences can be listed briefly, since these issues and their consequences have already been dealt with above[79]: The subject of faith is named explicitly in the Septuagint ('Αβράμ), which gives the pronoun αὐτῷ an unambiguous point of reference and excludes a reflexive meaning in favor of the demonstrative sense. Also, what is meant by the suffix *ha* in וַיַּחְשְׁבֶהָ is clearly expressed through the passive ἐλογίσθη. The rendition of the active through the passive entails the use of the term δικαιοσύνη in the accusative. Since the Septuagint by and large renders חשב plus prepositional expression with εἰς,[80] one might infer that the translator(s) read לצדקה and not צדקה as in the Masoretic Text.[81] It should be noted that the passive does not serve to avoid the direct reference to God,[82] but it presumably goes back to the elevated royal style at court, which says that an inferior is exposed to the ruler's exertion of power – with positive or

---

[76] Gen 15:1: ἐγενήθη ῥῆμα; 15:4: φωνὴ ἐγένετο.

[77] Against that, LXX Gen 15:1.4.8 etc. translate the tetragrammaton with κύριος. There is only one occurrence of אמן *hiphil* with the prepositional expression בַּיהוָה, Ex 14:31 (though there are additional instances that read בַּיהוָה אֱלֹהִים: Deut 1:32; 2Chr 20:20). There יהוה is also translated by θεός.

[78] Cf. D.-A. Koch 1986, 84n.2. – On the issue of the κύριος-title in Jewish theology, see also J.A. Fitzmyer 1975, 119-123.

[79] See above chapter III.C.II.1.

[80] Cf. R. Mosis 1989, 90. The only exception is Job 41:19 – and Gen 15:6, if in this respect the Septuagint's *Vorlage* of Gen 15:6 were to be identical with the Masoretic Text; but this is to be questioned.

[81] As for the question why Gen 15:6 lacks the preposition, H. Cazelles reasons that it is "stylistiquement difficile de le répéter après le lamed devant suffixe" (1962, 334n.57; see however, e.g., Ps 106:31).

[82] Against F. Blass/A. Debrunner/F. Rehkopf 1979, §130,1.

negative consequences.[83] Interestingly, this explanation complies with the above analysis of the term חשב where the situation of Abraham before God is compared to the situation of an inferior before the king.[84] As regards the textual history of LXX Gen 15:6, the introduction of the passive is more likely to be attributed to a Hebrew *Vorlage* diverging from the Masoretic tradition, and not to the translator(s). Later on we will discuss the Qumran fragment 4QPseudo-Jubilees[a],[85] which might allow us to hypothesize further about the possible wording of the Hebrew text on which the Septuagint relies. For now one can assume that it might have read: ויאמין אברהם באלוהים ותחשב לו לצדקה.[86]

It needs to be reckoned with the fact that by means of the translation into Greek, the semantic contents of the translation words influence the meaning of the whole and import into it different and new nuances, or remove aspects of meaning that have been present in the original. This principle can be verified in the light of the Septuagint translation of Gen 15:6. However, it certainly does not promote any clear-cut distinction between a "Hebrew" and "Greek" meaning that a certain "concept" (such as faith) might take on.[87] Therefore, one has to be cautious to speak of a fundamental, deliberate re-interpretation of the original text,[88] since the shifts of meaning, caused by the efforts of translation, come into being simply on grounds of the factual lack of a translation word or syntactical construction, which contains or expresses precisely the same as the original. The differences of meaning are in the nature of things and not avoidable, but the more the translation uncouples itself from the original – i.e., the smaller the ability or opportunity to verify a translation on the basis of the original –, the greater becomes the weight and influence of those differences. Hence, one should address the described phenomenon as potential modification of contents of meaning.[89]

Above, we discussed the range of meaning of the Hebrew verb חשב and criticized the view that it is generally to be subsumed under the category "commercial language,"[90] that it always denotes technical-objective preci-

---

[83] Cf. C. Macholz 1990. In our case the avoidance of the divine name would not be necessary, since Gen 15:6 (MT) does not use it.

[84] See above pages 122f.

[85] See below chapter IV.F.

[86] Rather than a diverging *Vorlage* B. Johnson presumes the "influence of Aramaic" to be determinative for the Greek translation (1986/1987, 110). See also below note 376.

[87] Cf. again with regard to "faith(fulness)," J. Barr 1961, 161-205.

[88] Thus apparently M. Oeming 1983, 195, and in a very pronounced way H.-W. Heidland 1936, 95-98.

[89] Cf. G. Ebeling 1958, 83: "[D]er Übersetzungsvorgang ins Griechische [tangiert] selbstverständlich auch die Bedeutungsgeschichte."

[90] Against K. Seybold 1982.

sion. Rather, as the analysis of the חשׁב-occurrences has sought to demonstrate, several instances – among which is Gen 15:6 – demand the understanding of חשׁב as a subjective-voluntary, free act of evaluation performed by a person who has authority over the person who or whose act is assessed. It appears that this component of meaning is not existent and innate in the Greek λογίζεσθαι and that compared to the Hebrew חשׁב the semantic range of its Greek equivalent is narrower and displays a rationalizing tone: What has been rejected with respect to חשׁב, generally applies to λογίζεσθαί τι εἴς τι: Since it stems from the language of business,[91] it denotes a rational converting of a value into a value measure,[92] sometimes even depositing in someone's account.[93] Though it is true that "in the LXX it comes to have further connotations as a result of the fact that it is used to represent the Hebrew חשׁב,"[94] one cannot deny that the used Greek term and its history of meaning influences theological concepts.

The second significant keyword of Gen 15:6, צדקה is rendered – as is usually the case – by δικαιοσύνη.[95] Here too the Old Testament subject matter had to be carried into the sphere of the Greek language. As the word צדקה in the Hebrew text of the Old Testament, the Septuagint translation word δικαιοσύνη has in most instances the connotation of a salvation-giving, faithful act of God, but occasionally takes on the classical Greek juridical meaning of an act of justice.[96] Aspects of both connotations are

---

[91] Cf. U. Wilckens 1978, 262.

[92] H.-W. Heidland 1936, 96 ("vernunftgemäßes Umrechnen eines Wertes in ein Wertmaß"). Heidland however goes too far when he assumes that this new, Greek meaning was deliberately and intentionally carried into the term חשׁב already in biblical or, more precisely, post-exilic times: "[D]as nachexilische Judentum *wollte* ja gerade dem alten Zusammenhang einen anderen, neuen Sinn geben. Der Endredaktor von Gn 15 und der Verfasser von Ps 106 hatten dies, soweit es ihnen bei חשׁב möglich war, versucht. Jetzt, in der LXX, erst ist es geglückt, auch in der Form das zu sagen, worauf der Inhalt hinaus wollte" (97; italics added). Equally overstated is his characterization of early Judaism as "Abfall vom AT" (98). This generalizing negative assessment of the post-exilic period – going back to J. Wellhausen (cf., e.g., 1958, 283f.) – no longer appears in the exegetical discussion.

[93] Cf. L. Gaston 1980, 50 with n.42. Gaston deems the preposition εἰς to be very significant in this case and refers to M. Black 1973, 47: "The view that Abraham's 'faith' was 'reckoned to him' as *equivalent* to 'righteousness' is less convincing than to take 'for righteousness' as meaning that Abraham's faith was counted to his credit 'with a view to the receiving of righteousness'." However, the form and the use of εἰς as such should not be overrated, since – as noted – the Septuagint is consistently in accord with the Masoretic Text as regards the translation of a preposition following on חשׁב. Rather, both the tradition-historical background and the respective context of λογίζεσθαι are decisive.

[94] C.E.B. Cranfield 1975, 230n.6.

[95] The exceptions are Gen 19:19; Isa 63:7 (for חסד); Mal 2:17 (for משׁפט); Isa 38:19; Dan 9:13 (for אמת); Dan 9:9 (for רחם).

[96] P. Stuhlmacher 1966, 110.

combined in the Septuagintal rendering of Gen 15:6: In combination with the term λογίζεσθαι, a juridical element is introduced into the statement, and "righteousness" receives the meaning of a righteous act of God which is the result of a judicial judgment based on the facticity of Abraham's faith. While in the Masoretic version of Gen 15:6, "righteousness" primarily qualifies Abraham's faith on grounds of the personal relationship between God and Abraham, in the Septuagint it tends to qualify Abraham's single act of faith, which necessarily confers on him a right status before God, the judge. The former remains contingent to Abraham's actual life-history and that of his descendants, while the Septuagint opens up the horizon towards an apocalyptic-eschatological thinking in terms of Abraham's acceptance with God in the final judgment.[97]

Not only λογίζεσθαι and δικαιοσύνη, but also the form and function of πιστεύειν in the Septuagint version of Gen 15:6 requires closer analysis.[98] As noted, the translation does not reflect the peculiar perfect form of the Masoretic Text with its stativic-durative connotation, but rather – probably on the basis of an alternate *Vorlage* – uses the aorist tense.[99] Thus, due to this narrative style, Abraham's faith is portrayed as a onetime, outstanding act in the past, with which he reacts on God's promise, whereas the Hebrew text stressed to a greater degree its general and permanent character.[100] As a consequence, also in this case the connotation of the Hebrew אמן *hiphil* with a prepositional object experiences a modification of meaning: The semantics changes from an internal-transitive into a declarative-estimative connotation. Instead of the relational "he fastened himself" or "he gained firmness" in Yahweh, it is said in a more formal and intellectualistic manner that "he gave credence" to the words that God has spoken. The difference is basically that between *credere in deum* and *credere deo*.[101] Even though this rendition concurs with the customary translation practice of the Septuagint,[102] the shift of the meaning and emphasis deserves consideration.

---

[97] Cf. M.A. Seifrid 2004, 52.

[98] Generally, one should note the phenomenon that πιστεύειν consistently represents אמן *hiphil* (45 times; cf. R. Bultmann 1959, 197f. with n.149).

[99] The Greek imperfect would be the most adequate to describe a permanently given disposition ("Haltung") that becomes concrete in a certain situation ("Verhalten") (cf. F. Blass/A. Debrunner/F. Rehkopf 1979, §325).

[100] See above chapter III.D.IV.1 on the analysis of וְהֶאֱמִן.

[101] On the distinction between a Hebrew and a Greek-Christian concept of faith, see especially M. Buber 1950. He believes that the influence of Greek thinking produced a rationalistic understanding of faith (656f.). But see the critical discussion of Buber in E. Lohse 1977 (see above chapter II.G.II); G. Ebeling 1961; L.H. Silberman 1990.

[102] This is why R. Mosis contends that this phenomenon should not be overestimated, because in the Pentateuch the Septuagint translates all appearances of אמן *hiphil* with *be*

This line of reasoning, based on a contextual and syntactical analysis, can be confirmed, but also specified by linguistic observations: While in later Greek usage, in contrast to Plato and probably in reaction to the increasing religious skepticism, the meaning of πιστεύειν generally[103] approached the meaning of νομίζειν, i.e., the intellectual affirmation that there are gods,[104] the Septuagint did establish the notion of "trust" within the semantic field of πιστεύειν by association with אמן *hiphil*. Yet even if it "does indeed signify an action-modifying trust, it does not necessarily have the base meaning of 'to stand firm', which is extremely important in האמין."[105]

In sum, even if the variations of the Septuagint can be attributed first to the general problem of translation and second to the probable existence of a different *Vorlage*, they represent a shift of the hermeneutical horizon that shone through in the reception of Gen 15:6 in Ps 106:31 and that will find its further expression in subsequent Jewish tradition: Gradually, faith is placed alongside (other) deeds and is viewed as part of keeping the Torah.[106] As has been seen, a soteriological aspect is not inherent in the semantics of the words *per se*, which does not exclude the possibility that it has been carried into the meaning of the verse within a broader theological framework. Thus, after the exile the concept of the righteousness of God started to incorporate eschatological and soteriological dimensions.[107]

D. Sirach 44

The significance of Ben Sira's sapiential writing – a work at the "borders of the canon"[108] – lies undeniably in its elucidating the religious, social,

---

or *le* with πιστεύειν τινί (cf. Ex 4:1; 14:31; 19:9; Num 14:11; Deut 1:32; 9:23; see also Jonah 3:5). Only outside of the Pentateuch one can find the formulation πιστεύειν ἐν (cf. Mi 7:5; Ps 78:22.32; 2Chr 20:20) (cf. R. Mosis 1999, 98).

[103] However, as we have seen, D.R. Lindsay makes the case that "to trust" was an element already of the Classical Greek πιστεύειν (1993, 108f.; see above chapter II.G.VII). See also J.H.H. Schmidt 1889, 692f. (quoted in L.H. Silberman 1990, 101): "Πιστεύειν heißt einer Person oder Sache *vertrauen* oder von einer Sache überzeugt sein" (italics original). Silberman however uses Schmidt's findings to assert a factual identity of Greek and Hebrew meaning (against M. Buber), which is clearly an overstatement.

[104] Cf. R. Bultmann 1959, 179.

[105] D.R. Lindsay 1993, 114; cf. 117.

[106] Cf. M. Oeming 1983, 196.

[107] Cf. K. Kertelge 1971, 24.

[108] This is the title of an essay by H.P. Rüger (1984): "Le Siracide: un livre à la frontière du canon."

and national circumstances at the eve of the Maccabean period.[109] Though both his attitude towards Hellenism and his inner-Jewish affiliation to one specific group remain disputed, one can arguably claim that he seeks to combine trans-national wisdom traditions with traditional-Jewish piety.[110] Compared to previous wisdom literature, the work of Ben Sira applies new methods, as it expressly and extensively includes Israelite history.[111] The only concrete datum that allows for a specification of the date of composition is given in the prologue which mentions the book's translation from Hebrew into Greek by Ben Sira's grandson, who came to Egypt in the 38th year of the king Euergetes, i.e., around 132 B.C. This insinuates the beginning of the second century B.C. as date of composition, i.e., around 190 B.C.[112]

The Praise of the Fathers, Sirach 44,[113] represents the most extensive literarily and materially coherent entity within the book Sirach.[114] In it, the second of the abovementioned aspects, i.e., the traditional-Jewish side, comes to the fore when Ben Sira glorifies the national-religious heroes of the past.[115] Amidst the Jewish search for identity, he attempts a fresh approach of Israelite history, which could be called "a mythic etiology of Second Temple Judaism centered in the covenants that undergird the priesthood."[116] Announced in the first person: "Let us now sing the praises of honorable men" (44,1), this poem venerates the honor and glory of pious men like Abraham, who is the third member in the long row of national heroes of faith from Noah to Simon. They all "were honored in their generations, and were the reason for boasting (καύχημα/תפארת) of their times" (44,7).

In the verses on Abraham, various elements of the Old Testament Abraham cycle are placed side by side; in fact, these verses embrace in concise form nearly all elements that play an eminent role in the post-Old Testa-

[109] Cf. F.M. Abel 1952, 100 (quoted in J. Marböck 1977, 149): "Lire l'Ecclésiastique c'est s'insinuer dans le milieu complexe où se déroulera l'histoire maccabéenne, dans l'âme des différentes classes de la société aux prises dans le conflit religieux et national."
[110] M. Hengel 1988, 455.
[111] Cf. J. Marböck 1977, 151.
[112] Cf. recently on question regarding *Einleitung*, G. Sauer 2000, 17-35.
[113] On the "Praise of the Fathers" see T. Maertens 1956; B.L. Mack 1985.
[114] The book Sirach developed in the course of a long and intricate process. Its overall arrangement suggests that the Praise of the Fathers came into being as an independent entity, which incorporates and uses older traditions of historical summaries, but which also clearly shows "die Hand des Siraziden" (J. Marböck 1977, 152). B.L. Mack contends that the Praise of the Fathers was written around 180 B.C. (1985, 1), but one should not neglect the long tradition-historical process standing behind the final form.
[115] Cf. O. Schmitz 1922, 100.
[116] B.L. Mack 1985, 6.

ment view of the figure of Abraham.[117] The intention and interest of the author are transparent: Amidst the challenges of Jewish religion brought about by the influence of Hellenistic thought, the value of tradition is highlighted and Abraham presented as pedagogic example,[118] who "fulfilled the Torah in a general and comprehensive sense"[119]:

	Sir 44,19-21 (B)[120]	Sir 44,19-21 (LXX)[121]
(19) Abraham became a great father of a multitude of nations, and no one has been found like him in glory.	(19) אברהם אב המון גוים לא נתן בכבודו מום	(19) Αβρααμ μέγας πατὴρ πλήθους ἐθνῶν καὶ οὐχ εὑρέθη ὅμοιος ἐν τῇ δόξῃ
(20) He kept the law of the Most High, and entered into a covenant with him; he certified the covenant in his flesh, and when he was tested he was found faithful.	(20) אשר שמר מצות עליון ובא בברית עמו בבשרו כרת לו חק ובניסוי נמצא נאמן	(20) ὃς συνετήρησεν νόμον ὑψίστου καὶ ἐγένετο ἐν διαθήκῃ μετ' αὐτοῦ ἐν σαρκὶ αὐτοῦ ἔστησεν διαθήκην καὶ ἐν πειρασμῷ εὑρέθη πιστός.
(21) Therefore the Lord assured him with an oath that the nations would be blessed through his offspring; that he would make him as numerous as the dust of the earth, and exalt his offspring like the stars, and give them an inheritance from sea to sea and from the stream [Euphrates] to the ends of the earth.	(21) על כן בש[..]עה הקים לו להנחילם [.]ים ועד ים ומנהר ועד אפסי ארץ	(21) διὰ τοῦτο ἐν ὅρκῳ ἔστησεν αὐτῷ ἐνευλογηθῆναι ἔθνη ἐν σπέρματι αὐτοῦ πληθῦναι αὐτὸν ὡς χοῦν τῆς γῆς καὶ ὡς ἄστρα ἀνυψῶσαι τὸ σπέρμα αὐτοῦ καὶ κατακληρονομῆσαι αὐτοὺς ἀπὸ θαλάσσης ἕως θαλάσσης καὶ ἀπὸ ποταμοῦ ἕως ἄκρου τῆς γῆς.

The designation "father of a multitude of nations" derives from Gen 17:5. The "law of the Most High" not only includes all the divine commandments given to Abraham from Gen 12:1 onwards,[122] but also the whole of God's νόμος, which was later written down by Moses.[123] As in Gen 26:5 the mention of his keeping the divine law summarizes his entire conduct before God. Abraham's obedience resulted in the covenant (cf. Gen 15:18; 17:2.4.7), which he himself certified by means of circumcision (Gen

---

[117] F. Hahn 1971, 95. – See further G. Sauer 1996.

[118] Cf. B. Ego 1996, 26; M. Oeming 1998, 84.

[119] S.J. Gathercole 2002, 238.

[120] See P.C. Beentjes 1997, 78. The relevant chapter is only preserved in the Ben Sira Manuscript B.

[121] See J. Ziegler, 1965, 334.

[122] Thus F. Hahn 1971, 95.

[123] Cf. B. Ego 1996, 25.

17:10-13); and he confirmed his faithfulness when he was tested (Genesis 22). It is noteworthy that and how Sir 44,20 emphasizes Abraham's action[124]: He remains the syntactical subject throughout the verse: He obeys the commandments, enters and certifies the covenant, and is found faithful. The two middle elements signify a contrast and reinterpretation compared to the presentation of the Abrahamic covenant and circumcision in Genesis. The Genesis account clearly names Yahweh as the one who takes the initiative and Abraham as the one who reacts and accepts: "Yahweh made a covenant with Abraham" (Gen 15:18), "I will establish my covenant between me and you" (Gen 17:7).[125] Only the theological passive נמצא/εὑρέθη confers to God implicitly an active role. Compared to Neh 9:8, a text that displays a similar synopsis of elements of the Abraham narratives, the one-sidedness of Ben Sira regarding Abraham's conduct is remarkable. Partly, it can be explained by the genres of the texts, the one being a prayer to God, the other being a praise of a person, but nevertheless the contrast between Abraham's passivity in Nehemiah 9 and emphasis on his initiative in Sirach 44 is striking.

A second distinctiveness of the text shows itself in the manner how Abraham's action, his obedience and his entering the covenant, are linked to the following divine promises. The conjunction כי על/διὰ τοῦτο implies a conditional connection between Abraham's righteous deeds and his being rewarded through Yahweh's promises,[126] which consist in the blessing of the peoples through his descendants (Gen 12:3; 18:18; 22:18), their great number like the dust of the earth (Gen 13:16) or the stars in heaven (Gen 15:5; 22:17) and their possession of land (Gen 12:7; 13:15; 15:7.18; 17:8; 22:17). Above we have seen that in essence such an understanding had already been present in the redactional supplement to the Aqedah-narrative, Gen 22:15-18.[127]

Both the emphasis on Abraham's action and the conditional relationship to Yahweh's promises provide an interesting insight in the notion of "deed" and "reward" in the theology of Ben Sira: What Abraham accomplished led to honor, boasting, and blessing; the descendants of the Fathers

---

[124] Cf. already R. Smend 1906, 423.

[125] Cf. Gen 17:13, and with regard to Isaac 17:19.21. In Luther's translation of Sirach, for instance, this discrepancy is eliminated; there, God is made the subject of the two elements covenant and circumcision. J. Marböck reasons: "Vielleicht ist die 'Initiative' Abrahams von der Annahme der Bundeszusage (Gen 17,2.4.8) durch die Beschneidung zu verstehen" (1993, 110). Apart from the Masoretic Text, the Samaritan Pentateuch, the Septuagint, and the Ethiopic version (17,26) have the passive form; "Latin Jubilees uses a reflexive verb, while Syriac Genesis and [Targum Jonathan] have active verbs" (J.C. VanderKam 1989, 91).

[126] Cf. M.W. Yeung 2002, 250.

[127] See above chapter III.E.II.

and again their children remained in the covenants for the sake of the Fathers (δι' αὐτούς) (Sir 44,11).[128] And for that reason, the nations are blessed through Abraham's offspring (44,21), and Isaac received the same blessing as Abraham,[129] for Abraham's sake (בעבור אברהם/δι' 'Αβραάμ) (44,22).[130]

While several aspects of Genesis 15 reappear in Sir 44,19-21, one misses an explicit reference to Abraham's faith. Obviously, Ben Sira regards Abraham's obedient attitude towards the divine law (מצוה/νόμος)[131] and his being faithful (נאמן/πιστός)[132] under ordeal as a conduct that embraces the aspects that Gen 15:6 calls "faith." Similar to Neh 9:8, therefore, Gen 15:6 and Genesis 22 are viewed under one generic term, namely faithfulness,[133] but the main concentration lies undeniably on the narrative of the sacrifice of Isaac; this is shown by the keyword connection between Gen 22:1 (נִסָּה) and Sir 44,20 (בניסוי/ἐν πειρασμῷ). The connection to Gen 15:6 is established through the common use of the root אמן. Hence, in analogy to Neh 9:8, the remark of Yahweh's considering Abraham's faith as righteousness (Gen 15:6b) is replaced by the statement that Abraham "was found faithful," though here Abraham's obedience to God's will receives

---

[128] The extant Hebrew manuscripts did not preserve this passage.

[129] Through combinations like Abraham-Isaac and the like, Ben Sira always seeks "to create a sense of sequence and succession" (B.L. Mack 1985, 45) and to emphasize real historical continuity.

[130] The expression בעבור אברהם recalls Gen 26:24. See also Sir 47,12: Solomon lived in security because of David (בעבורו/δι' αὐτόν). – It should be noted that, with respect to the duration, the covenant with Abraham is surpassed by the *eternal* covenants granted to Noah (44,18), to Aaron and his offspring (45,15), and to Phinehas (45,24), who is praised for his being zealous in the fear of God (cf. Ps 106:31) and who together with his descendants will hold the priesthood forever. The covenant with Phinehas embraces the Davidic covenant (Sir 45,25) and is consequently superior to it. The climax of the covenant, however, is reached with the high priest Simon, who receives the highest praise and admiration. Yet even this covenant is not invulnerable to threats, and thus the pleas for wisdom for Aaron's successors indicate the beginning of problems among the sons of Simon (cf. M. Hengel 1988, 244f.).

[131] One should note the translation of מצוה with νόμος. One would rather expect ἐντὸ λαί as translation (cf. E. Gräßer 1998, 13n.52, but also E. Lohmeyer 1929a, 183).

[132] On the side one may refer to another occurrence of the root אמן in the *niphal*, Sir 44,11: עם זרעם נאמן טובם ("their [*sc.* the fathers'] good will remain with their descendants"). This verb form, third person masculine singular perfect, appears in the Hebrew Bible only in 2Sam 7:16, which is part of Nathan's words on God's covenant with David.

[133] The factual identity of faith and faithfulness for Ben Sira is also stressed in M. Dibelius/H. Greeven 1984, 209: "Wenn es heißt εὑρέθη πιστός Sir 44,19-21 1Makk 2,52, so kann man wie übrigens auch bei den entsprechenden hebräischen, aramäischen und äthiopischen ... Ausdrücken zwischen der Übersetzung 'gläubig' und 'treu' wählen." Cf. H. Moxnes 1980, 129; G.W. Hansen 1989, 180.

clear prevalence over against his faith in the context of the promise of descendants.

Both the equivalence of faith and faithful deeds and their immediate fruition in terms of reward are expressed in two verses, one from the beginning and one from the very end of the book. Both Sir 2,8 and the final verse 51,30 display clear evidence for a certain divine economy, from two perspectives: "Believe him (πιστεύσατε αὐτῷ), and your reward (μισθός) will not be lost," and: "Do your work (ἐργάζεσθε τὸ ἔργον ὑμῶν) in due time, and in his own time God will give you your reward (μισθός)."[134]

The Greek version of Sir 44,10 provides another general expression for the conduct of the Fathers: They all performed righteous deeds, δικαιοσύναι, which will never be forgotten. Also the Hebrew manuscript B contains a similar thought in 44,13 where it reads that the patriarchs' deeds of righteousness ([.]ןקדצ) will never be blotted out.[135] A comparison with the second Hebrew manuscript preserving this verse, the Ben Sira Scroll from Masada, which has כבוד instead of צדקה, reveals an interesting correlation between righteous deeds and glory.[136]

One other passage in Sirach resembles so strongly the phrase from Sir 44,19: "no one has been found like him in glory" that one cannot fail to briefly comment on it. Sir 31,5-11 offers a discourse on wealth and the danger of insatiable greed, praising the one who does not succumb to the materialistic corruption[137]: "He who loves gold shall not be justified... Who has been tried in this, and been found perfect? Then let him boast (καύχησις)." This is "one of the clearest examples where boasting – the ability to declare that one has overcome sin and is therefore secure in the face of judgment – is set within the framework of justification."[138]

This quotation however may not be taken as evidence for the idea of "personal afterlife" in Sirach.[139] Rather, the beneficial and salvific blessings of a life conducted in obedience materialize in time and space, though within these dimensional limitations the temporal and spatial borders are indeed reached: The impact of the covenant granted to Abraham goes beyond one's imagination and has infinite measurements. It is all the more interesting however that later, "[i]n the stage of the Greek redaction the

---

[134] The key idea of deed and reward is frequent in Sirach, both explicitly (11,26; 17,23; 35,22) and implicitly throughout.

[135] The text is partly destroyed, so that its reconstruction has to be conjectured with the help of the Septuagint.

[136] Also the Septuagint has δόξα.

[137] On this passage and its socio-economic relevance in Sirach, see B.G. Wright/C.V. Camp 2001.

[138] S.J. Gathercole 2002, 191.

[139] S.J. Gathercole 2002, 38.

theology of free will was set in an eschatological soteriology."[140] The eschatological skepticism[141] of Ben Sira is corrected intriguingly by the establishment of a doctrine of punishment (Sir 7,17; 11,26; 48,11) and can be attributed to the temporal and geographical proximity of the translation to the Wisdom of Solomon: around 120 B.C. in Alexandria.[142] Nevertheless, the permanence of God's covenant with Abraham, though this-worldly, carries within itself the potential of an eschatological widening.

Looking back on Ben Sira's general outlook and his view of the patriarch, it has become obvious that the conduct of the pedagogic model Abraham can be subsumed under the umbrella of "obedience." Accordingly, the author accomplished a terminological and conceptual fusion of Genesis 15 with 22, which mirrors an essential identification of "faith" and "faithful deeds" in terms of their outcome, namely, their "this-worldly" reward (cf. Sir 2,8; 51,30).[143]

E. Jubilees

Scholars have proposed different dates for the time when this extra-canonical Jewish writing was composed,[144] but above all since R.H. Charles's contributions to and edition of *Jubilees*, the majority of scholars dates the composition of *Jubilees* into the second century,[145] or more precisely, around the middle of the second century,[146] i.e., a few decades later

---

[140] T. Eskola 1998, 47f.

[141] Cf. J.J. Collins 2000a, 335.

[142] This is pointed out by S.J. Gathercole (2002, 38n.3), with reference to A.A. Di Lella (1966).

[143] Almsgiving in particular brings good fruits: Having stored almsgiving in one's treasury rescues from every disaster (29,12) and remains for eternity (40,17).

[144] See the overview in J.C. VanderKam 1977, 207-213. The dates range from the fifth or fourth century B.C. to the first century A.D.

[145] Cf. R.H. Charles 1902, lxiii-lxvi. Charles narrowed this period down to the time between 109 and 105 B.C. on grounds of alleged allusions to John Hyrcanus's destroying of Samaria in 109 B.C. and on the other hand on grounds of the author's not mentioning the break between the Pharisees and John Hyrcanus or Alexander Jannaeus. See however the following note on the new *communis opinio*.

[146] Cf. J.C. VanderKam 1977, 287 (161-152 B.C.); 1989, v-vi; 1997a, 20: "[O]ne can date the book fairly narrowly to between 160 and 150 BCE." G.W.E. Nickelsburg 1981, 78f. (before 167 B.C.); K. Berger 1998, 33 (160-135 B.C.). Berger however concurs with H. Stegemann that it is also possible to think of a substantially older age, namely, the fifth century B.C., because *Jubilees* ends with Israel's taking the possession of the land and could therefore serve as a theological preparation for a new land in the early post-exilic period. However, *inter alia* the use of Gen 15:6 in *Jubilees* seems to point to a later stage in the Jewish history of theology (see also below the appendix chapter IV.K.II).

than Sirach and after the death of Judas Maccabeus. Nowadays, scholars also agree "that it was composed in Hebrew and that from Hebrew it was translated into Greek,"[147] from which finally the Latin and Ethiopic translations derive; only the Ethiopic version preserves the entire text of *Jubilees*.[148] The oldest verifiable title of *Jubilees* is found in the Damascus Document and reads: "The book of the divisions of the periods according to their jubilees and their weeks."[149] In patristic times, *Jubilees* was called Λεπτογένεσις, "Little Genesis," since it recounts stories from the book of Genesis[150] within a framework of jubilee years. Its close adherence to the biblical text, both regarding its macro-structure as well as its wording,[151] assigns *Jubilees* to the genre "Rewritten Bible."[152]

Three sections in particular are of interest in our quest for the interpretation of Gen 15:6 in Jewish theology: (1) *Jub* 14,4-7.18, (2) 30,17, and (3) 31,23. The first is the most significant one:

I. Jubilees 14,4-7.18[153]

 (4) And he brought him outside and said to him: "Look at the sky and count the stars, if you can count them."

(5) And he looked at the sky and saw the stars. And he said to him: "Your descendants will be like this."

(6) And he believed in the Lord, and it was credited to him as something righteous.

(7) And he said to him: "I am the Lord who brought you from Ur of the Chaldeans to give you the land of the Canaanites to occupy forever and to become God for you and your descendants after you."

(18) On that day the Lord concluded a covenant with Abram with these words: "To your descendants I will give this land from the river of Egypt as far as the great river, the Euphrates River…

Even though in rewriting the Genesis story *Jubilees* is generally rather faithful to the outline of the Masoretic Text, some differences are worth mentioning in our context. One aspect that immediately strikes the eye is

---

[147] J.C. VanderKam 1989, vi. Due to the discovery of several Hebrew manuscripts of *Jubilees* at Qumran, "Hebrew must be regarded as the only serious candidate for the original language of Jubilees" (vi-vii). Cf. K. Berger 1981, 285-287. Already before the Hebrew fragments were found, some commentators argued that *Jubilees* was originally written in Hebrew and that the Ethiopic version renders the Greek translation of the Hebrew *Urtext* (cf. already E. Littmann 1900, 31).

[148] In the Ethiopic church *Jubilees* is counted to the canon (cf. K. Berger 1998, 36f.).

[149] Cf. F. García Martínez/E.J.C. Tigchelaar 1997/1998, 565.

[150] Actually, it retells Genesis 1 until Exodus 12.

[151] Cf. J.C. VanderKam 1977, 214-285.

[152] Cf. G. Vermès 1961, 95; M. Müller 1996, 240.

[153] See J.C. VanderKam 1989, 84 (the following quotations also adhere for the most part to VanderKam's translations); cf. also K. Berger 1981; R.H. Charles/C. Rabin 1984.

the change of the active verb form וַיַּחְשְׁבֶהָ of Gen 15:6 into the passive voice in *Jub* 14,6, by virtue of which Abraham is clearly signified as the recipient of righteousness. Besides that, there are some additions that point to more or less subtle tendencies which undergird the picture of the patriarch in *Jubilees*; the larger context of its re-narration of the Abraham material has to confirm these tendencies.

The author provides Abraham's immediate obedient reaction to God's command "Look at the sky…!"[154]: "And he looked…" It is not by accident that this supplement appears in this context, for a like situation will recur at only one other passage within the Abraham stories that similarly portrays his instantaneous compliance with regard to a divine instruction[155]: at the introduction to the Aqedah. God says: "Take your son…!", and "Abraham got up… and took…" (18,2-3).[156] Hence, with respect to Abraham's uncompromising obedience, *Jubilees* confers the same character to the re-narration of both Genesis 15 and 22. In like manner, Abraham's faith is reported as immediate reaction to the promise of innumerable descendants.

On the basis of the attestation of Abraham's faith, the narrative finds its progression, and in line with the outline of Genesis, the promise of land follows. However, *Jubilees* not simply repeats its *Vorlage*, but incorporates other elements from a related promise that is even wider in scope and sheds a different light on the promise: Influenced by Gen 17:7, the author describes the land donation as having everlasting validity for Abraham and his descendants.[157] Moreover, God not only binds himself permanently to his promise, but – as the author of *Jubilees* stresses – he also binds himself

---

[154] In contrast to the Qumran text of 4QPseudo-Jubilees (see below chapter IV.F), *Jubilees* does not add to the star image of Gen 15:5 by drawing on similar promises to the patriarchs (sand, dust), but remains within the scenery of the nightly firmament.

[155] The decisive characteristic of the two parallel instances is that both take up the verb of the divine command when reporting Abraham's reaction and thereby demonstrate the immediateness of Abraham's act. On Abraham's obedience, see also *Jub* 15,23; 17,8.

[156] Coming from the narratives in Genesis, there is yet another passage that comes to mind with a similar structure, namely Gen 12:1-2: God says "Go from you country…!" "And Abraham went…" (cf. B. Ego/A. Lange 2003, 184). In the parallel passage in *Jubilees* (*Jubilees* 12), however, the "six rainy months" – the time in which Abraham studied Hebrew – are in between God's command and Abraham's actual leaving his homeland, so that here no real analogy exists. – On the other hand, the structure of command-obedience recalls a story of Abraham's youth reported in *Jub* 11,18-19 (possibly this story with its mention of the birds anticipates Genesis 15; thus G. Stemberger 1976, 232n.8): At the age of 14, Abraham – already praying to the creator (*Jub* 11,17) – has to prevent ravens from coming down and eat the seed (cf. 14,12), and he succeeds, since the ravens obeyed him instantly: "He would say: '… Return to the place from which you came!' And they returned."

[157] Later, the author of *Jubilees* will extend the measurement of the land-promise to the whole world (*Jub* 17,3; 19,21; 22,14; 32,19; cf. also Sir 44,21).

to Abraham's family as their God. Insofar, he responds to Abraham's fastening himself to the assurance that had just been uttered by attaching his presence to the contents of his assurance, i.e., to the promised land, and to those who will inhabit it, Abraham and his seed. Thus, Abraham's faith finds its counterpart in God's declared faithfulness.

At the end of the subsequent covenant rite, Abraham's faith is again confirmed and accentuated: Initially caused by the assurance of offspring, it did not cease after his encounter with God; rather, following on the establishment of the covenant, we read: "Abram was very happy[158] ... He believed that he would have descendants" (*Jub* 14,21). His faith is a constant disposition and deep-rooted, not dependent on outer appearances. The reader reaches this conclusion inevitably, for right after this reiteration of Abraham's faith, the text continues: "But she [*sc.* Sarai] continued not to have a child." Even if those two statements, Abraham's faith and Sara's barrenness are not put into a direct relationship, the reader has to acknowledge with admiration this curt contrast.

This episode of the life of Abraham, his unwavering faith in God's promise in the face of all contrariety, is taken up a few chapters later where the most challenging situation for Abraham's relationship to God is recounted: the Aqedah. Some terminological and contextual bridges draw attention to the close affiliation of Genesis 15 and Genesis 22 from the perspective of *Jubilees*: Abraham's faith/faithfulness towards the word of God (*Jub* 14,6.21 and 17,15-18),[159] its permanence in spite of difficulties (14,21 and 17,15.17), and his joy about Isaac (14,21 and 17,16). The section that treats the sacrifice of Isaac, *Jub* 18,1-17,[160] adheres to a great degree to the biblical version, though there are occasional minor extensions and abbreviations.[161] The author of *Jubilees* gives the date of the intended sacrifice, the day of Passover, and he creates (possibly for the first time in Jewish literature[162]) a Job-like setting for the following test.[163] There, the

---

[158] Cf. *Jub* 15,17; 16,19.27; 17,2.3.4(.16).

[159] Whereas VanderKam chooses to use the term "faithful," Berger employs the word "glaubend," which is closer to "faith" ("Glaube") than to "faithfulness" ("Treue"). See the remark of M. Dibelius quoted above note 133.

[160] On the re-narration of the Aqedah in *Jubilees*, see, e.g., J.C. VanderKam 1997; J.A. Fitzmyer 2002, 213-215; L.A. Huizenga 2002.

[161] Cf. J.C. VanderKam 1997, 243, 256. The most obvious insertion of the author is *Jub* 18,9 where the angel reports about his direct contact with Abraham.

[162] See however 4QPseudo-Jubilees, which most likely stems from about the same period of time and which provides a similar detail. This analogy between *Jubilees* and 4QPseudo-Jubilees points to an even earlier tradition.

[163] The book of Job provides an Old Testament comparison to the depicted court-room situation (Job 1:6); also the titles of the respective adversaries of Abraham and Job are associated: "Satan" and "the Prince of Mastemah." Furthermore, Abraham's character is similar to Job's: Abraham is faithful in all trials and loved by the Lord (*Jub* 17,15-16),

narrating Angel of the Presence, begins his report by highlighting – on different communicative levels – no less than six times Abraham's being faithful (*Jub* 17,15-18). Rumors[164] of his faithfulness even reached heaven (17,15), which led the Prince Mastemah[165] to provoke God to test Abraham by commanding him to offer his son Isaac; then God "will know whether he is faithful in everything through which you test him" (17,16).[166]

The next verse lists six[167] tests of Abraham before Mastemah's assault, in which Abraham was found faithful: "his land [Genesis 13] and the famine [Genesis 12]; ...the wealth of the kings [Genesis 14]; ... his wife when she was taken forcibly [Genesis 12; 20], and ... circumcision [Genesis 17]; ... Ishmael and his servant girl Hagar [Genesis 16]." God's demand to sacrifice his son, is therefore not the first one, but the "significant seventh in the divine pedagogy of Abraham."[168] Abraham however passes this most difficult seventh test, and God can state that "you are faithful to me in eve-

---

while Job is a "blameless and upright man who fears God and turns away from evil" (Job 1:8). Both also are exposed to most difficult tests regarding their son or children respectively; Job in fact had endured the loss of all of his children. – On the issue of "Job versus Abraham" in rabbinic tradition, see J. Weinberg 1994.

[164] The "rumors in heaven" go back to the introduction of Genesis 22: וַיְהִי אַחַר הַדְּבָרִים הָאֵלֶּה (cf. Gen 15:1), whereby הַדְּבָרִים is interpreted as "words" and not as the expected "things" (the rendering of Gen 15:1 in *Jub* 14,1, on the other hand, reads "After these things"). The translation with "voices" (*Jub* 17,15) in J.C. VanderKam 1989, 105 is therefore not entirely adequate in this context, as he himself concedes (1997, 249 with n.19). In an extension of this tradition in Pseudo-Philo's *Liber Antiquitatum Biblicarum*, it is the angels' jealousy that leads God to test Abraham (32,1-2) (see H. Jacobson 1996, 149). F. García Martínez further refers to *bSanh* 89b and *GenR* 55,4 which contain similar interpretations (2002, 50f.).

[165] As mentioned, the introduction of the Prince Mastemah constitutes a parallel to the book of Job: His heavenly adversary is שָׂטָן, a name which is related to the root שטם, and God's assaults on Job are characterized by the verb שטם (Job 16:9; 30:21), on which the term משטמה is based. If W. Kornfeld is right when he says: "Mastema n'est pas un nom propre, mais doit être compris comme une appellation significative" (1992, 21f.) then the designation "Prince Mastemah" as proper name in *Jubilees* is due to a misinterpretation. In *Jubilees*, the "Prince Mastemah" only appears in the context of the Aqedah (*Jub* 17,16; 18,9.12) and in the reports on the events leading up to the exodus (48,2.9.12.15); thus, there must have been an association of the Aqedah and Passover/exodus (cf. J.C. VanderKam 1997, 248, 254f.). On "Mastemah," see also M. Müller 1996, 246n.20; J.W. van Henten 1999.

[166] The author of *Jubilees* however makes clear that God already knew that Abraham would prove his faithfulness – only the Prince of Mastemah needed to be educated.

[167] It is not clear whether from the perspective of *Jubilees* there are six or seven tests that precede the Aqedah – it depends on the question if Ishmael and Hagar constitute one test or rather two. K. Berger decides for the latter option (1972, 373; see also C. Rose 1994, 204; B. Ego/A. Lange 2003, 186), while J.C. VanderKam opts for the other possibility (1997, 250n.24).

[168] J.C. VanderKam 1997, 250.

rything that I have told you" (*Jub* 18,16). In 19,8 the author mentions *en passant* that the actual number of tests was ten; this shows that the tradition of the ten tests, which will become prominent in later Midrashic literature, is already known to *Jubilees*.[169] In all of these tests, Abraham "was found to be faithful" (19,8 and 9).[170]

Added up, Abraham's faithfulness appears nine times in the Jubilees stories that recount the life of the patriarch, the first time in the enumeration of tests in the context of the decisive seventh test (17,16-18), and for the last time with respect to the events surrounding Sara's death (19,9). Both passages provide a more concrete characteristic of the attitude connected to Abraham's faithfulness: He did not grow impatient (17,18 and 19,8), neither in the first six tests (17,18) nor in regard to the promise of the land (19,9).[171] Hence, the deed character of Abraham's conduct is embedded in and embraced by his continuous trust and faithfulness towards God. This relationship is tested, proved, and confirmed in various situations that require the repeated commitment to God and his promise.[172] One could also say that the author correlates and identifies deed and disposition of Abraham. In the words of *Jubilees*: He was faithful and ready to act (17,18).

Commencing with Abraham's faith (14,6), the author gives insight into the soul of Abraham and his relationship with God, and he draws the line further to the enumeration of events in which Abraham proved to be faithful (17,16-18) and finally to the last test after Sara's death (19,8-9). Within the context of *Jubilees*, therefore, Abraham's trust in the assurance of descendants has paradigmatic significance, as it stands at the beginning of this row, even if actually several of the other tests precede it chronologically.[173] However, it is not only the description of Abraham's attitude to God that embraces the series of episodes, but also God's response: Abraham's faith was "credited to him as something righteous" (14,6) and due to his faithfulness he "was recorded on the heavenly tablets as the friend of the Lord" (19,9). In a fictionalized monologue Abraham attributes to him-

---

[169] Cf. *Pirqe Rabbi Eliezer* 26-31; *'Abot de Rabbi Nathan* A 33; *'Abot* 5,3. See K. Berger 1972, 373; M. Dibelius/H. Greeven 1984, 208 with n.2; B. Ego/A. Lange 2003, 186n.64 (with further references to rabbinic literature).

[170] The phrasing and contents of *Jub* 19,8-9 recalls the contents of Neh 9:8, for both passages connect Abraham's faithfulness with the promise of the land. Cf. J.H. Newman 1999, 73.

[171] Cf. *Jub* 19,3. This aspect recurs in the later Targum *Pseudo-Jonathan*, which – as the only one among the Targums – paraphrases Gen 15:6: "... he did not argue against him [*sc.* God] with words."

[172] Cf. M. Oeming 1998, 26.

[173] Cf. B. Ego/A. Lange 2003, 186.

self his striving to walk uprightly in all his ways (21,1-3)[174]; this self-assessment is confirmed after the notice of his death: "Abraham was perfect with the Lord in everything that he did" (23,10).[175] Even if he lived in pre-Mosaic times, he observed the "Festival of Weeks" (14,20; 15,1), the "Festival of Booths" (16,21) and Passover (18,18) and presented to God all forms of offerings.[176] This proves his full obedience to the divine law, or, in the language of *Jubilees*: to the "testimony of the heavenly tablets" (16,28).

Abraham's enduring faithfulness and his obedience to the testimony of the heavenly tablets and to the covenant eventually led to his name being written on the heavenly tablets as God's friend.[177] What consequence does this have? In the view of the author of *Jubilees*, the righteous will experience a spiritual resurrection (23,22.31)[178]; so to be recorded on the tablets as friend of God based on one's righteousness clearly has eschatological dimensions. It confirms a life in accordance with the covenant and anticipates the favorable divine judgment at the time of death.[179]

II. Jubilees 30,17

At a later point in *Jubilees*, a reference to the heavenly tablets will recur, together with an allusion to Gen 15:6b, which sheds a remarkable light on the question how a positive divine judgment on a person's conduct can be attained. The zealous act of Jacob's sons, Simeon and Levi, who killed the Shechemites in revenge for the rape of their sister Dinah (Genesis 34), "was recorded as a just act for them," according to *Jub* 30,17.[180] This just act was nothing else than carrying out the punishment that had been de-

---

[174] On this passage, see S.J. Gathercole 2002, 177, 240, who also refers to *Jub* 7,34 and 35,2 where a character such as that of Abraham is said to entail honor, greatness, and righteousness.

[175] Cf. B. Ego 1996, 25, 37.

[176] Cf. F.E. Wieser 1987, 167f. This makes Abraham "the model ... of strict adherence to the Mosaic law" (G.W. Hansen 1989, 181).

[177] On the concept of the heavenly tablets, which occurs twenty times in *Jubilees*, see F. García Martínez 1997. On the idea of Abraham as "friend of God," see M. Dibelius/H. Greeven 1984, 203-206, 207, 212.

[178] G. Davenport wants to limit the restoration imagery of this passage to the historical (1971, 40), but as S.J. Gathercole points out, this approach itself is a limitation of the world of thought of *Jubilees* (2002, 59).

[179] How the author of *Jubilees* deals with the figure of Abraham in general is elaborated in M. Müller 1996.

[180] The allusion to Gen 15:6 cannot be accidental, given the quotation of Gen 15:6 in *Jub* 14,6. The Latin version of *Jubilees* has "conputatum est," which is strongly reminiscent of the Genesis-verse and goes back to the Greek ἐλογίσθη, which in turn is a translation of ויחשבה (thus also S.J. Gathercole 2002, 61n.108). On the other hand, the Ethiopic translation reads "it was written down for them as righteousness."

creed in heaven (30,5), and "it was recorded as a blessing" (30,23). As a consequence, God elected Levi and his offspring to become Israel's priesthood, and he blessed them in eternity (30,18). "So blessing and justice before the God of all are entered for him as a testimony on the heavenly tablets" (30,19).[181] Just as Abraham (19,9), also Levi (30,20) and every Israelite who keeps and obeys the covenant, will be recorded on the tablets as God's friend (30,21). But those who break the covenant will be recorded as enemies (30,22).

As in Ps 106:31, which undoubtedly stands in the background of *Jub* 30,17-23, there exists an interesting correlation between zeal and eternal, priestly blessing, but even more striking is the fact that both passages link those ideas with God's response to Abraham's faith by virtue of the quote from Gen 15:6. Neither of the two instances perceives a qualitative difference between faith, faithfulness, and zeal; rather, with regard to a person's standing before God, these passages presuppose the equivalence of their value and effect.[182] Both in Ps 106:31 and *Jub* 30,17-23, the purity of the covenant people is central.

III. Jubilees 31,23

Similar thoughts pervade the continuation of the stories surrounding Levi. He, together with his brother Judah, receives the blessing of both Rebecca and Isaac, who assure him that he will carry on the blessing of Abraham (31,7) and receive honor and greatness throughout all ages (31,13-14). After Isaac had given his blessing to Jacob's two sons Levi and Judah, it is reported that he made them sleep, "one on his right, one on his left; and it was credited to him as something righteous" (31,23). This allusion to Gen 15:6b – also in the passive voice – which recalls both *Jub* 14,6 and 30,17, stands out from its context as an unexpected statement that is connected in an unharmonious manner to the preceding; it is difficult to say why it has been inserted precisely here. In spite of the obscurity of this passage the context elucidates the nature of righteousness both as obedient and righteous human deed as well as a gracious and righteous gift of God. A few lines below we read: "Isaac blessed the God of his father Abraham who had not put an end to his mercy and righteousness for the son of his servant Isaac" (31,25); and further, when Rebecca admonishes Jacob to honor his father and his brother all his life, he agrees to do so since this is "an honor and a greatness and a righteousness for me before the Lord" (35,2).

---

[181] See the other interpretations of the zeal of Simeon and Levi in Jdt 9,2-4 and *TestLev* 6,3 (cf. M. Hengel 1976, 182f.).

[182] L. Gaston argues for another analogy between Ps 106:31 and *Jubilees* 30: Both contain elements that are linked to the idea of the "merit of the fathers" (1980, 50, 64 with n.43).

F. 4QPseudo-Jubilees (4Q225)

Only in recent times, since the edition of the Qumran writings on Micro-fiche,[183] some texts became accessible that are relevant for the reception history of Old Testament texts. Although no Qumran manuscript that is extant among the biblical texts found in the caves contains Genesis 15, there is one parabiblical text that cites Gen 15:6. 4QPseudo-Jubilees[a] (4Q225) is one of three manuscripts (4QPseudo-Jubilees[a-c] [4Q225-227])[184] from cave four of Qumran, "perhaps the most interesting para-phrase of the story of Abraham,"[185] whose paleographical analysis suggests that it has been produced in Herodian times, around 30 B.C. to A.D. 20.[186] It consists of three partly destroyed text fragments[187] with five columns that center predominantly on the following topics: the promise of a son to Abraham, the birth of Isaac, and the binding of Isaac.[188] Especially the lat-ter aspect drew much attention to the manuscripts – above all to 4Q225 2 i and ii – since there we find "the earliest known interpretive account of Genesis 22 which offers an explanation for God's command that Abraham sacrifice Isaac."[189]

---

[183] See E. Tov 1993.

[184] If not otherwise noted, text and translation are taken from J.C. VanderKam/J.T. Milik 1994, 141-155 (4Q225), 157-169 (4Q226), 171-175 (4Q227). A comparison bet-ween 4Q225 2 ii and 4Q226 7 reveals several notable parallels; "bei 4QPsJub[a-b] handelt es sich somit um zwei Handschriften eines Textes" (B. Ego/A. Lange 2003, 173). 4Q227 2 resembles *Jub* 4,17-23, but despite this similarity, "the differing order of the presenta-tion demonstrates that the fragment is not part of a copy of *Jubilees*" (J.C. Vander-Kam/J.T. Milik 1994, 174).

[185] C.A. Evans 2000, 3.

[186] J.C. VanderKam/J.T. Milik 1994, 141, 157, 171 (referring to F.M. Cross's dating and describing of scripts similar in character: "early Herodian round semiformal" [F.M. Cross 1961, 138, 176; cf. 1998, 388]).

[187] Against the order of the fragments 1 and 2 in J.C. VanderKam/J.T. Milik 1994, see J.C. VanderKam 1997, 254: "[T]here is no convincing reason for locating it [*sc.* frag. 1] there rather than after frag. 2 where it seems more logically to belong." This alternate view has been substantiated in R.A. Kugler/J.C. VanderKam 2001. In the 1994 edition, VanderKam followed the order determined by Milik, for the fragments of 4QPseudo-Jubilees belonged to the manuscripts originally assigned to Milik for publication.

[188] The appearance of the Aqedah in a Qumran text is noteworthy, as J.A. Fitzmyer points out (2002, 215), for scholars thought at times that this important Jewish theme "soit passé sous silence dans ce que nous connaissons de la *littérature qumrânienne*" (R. Le Déaut 1963, 184n.134; italics original). And in fact, in the twenty-two occurrences of the name "Isaac" in Qumran literature that F. García Martínez counts, "we do not learn anything substantial about Isaac, and of course, nothing about the *Aqedah*" (2002, 44).

[189] R.A. Kugler/J.C. VanderKam 2001, 109.

The motifs and language employed in 4QPseudo-Jubilees resemble to some extent those known from the Book of *Jubilees* – hence the designation "Pseudo-Jubilees."[190] Yet the text of the fragments differs from the text of *Jubilees* to such a degree that they cannot be considered as witnesses to that writing; nor is it necessary to assume a dependency of "Pseudo-Jubilees" upon *Jubilees*. Rather, "Pseudo-Jubilees" appears as an autonomous work that indeed shares some characteristic language and traditions of interpretation with *Jubilees*, but incorporates them independently and differently from *Jubilees* and, furthermore, draws on the biblical stories in a much more liberal manner than does *Jubilees*.[191] Due to the strongly corrupted condition of the manuscripts and the uncertain relationship between *Jubilees* and 4Q225-227, the date of origin of "Pseudo-Jubilees" can only be hypothetically discerned: The period between the middle of the second century and the first century B.C. seems most probable.[192] A Qumran origin of the composition is not likely due to the general avoidance of the tetragrammaton; it only appears twice, namely, in the two parallel (liturgical) passages 4Q225 2 ii 10 and 4Q226 7 2, and those read

---

[190] The name goes back to J.T. Milik (cf. J.C. VanderKam/J.T. Milik 1994, 142).

[191] Cf. J.C. VanderKam/J.T. Milik 1994, 142; G. Vermès 1996, 140. Rather than as different versions of the same basic text, both "Pseudo-Jubilees" and *Jubilees* could be considered as belonging to the same genre, namely that of the "Rewritten Bible" (cf. B. Ego/A. Lange 2003, 173, with reference to the phrase following on an address directed to Moses: "the creation until the day of the [new] creation" [4Q225 1 7; cf. *Jub* 1,27.29]). This common designation, however, underrates the fact that while *Jubilees* generally adheres closely to the biblical text, the remains of "Pseudo-Jubilees" demonstrate far more liberty in handling the biblical narrative. For instance, in retelling Genesis 22, *Jubilees* follows largely the order of the Genesis-text, while 4QPseudo-Jubilees seems to reproduce its *Vorlage* more freely by including references to other books (cf. the allusion to the burning bush, 4Q226 1 [cf. Ex 3:2-4]; the crossing of the Jordan, 4Q226 6 4.6; 4Q225 1 6[?] [cf. Exodus 14]) and by focusing selectively on the theme of Abraham's progeny (cf. J.C. VanderKam 1997, 252f., 260f. VanderKam there lists other differences to *Jubilees*). Also, while the Angel of the Presence is the narrator of *Jubilees*, the story of 4QPseudo-Jubilees is apparently told by an anonymous narrator. In VanderKam's view, therefore, *Jubilees* and 4QPseudo-Jubilees "appear to be markedly different kinds of compositions"; there is "no justification for classifying the cave 4 text as 'Pseudo-Jubilees' because it is not, as nearly as we can tell, pretending to be the work of this author, nor is there any indication that anyone thought it was" (1997, 261; cf. 242). See also the following argumentation, which will specify VanderKam's point.

[192] G. Vermès, who acknowledges a literary connection between "Pseudo-Jubilees" and *Jubilees*, contends that "the actual composition, just as the traditional form of *Jubilees*, is likely to have originated in the middle of the second century B.C.E." (1996, 140). J.C. VanderKam is skeptical regarding such dependence, but still deems the origin of 4QPseudo-Jubilees rather late, "perhaps in the first century BCE" (1997, 241; cf. F. García Martínez 2002, 45: "around the end of the first century BCE or the beginning of the first century CE"; A. Lange/B. Ego 2003, 173f.: around 150 B.C., due to the general lack of the tetragrammaton).

אל יהוה, whereby the divine name is not written in palaeo-Hebrew, but in the same script as the rest of the fragment.[193]

The second fragment of 4QPseudo-Jubilees consists of two relatively well preserved columns that deal with some episodes in Abraham's life. Particularly 4Q225 2 i 7-8 is significant, for it provides a modified quotation of Gen 15:6. It is preceded by Abraham's lament that he is without heir and by God's promise of descendants as numerous as the stars in heaven or the sand on the seashore, the dust of the earth. This paraphrase of Gen 15:1-6 is followed by the retelling of another central Abrahamic text, the sacrifice of Isaac, which the largest amount of space is devoted to in the preserved columns.[194] Thus, in the narrative structure of 4Q225 2, Gen 15:6 represents the connecting link that binds together thematically and compositionally the mention of God's promise to Abraham with the account of the sacrifice of Isaac.

Due to the partly corrupted text, some readings of the Gen 15:6 quotation are uncertain and have been reconstructed differently[195]:

B.Z. Wacholder/M.G. Abeg[196]

(7) ויא[מ]ין
(8) ... ב[אל]והי[ם >ו<יתחשב לו צדקה

J.C. VanderKam/J.T. Milik[197]

(7) ויא[מ]ין
(8) [אברהם ב[אלו]הי[ם ותחשב לו צדקה

F. García Martínez/E.J.C. Tigchelaar[198]

(7) ויא[מ]ין
(8) [אברהם] אלו]הי[ם ותחשב לו צקרה

M. Oeming[199]

(7) ויא[מ]ין
(8) [אברהם ב[אל]והי[ם וי]>ת?<ח[שב לו צדקה

R. Mosis[200]

(7) ויא[מ]ין
(8) [אברהם ב[אל]והי[ם ות]ח[שב לו צדקה

---

[193] Cf. A. Lange/B. Ego 2003, 173f.; F. García Martínez 2002, 56; see A. Lange 1997, 46, and 2003 on criteria for the identification of Essenic texts.

[194] However, despite the breadth of description and several supplements to Genesis 22, "most of the details of the Biblical text ... are not mentioned (F. García Martínez 2002, 47).

[195] Cf. the photographs in E. Tov 1993 with the PAM-numbers 41.517, 41.718, 42.361 (printed in R. Mosis 1999, 103), and 43.251 (printed in J.C. VanderKam/J.T. Milik 1994, table 10). – On a detailed and, regarding its results, convincing analysis of the text-critical issues, see especially R. Mosis 1999, 102-111.

[196] B.Z. Wacholder/M.G. Abegg 1992, 205.

[197] J.C. VanderKam/J.T. Milik 1994, 145.

[198] F. García Martínez/E.J.C. Tigchelaar 1997/1998, 478.

[199] M. Oeming 1998, 86, preferring the reading וישב (88).

[200] R. Mosis 1999, 109.

Problems pertinent to our discussion arise especially regarding the question of the (non)existence of the preposition before אלוהים and the transcription of the verb חשב; the solution to those text-critical issues significantly bears on the question how the author of "Pseudo-Jubilees" comprehended Gen 15:6. With greatest probability one can reconstruct the verb ויאמן at the end of line 7.[201] Hence, instead of using the conspicuous perfect tense as in the Masoretic וְהֶאֱמִן, the author of "Pseudo-Jubilees" inserted the statement on Abraham's believing directly into the narrative structure by employing a narrative form. As in the Septuagint, where the aorist tense appears, Abraham's faith is understood in terms of an immediate reaction to God's promise, a onetime act. Moreover, in contrast to the Masoretic Text, yet again in line with the Septuagint, the subject of ויאמן, Abraham, seems to be mentioned. In fact, the context does not allow for another solution than to fill the lacuna at the beginning of line 8 with the name אברהם.[202] In order to determine how the sentence continues, one has to compare the loss of text on the right margin in line 8 with the suggested reconstructions of the previous and following lines. There is some significance attached to this issue, as the space that is used up by the five letters for "Abraham" plus the space to the next word determines the degree of probability for a preposition before אלוהים[203] – which in turn bears on the author's use and theological understanding of אמן *hiphil*.[204] The fact that אמן *hiphil* in biblical Hebrew presupposes a preposition when the object of

---

[201] Cf. J.C. VanderKam/J.T. Milik 1994, 147.

[202] It is almost certain that one has to reconstruct אברהם rather than אברם (cf., e.g., 4Q225 2 i 3.5.11).

[203] The reading אלוהים is almost sure (cf. J.C. VanderKam/J.T. Milik 1994, 147).

[204] The "instruction-like" text 4Q424 1,7-8 seems to present two instances in which אמן *hiphil* has a direct object, without preposition (cf. D.J.A. Clines 1993, 316): איש תלונה אל ת[א]מין ... איש לוז שפתים אל תאמ[ין...] ("Do not trust a contentious man... Do not trust a man with twisted lips...") (cf. F. García Martínez/E.J.C. Tigchelaar 1997/1998, 888f.). This is indeed surprising – also in view of the analysis of אמן presented above –, for one expects that if not used in the absolute, אמן always denotes the person or subject matter, to which faith is directed, by employing a prepositional expression with *be* or with *le*. Therefore, a text-critical comment by G. Brin seems interesting: Though not referring to this syntactical issue involved, he says regarding line 7 that the "correct reconstruction here, even though it has not been suggested by any of the various scholars, seems to be: אל תא[מין בו] ('do not trust in him')" (1997, 35). As for the second occurrence of the phrase, Brin does not make a like suggestion (36), but preserves the common reconstruction. On the other hand, S. Tanzer reconstructs the end of line 7 without employing a derivate of אמן: [תאמ]ר ממנו] ... (2000, 336, 339), but as for line 8 she contends that it can be restored to: תאמ]ין בו לעשות] ..., whereby the "the restoration תאמ]ין בו ... is almost certain" (340).

faith is mentioned, speaks in favor of the reading ויאמין אברהם באלוהים, despite the relatively little space that is available.[205]

This half sentence is followed by a word, which is mostly lost in the
hole in the manuscript, but which has surely to be reconstructed as a derivative of the verb חשב. The *Preliminary Edition* assumed a scribal error,
conjectured an additional *waw* at the beginning of the word and hence
transcribed the *hithpael* form ויתחשב.[206] This conjecture however is
unlikely, since *yod* and *waw* can be fairly clearly distinguished in this particular scribal hand – especially when they appear side by side[207] – so that
the remains of the word's first letter evidently have to be read as *waw*, not
as *yod*. In addition, the reading ויתחשב generates the syntactical irregularity
that the declaration of Abraham's faith would be taken up by a masculine
singular form, against the common tendency in the Hebrew and Aramaic
language of referring to preceding statements by a feminine singular
form.[208] The difficulties that arise with the assumption of a *hithpael*-form
with respect to the graphical, grammatical and contextual evidence disappear, if one reconstructs the feminine singular *niphal* ותחשב, as for instance
in Ps 106:31.

What remains in need of an explanation with this transcription is the
lack of the preposition *le* before צדקה, which concurs on the one hand with
the Masoretic Text of Gen 15:6b, but insinuates a syntactical deviation
from Ps 106:31 or from other passages that have a passive construction,
namely, the translation of the Genesis-verse in the Targum *Neofiti* or the

---

[205] F. García Martínez and E.J.C. Tigchelaar decide for the other option without
preposition and restore the reading ויא[מין] [אברהם] אלו[הי]ם (1997/1998, 478; cf. F. García
Martínez 2002, 48). As the above compilation of the different reconstructions shows, the
preposition *be* is rightly preferred over *le*. Not only the Masoretic Text suggests this
reading, but also the Targums.

[206] B.Z. Wacholder/M.G. Abegg 1992, 205; cf. J.T. Milik 1962, 225. In biblical Hebrew the *hithpael* form appears in Num 23:9 (יִתְחַשָּׁב) and stands for "to reckon oneself
among"; consequently, as regards the alleged reading in 4Q225 2 i 8 one has to presuppose that the *hithpael* in connection with the dative לו assumed passive meaning in this
linguistic stage of the Hebrew language, as is frequently the case. Cf. E. Qimron/J. Strugnell 1994, 84; W. Gesenius/E. Kautzsch 1909, §54e.

[207] Cf. 4Q225 2 i 4 (וירשני), 8 (ויולד), 9 (ויבוא), 10 (ויאמר). See B. Ego/A. Lange 2003,
175f., on the distinctive features of *yod* and *waw*. Moreover, it is unlikely that the scribe
accidentally omitted the *copula* in a series of succeeding narrative forms.

[208] Cf. R. Mosis 1999, 107f., who refers to E. König 1897, §346 a and b, W. Gesen-
ius/E. Kautzsch 1909, §122q, and P. Joüon/T. Muraoka 1991, §152b and c, and names
the following texts, all containing the verb חשב in the passive feminine singular, as evidence: Ps 106:31; 4QMMT^e; *TgNeof* Gen 15:6; Peshitta Gen 15:6; analogously, the feminine singular suffix *ha* in וַיַּחְשְׁבֶהָ (MT) refers to the aforementioned faith of Abraham.

Peshitta and the allusion to it in 4QMMT[e].[209] One might infer that here צדקה is the subject of this part of the verse so that one would have to translate "...and righteousness was reckoned to him."[210] Yet this rendition leads to several problems: (1) The construction of a double nominative and the predicative translation of it would be dissolved, which is however characteristic of numerous biblical occurrences of חשב and typical for the meaning of this verb as discerned above.[211] (2) The parallelism to the just mentioned allusions to and versions of Gen 15:6 that use the passive voice would be disbanded as well (even if they use the preposition in contrast to 4QPseudo-Jubilees).[212] (3) Finally, by neglecting the reference back to Abraham's faith expressed by the feminine singular form, one separates structurally Abraham's faith from the divine judgment, which counters the very intention of Gen 15:6 itself.[213] Hence, the more likely solution is to make Abraham's believing the subject of the feminine singular *niphal* verb form – in factual analogy to the suffix *ha* of Gen 15:6 – and to determine the noun צדקה as second nominative.[214] The parallel structure in Prov 27:14: a feminine singular *niphal* that refers to preceding actions, the object of the counting לו, and the indirect object without the preposition *le*, demonstrates the general syntactical openness for such a construction. The verse reads: קְלָלָה תֵּחָשֶׁב לוֹ – "it will be considered as cursing for him."

As a result of this text-critical analysis, one can claim with great probability that the quotation of Gen 15:6 in 4Q225 2 i 7-8 is to be reconstructed as follows: ויאמין אברהם באלוהים ותחשב לו צדקה. Lines 3-9 constitute the immediate context of this statement and will be reproduced as well.[215]

---

[209] On 4QMMT[e] see below chapter IV.G. – This difficulty leads M. Oeming to favor the reading ויחשב, i.e., masculine singular *qal* in the third person (1998, 87f.). However, considering the width of the lacuna his solution seems improbable, above all since remainders of all letters of the word in question are discernible in the lacuna.

[210] Thus J.A. Fitzmyer 2003, 266; J.C. VanderKam/J.T. Milik 1994, 147; J.C. VanderKam 1997, 253; F. García Martínez 2002, 47f.

[211] See above chapter III.D.I.2.

[212] As has been shown, there is no significant difference of meaning between a double nominative construction and a qualifying prepositional expression (*le* or *ke*) instead of the second qualifying nominative.

[213] See above chapter III.D.II.

[214] Cf. the same result in B. Ego/A. Lange 2003, 176.

[215] The reconstruction is identical to that in J.C. VanderKam/J.T. Milik 1994, 145. The translation follows mostly that in J.A. Fitzmyer 2003, 265f.

(3) [And A]braham [said] to God: "My Lord, look at me, going childless, and Eli[ezer]	(3) [ויאמר א]ברהם אל אלוהים אדני הנני בא עררי ואלי[עזר]
(4) is [the son of my household], and he will inherit me."	(4) [בן ביתי] הואה וירשני *vacat*
(5) [The Lo]rd [said] to A[b]raham: "Lift up (your eyes), observe the stars, and see	(5) [אמר אד]ני אל א[ב]רהם שא צפא את הכוכבים וראה
(6) [and count] the sands that (are) on the seashore and the dust of the earth, for if	(6) [וספור את]החול אשר על שפת הים ואת עפר הארץ כי אם
(7) these [will be num]bered, and ev[en] if not, so will your descendants be."	(7) [יהיו נמ]נים אלה וא[ף] אם לוא ככה יהיה זרעכה ויא[מין]
(8) And Abraham believed in God, and it was considered as righteousness to him. And a son was born af[ter] this	(8) [אברהם ב]אלו[הי]ם ותחשב לו צדקה ויולד בן אח[רי]כן
(9) [to Abraha]m, and he named him Isaac. And the Prince Ma[s]temah came	(9) [לאברה]ם ויקרא את שמו יסחק ויבוא שר המ[ש]טמה
(10) [to G]od, and he accused Abraham regarding Isaac.	(10) [אל אל]והים וישטים את אברהם בישחק

Hence, the formally ambiguous wording of the Masoretic Text is specified and clarified in 4QPseudo-Jubilees, thus agreeing with the translation found in the Septuagint; the passive voice in this *passivum divinum-*construction signifies God as the logical subject of ותחשב. Abraham's faith finds its verbal expression in the *imperfectum consecutivum* ויאמין, which is embedded in the narrative structure of the account. Notably, therefore, with the exception of the preposition before "God" and another preposition before "righteousness," the text of 4QPseudo-Jubilees concurs with that of the Septuagint against the wording of the Masoretic Text[216]:

(1) Both 4QPseudo-Jubilees and Septuagint name explicitly the subject of faith, "Abraham" (4QPseudo-Jubilees) and "Abram" (Septuagint), respectively. (2) By integrating the remark about Abraham's faith directly into the narrative and by thus replacing the anomalous perfect of the Masoretic Text, they express a onetime past act. (3) They both replace the tetragrammaton with a more general designation of God, אלוהים and θεός, respectively. (4) Finally, as already noted, by means of the change of the *genus verbi* into the passive voice, the Septuagint and 4QPseudo-Jubilees remove the vagueness of the Masoretic וַיַּחְשְׁבֶהָ and refer the personal pronoun לו and αὐτῷ, respectively, unambiguously to Abraham. Those observations suggest that the *Vorlage* of the translation preserved in the Septua-

---

[216] Cf. R. Mosis 1999, 109. Even though in his earlier essay Mosis rightly contended: "LXX hat bei der Übersetzung von חשב nur dann eine Präposition, wenn auch MT eine Präposition aufweist" (1989, 90; exception: Job 41:19), he does not mention the lack of the preposition *le* in 4QPseudo-Jubilees.

gint possesses a notable affinity to the version found in 4QPseudo-Jubilees; possibly, both texts, Septuagint and 4QPseudo-Jubilees, are dependent on the same or a similar Hebrew *Vorlage*.[217]

The unidentified narrator[218] begins[219] his account with the mention of Abraham's or Jacob's twenty-year stay in Haran,[220] and then continues immediately, i.e., without blank space, with Abraham's[221] concern that he would remain childless. Hence, the re-narration of God's promise of an heir in 4QPseudo-Jubilees starts with a condensed combination of Gen 15:2 and 15:3, without including the preceding divine assurance of Gen 15:1, which marked the Genesis text as salvation oracle. The author omitted Gen 15:4 and the first words of Gen 15:5 as well, but he extended in a Midrashic manner God's command to look at and count the stars, by adding the analogous images of the sand on the seashore and the dust of the earth, drawn from other passages about the patriarchal promises (Gen 22:17; 13:6).[222] He rephrases and re-interprets the logic of Gen 15:5 slightly,[223] but retains its point: Abraham's descendants will be as populous as the stars, the sand, or the dust.

As in Genesis 15, now the statement on Abraham's faith follows, even though in contrast to Genesis 15, the author creates a direct association to God's promise by means of the employed verbal form. Nevertheless, an intellectualistic understanding – in the sense of a mere "acceptance"[224] – is averted through the preposition *be*, as in the Masoretic Text: It is rather *credere in deum* than *credere deo*. Abraham fastens himself trustfully in

---

[217] Cf. J.A. Fitzmyer 2003, 267: "The Greek translation of the Septuagint would, then, be … probably dependent on a Hebrew *Vorlage*, which this Qumran text [*sc.* 4QPseudo-Jubilees] also uses."

[218] *Jubilees* on the other hand presupposes the Angel of the Presence as narrator.

[219] The fragment about a person "cut off from his people" which is preserved in line 1 could refer to Gen 17:14.

[220] The immediate context would suggest that the stay in Haran should be attributed to Abraham, yet this would counter *Jub* 12,12.28, which indicates a seventeen-year period (cf. also 12,15). On the other hand, Gen 31:38 and *Jub* 27,19; 29,5 mention that Jacob stayed in Haran for twenty years (cf. J.C. VanderKam/J.T. Milik 1994, 148).

[221] In contrast to Gen 15:2, the fuller form of his name is used here.

[222] On the star metaphor and its occurrence in further biblical passages, see above pages 89f. The "sand on the seashore" appears in Gen 22:17 with regard to Abraham (cf. כַּחוֹל אֲשֶׁר עַל־שְׂפַת הַיָּם [Gen 22:17] with החול אשר על שפת הים [4Q225 2 i 6]) and in LXX Dan 3:36 with regard to the three patriarchs Abraham, Isaac, and Jacob. The third image of the "dust of the earth" occurs besides Gen 13:16 (Abraham) also in Sir 44,21 (Abraham), Gen 28:14 (Jacob), and 2Chr 1:9 (Israel).

[223] A positive affirmation ("if these will be numbered"; cf. Gen 13:16) is combined with a negative affirmation ("even if not"; cf. 1QapGen 21,13) (see F. García Martínez 2002, 48).

[224] Against J.C. VanderKam 1997, 253.

Yahweh and, dependent on that, considers God's word reliable – against all appearances.[225]

God considers this kind of faith as righteousness. Despite the description of Abraham's faith as punctual, one-time event, its actual permanent character manifests itself in the following test. After quoting Gen 15:6, the re-narration of Genesis 15 ends abruptly and the author reports the birth of Isaac, i.e., the direct fulfillment of the promise (Gen 21:1-7), connected through the simple temporal specification אחרי כן.[226] Obviously, both the assurance of land and the establishment of the covenant are omitted (Gen 15:7-21)[227]; the covenant of circumcision (Genesis 17) lacks mention as well.[228] It is clear that from the perspective of narrative technique, reduction and selection concurs with the expressive emphasis of the selected items. Structurally, therefore, the statement on Abraham's faith represents the centerpiece of the two principal texts dealing with the themes of Abraham's attitude to God and God's dealing with Abraham: Genesis 15 and 22.

Without further ado, the narrator comes to the main object of his re-narration, the binding of Isaac (Genesis 22),[229] which takes the lion's share of the fragments 4Q225 2 i and ii,[230] and which he describes in a more picturesque way than the preceding part.[231] In a Joban interpretation of Genesis 22, he creates a court-room scene, in which the Prince of Mastemah as Abraham's "prosecutor"[232] – without being introduced[233] – brings accusa-

---

[225] On the meaning of אמן *hiphil* in connection with *be*, see above chapter III.D.IV.2.

[226] The scribe of the manuscripts did not even deem it necessary to interrupt the text through a *vacat*. At the end of the re-narration of the Aqedah, the summary of the results of the promise will follow in a like uninterrupted manner, namely, the lineage subsequent to Abraham's son Isaac: Jacob and Levi (4Q225 2 ii 11).

[227] This means that the author of "Pseudo-Jubilees" (in opposition to the author of *Jubilees*; cf. *Jub* 14,1-20) did not consider Gen 15:7-21 to be essential for his purpose.

[228] See however above note 219.

[229] On the re-narration of the Aqedah in 4QPseudo-Jubilees, see G. Vermès 1996; J.C. VanderKam 1997; F. García Martínez 2002; J.A. Fitzmyer 2002.

[230] Column ii continues the text of column i directly.

[231] The picturesque character does not derive from an abundance of details – in fact it is less detailed than Genesis 22, which itself presents concrete facts only sparingly (cf. T. Veijola 1988, 138) – but from elements like the "Prince of Mastemah," the "angels of Mastemah", and the "angels of holiness," as well as from creating a Job-like scenery. 4QPseudo-Jubilees stresses the presence of angels more explicitly than *Jubilees*; in the latter, the Angel of the Presence is the narrator who refers implicitly to other angels (*Jub* 18,14).

[232] The designation משטמה is a feminine abstract noun, meaning "opposition," and it is difficult to decide whether to translate the expression used for an angelic figure, שר המשטמה, as "Prince of (the) Mastemah" (thus J.C. VanderKam/J.T. Milik 1994) or as a name "Prince Mastemah" (as in several passages in *Jubilees*: see *Jub* 17,16; 18,9.12 [the binding of Isaac]; 48,2.9.12.15 [the context of the exodus]; for "Mastemah" see *Jub*

tions against Abraham in regards to Isaac,[234] and this provokes God's testing of Abraham. In a certain sense these elements concur with details in
Jub 17,15-18,19, but in sum 4QPseudo-Jubilees displays again a strong
abbreviating and selective tendency compared to *Jubilees*.

Out of the re-narration of the Aqedah, two related passages need to be
highlighted[235]: The first expresses (in a negative construction) the hope of
the angels of Mastemah[236] or the Prince of Mastemah that Abraham will be
found *not* faithful: [ואם לא ימצא נאמן א[ברהם לאלוהים ("and whether
A[braham] should not be found faithful [to God]," 4Q225 2 ii 8),[237] while
the second states positively that Abraham was in fact found faithful in his
testing: [נמצא אברהם נאמן ל[א]ל[הים ("Abraham was found faithful to Go[d],"
4Q226 7 1).[238] As with Neh 9:8 and the comparable passages, the question
arises if and how the expression מצא נאמן relates to Gen 15:6. In the case of
4QPseudo-Jubilees one cannot state an amalgamation of Genesis 15 and
22, since both narratives are retold as separate entities. Yet on the other
hand, Abraham's testing provoked by the Prince of Mastemah follows immediately on the birth of Isaac; all those events are integrated into a chain
of narrative forms: "And Abraham believed..., and a son was born..., and
the Prince of Mastemah came..." Thus, even though chronologically a gap

---

10,8.11; 11,5.11; 19,28). Cf. again Job 1 and 2 (on שָׂטָן), 16:9 and 30:21 (on שׂטם), and 1:6
(on the court-room situation).

[233] See differently *Jub* 17,15.

[234] Cf. in the same context *Jub* 17,16.

[235] The content of both fragments (4Q225 2 ii and 4Q226 7) overlaps several times so
that they mutually interpret each other.

[236] On the presence of the angels of Mastemah in 4QPseudo-Jubilees, see F. García
Martínez 2002, 54: "As far as I know, no other version of the story attests to the presence
of the wicked angels at the scene" (cf. *Jub* 18,12).

[237] J.C. VanderKam/J.T. Milik 1994, 149, 151. One should refrain from determining the
meaning of נאמן in this context from the adjective כחש (as in B. Ego/A. Lange 2003,
175f.), which appears four words earlier; for, the noun of reference of כחש is more likely
to be Isaac than Abraham (cf. G. Vermès 1996, 142nn.16f.). See also the following note.

[238] J.C. VanderKam/J.T. Milik 1994, 165. F. García Martínez suggests that Isaac
should be considered the subject of the first passage (4Q225 2 ii 8) (2002, 55), i.e., he
does not read נאמן א[ברהם], but נאמן [יצחק]; but the formal parallelism of the two passages
and their logical connection (negative – positive), as well as the existence of a set expression מצא נאמן with regard to Abraham counter his proposal (cf. also the multiple reference
to Abraham's faithfulness in *Jubilees*). – Notably, in later Jewish interpretation of Genesis 22, until the Middle Ages, it is not Abraham's obedience that stands in the center of
attention, but Isaac's willingness to serve as sacrifice to God (cf. E. Dassmann 2002, 2).
García Martínez suggests that already "Pseudo-Jubilees" "inaugurates ... the shift which
later on will led [*sic*] to consider Isaac (and not Abraham) the center of the story (for
example, in ... [Pseudo-Philo's] *Liber Antiquitatum Biblicarum* 32:2-4)" (2002, 50).

of several years exists between those events,[239] the author saw a logical and theologically relevant connection between them: The Prince of Mastemah seeks to disprove Abraham's faith in God and his promise by putting to the test Abraham's faithfulness to God. If he can substantiate his supposition that Abraham is not firm towards God in such a distressful situation, the evidence is clear that his trust in God regarding the promise was not veritable.

But there is yet another link between the two main sections of the Qumran fragment, which concerns the fulfillment of the promise of a son, i.e., Isaac.[240] The rationale of the Prince of Mastemah is not only to prove Abraham's unfaithfulness, but also on a different level to annihilate God's plan and promise of an offspring for Abraham, which is supposed to become as numerous as the stars, the sand, or the dust. This is why the angels of Mastemah rejoice at the prospect of Isaac's death and exclaim: "Now he will perish" (4Q225 2 ii 7).[241] At the end, however, God annihilates the adversary's plan – even reverses it[242] – and demonstrates his fidelity to the promise by blessing Isaac.[243]

In sum, also the present *relecture* of Genesis 15 and 22 reflects the significant development in Jewish tradition regarding the understanding of faith,[244] as it combines in a remarkably concise and selective manner the two notions of "faith" and "faithfulness" of Abraham and places them along with God's faithfulness to Abraham's offspring. On the one hand, the whole of 4QPseudo-Jubilees "is entirely concentrated within the framework of the testing of Abraham's 'fidelity'"[245] and his trust in God, but on a different level it is also about the fidelity and continuity of God's promise, which has as its content Abraham's offspring.[246] The central *scopos* in the re-narration of those eminent dimensions in 4QPseudo-Jubilees is provided through the triple use of the root אמן, once in the *hiphil* (ויאמין)

---

[239] The re-narration of Genesis 22 implies (as the Old Testament original itself) that Isaac is a youth who can carry wood and knows the meaning of a sacrifice.

[240] 4Q225 2 i 10 gives a first hint to the focus on Isaac where it mentions Mastemah's reason and motivation for provoking the test: בישחק.

[241] F. García Martínez even argues that this exclamation "expresses the main intention of our text's narrative" (2002, 55; cf. 51, but see 47 and 49: "[T]he point of the whole story is indeed to prove '…whether he [*sc.* Abraham] would not be found faithful").

[242] The earthly events of the binding of Isaac are overturned in heaven where the Prince of Mastemah is bound after Abraham proved his faithfulness. In the framework of its re-narration of the exodus, *Jub* 48,15.18 mentions as well the binding of Mastemah (see above note 165).

[243] Cf. Gen 22:17; *Jub* 18,15; and the parallel 4Q226 7 2.

[244] Cf. J.A. Fitzmyer 2003, 268.

[245] F. García Martínez 2002, 47; cf. 49.

[246] As in Genesis 15, therefore, one may speak of a convergence between human and divine action (see above page 129).

and twice in the *niphal* (נאמן), by means of which Gen 15:6 and Genesis 22 mutually interpret each other. The author achieves a similar, though less strong, effect by incorporating the metaphor of the sand (Gen 22:17) into the son promise. The consequences of Abraham's proven faith and faithfulness reach a cosmological dimension, for, with the binding of the Prince of Mastemah the negative powers are banned; and on an earthly level, it leads to life and blessing for generations to come. While in Gen 15:6 the latter was the consequence of God's considering Abraham's faith as righteousness, here the attitude and action of Abraham seem to stand in the foreground.

G. 4QMMT

Another striking evidence of the allusion to Gen 15:6 is found in the "halakhic"[247] letter 4QMMT^e.[248] This writing to some extent reopened the question of the origin and structure of the sect at Qumran, of the relationship or identity of the Essenes (as described by Philo, Josephus, and Pliny the Elder) and the Qumran covenanters. In the controversial halakhic issues dealt with in the letter, the writer generally takes a position that is stricter than the stance of the more lenient pharisaic-rabbinic tradition; his view comes close to that of the Sadducees in their debate with the Pharisees in the Mishnah.[249] On a number of occasions, the halakha of 4QMMT concurs with that of the Temple Scroll.[250] Based on these premises and the unique character of 4QMMT, some – first and foremost L.H. Schiffmann – claim "that the origins of the Qumran sect are Sadducean,"[251] while others maintain that "[d]espite its many peculiarities," 4QMMT "breathes the spirit of Qumran."[252]

With caution and in awareness of the controversial scholarly *status quaestionis*, one might maintain the following: 4QMMT is a letter of a

---

[247] This term, commonly applied to 4QMMT, must not create the (wrong) assumption that the rulings presented by the author would be precepts of an oral law (cf. O. Betz 1994, 183: "[T]he author of 4QMMT does not present *halakhoth* in the rabbinic sense.").

[248] It is the only (preserved) letter among the Qumran writings, and it deals with the responsibilities of the Jerusalem priests. Both these features account for the letter's unique style and terminology: It has official character and is addressed to a group outside the community and therefore does not apply the somewhat esoteric in-group language of Qumran.

[249] Cf. L.H. Schiffmann 1992; 1995. The language appears to have "elements of mishnaic Hebrew" (O. Betz 1994, 177).

[250] Cf. H. Lichtenberger 1996, 15, with some examples.

[251] L.H. Schiffmann 1992, 41.

[252] O. Betz 1994, 201; cf. 178.

Qumranic teacher – probably the "Teacher of Righteousness,"[253] who represents those who have separated (פרש) themselves from the mass of the people (C 7-8). It is addressed to the leader of a rival group located at the Jerusalem temple – probably the high priest.[254]

As for the date of the manuscripts, the editors in the "Discoveries in the Judean Desert"-series contend that "if we dismiss the scribe's idiosyncrasies" the features of the script "tend to support a date no later than the Herodian period."[255] If one agrees that the author of the letter is the Teacher of Righteousness and the addressee the Jerusalem high priest, some clues such as the allusion to the office of the king (C 23-25) suggest that "a Hasmonean priest king could be addressed; Alexander Jannaeus ... (103-76 B.C.) appears to be the first choice."[256] Hence, the date of the writing itself would fall into the first quarter of the first century B.C. On the other hand, "many researchers believe that the document dates to the earliest days of the Qumran sect (c. 160 B.C.)."[257]

For several reasons, the conclusion of the parenetic section of the letter (C 7-32) is of greatest interest to us: It provides a reference to the sin and forgiveness of David, clarifies the correlation between salvation and obedience to the law, names God as the one who assesses and judges deeds using the quotation of Gen 15:6 and/or Ps 106:31,[258] and finally presents the phrase "works of the law."

---

[253] Cf. E. Qimron/J. Strugnell 1994, 1.

[254] The addressee belongs to the "Sons of Aaron (בני אהרן)" (B 16-17) and is responsible for the proper handling of the sacrifices; his own welfare and the welfare of "your people (עמך)" Israel are interrelated (C 27.31-32). – 4QMMT shares with *Jubilees* a certain "Priesterdominanz" (M. Müller 1996, 244).

[255] E. Qimron/J. Strugnell 1994, 6.

[256] O. Betz 1994, 195; cf. R. Bergmeier 2000, 59.

[257] M.G. Abegg 2000, 709.

[258] On the relationship between Gen 15:6 and 4QMMT, see the extensive discussion in M.W. Yeung 2002, 241-249. If one asks why 4QMMT relates Abraham to David, one could think *inter alia* of the manifold associations between the two personages already in the Old Testament; "[sie] sind derart vielfältig, daß insgesamt nicht mehr von Zufall gesprochen werden kann, sondern mit einer gezielten Typologisierung zu rechnen ist" (W. Dietrich 2000, 51). This typology might have been sensed by the theologian composing the letter.

	4QMMT C 25-32[259]
(25) Think of David who was a man of righteous deeds/of the pious ones[260] and	(25) זכור [את] דויד שהיא איש חסדים [ו]אף
(26) who was (therefore) delivered from many troubles and was forgiven. We have (indeed) sent you	(26) היא [נ]צל מצרות רבות ונסלוח לו ואף אנחנו כתבנו אליך
(27) some of the works of the Torah according to our decision, for your welfare and the welfare of your people. For we have seen (that)	(27) מקצת מעשי התורה שחשבנו לטוב לך ולעמך שר[א]ינו
(28) you have wisdom and knowledge of the Torah. Consider all these things and ask Him that He strengthen	(28) עמך ערמה ומדע תורה הבן בכל אלה ובקש מלפנו שיתקן
(29) your will and remove from you the plans of evil and the device of Belial	(29) את עצתך והרחיק ממך מחשבת רעה ועצת בליעל
(30) so that you may rejoice at the end of time, finding that some of our practices/words are correct.	(30) בשל שתשמח באחרית העת במצאך מקצת דברינו כן
(31) And this will be counted as righteousness to you since you will be doing what is righteous and good in His eyes, for your own welfare and	(31) ונחשבה לך לצדקה בעשותך הישר והטוב לפנו לטוב לך
(32) for the welfare of Israel.	(32) ולישראל

Especially the phrase מעשי התורה gave rise to a major discussion in scholarship, concerning both its translation and its meaning.

(1) While some render this expression in a rather general way with "the precepts of the Torah"[261] or "legal rulings of the Torah,"[262] one can recognize an increasing agreement to regard it as the only secure occurrence of the momentous expression "works of the law" in Second Temple Judaism outside of Paul[263] – which however is not without roots in the Old Testa-

---

[259] See E. Qimron/J. Strugnell 1994, 62f. (translation adapted). Cf. F. García Martínez/E.J.C. Tigchelaar 1997/1998, 802f.

[260] The plural חסדים can either be translated as "righteous deeds" (e.g., E. Qimron/J. Strugnell) or as "pious ones" (e.g., F. García Martínez/E.J.C. Tigchelaar).

[261] E. Qimron/J. Strugnell 1994, 63.

[262] L.H. Schiffmann 1990, 67. Against that, see above note 247.

[263] Cf. among recent publications D. Flusser 1996; F. García Martínez/E.J.C. Tigchelaar 1997/1998, 803 (F. García Martínez here changed his mind; cf. J.D.G. Dunn 1997a, 150); M. Bachmann 1998; M.W. Yeung 2002, 241-243; J.D.G. Dunn 2002. – Another possible occurrence of this expression is found in 4QFlor 1,7 (4Q174 1); the contentious issue is whether one should read מעשי תורה or מעשי תודה. Yeung states that "it appears that the reading 'works of thanksgiving' receives increasing consensus among scholars" (241). Among those who support the reading מעשי תורה are J. Allegro 1968, 53f.; M.O. Wise 1991, 105; J.A. Fitzmyer 1993, 338; H.-J. Eckstein 1996, 25f., while the alternative reading מעשי תודה is supported in O. Hofius 1993, 158n.26; A. Steudel 1994, 13 (referred to in E. Gräßer 1998, 12n.50); J. Maier 1995, 104; F. García Martínez 1996, 24; F. García Martínez/E.J.C. Tigchelaar 1997/1998, 352f.; M. Bachmann 1998, 100; K. Haacker 1999, 84n.40. See also the discussion in J.C.R. de Roo 2000, 127-131, with n.45 for more proponents of the first reading, and n.44 of the second; she herself favors the מעשי-תורה

ment.[264] This opens up the question how the two occurrences relate to each other and how they mutually explain each other.

(2) The second issue, the precise meaning, contents, and implication of the "works of the law" in this Qumran writing, divides scholarship into at least two groups. On the one hand, there are commentators who contend that this expression denotes "that understanding of the law's requirements which distinguished the Qumran covenanters from their fellow Jews."[265] Against this primarily sociological understanding, others prefer a more general view of the expression: "[I]t denotes (the doing of) the works which the law requires, obedience to the law."[266] Not the distinction from the Jerusalem priests is of primary importance, but the standing of the members of the Qumran community before God.[267]

Since our task is an analysis of the use of Gen 15:6, we cannot engage in a deeper discussion of this question about the understanding of the "works of the law," but have to confine ourselves to a few remarks. To be sure, on first sight the meticulous details in the rulings on the handling of the sacrifices appear to support the first, more restrictive view. Yet the above cited conclusion of the letter opens up the perspective, as it binds the fulfillment of the "works of the Torah" to personal welfare, to the welfare of Israel, to God's positive judgment, and even to salvation at the end of times. Furthermore, the "entire concluding formula is perhaps influenced by Deut 6:24-25,"[268] i.e., by a passage that calls for the observance of Yahweh's whole commandment.[269] Other aspects confirm the compre-

---

reading. Ultimately, it seems that paleography cannot decide the issue (cf. M.G. Abegg 1999, 139n.3). – In addition one should refer to *2Bar* 57,2 which has the phrase "opera praeceptorum" ("praecepta" correlates to מִצְוֹת or ἐντολαί; but see above note 131: The Greek of Sir 44,20 reads νόμος for מצות). This passage from *2Baruch* talks about the time of the patriarchs when the still unwritten law was already being observed.

[264] See below note 269; also below chapter V.B.III.4 on the "works of the law."

[265] J.D.G. Dunn 1992, 103; cf. 1998, 376. ("the works of the law which distinguished the Qumran community's halakhah"). See also M.G. Abegg 1999.

[266] C.E.B. Cranfield 1991, 13.

[267] Thus, M.W. Yeung argues that "'works of the law' has a far greater *theological implication* than sectarian implication for the Qumran covenanters" (2002, 245; cf. 262). See also O. Hofius 1987, 85n.35; H.B.P. Mijoga 1999, 102; S. Westerholm 2004, 290.

[268] E. Qimron/J. Strugnell 1994, 63.

[269] Cf. Deut 6:25: עשה אֶת־כָּל־הַמִּצְוָה הַזֹּאת לִפְנֵי יְהוָה אֱלֹהֵינוּ with 4QMMT C 27.31: עשה מעשי התורה, i.e., היישר והטוב לפנו. On the side one should note the interesting fact that both the book of Deuteronomy and 4QMMT end with "Israel" and hence display another commonality (cf. E. Qimron/J. Strugnell 1994, 46). Other related Old Testament passages imply the obedience "to the totality of the Law" (S.J. Gathercole 2002, 95f.), in a way comparable to Deut 6:25, such as Deut 17:19; 27:26; 28:58; 29:28; 31:12; 32:46; Josh 1:7-8; 22:5; 23:6; 2Kgs 17:37; 21:8; 2Chr 14:3; 33:8; Ezra 7:10; 10:3; Neh 9:34; 10:30; they all combine the verb עשה with the noun תורה. In many of these instances, the noun כל denotes the totality of the law to be obeyed.

hensive scope of what is dealt with here: An expression related to מעשי
התורה is found in 1QS 5,21 and 6,18, which deal with a person's all-
encompassing theoretical understanding and concrete practice of the Torah
(שכל ומעשי בתורה).[270] Only the one who fulfills these criteria can join the
community of the "sons of truth," who will receive "eternal enjoyment
with endless life, and a crown of glory with majestic raiment in eternal
light" (4,7-8).[271] In both 4QMMT and 1QS, works of/in the law are connected to individual, eschatological blessing.[272] At the end, God will forgive in his judgment (4QMMT C 26; 1QS 11,14), and the faithful will rejoice in eternal salvation.[273]

The addressee of 4QMMT indeed has "wisdom and knowledge of the
Torah" (C 28), but still lacks the full understanding and practice of some
legal prescriptions. Through the observance of these points, he would show
his understanding (בין) of the Scripture (C 10) and take his place among the
leaders of Israel, who "feared the Torah (ירא את תורה)" and were "seekers
of the Torah (מבקשי תורה)," which is evident in their "deeds (מעשיהמה)" (C
23-24). God's history of salvation or curse is contingent on the holistic
human response to the normative authority of what is written in the Book
of Moses (C 6.10.11.12), for ultimately the Torah is God's[274] and seeking
the Torah is seeking God (C 28).[275] Real knowledge of the Torah leads to
obediently fulfilling it, and both lead to well-being and eschatological salvation. The overarching principle therefore is: "eternal life for the righteous."[276]

Besides the notion of the "works of the law," 4QMMT offers an interesting expression that derives from Gen 15:6 and/or Ps 106:31: וְנֶחְשְׁבָה
לך לצדקה. It shares with Ps 106:31 formally the passive voice (though not

---

[270] Cf. O. Betz 1994, 183; C. Burchard 1996, 411 with n.37. See also 1QS 5,23-24,
which states that (lack of) insight and practice result in (demotion or) promotion. 1QHᵃ
1,26 and 4,31 have the expression "works of righteousness" (מעשי הצדקה).

[271] See F. García Martínez/E.J.C. Tigchelaar 1997/1998, 76f. The requirements to join
the community are more than just repentance (against M.G. Abegg 1999, 143), and it is
true that "works are determinative at the final judgment" (S.J. Gathercole 2002, 97).

[272] Concerning 1QS 4, M. Philonenko speaks of "une eschatologie individuelle"
(1983, 214). – On the idea of resurrection and reward after death in the Dead Sea Scrolls
in general, see J.J. Collins 1997.

[273] The notion of joy (שמח) appears both in 4QMMT C 30 and 1QS 4,7.

[274] A "possible" reading of B 1 is ל[א תורת] (E. Qimron/J. Strugnell 1994, 46; they prefer however the reading ל[ישרא ...])

[275] Cf. O. Betz 1994, 185.

[276] J.J. Collins 2000, 43. Collins however adds that the "essential transition to eternal
life was made within the community itself" and thus places the sect's eschatology into
the category of "realized eschatology" (cf. 2000a, 336). Nevertheless, the phrase "end of
time" (4QMMT C 30) clearly denotes future eschatology, as does the notion of "endless
life" (1QS 4,7) (cf. 335).

the tense) and materially the aversion against "unholy mixture" in religious matters,[277] as well as the priestly outlook. As for the last-mentioned aspect, the assumed writer of the letter, the Teacher of Righteousness was a priest (cf. 1QpHab 2,7-8), who deemed himself and his colleagues to be inheritors of Zadoq, i.e., to be the genuine priests. Thus, "we must speak of a controversy between priests,"[278] between Zadoqites and the "Sons of Aaron." Both groups however have Phinehas in their line of succession,[279] and this might explain the author's reference to him and the call for righteous actions. The note on Phinehas's zealous act in Ps 106:31 and the appeal for obedience in 4QMMT both illustrate the perpetual consequences of God's acceptance of one's righteous deed, for the individual as well as for the entire community.[280]

While therefore the immediate appeal probably is to Ps 106:31, Gen 15:6 still constitutes the wider background, which is evident in the unique authority the "Book of Moses" possesses and in the fact that the writer would not mention God's judgment of Phinehas's act without an implicit reference to God's considering Abraham's faith as righteousness. It is even possible to go beyond that: Since the *relecture* of the Abraham narratives displays the tendency to link among others Genesis 15 and 22, one has to assume that both Abraham's faithfulness and Phinehas's zeal are placed before the addressee's eyes as models to be imitated. Abraham "has done this (עָשָׂה אֶת־הַדָּבָר הַזֶּה)," i.e., he has not withheld his son, and so the addressee is called to do these "things (דברים)" (B 1; C 30), i.e., the rulings given by the Teacher of Righteousness. This will be considered as righteousness at the end of time: "works (מעשׂי) of the law," i.e., "your doing (עשׂותך) [of] what is righteous and good in His eyes."

The combination of Gen 15:6 and Deut 6:24-25 is interesting. For, whether or not the author of Gen 15:6 sought to present a "counter program" to Deut 6:25,[281] its emphasis on "faith" is striking; and likewise, whether or not 4QMMT in turn deliberately reinterprets Gen 15:6 in terms of Deut 6:25, it provides a noteworthy nuance as to what finds acceptance in God's eyes: The aspect of "believing" (אמן) is not mentioned, but rather that of "doing" (עשׂה). The rich scriptural background of the letter creates a coherent picture concerning the right attitude and acts that will find a posi-

---

[277] M.W. Yeung 2002, 247.

[278] O. Betz 1994, 181.

[279] Phinehas is a grandson of Aaron (Ex 6:25; 1Chr 5:29-30) and Zadoq follows on Phinehas in the eighth generation (1Chr 5:30-35).

[280] See above pages 156f.

[281] This is the thesis of R. Smend (see above page 104). He argued that the Genesis-verse presupposes Deut 6:25 and reinterprets it by replacing Torah observance with faith in God (1967, 286f.) 4QMMT would again reverse this modification by replacing faith with Torah observance.

tive judgment with God. Another difference to Gen 15:6 is worth mentioning: In the Genesis passage God's considering Abraham's faith as צְדָקָה has consequences that are described as being basically confined to the earthly sphere – "you shall go to your ancestors in peace; you shall be buried in a good old age" (Gen 15:15). In other words there is no speculation or indication as to what happens to Abraham after the end of his physical life. This changes essentially in 4QMMT: The perfect tense with *wow consecutivum* relocates the situation of God's judgment from the *hic et nunc* to the "end of time" (C 30). It introduces an eschatological perspective and a soteriological component: Understanding and doing the "works of the law" leads to eternal salvation.[282]

The appeal to remember (זכר, C 25) is a characteristic Jewish motif, which we encountered already in the Praise of the Fathers (Sirach 44) and which will now recur very prominently in 1Maccabees 2.

H. 1Maccabees 2

Originally written in Hebrew, 1Maccabees describes the history of the beginning of the Hasmonean dynasty from its own perspective, naming it "the family of those men through whom deliverance was given to Israel" (1Macc 5,62). Like the judges and kings of past times, Judas and his brothers saved Israel from internal opponents as well as from the Seleucid armies; this demonstrates God's support and consent so that any concern which questions the legitimacy of the Hasmoneans as "leader," "high priest," and "governor" seems unfounded (14,41-42).

The date of composition lies between the beginning of John Hyrcanus's reign (134 B.C.) and Pompey's invasion into Jerusalem (63 B.C.),[283] i.e., around 100 B.C. Texts from Qumran and passages in Josephus indicate for that time a growing antipathy and opposition to the fusion of political, priestly, and military functions and against the claims of a non-Davidic dynasty and a non-Zadokite family of priests. To Josephus, the Greek

---

[282] Cf. L.H. Schiffmann 1990, 64 (though he is cautious about the eschatological implication); P. Stuhlmacher 1997, 341, with reference to 4QMMT (and *2Bar* 57,2): "'Werke des Gesetzes' sind nach frühjüdischem Sprachgebrauch die Erfüllungen von Geboten der Tora ..., die ihren Tätern im Endgericht zur Gerechtigkeit angerechnet werden" (cf. 326, 330). Hence, both, a restricted understanding of "works of the law" in terms of boundary markers (cf., e.g., J.D.G. Dunn 1992, 103), as well as a proposal of a "pattern of religion" in terms of "covenantal nomism" (cf. M.G. Abegg 1999, 142-146) do not seem to do full justice to the textual evidence of 4QMMT.

[283] It must have been before Pompeius's intervention, because the Romans are portrayed in a positive way.

translation of 1Maccabees was already at hand when he composed his *Antiquitates Judaicae*.

1Macc 2,50-52 offers a particularly illuminating Jewish interpretation of Gen 15:6, as regards the development of the concept of faith. The dying Mattathias entrusts his sons with the following legacy:

1Macc 2,50-52 (LXX)	
(50) Now, my children, show zeal for the law, and give your lives for the covenant of our ancestors!	(50) νῦν τέκνα ζηλώσατε τῷ νόμῳ καὶ δότε τὰς ψυχὰς ὑμῶν ὑπὲρ διαθήκης πατέρων ἡμῶν
(51) Remember the deeds of the ancestors, which they did in their generations! And achieve great honor and an everlasting name!	(51) καὶ μνήσθητε τὰ ἔργα τῶν πατέρων ἃ ἐποίησαν ἐν ταῖς γενεαῖς αὐτῶν καὶ δέξασθε δόξαν μεγάλην καὶ ὄνομα αἰώνιον
(52) Was not Abraham found faithful in trial, and it was reckoned to him as righteousness[284]?	(52) Αβρααμ οὐχὶ ἐν πειρασμῷ εὑρέθη πιστός καὶ ἐλογίσθη αὐτῷ εἰς δικαιοσύνην;

"The use of Abraham's name here is interesting, since it conflates two separate passages in Genesis."[285] (1) While in Neh 9:8 and Sir 44,20, the link to Genesis 15 was less explicit, it cannot be denied in this case, since Gen 15:6b is quoted literally in the words of the Septuagint.[286] Furthermore, the remark of Abraham's faith in the first half of the Genesis-verse (ἐπίστευσεν) is echoed in the reference to Abraham's faithfulness in trial (πιστὸς ἐν πειρασμῷ). (2) On the other hand it is more problematic to assign a single episode of the Abraham narrative in Genesis to the term πειρασμός. As the discussion of passages in the book of *Jubilees* has demonstrated, Jewish tradition knew of at least ten tests Abraham had to endure[287]; this is why several scholars suggest that "this verse [*sc.* 1Macc 2,52] could be a construal of the Abraham tradition in which a number of events in the life of Abraham are considered tests."[288] Against this proposal one has to take into consideration the employed singular form, which is not likely to refer to several events in the life of Abraham, but rather points to but one test, the most challenging one, namely, the sacrifice of Isaac. Another evidence of this view consists in the keyword connection

---

[284] J. Goldstein translates "...to his merit" (1976, 238).

[285] R.A. Harrisville 1992, 127.

[286] Cf., e.g, J.-N. Aletti 2003, 312.

[287] See below page 180.

[288] J.H. Newman 1999, 74; positively taken up in B. Ego/A. Lange 2003, 187 ("Gesamtschau der Abrahamsinterpretation").

established by πειράζειν or πειρασμός,[289] which occurs both in Gen 22:1 and 1Macc 2,52. The growing significance of the Aqedah in Second Temple Judaism finally confirms the concentration of the author on just one test.[290]

As a consequence, what has been in the offing in previous *relectures* of the Abraham cycle materializes in an explicit manner in Mattathias's last words. The scenes of Genesis 15 and 22 are for the first time completely merged. Abraham's faith, ἐπίστευσεν (Gen 15:6a) is replaced by his faithfulness in trial, πιστὸς ἐν πειρασμῷ, which notably falls under the category ἔργα (1Macc 2,51). Thus, Abraham's πίστις "was his 'faithfulness' under test, that is, his unquestioning obedience to God's command."[291] And thus, faith is an act that is temporally and conceptually defined, as it refers to a man's proving his fidelity in a certain situation[292]; this proving, however, receives a reward in the form of righteousness, which is attributed to Abraham according to a rational-necessary and commonly conceivable judgment: Abraham is evidently faithful, and God pronounces a descriptive verdict, saying that Abraham is righteous.

One idea that accounts for the combination of the two passages Genesis 15 and 22 is, that to the author of 1Maccabees, Abraham's faith showed itself most powerfully when he was prepared to sacrifice his son, and therefore indeed believed that God could nevertheless fulfill his promise of great offspring. Already Ramban's exegesis made this connection.[293] Yet apart from the trust in God's promise, the main focus is directed on the deed, which seeks to give everything to God and is able to suffer everything for him,[294] in other words, on the act of πιστὸν εἶναι.

There is a peculiar connection between the early Maccabean heroes, Phinehas, Elijah, and Abraham, as they all share the zeal for the law (1Macc 2,26.52.58) and therefore serve as prototypes for those Jews who are zealous for the law, stand in the covenant, and seek to achieve an everlasting name (2,27.50).[295] Considering what has been said on the notion of

---

[289] As in Sir 44,20, one can presuppose that the original Hebrew text of 1Macc 2,52 read for πειρασμός a derivate of the root נסה.

[290] See further arguments in M. Dibelius/H. Greeven 1984, 207f.

[291] J.D.G. Dunn 1998, 375; cf. J.A. Fitzmyer 2003, 259. This redefinition of "faith" concurs with a redefinition of "righteousness" (cf. G.W. Hansen 1989, 182).

[292] On the transformation of "faith" to "faithfulness" in 1Maccabees, see P. Billerbeck 1926, 200: "Die Umsetzung der gesamten Glaubenshaltung Abrahams beginnt bereits in der vorchristlichen Zeit. Den Anfang in dieser Richtung macht 1Makk 2,52." See also again above note 133 on M. Dibelius's view.

[293] See above page 139, but also pages 143f.

[294] Cf. A. Schlatter 1927, 16.

[295] As for the importance of the Phinehas figure in Jewish theology, W.R. Farmer points to rabbinic tradition that identifies Elijah as Phinehas *redivivus* (1952, 28).

zeal, righteousness, and the covenant in Ps 106:31, it is not unlikely that the reception of the Abraham tradition in 1Macc 2,52 is influenced by the Psalm.[296] In this regard, 1Maccabees converges with the just discussed 4QMMT.

Another connection exists between Abraham and Mattathias: In their zeal to fulfill the divine law, both are willing to sacrifice their children.[297] The reward for such zeal consists in great honor and an everlasting name – and this is at the same time the motivation to be faithful to the law (cf. 1Macc 2,64). However, the reward remains confined to the boundaries of this world. The factual absence of an eschatological soteriology and after-life in 1Maccabees, which stands in stark contrast to 2Maccabees, becomes evident in the political-military fervor of Mattathias. He made the severe decision to fight the attackers even on the Sabbath, rather than to accept martyrdom in expectation of future restoration; the earthly glory of Israel and its religion had priority (1Macc 2,41-48.51).[298]

Apparently the relationship between the sections in 1Maccabees 2 and Sirach 44 is close, as both seek to engrave the remembrance of the heroes into the minds of their contemporaries and show them the way to unending glory through Torah obedience; both have a strong notion of "this-worldly" reward, though the everlasting nature of the rewards has an innate potential towards an eschatological dimension. However, the underlying thought-pattern diverges: Here, it is zealous activism, there sapiential cir-cumspection.

I. Philo of Alexandria

In a final paragraph in our outline of the Jewish reception history of Gen 15:6, we turn to one representative of Hellenistic Judaism, Philo of Alex-

---

[296] B. Ego and A. Lange mention two representatives of this view (2003, 183n.56): D. Dimant 1988, 394; G.J. Brooke 1989, 280f.; but they themselves claim "daß eine Bezug-nahme auf Ps 106,31 unnötig erscheint." Their reasoning however is limited to text-historical arguments so that they neglect the keyword connection given through "zeal" and "righteousness."

[297] Cf. J. Goldstein 1976, 7.

[298] S.J. Gathercole (2002, 50, appealing to J. Goldstein 1976, 12, 26) points to this connection of "fighting on the Sabbath" and "denial of resurrection." "1 Maccabees's eschatological skepticism is connected to its politico-religious activism, 2 Maccabees's resurrection theology to its strict sabbatarianism" (57). – In contrast to Mattathias's deci-sion, Eleazar and a mother with her seven sons refused any compromise for the sake of "natural love of life" (2Macc 6,20). Out of love for the law they rather died, with the hope that "the king of the universe will raise us up to an everlasting renewal of life, be-cause we have died for his laws" (2Macc 7,9).

andria.[299] Some might argue that his idea of faith could be easily passed over, as it is strongly colored by his philosophical and apologetic interests.[300] The value of Philo's contribution for a biblical-theological study is oftentimes assessed with skepticism.[301] Nevertheless, the abundant references to Abraham and his faith, partly with explicit reference to Gen 15:6, require an analysis of what Philo conceives of as faith – not least since he has been called the first theologian of faith.[302]

A brief word should be said in this context on another Jewish writer who is generally mentioned together with Philo in one breath: Josephus. In notable contrast to Philo, Gen 15:6 does not play a role in Josephus's writings. Though the πιστ- group in general is very prominent,[303] his retelling the story of Genesis 15 lacks a reference to 15:6 and Abraham's faith. It would be an interesting task to find out why. Was it because of the shift that had taken place in Jewish theology regarding the concept of faith – from "faith" to "faithfulness"[304]? For Josephus directs his attention to highlighting Abraham's deeds. But these are hypotheses argued *e silentio*, and therefore we can leave this issue aside and turn to Philo.

The vast *Corpus Philonicum* preserves not only the greatest amount of scriptural interpretation within the early Jewish writings, but also the most comprehensive interpretation and *relecture* of the narratives surrounding the patriarch Abraham.[305] Philo's presentation of Abraham (and the other Fathers and Mothers of Israel) correlates to the life and status of the upper class Alexandrinian Jews[306]: They strive for the Hellenistic virtues, combine wealth and high education, experience God's help in enforcing their right of hospitality, aspire to full societal privileges, and conduct their lives according to Roman law. Overall, they seek to create a harmonization between Hellenistic ideals and Jewish identity.[307]

---

[299] On Philo's concept of faith, see especially E. Bréhier 1925, 206-225; A. Schlatter 1927, 60-80; M. Preisker 1936; H. Moxnes 1980, 155-164; D.M. Hay 1989, 463-468 (Hay lists additional literature, 463n.10); most recently M. Böhm 2004, 378, 391f.

[300] Cf. F. Neugebauer 1961, 162; J.D.G. Dunn 1988, 202.

[301] Cf. S.J. Gathercole 2002, 29.

[302] W. Bousset 1926, 447.

[303] On Josephus's use of the πιστ-stem, see A. Schlatter 1927, 582-585; D.M. Hay 1989, 468-470; and especially D.R. Lindsay 1993a.

[304] J.A. Fitzmyer considers this possibility (2003, 262).

[305] Cf. M. Böhm 2004, 378. She refers to the following passages: *Abr* 60-276; *Virt* 207.211-219; *Praem* 27-30.57-58.60; *VitMos* 1,7.76; *Leg* 2,59; 3,24.27.83-85; *Cher* 4-10.18.31.40; *Sacr* 5.43.59; *Det* 59-60.124; *Post* 17-18.27.62.75; *Ebr* 24; *Sobr* 17-18.56; *Conf* 79; *Migr* 1-225; *Her* 1-316; *Congr* 1-180; *Fug* 200; *Mut* 1-270; *Somn* 1,47.52.64-67.70.160-162.214; 2,226-227.244.255; *QuaestGen* 3,1-4,153.

[306] On the following, see M. Böhm 2004, 380f.

[307] Cf. S. Sandmel 1971, 106; G.W. Hansen 1989, 190: "Philo's primary goal was to prove that all the best elements of Greek philosophy are embodied in Abraham."

The above-mentioned study of D.M. Hay concluded that in Philo it is not the subjective "faith in God" which is prevalent in his use of πίστις, but the meaning "objective ground for subjective faith."[308] However, it is noteworthy that passages describing human faith by πίστις occur especially in relation to Abraham.[309] For our purpose, these passages are of primary significance. In several places and contexts and with different intentions, Philo refers to Gen 15:6, to Abraham's faith and – only occasionally! – to God's appraisal of it. The theme of faith is so prominent in Philo that "it reigns supreme in his theology,"[310] though not being the chief concept which encapsulates the totality of one's relationship with God.[311]

Philo interprets Scripture on two distinguishable levels, first according to the literary-historical sense and second according to the allegorical-universal sense. Three sets of his writings or commentary series on the Pentateuch correspond to these two levels: The *Expositio Legis*, the Allegorical Commentary, and the *Quaestiones et solutiones*.[312] In the following we will present the relevant references to Gen 15:6, classified among his commentary series.[313] The passages quoted are selective insofar as they comprise Philo's direct comments on the patriarch's faith. Below we will also take into account Philo's more extensive elaborations.

(1) Of the *Expositio*, possibly "written for a wider Jewish audience,"[314] twelve of the fifteen books are preserved in Greek; in this rather systematically organized work Philo adopts a literal interpretation. Abraham's faith appears in the following passages, either in the form of a quote of Gen 15:6a or as allusion to it.

Abr 262.268.273[315]	
(262) ... "he believed God" ...	(262) ... ἐπίστευσε τῷ θεῷ ...
(268) Faith towards God, then, is the one sure and infallible good ...	(268) μόνον οὖν ἀψευδὲς καὶ βέβαιον ἀγαθὸν ἡ πρὸς θεὸν πίστις ...
(273) That God marvelling at Abraham's faith in him, repaid him with faithfulness	(273) ὃς τῆς πρὸς αὐτὸν πίστεως ἀγάμενος τὸν ἄνδρα πίστιν ἀντιδίδωσιν αὐτῷ, τὴν

---

[308] D.M. Hay 1989, 465; cf. 470. He also states that "in the vast majority of instances Philo does use the term in some relation to his religious convictions." Humans require objective foundations of faith, namely, "revelatory signs from God." Expressions parallel to πίστις are ἀπόδειξις, δεῖγμα, and τεκμήριον (468). Hay thus seeks to correct interpretations of Philo's concept of faith that connect it to his mysticism and inwardness. See however below note 333.

[309] Cf., e.g., D.M. Hay 1989, 464n.11.

[310] J.B. Lightfoot 1896, 160.

[311] Cf. A. Schlatter 1927, 74.

[312] Cf. G.E. Sterling 2000, 790f.

[313] See the "Scripture index" in J.W. Earp 1962, 202 (also A. Schlatter 1927, 579).

[314] G.E. Sterling 2000, 791.

[315] See F.H. Colson 1935, 128f.

by confirming with an oath the gifts which He had promised, and here He no longer talked with him as God with man but as a friend with a familiar.	δι' ὅρκου βεβαίωσιν ὧν ὑπέσχετο δωρεῶν, οὐκέτι μόνον ὡς ἀνθρώπῳ θεός, ἀλλὰ καὶ ὡς φίλος γνωρίμῳ διαλεγόμενος.

Virt 216.218[316]

(216) ... He [sc. Abraham] is the first person spoken of as believing in God, since he first grasped a firm and unswerving conception of the truth ... And having gained faith, the most sure and certain of the virtues, he gained with it all the other virtues, so that by those among whom he settled he was regarded as king.	(216) ... πιστεῦσαι λέγεται τῷ θεῷ πρῶτος, ἐπειδὴ καὶ πρῶτος ἀκλινῆ καὶ βεβαίαν ἔσχεν ὑπόληψιν ... κτησάμενος δὲ πίστιν τὴν τῶν ἀρετῶν βεβαιοτάτην, συνεκτᾶτο καὶ τὰς ἄλλας ἁπάσας, ὡς παρὰ τοῖς ὑποδεξαμένοις νομίζεσθαι βασιλεύς
(218) ... he who believed nothing created rather than the Uncreated and Father of all ...	(218) ... πιστεύσαντα δὲ μηδενὶ τῶν ἐν γενέσει πρὸ τοῦ ἀγενήτου καὶ πάντων πατρός ...

Praem 27[317]

The leader in adopting the godly creed, who first passed over from vanity to truth, came to his consummation by virtue gained through instruction, and he received for his reward belief towards God.	ὁ μὲν οὖν ἡγεμὼν τῆς θεοφιλοῦς δόξης, ὁ πρῶτος ἐκ τύφου μεθορμισάμενος πρὸς ἀλήθειαν, διδακτικῇ χρησάμενος ἀρετῇ πρὸς τελείωσίν ἄθλον αἴρεται τὴν πρὸς θεὸν πίστιν.

(2) The Allegorical Commentary offers a running interpretation of Gen 2:1-41:25 distributed into around thirty-one books, of which twenty are extant in Greek and a fragment of another in Armenian. With this allegorical exposition Philo probably addressed advanced students of the Greek Bible.

Leg 3,228[318]

"Abraham believed God and was held to be righteous."	Ἀβραάμ γέ τοι ἐπίστευσε τῷ θεῷ, καὶ δίκαιος ἐνομίσθη

Migr 43-44[319]

(43) [Gen 12:1 is] a testimony to the faith with which the soul believed God, exhibiting its thankfulness not as called out by	(43) μαρτυρία[.] πίστεως ἦν ἐπίστευσεν ἡ ψυχὴ θεῷ, οὐκ ἐκ τῶν ἀποτελεσμάτων ἐπιδεικνυμένη τὸ εὐχάριστον, ἀλλ' ἐκ

---

[316] See F.H. Colson 1939, 294-297.
[317] See F.H. Colson 1939, 326-329.
[318] See F.H. Colson/G.H. Whitaker 1929, 456f.
[319] See F.H. Colson/G.H. Whitaker 1932, 156f.

accomplished facts, but by expectation of what was to be.
(44) ... it [*sc.* the soul] found as reward faith, a perfect good. For it says a little later: "Abraham believed God."

προσδοκίας τῶν μελλόντων.

(44) πίστιν, ἀγαθὸν τέλειον, ἆθλον εὕρεται· καὶ γὰρ αὖθις λέγεται, ὅτι ἐπίστευσεν Ἀβραὰμ τῷ θεῷ.

Her 90-95[320]

(90) The words "Abraham believed God" are a necessary addition so speak the praise due to him who has believed. Yet, perhaps it may be asked, do you consider this worthy of praise? When it is God who speaks and promises, who would not pay heed ...?
(92) ... to believe God alone and join no other with Him is no easy matter ...
(93) ... to believe God alone, even as He alone is truly faithful – this is a work of great and celestial understanding ...
(94) And it is well said "his faith was counted to him for righteousness," for nothing is so righteous than to have a faith towards God which is pure and unalloyed.

(90) Ἀναγκαίως οὖν ἐπιλέγεται ἐπίστευσεν Ἀβραὰμ τῷ θεῷ πρὸς ἔπαινον τοῦ πεπιστευκότος. καίτοι, τάχα ἄν τις εἴποι, τοῦτ᾽ ἄξιον ἐπαίνου κρίνετε; τίς δὲ οὐκ ἄν τι λέγοντι καὶ ὑπισχνουμένῳ θεῷ προσέχοι τὸν νοῦν...;
(92) ... μόνῳ θεῷ χωρὶς ἑτέρου προσπαραλήψεως οὐ ῥᾴδιον πιστεῦσαι ...
(93) ... μόνῳ δὲ πιστεῦσαι θεῷ τῷ καὶ πρὸς ἀλήθειαν μόνῳ πιστῷ μεγάλης καὶ ὀλυμπίου ἔργον διανοίας ἐστί ...
(94) εὖ δὲ τὸ φάναι λογισθῆναι τὴν πίστιν εἰς δικαιοσύνην αὐτῷ· δίκαιον γὰρ οὐδὲν οὕτως, ὡς ἀκράτῳ καὶ ἀμιγεῖ τῇ πρὸς θεὸν πίστει κεχρῆσθαι.

Mut 177.186[321]

(177) "And Abraham believed God and it was counted to him as righteousness."
(186) "Abraham then has believed God," but he believed only as a man, so that you may recognize the weakness, the distinctive mark of the mortal ...

(177) ἐπίστευσε δὲ Ἀβραάμ τῷ θεῷ, καὶ ἐλογίσθη αὐτῷ εἰς δικαιοσύνην.
(186) πεπίστευκεν οὖν Ἀβραὰμ τῷ θεῷ, ἀλλ᾽ ὡς ἄνθρωπος πεπίστευκεν, ἵνα τὸ ἴδιον τοῦ θνητοῦ γνῷς ...

Immut 4[322]

He brings to God the dearly loved, the only trueborn offspring of the soul... [He had] knowledge of the unwavering steadfastness that belongs to the Existent; for in this we are told he had put his faith.

ὃς τὸ ἀγαπητὸν καὶ μόνον τῆς ψυχῆς ἔγγονον γνήσιον... τὴν περὶ τὸ ὂν ἀνενδοίαστον ἔγνω βεβαιότητα, ᾗ λέγεται πεπιστευκέναι.

---

[320] See F.H. Colson/G.H. Whitaker 1932, 326-329.
[321] See F.H. Colson/G.H. Whitaker 1934, 232f., 236f.
[322] See F.H. Colson/G.H. Whitaker 1930, 12f.

(3) In the third commentary series, the twelve-book *Quaestiones*,[323] Philo presents his exposition of Gen 2:4-28:9 and Ex 6:2-30:10 in a dialogic question-answer style. The brief answers contain both literal and allegorical interpretations and could have been intended for the larger Jewish community.[324] Ten books are preserved in the Armenian translation and in some Greek fragments. No comment is extant on Gen 15:6 and on Abraham's faith. Possibly, those parts of the commentary that deal with Gen 11:26-15:6 have been lost, but on the other hand in this writing Philo has not elaborated yet the correlation between learning and the reward of learning: faith, which we encounter in the other two sets of commentaries.[325] Nevertheless, some hints as for the character of Abraham's faith are discernible: Abraham believes without doubt (*QuaestGen* 3,2) and without ambiguity and hesitation (*QuaestGen* 3,58); "to him who has faith in God all uncertainty is alien" (*QuaestGen* 4,17).

Philo not only recounts and embellishes the narratives of Genesis, but also paints over them with his own philosophical and theological insights. While it is true that adequate attention is to be given to the differences between Philo's three sets of commentaries, his presentation and interpretation of Abraham's faith appears to be fairly consistent, so that a comprehensive portrayal is justified.[326] How, according to Philo, is faith attained, what is faith, what is faith not, and what does faith entail?

(1) Abraham never ceased to seek for the "father of all things," until he received a clear vision of his existence and providence (*Virt* 214-215). He also "crave[d] for kinship with him" (*Virt* 218). Therefore, faith is a great work of understanding (ἔργον διανοίας, *Her* 93) and a reward and recognition for successful learning and piety (*Praem* 27).[327] It is the transition "from vanity to truth" (*Praem* 27).

(2) Hence, faith is a "firm and unswerving conception of the truth" (*Virt* 216). The one who believes does so "firmly and without wavering" (*Her* 101; cf. 95), without doubt, hesitation and uncertainty (*QuaestGen* 3,2.58; 4,17).[328] The occasional use of the perfect tense (πεπίστευκεν) conveys the continuance of Abraham's faith (*Her* 90; *Immut* 4; *Mut* 177.186.218). Philo famously characterizes faith as "the most sure and certain of the virtues" (*Virt* 216) the "queen of virtues (βασιλὶς τῶν ἀρετῶν)" (*Abr* 270),

---

[323] See R. Marcus 1953.

[324] Cf. G.E. Sterling 2000, 790.

[325] *QuaestGen* 3,1 begins with Gen 15:7 (cf. M. Böhm 2004, 392 with n.51).

[326] See however M. Böhm 2004, 384.

[327] Elsewhere, Philo says that humans are also free to reject in disbelief the evidence of God and his will (cf. D.M. Hay 1989, 468, referring to *Spec* 1,273; *Prov* 2,72).

[328] But see *Mut* 182-183.

the "most perfect of virtues (ἡ τελειοτάτη ἀρετῶν)" (*Her* 91) a "perfect good" and a "reward (ἆθλον)" (*Migr* 44).[329]

The fact that faith is counted as righteousness is by no means a paradox, but rather follows nature (φύσις); when people marvel at this correlation between faith and righteousness it is in fact a proof for their unbelief (ἀπιστία), for faith is merely an act of righteousness (δικαιοσύνης ἔργον) (*Her* 95). The natural logic that is inherent in the correspondence of faith and righteousness might explain the interesting observation that in quoting or alluding to the Genesis-verse Philo limits himself mostly to referring to Abraham's faith in the first half of the verse, while leaving aside the second. Likewise, the modification of the quote from ἐλογίσθη to ἐνομίσθη in *Leg* 3,228 indicates that apparently Philo does not lend much weight to the term λογίζεσθαι[330] and that the second part of the verse presents itself to him as a self-evident result of the first.[331]

Faith contains also the component of hope in promised, future things (τὰ μέλλοντα). Though they are not physically present yet, they are in fact already there due to the steadfastness of the one who promises (*Migr* 43-44); that the promise will come to pass is beyond question or doubt (*Her* 101; *QuaestGen* 3,2; *Mut* 177).

Time and again Philo stresses that faith can *per definitionem* only be directed to God – belief in God is belief in the "Uncreated" (*Virt* 218), the "Existent" (τὸ ὄν, *Abr* 270; *Praem* 27; *Her* 95).

(3) Therefore, on the other hand, faith cannot be directed to anything else other than God. All created things are in themselves wholly untrustworthy (ἄπιστος, *Her* 93), such as "high offices or fame and honours or abundance of wealth and noble birth or health and efficacy of the senses or strength and beauty of the body" (*Abr* 263; *Virt* 218),[332] "the bodily and the external (τὰ σωματικὰ καὶ τὰ ἐκτός)" (*Abr* 269), "our dim reasonings and insecure conjectures" (*Leg* 3,228). Those who have set their faith in these things disbelieve God, and those who disbelieve in them have set their faith in the supreme being, which is God (*Abr* 269).[333]

---

[329] R. Bultmann 1958, 317, with a quote from A. Schlatter 1927, 67: "[Philo] versteht die πίστις als eine διάθεσις der Seele, als deren vollkommene Verfassung, als eine ἀρετή. Sie steht bei ihm deshalb am Ende, 'als Ziel der auf Gott gerichteten Lebensbewegung'."

[330] Cf. H.-W. Heidland 1936, 101.

[331] Cf. A. Schlatter 1927, 66: "[Gen 15:6b gilt] ihm als die mit dem ersten [Versteil] gegebene Folge, die im Glauben selbst begründet ist." – On the theological necessity of the divine act of λογίζεσθαι, see however above page 129.

[332] Cf. the sequence of fateful objects of faith in *Her* 92: "riches and repute and office and friends and health and strength and many other things."

[333] Cf. F.E. Wieser 1987, 163. See also O. Schmitz 1922, 114 ("mystische Versenkung der Seele in das eine reine Sein Gottes"); A. Schlatter 1927, 66f.; R. Bultmann 1959,

Despite the certainty of faith, Philo makes one qualification: The fact that human beings are created, mortal, perishable – simply human – requires a qualitative differentiation between human πίστις and God's πίστις: His is "sound and complete in every way" (*Mut* 182), while human's is but an "image (εἰκών)" of the "archetype (ἀρχέτυπος)" (*Mut* 183).

(4) The fruits of faith are manifold and magnificent: "life-long joy, the perpetual vision of the Existent – what can anyone conceive more profitable or more august than these?" (*Praem* 27). Together with the virtue of faith Abraham gained all the other virtues and was regarded as king (*Virt* 216); God, the "friend of virtue," rewards faith with all other virtues and powers (*Virt* 218), but also with his faithfulness (*Abr* 273).[334]

It is apparent that Philo has utmost respect for the faith of the patriarch. He expresses this in the context of his explanation of Gen 15:6 when he calls Abraham the friend of God (*Abr* 273), "the perfect (ὁ τέλος)" (*Immut* 4) or "the virtuous (ὁ ἀστεῖος)" (*Mut* 180).[335] Philo rebukes the objection that Abraham's faith is something self-evident, a necessary and inevitable reaction to a promise given by God. No, it is indeed worthy of great praise (ἔπαινος). The admiration of Abraham's faith is due the empirical observation that faith is nothing patently obvious – rather, disbelief (ἀπιστία) reigns in general; on the other hand there is no need to marvel at it since it simply a natural act of righteousness, which God rewards according to the principles of nature (*Her* 90-95).[336]

However, there is yet another episode in Abraham's life that receives like admiration by Philo: the sacrifice of Isaac. Compared to the elaborate literal and allegorical expositions on Abraham's faith, however, he seems to give less attention to Abraham's readiness to sacrifice Isaac. Yet the main section narrating this event (*Abr* 167-207) begins with these words: "For I might almost say that all the other actions which won the favor of God are surpassed by this." Hence, for Philo, there is a close structural correlation between Abraham's faith in God's promise of a son and his obedience to God's command to sacrifice his son. Both find God's momentous, far-reaching approval.

This correlation between Genesis 15 and 22 can be confirmed textually: In *Quod Deus immutabilis sit*, the reader is told why the "perfect Abraham" presumably bound the feet of his son (*Immut* 4; cf. Gen 22:9): "It

---

202f.: "Die πίστις ist also im Grunde die Festigkeit, die Unerschütterlichkeit des Menschen, die im Sich-Verlassen auf das einzig Feste, das einzig Seiende begründet ist."

[334] Both "faith" and "faithfulness" are represented through πίστις. This means that this term once denotes Abraham's faith or trust in God, then it refers to God's faithfulness in keeping his promise to Abraham.

[335] See also J.W. Earp 1962, 271, for a list of other attributes that Philo gives to Abraham.

[336] Cf. M. Dibelius/H. Greeven 1984, 216f.

may be that he was taught to see how changeable and inconstant was creation, through his knowledge of the unwavering steadfastness that belongs to the Existent; for in this we are told that he had put his trust." Accordingly, binding Isaac's feet is an expression of faith. In a more illuminating passage from Philo's most important work on the history of Abraham, in *De Abrahamo*, right after mentioning Abraham's faith, he refers to the climax of the Aqedah narrative, the oath that God swore (Gen 22:16) and adds the "crowning saying of Moses" (*Abr* 275) from Genesis 26 that Abraham did the divine law and the divine commands (Gen 26:5).[337] He concludes his treatise by saying: "And when they have God's promises before them what should men do but trust in them most firmly? Such was the life of the first, the founder of the nation, one who obeyed the law, some will say, but rather ... himself a law and an unwritten statute" (*Abr* 275-276). At another place Philo explains that nature itself is the oldest precept, and the law given by Moses is nothing but a commentary on the life of these men (*Abr* 3-5)[338] Hence, in the quintessence of his re-narration of the story of Abraham, Philo joins very closely, both thematically and contextually, zealous submission to the impulse of "unwritten nature" or "unwritten statute" with faith in God's promises. Abraham was the first to accomplish both and thus represents implicitly the model to be followed.

We have seen that the combination of Genesis 15 and 22 is a common strand in Jewish tradition. Philo adds another nuance to it: He retains a clear borderline between the inner, psychological function of faith and the outward proof of faithfulness, thus avoiding a complete amalgamation such as that of 1Macc 2,52.[339] But both aspects are connected in that both faith in the promise and obedience to the command follow the power and principle of nature. Since they are bound to the "unwritten nature" or "unwritten statute," both faith and obedience are considered a "work" ($\check{\epsilon}\rho\gamma o\nu$). As both comply with nature, they do not bring about a claim for merit before God, but carry within themselves God's favor and approval – for God and nature are in harmony. An additional divine act of counting is not required.

J. Summary

The foregoing overview of the interpretation of Gen 15:6 in Jewish theology has yielded a wide array of results and by no means a straightforward

---

[337] Cf. J.D. Levenson 1987, 59.

[338] Without being taught, pious men like Abraham, Enoch, or Noah listened to their inner voice and followed the order of nature.

[339] Cf. H.-W. Heidland 1936, 94.

line of development in the way how the authors conceived of Abraham's faith and God's judgment on it. If we now seek to recapitulate the results we have to be aware of several, mostly interrelated, issues that have an influence as to how Gen 15:6 has been viewed and used: genre, interest of reception, date of composition, historical and theological background, etc.

The different kinds of literature dealt with comprise a historical psalm (Psalm 106), a penitential prayer (Nehemiah 9), a retrospective on the great ancestors in a wisdom framework (Sirach 44), a stylized legacy of a revolutionary (1Maccabees 2), a "Rewritten Bible" (*Jubilees* 14), a free paraphrase of biblical material (4QPseudo-Jubilees), a halakhic letter of a religious "fundamentalist" (4QMMT), and apologetic-philosophical treatises (Philo). In two cases, the context is a non-Abrahamic one (Psalm 106; 4QMMT[340]). The time period covered ranges from not long after the exile until New Testament times and consequently presupposes greatly differing circumstances, such as the still existing dispersion of the people after the catastrophe of the exile in Persian times (Psalm 106; Nehemiah 9), the beginning of (Sirach 44) and the time amidst the Maccabean period (1Maccabees; *Jubilees*; 4QPseudo-Jubilees; 4QMMT) in its confrontation with Hellenism, as well as the combination of Jewish religious traditions with Hellenistic thought (Philo).[341]

Despite this complex situation it is worthwhile to schematize the obtained results in a systematic manner in order to find distinct trajectories of tradition and multiple attestations of single traditions. On several occasions, the texts make mention of Abraham in a retrospective account of Israel's history, and he appears either as the one whose faithful conduct parallels the perpetual faithfulness of God – as opposed to Israel's unfaithfulness (Nehemiah 9[342]) –, or he is listed in a row of Israel's heroes and serves as a model of faithfulness (Sirach 44; 1Maccabees 2). The mention of faith/faithfulness and God's acceptance of it is generally embedded in the idea of God's faithfulness and righteousness in relation to Israel throughout its history: He stopped the plague after Phinehas's intercession (Ps 106:30) and always acted in love according his covenant (106:45); he is righteous (Neh 9:8.33) and keeps covenant and love (9:32). However, there is a growing tendency – already discernible in the just mentioned passages – to link and interconnect God's act towards his people to the faithful and righteous conduct of the individual: Thus it is said that Abra-

---

[340] See also *Jub* 30,17.

[341] At the same time, this time-frame marks not only "a period of many-faceted exegesis," but also of "scripture production." "During this period, the history of interpretation is also the history of the canon" (M. Hengel 1994, 158).

[342] Similarly, the zealous faithfulness of Phinehas in Psalm 106 interrupts the line of Israel's disobedience throughout history.

ham "entered into a covenant with God" (Sir 44,20) and even that one is to give one's life "for the covenant of our ancestors" (1Macc 2,50); "doing what is righteous and good in His eyes" leads to righteousness (4QMMT C 31). Consequently, Abraham's obedient faithfulness – it is mentioned almost ten times in *Jubilees* – and its paradigmatic function receive more and more attention.

The most obvious materializing of this tendency is the connection of Genesis 15 with Genesis 22, which begins in a still subtle manner in Neh 9:8 through the change of the mode of אמן from *hiphil* (Gen 15:6) to *niphal*, becomes more obvious in Ben Sira's statement about Abraham's being πιστός ἐν πειρασμῷ (Sir 44,20), then shows itself structurally in the arrangement of both Abraham narratives in 4QPseudo-Jubilees, and culminates in the full conflation of the essence of both narratives in 1Macc 2,52. Philo, on the other hand, unites both Abraham's faith and his faithfulness by associating both to "unwritten nature."

All this conforms to the observation of an "emerging importance of the Aqedah in Jewish theologizing"[343] and the ensuing glorification of the patriarch.[344] Overall, one considers as a unity faith and faithfulness, trust and obedience, "Vertrauen" and "Treue."[345] The tradition of regarding Abraham's faith in the light of the sacrifice of Isaac became a common property.[346]

However, though Abraham's readiness to sacrifice his son symbolizes the climax of his faithfulness, it is but *one* aspect of his general compliance to the νόμος ὑψίστου (Sir 44,20), it is *one* part of his ἔργα (1Macc 2,51), *one* proof of his faithfulness – though the most significant one – (*Jub* 18,16), and ultimately *one* part of the "works of the law," of keeping God's precepts.[347] Consequently, the underlying understanding is that in all that Abraham did, he observed and fulfilled the whole Torah without compromise; the Torah, consequently, becomes a trans-temporal pre-Mosaic entity.[348] Hence, he is model for all his descendants, i.e., for all members of

---

[343] J.D.G. Dunn 1998, 375.

[344] Cf. O. Schmitz 1922, 115.

[345] Cf. M. Dibelius/H. Greeven 1984, 209, on the rationale of the merging of Genesis 15 and 22: "Trotz der Versuchung bleibt er seinem Gott treu – darin zeigt sich sein Glaube; und weil er Gottes Willen vertraut, hält er auch in der schwersten Versuchung stand – so erklärt sich seine Treue."

[346] Cf. K. Haacker 1993, 134. See also Jas 2:21-24 and Heb 11:17-19.

[347] Cf. CD 3,2-4 (see following note) with 4QMMT. On the notion of the offering of Isaac as ἔργα νόμου, see J.D.G. Dunn 1997, 270.

[348] See also CD 3,2-4, which shows overlaps to the Abraham image of *Jubilees*: "Abraham ... was counted as a friend for keeping God's precepts (בשמרו מצות אל) and not following the desire of his spirit. And he passed (them) on (וימסור) to Isaac and to Jacob, and they kept (them) and were written up as friends" (see F. García Martínez/E.J.C. Tig-

the covenant to do "all the commandments" (Neh 10:30), to keep the law entirely (Sir 44,20)[349] – even to the degree of fulfilling the law with zeal (ζηλοῦν), that is, if called for, through bloodshed and self-sacrifice (1Macc 2,50[350]). Already before, but even more prominently after the victory of the Maccabeans, obedience to the law gained central significance. That this process has its roots already in the Abraham narratives of Genesis has been shown above,[351] yet the intensification and radicalization is a later development.[352] A distinct motif of remembrance makes the heroes of the past function as examples: "The righteous deeds [of the Fathers] will not be forgotten" (Sir 44,10); the community is called to "remember David, a man of righteous deeds" (4QMMT C 25) and to "remember the deeds of the ancestors" (1Macc 2,51).

Together with the tendency to concentrate on the human preconditions for the acceptance with God, there has been a development towards the "eschatologizing" and "soteriologizing" in the Jewish interpretation of Gen 15:6. In contrast to certain prominent, modernistic trends in biblical scholarship, especially the dimension of eschatology and the notion of final judgment in Second Temple Jewish writings need to be brought to the fore again.[353] With regard to Abraham, Genesis 15 itself does not transcend history; Abraham will have a long life, but die (15:15), and the blessings of the covenant will be transferred to his descendants, but remain within time

chelaar 1997/1998, 554f.). Notably, Abraham is portrayed here even as teacher of the law, which is also a topic, for instance, in *TestBen* 10 (cf. Gen 18:19). That Abraham kept the whole (unwritten) Torah before it was given at Mount Sinai is also expressed by Philo (*Abr* 275) as well as in *mQid* 4,14 (both with reference to Gen 26:5) and *mNed* 3,11 (see B. Ego 1996, 25f., 37, with further passages from rabbinic literature). The text of the Damascus document that follows on the quoted passage, states that God established a covenant with Israel forever (CD 3,13) and built a "safe home" in Israel (בית נאמן, 3,19; cf. 2Sam 7:16), but also that only the one who lives according to God's will live (3,16; cf. Lev 18:5) and who remains steadfast in the "safe home" "will acquire eternal life (חיי נצח)" (3,20) (see on these passages E.P. Sanders 1977, 295, who interprets them in terms of "covenantal nomism" – based on God's initiative to build a "safe home" –, but also S.J. Gathercole 2002, 100-102 [cf. also 2004], who rightly sees a causal connection between obedience and final salvation).

[349] Since the ending of 4QMMT is reminiscent of Deut 6:25 ("to observe this entire commandment") one could appeal to this passage as well. See also *Jub* 15,1; 16,21; 21,5, where it is reported that Abraham even observed the details of the festival calendar.

[350] Implicitly also in Ps 106:30-31.

[351] See above chapters III.E.II, III.E.III, III.E.IV, but also IV.A and IV.B.

[352] Cf. the term "Toraverschärfung" coined by H. Braun (see also M. Hengel 1976, 231f.).

[353] Especially the New Perspective seems to minimize these elements. See P. Stuhlmacher 2001, 353f. and especially S.J. Gathercole 2002, 23f., with reference to T. Laato 1995, 156; M. Hengel/R. Deines 1995, 4, against E.P. Sanders, J.D.G. Dunn, and N.T. Wright. See also the discussion in H.-M. Rieger 1996.

and space; the notion of continuous blessing shows that the idea of "soteriology" is nonetheless present, though understood in historical and not eschatological terms. There is still no clear notion of personal eschatology in Sirach and 1Maccabees, which speak of earthly, but everlasting glory (Sir 44,19) and "great honor and an everlasting name" (1Macc 2,51), grounding in Abraham's faithfulness.[354] Obviously, the gap between such "this-worldly"-thinking and individual eschatology is not unbridgeable; rather, the texts basically contain eschatology *in nuce* due to their recurring idea of "eternity." And indeed, already the Septuagint – if its broader theological framework is taken into account – makes Abraham cross the boundary to the "other world" and receive the positive verdict of righteousness in the final judgment, based on his act of faith. When *Jub* 19,19 says that Abraham was "recorded on the heavenly tablets as the friend of the Lord," this carries within itself the idea of afterlife, based on faithfulness. Or, as 4QMMT states, the one who reenacts Abraham's faithfulness will "rejoice at the end of time" (C 30).

K. Appendix

I. The Passive Voice in Genesis 15:6

We have seen that several passages that quote, translate, allude to Gen 15:6 use the passive voice instead of the active וַיַּחְשְׁבֶהָ of the Masoretic Text. The use of the passive resolves the ambiguity of the syntax regarding the subject of this verb. Regardless of what exegetical solution is given in determining the meaning of Gen 15:6b – is it Abraham or God who "considers"? – one might ask the question how the remarkable change from active to passive came about, or, going beyond this question: which was the original wording?

The *opinio communis* – expressed more or less explicitly – used to attribute the change into the passive voice in the Septuagint (plus the addition "Abram" in Gen 15:6a) to the translator(s), who sought to confer to the verse an unambiguous syntactical organization. Hence, it has been assumed that the translator(s) worked with a Hebrew *Vorlage* which is either identical to or at least essentially congruent with the Masoretic Text. Notwithstanding this unanimity, with respect to other evidence, this view is to be challenged; instead, there are signals for the existence of a further, rather widespread Hebrew text that is at variance to the Masoretic Text and might have served as *Vorlage* for at least some of the following texts.[355]

---

[354] Ps 106:31, too, includes the notion of everlasting fame.
[355] Cf. especially R. Mosis 1989, 89-93.

The extant Greek text of 1Maccabees, generally and persuasively regarded as a translation of a Hebrew original, has in 2,52 the passive ἐλογίσθη, which is customarily attributed to the Septuagint-translation of Gen 15:6. More likely, however, the *Vorlage* used by the translator of 1Maccabees read something like וַתֵּחָשֶׁב לוֹ לִצְדָקָה.[356] This expression now is literally found in Ps 106:31, whose Septuagint version is identical both to LXX Gen 15:6b and 1Macc 2,52: καὶ ἐλογίσθη αὐτῷ εἰς δικαιοσύνην. Since Psalm 106 is dependent on and draws its statements from a version of the Pentateuch that comes close to its final form, one could assume that the Hebrew passive wording in Ps 106:31 is connected with and due to an alleged, originally passive version of Gen 15:6b.[357] Alternatively, it could be argued that the psalmist changed his Hebrew quote of Gen 15:6 into the passive voice and that the "use of the passive in the Septuagint may be influenced in part by the similar ascription of righteousness to Phinehas in Ps 106:30-31."[358] The second explanation appears less likely on first glance,[359] but further evidence has to tip the scale in one direction or the other.

The book of *Jubilees*, whose extant Ethiopic version most probably derives from a Hebrew *Urtext*, has the passive wording both in 14,6 (about Abraham)[360] and 31,23 (about Isaac). Unfortunately, those two passages are apparently not among the Hebrew text pieces of *Jubilees* found at Qumran, so that one can only hypothesize about how the passive was introduced into the text: Either, the Septuagint tradition is responsible for this alteration or the Hebrew original read again וַתֵּחָשֶׁב לוֹ לִצְדָקָה.[361] One significant document now presents a quotation of Gen 15:6 in Hebrew: 4QMMT. While Ps 106:31 used a narrative form, 4QMMT has a perfect form with *waw consecutivum* to indicate the orientation "to the end of time" (C 30); it reads וְנֶחְשְׁבָה לְךָ לצדקה. This statement might have as its immediate background Ps 106:31,[362] and this would pose again the question how the passive voice found its way into the Psalm. On the other

---

[356] R. Mosis observes that in its translation of חשב the Septuagint only uses a preposition if the original has one, with the exception of Job 41:19 (1989, 90). This is why one has to assume for the original of 1Macc 2,52 a preposition *le* before צְדָקָה, which was rendered with εἰς.

[357] Cf. R. Mosis 1989, 90.

[358] J.A. Fitzmyer 2003, 261n.7. Cf. L. Gaston 1980, 50: Presumably, "the wording of Ps 106:31a ... has influenced the rendering of Gen 15:6b in the LXX."

[359] Cf. R. Mosis 1989, 90f.n.94: "[D]aß eine Bemerkung zu Pinhas die Wiedergabe eines für wichtig angesehenen Textes zu Abraham beeinflußt haben sollte, ... ist sehr unwahrscheinlich."

[360] Cf. J.C. VanderKam 1977, 159.

[361] The latter position is taken in R. Mosis 1989, 92.

[362] Cf., e.g., M.G. Abegg 1994, 52-55 (referred to in M.W. Yeung 2002, 247).

hand, one could assume a direct dependence to Gen 15:6[363] so that the passive voice would be due to a modification from the hand of the letter's author – if there has not been a passive reading of Gen 15:6 –, or it would derive from an alleged Hebrew passive *Vorlage* of Gen 15:6.

Furthermore, the Targum *Neofiti*, stemming from fourth-century Palestine, but containing much earlier tradition, also has the passive voice in its paraphrase of Gen 15:6b (and furthermore it inserts the subject of the first half-verse, "Abram").[364] Again, this could be attributed to the Septuagint[365] or to an already passively formulated alternative Hebrew version. Similar to the Targum, the Syriac translation of Genesis, the Peshitta, has the passive (and in addition writes the *appellativum 'lh'* for God and integrates the mention of "Abram").

None of these instances represented a primary evidence for a Hebrew passive wording in an Abrahamic context.[366] In turn, those that stand in the framework of the Abraham narratives are only preserved in a language other than Hebrew so that their alleged Hebrew *Vorlage* can only be reconstructed hypothetically. With the publication of 4QPseudo-Jubilees, however, a direct testimony of this variation is given; there Gen 15:6 is quoted as ויאמין אברהם באלוהים ותחשב לו צדקה, i.e., the verb חשב appears as a third person narrative form in the *niphal* (and besides, "Abraham" is mentioned as the subject of faith and "God" – not "Yahweh" – as the one to whom his faith is directed). It is principally this Qumran fragment and its extensive textual conformity with the Septuagint in contrast to the Masoretic Text[367] that counters the widely held view that the change of the *genus verbi* is to be attributed to the Septuagint. Indirectly then, LXX Gen 15:6b, too, proves to be a witness for a passive Hebrew form of חשׁב.[368]

How is this evidence to be explained? Considering the fact that the passive occurrences are distributed among a broad array of traditions that are to a great degree independent from each other, one can hardly make responsible the translation of the Septuagint for the change from active to passive. Rather, it is not unlikely that "the passive form of the verb in Gen 15:6 was known in pre-Christian Judaism along with the active form that is preserved in the Masoretic tradition."[369] Possibly even, the passive form

---

[363] Cf., e.g., J.D.G. Dunn 1998, 376.

[364] *TgNeof* Gen 15:6 reads: והיימן אברם בשם ממרא דייי ואתחשבת ליה לזכו ("And Abram believed in the name of the Memra of the Lord and it was reckoned to him as a meritorious deed"). See A. Dièz Macho 1968, 79; M.J McNamara 1992, 95.

[365] Cf. J.A. Fitzmyer 2003, 264.

[366] Ps 106:31 and 4QMMT have the passive form in another context.

[367] See the details above chapter IV.C.

[368] Notably, already H.B. Swete suggested that the translators of the Septuagint used a Hebrew manuscript which had the same wording as Ps 106:31 (1914, 331).

[369] J.A. Fitzmyer 2003, 267.

represents an alternative to the Masoretic form, which was not just a marginal text tradition and therefore eliminated by the Masoretes, but which in wide parts of Judaism and over a long period of time was better known and received than the version which later became canonical.[370] For, at the time of the translation enterprise of the Septuagint – around 275 to 150 B.C. – "the MT manuscripts were embraced by certain circles only, while others used different, often older, manuscripts."[371]

Whether in our case the Septuagint version is indeed earlier has yet to be determined. And more significantly: Did the two alternate versions just co-exist, or did they compete with each other on grounds of their respective theological implications? It seems that the stronger arguments speak for the solution that the Masoretic Text represents the earlier version: (1) The perfect form וְהֶאֱמִן, which caused many difficulties for its interpreters,[372] is hardly due to an intentional change from an obviously more fitting narrative form (as in 4QPseudo-Jubilees), but seems to represent the *lectio difficilior*. (2) With regard to the other verb of Gen 15:6, וַיַּחְשְׁבֶהָ, the reason for an alteration from active to passive could lie in the ambiguous formulation, which theoretically allows for two possibilities of understanding: Abraham as subject of the act of "considering," or God.[373] With this syntactical clarification, one could combine a theological effect, which in later periods of Israel's history of theology became important: Primarily, the use of the passive serves the purpose – not to avoid the divine name or to emphasize God as the one who acts – but to speak of a divine action in a reverential way. An alteration from the passive to the active is not likely, therefore.[374]

However, it is not necessary to assume a *Tiqqun Soferim* that alters the text for theological concerns, since the hypothesis of such a procedure presupposes that the wording in the context is openly and dangerously misleading in theological matters. As the exegesis of Gen 15:6 and a glance on the Jewish reception history can prove, this hypothesis is unfounded – not on formal-grammatical, but on exegetical-theological grounds. Thus, the co-existence of the two textual traditions does not require a theologically heavy loaded explanation, but could equally well be due to two independent strands of tradition that are separated from each other by a merely for-

---

[370] Cf. R. Mosis 1989, 92f.; 1999, 118.

[371] E. Tov 2003, 142f.

[372] See above chapter III.D.IV.1.

[373] cf. R. Mosis 1989, 92f.; 1999, 116f.

[374] Cf. B. Ego/A. Lange 2003, 191.

mal difference – which is the case with the majority of variants in the Hebrew Bible.[375]

In sum, the evidence points to a parallel occurrence of both an active and a passive Hebrew version of Gen 15:6b, of which the first (and earlier) led to the canonical text form, while the second constituted the basis of the other passages mentioned[376]; both versions need to be interpreted with equal rights.[377] Furthermore, it provides a Palestinian Jewish background of Paul's quotation of Gen 15:6 in Romans 4 and Galatians 3, as well as of the different use of Gen 15:6 in James 2[378]; it shows that these texts do not merely draw on a version of Gen 15:6 that circulated in Hellenized or Greek-speaking Judaism, but one that was in use in Palestine.

II. Genesis 15:6 a Set Expression?

Besides the occurrences on Abraham's faith within translations or paraphrases of the Abraham narratives, there are texts that quote (parts of) Gen 15:6 in other contexts, i.e., in contexts where the direct reference to Abraham is not given. With regard to these passages one has to ask, if at a certain point in Jewish tradition the phrase detached itself from its original setting and became an independent, fixed expression that was employed in various ways and contexts.

The first indication of such a development is Ps 106:31 where the phrase is used in the context of the Phinehas story, and some exegetes argue that already at the time of this Psalm's composition, it had become a commonly used idiom.[379] Yet the presumably small temporal gap between the composition of Gen 15:6 and Ps 106:31 rather speaks in favor of a con-

---

[375] As to the difference between the Septuagint and the Masoretic Text, F. García Martínez argues that it "does not need to be interpreted as a theological explanation, but it is most probably the result of the use of a different Hebrew *Vorlage*" (2002, 48).

[376] One should also take note of the hypothesis of R.T. McLay: "[T]he use of the passive voice in the Greek may also originate from both the OG translator and Paul reading ויחשב *it was reckoned* in an unvocalized Hebrew text. The only difference is the omission of the final ה, which could have occurred in the transmission of the Hebrew texts" (2003, 42). However, as has been seen, one would rather expect the feminine form ותחשב instead of ויחשב.

[377] Cf. D. Barthélemy 1984, 39 (referred to in E. Tov 2003, 143n.64): "Souvent cet état [*sc.* littéraire autonome et distinct du TM] est plus ancien que celui qu'offre le TM. Parfois il est récent. Mais cela ne saurait amener à préférer l'un à l'autre. LXX et TM méritent d'être traits comme deux formes bibliques traditionnelles dont chacune doit être interprétée pour elle-même."

[378] Cf. F. García Martínez 2002, 48; J.A. Fitzmyer 2003, 267.

[379] H.-W. Heidland assumes that since Ps 106:31 quotes Gen 15:6 from memory, it must have been "ein geläufiges Wort" already at that time (1936, 84). Cf. W.R. Farmer 1952, 27. These authors certainly start from the assumption that Gen 15:6 belongs to one of the old Pentateuchal sources.

scious allusion, through which it is expressed that *coram deo* Phinehas's zealous act is not categorically different to Abraham's faith. In this constellation, that is, under the condition that God's positive judgment is applicable to both aspects of the human conduct, the phrase had the potential of being utilized for a broad array of expressions of a person's attitude towards God and consequently to become more and more independent. Thus, the quotation of Gen 15:6 in *Jub* 31,23 makes the impression of being secondarily inserted and not organically connected to the context. The degree of its independence from the Abraham narrative of Genesis 15 indicates that at the time of the composition of *Jubilees*, the expression had attained the character of a catchphrase with a "fairly long history."[380] The application of Gen 15:6b in 4QMMT which also occurs in an extra-Abrahamic context, confirms this observation.

The fact that Gen 15:6 had become a "quotable" *dictum* for some centuries in Jewish theology correlates to its isolation and dissociation from its immediate context.[381] Abraham's faith and his righteousness have been related to his whole life, especially to the principal test of his faith, to the Aqedah, and from his life-example the community could discern and learn what leads to righteousness and to the favor of God. In the following chapter, we will witness the apostle Paul's effort to contextualize and re-direct the statement of Gen 15:6 to the life story of the patriarch, but also to exploit his exegetical results theologically. In Romans 4 he proceeded to dissolve (implicitly) the fusion of Genesis 15 and 22 and reflect (explicitly) on the relationship between Genesis 15 and 17 – certainly being familiar with the Jewish Abraham tradition and the theology of his contemporaries.

---

[380] W.R. Farmer 1952, 27. Cf. R. Mosis 1989, 91n.96: Gen 15:6 acquired such an importance that it was "als eine Art Merksatz ... zitierfähig." See also J.B. Lightfoot 1896, 159: "[T]here is ... sufficient evidence to show that at the time of the Christian era the passage in Genesis relating to Abraham's faith had become a standard text in the Jewish schools ... in both the great schools of Jewish theology, in the Alexandrian ... and the Rabbinical" (cf. 164). M.W. Yeung 2002, 248: The phrase "has apparently become a set expression by the Second Temple period."

[381] Cf. M. Dibelius/H. Greeven 1984, 209.

Chapter V

Romans 4 and Its Context

A. Introductory Matters

Notable, there is no Old Testament personal name in the New Testament except that of Moses that appears as often as the name "Abraham"[1] – and the patriarch is mentioned not only in passing, but in extended and eminent arguments. In Paul, out of the eleven quotes from Genesis eight derive from narratives about Abraham.[2] The goal of the following is not so much to present a detailed verse-by-verse exegesis of Romans 4,[3] but to analyze how Paul employs the significant statement of Gen 15:6 on Abraham's faith and God's response to it, whereby the underlying question is that of the meaning and position of the concept of faith. One continuous criterion in the background is the Jewish interpretation of Gen 15:6 and of Abraham, as presented in the previous chapter. It serves to demonstrate both Paul's continuity and contrast compared to the Jewish Abraham tradition and point to the junctures at which their ways part.

However, the fourth chapter in Paul's letter to the Romans, which undoubtedly has a key position in this writing,[4] cannot be understood without a thorough exegesis of Rom 3:21-31 and an outline of Paul's basic line of argument up until Romans 4, especially if the theme of faith stands in the center of interest. But at first, we will present the theme and theology of Romans 4 in light of previous scholarship.

---

[1] Abraham appears 73 times, Moses 80 times, and David 59 times (cf. J. Lambrecht 1979, 4n.5).

[2] Cf. G. Mayer 1972, 119.

[3] On the side one should note the interesting fact that there is hardly any separate treatment of Romans 4 until M. Neubrand's monograph from 1997; she contends that the reason for this negligence lies in the commonly drawn connection between Romans 4 and 3:21-31 which assigns to the Abraham-chapter a merely confirming or explicating function (M. Neubrand 1997, 2; cf. P. Müller 1999, 133: "Solange die Rechtfertigung als 'die Mitte' des paulinischen Denkens angesehen wird kommt anderen paulinischen Aussagen die Funktion der Bestätigung und Beglaubigung zu. Und der Verweis auf Abraham wird dementsprechend als Schriftbeweis angesehen für die Rechtfertigung, die bereits in Röm 3,21ff. formuliert ist.").

[4] Cf. E. Käsemann 1969, 140.

I. Faith or Fatherhood? The Theme of Romans 4 in Recent Scholarship

A brief glance through recent studies on the Abraham figure in Paul reveals that there can be no talk of unanimity in Pauline scholarship regarding the argumentative purpose of Paul's appeal to the patriarch. The thematic of Romans 4 is complex indeed, and various overall topics have been suggested[5]: the righteousness of God now revealed, the universality of God's grace, the significance of faith, the order of salvation, etc. – or: the inclusion of Gentiles, the religio-sociological dimension of the Christ-event, the two equivalent elections of both Jews and Gentiles, etc. This enumeration insinuates that the central issue of the controversial assessments of Paul's intention can be narrowed down to two poles, the first of which is signified with the phrase "justification by faith," the second with "inclusion of Gentiles." More pointedly and more pertinent to our overarching focus on Abraham, the "alternatives" are "faith" or "fatherhood."[6] However, "[i]t is not, of course, that simple,"[7] for, obviously, the structure of the Abraham-chapter itself gives rise to the two different focal points suggested: Generally, the first and last part (4:1-8.19-25) center on faith, while the middle part (4:9-18) deals with Abraham's universal fatherhood. Only an exegesis that accomplishes to integrate both elements can do justice to the text. A brief overview of various interpretations of Romans 4 – divided up into "faith" and "fatherhood" – will point to the contentious issues connected to the exegesis of the Abraham-chapter.[8]

1. Abraham's Faith

a) Abraham's Faith and Salvation History

No discussion of Romans 4 can ignore the debate between U. Wilckens and G. Klein, who quarreled over the necessity or illegitimacy of a salvation-historical interpretation of Paul: Does Paul think in terms of "Erwählungsgeschichte" or "Individualgeschichte"?[9]

According to Wilckens, the justification of Abraham stands at the beginning of "election history."[10] From this starting point onwards, there is a

---

[5] Cf. G. Klein 1963, 150n.20.

[6] In a somewhat analogous manner, F.E. Wieser distinguishes between two models in the New Testament use of the Abraham figure: the paradigmatic model ("faith") and the election-historical model ("fatherhood") (1987, 35). He oversystematizes however when he assigns Romans 4 solely to the first (65-67).

[7] L.H. Silberman 1990, 103.

[8] See the comprehensive history of scholarship in M. Neubrand 1997, 32-79.

[9] Apart from M. Neubrand, see especially K. Berger 1966, 75-77; R. Schmitt 1984, 38-58; D.-A. Koch 1986, 312-315.

[10] U. Wilckens 1961, 45; cf. similarly O. Schmitz 1922, 99 with n.1; A. Schlatter 1927, 396; O. Cullmann 1965, 111 ("Ausgangspunkt einer *Entwicklung*"; italics origi-

historical-real ("geschichtlich-*wirklich*") continuity that leads in historical concreteness to the present time of the apostle: God's election involves Abraham, Isaac, the Israelites, Christ, Paul, and finally the Gentiles.[11] However, the *factual* non-fulfillment of the law, sin, prevented the full effectiveness of God's election.[12] Only through faith in Christ, which correlates to Abraham's faith, is the factual distance bridged and the justification of the sinner made possible.[13] Abraham therefore witnesses both to God's faithfulness and to justification by faith; the appeal to Abraham serves to disclose the Christ-event as fulfillment of God's "election history."[14] Thus, faith is not an individual, general possibility, but is located comprehensively in God's history.[15]

Against this idea of continuity, Klein states a sharp discontinuity between the law-free era (Abraham) and the period of the law, since according to Paul the empirical Israel is radically cut off from the sonship of Abraham.[16] In other words, before the Christ-event, more precisely: his crucifixion, the righteousness of God could not have and has not been revealed.[17] As a consequence, Paul necessarily has to desacralize and profanize Israel's history in order to create a theological indifference of Jews and

---

nal). Wilckens uses the terms "Heilsgeschichte" and "Erwählungsgeschichte" almost synonymously, but claims that the latter correlates more precisely with Paul's thought (1964, 66; cf. U. Luz 1968, 179). However, in the following the conventional term "Heilsgeschichte"/salvation history is preferred.

[11] U. Wilckens 1961, 45 (italics original). Against such a line of development from Abraham to Christ, see – apart from G. Klein – U. Luz 1968, 182; J. Roloff 1990, 252.

[12] Cf. U. Wilckens 1969, 94; 1978, 132f., 145f., 152f. Hence, Wilckens interpretation of Paul's view of the law plays a significant role in the discussion. Despite the existence of a "geschichtlich-*wirklich[e]*" continuity (1961, 45), there is no "faktisch-geschichtliche" continuity (1978, 266) due to the human sin.

[13] U. Wilckens 1978, 266 ("… wenn man wie Abraham glaubt").

[14] U. Wilckens 1961, 42.

[15] U. Wilckens 1961, 45. He continues: "[Glaube] gründet sich in Geschichte, er steht selbst in Geschichte und er vertraut in Geschichte." Wilckens highlights continuously the "erwählungsgeschichtliche Kontinuität" (43; cf. 49n.27), which is determined through the divine promise "von jenem Damals her … bis zum Christusgeschehen" (69). D.-A. Koch (1986, 313) criticizes that Wilckens has to fill the gap between Abraham and the presence with the aid of other texts (Rom 9:4-13; 11:13-16) in order to receive an intact historical continuity in Romans 4. But if one seeks to integrate the missing history of Israel – thus going beyond Romans 4 – one could say, according to Koch, that in Abraham the line of election has begun, but until the Christ-event it remained concealed under Israel's disobedience and God's rejection of it (314f.; in this regard, therefore, Koch's position is similar to that of Wilckens).

[16] G. Klein 1963, 159.

[17] G. Klein 1963, 148. For Klein's interpretation of Paul's concept of the law this implies (against Wilckens) that *independent* from the fulfillment of the law, the law cannot effect righteousness (cf., e.g., 1984, 71).

Gentiles.[18] He has to detach the patriarch from the context of Jewish history and from Judaism so that the Abraham figure can become proof for the righteousness *post Christum crucifixum*. There is however continuity between Abraham (as historical figure) and the present, but this kind of continuity cannot be verified historically. It materializes only, if and when one believes as Abraham believed.[19] Thus, faith itself establishes this (theological) continuity, which consequently, in turn, is itself part of faith.[20]

A somewhat mediating position between Wilckens and Klein is taken by K. Berger, who contends that Paul neither intended to provide a systematic-coherent historical portrait, nor cut off the Abraham figure from its bond to history in order to use it as general truth.[21] Rather, the continuity consists in the identity of God's act, in his always analogous election, and the paradigmatic character lies in the event of faith and reckoning, not in Abraham's faith as such.[22] Nevertheless, there is identity between Abraham and the Christians in faith.[23] Basically, Paul seeks to legitimate his theses (Rom 1:16-17; 3:21-31) through a salvation-historical foundation.[24] Berger also points to Paul's universalistic view in his quotation of Gen 15:6: Jews and Gentiles alike are Abraham's seed, since his justification precedes the differentiation into Jew and Gentile – and only the way of faith leads to salvation, for all.[25]

Similarly to Klein, U. Luz wants to see Abraham not as a part of history that extends to both past and future, but as unique individual of a contingent past time and thus as example for a certain subject matter.[26] That

---

[18] G. Klein 1963, 149, 163; affirmed in H. Boers 1971, 76f. Jews and Gentiles are all subsumed under the category ἄνθρωπος.

[19] G. Klein 1963, 157: "Abraham *ist* niemandes Vater, – er *wird* zum Vater, im und durch den Glauben" (italics original; cf. 1964, 175n.14). This is why the appeal to Abraham does not serve the construction of a salvation-historical development, but its destruction (1963, 164).

[20] G. Klein 1963, 157-164. Again, D.-A. Koch disapproves of the systematized isolation of Romans 4 that does not allow for an "Abrahamssohnschaft ... ante Christum" (1986, 313f. with a quote of G. Klein 1964, 203).

[21] K. Berger 1966, 74f. with n.58.

[22] K. Berger 1972, 375. Cf. similarly D. Zeller 1973, 108: Paul's intention is not simply to present Abraham as "Vorbild," but to underscore the identity of God, as he reveals himself in the Old Testament and to the believer.

[23] K. Berger 1972, 379.

[24] K. Berger 1966, 63.

[25] K. Berger 1966, 63, 67.

[26] U. Luz 1968, 180, with reference to G. Klein 1963, 157. The exemplary character of Abraham is common to Paul and rabbinic Judaism. Cf. similarly K. Kertelge 1971, 193: "[Paulus] bietet ... keine 'heilsgeschichtliche' Konstruktion"; E. Gräßer 1981, 190n.4 (Abraham as "geschichtsloser Typos").

Abraham is not simply a timeless, exchangeable example is indicated by Paul when he calls Abraham "father" and refers to his justification as an analogy-less event that has an effect for the present, for us (Rom 4:23-24), as it involves God's free deed.[27] But Abraham is a temporally isolated example for Paul, since he shows no interest in the prehistory of faith before Abraham or in the history from Abraham to the law and from the law to Christ (in contrast to Romans 9). Positively said, the lack of a theology of history in Romans 4 emphasizes the free, independent divine deed.[28]

Finally, H. Boers affirms Klein's contention that Paul desacralizes Israel's history, but denies that "Paul was consciously facing up to an historical problem,"[29] consisting in the fact that Abraham is obviously historically excluded from the (christologically determined) faith-righteousness. For, "that Abraham was justified by faith was beyond doubt for Paul as a result of Gen. 15:6."[30] Boers also denies a lack of difference of Jews and Gentiles, for "Paul presupposes all through the letter" "the advantage of the Jew."[31] Paul's "positive interest in Abraham" was determined by his reflecting on the "relation between Abraham's faith and the faith of the believer," both of which are connected through "the fact that it is the same God who is the object of ... faith."[32]

b) Abraham's Faith and Typology

L. Goppelt's view of a salvation-historical thinking in Paul[33] is subsumed under his concept of typology: God establishes in and through history a connection of promise and fulfillment, of *typos* and *antitypos*; but this connection remains concealed and only conceivable for faith.[34] Even if Paul uses apocalyptic terminology to express the eschatological character of the Christ-event, he factually understands and explains it as realization of the promise and as fulfillment of the prevenient salvific act of God.[35] Consequently, Abraham is the *typos* through whom Paul interprets the

---

[27] U. Luz 1968, 181.

[28] U. Luz 1968, 182.

[29] H. Boers 1971, 77.

[30] H. Boers 1971, 78.

[31] H. Boers 1971, 92.

[32] H. Boers 1971, 76, 84.

[33] Salvation history is "das entscheidende Interpretationsprinzip" of Paul, which requires from his modern interpreters to apply it as "das maßgebende hermeneutische Prinzip" (L. Goppelt 1966/1967, 233). – On the theme of "typology" see also Goppelt's landmark work from 1939.

[34] L. Goppelt 1966/1967, 227f.; cf. 1939, 29f.: The Abraham passages in Paul in fact constitute the test case for the understanding of typology. Wilckens's "geschichtlich-wirklich[e]" continuity does not apply here. E. Käsemann criticizes the perspective of promise and fulfillment (1969, 171).

[35] L. Goppelt 1966/1967, 223.

Christ-event.[36] Within the framework of his typological hermeneutics, Goppelt holds that Abraham's faith has the same structure, but a different content compared to the Christian faith[37]: Abraham believed in the face of his infertility that God would give him descendants, while the Christians believe in the face of the cross that God has raised Christ. In sum, the Abraham passages in Paul become the test case for the conception of typology.[38]

A broad description of salvation history is offered by E. Käsemann,[39] into which he places Paul's typological interpretation of Abraham. Paul thinks in terms of the apocalyptic scheme of the two eons, of "Urzeit" and "Endzeit"[40] and possesses therefore cosmic dimensions. Within this scheme Abraham is the "prototype" or *Urbild* of Christian faith who prefigures Christian faith.[41] The Abraham-story anticipates the Christ-story and makes therefore possible the Pauline statement of the identity of Abraham's faith and that of Christianity which conceives of the justification of the ungodly as *creatio ex nihilo* and as anticipation of the resurrection of the dead.[42] Thus, Abraham is both inexchangeable bearer of the promise and cosmic bearer of fate, who anticipates the eschatological reality.[43] Salvation history therefore does not stand for the continuity of a develop-

---

[36] Cf. L. Goppelt 1991, 384. Through Abraham, Paul illuminates the "election history," while through Adam he interprets the whole history of humanity.

[37] L. Goppelt 1966/1967, 231. Against this position U. Luz holds that Paul speaks only of *one* faith, whose contents and structure belong together; Goppelt's view is dependent on his typological interpretation that requires an *antitypos* (1968, 114n.369).

[38] L. Goppelt 1964, 252.

[39] E. Käsemann 1969a, 116. Salvation-historical thinking means to structure universal history into the epochs of Adam, Abraham, Moses, and Christ and to regard creation as proceeding towards the final judgment through fall and salvation.

[40] E. Käsemann 1969, 169, 171, 173.

[41] E. Käsemann 1969, 141. By making Abraham the *Urbild* of the Christian faith, Paul bridges the time difference with extraordinary audacity (167). Käsemann takes up positively the pointed statement of F. Neugebauer: "Abraham [ist] der Typus des neuen Gottesvolkes ... gewissermaßen das präexistente Glied der Ekklesia, er ist eine ekklesiologische Gestalt" (1961, 168f.). Nevertheless, faith is no ecclesiological, but an anthropological term (E. Käsemann 1980, 103).

[42] E. Käsemann 1969, 172f. The more narrow description of typology (proposed for instance by U. Luz) does not comprise anticipation, but requires an antithesis; against that Käsemann subsumes both categories under "typology," anticipation (e.g., Romans 4) and antithesis (e.g., Romans 5). He also demarcates his view of "typology" from the salvation-historical schema of analogy or fulfillment (against O. Cullmann), as well as from the history-of-religions idea of cyclic repetition (against R. Bultmann; cf., e.g., R. Bultmann 1950, 369, 377).

[43] E. Käsemann 1969, 173.

ment,[44] but for the correlation or contrast between beginning and end, i.e., between the two poles of history.[45] This excludes both, an a-historical isolation (G. Klein) and theology-of-history speculation (U. Wilckens).[46]

Against any typological view of Paul's presentation of Abraham, R. Bultmann argues that since the idea of cyclic repetition is missing, one should speak of Abraham as *Urbild* or *Vorbild* of the believers (as does Judaism), but not as *typos*.[47] As we have seen, Bultmann has a distinctive view of the correlation of Abraham's faith and Paul's concept of πίστις in general: The weight he assigns to the elements obedience and confession diminish that dimension of πίστις that denotes the trust in the fulfillment of the divine promise, in God's miraculous power, as in Romans 4.[48] The Old Testament-Jewish notion of trust only prevails in passages dominated by Old Testament texts and tradition, such as Rom 4:3.

c) History and Story

Many arguments of the debate on "salvation history" in Paul recur in the current discussion on the topic of "narrative dimensions," which in effect comes close to "a refurbishing of the older salvation history model."[49] An implicit grand, all-encompassing narrative in Paul would correspond to "a linear *Heilsgeschichte*."[50]

Some exegetes have uncovered "a story about Jesus Christ"[51] or a "story of God's righteousness"[52] as narrative substructure which governs Paul's reasoning. R.B. Hays employs a "narrative hermeneutic"[53] and seeks to identify "Paul's allusions to his story of Jesus Christ," which "provides the foundational substructure upon which Paul's argumentation is constructed."[54] According to Paul's narrative logic, "[t]he Abraham story is for Paul taken up into the Christ-story" in which we too "are included" in terms of a participatory soteriology.[55]

---

[44] Cf. E. Käsemann 1969, 153f. There is no uninterrupted continuity between Abraham and Christ according to the scheme "promise-fulfillment."

[45] E. Käsemann 1969, 171.

[46] With some irony, J.D.G. Dunn calls Käsemann's exposition of Abraham's faith "almost lyrical ... Lutheranism" (1988, 203).

[47] R. Bultmann 1950, 377. Against that L. Goppelt 1964, 251.

[48] R. Bultmann 1959, 207; 1984, 320f. A similarly secondary character Bultmann assigns to fear and hope (see above page 42).

[49] This is the formulation of J.D.G. Dunn 1998, 20n.62.

[50] I.H. Marshall 2002, 212.

[51] R.B. Hays 1983, 6.

[52] A.K. Grieb, 2002 (title).

[53] Cf. R.B. Hays 1989, 157. See also above chapter II.H.IV.

[54] R.B. Hays 1983, 6f.

[55] R.B. Hays 1983, 196f.

Within such an "implicit overall narrative"[56] A.T. Lincoln is interested in the "stories of predecessors and inheritors" of the Pauline gospel and investigates the "narrative world" of Romans (and Galatians).[57] In result, Paul's Abraham-story is "shaped decisively in the light of the gospel story of God's actions in Christ and formulated with the stories of the readers in view, so that ... there is an intricate interplay of all three stories."[58] Importantly, all these stories are in need of interpretation, and "the highly effective vehicle" of this interpretation is "the epistolary form with its theological argument and paraenesis."[59]

Critical of the heuristic value of the category of narrative for the interpretation of Paul's argumentation, I.H. Marshall argues that the purpose of Paul's use of the Abraham-story is basically to reveal "real parallels" between the life and experience of Abraham and Christian believers.[60] Nevertheless, on grounds of a common strong tendency "toward unification and synthesis" "Paul does have a sense of an ongoing, underlying story,"[61] of which he makes use in his argumentation.

Despite the differences in the views presented in chapter V.A.I.1, almost all presuppose that Paul refers to the Abraham figure with the intention to expound on the notions of Abraham's faith and God's act of justification.[62] Many other voices could be added to this choir, claiming that in Romans 4 Paul is predominantly concerned with Abraham's faith and its relevance for the doctrine *sola fide*, particularly those who deal in a more general way with the theme of "faith," i.e., many of those listed in the chapter on the history of scholarship,[63] but also other monographs, essays,

---

[56] A.T. Lincoln 2002, 201.

[57] A.T. Lincoln 2002, 173. Lincoln has "chosen simply to accept initially the category of 'story' as a heuristic device for interpreting the material about the figures and groups to be highlighted" (173). He "employ[s] the category of story loosely" and restricts himself to the "referential-contextual narrative world of the letter[s]" (197 with n.29).

[58] A.T. Lincoln 2002, 189. Elsewhere, Abraham is perceived as "a character in an implied story line in which God is the main actor" (201).

[59] A.T. Lincoln 2002, 200.

[60] I.H. Marshall 2002, 210.

[61] I.H. Marshall 2002, 212f.

[62] Cf. for example H. Boers 1971, 97: Paul's "real concern is the justification by faith without works."

[63] Some may be mentioned exemplarily: According to A. Schlatter, the one who has "real faith" ("reeller Glaube") is set into a relationship with God analogously to Abraham; there is an inner connection of the believer with the patriarch (1927, 396n.2) based on a deed of decision (336n.1, 347). In W.H.P. Hatch's view, Paul uses Abraham's faith as an "illustration and confirmation of his doctrine that the believer is justified through faith"; however, the "Christian has faith in a much deeper sense than Abraham had it" (1917, 58; Hatch does not say what he understands by "deeper"). H. Binder 1968, 42f.; E. Lohse 1977, 158; D.M. Hay 1989, 472.

and commentaries.[64] Though we find accentuations of different aspects, the tenor remains basically the same.

2. Abraham's Fatherhood

a) Exclusive Soteriology[65]

The other, "new perspective" basically grounds in an old view that positions Paul's doctrine of justification by faith at the margins of his theology and places the idea of "participation" into its center. To this aspect correlates a renewed understanding of Judaism, which more or less explicitly seeks to distance itself from the so-called "Lutheran" perspective that regards Judaism as "works religion" and its way to salvation as "works-righteousness." In addition, there is always a certain antipathy against an alleged individualistic and existential Reformation interpretation of Paul's doctrine of justification.[66]

Already G.F. Moore credits the Christian prejudice against the idea of good works and their reward and merit to Luther's struggle with Catholicism, but also to Paul's assertion that the Jewish religion cannot provide salvation. In contrast to C.G. Montefiore, who attributes Paul's pessimism towards Judaism to a Hellenistic diaspora Judaism rather than to rabbinic Judaism,[67] Moore blames Paul himself for painting a questionable picture of Judaism.[68] H.-J. Schoeps welcomes the "de-lutheranization" of Paul that in his view began with W. Wrede and his talk of Paul's "Kampfeslehre."[69] He calls Paul an "Assimilationsjude" of the diaspora who got estranged from the faith of his fathers, culminating in his tearing apart law and faith in the promises[70]: To make law and faith two antithetic poles contradicts

---

[64] See only C. Dietzfelbinger 1961, 18; J. Jeremias 1970, 51; K. Kertelge 1971, 193; F. Hahn 1971, 103 ("Wesen des Glaubens Abrahams"), 107; H. Boers 1971, 83, 91 ("the structure of faith"); H. Schlier 1977, 135; O. Michel 1978, 162; J.-N. Aletti 1989, 245: "Rm 4 est sans doute le passage qui parle le plus de l'acte de croire." R.A. Harrisville 1992, 154-159; D.J. Moo 1996, 255.

[65] An alternate label for "exclusive" and "non-exclusive" soteriology is "one-way" and "two-ways" salvation (cf. P. Eisenbaum 2004, 672n.3).

[66] With the exception of M. Neubrand's study (1997), Romans 4 has not been subject to a larger treatment governed by those new paradigms, though the Abraham-chapter always played a role in these interpretations (cf. especially M. Cranford 1995).

[67] C.G. Montefiore 1914, 17-22.

[68] G.F. Moore 1927-1930.

[69] Cf. H.-J. Schoeps 1959, 206f. and W. Wrede (1907, 72; see above page 12).

[70] H.-J. Schoeps 1959, 278. To state the powerlessness of the Torah is a heresy in the biblical understanding (196). Hence, Paul misunderstood his paternal religion, and Paul's interpreters misunderstood him in turn, so that eventually Pauline theology is "die Theologie des potenzierten Mißverständnisses" (279).

the context of the biblical Abraham narrative and therefore remained in-comprehensible to Jewish thinking.[71]

The famous study on the patterns of religion of (Palestinian) Judaism and (Pauline) Christianity by E.P. Sanders maintains some essential distinctions between the two: According to Sanders, in Judaism righteousness is what keeps one in the covenant, while for Paul justification is what brings one into the covenant.[72] Paul teaches an exclusive soteriology, and his problem "with the law, and thus with Judaism, is that it does not provide for God's ultimate purpose, that of saving the entire world through faith in Christ, and without the privilege accorded to Jews through the promises, the covenants and the law."[73] Judaism's "pattern of religion" is first election and then obedience ("covenantal nomism"), while for Paul it is the union with, and participation in Christ, which will be fulfilled at Christ's return.[74]

J.D.G. Dunn concurs with Sanders's assessment of Judaism as "covenantal nomism," but develops this thesis further in terms of the "works of the law,"[75] i.e., particularly food laws and circumcision as sociological-national "identity and boundary markers." The function of the law was twofold: demarcation from other nations and strengthening of the own identity. Paul fights against this inherent separation of Jews and non-Jews and refutes the Jewish notion of being privileged – in short: He reacts against "Jewish exclusivism," though not against "the fundamental belief in Israel's election as such."[76] Positively said, God's "covenant righteousness extends to believing Gentile as well as to Jew without regard to national identity as determined by the law."[77] "'Justification by faith' was Paul's answer to the question: How is it that Gentiles can be equally acceptable to God as Jews,"[78] and consequently "the example of Abraham in particular was treated not only as typical and normative, but also as relativizing those subsequent Scriptures which emphasize Israel's special place with God's affections."[79]

---

[71] H.-J. Schoeps 1959, 212.

[72] E.P. Sanders 1977, 544.

[73] E.P. Sanders 1983, 47. See his pointed *dictum*: "In short, this is what Paul finds wrong in Judaism: it is not Christianity" (1977, 552).

[74] E.P. Sanders 1977, 548f. Sanders calls this kind of participation therefore "participationist eschatology" (548f.). In placing "participation in Christ" into the center of Paul's soteriology and theology, Sanders has famous precursors, A. Schweitzer being the most prominent one.

[75] See the *excursus* below chapter V.B.III.4.

[76] J.D.G. Dunn 2002, 277f.

[77] J.D.G. Dunn 1988, 227 (in his exposition of Abraham in Romans 4).

[78] J.D.G. Dunn 1998, 340.

[79] J.D.G. Dunn 1983, 202.

The third of the "three musketeers of the so-called 'New Perspective',"[80] N.T. Wright, similarly argues that justification by faith is "a polemical doctrine, whose target is not the usual Lutheran one of 'nomism' or '*Menschenwerke*,' but the Pauline one of Jewish national pride."[81] Hence, Paul does not seek to counter a Jewish image of Abraham as a "good moralist," who earned righteousness through good works. What he says regarding work and reward (Rom 4:4-5) is not intended to reflect the theology of his contemporaries.[82] Rather he speaks of "works" in the sense of the "badges of Jewish membership (Sabbath, dietary laws, circumcision) which kept Jews separate from Gentiles."[83] Wright however reformulated the problematic issue at stake: Paul's concern is not so much the inclusion of the Gentiles,[84] but the sentiment that caused the Gentiles to exclude the Jews from membership in the community.[85]

The argumentative force of this position – which of course has pre-Sanders forerunners[86] – has convinced many participants in the debate centering on the main threats of Paul's theology in general and on his use of Abraham in particular. With different intentions and goals many other scholars seek to place Abraham's "faith" into the periphery of Paul's argument to the benefit of Abraham's "fatherhood."

---

[80] S.J. Gathercole 2002, 16.

[81] N.T. Wright 1978, 71; cf. 1991, 261. On the problematic ethnic notion of these formulations, see F. Avemarie 2001, 285n.13. – Sanders, Dunn, and Wright all agree that Luther significantly misunderstood Paul (cf., e.g., E.P. Sanders 1977, 44, 49, 492n.57; J.D.G. Dunn 1983, 185-187; N.T. Wright 1991, 258f.; 1997, 120; also K. Stendahl 1963, 83; T.L. Donaldson 1997, 111). One should note however opposing views as well. Cf., e.g., O. Michel 1978, 94: "Kein Ausleger [hat] Paulus in seinen tiefsten Intentionen so gut verstanden wie M. Luther." M. Hengel 1991, 86: "Although people nowadays are fond of asserting otherwise, no one understood the real essence of Pauline theology, the salvation given *sola gratia*, by faith alone, better than Augustine and Martin Luther." See also H.D. Betz 1979, xv: "Luther speaks as Paul would have spoken had he lived at the time when Luther gave his lectures [on Galatians]." S. Westerholm 2004, 400: "It seems fair to say that all the essential features of the 'Lutheran' Paul find support in Romans, though the emphases of the Reformer are not always those of the apostle."

[82] Cf. N.T. Wright 1995, 41.

[83] N.T. Wright 1991, 240.

[84] Cf. N.T. Wright 1995, 154f.: "Gentiles simply come in, from nowhere; Jews have their membership renewed ... by sharing the death and resurrection of their Messiah."

[85] N.T. Wright 1995, 34f.

[86] See already E. Jacob 1962, 154: "[L'apôtre Paul] attache moins d'importance à la foi et à l'obéissance d'Abraham qu'à sa fonction de père inaugurant une histoire qui est celle du salut de toute l'humanité." Despite polemics in Paul's use of Abraham, "l'ancêtre reste à l'abri de toute polémique; il reste le père" (154). "En mettant au centre de la figure d'Abraham la fonction de père, nous arriverons à surmonter l'antithèse entre foi et œuvres et l'opposition entre Paul et Jacques" (155).

Thus, R.B. Hays asserts: "The chapter as a whole revolves around the issue of Abraham's status as a father"[87]; Abraham has "*symbolic* significance" as a "*representative* figure whose destiny 'contains' the destiny of others."[88] Overall, the "fundamental problem" of Romans "is *not* how a person may find acceptance with God" but "to work out an understanding of the relationship in Christ between Jews and Gentiles."[89]

With a very provocative underlying program of "de-lutheranizing Paul" (H.-J. Schoeps) and of offering a non-theological reading of Paul,[90] F. Watson takes a sociological approach through which he wants to show that the group of Jewish-Christian converts developed from a reform movement to a sect, i.e., to a "single 'Pauline' congregation in Rome."[91] Paul's letter to the Romans is directed to Jewish-Christians, for whom he attempts to give reasons for the necessity for this separation. He uses denunciation, antithesis, and reinterpretation as argumentative means. His antithesis between faith and works, however, "does not express a general theoretical opposition between two incompatible views of the divine-human relationship. It merely expresses Paul's conviction that the church should be separate from the Jewish community."[92] Romans 4 "is a far reaching reinterpretation of the figure of Abraham with important sociological implications, and not purely theoretical argument."[93] Paul asserts "that Abraham in fact justifies the way of life and beliefs of 'Pauline' Jewish and Gentile congregations."[94]

Comparable ideas motivated the study on Romans 4 by M. Cranford, who claims that "Abraham's faith is meant not as an example of Christian faith ... but rather as the reason why uncircumcised Gentiles can receive the forgiveness reserved for those in the covenant,"[95] "why Gentiles can be

---

[87] R.B. Hays 1985, 93.

[88] R.B. Hays 1985, 90 (italics original).

[89] R.B. Hays 1985, 84 (italics original); cf. 1997, 285: Paul does not look for "models of faith" nor does he explain in a general way "how justification takes place"; rather he gives a "*scriptural* warrant for the claim that God will justify Jews and Gentiles alike." Yet see 290 (cf. 1985, 97f.): "*[B]oth* Abraham and Jesus are paradigms for Christian faith."

[90] Cf. F. Watson 1986, 48: "This combination of historical and sociological perspectives seems to offer a more appropriate approach to the interpretation of Paul's view of Judaism than the exclusively theological models so often propounded."

[91] F. Watson 1986, 98.

[92] F. Watson 1986, 64; cf. 134: "*Faith is incompatible with works because participation in the life of a Pauline Gentile Christian congregation is incompatible with continuing membership of the Jewish community*" (italics original).

[93] F. Watson 1986, 139.

[94] F. Watson 1986, 136.

[95] M. Cranford 1995, 83.

considered members of God's people,"[96] "why Gentiles can be considered his progeny as much as Jews."[97] Not the "Lutheran" reading of Abraham does justice to Paul, but that reading which concentrates on the circumstances of faith: Abraham received the promise as an uncircumcised, ungodly man – and this marked the beginning of salvation history.[98]

b) Non-Exclusive Soteriology

All of the scholars just mentioned (seem to) agree with the basic contention that in his soteriology Paul retains no difference between Jews and Gentiles, insofar as there is categorically no salvation apart from faith in Christ. In more recent scholarship, those voices become more vocal that – in dependence on the renewed understanding of Judaism – propagate a comprehensive revision of Paul's allegedly exclusive soteriology, which bases salvation solely on Jesus Christ for both Jews and Gentiles. In their view Paul continuously presupposes a religious-sociological distinction of the two groups, a "soteriological dualism,"[99] or a Jewish "Sonderweg."[100] His intention is not to integrate Jews into the sphere of the christologically determined faith-righteousness, but rather to include Gentiles into the sphere of divine election which was initially only granted to Jews.

Thus, K. Stendahl comprehends Paul's letter to the Romans not as polemics against Judaism, but as apologetic for his Gentile mission. His gospel does not center on the doctrine of justification, but on the relation between Jews and Gentiles. "The doctrine of justification by faith was hammered out by Paul for the very specific and limited purpose of defending the rights of Gentile converts to be full and genuine heirs to the promises of God to Israel."[101]

Along this "unique rather than universal"-line of thought, L. Gaston starts from the assumption that Paul "interprets the figure of Abraham not

---

[96] M. Cranford 1995, 73.

[97] M. Cranford 1995, 76. Cranford also refers to G. Howard 1990, 55f., 88.

[98] See also, with reference to Cranford, J.-N. Aletti 2003, 323: "...ce n'est pas l'acte de foi du patriarche qui est de soi typique, mais l'ensemble des données qui constituent la situation dans laquelle il se trouvait alors (son status d'incirconcis, l'absence d'œuvres, sa foi, etc.) et qui est celle-là même des non juifs adhérant à l'Évangile" (cf. 319f. with n.35). J.S. Siker 1991, 75: "The emphasis on Gentile inclusion provides *the* constant feature in Paul's use of Abraham" (italics original); A.T. Lincoln 1992, 167-170.

[99] Cf. D.A. Campbell 1992a, 94n.9.

[100] On the idea of Israel's "Sonderweg," see D. Zeller 1976, 245; F. Mußner 1976, 251: Israel will be saved through Christ, through the gospel, *sola gratia*, not through works of the law – but without "conversion" to Christianity. Cf. the title of F. Mußner's essay (1981): "Heil für alle," i.e., inclusion of all humans in the messianic salvation revealed in Christ (37).

[101] K. Stendahl 1976, 2. In a more recent publication, Stendahl seems to withdraw from the idea of Paul's non-exclusive soteriology (cf. 1995, 7).

against but with the traditional understanding."[102] His theological concern is not justification by faith, but "the justification of the legitimacy of his apostleship to ... the Gentiles."[103] For Paul, the initial and ultimate goal of the Torah is the inclusion of the Gentiles, i.e., Abraham's fatherhood for Gentiles.[104] And through Christ this goal is realized – he is "the fulfillment of God's promises concerning the Gentiles."[105] As a consequence "Rom 4 is not about Christian faith but about grace ... to Abraham's heirs" and "Abraham is understood in Rom 4 not primarily as the *type* of the later believers but as the *father* of later believers."[106]

In accordance with Gaston, J.G. Gager believes the inclusion of Gentiles to be Paul's major concern. Jews remain obliged to the Torah, while non-Jews do not need to enter God's covenant with Israel. The first group is justified through the Torah, the second through Christ,[107] but the religious status of both groups is the same; through his appeal to Abraham, Paul seeks to prove that he does not overthrow the law on the one hand, but that there is "fundamental parity of Jews and Gentiles" on the other.[108]

An opposition against the so-called Lutheran Paul, similar to that of F. Watson, figures in S.K. Stowers's works in which he claims that Paul's concern is "not that the sinner is saved by faith rather than works but that God has shown his righteousness and truthfulness to the Abrahamic promise."[109] The promise itself, as well as the covenant and the law, were given to Abraham "on the basis of his faithfulness."[110] While these ideas comply fully with Jewish theology, the originality of Paul lies in his belief that

---

[102] L. Gaston 1980, 53, 59. He mentions G. Howard's work (1979) as "an important beginning in this direction" (L. Gaston 1980, 65n.55). Even Sirach 44 belongs to the exegetical tradition to which Paul also adheres, according to Gaston (54).

[103] L. Gaston 1980, 53.

[104] Cf. the title of the essay "The Inclusion of Gentiles as the Ultimate Goal of Torah in Romans" (L. Gaston 1987).

[105] L. Gaston 1986, 66. The result of Paul's encounter with Christ on the road to Damascus was his insight that non-Jews receive God's righteousness apart from the law. Notably, however, Jesus is not "the messiah nor the climax of God's dealing with Israel."

[106] L. Gaston 1980, 57; cf. 54: "If Paul was concerned to find his gospel of salvation for Gentiles prefigured in the Torah, there is no other figure to whom he could turn but Abraham. If in addition he wanted to find the righteousness of God applied to the salvation of Gentiles, there is no other passage in the Torah to which he could have turned but Gen 15:6."

[107] Cf. J.G. Gager 1975, 263f.: "God's promise of righteousness leads in two separate directions, each according to its own time": In Moses the promise to Abraham as the father of the circumcised is fulfilled, and in Christ the promise to Abraham as the father of the uncircumcised.

[108] J.G. Gager 1975, 218.

[109] S.K. Stowers 1989, 667, with reference to S.K. Williams 1980; K. Stendahl 1976; G. Howard 1970.

[110] S.K. Stowers 1989, 673.

"the scripture establishes a way for Gentiles to be justified through the promise to Abraham that all the Gentiles would be blessed in his seed."[111] In sum, "Romans does not wrestle with the problem of how God goes about saving the generic human being. Rather, it asks how families of people establish a kinship with God and with one another."[112]

M. Neubrand's monograph is the first study that attempts to take into account the religious-sociological relevance of Paul's statements in Romans 4.[113] In biblical and early Jewish writings, Abraham is the figure that constitutes identity, and the analogous use of terms relevant for identity ("father," "descendants") in Rom 4:9-18 indicates the *scopos* of the whole argumentation: Paul seeks to place the new and equivalent election of non-Jews, which is based on God's dealing with Jesus Christ, at the side of the election of the Jewish people.[114] The non-Jewish believers too receive the honorable title σπέρμα 'Αβραάμ. Paul does not argue against the Jewish identity; to him the "identity and boundary markers" remain connected with the Jews. What he refutes is that the "works of the law" – primarily circumcision – become compulsory for non-Jews. Unified through Abraham's fatherhood, the peoples stand side by side with Israel; he becomes the figure of identification for both Jews and Christian believers.[115] The framework of Paul's argumentation is to be seen in his circumcision-free Gentile mission.[116] Within the existing and propagated difference between Jews and Gentiles, faith is the common bond of unity.[117]

Finally, P. Eisenbaum is "bothered by a question that is largely by others": "*Why* did Paul associate the death and resurrection of Jesus with transcending distinctions between people, particularly the Jew-Gentile distinction?"[118] In her eyes, Paul's turn toward Gentiles is not adequately explained through the "eschatological pilgrimage tradition"[119] or related hypotheses, but rather through a theory concerning patrilineage and sacrifice: "Jesus' death is the kind of filial sacrifice that has the power to rearrange

---

[111] S.K. Stowers 1989, 669f.

[112] S.K. Stowers 1994, 227.

[113] Cf. M. Neubrand 1997, 79.

[114] M. Neubrand 1997, 78, 223, 291 *et passim*.

[115] Cf. M. Neubrand 1997, 66. The theme of "justification by faith" is subordinated to this primary concern of Paul (73). – Against Gaston and Gager, Neubrand contends that Jesus is for Paul the Messiah for Israel as well (72).

[116] M. Neubrand 1997, 291.

[117] M. Neubrand 1997, 97.

[118] P. Eisenbaum 2004, 672 (italics original). Eisenbaum does not position herself explicitly either on the "exclusive" or "non-exclusive" side (672n.3), though she notes that Jews and Gentiles "are being integrated through Christ into a single 'family' that has as its head a single paternal God" (696).

[119] P. Eisenbaum 2004, 675 (against J. Munck and E.P. Sanders).

genealogical relationships, in this case, the relationships between Jews and Gentiles and God."[120] "What Gentiles need is not Torah but reception into the lineage of Abraham,"[121] and therefore, Paul's point in Romans 4 "is to demonstrate that Abraham is the common progenitor of Jews and Gentiles, not that he is an example of how to justified by faith."[122]

II. Reasons and Intention of Paul's Letter to the Romans

Before turning to the issues arising from the foregoing portrayal of the various scholarly positions regarding Romans 4, but also from the history of scholarship on the Pauline faith presented above in chapter II, it is indispensable to reflect briefly on some questions regarding the origin and purpose of Romans, on the circumstances of the Roman congregation and on Paul's own personal situation, because these factors are crucial for our understanding of how the letter was received, what stood behind its composition, and what was Paul's intention.[123]

The date of Romans is hardly disputed: 56 B.C. – yet already here the basic consensus ends. The famous Claudius-edict of 49 B.C.[124] presupposes conflicts between Jews and Christians in Rome about a certain "Chrestus," which testifies to the success of Christian mission in the syna-

---

[120] P. Eisenbaum 2004, 702.

[121] P. Eisenbaum 2004, 700; cf. 698. According to Eisenbaum, Paul places much value on "genealogy or genealogical status" (693), especially in relation to the "divine patrimony" (694), but she remains vague concerning the relationship between Jesus' filial sacrifice, Abraham's fatherhood and God's patrimony.

[122] P. Eisenbaum 2004, 687. Apart from Romans 4, Eisenbaum appeals to instances of Jewish sacrificial language in Romans such as 3:25; 5:8; 12:1; 15:16 (685n.46) and to the sacrificial framework of 8:3-4 (700f.). However, it is one thing to acknowledge sacrificial language in Paul, but another to make "sacrifice" the *one* key of Paul's thinking and mission. Certainly, in Paul atonement and justification are integrally related (cf. S.J. Gathercole 2004, 168-183), but concerning his idea of sacrifice one has to account for the fact that, first, Paul consciously reinterprets and refocuses traditional elements (see only the addition of διὰ [τῆς] πίστεως in 3:25; see below chapter V.B.III.2.b.[b]), second does not assign much space to the theme of "the blood of Christ" (only 3:25; 5:9; 1Cor 10:16; 11:25), and third alludes only scantly to the sin offering in Rom 8:3-4 and does not deem it crucial enough to elaborate it any further (Eisenbaum simply presupposes the sacrificial interpretation of this passage, a view which is supported for instance by Origen, Thomas Aquinas, F.F. Bruce, P. Stuhlmacher, N.T. Wright, M.D. Greene, W. Kraus; others prefer a more general interpretation, such as M.J. Lagrange, O. Michel, C.E.B. Cranfield; references in C.E.B. Cranfield 1975, 382nn.3f.; K. Haacker 1999, 152n.15).

[123] Cf., e.g., apart from the commentaries and the collection of essays in *The Romans Debate* (edited by K.P. Donfried, 1991), the overview of scholarly positions in M. Kettunen 1979, 7-26; M. Theobald 1983; A. Reichert 2001, 13-75. With special regard to Romans 4, see M. Neubrand 1997, 80-97.

[124] This date, too, seems sure, though it is disputed in G. Lüdemann 1980, 183-195. See the discussion in A.J.M. Wedderburn 1988, 54-59.

gogue. The consequences of the edict were first the final separation of the Christian community from the synagogue, and second the fact that Gentile-Christians constituted from that time on the majority within the community – i.e., already at the time when the letter was composed. The size of the congregation, which was organized in several house churches (cf. Rom 16:5.14.15),[125] must have been considerable, since Paul apparently expected substantial material and personal support for his projected mission in the West (cf. Rom 15:24).

Still unknown to most of the Roman Christians, he exposes his theology as extensively as in no other letter. Apart from the expected help from Rome, there are several other factors that determine, in their combination and mutual influence, the cause and purpose of Romans[126]: Paul's request of intercession and support in the context of the collection for the Jerusalem congregation,[127] through which the bond between Jewish and Gentile-Christians was supposed to be strengthened (Rom 15:25-32); the agitation of Judaizing opponents both in Jerusalem and Rome and the conflict with the state being in the offing; problems with some aspects of Paul's theology that potentially led to misunderstandings and allegations.

Dependent on which of the mentioned elements purportedly prevails, commentators made different suggestions as to the reasons for the letter's composition. The classic position is that of F.C. Baur, who assumed a particular situation in Rome to which Paul felt coerced to respond: An anti-Pauline, Jewish-Christian party opposed to the universalism of Paul's gospel and sought to exclude Gentiles from salvation.[128] Hence, the letter was addressed to Jewish-Christians,[129] and at the same time – Rome being the capital of the empire – to the head of all Jewish-Christians of the Gentile world. Paul's aim was to present a general foundation of his universalistic theology against Jewish particularism. According to Baur this is the proper subject of Paul's epistle – not the Lutheran "Justifikationsprozess."[130]

Today, many scholars follow Baur in regarding the Roman Jewish-Christians to be the primary dialogue partners of Paul; his letter possesses dialogic character throughout and consequently it is not a dogmatic trea-

---

[125] Cf. H.J. Klauck 1981.

[126] Cf. the succinct summary in U. Schnelle 2002, 132.

[127] The collection for Jerusalem seems to refute F. Watson's thesis (see above page 232). It is hardly conceivable that Paul sought to separate the Jewish-Christians from the synagogue and simultaneously tried to secure Jerusalem's approval of his mission through the collection of money (1986, 174-176).

[128] F.C. Baur 1836.

[129] According to Baur, Jewish-Christians constituted the majority of the Roman congregation (1866, 370).

[130] F.C. Baur 1866, 349.

tise, but grown from a continuous "Dialogus cum Iudaeis."[131] Others claim that the letter to the Romans is to be understood as great apologetic letter directed against Paul's Judaizing opponents, who followed him everywhere and have started to agitate against him in Rome. It is "a document of an inner-Christian dispute over the Pauline Gospel from the perspective of the missionary task to Gentiles and Jews which still remained largely unfulfilled."[132] Therefore, he has to refute objections against his theology and mission and win the Roman congregation for his plans.[133] Again others read between the lines that in reality Paul composed his letter as apologetic speech, which he planned to give in Jerusalem. The *raison d'être* for this course of action was his concern that the collection might be refused in Jerusalem at the instigation of the Judaizers.[134] The tendency in more recent years to regard the "inclusion of the Gentiles" to be the main concern of Paul, is obviously also prefigured in Baur's seminal work.[135] – All these approaches agree in acknowledging the "'occasional' character"[136] of Paul's letter to the Romans and its dependence on "a cluster of different interlocking factors."[137]

Nevertheless, with P. Melanchthon as a famous authority, scholars occasionally seek to disconnect to a certain degree the message of Romans from this historical variability and regard it "Christianae doctrinae Compendium"[138] or as (timeless) sum of the gospel.[139] This "great document" of Paul "elevates his theology above the moment of definite situations and conflicts into the sphere of the eternally and universally valid."[140]

---

[131] J. Jeremias 1953, 271.

[132] P. Stuhlmacher 1986/1987, 88. – The most recent larger treatment on the purpose of Paul's letter to the Romans, the monograph of A. Reichert, also takes into account Paul's missionary plans: Through his letter he sought to organize the multifaceted structure of the Roman congregation into a Pauline congregation, in order to enable them to carry out his plans in the case of his disability (2001, 321).

[133] Cf., apart from Stuhlmacher, M. Kettunen 1979.

[134] Cf. the title of J. Jervell 1971: "Der Brief nach Jerusalem"; U. Wilckens 1974, 167: "Paulus legt der römischen Gemeinde sein Evangelium so dar, wie er es demnächst in Jerusalem zu vertreten gedenkt."

[135] See above chapter V.A.I.2. Apart from the scholars mentioned there, see H.-W. Bartsch 1968, 42; W. Schmithals 1975, 12f.; F. Siegert 1985, 110.

[136] R.B. Hays 1983, 1.

[137] A.J.M. Wedderburn 1988, 142; cf. K.P. Donfried 1991, lxx.

[138] P. Melanchthon (quoted in U. Wilckens 1974a, 9).

[139] Cf. E. Lohse 1993; 2003, 46 ("Summe des Evangeliums"); U. Wilckens 1978, 41; C.E.B. Cranfield 1979, 817 ("a serious and orderly summary of the gospel"); D.J. Moo 1996, 29f.: "The theme of the letter is the gospel."

[140] G. Bornkamm 1963, 27f.; cf. J. Becker 1992, 351-394; C. Song 2004, 122: "[Paul's] teaching was not directed to a specific group of people ... but rather intrinsically universalized."

However, principally, both approaches – the one that considers the letter as contingent upon various concrete-historical factors, as reaction to the "need of the moment"[141] and the other that points to its general, "eternal" character – should be seen together: The specific challenges to Paul and his message called for and caused a universally valid response. It is situational in that it is addressed to a fractionalized and diverse Roman community[142] and deals with those theological issues pertinent to its situation; but it is universal in that it seeks to establish the prerequisites for a peaceful Christian unity of Jewish-Christians and Gentile-Christians and to give conclusive and final answers to the issues dealt with.[143]

In concreto, Paul's argumentation followed a strategy with multiple dimensions: The primary addressees of his letter are the Gentile-Christians of the Roman congregation,[144] whom he, on a second communicative level, involves in the (fictitious?) dialogue with his opponents.[145] As will be detailed below, the specific stumbling stone is Paul's contention of the soteriological exclusivity of πίστις Χριστοῦ, which is severely challenged by those upholding the soteriological value of the law and taking issue with Paul's pointed exclusion of it (χωρὶς νόμου).[146] In this two-sided communicative situation and with respect to the particular theological problems, Paul endeavors to expound his own position, to preclude misunderstandings, and to win his addressees' assent and support. But since the proposed and defended exclusivity of πίστις Χριστοῦ concurs with its universality, the situational element of the epistolary communication is seconded by a universal element.

---

[141] J.C. Beker 1980, 25.

[142] On the constitution of the Roman Christians with its several fractional communities, see P. Lampe 1989.

[143] K. Barth gives clear prevalence to the second aspect and begins his preface to the first edition of his commentary: "Paulus hat als Sohn seiner Zeit zu seinen Zeitgenossen geredet. Aber *viel* wichtiger als diese Wahrheit ist die andere, daß er als Prophet und Apostel des Gottesreiches zu allen Menschen aller Zeiten redet" (1922, xi). See also, for instance, A. Nygren 1951, 6-8; G. Klein 1969, 144; R.E. Brown 1998, 563f. – The early collection of Paul's main letters in the first half of the second century (cf. 2Pet 3:16) or even earlier (cf. the proposal of D. Trobisch [1989] that Paul himself edited his letters to the Romans, Corinthians, and Galatians) also presupposes a less polarized view of situational vs. universal. The *Sitz im Leben* of the congregation to which the letters were addressed was at the same time matrix for any possible situation of the church.

[144] See especially Rom 1:5-6.13; 11:13; 15:16.

[145] See below chapter V.B.IV.2.

[146] Cf. M. Theobald 1999, 292f.

B. Faith in Romans 1-3 and in Romans 4

By exploring the context and usage of the stem πιστ- in Romans 1-3 and then in Romans 4, it will become apparent that "faith in the New Testament is a polymorphous concept"[147] and that one has to consider various nuances and distinctions in the way Paul phrases his statements. One is confronted with the question whether or not those who read or listened to the letter were capable of recognizing or understanding more or less subtle distinctions, plays on words, rhetorical challenges to opponents, references to preceding statements, allusions to the Old Testaments, to pre-formed doctrinal elements etc. Furthermore, one has to ask: What stood in the back of Paul's mind when he formulated and dictated his letter? What was his concrete argumentative purpose? Which impression were his words supposed to make.[148]

Our exegesis is divided into four principal parts, setting off with the puzzling expression ἐκ πίστεως εἰς πίστιν in Rom 1:17 (chapter V.B.I), proceeding to the portion of the letter that is remarkably silent on faith and that illustrates the sphere χωρὶς πίστεως, as it were (1:18-3:20) (chapter V.B.II), and finally discussing the coming of faith, first in the dimension of an eschatological power (ἐκ πίστεως,[149] 3:21-31) (chapter V.B.III) and second in the dimension of an individual gift (εἰς πίστιν, 4:1-25) (chapter V.B.IV).

I. Romans 1:16-17: Faith as the Theme of Romans:
ἐκ πίστεως εἰς πίστιν

Oftentimes, the powerful and complex verses in the first chapter of Paul's letter to the Romans, at the beginning of his doctrinal expositions are con-

---

[147] A.C. Thiselton 1980, 409; cf. O. Kuss 1956, 195 ("innere Beweglichkeit des Begriffes"); J. Barr 1961, 202; K. Haacker 1984, 290; D.M. Hay 1989, 475; S. Ota 1997, 65; R.B. Matlock 2000, 6-20; also E.P. Sanders 1977, 490f. As noted, K. Barth speaks of the "Schillern des Begriffs" (1922, xxiv). – We have seen that also Philo (e.g., *Abr* 273) displays a similar multivalent use of πίστις (see above chapter IV.A, especially page 210; also D.A. Campbell 2005, 179 with n.4).

[148] W. Dabourne carries out a distinction between "teleological" and "causal" exposition; the one asks "Where was this text going *to*?" and the other "Where was this text coming *from*?" (1999, 22; italics original). A. Ito, who refers to these statements, puts this concern in other words: One has to "distinguish what Paul intends to convey to the reader/hearer at a certain point of his argumentative flow from what he has in mind on the whole: the former concerns his rhetoric and the latter his theology" (2003, 239).

[149] Statistically, "ἐκ πίστεως is found only in Galatians (9 times) and in Romans (12 times). At the same time it may be recalled that in these two letters Paul employs the Habakkuk quotation… In the LXX there is only one occurrence of the words ἐκ πίστεως and that is precisely in Hab 2:4" (B. Corsani 1984, 87).

ceived of as a programmatic thesis underlying the letter.[150] Every word deserves due consideration[151] – particularly words occurring repeatedly like πίστις/πιστεύειν. From a rhetorical perspective these verses conclude the *proemium*[152] and at the same time constitute the *propositio* containing the basic elements of the following *argumentatio*.[153]

The term τὸ εὐαγγέλιον is the keyword, which constitutes the objective ground for the subjective missionary enterprise of the apostle (Rom 1:13-15); in 1:16b-17 he explicates his gospel in terms of its effects.[154] Already here the stem πιστ- receives central significance, as it appears four times, tying closely together the different elements that define the "gospel."[155] What Paul says about the "righteousness of God" and the "power of God" as undisputed components and characteristics of the salvation-giving gospel is essentially bound to faith. Hence, Paul assigns to faith the function and the capability to integrate and give meaning to the great themes of his message. Accordingly, faith can be shown to be the key-term of the entire letter[156] and at the same time the point at stake[157] – possibly even more so than "God's righteousness"[158]: Here, in 1:16-17 it appears in still "unmodi-

---

[150] Cf., e.g., K. Haacker 1999, 36; C.L. Quarles 2003, 1, 13. On the function of Rom 1:16-17 for the whole of Romans, see J.N. Vorster 1993; E. Lohse 1998; M. Theobald 1999.

[151] Cf. E. Käsemann 1980, 27.

[152] Cf. D.-A. Koch 1986, 275

[153] Cf. J.-N. Aletti 1989, 245 with n.43; M. Theobald 1999, 289.

[154] On the other hand, in Rom 1:3-4 Paul declares *who* is in the center of his gospel. – O. Hofius (1990, 150-154) strongly disagrees with R. Bultmann's contention that εὐαγγέλιον is technical term for the Christian proclamation (1958, 89; similarly U. Wilckens 1978, 74). Gospel and proclamation have to be distinguished, but belong innately together: "Das Menschenwort der Predigt steht ... im Dienst des Evangeliums, und das Evangelium ergeht nirgends anders und wird nirgends anders vernommen als in diesem Menschenwort" (O. Hofius 1990, 153).

[155] M. Theobald points to the "Definitionsstil" of Rom 1:16b-17: dominance of abstract nouns, lack of article, defining ἐστίν (1999, 282; cf. also F. Blass/A. Debrunner/F. Rehkopf 1979, §252n.6). On the other hand, K. Haacker questions the use of the term "definition" due to a lack of an "Oberbegriff" and a demarcation from other realities (1999, 37).

[156] Cf. R. Bultmann 1959, 218.

[157] Cf. E. Lohmeyer 1929, 115; M. Theobald 1999, 283 *et passim* ("der 'strittige Punkt'"). It is not true therefore that "righteousness by faith" is an undisputed element of Paul's theology (against M. Neubrand 1997, 191; cf. 137-139). Rather, only the theme δικαιοσύνη θεοῦ can be called undisputed; considering Jewish tradition, God's righteousness has to be part of Paul's gospel – even if it goes too far to label it *terminus technicus* (thus P. Stuhlmacher 1966, 73, 80; see however 1981, 105f.n.16). The bone of contention is πίστις.

[158] Mostly, "God's righteousness" is regarded as key-term of the letter (cf., e.g., P. Stuhlmacher 1981, 105; F. Hahn 1993; U. Schnelle 2003, 348).

fied" form as πίστις, while later, as πίστις Χριστοῦ, it will receive its full controversial character.[159] For the interpretation of Romans this suggests that the "faith"-theme should be expected – implicitly or explicitly – at every significant assertion and turn in Paul's line of reasoning, and for the content of the letter itself it implies that Paul's greatest interest is to clarify the meaning and significance of faith,[160] as the concept of faith constitutes, as it were, the *articulus stantis et cadentis euangelii (Pauli).*[161]

The distinct, but also complex formulation of the theme makes the attentive reader and hearer aware that whenever Paul brings in the topic of faith in his line of reasoning throughout the letter, special attention is required as to how it relates to the whole of his gospel. Some attempts have been made to find a structural correlation between (parts of) the initial *propositio* and the composition of the following argument, i.e., the *partitio*. An indeed attractive suggestion is that of A. Nygren[162] and A. Feuillet,[163] who point to the organizing function of the Habakkuk quote for Romans 1-8: The first part of the quote ("the righteous by faith") refers to Romans 1-4, the second part ("will live") to Romans 5-8.[164] Detailed reasons in favor of and against this thesis cannot be presented here,[165] but it seems more adequate to interpret Paul's assertion and scriptural quote of Rom 1:17 in terms of a compositionally elevated introduction to Rom 1:18-4:25.[166] This first part of Romans is structured as ring composition

---

[159] Cf. M. Theobald 1999, 291f. – Even the unmodified form πίστις means for Paul faith in relation to Christ (cf. G. Friedrich 1982, 105, referring to H. Cremer 1900, 316).

[160] M. Theobald follows these critical turns in the letter (1999, 295-298): the expression ὑπακοὴ πίστεως (Rom 1:5) in the prescript 1:1-7, the explication of the Pauline key phrase 3:28 in 1:18-4:25, (the application of faith in 6:1-8:39,) the offensiveness of faith for Israel in 9:1-11:36, faith as criterion in the paraenetical part 12:3-8 and the ecclesiological admonition 14:1-15:6, and finally, faith in the epilogue 15:7-13. – Generally, the repetition of ὑπακοὴ πίστεως in 16:26 is considered as part of a post-Pauline addition. But see J.-N. Aletti 1989, 247n.46: "[L]e syntagme *hypakoè pisteôs* apparaît dans l'*exordium* (1,5) et la *peroratio* (16,25 [*sic*]) de Rm. En bonne rhétorique, cela signifie qu'il s'agit d'un thème développé dans le corps de la lettre."

[161] Even statistics support this: Πίστις appears 91 times, πιστεύειν 42 times; taken together they are the most frequent terms relating to salvation, followed by πνεῦμα (with 120 occurrences).

[162] A. Nygren 1951, 86f.

[163] A. Feuillet 1959/1960. "Ces chapitres [*sc.* Rom. i-viii] ... ne veulent être qu'un commentaire du texte d'Habacuc ii. 4 cité au début" (76).

[164] Cf. also with different nuances C.E.B. Cranfield 1975, 102; O. Michel 1978, 43-45. See against this solution U. Luz 1969; E. Käsemann 1980, 29 ("künstlich").

[165] C.E.B. Cranfield summarizes and notes "that in 1.18-4.25 πίστις occurs nineteen times and πιστεύειν eight times, whereas in 5.1-8.39 they occur only twice and once respectively; and that whereas in 1.18-4.25 ζωή occurs only once and ζῆν not at all, each of them occurs twelve times in 5.1-8.39" (1975, 102).

[166] Cf., e.g., S. Lyonnet 1951.

with two quotes from Scripture at the beginning (Hab 2:4) and the end
(Gen 15:6), both with the pronounced occurrence of πίστις/πιστεύειν and
δίκαιος/δικαιοσύνη.[167] The second main part (chapters 5-8) builds on 1:18-
4:25, especially on 4:24-25, and inaugurates a new line of reasoning, presupposing what has been argued previously.[168] Reasons for this view will
be given in the following; they relate to the main thesis of this exegesis,
according to which the prepositional expressions ἐκ πίστεως and εἰς
πίστιν correspond to Paul's elaborations in 3:21-31 and 4:1-25.

1. The Phrase ἐκ πίστεως εἰς πίστιν[169]

Much is dependent on the interpretation of the double recurrence of πίστις
in this verse with the two prepositions ἐκ and εἰς, which already troubled
commentators of the Early Church[170] and "continues to baffle interpreters."[171] Possibly, the interpretation of this phrase mirrors the understanding
of faith of the entire history of theology.[172] Two basic questions are debated. First, from a syntactical view: Do those prepositional expressions ἐκ
πίστεως and εἰς πίστιν refer to the verb ἀποκαλύπτεται[173] or to δικαιοσύνη
θεοῦ[174]? Second, on rhetorical-argumentative grounds: Is the double πίστις
to be assigned to two different subjects of faith[175] or does πίστις take on
two distinguishable meanings[176]; does the construction simply indicate a
rhetorical intensification[177] or does it designate growth of faith[178] or the
foundation and goal of faith[179]?

---

[167] Cf. D.-A. Koch 1986, 276.

[168] Cf. Rom 5:1: Δικαιωθέντες οὖν ἐκ πίστεως. See J.A. Bengel 1773, 562 (*"summa[.] praecedentium"*; italics original); H. Lietzmann 1928, 58: "Das Thema von 1,17 ist
erwiesen. Es folgt die Weiterführung des Gedankens."

[169] See on this phrase, apart from the commentaries, especially A. Fridrichsen 1948
and recently C.L. Quarles 2003; R.M. Calhoun 2006.

[170] See the references and discussion in K.H. Schelkle 1956, 44-46; O. Kuss 1963, 22-
24; C.E.B. Cranfield 1975, 99nn.2f.; K. Haacker 1999, 42nn.87f.; C.L. Quarles 2003, 2f.

[171] C.L. Quarles 2003, 1. A few textual conjectures resulted from this puzzling expression by A. Pallis and J.H. Michael (cited by Quarles [5]).

[172] Thus H.W. Schmidt 1966, 28; also W. Schenk 1972, 166.

[173] Cf., e.g., M.A. Seifrid 1992, 218; K. Haacker 1999, 43.

[174] Cf., e.g., U. Wilckens 1978, 204f. (but see his translation, 76); M. Neubrand 1997,
109.

[175] Cf., e.g., Chrysostom, *Homiliae in epistulam ad Romanos* 2 (from the faith of the
Old Testament saints to the New Testament believers); Augustine, *De Spiritu et Littera*
11,18 (from the faith of the preachers to the faith of the hearers). – Chrysostom's explanation has been revived by C.L. Quarles (2003, 18-21), though R.M. Calhoun criticizes
"that Quarles has not accurately represented what John says" (2006, 131).

[176] Cf., e.g., Tertullian, *Adversus Marcionem* 5,13 (from the faith of the law to the
faith of the gospel).

[177] The following exegetes offer the equation ἐκ πίστεως εἰς πίστιν = *sola fide*: H. Lietzmann, A. Nygren, C.E.B. Cranfield, J.A. Ziesler, D.J. Moo, B. Byrne, J.A. Fitzmyer,

Theologically, the first question pertains to the problem whether human faith can be causally connected to the revelation of God's righteousness. This problem will recur in Rom 3:22.[180] Yet only a limited and systematically pre-formed understanding of faith will raise the concern of such inappropriateness. Since it is imperative to conceive of faith also in "apocalyptic" or eschatological terms, there is good reason to prefer the first solution: ἐκ πίστεως εἰς πίστιν qualifies ἀποκαλύπτεται.

An increasingly popular interpretation also answers the former question in terms of the first option and finds, concerning the second question, both a change of subjects and of meaning: Following K. Barth and others,[181] J.D.G. Dunn writes that the "phrase can and probably should be taken as a play on the ambiguity of the word faith/faithfulness, in the sense 'from *God's* faithfulness (to the covenant promises) to man's response of faith'."[182] Alternatively, one argues with S.K. Stowers, who is preceded for instance by J. Haußleiter, that the "key question is not the believer's faith but Jesus Christ's faithfulness in which the believer shares"; i.e., ἐκ πίστεως denotes Christ's faithfulness.[183]

However, Paul does not indicate in this context any such changes, either of subject or of meaning. If this view should be correct, it has to prove plausible throughout his *argumentatio*. Our criterion therefore is not whether or not the reader/hearer was able to understand Paul's intention on first reading or hearing, but we first ask the question: "Where was this text

---

T.R. Schreiner (referred to in C.L. Quarles 2003, 4); J.A. Bengel 1773, 543; A. Schlatter 1935, 42; A. Fridrichsen 1948; H. Ridderbos 1970, 126; E. Käsemann 1980, 27f.; O. Hofius 1990, 159n.78; E. Lohse 2003, 78. – Quarles challenges this solution by exploring analogous constructions with ἐκ – εἰς in extra-biblical Greek, in the Septuagint (above all LXX Ps 83:3: ἐκ δυνάμεως εἰς δύναμιν), and in Paul (2Cor 2:16: ἐκ θανάτου εἰς θάνατον ... ἐκ ζωῆς εἰς ζωήν; 2Cor 3:18: ἀπὸ δόξης εἰς δόξαν). In none of these places ἐκ – εἰς appears to "function as an idiom of emphasis" (13; cf. 8, 11).

[178] Cf., e.g., J. Calvin and M. Luther, but also W. Sanday/A.C. Headlam 1895, 28; W.H.P. Hatch 1917, 48n.4 (cf. 2Cor 10:15; 2Thess 1:3). H. Binder renders somewhat awkwardly: from small beginnings to all peoples (1968, 50).

[179] H. Schlier 1977, 45; O. Michel 1978, 54; U. Wilckens 1978, 88; M. Theobald 1999, 292n.49.

[180] See below pages 274f.

[181] Cf. K. Barth 1922, 17f. and G. Hebert 1955, 375; T.F. Torrance 1956/1957; J.J. O'Rourke 1973, 189; see in addition K. Haacker 1999, 43, but also J.A. Bengel 1773, 543: "[E]x fide Dei offerentis in fidem hominum accipientium"; Ambrosiaster, *Commentaria* 56: "[E]x fide Dei promittentis in fidem hominis credentis" (cited in C.E.B. Cranfield 1975, 99n.7).

[182] J.D.G. Dunn 1988, 48; cf. 37, 43f.; 1987, 2837f. The analogy between Rom 1:17 and 3:21-22 speaks against Dunn's suggestion.

[183] S.K. Stowers 1994, 202; cf. M.D. Hooker 1989, 180, 183; D.A. Campbell 1994; 2005, 191f.

coming *from*?,"[184] what could have stood before the eyes of the apostle when he formulated this expression, presupposing he had in mind the disposition of his letter in this carefully and intricately constructed *propositio*.

One should give closer attention to E. Lohmeyer's distinction between faith as "metaphysical principle" (ἐκ πίστεως) and faith as "deed" (εἰς πίστιν)[185]; unfortunately, it remained largely unnoticed probably due to his cryptic and philosophically colored style.[186] A different, more satisfactory terminology is called for, since on the one hand, "principle" evokes the notion of an objective law that could be freely accepted, applied and utilized, and since, on the other hand, "deed" brings to mind the idea of such free, synergistic acceptance, application and utilization within the conditions of the "principle."[187] Other terms (which of course might raise other questions) could be: universal-eschatological sphere of power, new salvation-historical reality, and new ground and possibility of existence for ἐκ πίστεως,[188] and access into that sphere, participation in that new reality, and founding one's existence on that new ground for εἰς πίστιν. Through this way of interpretation, A. Schlatter's thesis assumes an unexpected meaning: He claimed that the deeper one understands the causal weight of ἐκ and the teleological of εἰς, the more meaningful the phrase ἐκ πίστεως εἰς πίστιν becomes.[189]

The proposed language seeks to do justice to the dynamic-historical structure of Pauline thinking, as opposed to the subject-object scheme[190]; it

---

[184] W. Dabourne 1999, 22 (see above note 148).

[185] Cf. E. Lohmeyer 1929, 115-125 (faith as "principle"), 125-133 (faith as "deed") (see above chapter II.F.II). Lohmeyer supports his analysis through linguistic observations: The noun occurs much more often than the verb, typically without possessive pronoun; in genitive constructions "Christ" appears most often, though on the whole the absolute use prevails. In verbal expressions the form "I believe" never appears, and also other personal pronouns are used infrequently (115f.; cf. 118, 147). Consequently, the first impression is the notion of faith as a "gegenständliche[r] Sachverhalt" (115).

[186] The one who acknowledges the force of Lohmeyer's presentation of faith, is F. Neugebauer, though he also notes that one has to understand Lohmeyer better than he expressed himself (1961, 156).

[187] What K. Barth says regarding God's grace pertains to our problem as well: "[Die] Gnade Gottes [ist] kein Prinzip, das man als solches einsehen, bejahen und sich aneignen könnte und dann nur konsequent zu entfalten und anzuwenden brauchte ... Sie ist vielmehr frei herrschende Macht und frei sich eröffnende Wahrheit" (1959, 808f.). – On the use of the term "principle" with regard to faith, see above note 306 in chapter II.

[188] Cf. above all the works mentioned above chapter II.F.

[189] A. Schlatter 1935, 42. See also B. Corsani 1984, 92f.

[190] Cf. R. Gyllenberg 1936, 619; F. Neugebauer 1961, 41; H. Binder 1968. D.M. Hay's formulations "objective ground for subjective faith" (1989, 465) or "objective ground and subjective response" (475) run the risk of maintaining this subject-object scheme; it is better to speak of the "divine and human dimensions of Christian faith" (475). See also J.D.G. Dunn 1988, 43; B.S. Childs 1992, 607.

also incorporates the participatory character of faith,[191] i.e., the individual takes part in this new realm. To preclude a misunderstanding: If in the following there is mention of individual appropriation of faith and like expression, the relational, social or intersubjective aspect of faith, i.e., the community of believers (ἐκκλησία), the unity of the body of Christ is always included.

Whether or not this overall thesis bears closer examination, will show itself in due course. It will be argued below that in Rom 3:21-4:25, Paul will develop and elaborate this very schematic expression ἐκ πίστεως εἰς πίστιν in a way that 3:21-26(.27-31) expounds on the first part (ἐκ πίστεως) and 4:1-25 on the second (εἰς πίστιν) – with 5:1 as summary. Thereby, 3:22, which together with 3:21 takes up 1:17,[192] also presents both aspects and hence anticipates the second: God's righteousness has set in through the eschatological, salvation-historical event of faith (διὰ πίστεως),[193] and it is appropriated by all those who believe and take part in this reality (εἰς πάντας τοὺς πιστεύοντας). Likewise, in Gal 3:22 Paul argues that those who believe (οἱ πιστεύοντες) participate in the new reality of faith (ἐκ πίστεως) insofar as they receive the promise given on the basis of this reality.

One difference between Rom 1:17 and 3:21-22 should be noted that concerns the tenses of the verbs ἀποκαλύπτεται (present) and πεφανέρωται (perfect) respectively[194]: At the beginning of his letter, Paul speaks of the present effect and dynamics of his gospel and of the process following on its proclamation (εἰς πίστιν), based on the event of faith (ἐκ πίστεως); hence, God's righteousness is said to be revealed both in terms of salvation history and individual history. In the course of his exposition of this theme, from 3:21 onwards, Paul at first concentrates on the former dimension, on the revelation of God's righteousness once and for all through faith; the implication for the present and the individual he anticipates in 3:22 ("all who believe"), but will develop it later in the Abraham-chapter.[195] In addition, the difference in number – compare πᾶς ὁ πιστεύων (1:16) with

---

[191] Cf. A. von Dobbeler 1987: "Glaube als Teilhabe" – though he understands "participation" in terms of being part of a group and of a new community-understanding.

[192] Cf., e.g., J. Murray 1959, 31f.; D. Hill 1967, 157; W. Schenk 1972, 168 ("genaue Entsprechung zwischen 1,17 und 3,22"); O. Michel 1978, 90. The dismissal of this view by C.L. Quarles (2003, 15) is unconvincing; the dense, programmatic language accounts quite naturally for the abbreviating style.

[193] The prepositional expressions ἐκ πίστεως and διὰ πίστεως are practically synonymous (cf. D.A. Campbell 1992a, 95; see below pages 307f. on Rom 3:30), for in the framework of the salvation-historical dimension of faith, causality ("on the basis of faith") and instrumentality ("through the mediation of faith") are virtually identical.

[194] Cf. with different nuances O. Hofius 1990, 150n.10.

[195] Cf. U. Wilckens 1978, 185.

πάντες οἱ πιστεύοντες (3:22) – strengthens the observation of distinctive perspectives, one of the missionary proclamation (1:16-17) and the other of general salvation-historical facts (3:21-22).

Already here we can anticipate that the distinction between universal and participatory is not limited to the aspect of faith. The correlate of faith in 1:17, "God's righteousness," also comprises these two dimensions[196] with an emphasis on the first. Analogously, as Paul shows especially in 1:18-3:20, also sin, i.e., unrighteousness and ungodliness (1:18), and its correlate "God's wrath" can take on both aspects.[197] Which aspect prevails in the respective context, can only be determined with the help of the context. In 1:17, "the righteousness of God ... is his saving righteousness,"[198] understood as soteriological-eschatological power. This is indicated by the ideas of "revelation" and "power"[199] and the concept of the salvation-historical force of faith (ἐκ πίστεως). But the participatory level is present as well on a second level, suggested by the present tense of ἀποκαλύπτεται, i.e., the "on-going proclamation of the gospel,"[200] and the notion of the individual appropriation of faith (εἰς πίστιν).[201] When we later turn to 3:22 and discuss the relationship between δικαιοσύνη θεοῦ and πίστις Χριστοῦ, further arguments will be added.[202] To be sure, no clear-cut distinction between "universal" and "participatory" is advocated; rather these dimensions are two poles of an ellipsis.

After these remarks, we have to return to the phrase ἐκ πίστεως εἰς πίστιν. Lohmeyer's interpretation failed to recognize that Paul's *argumentatio* (3:21-4:25) draws on the two aspects of faith that he introduced in 1:17 in a schematic way. The related, more radical view of H. Binder also falls short; he says that Paul *never* used πίστις in a "verbal" – in our termi-

---

[196] Cf. U. Schnelle 2003, 352. See also Rom 10:3, where Paul accuses the elect people that it did not submit to the righteousness of God, but sought to establish their own. As in 1:17, δικαιοσύνη θεοῦ implicates "die sich als eschatologische Schöpfergewalt betätigende, die Geschichte und Geschicke lenkende Gottesmacht" (P. Stuhlmacher 1966, 93), but on a second level also "God's proffered gift of a status of righteousness in His eyes" (C.E.B. Cranfield 1975, 515).

[197] Just as with "faith," E. Lohmeyer carries out a distinction concerning "sin" in terms of force and deed (1929, 138f.; cf. also 1930). – In Rom 1:18, "wrath" in connection with ἀποκαλύπτεσθαι denotes primarily the universal-eschatological aspect (cf. P. Stuhlmacher 1966, 80f.: "richtende Gottesmacht"), while 2:8, for instance, emphasizes the individual element.

[198] G.N. Davies 1990, 37.

[199] Cf. P. Stuhlmacher 1966, 78-81.

[200] C.E.B. Cranfield 1975, 109.

[201] Cf. D. Zeller 1985, 43, whose formulation also incorporates both aspects: God's righteousness if offered in the gospel now with eschatological validity.

[202] See below chapter V.B.III.1.e.

nology: participatory – sense,[203] which is incorrect considering the second occurrence of πίστις in 1:17. On the contrary, since R. Bultmann never speaks of faith apart from the believing person, he factually comprehends πίστις *exclusively* as abstract noun of πιστεύειν and neglects the event-character of faith.[204] Rather, Paul is not much concerned with proving or disproving that faith can take on hypostatic nature existing apart from the person,[205] but he is eager to show that faith cannot be separated from Jesus Christ (πίστις Ἰησοῦ Χριστοῦ)[206] – implicitly already here in 1:17, and explicitly in 3:22 (and Gal 3:22).[207] This christological characterization of faith is still to be specified.[208]

2. The Habakkuk Quote

When Paul quotes Hab 2:4 in order to show the compatibility of his thesis with Scripture, he leaves the exegete with two puzzles: First, is there a reason why he abbreviates the quote, omitting the possessive pronoun or suffix of "faith(fulness)"? As is well known, while the Hebrew reads בֶּאֱמוּנָתוֹ, speaking of the person's faith(fulness), the Greek has ἐκ πίστεώς μου, implying God's faithfulness. Second, what is Paul's intention with the ambiguous formulation ὁ δὲ δίκαιος ἐκ πίστεως ζήσεται, in which ἐκ πίστεως could be the point of reference of the verb ζήσεται[209] or of the subject ὁ δίκαιος[210]? In trying to answer these questions, we cannot deal with

---

[203] H. Binder 1968, 11.

[204] See above chapter II.E.I on Bultmann's reluctant comments on the eschatological dimension of faith; cf. E. Käsemann 1980, 20, 103 (faith as "ein anthropologischer ... Begriff"). See the critique in H. Binder 1968, 84. Basically, therefore the substantive and verbal connotations are not identical (cf. G. Friedrich 1982, 104), but the substantive can contain the verbal idea.

[205] Against D. Georgi 1991, 43.

[206] According to E. Käsemann, the emphasis in genitival constructions describing divine eschatological gifts principally falls on the genitive (1980, 26, on δικαιοσύνη θεοῦ).

[207] All this does not exclude that Paul also deliberately allowed for another meaning on the first hearing or reading, which of course does not contradict the other level just discerned: God's righteousness is revealed and happens there, where faith is both beginning and end (cf. H. Schlier 1977, 45); it is founded through faith and aims at faith (U. Wilckens 1978, 88).

[208] See especially below chapters V.B.III.1 and VI.A.VI.

[209] Cf., e.g., NRSV; M. Luther; W. Sanday/A.C. Headlam 1898, 28; T. Zahn 1925, 85; A. Schlatter 1935, 43f.; O. Michel 1978, 90; H. Schlier 1977, 45f.; H.C.C. Cavallin 1978; R.M. Moody 1981; J. Lambrecht 1986, 116f.; M.A. Seifrid 1992, 218; J.A. Fitzmyer 1993, 265.

[210] Since Beza this interpretation exists and is maintained by, e.g., E. Kühl 1913, 40; H. Lietzmann 1928, 30; E. Jüngel 1962, 43; O. Kuss 1963, 22f.; H. Binder 1968, 40; C.E.B. Cranfield 1975, 101f.; U. Wilckens 1978, 89f.; E. Käsemann 1980, 27-29; B. Corsani 1984, 89; D.-A. Koch 1986, 290f.; O. Hofius 1993, 158n.25. Passages that seem to confirm this view are Gal 2:16; 3:8.24; 5:5; Rom 3:22.28.30; 4:11; 5:1.9-10; 9:30;

the text-critical issues involved[211] nor with the meaning of the quote in the original[212] and with its traditional interpretation in Judaism,[213] but have to confine ourselves to the Pauline context – which is difficult enough.[214]

By changing the wording of his *Vorlage* (Septuagint or Masoretic Text) and omitting the genitive pronoun/suffix that defines the subject of "faith(fulness)," Paul made a deliberate choice. Again, for Paul πίστις is at first and above all christologically defined,[215] and certainly neither of the *Vorlagen* that he might have had at his disposal expressed what he intended to convey.[216] According to the whole thrust of Paul's thought, righteousness is contingent on πίστις Χριστοῦ, i.e., on faith that is connected to and belongs to the Messiah. Hence, he is not primarily concerned with the person's faith[217] or faithfulness[218] (πίστις αὐτοῦ), nor with God's

---

10:5. – K. Haacker cites numerous references for both solutions (1999, 44n.100 and n.99). Following H. Lietzmann, J. Jeremias thinks that the pre-Christian Paul read Hab 2:4 in terms of the first alternative, while after his conversion he understood it in the second way (1954/1955, 369).

[211] See the discussion in D.-A. Koch 1984.

[212] On this set of questions, see apart from the commentaries J.A. Emerton 1977; J.M. Scott 1985.

[213] This text received much attention in Judaism before, beside and after Paul (cf. A. Strobel 1961). – One significant interpretation is worth mentioning: 1QpHab 7,17-8,3. It says: "Its interpretation concerns all observing the Law (כול עושי התורה) in the House of Judah, whom God will free from the house of judgment on account of their toil and of their loyalty (אמונה)" (see F. García Martínez/E.J.C. Tigchelaar 1997/1998, 16f.). – Heb 10:38 has ὁ δὲ δίκαιός μου ἐκ πίστεως ζήσεται (on the concept of faith in Hebrews, see with greatly differing emphases E. Gräßer 1965; D. Hamm 1990; G. Schunack 1999a; V. Rhee 2001. The two most recent works stress against Gräßer's ethical interpretation the inherent christological substance of faith in Hebrews).

[214] Cf., e.g., A. Merk 1922; J.A. Sanders 1959; D.M. Smith 1967; W.B. Wallis 1973; H.C.C. Cavallin 1978; J.A. Fitzmyer 1981; R.M. Moody 1981; S.-J. Oh 1992; D.A. Campbell 1994; J.L. Martyn 1997a; G. Bodendorfer 1998; R.E. Watts 1999; M.W. Yeung 2002, 196-225.

[215] Cf. W. Schenk 1972, 169. The question of Christology does not recede into the background (against P. Stuhlmacher 1966, 84), but is always present.

[216] H. Binder claims that Paul left aside a subject of πίστις, since in itself it is subject, event, and activity (1968, 40). – In any case, one should not speak of a deliberately ambiguous reading (against M. Neubrand 1997, 110), but of a deliberately open reading that Paul intends to fill with meaning in due course. As for the mode of how Paul uses the quote, P. Vielhauer even argues: "Paulus übernimmt aus Hab 2,4 nur die Vokabeln, füllt sie aber mit ganz anderem Sinn" (1969, 214; cf. E. Lohse 2003, 82).

[217] Cf. the translation of M. Luther: "der Gerechte wird seines Glaubens leben." – Notably, Paul uses πίστις αὐτοῦ only in Rom 4:5, i.e., in that part of Romans that according to our analysis is concerned with the individuation of faith.

[218] See the just mentioned Qumran *pesher*. Much could be said on the relation between Paul's view of Hab 2:4 and the Qumran writing. Especially noteworthy is the Pauline antithesis of "faith" and "works of the law" in contrast to the Qumranic equation

faithfulness (πίστις θεοῦ),[219] but with "Christ-faith" (πίστις Χριστοῦ).[220] The way how Paul employs the quote from Scripture suggests that he regards it as summary and conclusion of the letter's theme.

What he expressed in his complex, programmatic language could be disentangled as follows: The quote confirms and repeats at first the already employed phrase ἐκ πίστεως[221]: Πίστις constitutes the grounds of possibility on which any realization of righteousness happens; without πίστις no righteousness is revealed, either in a general salvation-historical dimension or in the reality of life of the individual. The latter point gives the reason why, on a second level, the quote explicates εἰς πίστιν, which is at the same time equivalent with the expression πᾶς ὁ πιστεύων: Righteousness is revealed "to faith," i.e., to all who believe, which means in turn that the one who believes is the one who is righteous (ὁ δίκαιος).[222] The references to eternal life and salvation form an inclusion and present the final goal of the process of "justification by faith": salvation to the believer, life to the righteous.[223] Thus, righteousness is essentially, not secondarily, soteriological.[224] Having in mind that both πίστις and δικαιοσύνη can assume

---

of "faithfulness" and "doing the law." O. Michel writes therefore: "*Das antike Judentum kann also aus dem Zitat gerade die von Paulus bekämpfte Meinung herauslesen*" (1978, 90n.40; italics original).

[219] Cf. K. Barth 1922, 18.

[220] The christological view of faith is also present in the other Pauline Habakkuk quote, in Gal 3:11 (cf. D.A. Campbell 1994, 279).

[221] The correlation of the two ἐκ πίστεως-occurrences in Rom 1:17 is important (cf., e.g., W. Schenk 1972, 167; O. Michel 1978, 90).

[222] It is rather unlikely that Paul understood the Habakkuk quote as messianic prophecy, as it was the case in some traits of Jewish theology (cf. already J. Haußleiter 1891, 212f., and more recently A.T. Hanson 1974, 42-45; R.B. Hays 1983, 134-138; 1997, 278-281; D.A. Campbell 1992; 1994; 2005, 219; S.K. Stowers 1994, 198-202; but see against this view, e.g., M. Neubrand 1997, 110n.49; R.E. Watts 1999; C.L. Quarles 2003, 17f.). – *Inter alia* the equation of ὁ πιστεύων and ὁ δίκαιος ἐκ πίστεως counters this suggestion. Furthermore, one should take into consideration O. Betz's suggestion (1991, 72), taken up extensively by M.W. Yeung (2002), that Jesus' saying ἡ πίστις σου σέσωκέν σε has close affinities to Paul's interpretation Hab 2:4, which would also weaken the case for a messianic understanding of the prophecy.

[223] This structural parallelism of σωτηρία and ζῆν and the association of both terms with δικαιοσύνη appears to convey a principally soteriological-forensic perspective. This again counters the proposal to regard ἐκ πίστεως as modifier of ζήσεται and read into the formulation a primarily ethical perspective (against G.N. Davies 1990, 38). That for Paul God's righteousness "calls to a life of obedience" (M. Brauch 1977, 540) is beyond dispute, but was his first intention to argue for the ethical implications of God's righteousness in Rom 1:16-17? See also below pages 397-399 on the expression ὑπακοὴ πίστεως.

[224] Nevertheless D. Hill's distinction is still correct: God's righteousness "brings about salvation, but is not equated with it" (1967, 156; cf. S. Westerholm 2004, 285).

both a super-individual and an individual perspective, one can extrapolate two traits in 1:16-17:

(1) "universal trait": ἐκ πίστεως – ἐκ πίστεως – δικαιοσύνη θεοῦ

(2) "individual trait": πᾶς ὁ πιστεύων – εἰς πίστιν – δικαιοσύνη θεοῦ/ὁ δίκαιος

Consequently, to answer the questions posed above: First, in quoting Hab 2:4 Paul had to use πίστις in the absolute sense, since it served the development of his own formulation ἐκ πίστεως εἰς πίστιν[225] – and will function as "linguistic template" for the following ἐκ πίστεως-expressions[226] –, but on second glance it becomes obvious that already here the expression ἐκ πίστεως Χριστοῦ stood before the apostle's eyes,[227] which will become so important later. Second, the brief analysis of the quote in Paul's line of reasoning showed that most likely ἐκ πίστεως modifies ὁ δίκαιος, so that just as δικαιωθεὶς ἐκ πίστεως (5:1) summarizes 3:21-4:25, δίκαιος ἐκ πίστεως introduces it. However, text and theology are generally open to both alternatives, and the suggested solution is not subjected to a rigid either-or exegesis[228]; nevertheless the most probable primary reference needs to be highlighted.

II. Romans 1:18-3:20: The Opposite Side of Faith[229]

1. The Wrath of God over Human Sinfulness

Paul inserts into the flow of his thought a large "parenthesis,"[230] which deals with the revelation of the wrath of God (ὀργὴ θεοῦ) over human ungodliness and sinfulness. This arrangement has a theological purpose: He interrupts the thetical presentation of the content of his gospel, i.e., the revelation of God's righteousness from faith to faith, by a portrayal of the

---

[225] Cf. D.-A. Koch 1986, 128.

[226] D.A. Campbell 1992a, 101.

[227] Cf. W. Schenk 1972, 168.

[228] An open reading is also suggested in C.K. Barrett 1957, 31; G.N. Davies 1990, 41; R.L. Brawley 1997, 293.

[229] On this part of Romans, see J.-N. Aletti 1988 (cf. 1992, 362f.); R.H. Bell 1998 (but see also the critique of Bell by S.K. Stowers [2000, 370: "unconvincing"]). – A discussion of the text-historical issues cannot be accomplished here. The carefully structured arrangement makes Pauline authorship most likely (against those who judge Rom 1:18-2:29 as foreign element, as Hellenistic-Jewish "synagogue sermon" inserted by Paul [E.P. Sanders 1983, 123-135] or as non-Pauline interpolation [W.O. Walker 1999]). Furthermore, we can only state the difficulties contained in this section: 2:17-29 is written in a diatribe-style with an imaginary Jewish interlocutor (S.K. Stowers 1981, 79-115), but is 2:25-2:29 directed against Judaism (O. Kuss 1963, 90; O. Michel 1978, 134) or is it merely an inner-Jewish critique (W. Schmithals 1988, 96-101; M. Neubrand 1997, 114)?

[230] Cf. D.-A. Koch 1986, 275. It is insofar parenthesis, as God's wrath is not part of and does not derive from the gospel (cf. J. Becker 1992, 372).

reality of the sphere outside of πίστις. Only the knowledge of the disclosure of God's righteousness in the gospel opens the eyes for the full dimension of the catastrophe of the other side, of God's wrath.[231]

This can be verified rhetorically: After the dominance of πίστις in Rom
1:16-17, Paul generates a "vacuum" by being silent on "faith" and on the
one to whom faith belongs, Jesus Christ.[232] Thus the vacuum is characterized by the fact that neither faith nor Christ is present; it is a global state of
calamity of *all* of humanity.[233] God's charge of human sinfulness is inescapable; there is not even an (ethical) imperative in 1:18-3:20 that would
call for the avoidance of sins.[234] The force created by this contrast is positively taken up by Paul in 3:21-4:25 where he will clarify what (participation in) that πίστις Χριστοῦ means. Hence, the revelation of God's wrath
is no separate revelation,[235] but the *negativum* effected by the revelation of
God's righteousness through faith.

The truth that Paul seeks to convey so powerfully in 1:18-3:20 is that
"everybody without exception is a sinner, as Scripture attests"[236]: Πάντες
γὰρ ἥμαρτον (3:23) – *non posse non peccare*. But Paul not only aligns
himself with the Jewish and early Christian notion that ἁμαρτία means the
single deed of transgression, but he also radicalizes and "globalizes" this
idea[237]: Sin is a trans-individual, cosmic power, which enslaves all of humankind.[238] Hence, he can also say: πάντες ὑφ' ἁμαρτίαν εἰσίν (3:9; cf.

---

[231] Cf. C.E.B. Cranfield 1975, 104n.1. – Normally, it is argued that "[a]lthough God's
wrath has an eschatological dimension (2.5), it is always present where sin is operative"
(G.N. Davies 1990, 46; cf. C.E.B. Cranfield 1975, 110; see in addition the numerous
exegetes mentioned in H.-J. Eckstein 1987, 21-28). The antithetical parallelism connecting the two verses is indeed apparent (cf. P. Stuhlmacher 1966, 80). However, due to the
difficulty of integrating into this view the expression ἀπ' οὐρανοῦ, H.-J. Eckstein (1987)
and M. Theobald (2001a) developed an insight already articulated by Irenaeus that the
present tense of the verb ἀποκαλύπτεται has a futuric meaning and refers to the "*universale Zorngericht Gottes am Ende der Zeit*" (M. Theobald 2001a, 96; italics original; cf.
also O. Hofius 1993, 156n.11; 1997, 39; J. Woyke 2001, 197n.47, 200). A closer discussion of this specific interpretation cannot be offered here, but as the following argument
shows, prevalence is given to the more common view. See against this proposal also E.
Lohse 2003, 86 with n.4.
[232] Apart from Rom 3:2-3 there is no mention of πίστ-, and apart from 2:16, Paul fails
to mention Jesus Christ.
[233] Cf. J. Becker 1992, 373.
[234] Cf. O. Michel 1978, 95.
[235] Cf. G. Bornkamm 1935, 10, 30-33.
[236] I.H. Marshall 2004, 309, and many others.
[237] Cf. R. Bultmann 1958, 244f.; H. Conzelmann 1967, 217; E. Gräßer 1998, 19-22.
[238] While G. Röhser's work on sin and its personification in Paul speaks of a personified "Tatbegriff" (cf. 1987, 142), H. Umbach points to the power-character of sin (cf.
1999, 127: "widergöttliche[.] dämonische[.] Macht"), which transcends and signifies
more than the sum of human transgressions (17) and which stands opposite to the

Gal 3:22). Linguistic evidence for this view offers itself in the fact that ἁμαρτία is used almost always in the absolute[239] and in the singular.[240] Thus, for sin to be an effective force, it is not dependent on human deeds,[241] but rather, everybody's inevitable participation and being in that calamitous reality is unavoidably connected to sinful deeds.[242] Apart from the righteousness of God revealed through πίστις Χριστοῦ (Rom 3:21-22), all live in this reality and facilitate a historical realization of the power of sin. Especially the verbal expressions, such as to be under sin (3:9), serve sin (6:6), have sin dwell in oneself (7:17), point to the double character of sin for Paul. Sin came into the world "through one man," and as a consequence all have sinned (5:12),[243] since the power of sin determines *a priori* a person's being and causes concrete sinful acts.[244] The first aspect (being) has been called the "qualitative," the second (doing) the "quantitative"

"Machtbereich" of righteousness (265). Cf. E. Lohse 2003, 122. Today, the view that ἁμαρτία denotes some kind of power is rather common, but see against this the perspective of F.C. Baur, normative for a long time: He claimed that "die Sünde wesentlich nur in dem Bewußtsein existiert, das man von ihr hat" (referred to in E. Lohmeyer 1930, 89).

[239] Cf. E. Lohmeyer 1930, 79f. with nn.1f. According to Lohmeyer, the exception to this rule is found in Old Testament quotations (Rom 4:7 [see below chapter V.B.IV.4.d]; 11:27) and passages in the context of traditional pieces (1Cor 15:3.17; 1Thess 2:16), or in a greeting formula (Gal 1:4). Rom 7:5 is no counter-example. In contrast, the term παράπτωμα often takes a personal genitive.

[240] In Romans, the plural only occurs in 4:7; 7:5; 11:27, i.e., in passages in which Paul draws on tradition. Otherwise, the singular is used (not all these passages, though, emphasize the power-character of sin): see Rom 3:9.20; 4:8; 5:12(*bis*).13(*bis*).20.21; 6:1.2.6(*bis*).7.10.11.12.13.14.16.17.18.20.22.23; 7:7(*bis*).8(*bis*).9.11.13(*ter*).14.17.20.23. 25; 8:2.3(*ter*).10; 14:23.

[241] Cf. E. Lohmeyer 1930, 79f.; H. Umbach 1999, 207n.535: Sin stands "jenseits vom menschlichen Fehlverhalten." See differently U. Wilckens 1978, 317 (see also above pages 222f.): "Wo 'alle gesündigt haben,' herrscht 'die Sünde' in der Welt." Lohmeyer overdoes it however, when he makes an Aristotelian distinction between *substantia* and *forma* (80) and labels sin as "mythisch-metaphysische Macht" (81; cf. 84).

[242] According to O. Hofius (1996, 69nn.23 and 31), sin is regarded as personified power in Rom 3:9.20; 5:12.21; 6:1-2.6-7.10-14.16-18.20.22-23; 7:7-9.11.13-14.17.20.23; 8:2-3.10 (also 1Cor 15:56); and as deed in Rom 4:8; 5:13.20; 14:23.

[243] R. Bultmann's often quoted statement that through sinning sin came into the world (1958, 251) is *only* valid for Adam.

[244] The verb ἁμαρτάνειν, which occurs rather infrequently, is certainly used exclusively for the deed-character of sin, and hence appears predominantly in parenetic sections (1Cor 6:18; 7:28.36; 8:12; 15:34). – In this context E. Lohmeyer anticipates what others called the "robust conscience" of the apostle: "Das Problem der Sünde ist also ... für Paulus nicht aus der Erfahrung des eigenen Herzens aufgestiegen" (1930, 85; cf. 1929a, 68: Paul knows nothing of a "Ringen und Verzweifeln an dem eigenen Ich" as Luther did). This is clearly one-sided, for theological ideas are never disconnected from one's life experience.

character of sin,[245] but it is important to remember that for Paul the person's being under the prevenient power of sin and the person's actual sinning are mutually dependent. In Paul, the theological necessity of sin (being "under sin," 3:9) and the empirical factuality of sin ("all have sinned," 3:23) correlate, though he knows to distinguish both aspects. Also, Paul does not ponder the question if "sin" could exist in an a-historical, mythical way. Its power is visible in sinful deeds, and sinful deeds make apparent its power.[246] Hence, there is also no tension for Paul in the relationship between "sin as inevitable predicament" and "sin as responsible deed."[247] Overall, however, the crucial point for Paul is God's will to rescue humanity from their sinful state and deeds, which is why he handed Christ over to death, while we still were sinners (4:25; 5:6.8).

Paul's hermeneutics and rhetoric of faith opens the eyes for the tragedy caused and represented by the power of sin. But before dealing with Paul's portrayal of the way out from this tragedy, πίστις Χριστοῦ, we have to ask what these findings on "sin" have to do with the structure of "faith"? E. Lohmeyer noted that ultimately there are two foundations of "being," faith and sin; and everything that is historical originates from these foundations and is accordingly called faith and sin.[248] That means that in Paul's thinking, sin and faith, both in their trans-individual power and their individual appropriation, display a similar structure. Thus, the force of faith is visible in a believing attitude, and a believing attitude makes apparent its force. In Rom 14:23, he connects the participatory aspect of both terms explicitly: "For all that is not from faith is sin." Similar to ἁμαρτία, πίστις is regularly used in the absolute and appears only in the singular.[249] Just as the power of sin determines a person's existence and its outcome: death (cf. 5:12; 6:23), the power of faith determines the person's existence and its outcome: life (cf. 1:17). While Adam is the mediator of the cosmic power of sin: "Sin came into the world through one man" (5:12), Christ is the mediator of faith: "[W]hen Christ came faith came."[250] However, while both Adam and Christ are mediators, only Christ is also origin and originator. Paul notably does not say through whom/what sin originated.[251] In a re-

---

[245] On the terms "qualitative" and "quantitative" here, see J. Lambrecht 1986, 243f.

[246] Some highlight the former aspect: The power of sin determines the existence of everybody (e.g., O. Hofius 1987, 81; H. Umbach 1999), while others stress the latter: The power of sin is the manifestation of the sin of all humans (e.g., G. Röhser 1987; M. Theobald 2000, 153f.).

[247] On this problem, see E. Käsemann 1980, 138; U. Wilckens 1978, 316f.

[248] Cf. E. Lohmeyer 1929, 138f.; 1930, 82.

[249] See above note 185.

[250] M. Barth 1970, 204, with regard to Gal 3:19-26.

[251] Cf. E. Lohmeyer 1930, 86f.

markable line of thought, however, he links sin with the law.[252] It would lead us astray here to tackle this most difficult problem of the relationship between sin and law, but some aspects will become pertinent in due course.

2. The Faithfulness of God versus Human Disbelief

After these remarks on God's wrath as his righteousness apart from and without Christ,[253] we now briefly turn to "a passage that has been the despair of many,"[254] Rom 3:1-8, where Paul – possibly in dialogue "with a fellow Jew,"[255] possibly in a theoretical reflection[256] – explicates how God deals with a covenant partner who has broken the covenant.[257] The text presumes "a lawsuit between two parties"[258]: God as the "true" judge against his "lying" covenant partner; the creator against the unreasonable creature. Clearly, God wins the case.

The passage centers on the truthfulness and righteousness of God's words: He is the judge who utters words of judgment and he is the creator who creates through his words. Surely, therefore, ἀπιστία is a lack of human faithfulness that radically opposes to God's covenant faithfulness.[259]

But it also likely that Paul here anticipates what he will further develop through his reference to Gen 15:6 and more generally to the Abraham figure. Ἀπιστία is not only unfaithfulness, but also rejection of faith[260] and hostility against God. The consequence of ἀπιστία, of disbelief in God's words, is ἀδικία, an unrighteous standing before God,[261] while on the other hand God judges Abraham's πίστις, his faith in his words, as δικαιοσύνη, as right standing before God. Abraham did not oppose in disbelief (ἀπιστία) to God's promise, but he became strong in faith (πίστις) and

---

[252] In the context of the discussion on ἔργα νόμου and καυχᾶσθαι, we will see that for R. Bultmann, this connection is central: The law triggers the central sin: boasting (1958, 242). See below pages 294f. and 332f.

[253] Cf. K. Barth 1922, 20: "Gottes Zorn ist Gottes Gerechtigkeit außer und ohne Christus."

[254] A.J.M. Wedderburn 1988, 112.

[255] S.K. Stowers 1984.

[256] Cf. E. Käsemann 1980, 73, with reference to R. Bultmann 1958, 110f.

[257] Often scholars point to the parallelism of ἡ πίστις τοῦ θεοῦ, θεοῦ δικαιοσύνη, and ἀλήθεια τοῦ θεοῦ (cf. P. Stuhlmacher 1966, 86; R.B. Hays 1980; 1997, 282; S.K. Williams 1980, 268 ["virtual equivalents"]; M. Neubrand 1997, 115n.76). This potential synonymity of πίστις and ἀλήθεια is endorsed by the fact that while the Septuagint consistently translates אֱמוּנָה with ἀλήθεια, Aquila and Symmachus prefer πίστις (cf. H. Ljungman 1964, 14n.1).

[258] H. Ljungman 1964, 21.

[259] Cf. P. Stuhlmacher 1966, 85.

[260] Cf. O. Michel 1978, 138.

[261] In 2Cor 4:3-4 Paul parallels οἱ ἄπιστοι and οἱ ἀπολλύμενοι.

gave glory to God (Rom 4:20). "Πίστις is thus linked to the fact that God is found 'truthful,' 'has right' (in his words)."[262] Furthermore, πίστις is also the creature's acceptance that God justifies through his word of creation which "calls into existence the things that do not exist" (4:17; cf. 4:3-5.24-25).[263] Such acceptance also happens through a "word-event," namely, by way of confession (10:9-10).

Upon first reading or hearing Rom 3:1-8, this suggested anticipation of the Abraham-chapter does not stand out as obvious, but the first occurrence of a derivate of πιστ- after the presentation of the theme of the letter (1:16-17) in 3:2 catches eye and ear and creates an expectation as to how human disbelief (ἀπιστία) and unrighteousness (ἀδικία) can be overcome, how salvation (σωτηρία) (1:16) and righteousness (δικαιοσύνη) are received, and how God averts his wrath (ὀργή) (3:5; cf. 1:18).[264] And indeed, following on the pointed restating of the general sinfulness of humankind 3:9-20, Paul precisely describes God's righteousness revealed through faith (3:21-31),[265] and God's conferring righteousness to Abraham who believed (4:1-25).

The verse concluding this Pauline "parenthesis" summarizes the basic facts (3:20): Alluding to Ps 143:2 (LXX Ps 142:2),[266] the apostle denies any grounds of righteousness before God based on the "works of the law" and continues in a doctrinal thesis[267]: The (salvation-historical reality of the) law brings knowledge of (the power of) sin; it cannot reveal righteousness, for righteousness comes through the (new, eschatological power of) faith.

Paul refers to this Psalm-verse in Gal 2:16 and Rom 3:20, but in each case one decisive modification occurs[268]: The inclusion of ἔργα νόμου specifies the negative side of his doctrine of justification.[269] Below, this unique Pauline expression will be dealt with in greater detail,[270] but we have to note the often neglected explosiveness of the opposition between ἔργα νόμου and πίστις in Paul's thought, breaking forth in various con-

---

[262] H. Ljungman 1964, 35.

[263] Cf. P. Stuhlmacher 1966, 227.

[264] E. Brandenburger (1988, 165, 186) points to the correlation between πίστις, σωτηρία, and ὀργή.

[265] Also H. Ljungman states that Rom 3:3-5 and 3:21-31 mutually explain each other (1964, 37).

[266] See R.B. Hays 1980 on the significance of LXX Ps 142:1-2 for the argument of the entire chapter 3.

[267] Cf. O. Michel 1978, 145 with n.9.

[268] Cf. D.-A. Koch 1986, 18. Minor changes are πᾶσα σάρξ for πᾶς ζῶν and the third person (ἐνώπιον αὐτοῦ) for the second (ἐνώπιον σοῦ).

[269] Cf. E. Lohse 2003, 125.

[270] See below the *excursus* chapter V.B.III.4.

texts. Modifications of traditional texts are paradigmatic: Here, in 3:20, he inserts ἔργα νόμου into an allusion to Psalm 143, while in Rom 3:25 he will insert πίστις into a traditional paradosis. What does this imply? Formally, it reinforces the opposition between the two entities ἔργα νόμου and πίστις.[271] When dealing with 3:25 the question will become pertinent, whether the opposition is characterized in terms of a juxtaposition of futile human activity with the gracious divine initiative[272] or in terms of two "alternatives on the human side on the basis of which ... one might hope to be justified"[273] – or, if there is a third solution that reconciles both suggestions through reconsidering the common understanding of "faith." O. Michel asks whether the phrase διὰ πίστεως (3:22) might be the part in this section that is most important to Paul (3:21-31).[274] This endeavor of re-examining a pre-formed understanding of faith and of answering Michel's question constitutes the main part of the following chapters.

III. Romans 3:21-31: The Salvation-Historical Reality of Faith:
ἐκ πίστεως

1. Romans 3:21-22b: πίστις Ἰησοῦ Χριστοῦ

In Rom 3:21-22 Paul picks up the thread of his introductory programmatic thoughts on the "righteousness of God" and on "faith," which he interrupted through the "parenthesis" on God's wrath. Now, he turns his perspective from the human plight to the divine solution,[275] which, corresponding to the inescapability of sin, has to consist in "an (apocalyptic!) transformation of the conditions of human existence."[276] Despite the minor differences to 1:16-17,[277] the function of this new paragraph (νυνὶ δέ) is to affirm the main thesis uttered at the beginning of the letter by creating an antithesis to 1:18-3:20, but also to introduce decisive new aspects.[278]

While 1:18-3:20 and 3:27-31 are marked by the style of the diatribe, one could describe the style of 3:21-26 as "proklamatorisch."[279] However, the

---

[271] In a more concise syntactical unit both elements appear in Gal 2:16, too: ἔργα νόμου and πίστις Ἰησοῦ Χριστοῦ.

[272] R.B. Hays 2002, xlvii.

[273] J.D.G. Dunn 1997, 261; cf. 270; R.B. Matlock 2000, 21f.

[274] O. Michel 1978, 146f. He does not answer his question though.

[275] Cf. F.S. Thielmann 1989; E. Adams 1997, 49.

[276] S. Westerholm 2004, 373; cf. 280f. with n.46.

[277] Cf. especially the difference in tense of the verbs (ἀποκαλύπτεται [1:16] and πεφανέρωται [3:21]), but also the difference in number of the noun πᾶς (πᾶς ὁ πιστεύων [1:16] and πάντες οἱ πιστεύοντες [3:22]).

[278] Cf. J. Woyke 2001. For argumentative and stylistic reasons, it cannot be denied that Rom 3:21 begins a new section (against R.B. Hays 1980; 1985, 83n.26; S.K. Stowers 1981, 155-174); it is a "Schlüsselstelle und Wendepunkt" (J. Woyke 2001, 206).

[279] O. Michel 1978, 146; cf. G. Klein 1963, 146.

theme and the line of argument remain the same: For Paul, the Christ-event that has disclosed God's saving righteousness is the decisive, eschatological consequence of the fact that no human being is justified by works. The law and the prophets testify to this revelation of God's righteousness.[280]

With the revelation of God's righteousness through πίστις Χριστοῦ, a new salvation-historical era has begun, the eschatological "time" has set in.[281] Νυνὶ δέ, therefore, signifies both logical antithesis and eschatological turning-point.[282] In 3:22, Paul has in mind not only Gentiles,[283] thinking in religious-sociological categories; but what he says is valid "for Israel and for the nations,"[284] since he argues in an all-embracing theological framework. Just as the law is not merely an identity or boundary marker of a certain group living within certain "national and religious parameters,"[285] faith is not primarily the most characteristic attribute of another group that would distinguish it "more than anything else." Such a view would equal a fatal reduction of Paul's thought. Rather: For Paul, both, the law and faith are theological and soteriological categories that have their validity beyond sociological boundaries. To be sure, Paul's words were "shocking" to any Jew, to whom the righteousness of God was intrinsically connected to the law[286]; yet for Paul the Christ-event broke apart this connection: Now, God's righteousness belongs to faith ("faith-righteousness"[287]), i.e., faith is the divine means through which his righteousness is revealed.

But what is the meaning of the enigmatic genitival construction πίστις Ἰησοῦ Χριστοῦ, which, in the letter to the Romans, occurs in 3:22 for the

---

[280] For Paul as for all Jews, in no other mode than testimony certitude arises (Rom 3:21.31; cf. W. Brueggemann 1997, 714n.20).

[281] The *passivum divinum* πεφανέρωται in the perfect tense signifies "die Dauer des Vollendeten" (O. Kuss 1963, 112), not merely a past event in history.

[282] Cf. E. Käsemann 1980, 86, 177; C.E.B. Cranfield 1975, 201; U. Wilckens (1978, 184f., with reference to Rom 3:26; 5:9-11; 6:21; 7:6; 8:1; 11:30-31; 13:11). Against J. Woyke 2001, 206, who denies an eschatological or salvation-historical understanding. Woyke recapitulates the scholarly debate over the particle νυνὶ δέ, lists 19th century interpreters who also contested the temporal meaning (185f.; W.M.L. de Wette, H.A.W. Meyer, F. Godet), and proves the current dominance of the eschatological or salvation-historical view (186 with nn.11f.; apart from Käsemann, Wilckens, and Cranfield: O. Kuss, A. Viard, H. Schlier, R. Pesch, J.D.G. Dunn, W. Schmithals, J.A. Fitzmyer, D.J. Moo, T.R. Schreiner), partly with the explicit or implicit assumption of the apocalyptic scheme of the two eons (187 with n.13; W. Sanday/A. C. Headlam, A. Nygren, P. Althaus, H. Schlier, O. Michel, U. Wilckens, E. Käsemann, J.D.G. Dunn, W. Schmithals, J.A. Fitzmyer).

[283] Against, e.g., S.K. Stowers 1989, 669.

[284] S.J. Gathercole 2002, 225.

[285] Thus, J.D.G. Dunn 1988, 165, 178.

[286] J.D.G. Dunn 1988, 165.

[287] See below pages 357f. on Rom 4:11.

first time[288]? It seems appropriate to enter the debate at this point and to scrutinize the basic arguments of the subjective understanding.[289] The following points are claimed to support the view that Paul uses this phrase to denote Christ's faithfulness:

(1) In Romans there is no statement that names unambiguously, from a grammatical and contextual perspective, Christ as the one to whom faith is directed – contrary to Gal 2:16[290] and Phil 1:29. – We will see that the customary clear-cut distinction of Christ as object or subject of faith misses the complex semantics of πίστις Χριστοῦ, both from a grammatical and contextual perspective.

(2) Also, particularly the Abraham-chapter lends to the theme of faith in Romans a distinctive theocentric character; this is claimed to stand in contradiction to the christocentric faith of the traditional understanding. – It will be shown that and how the theocentric character of Romans 4, but also of Rom 3:21-31 can be meaningfully integrated into Paul's Christology.[291]

(3) Furthermore, one has to account for the formally parallel constructions πίστις τοῦ θεοῦ (3:3), πίστις Ἰησοῦ (Χριστοῦ) (3:22.26), and πίστις (τοῦ πατρὸς ἡμῶν) Ἀβραάμ (4:12.16). – As has been and will be seen, the structure of Romans 3 and 4 gives clues as to how one is to understand the (different) meaning(s) of πίστις in the respective context.

(4) Just as Gal 3:22, Rom 3:22 has a noteworthy double occurrence of πιστ- where Paul juxtaposes the noun πίστις and the verb πιστεύειν: "Through πίστις Ἰησοῦ Χριστοῦ for all who believe." There are two options to explain this puzzling verse: Either it is a redundancy of expression, "a tautology, a senseless repetition, resembling the diction of verbose ministers whose sermons will never end,"[292] or it signifies a distinction of two

---

[288] The formula πίστις Χριστοῦ and its equivalents appears seven times in Paul:

πίστις Ἰησοῦ Χριστοῦ	Rom 3:22; Gal 3:22
πίστις Ἰησοῦ	Rom 3:26
πίστις Χριστοῦ Ἰησοῦ	Gal 2:16
πίστις Χριστοῦ	Gal 2:16; Phil 3:9
πίστις τοῦ υἱοῦ τοῦ θεοῦ	Gal 2:20

See also the *varia lectio* (P[46]) in Gal 3:26, which has πίστις Χριστοῦ and in addition Eph 3:12, which reads πίστις αὐτοῦ [*sc.* Χριστοῦ Ἰησοῦ]. The genitive of the verse from Ephesians is determined as subjective for instance by M. Barth (1981, 347) and I.G. Wallis (1995, 128-132). – On the grammatical issue in general, see N. Turner 1963, 211.

[289] On Rom 3:21-26, see especially L.T. Johnson 1982; R.B. Hays 1983, 156-161.

[290] Cf. R.B. Hays 1983, 156. This is why Hays deems Galatians to be "the more difficult case" (1997, 277n.10). See however the already mentioned interpretation by G. Kittel (1906, 428f.) and S.K. Williams (1987, 434f.) (see above note 454 in chapter II).

[291] L.E. Keck formulates: "Paul's theology in Romans is theocentric but christomorphic" (2005, 141).

[292] M. Barth 1970, 203.

different aspects of "faith." – That the verse is by no means tautological, but rather carefully formulated, can be demonstrated.

(5) The problem of the final issue arose already in 1:17[293] and concerns the relationship between πίστις Ἰησοῦ Χριστοῦ and δικαιοσύνη θεοῦ and the question: Is it imaginable that human faith can bring about the revelation of God's righteousness? – The detachment of πίστις Χριστοῦ from the misleading subject-object pattern and its redefinition in terms of a salvation-historical reality will render this question a wrongly posed question.

The brief overview of scholarly positions that favor the subjective reading[294] has indicated the implications of such a view, which pertain to questions of soteriology, Christology, the doctrine of justification and others.[295] Our quest is put into perspective, if one realizes that the question: "Whether or not in Christ there was faith (Utrum in Christo fuerit fides)" has always been part of scholastic *quaestiones*.[296]

The following argumentation will be arranged according to the five points just enumerated.

a) Grammatical and Cultural Conditions – Context

It is true that the formulation εἰς Χριστὸν Ἰησοῦν πιστεύειν in Gal 2:16 and Phil 1:29 is exceptional in Paul, but passages like Rom 9:33, 10:11, 10:14, and Phlm 5 surely reduce the difficulty of identifying the direction of human faith with Christ.[297] In turn, as especially A.J. Hultgren pointed out, the subjective understanding is confronted with a grammatical diffi-

---

[293] See above page 244.

[294] See above chapter II.H.

[295] Among those who propose a subjective interpretation or Rom 3:22 are, e.g., H.W. Schmidt 1966, 64: "Christi Opfertod wird als Glaubenstat verstanden." 66; S.K. Williams 1980, 276; 1987; S.K. Stowers 1989, 669; 1994, 194-202; D.A. Campbell 1992, 58-69 (with a discussion of the *état de question*); M. Neubrand 1997, 118f., and the other scholars enumerated in chapter II.H. Stowers goes so far as to argue that "Paul consistently applies διὰ τῆς πίστεως to the redemption of the Gentiles" (1989, 672), i.e., even in Gal 2:16 and Phil 3:9.

[296] See, for instance, Petrus Lombardus, *Sententiae* 3,26,4: "Christus, in quo fuerunt bona patriae, credidit quidem et speravit resurrectionem tertia die futuram, pro qua et Patrem oravit; nec tamen fidem-virtutem vel spem habuit, quia non aenigmaticam et specularem, sed clarissimam de ea habuit cognitionem, quia non perfectius cognovit praeteritam, quam intellexit futuram. Speravit tamen Christus, sicut in Psalmo ait: 'In te, Domine, speravi'; nec tamen fidem vel spem-virtutem habuit, quia per speciem videbat ea quae credebat." Thomas Aquinas, *Summa Theologica* 3,7,3: "[E]xcluso quod res divina sit non visa excluditur ratio fidei. Christus autem a primo instanti suae conceptionis plane vidit Deum per essentiam … Unde in eo fides esse non potuit" (quoted in G. Ebeling 1958, 97f.n.1; see also I.G. Wallis 1995, 1). Ebeling himself concludes: "[E]s dürfte unmöglich sein, angesichts der Art und Weise, wie Jesus vom Glauben redet, ihn selbst vom Glauben auszunehmen" (1958, 97; cf. D.A. Campbell 2005, 193).

[297] See also Eph 1:15; Col 2:5. Cf. even D.A. Campbell 2005, 221f.n.19.

culty: When πίστις is accompanied by a subjective genitive, the definite article is "invariably present."[298] Though the formulation "invariably" is too strong, considering Rom 4:16, the argument is to be taken seriously.[299]

Furthermore, one could enumerate some instances of comparable genitival constructions, which suggest an "objective" meaning: First, the expression ἡ γνῶσις Χριστοῦ Ἰησοῦ in Phil 3:8, which stands in close proximity to one of the occurrences of the phrase in question (Phil 3:9)[300]; second, Jesus' admonition in Mk 11:22: ἔχετε πίστιν θεοῦ[301]; third, some (possibly) analogous phrases in 2Thess 2:13, Col 2:12, Jas 2:1, Rev 2:13 and in Acts 3:16, Phil 1:27, Rev 14:12.[302]

Yet the problem lies deeper: It is above all necessary to remove the current discussion from the unprofitable subjective-objective diastase and to recognize the peculiar character of the Greek genitive.[303] It is worthwhile to reconsider the comments in older exegesis as there the sensibility to this problem seems to have been greater. Already A. Deißmann argued that the use of cases in Greek and the originality of Paul's language bring about a plethora of interesting problems, which oftentimes cannot be expressed through conventional technical terms.[304] To indicate the problem, Deißmann himself coined the expression *genitivus mysticus*. Also O. Schmitz assigns to the phrase πίστις Χριστοῦ a mystical connotation and regards the genitive as characterizing genitive: Christ-faith.[305] A. Schlatter on the other hand moved the discussion to a different level, leaving aside the mystical preoccupation of his contemporaries. He contends that Jesus

---

[298] A.J. Hultgren 1980, 253. Against this point R.B. Hays notes that if the expression ἐκ πίστεως from Hab 2:4 constitutes the point of reference of the further elaboration, the absence of the article becomes irrelevant (1997, 295; but see S.K. Stowers 1989, 672n.37).

[299] Cf. K. Haacker 1983, 291; J.D.G. Dunn 1997, 253; U. Schnelle 2003, 601; but also E.D. Burton 1921, 482.

[300] Cf. J.D.G. Dunn 1997, 251; see also Rom 10:2: ζῆλος θεοῦ. Doubts against the objective understanding of Phil 3:8 are raised in I.G. Wallis 1995, 122f.

[301] Even R.B. Hays understands this phrase as objective genitive (1983, 149; against that D.W.B. Robinson 1970, 71f.; G. Howard 1990, 759).

[302] D.B. Wallace qualifies the first set of passages as "clear instances" of the objective genitive, the second as "ambiguous" or "debatable" (1996, 116).

[303] Cf. for secular Greek R. Kühner/B. Gerth 1898, 334.

[304] A. Deißmann 1925, 126f.n.4. (on this and following references, see above the respective chapters in the history of scholarship). – E. Käsemann argues similarly concerning the Greek genitive: "Sprachregelungen hüllen im technischen Zeitalter nicht selten die Sachprobleme in dichten Nebel" (1980, 25). Also J.H. Moulton 1908, 72: The "question is entirely one of exegesis, not of grammar." M.D. Hooker 1989, 165. Though citing Moulton, R.B. Matlock seeks to acquire a "neutral" "set of terms and principles for the analysis of word-meaning," which he obtains through "lexical semantics" (2000, 2).

[305] O. Schmitz 1924, 230.

Christ is not just the passive object for the believers, but rather he is origin, content, and goal, and all these connections are produced by the genitive.[306] In other words, faith clings to Christ.[307] Finally, E. Lohmeyer also leaves behind an exclusivist grammatical determination of the genitive and notes: The phrase is a subjective genitive, since faith comes through Christ, it is objective genitive since faith is directed to Christ, and it is qualitative genitive, since Christ is this faith.[308] Particularly the latter category is central to Lohmeyer; faith is revelation just as Christ is revelation.[309]

Other suggestions transcending the customary grammatical designations apart from *genitivus mysticus* or *qualitatis* derive from H. Binder, who proposes either *genitivus possessivus*, denoting the idea that Christ is the Lord of faith, or *genitivus identificationis*, meaning that Christ is the representative of faith.[310] Faith and Christ are no synonyms, but they represent the same sphere; ἐν Χριστῷ correlates with ἐν πίστει, while the center of both realms is Christ himself – in consequence Christology and faith belong together.[311] J.A.T. Robinson comes to a similar conclusion, though he starts his considerations from the theme of the "body of Christ": Πίστις Χριστοῦ is "the faith *of* Christ, which has now been communicated to him [*sc.* the Christian] as part of His body."[312]

Hence, the most adequate description both incorporates and transcends the classical grammatical categories. The current "faith of Christ"-discussion apparently falls prey to a narrow, pre-formed understanding of the modification "subjective," but also of the meaning of πίστις as faithfulness. Yet where does this originate?

If today J. Haußleiter or G. Kittel are commonly named as precursors of the nowadays so popular view that Paul's expression πίστις Χριστοῦ highlights Jesus' faithfulness, one gets the impression upon closer reading that the wrong pillars are appealed to for support. Haußleiter disapproved of the designation "objective," since it implicates a distance between the believer and Christ; rather, faith means the mystical bond between the two. Also, Kittel dealt with the πίστις Χριστοῦ-question in the context of the broader issue "mysticism in Paul."[313] Hence, the notion of Christ's faithfulness, so dominant in current exegesis, only entered the discussion

---

[306] A. Schlatter 1927, 587.

[307] A. Schlatter 1927, 607 ("haften").

[308] E. Lohmeyer 1929a, 74. Cf. W. Schenk 1972, 170.

[309] E. Lohmeyer 1929, 121. Cf. M. Barth 1970, 204.

[310] H. Binder 1968, 63.

[311] Cf. H. Binder 1968, 59f.; F. Neugebauer 1961, 171-174.

[312] J.A.T. Robinson 1952, 63n.1 (on Rom 3:22.26); cf. N. Turner 1963, 212 ("faith exercised within the Body [of Jesus Christ]"); M.D. Hooker 1989, 185.

[313] Cf. also O. Schmitz 1924, 108.

through the contributions of A.G. Hebert and T.F. Torrance, who following K. Barth understood πίστις Χριστοῦ in terms of "the faithfulness of God manifested in Christ's human faithfulness."[314] However, in a subtle, but far-reaching way Barth is re-interpreted, as instead of the sole emphasis on *God's* faithfulness in Jesus Christ,[315] the *human* possibilities of the incarnate are highlighted.[316] The end of these by no means straightforward trajectories is the conclusion that Paul's soteriology depends on the notion of Christ's human faithfulness; this *en vogue* position culminates in the statement that Jesus, like Abraham, was a "hero of faithfulness,"[317] and as such model for our own faithfulness.

In sum, the alternatives "objective" or "subjective" cannot convey satisfactorily the complexity of the Greek genitive in the phrase in question. Πίστις Χριστοῦ is "subjective" in that faith has its origin in Christ, in what God has done in Christ, and so belongs to Christ – but not in its denoting Christ's character. It is "objective" in that it has its goal in Christ, in what God has done in Christ *pro nobis*, and so also belongs to Christ – but not in signifying Christ as a motionless, disposable object.[318] If one is to find a suitable grammatical term to express these facts, the term *genitivus relationis* could be suggested.[319] Faith relates to Christ insofar as it only exists in relation to Christ – faith came with Christ, and it establishes a relation to Christ – we come to faith. The universal power-character of faith is weakened if one argues that with Christ merely the existential possibility of faith is disclosed, since this defines faith from the situation of the human being. For the sake of clarity and objectivity, the literal translation "Christ-faith" would probably be most precise. The relationship of the believer's "I" to the Christ-event is so intimate that "it is no longer I who live, but it is Christ who lives in me" (Gal 2:20).[320] Again, objectivity and subjectivity, universalism and individuation constitute a coherent unity.

---

[314] A.G. Hebert 1955, 376.

[315] Cf. K. Barth 1922, xxiv, and the translation of διὰ πίστεως Ἰησοῦ Χριστοῦ (Rom 3:22) with "durch seine [*sc.* Gottes] Treue in Jesus Christus" (72).

[316] Against that, see K. Barth 1922, 78: Christ sacrificed *all* human possibilities, and this is his obedience.

[317] Cf. S.K. Stowers 1989, 674; 1994, 230. See again against this highly questionable statement K. Barth 1922, 78: Jesus is "keinesfalls Held."

[318] See against that also E. Käsemann 1969, 146. The language of "object" or "content" is deeply inadequate and confusing, since Christ the Lord is pressed into the category of a disposable neuter.

[319] K. Haacker mentions this category for instance with respect to the phrase δι καιοσύνη θεοῦ (1999, 39 with n.63).

[320] On this passage, see R. Bultmann 1946, 125, but also A. Schlatter 1927, 335. K. Barth calls it the demythologization of the "I" (1960, 846).

The contention that an "objective" genitive construction with πίστις cannot be found in Paul[321] is somewhat circular, for the main form to be expected in Paul as evidence is the phrase under debate.[322] The absence of phrases that speak of "faith in Christ" in the undisputed Pauline letters (with the exception of Phlm 5) in contrast to the deutero-Paulines suggests that the expression πίστις Χριστοῦ filled that function for Paul[323] – notwithstanding the fact that πίστις Χριστοῦ encompasses more than simply personal faith in Christ.

Another array of questions concerns the semantic and cultural background of Paul's πίστις Χριστοῦ expression[324]: Could Paul presuppose that the recipients of his letter in Rome would understand the phrase as well-known abbreviation[325]? Otherwise, why would he refrain from any clarification[326] and use both πίστις and πίστις Χριστοῦ frequently and obviously without feeling the need to give precise definitions[327]? There can be no doubt that the faith terminology of the New Testament authors and also of the early Christian tradition incorporated by them roots predominantly in the Old Testament[328] and has been mediated through (Hellenistic) Judaism. There, the intensity of the concept of faith increased, and "faith" acquired a central status as a term for the basic religious relationship.[329] Nevertheless, religious usage of πίστις and πιστεύειν in pagan Greek language contributed to the cultural repertoire of the readers/hearers of the New Testament writings. Particularly depictions of sermons and missionary dialogues in Acts seem to presuppose that the faith language has been understand-

---

[321] Thus R.B. Hays 1983, 149.

[322] This is observed also in J.D.G. Dunn 1997, 252n.14. Cf. S. Westerholm 2004, 305n.18.

[323] Cf. A.J. Hultgren 1980, 254; J.D.G. Dunn 1997, 256.

[324] See above chapter II.G, but also, with regard to R.B. Hays's work, page 74 with note 500.

[325] Cf. with different nuances, e.g., E. Wißmann 1926, 32 ("eine bekannte Größe"), 68-70, referring also to G.P. Wetter 1916, 136; W. Kramer 1963, 42; W. Schenk 1972, 170; R. Bultmann 1958, 91-93; F. Neugebauer 1961, 168; J.M.G. Barclay 1988, 78n.8. R.B. Hays counters this argument stating that "since Paul was writing to a congregation where he had never visited in person ... fewer things could be taken for granted" (1983, 157; cf. 1997, 277).

[326] Cf. again E. Wißmann 1926, 32.

[327] Cf. P. Stuhlmacher 1966, 81.

[328] Cf. already E.D. Burton 1921, 478: "The words are Greek, the roots of the thought are mainly in the experience and writings of the Hebrew prophets and psalmists."

[329] Cf. G. Ebeling 1958, 84-86, who refers to statements of A. Meyer, H. Windisch, P. Billerbeck (1926, 187), E. Wißmann (1926, 41). It is an oversimplification, however, to call early Judaism "eine Religion des Glaubens" (H. Windisch) and to label faith a "Fachausdruck für die Frömmigkeit" (E. Wißmann). – See on the Old Testament and Jewish roots of the New Testament concept of faith also the position of D. Lührmann (see above chapter II.G.I).

able,[330] even if in pagan use the πιστ-group does not qualify the totality of the human relationship to the gods.[331] But drawing on a common cultural repertoire does not inhibit, but rather solicits "revisionary interplays," interpretative "twists,"[332] and linguistically creative developments[333]; thus, new, sometimes unexpected facets of meaning emerge.

These are perceivable already formally: The astonishing and hitherto unparalleled quantitative frequency of πίστις and πιστεύειν throughout all layers of the New Testament points to a qualitative eminence of faith from early Christian times onwards. New and unique syntactical phenomena such as the prepositional construction πιστεύειν/πίστις εἰς and the genitive Χριστοῦ add to this picture[334] and underline the christological substance of faith, for, significantly, these new grammatical possibilities appear consistently in relation to Christ.[335]

Most likely Paul could draw on the connection of faith and Christ, as it had come into use in the Jerusalem congregation[336] and had found its verbal expression in the old confessional formula Rom 10:9.[337] As a result of theological disputes, he intensified this usage, assigned to it greatest prominence, and universalized it by construing πίστις as the new time of salvation and the exclusive way and mode of salvation for *both* Jews and Gentiles.[338] As for the semantics of the theologically controversial πίστις Χριστοῦ[339] it is conceivable that Paul – whether or not he coined the phrase – developed his understanding in conscious analogy to the fundamental and theologically outstanding concept δικαιοσύνη θεοῦ. The relationship of

---

[330] See especially Acts 10:43; 13:39; 16:31; 20:21; 24:24. Cf. G. Barth 1982, 125; K. Haacker 1993, 130f.; against that D. Lührmann 1985, 104n.44.

[331] Cf. R. Bultmann 1959, 179; D. Lührmann 1985, 94.

[332] Cf. R.L. Brawley 1997, 297. Such characteristic revisions Paul will also carry out with the Abraham-story.

[333] Cf. G. Barth 1992, 218.

[334] Cf. R. Bultmann 1959, 203. If the Markan phrase πίστις τοῦ θεοῦ (Mk 11:22) really is best explained through the missionary situation for which the gospel has been written (thus G. Ebeling 1958, 91n.2), we would have a second author apart from Paul who presupposed the comprehensibility of a genitive after πίστις.

[335] Cf. G. Ebeling 1958, 79n.2.

[336] Paul seems to presuppose this use in 1Cor 15:11 and Gal 2:16. See E. Brandenburger 1988, 197, who however adds that the Jerusalem congregation most likely did not introduce and use the technical phrase "to come to faith."

[337] W. Kramer introduces the form-critical label "Pistisformel" for passages such as Rom 10:9 (1963, 16f.).

[338] E. Brandenburger hypothesizes that it was Paul who extended the use of the faith terminology in the sense of "conversion" also to Jews, at the latest in the context of the conflict with Peter in Antioch (Gal 2:15-16). Traditionally, only Gentiles have to "come to faith" (E. Brandenburger 1988, 195).

[339] See above pages 241f.

the two ideas will occupy us below,[340] but we can anticipate some of the commonalities: the patent inappropriateness of the alternative subjective/objective genitive,[341] the accent on gift and giver, the structure of power and gift, and the nature as revelation. While the grammatical disputes have just been reviewed, there is an interesting point to make regarding the second element of analogy. The progression of thought and the context of Pauline theology in general give clues as to what Paul seeks to articulate through the respective expressions: In both cases he moves together gift and giver so closely that he can almost identify God and righteousness (Rom 6:18.22),[342] Christ and faith (Gal 3:23.25).[343] Concerning the third analogous item one has to recall Paul's liberty to transform handed down ideas and to go beyond presupposed conceptions[344]: Taking δικαιοσύνη θεοῦ as paradigm, he extends the common understanding of faith and "globalizes" it in terms of a powerful reality – just as he "globalizes" the idea of "sin" and understands it, in contrast to conventional thinking, as powerful dominion.[345] Hence, the debate carried out some 40 years ago on the question whether to give priority to the history of a concept[346] or to the interpretation of the context[347] presupposes wrong alternatives. With regard to all these central Pauline terms, a one-way solution is unsatisfactory; concept and context inform and verify each other,[348] but also help interpreting corresponding ideas. The fourth aspect will become important below, where we will also seek to resolve some of the exegetical difficulties surrounding Gal 3:23-26. For now it suffices to say that both

---

[340] See below chapter V.B.III.1.e.

[341] As for δικαιοσύνη θεοῦ, see P. Stuhlmacher 1981, 105f.n.16, quoting H. Graf Reventlow.

[342] Cf. E. Käsemann 1980, 25, 172, 177.

[343] Cf. K. Stendahl 1976, 21; D.M. Hay 1989, 470; S. Ota 1997, 70. See in addition for instance, the parallel structure of Gal 3:14, but also the correlation of ἐν Χριστῷ and ἐν πίστει. From this perspective, the labels characterizing genitive (O. Schmitz), qualitative genitive (E. Lohmeyer), or identifying genitive (H. Binder) have their right.

[344] Cf. also D.A. Campbell 2005, 182.

[345] See above pages 252f. and below pages 353f.

[346] Cf. E. Käsemann 1962, 105 note: "[E]inige müssen in der gegenwärtigen Hochflut der 'Interpretation' der Nachlaß-Verwaltung der Historiker sich widmen, schon um die Interpreten zu beunruhigen." P. Stuhlmacher 1970, 179n.28.

[347] Cf. G. Klein 1967, 227 ("Priorität der Interpretation vor der religions- und traditionsgeschichtlichen Methode"; with reference to H. Conzelmann 1966, 247: "Entscheidend ist nicht die Begriffsgeschichte, sondern der Kontext.").

[348] Cf. W. Schenk 1972, 163.

δικαιοσύνη θεοῦ and πίστις Χριστοῦ are uniquely connected to the verb ἀποκαλύπτειν.[349]

b) Theology and Christology

The discussion of the seeming discrepancy between "faith in Christ" and "faith in God" has to be postponed to a later chapter.[350] Yet some things can be said on the alleged incongruity between the "christocentrism" of the objective understanding of πίστις Χριστοῦ and the "theocentrism" of the Abraham-chapter (and the whole of Romans),[351] based on the considerations already offered. In Rom 3:21-31, it is God who acts: He has revealed his righteousness (3:21), he justifies (3:24.26.30), and he put forward Christ as a ἱλαστήριον. Especially the latter aspect receives detailed attention further below.[352] But at the same time 3:24-26 shows that Paul's doctrine of justification is the climactic development of the christological kerygma.[353]

God himself accomplished atonement through Jesus Christ and thus proved his righteousness; it is not Christ, who utilizes his own righteousness – achieved through his faithfulness – to cover for the lack of human righteousness.[354] God establishes faith in its multiple dimensions (as πίστις Χριστοῦ), and he also counts a person's faith as righteousness. God therefore creates the original, "ursprünglich" relationship to the human being,[355] and only what he himself creates is right for him.[356] It is not our achievements through works and not self-accomplished faith, which bring about this relationship. For Paul, God's work produces God's work[357] – and insofar both Christology and theo-logy constitute a harmonious whole.

c) The Uniqueness of the "Obedience of the One"

Above we already dealt with the opposition in Romans 3 between God's faithfulness (πίστις) and human disbelief (ἀπιστία) (3:3).[358] In Romans 5 Paul contrasts Adam's disobedience (παρακοή) with Christ's obedience

---

[349] Cf. H.-S. Choi 2005, 476n.53. Paul generally uses the verb ἀποκαλύπτειν in terms of a divinely effected revelation (cf. Rom 1:17.18; 8:18; 1Cor 2:10; 3:13; 14:30; Gal 1:16; 3:23; Phil 3:15; 2Thess 2:3.6.8).

[350] See below chapter VI.A.VI.

[351] Cf. R.B. Hays 1983, 156f.; W. Baird 1988, 378. Against that, e.g., A. Feuillet 1959/1960, 79.

[352] See below page 289.

[353] G. Eichholz 1972, 196.

[354] Cf. J. Becker 1992, 373.

[355] Cf. K. Barth 1922, 112.

[356] Cf. P. Stuhlmacher 1966, 82.

[357] A. Schlatter 1935, 38.

[358] See above chapter V.B.II.2.

(ὑπακοή) – the obedience of "the one" (5:19). He does not, however, make the antithesis between Christ's faith(fulness) and Adam's faithlessness – even if "he ought to!,"[359] nor does he create a parallel between Christ's faith and Abraham's faith[360] – not even a "less obvious[.]" one,[361] nor does he speak anywhere of the "believing Christ"[362] – "reasons unknown"[363]!? Nevertheless, L.T. Johnson regards Rom 5:15-21 as plain explication of the "the faith of Christ" in 3:21-26.[364]

A "representative christology" (R.B. Hays) or an "interchange soteriology" (M.D. Hooker) in the framework of Paul's Abraham-chapters in Romans and Galatians leads ultimately to the conception that our participation in Christ's faith(fulness) somehow transfers his faith to us. For, since Abraham had faith, also his true son, Christ, had faith (Gal 3:16), and to share in that sonship means to share in the faith of the one true seed.[365] According to this logic, our faith(fulness) becomes somehow (metaphorically?) analogous to Jesus' faith, and "his death and resurrection define a pattern for our obedience as well."[366] In this way, one deems to arrive at an ethics that is christologically grounded, insofar as Christ's faith-obedience calls the Christian community to follow his example. And this has significant consequences regarding soteriology.[367]

---

[359] M.D. Hooker 1989, 168.

[360] Cf. E. Käsemann 1969, 142: There is no comparison between Christ and Abraham, and Christ "ist nicht wie Abraham Urbild des Glaubens."

[361] D.A. Campbell 2005, 205.

[362] Christ never receives the predicate πιστός (K. Haacker 1999, 87).

[363] M. Barth 1970, 204.

[364] L.T. Johnson 1982, 87-89. According to this line of thought, Romans 4 "seems something of an intrusion" (M.D. Hooker 1989, 169; cf. 170). – As for πίστις Χριστοῦ in Gal 2:16 and Phil 3:9, B. Witherington argues that Gal 2:19 and 2:21 (Christ's crucifixion) and Phil 2:5-11 (Christ's "faithful obedience … even unto death") "unpack what he [*sc.* Paul] means by this phrase" (1998, 179f.; against J.D.G. Dunn's claim that Paul never unpacks the notion of "the faithfulness of Christ"). It is however hardly legitimate to call Rom 5:15-21, Gal 2:19.21, and Phil 2:5-11 a clear unpacking of Christ's πίστις.

[365] Cf. R.B. Hays 1983, 204; M.D. Hooker 1989, 173-175; cf. 166f., 180f., 184; E.R. Goodenough 1968, 45; J.L. Martyn 1997, 362, 276: "Christ's faith is not only prior to ours but also causative of it."

[366] R.B. Hays 1997, 287; cf. 294. See however the careful remarks that describe the relationship between our faith and Christ's faith as "not strictly isomorphic," but "metaphorical" (297) and also the statement that "[w]e are saved by Christ's faith(fulness), not by having a faith like his" (1983, 158n.135). D.M. Hay rightly states that Hays's distinction between "imitation and participationist reenactment of a pattern grounded in Jesus seems neither wholly clear nor readily justifiable on the basis of Pauline texts" (1989, 474).

[367] Parenthetically, one might note that some exegetes who refute that Paul intended to say "faith of Christ" still concede that this notion would be fully "consistent with other emphases" in Paul's theology and that it is "an attractive variant on the Adam motif of

There is no passage in Paul – we leave aside the phrase under discussion – where he describes Jesus' obedience or generally his conduct as faith or trust or faithfulness.[368] The secondary combination of these terms remains a hypothesis.[369] Jesus' faith does not play such a role in Paul's Christology that he deems it worth mentioning, let alone explicating; it would intrude here into the flow of the letter without any previous signal.[370] Furthermore, no passage indicates that Paul expects the Romans to strive for a faith(fulness) that is (metaphorically) comparable to the faith(fulness) Jesus had; the correlation of Jesus' πίστις and human πίστις does not play a role in Paul's ethics.

This statement requires some comment: Notably, Paul frequently insists that the believers should follow his own example,[371] and twice he names himself and Christ as those to be imitated.[372] But indeed, in Paul there is a strong notion of "putting on the Lord Jesus Christ" (Rom 13:14), of "living in accordance with Christ Jesus (κατὰ Χριστὸν Ἰησοῦν)" (15:5) and "the law of Christ" (Gal 6:2). It is true that one ought to place more emphasis on Paul's – sometimes hidden – references and allusions to the life and ministry of Jesus and his function as example.[373] Older exegesis used to draw a connection between the earthly Jesus and the Christian community in terms of an ethical example,[374] but this view has been effectively contested by prominent exegetes such as R. Bultmann. They consider Paul's talk of Christ's ὑπακοή to denote the obedience of the pre-existent, not a characteristic of the historical Jesus.[375] Yet Paul and the tradition he is

---

Christ's obedience" (J.D.G. Dunn 1997, 269). Hence, though exegetically unfounded it would be a theologically true reading. Yet even this position is doubtful as the subsequent discussion seeks to show.

[368] Cf. T. Zahn 1925, 177n.2.

[369] One would have to prove conclusively the identity of πίστις and ὑπακοή, as attempted by R.B. Hays 1997, 286 (against C.H. Cosgrove 1988, 55f.): "[I]t is difficult to suppose that this terminological difference [*sc.* between πίστις and ὑπακοή] is particularly significant." As noted, Hays's identification of πίστις and ὑπακοή comes close to the position of his adversary R. Bultmann (see above page 75). The interpretation of the phrase ὑπακοὴ πίστεως is decisive in this regard. See below pages 397-399.

[370] Cf. again T. Zahn 1925, 177n.2.

[371] 1Cor 4:16; Gal 4:12; Phil 3:17; 4:9; 2Thess 3:7.9. See especially W.P. De Boer 1962; E.A. Castelli 1991.

[372] 1Cor 11:1; 1Thess 1:6; see also Eph 5:1; Heb 13:7. On the concept of "imitation," see the concise account in G.L. Green 2002, 97f.

[373] Cf. J.D.G. Dunn 1998, 654-658. "[T]he conclusion becomes increasingly persuasive that knowledge of and interest in the life and ministry of Jesus was an integral part of his theology albeit referred to only *sotto voce* in his written theology" (195). See also E. Käsemann 1969, 142; P. Stuhlmacher 1983.

[374] W. Schrage (1989, 214) refers to P. Feine and W.D. Davies.

[375] Cf. R. Bultmann 1929a, 213; see also, e.g., W. Schrage 1989, 214-217.

adapting do not separate Jesus Christ's *kenosis* (Phil 2:7) and his obedience to the cross (2:8) in such a way that the first would refer to the preexistent Christ and the latter to the earthly Jesus.

But what are the concrete instructions in which Jesus Christ functions as pattern for our conduct – implicitly or explicitly[376]?

(1) Most often they concern the fellowship within the community, the life in and for the community: In fulfilling the love commandment, the whole law is fulfilled (Rom 13:8-10; Gal 5:14) – this is reminiscent of Jesus' own teaching and Jesus' own living out this command.[377] *In concreto*, living out the love commandment means to bear another's burdens (Gal 6:2), which takes also Jesus as example; it also means to "welcome one another, just as Christ has welcomed you" (Rom 15:7), to seek not one's own advantage, but that of many, so that they may be saved (1Cor 11:1), and ultimately to suffer for one's faith in order to become a model for others (1Thess 1:6).[378] In sum, it is a life to the interest of others (Phil 2:4).

(2) But the instructions that Paul derives from Jesus also concern one's inner attitude as a member of the community: In accordance with Christ Jesus, one is not to please oneself (Rom 15:3.5), but rather to take an attitude of humility (ταπεινοφροσύνη, Phil 2:3[379]). Hence, Paul can appeal to Jesus as "antidote to communal disaffection."[380]

Overall, it appears that Paul's appeals to Jesus are interested in his relationship to humans or in his "inner" attitude that pertains to this relationship.[381] In this regard, Jesus becomes a model of what it means to live in and for the Christian community according to the "law of Christ."[382]

---

[376] Cf., e.g., E. Larsson 1962 (also the literature noted in R.B. Hays 1983, 223n.36). The issues concerning the topic *imitatio Christi* fill thousands of pages in books and essays. They are especially pertinent in the Christ-hymn Phil 2:6-11, including Paul's admonition 2:5: "Let the same mind be in you that was in Christ Jesus." See the succinct discussion in G. Hawthorne/R.P. Martin 2004, 104-109, who apart from the commentaries refer to and engage in a dialogue with the views of scholars such as M.S. Enslin, L. Cerfaux, E. Käsemann, E. Larsson, V.P. Furnish, L.W. Hurtado, E.A. Castelli, R.B. Hays, S.E. Fowl, etc.

[377] Cf. H. Schürmann 1974.

[378] Cf. Col 3:13: "Just as the Lord has forgiven you, so you also must forgive."

[379] Cf. D.M. Hay 1989, 473.

[380] J.D.G. Dunn 1998, 194.

[381] What G. Hawthorne and R.P. Martin say regarding the Christ-hymn of Philippians is true for the other mentioned passages as well: They all present Jesus "as the supreme model of the humble, obedient, self-sacrificing, self-denying, self-giving service" (2004, 104).

[382] On "the law of Christ," see M. Winger 2000, who lists the relevant interpretations of this phrase: It has been said to denote the ordinances of Christ (C.H. Dodd), the example of Christ (R.B. Hays), or the commandment of Lev 19:8 (M. Luther, E.D. Burton, V.P. Furnish, H.D. Betz, J.L. Martyn). Winger himself takes Paul's use of the "law" "in a

While, therefore, on the one hand Jesus provides a pattern which is supposed to guide life in the community, on the other hand, he does *not* prefigure or predetermine our relationship to God. His obedience, his faith(fulness) to God are never perceived as being a model for any human participatory reenactment or as an *imitatio Christi*. Jesus' completely binding himself to and being wholly dependent on God's will, and his salvific, self-sacrificing mission shows his categorical and qualitative distinction from humans. It is impossible to claim on these grounds any human "imitation" of certain patterns of Jesus' conduct (faith/obedience), be it as participatory reenactment or as an *imitatio Christi*.[383] Thus, Christ's obedience on the cross is for Paul *not* "the paradigm for [our] faithfulness to God."[384] Since Christ's relationship to God is singular, Paul never refers to Christ's faith(fulness) or obedience as example or archetype of the believers' lives – even if he ought to.[385] Rather than *Urbild* of the community's faith, Christ is the Lord of the community.[386] "The thrust is not 'here is a model to be followed' so much as 'here is a Master to be obeyed'."[387]

Furthermore, there are two related tenets in Paul's theology that weaken the case for the subjective understanding significantly: While Christ's obedience on the cross leads to an absolute *negativum*, to his abandonment by God,[388] our faith leads to an absolute *positivum*, our acceptance by God (Rom 4:3). On the other hand, while Christ was obedient in total sinlessness, our faith is fundamentally connected to forgiveness of sin (Rom 4:3-

---

somewhat looser sense, not as identifying any specific, legal instruction, but as referring to the way Christ exercises his lordship over those called by him" (544), i.e., "to the practice which ... should govern the community of believers" (538).

[383] Cf. again D.M. Hay 1989, 474.

[384] Against R.B. Hays 1996, 197; cf. M.D. Hooker 1989, 167; D.A. Campbell 2005, 201, 229.

[385] Terminological overlaps in the description of a certain conduct, particularly that of obedience, do not presuppose a correlation in terms of *imitatio* or *Vorbild-Abbild*. It is not without purpose that Paul in Rom 5:19 highlights the obedience of "the one" (ὑπακοὴ τοῦ ἑνός). His obedience did not result in the obedience "of the many," but in the grace for many (5:15). Furthermore, the language of being crucified with Christ (Gal 5:24; 6:14), dying with Jesus (2Cor 4:10-12), being conformed to Christ's death (Phil 3:10) refers first and foremost to our spiritual death and resurrection and eventually to our being conformed to the image of the Son (Rom 8:29; 2Cor 3:18), i.e., to our being with God. – 2Cor 5:16 should no longer be taken as evidence for Paul's indifference towards Jesus' life and ministry and consequently not as evidence against the subjective understanding of πίστις Χριστοῦ (against F. Neugebauer 1961, 168n.69).

[386] Cf. E. Käsemann 1969, 142. In Romans 4, this is expressed in 4:24.

[387] G.F. Hawthorne/R.P. Martin 2004, 135. They continue: "The latter joins the soteriological with the ethical, grounding the ethical in both the salvation act and the call to obey the obedient One."

[388] Cf. K. Barth 1922, 78: "Er [*sc.* Jesus] ist auf der Höhe, am Ziel seines Weges eine rein negative Größe."

8)[389] and justification means the new creation of the ungodly sinner (Rom 4:5.25).[390] This is Paul's "interchange soteriology": Christ was sinless and obedient to the cross; through this self-humiliation and godforsakenness he was exalted and became Lord. We acknowledge and confess our sinfulness in faith, are therefore accepted by God and become the Lord's servants. "For our sake he made him to be sin who knew no sin, so that in him we might become the righteousness of God" (2Cor 5:21).

One other major critique needs to be raised: The factual identification of πίστις with obedience or noncognitive trust leaves aside essential components of Paul's concept of faith. It reduces faith to the execution of a certain disposition, in Augustinian terms: to the *fides qua creditur*. Equally significant for Paul is the assent to the missionary kerygma, to the content of faith, as the phrase πιστεύειν ὅτι (1Thess 4:14; Rom 10:9) sufficiently demonstrates. Knowledge of and confession to the *fides quae creditur* is for Paul an important and indispensable aspect of faith.[391]

Having clarified the relationship between πίστις Χριστοῦ and our faith, we have to briefly look at the alleged parallelism between Abraham's faithfulness and Christ's faithfulness. The above analysis of central Jewish texts[392] leaves no doubt that the crucial proof of Abraham's faithfulness is the sacrifice of his son. Yet there is but one passage in Paul in which he clearly alludes to the Aqedah, namely, Rom 8:32[393]: God "did not withhold his own Son, but gave him up for all of us." But Paul's point is to give "testimony to the faithfulness of God";[394] for him "the Aqedah served more as a type of *God's* faithfulness ... rather than of Abraham's."[395] Consequently, Paul is not concerned with elevating Abraham's faithfulness, or with creating an analogy between Abraham's faithfulness and Christ's

---

[389] Cf. C.E.B. Cranfield 1998, 96f. (affirmed by S. Westerholm 2004, 281n.47): "Faith is the attitude of one who knows and confesses that he is a sinner"; therefore, if πίστις "was in Paul's mind as strongly associated with the situation of the sinner who knows that he has no ground on which to stand before God except God's own sheer grace in Jesus Christ as I think it was, then this would suggest that it would not be likely to come at all naturally to him to speak of Jesus Christ's πίστις."

[390] Cf. P. Stuhlmacher 1975, 134.

[391] Cf. E. Wißmann 1926, 38; W. Mundle 1932, 41-43, 50; E. Lohse, 1977, 152; G. Barth 1982, 122; B.S. Childs 1992, 606. See also K. Barth's analysis of faith as "Anerkennen," "Erkennen," and "Bekennen" (1960, 847; cf. 846-872).

[392] See above chapter IV.

[393] An allusion to the offering of Isaac in Romans 8 seems patent (cf. the opposition of opinions in G. Vermès 1961, 193-227; 1996; P.R. Davies/B.D. Chilton 1978; see further, e.g., H.-J. Schoeps 1946, who finds some allusions to the Aqedah in Paul's theology; C.T.R. Hayward 1981; A.F. Segal 1984; 1996; L. Kundert 1998 and the bibliographical data provided in G. Vermès 1996, 143n.23 and J.A. Fitzmyer 2002, 211n.1).

[394] B.S. Childs 1992, 334.

[395] J.D.G. Dunn 1998, 225 (italics original).

faithfulness, which in turn would prefigure ours. The patriarch's faithfulness is neither highlighted in Rom 8:32, nor is it at all thematized in the Abraham-chapter. "Those who see the meaning of 'the faith of Christ' as stressing obedience ... find little support in Romans 4."[396]

d) "Principle" and Act of Faith

One of the primary arguments for a subjective understanding of πίστις Χριστοῦ in Rom 3:22 is the already mentioned impression of a "ponderous redundancy,"[397] tautology,[398] or pleonasm[399] prompted by the occurrence of both πίστις and πιστεύειν. It stands parallel to Gal 3:22 which also combines both verb and noun. Is it true, here and there, that "another reference to the faith of believers would be redundant in a sentence which already refers to those who believe"?[400]

Our verse in Romans – not the one in Galatians[401] – features a notable keyword, which partly explains the intention of the "redundant" occurrence of the verb in the present participle construction: It is the significant keyword πᾶς,[402] which emphasizes that "*all* who believe" will be the recipients of God's righteousness.[403] It contrasts the adjacent statements that no human being (πᾶσα σάρξ) is justified by the works of the law (Rom 3:20) and that all (πάντες) have sinned (3:23). In the context of πίστις, Paul puts much weight on the keyword πᾶς[404] and even inserts it into the Isaiah quote (Isa 28:16) in Rom 10:11.[405]

But more importantly, Paul seems to carry out a careful distinction between πίστις and πιστεύειν in this context. With regard to the analogous passage Gal 3:22, H. Schlier notes that faith as the new "principle" of salvation actualizes itself in each act of faith of the individual.[406] Though the term "principle" is open to misunderstandings, the intention of Paul is fittingly detected. Hence, in Rom 3:22, faith is understood as a universal, salvation-historical force with an eschatological implication which be-

---

[396] W. Baird 1988, 378.

[397] R.B. Hays 1983, 158; cf. D.A. Campbell 2005, 192.

[398] M. Barth 1970, 203; J.J. O'Rourke 1973, 189.

[399] H.W. Schmidt 1966, 66.

[400] M.D. Hooker 1989, 173.

[401] See however Gal 3:26-28.

[402] As in Rom 1:16, πᾶς refers to Jews and non-Jews (cf. M. Neubrand 1997, 101).

[403] Cf. J.D.G. Dunn 1997, 264.

[404] In relation to πίστις, πᾶς appears in Rom 1:5.16; 4:11.16; 10:4.11-13.16. See also below pages 363f. on Rom 4:11-12 and page 374 on Rom 4:16.

[405] Cf. D.-A. Koch 1986, 133.

[406] H. Schlier 1965, 165: "Der Glaube als das neue Heilsprinzip [πίστις] aktualisiert sich im jeweiligen Glaubensakt des Einzelnen [πιστεύειν]."

comes real in the existence of the individual believer.[407] R.B. Hays, who refers to Schlier's statement, argues that "[t]his interpretation ... seems contrived; could Paul have expected his readers to make such a distinction between *Heilsprinzip* and *Glaubensakt?*"[408] Yet, instead of two different meanings of πίστις ("principle" and act), Hays has to assert two different meanings (faithfulness and faith) and two different subjects (Christ and the believer). Which exegesis is more contrived?

Gal 2:16 places before us a similar combination of noun and verb, which again is no "wooden redundancy,"[409] but the differentiation between πίστις as general order of salvation and πιστεύειν as concretization.[410]

e) "Christ-Faith" and "God-Righteousness"

It is noteworthy that already Augustine in his comments on Rom 3:22 finds a connection between the phrases πίστις Χριστοῦ and δικαιοσύνη θεοῦ, arguing that just as Paul did not mean the faith with which Christ himself believes, he also did not mean the righteousness whereby God is himself righteous.[411] As is obvious, both statements are challenged by many modern commentators, but at least his insight regarding their correlation proves valuable. Neither phrase can be explained without the other.

The proponents of the subjective understanding claim that the human act of believing in Jesus Christ cannot be, in Paul's view, the reason for God's manifestation of his righteousness – rather, an act of God is required.[412]

First of all, this critique presupposes that πίστις Ἰησοῦ Χριστοῦ refers to the revelation of God's righteousness[413] rather than to δικαιοσύνη θεοῦ itself.[414] Considering our interpretation of 1:17 this understanding appears to be correct.[415] But the actual problematic issue lies in the critique's presupposition of a particular concept of faith – possibly derived from a (mis)reading of R. Bultmann – that regards the divine righteousness as

---

[407] Thus, the relationship of the prepositions διά and εἰς is parallel to the one discovered for ἐκ and εἰς in Rom 1:17 (cf. A. Schlatter 1935, 140).

[408] R.B. Hays 1983, 142n.80.

[409] L.E. Keck 1989, 545; cf. S.K. Williams 1980, 273f.

[410] Cf. similarly G. Friedrich 1981, 104.

[411] Augustine, *De Spiritu et Littera* 9,15 (referred to in R.B. Hays 2002, 1).

[412] Cf. R.B. Hays 1983, 159; 1997, 283; see however, slightly modified, 297: "[W]e receive the promise through [both], Christ's faithfulness ... [and] through our faith." M. Neubrand 1997, 118; D.A. Campbell 2005, 197: "The key point is simply this: human 'faith' *cannot function instrumentally within a process of divine disclosure*" (italics original). H.-S. Choi 2005, 471.

[413] Cf., e.g., O. Kuss 1957, 113, and, by implication, those who offer the critique against the objective understanding.

[414] Cf., e.g., U. Luz 1968, 170n.130; U. Wilckens 1978, 187.

[415] See above pages 244f.

incompatible with an individualized act of believing. It is argued that there cannot be a one-way causal connection between a human and a divine act. One criticizes the more common interpretation of 3:22, according to which through our faith God's righteousness becomes effective,[416] comes to expression,[417] imparts itself,[418] or is bestowed to us as a gift.[419] In any case, the *particula veri* of this objection lies in the fact that due to the argumentative connection between 3:21 and 3:22, one has to account appropriately for the context's "apocalyptic" horizon, in particular the verb πεφανέρωται, which is the implicit predicate of 3:22 as well.[420]

In order to navigate between these two mutually exclusive views and in order find a common ground that could accomplish the synchronization of their intentions (not results), we have to take into account some disputed scholarly perspectives on the expression δικαιοσύνη θεοῦ and steer from there to a redefinition of Paul's concept of faith. Mainly based on Phil 3:9, R. Bultmann and H. Conzelmann interpret "God's righteousness"[421] anthropologically in terms of its gift-character, as righteousness transferred to the "isolated" individual through faith – as "my righteousness."[422] In consequence and in like manner, faith is understood as radical individualization and isolation – as "my faith."[423]

With A. Schlatter's work as a decisive impulse,[424] E. Käsemann and P. Stuhlmacher have sought to describe "God's righteousness" in terms of its power-character, as righteousness with eschatological-soteriological force. Paul's theology and idea of history is not oriented toward the individual,[425]

---

[416] Cf. U. Luz 1968, 170; U. Wilckens 1978, 187; M. Theobald 1992, 97.

[417] Cf. J.D.G. Dunn 1988, 167.

[418] Cf. P. Stuhlmacher 1966, 87.

[419] Cf. O. Michel 1978, 148.

[420] Cf. W. Schenk 1972, 170. His essay makes the attempt of a "Verhältnisbestimmung" of "God-righteousness" and "Christ-faith" (see above chapter II.F.IV).

[421] On an extensive history of scholarship on this topic, see M.A. Seifrid 1992, 1-75 (cf. 2000). Also G. Klein 1967; M.T. Brauch 1977.

[422] Cf. R. Bultmann 1958, 280f.; H. Conzelmann 1967, 243. See also G. Klein 1967, 235f.; H.-W. Bartsch 1968, 49n.10.

[423] Cf. R. Bultmann 1954, 102: "Die entscheidende Geschichte ist nicht die Weltgeschichte, die Geschichte Israels und der anderen Völker, sondern die Geschichte, die jeder Einzelne selbst erfährt." 1959, 219; G. Klein 1967, 235; H. Conzelmann 1967, 193 ("radikale *Individualisierung*"), 243: "Der Glaube führt in die Vereinzelung." – Contrast the deliberations in K. Barth 1960, 844-846 on the individualism and subjectivity of faith ("Ich-Glaube"); the "I" has to be demythologized (846). Also S. Kierkegaard speaks of the "absolute isolation" of the believer: "Der Glaubensritter" Abraham, whose faith is about to be tested, "hat einzig und allein sich selber." But he goes on: "[D]arin liegt das Furchtbare" (quoted in M. Buber 1952, 591).

[424] Cf. A. Schlatter 1935, 36 (God's righteousness as act of God; God as creator).

[425] E. Käsemann 1961, 188. See also Bultmann's reaction to Käsemann (1964).

so that when he speaks of righteousness he has in mind a powerful word-event with eschatological implications and the idea of creation.[426] Correspondingly, in critique of an individualistic limitation of "faith," H. Binder offered an alternative that elevates the event of faith beyond any subjectivity.[427]

With regard to neither of the terms, δικαιοσύνη θεοῦ and πίστις Χριστοῦ, is a polarization towards either "anthropological-individual" or "eschatological-cosmic" helpful.[428] It is crucial that in each case both poles are addressed and considered as two components of a unity.[429]

Nevertheless, Paul's "Christian" language knows neither an individualizing, isolating "my righteousness"[430] nor an individualizing, isolating "my faith,"[431] for righteousness belongs to God, and faith belongs to Christ. But

---

[426] P. Stuhlmacher 1966, 98, 236. See also C. Müller 1964.

[427] See above chapter II.F.III. Stuhlmacher's description of faith as "überindividuelle[s] Gesamtphänomen" (1966, 81) has been attacked from two sides, from both H. Binder (1968, 57n.17) and E. Käsemann (1980, 20).

[428] Cf., e.g., P. Stuhlmacher 1966, 81 (but see 42); E. Käsemann 1980, 20 (on σωτηρία): "Universalismus und äußerste Individuation sind hier Kehrseiten desselben Sachverhaltes." 30 (on Rom 1:18-3:20): "Die Spannung von Kosmologie und Anthropologie charakterisiert paulinische Theologie im ganzen." To be sure, Käsemann does not apply his insight to Paul's concept of πίστις Χριστοῦ (cf. 20), even though he notices the structure power – gift in principally all genitival phrases that speak of eschatological gifts (26). – O. Cullmann, too, does not perceive a tension between the Christian existence and *Heilsgeschichte* (1965, vi).

[429] The bipolar structure of *both* righteousness and faith makes the dispute between E. Käsemann and G. Bornkamm and their pupils (P. Stuhlmacher and F. Hahn/E. Brandenburger) appear in a new light. Bornkamm criticized (1969, 156) that the unique Pauline correlation between righteousness and faith is put into the background in an awkward manner due to Käsemann's emphasis on the power-character of God's righteousness (see Käsemann's response in 1969a, 139; also Stuhlmacher 1970, 178f.n.28). If one concedes that universalism and individuation are two sides of both δικαιοσύνη θεοῦ and πίστις Χριστοῦ, then both correspond harmoniously.

[430] Notably, the phrase ἡ ἐμὴ δικαιοσύνη (Phil 3:9) refers to the time before his call.

[431] Paul never uses the form πιστεύω and only occasionally first and second person plural or third person plural (only with regard to Abraham). In nominal constructions, Paul refers to Abraham's faith three times (Rom 4:5.12.16); once he writes πίστις ὑμῶν τε καὶ ἐμοῦ (1:12), once ἡ πίστις σου (*sc.* Philemon's) (Phlm 6), while the expression ἡ πίστις ὑμῶν is more frequent (Rom 1:8.12; 1Cor 2:5; 15:14.17; 2Cor 1:24; 10:15; Phil 2:17; 1Thess 1:8; 3:2.5.6.7.10). In Rom 14:22, πίστις comes close to the meaning "conviction" (cf., e.g., K. Haacker 1999, 290). – While H. Binder has to explain away these passages in order to come to his "non-anthropocentric" conclusions on the Pauline faith (1968, 69), K. Barth offers a comparatively brief, polemical paragraph at the end of his doctrine of reconciliation (1960, 826-872), which is supposed to counter the "Unbescheidenheit" and "Wichtigtuerei" of the Christian individual (828; some call Barth's chapter listless [cf. D. Lührmann 1976, 15; 1992, 18; W. Schenk 1982, 69] and feel forced to give a sharp response [G. Ebeling 1958, 65n.1], but the provocation is some-

Paul's theology indeed knows the idea that what belongs to God and Christ is transferred to humans. Thus, both "God-righteousness" and "Christ-faith" are salvation-historical realities having power-character, but both also contain within themselves the dimension of individual participation and appropriation, hence having gift-character.[432] Both grammatical phenomena, "God-righteousness" and "Christ-faith," could be described through the label *genitivus relationis*.[433]

As for our passage Rom 3:21-22, on the one hand, both dimensions of "faith" occur in Rom 3:22, expressed through noun and verb, and on the other hand Paul's talk of the revelation of righteousness (3:21) stresses the universal horizon, while the idea of righteousness for all believers (3:22) brings to the fore the participatory aspect.[434] Just as the concept δικαιοσύνη θεοῦ "informs us not only of God's righteous activity ..., but also of the resultant state of those who are ... accorded the description of 'righteous',"[435] thus also the concept πίστις Χριστοῦ describes not only Christ's bringing about faith in his coming, but also the resultant state of those who receive that faith and are called "believers." Power and gift, giver and gift form a remarkable unity in both conceptions, righteousness and faith.[436]

---

what alleviated if his concept of faith is seen in the context of his whole dogmatics [see especially K. Barth 1932, 239-261: "Das Wort Gottes und der Glaube"; also M. Seils 1996, 210]). In any case, faith does not owe itself to a common anthropological "Anknüpfungspunkt" between God and humans (K. Barth 1932, 251) nor is it attached to an autonomous place in the human being so that it would become a possession (cf. E. Jüngel 1962, 43f.). Against that, see for instance J. Jeremias 1954/1955, 369: "Faith is nothing else than the *organon lepticon*."

[432] Cf., with regard to "faith" in Rom 3:22, A. Schlatter 1927, 607: The righteousness that originates from God is mediated to the person "durch das an Jesus haftende Glauben, weil und sofern er [*sc.* der Mensch] in seinem eigenen Verhalten ein Glaubender geworden sei." With regard to "righteousness" in Rom 3:22, cf. E. Käsemann 1961, 185f.; U. Schnelle 2003, 351: "Erscheint die Gerechtigkeit Gottes in V. 21 als universale Macht Gottes, so dominiert in V. 22 der Charakter der Gabe."

[433] See above page 263.

[434] Mostly, the two dimensions are not distinguished in Rom 3:21-22. Thus, some focus on the "gift-character" – such as C.E.B. Cranfield (1975, 202: "God's gift"); others stress that God's righteousness "is a righteousness of divine property and characterized by divine qualities" (J. Murray 1959, 30f.); again others note that δικαιοσύνη θεοῦ "seems to denote a divine act rather than a divine attribute" (S.J. Gathercole 2002, 224; cf., e.g., K. Kertelge 1971, 305: "[Δ]ικαιοσύνη θεοῦ [bezeichnet] nicht eine Eigenschaft Gottes, auch nicht eine Eigenschaft des Menschen vor Gott, sondern das Handeln Gottes am Menschen.").

[435] G.N. Davies 1990, 38.

[436] One of the few commentators who saw this analogous structure is P. Stuhlmacher: "Für die theologische Begrifflichkeit des Paulus ist es weithin charakteristisch, daß in ihr Macht und Gabe eine spannungsvolle Einheit bilden. Es gilt zu sehen, daß hiervon auch der Glaubensbegriff nicht ausgenommen ist" (1966, 81).

The emphasis on the power-character of πίστις derives from Paul's sal-vation-historical, dynamic structure of thinking. His thesis of God's right-eousness being revealed through faith has its counterpart in the significant formulations that "faith came" and "has been revealed" (Gal 3:23.25). "Galatians 3:23-26 is probably one of the decisive texts for the πίστις Χριστοῦ debate,"[437] for the use of πίστις here "seems to require that it bear a primarily objective sense."[438] Based on our previous deliberations on the bipolar structure of πίστις Χριστοῦ, our own interpretation of this passage will understand itself as a development and modification of the views es-poused by R. Gyllenberg, E. Lohmeyer, H. Binder, W. Schenk presented above,[439] which are also mirrored in statements of F. Neugebauer, P. Stuhlmacher, and H. Schlier.[440] Others, too, have noted that Paul here talks of πίστις as "historical phenomenon,"[441] as "God's eschatological action in Christ,"[442] or as eschatological event.[443] In striking analogy to δικαιοσύνη θεοῦ, it is "a new element in the situation,"[444] "a redemptive historical ... apocalyptical event,"[445] an "entity which is said to appear on stage at a specific point in the unfolding of the salvation-historical drama"[446]; a "sin-gle massive event at the centre of history seems to be in view."[447] The coming of πίστις marks the beginning of a new time[448] and represents the new divine "Heilssetzung."[449]

---

[437] H.-S. Choi 2005, 473. Choi remarks that "[m]ost commentators hold that the defi-nite articles with πίστις in 3:23-26 refer back to the πίστις Ἰησοῦ Χριστοῦ 3:22" (472f.n.26, with reference to F.F. Bruce, E.D. Burton, J.D.G. Dunn, R.Y.K. Fung, R.N. Longenecker, F. Matera, and S.K. Williams).

[438] D.M. Hay 1989, 470.

[439] See above chapter II.F.

[440] We may recapitulate some of their descriptions of πίστις: "metaphysisches Prin-zip" (E. Lohmeyer), "göttliche Geschehenswirklichkeit" (H. Binder), "eschatologisches Heilsereignis" (F. Neugebauer), "überindividuelles Gesamtphänomen" (P. Stuhlmacher), "Heilsprinzip" (H. Schlier 1965, 165). See also the interesting statements by S. Ota: "[T]he absolute use of πίστις ... in Paul refers to an *objective dispensation or system of salvation by God* comparable with the Torah of Judaism" (1997, 76; italics original), to "a new reality coming from God as a superindividual total phenomenon" (71), "to the superindividual, collective-communal reality of God's grace now revealed" (82).

[441] H.D. Betz 1979, 176n.120.

[442] C.H. Cosgrove 1988, 57f.

[443] O. Michel 1978, 76 ("eschatologisches Ereignis").

[444] M.D. Hooker 1989, 173.

[445] H.-S. Choi 2005, 475f.

[446] R.B. Hays 1983, 200.

[447] D.A. Campbell 2005, 214. To be sure, for Hooker, Choi, Hays, and Campbell this event is Christ's faith(fulness) or trust.

[448] F. Mußner 1981a, 257f.; similarly E. Lohse 1977, 162f.

[449] A. von Dobbeler 1998, 34.

Through these descriptions of πίστις, others are excluded or qualified: They are thoroughly incompatible with the subjective reading, which holds πίστις to be the faith or faithfulness of Christ, even if both interpretations agree on Paul's notion of the eschatologically qualified appearance of πίστις at "the turning point in salvation history"[450] (cf. Rom 3:21-22). Moreover, one would expect an adequate explanation of the logical and temporal relationship between the following ideas: Christ's faith(fulness) to the cross is a "single massive event." Faith is "that life-stance which he actualized and which, because he lived and died, now characterizes the personal existence of everyone who lives in him."[451] "[F]aith has now arrived with the advent of Christ."[452] "Abraham trusts God, Christ trusts God, and Christ enters the world."[453] There is also disagreement within this paradigm, whether one should interpret πίστις "messianically": Πίστις denotes Christ, "the Faithful One"[454] or "paradigmatically": Human faith is prefigured, actualized, and exemplified by Christ.[455]

The innate attachment of faith to Christ rules out that it becomes "an abstract principle or impersonal, historical phenomenon."[456] This speaks against the view of a (Gnostic-like) "hypostatization of *pistis*" which regards "faith" as "savior figure."[457] Πίστις is no hypostasis, but not primarily because its existence and reality would depend on human beings,[458] but because it essentially exists in connection with Christ, the savior. Likewise, Paul does not talk of faith in a metaphorical-personifying manner,[459] since for him πίστις is a sphere of power which brings about a real and

---

[450] H.-S. Choi 2005, 475, with reference to analogous occurrences of ἔρχεσθαι in Paul (Rom 7:9; Gal 3:19; 4:4).

[451] S.K. Williams 1987, 446; cf. J.L. Martyn 1997, 362.

[452] J.L. Martyn 1997, 23.

[453] D.A. Campbell 2005, 230 (his construal of Gal 3:22). – H.-S. Choi (2005, 473 with nn.30f.) lists other advocates of the subjective reading of Gal 3:23.25: G. Howard, R.N. Longenecker, R.B. Hays, F. Matera, I.G. Wallis, B.W. Longenecker). Notably, in his essay on Gal 3:23-25 A. von Dobbeler does not even mention this solution (cf. his brief review of suggested interpretations [1998, 16]).

[454] Cf. D.A. Campbell 2005, 214. Campbell reaches this conclusion through a messianic interpretation of Paul's quote of Hab 2:4.

[455] Cf. R.B. Hays 1983, 204; S.K. Williams 1987, 438; J.L. Martyn 1997, 362.

[456] G.W. Hansen 1989, 135.

[457] Thus D. Georgi 1991, 43 with n.32. "This hypostatization of *pistis* has received far too little attention." Cf. even E. Käsemann 1980, 88 ("hypostasierend"), 103.

[458] Thus E. Käsemann 1980, 103.

[459] Cf. R.B. Hays 1983, 200; G.W. Hansen 1989, 133; A. von Dobbeler 1998; H.-J. Eckstein 2000, 5. Von Dobbeler evaluates passages that use πίστις as personification, both in pagan (1998, 24-26) and early Christian texts (26-28), and applies his findings to Gal 3:23.25. – Above, regarding Paul's concept of sin, we have noted an analogous difference in opinion: G. Röhser speaks of a personifying talk of sin in Paul, while H. Umbach stresses its power-character (see above note 238).

ontological transformation of the cosmos.[460] The same critique applies to those suggestions that discern an objectifying use of πίστις in terms of "Christianity,"[461] the salvific significance of subjective faith,[462] the proclamation of faith,[463] the gospel,[464] or the epistemological "basis of Christian faith-knowledge."[465]

On the other hand, a subjective-anthropological understanding neglects the overtly objective and transformative character of πίστις, regardless whether one construes it generalizing as "personal response of faith"[466] or contextualizing as the faith of the Galatians.[467] Faith is not to be imagined in existential-philosophical terms as "general possibility for mankind,"[468] as "new possible mode of disposing one's self toward God,"[469] but in salvation-historical terms[470]: Πίστις "stands for the new order of eschatological salvation" and is at the same time "the principle (and means) of salvation."[471] Christ's incarnation, death, and resurrection have once and for all disclosed the possibility to become part of the realm of faith.

In sum, an anthropocentric narrowing of Paul's concept of faith is averted through the reference to its salvation-historical, trans-subjective character, whereas on the other hand a one-sidedly objectified view is corrected through the participatory aspect of faith. The distinction between a correct christological (subjective genitive) and a wrong anthropological reading (objective genitive) is inadequate.[472]

---

[460] Cf. K. Barth 1960, 836.

[461] W. Mundle 1932, 93.

[462] H. Lietzmann 1933, 23.

[463] J. Becker 1992, 398.

[464] F.F. Bruce 1982, 181.

[465] D.M. Hay 1989, 473.

[466] G.W. Hansen 1989, 135; cf. F. Mußner 1981a, 254f.

[467] Cf. D. Lührmann 1976, 58.

[468] H.D. Betz 1979, 176. Cf. G. Klein 1963, 163; P. Bonnard 1972, 75 (quoted in R.B. Hays 1983, 202n.22): "La venu de Jésus-Christ a … donnée la possibilité de la foi." G. Friedrich 1982, 104; A. von Dobbeler 1998, 34. See the critique in D.M. Hay 1989, 472; D.A. Campbell 2005, 227f.

[469] R.B. Hays 1983, 204. Hays however adds that "this mode is possible precisely because it was first of all actualized in and by Jesus Christ." Similarly S.K. Williams 1987, 438.

[470] Notably, this salvation-historical qualification of the idea of the "possibility of faith" is present also in R. Bultmann (1958, 319f., 330f.; 1959, 218; on the term possibility in Bultmann, which can only be appraised against the background of his entire theological-philosophical "system," see also 1958, 253, 275, 302, 348f.), yet his description of πίστις as decision reduces the reference of this qualification to a "je für mich" (1959, 219). "[D]ie konkrete Realisierung der Glaubensmöglichkeit des Einzelnen ist selbst eschatologisches Geschehen" (1958, 330).

[471] R.Y.K. Fung (quoted in H.-S. Choi 2005, 474n.38).

[472] Against R.B. Hays 1997, 277; also D.A. Campbell 2005, 178-207, 208-232.

2. Romans 3:22c-26: God's Atoning Act in Christ through Faith

In the following verses, after restating the disastrous human plight: "all have sinned" (Rom 3:23), Paul depicts Christ's saving activity as an act of God, using traditional motifs and formulations. The πίστις Χριστοῦ-issue will accompany us also in this section, but at first some clarifying remarks on the subject of "typology" will be made, as this thematic will become important in what follows.

a) Excursus: Typos and Typology

The problem of typology[473] has occupied numerous generations of scholars, mostly in terms of a Christian hermeneutics, according to which historical persons or motifs from the Old Testament are superseded through the New Testament which presents Christ's salvific work. Especially, L. Goppelt's work on typology shaped this still more or less normative description. Generally, the relationship between these two objects is defined in terms of an antithesis, as that of *typos* and *antitypos*.[474] Two related problems arise with any attempt to characterize the phenomenon of *typos* or typology: First, the subject-matter is relatively independent from the terminology, i.e., a typology can be present even if the word *typos* is missing, and *vice versa*.[475] Second, the New Testament offers no account of what should be understood by the concept of typology[476]; it has not become yet a distinct method of interpretation.[477]

Others have corrected and supplemented Goppelt's definition, but most consider the basic thrust of his argument as satisfactory. Yet scholars such as E. Käsemann have pointed out against Goppelt that the element of antithesis is *not* constitutive for "typology," for anticipation is an equally adequate relationship.[478] Also, for Käsemann the progress from *typos* to

---

[473] See also above chapter V.A.I.1.b.

[474] L. Goppelt 1939, 18f. U. Luz summarizes Goppelt's analysis and gathers the chief elements that define typology (1968, 52f., following L. Goppelt 1939, 2 *et passim*): (1) typology contrasts two historical facts, i.e., (2) events (not words, promises, etc.); (3) the *typos* is superseded by the *antitypos* that (4) follows on the *typos* chronologically; (5) generally only facts that are causally related to God become the subject of typological considerations.

[475] Cf. K.-H. Ostmeyer 2000, 112f.

[476] The term τύπος can appear where no typology is intended (e.g., 1Pet 5:3), while a typology can be present when the term is not mentioned (e.g., Gal 4:21-31). Therefore, U. Luz points out that any definition remains circular (1968, 52n.53).

[477] Cf. D.-A. Koch 1986, 216f. with n.12.

[478] E. Käsemann 1969, 173. Likewise, J. Roloff contends that to require the notion of an expressive antithesis is too narrow a definition and irreconcilable with the Pauline idea of history (1990, 243n.27)

antitypos is normal, but not indispensable.[479] All however agree on the significance of history.

A more recent study by K.-H. Ostmeyer also challenges Goppelt's findings, for the first time utilizing new research possibilities available through the *Thesaurus Linguae Graecae*. He comes to the conclusion that behind the multifaceted use of the term τύπος in antique literature, one understanding is consistent: It describes the relation between two entities by pointing to the identity of the comparative aspects; insofar, it is a "Relationsbegriff"[480] or "Funktionsbegriff,"[481] which does not require a counter-term such as ἀντίτυπος. In fact, a superseding or superseded τύπος is in Ostmeyer's view a *contradictio in adiecto* and any hierarchical view of typology does not correspond to the philological facts.[482]

In evaluation of this new approach one should agree that typology in the New Testament presupposes some kind of identity of certain aspects, but not in terms of an absolute identity. Since with Christ God indeed sets a new, "more fulfilled"[483] salvation-historical reality at the fullness of time, the identity consists in a relative or anticipatory sense, though not less valuable or valid.[484] The following analysis of Paul's calling Christ the ἱλαστήριον does not deprecate the Old Testament atonement or question its full value and validity, but now, through Christ, it is "more fulfilled." The issue is not a "worse-better" or "shallower-deeper" relationship, but one of "then-now," wholly based on God's decision to send Christ.

Likewise, as we will see below, Abraham's faith has full value and validity for Paul, but is at the same time anticipatory for the full, eschatological realization of πίστις through Christ. Such christological realization opens up the *sensus plenior* of what has been done and written in the old covenant.[485]

b) Faith and Atonement

From an argumentative-rhetorical perspective one notes that Paul does not offer any supportive line of reasoning for the interpretation of Jesus' aton-

---

[479] This aspect is the fifth of Käsemann's definition of typology; the others are (1969, 169-171): Typology is (1) bound to Scripture, (2) though not to a text primarily, but to an event; (3) there is no *a priori* relationship to the future (in contrast to "promise"); (4) history has an own reality and significance (in contrast to allegory) and relates to the presence either as anticipation or as antithesis.

[480] K.-H. Ostmeyer 2000, 128.

[481] K.-H. Ostmeyer 2000, 129.

[482] K.-H. Ostmeyer 2000, 129, 131.

[483] Cf. H. Binder 1968, 41 (πίστις as "erfülltere Heilsgestalt"); W. Mundle 1932, 109 ("größere[.] Offenbarung Gottes").

[484] On the relationship of typology and salvation-history, see O. Cullmann 1965, 114f.

[485] Cf. K. Haacker 1999, 110.

ing death.[486] Its core appears to be an undisputed reality, for the (Jewish-Christian) circles in which this text unit presumably originated, for Paul, who incorporated it into his letter, as well as for the recipients of the letter.

Nevertheless, to the modern reader, the section Rom 3:24-26 poses several questions that concern predominantly tradition-historical and redactional aspects, and these questions have received even more different interpretations. Many exegetes agree that the compact style[487] and for Paul unusual terminology[488] suggest that in 3:(24.)25-26 Paul took up and commented on a traditional Jewish-Christian soteriological formula – possibly a baptismal text.[489] The exact extent and form of what Paul adopted is disputed, but this issue does not need to be discussed here extensively.[490] Most of these exegetes understand the expression διὰ [τῆς] πίστεως to be inserted by Paul into this traditional text piece[491] and the second ἔνδειξις phrase (3:26b) as an explanatory addition to the first occurrence of ἔνδειξις in 3:25.[492] Hence, in sum, the text used and supplemented by Paul reaches from 3:25 until 3:26a.[493] In the course of the exegesis of this passage, we

---

[486] Cf. M. Neubrand 1997, 117. Only from Rom 3:27 onwards does he resume the argumentative style.

[487] Cf. already M. Luther 1515/1516, 238: "Textus obscurus et confusus."

[488] Cf. the unique meaning of προτίθεσθαι (different from Rom 1:13) and the *hapaxlegomena* ἱλαστήριον, πάρεσις, and προγίνεσθαι. The theme of "the blood of Christ" only appears in the context of the Lord's Supper (1Cor 10:16; 11:25) and in Rom 5:9 which however refers back to 3:25.

[489] Cf. especially U. Schnelle 1986, 67-72, 197-201. Alternatively, O. Michel (1978, 153n.16) and E. Käsemann (1980, 94) suggested the liturgy of the Lord's Supper as *Sitz im Leben* of Paul's *Vorlage*. In any case, one is left with some uncertainty (E. Lohse 2003, 133n.18).

[490] On the different solutions see especially P. Stuhlmacher 1975; cf. also R. Bultmann 1958, 49. Against E. Käsemann's proposal that the traditional text starts with Rom 3:24 (1950/1951; cf., e.g., K. Kertelge 1971, 48-53; D. Lührmann 1965, 150), K. Wengst contended that the progression of syntax from 3:23 to 3:24 is nothing unusual in Paul (1972, 87; cf., e.g., U. Wilckens 1978, 183f.; M. Theobald 1992, 99).

[491] Following R. Bultmann (cf. 1958, 49), E. Käsemann argues that Paul added the expression διὰ [τῆς] πίστεως, since it appears forced and disruptive (1950/1951, 100: "höchst gewaltsam und störend"; cf. U. Wilckens 1978: "gewaltsame paulinische Einfügung"). Notably, the Alexandrinus (A) lacks the expression διὰ [τῆς] πίστεως. See B.F. Meyer 1983 for further details, but also A. Pluta 1969, 36f., 45-56; S.K. Williams 1975, 41-51.

[492] Thus, through πρὸς τὴν ἔνδειξιν τῆς δικαιοσύνης αὐτοῦ Paul explains εἰς ἔνδειξιν τῆς δικαιοσύνης αὐτοῦ (3:25) to balance and broaden the gist of what he took over (cf. J.D.G. Dunn 1988, 164). Among those who defend Pauline authorship of these verses are O. Kuss 1963, 160; C.E.B. Cranfield 1975, 200f.; H. Schlier 1977, 107. Others want to identify Rom 3:24-26 as "non-Pauline fragment," i.e., post-Pauline gloss (C.H. Talbert 1966).

[493] Cf. P. Stuhlmacher 1975, 134.

have to take into account the relationship of Paul's interpretation to the existing tradition.

(a) Ἱλαστήριον

But at first we have to deal with the much discussed tradition-historical and history-of-religions background of the term ἱλαστήριον, as well as with its meaning and implication in the present context. Apart from Rom 3:25, ἱλαστήριον only appears in Heb 9:5 in the New Testament, but it is the common translation word for the Hebrew כַּפֹּרֶת in the Septuagint.[494] In the Old Testament כַּפֹּרֶת denotes the "mercy seat," the "place of expiation" on the Ark of the Covenant, on which a blood rite was carried out at the Day of Atonement.

The debate concerns the question whether Paul takes recourse to a later Jewish line of tradition that interprets the martyr death with the term ἱλαστήριον in the framework of the idea of atonement (especially 4Macc 17,20-22[495]) or whether he rather identifies Jesus with the "atonement cover" and alludes to the Day of Atonement (especially Leviticus 16; cf. Ezekiel 43[496]). It is mainly E. Lohse's work on the martyr-idea in Jewish theology that is linked to the first interpretation and that gained great influence in New Testament scholarship.[497] On the other hand, P. Stuhlmacher's step-by-step critique of Lohse's arguments brings to the fore weaknesses in his method and line of thought.[498]

---

[494] Cf. P. Stuhlmacher 1975, 121. – On ἱλαστήριον, see S. Schreiber 2006, discussing *inter alia* recent works of M. Gaukesbrink, T. Knöppler, D. Stökl Ben Ezra, and T. Söding.

[495] See the analysis of this idea in W. Kraus 1991, 33-44 (on 2Macc 7,37-38; LXX Dan 3:40; 4Macc 6,28-29; 17,21-22).

[496] These two chapters are also broadly discussed in W. Kraus 1991, 45-59, 59-63.

[497] Apart from the exegetes mentioned in P. Stuhlmacher 1975, 120 – H. Conzelmann, W. Schrage, K. Wengst, G. Delling, G. Klein, E. Schweizer, U. Wilckens (who later modified his view), and G. Eichholz (at first also P. Stuhlmacher himself; cf. 1966, 86f.) – see, e.g., S.K. Williams 1975, 47-51; R.B. Hays 1983, 160; J.W. van Henten 1993; K. Haacker 1999, 90f. Lohse has to conjecture that Paul had as *Vorlage* ἱλαστήριον θύμα (adjective), which he changed into ἱλαστήριον διὰ πίστεως (noun). This hypothesis emerges on grounds of the following observations: (1) the typological identification of Jesus and the "atonement cover" is not understandable for non-Jewish-Christian readers (E. Lohse 1963, 151); (2) the article is missing (in contrast to the use in the Septuagint) (151); (3) the public installing of Jesus contradicts the place of the ark in the *sanctum sanctorum* (151); (4) the image that Jesus stands for the כַּפֹּרֶת, onto which his blood is dashed at the same time, appears incomprehensible. See also E. Lohse 2003, 134f.

[498] Cf. P. Stuhlmacher 1975; 1989, 55-58, and following him more or less: U. Wilckens 1978, 190-194; M. Theobald 1992, 99f.; W. Kraus 1991, 152-154; 1999; D.P. Bailey 1999. Against the points of Lohse, Stuhlmacher argues: (1) later writings (1Peter; *1Clement*; *Hermas*) confirm that the Roman congregation must have been capable of understanding the meaning of the Jewish-Christian *paradosis*, especially if one considers the significance of the atonement and the Day of Atonement in post-exilic Jewish theolo-

As an alternative to a linear tradition-historical trajectory, others understand ἱλασήριον in Rom 3:25 as "dedication of the eschatological sanctuary,"[499] or, in a wide, general sense as "means of atonement,"[500] or, still
weaker as salvation-giving presence of God.[501]

In evaluation, both Lohse's and Stuhlmacher's explanations[502] seek to
and are able to account for the notion of αἷμα, which in Paul refers to Jesus' death on the cross[503] – for Lohse it is associated with the self-sacrifice
of the martyrs, for Stuhlmacher with the sin offering. Yet only the reference to Leviticus 16 can do justice to (1) to the fact that it is God himself
who provides for the atoning means (cf. Lev 17:11)[504]; (2) the singularity
of God's atoning act in Christ; (3) to its unrepeatable "once and for all"-
character; and (4) to the Jewish-Christian origin of the text in conjunction
with Paul's concern that what he asserts is sanctioned by the law and the
prophets (Rom 3:21). As will be seen later, the atonement also establishes
a link to the context of 4:3-8 and 4:25.

The language is metaphorical-typological. But what are the implications
of this language[505] in the present context? Some see in these phrases the

---

gizing (1975, 124); (2) the noun ἱλαστήριον is used as a *praedicativum* and therefore
does not require an article (125); (3) and (4) the highly complex and abstract idea of the
theology of the ark – the ark was no longer present in the second temple – does not allow
for demanding direct equivalences. As in Rom 3:25 where both the "atonement cover"
and the blood are referred to Jesus, in Hebrews Jesus is portrayed as both sacrifice and
high priest (127). – Furthermore, the date of composition of 4Maccabees might well be
later than Paul's letters. See also the concerns against 4Macc 17,20-21 as background for
Rom 3:25 in W. Kraus 1991, 39-41, 151f.

[499] W. Kraus develops and critiques insights of Stuhlmacher (1991, 152-154, 194-
199), concluding: "Jesus [wurde] in seinem Kreuzestod von Gott als eschatologisches
Heiligtum eingesetzt," and this sanctuary is the place of atonement and divine epiphany
(1991, 163).

[500] Cf. H. Lietzmann 1928, 49f.; U. Schnelle 2003, 509.

[501] Cf. G. Wiencke 1939, 52; also D.A. Campbell 1992, 113; M. Neubrand 1997, 121.

[502] J.D.G. Dunn argues against a "clear-cut either/or" (1988, 171), but goes on that "it
is more likely that 4Macc 17.21-22 ... and Rom 3:25 are parallel extensions of the same
cultic language" (180).

[503] According to Lev 17:11-12, the blood is the medium provided by Yahweh through
which cultic atonement is performed. The notion of "blood" speaks against a connection
to Hellenistic gifts of atonement (cf. U. Wilckens 1978, 192, against A. Deißmann 1903;
S. Schreiber seeks to revive Deißmann's interpretation [2006,100-102]).

[504] This idea differs greatly from the idea of the atoning blood of the martyrs (cf. P.
Stuhlmacher 1975, 131n.57).

[505] Even in Second Temple Judaism the mention of the "mercy seat" had metaphorical
meaning, since the physical ark was no longer present (cf. P. Stuhlmacher 1975, 127). On
the other hand the language is typological, insofar as it describes the relative identity of
the effects of the ἱλαστήριον, both of the Old and New Testament, namely, the forgiveness of sins.

abrogation of the temple cult and the factual substitution of the Day of Atonement through the Christian Good Friday, i.e., the break between the early Christian and the contemporary Jewish religion[506]; the atonement through Christ is the *antitypos* superseding the atonement of the old covenant.[507]

Above we noted some corrections to the *typos-antitypos* model. Rather than propagating a climactic-hierarchical progression from type to antitype, a concentration of identical aspects is more adequate: Both, the rite surrounding the atonement cover and Christ's death on the cross, offer forgiveness of sins, but for Paul the former happened in anticipation of the latter, until God, at the fullness of time – i.e., "at the present time" (Rom 3:26)! – would initiate a new, "more fulfilled," and more universal means of expitiation. Yet the essence of both is the same.[508]

But also an open, non-concrete metaphorical explanation[509] falls short by its "thin" understanding of metaphor: By definition, the correlations that a metaphor creates between two entities entail a fresh description of existence and a new vision of reality.[510] The new dimension that a metaphor lays on an "old" term may not be suppressed. For Paul and his addressees, therefore, Jesus' being the ἱλαστήριον establishes a new reality in which no other atonement rites are required; God's act has set a new time with a christological-eschatological and universal dimension – he put forward Christ as redeemer, once and for all, publicly[511] and not secluded in the *sanctum sanctorum*.[512] God is the one who acts; he is the subject of

---

[506] Cf. U. Wilckens 1978, 240; see also P. Stuhlmacher 1975, 131f.; 1989, 56; W. Kraus 1991, 163; M. Theobald 1992, 101f.

[507] Cf. L. Goppelt 1939, 179; T.W. Manson 1945; S. Lyonnet 1959.

[508] K.-H. Ostmeyer 2000, 131.

[509] Such as that of D.A. Campbell 1992, 113.

[510] P. Ricœur 1974, 45 ("Neubeschreibung der Existenz"). The talk of an "analogy" is therefore insufficient (against M. Neubrand 1997, 122).

[511] The translation of προτίθεσθαι as "install publicly" is to be preferred (cf., e.g., P. Stuhlmacher 1975, 130; 1997, 193; U. Wilckens 1978, 192 with n.537) over against "predetermine" (cf., e.g., K. Haacker 1999, 91; see K.H. Schelkle 1956, 116, for evidence from authorities of the early church, where this understanding prevails). Though the latter meaning would be supported by passages like Rom 8:28, 9:11, and especially Eph 1:9-11, where the noun πρόθεσις is used, the universalism and publicity of Paul's proclamation speaks for the former alternative. One could explain προτίθεσθαι within the framework of a cultic setting (which is also suggested by the term ἱλαστήριον), namely, as *terminus technicus* for the public installing of the Bread of the Presence (cf. LXX Ex 29:23; 40:23; Lev 24:8; 2Macc 1,8.15).

[512] Cf. U. Wilckens 1978, 191n.534.

what happens, as he prepares in Jesus Christ the means of salvation and of the forgiveness of sins.[513]

The next question that poses itself concerns the group of people, who are – in Paul's view – affected by the consequences of Jesus' atoning death, i.e., who are absorbed in this new reality. Does Paul attain a collective, universal perspective or does he distinguish between Jews and Gentiles[514]? Those who argue that Paul has in mind Gentile sin and atonement of Gentile sin[515] fail to account for Jewish-Christian provenance of the text piece, which in its original certainly spoke of the Jewish people, but more importantly they neglect the generic and universal statement: "There is no distinction, since all have sinned" (3:22-23).[516]

In sum, with his inclusion of the traditional, Jewish-Christian formula into the context of chapter 3, Paul takes up the basic thrust of this paradosis (proving that he deems equally valid a Christology with a different outlook than his own): By putting forward Jesus as ἱλαστήριον, God constitutes a holy, new, eschatological people and thus fully realizes and transcends what was anticipated in the sacrifice described in Leviticus 16.[517] In his righteousness, he is faithful to his covenant, renewing and fulfilling the relationship to his people.[518] As already indicated, Paul now gives to it his own impressive theological twist and extends it by means of two aspects[519]: first, the universal-eschatological reality of God's salvation, and second the notion of faith as universal means of salvation. To the latter we now turn.[520]

(b) Διὰ [τῆς] πίστεως

Above, the unexpected insertion of διὰ [τῆς] πίστεως has been highlighted, and it deserves some consideration. Already in his *propositio* Paul had shown that "faith" would constitute the cornerstone of his letter and made his reader/hearer aware that his crucial theses have to be appreciated from

---

[513] Cf. the remarkable way how God is named the subject of reconciliation as 2Cor 5:19: "In Christ God was reconciling the world to himself, not counting their trespasses against them."

[514] See above the distinction between proponents of an exclusive soteriology (chapter V.A.I.2.a) and those of a non-exclusive soteriology (chapter V.A.I.2.b).

[515] Cf. S.K. Williams 1975, 25-34; J.G. Gager 1985, 216; S.K. Stowers 1989, 668-670; M. Neubrand 1997, 122.

[516] Cf. J.D.G. Dunn 1988, 173. Paul's view is different from that of 2Macc 6,12-16.

[517] This tenet is related to the words of the Lord's Supper, especially to 1Cor 11:25; Lk 22:20.

[518] Cf. P. Stuhlmacher 1975, 132; G. Eichholz 1972, 194.

[519] While G. Klein sees in Paul's use of the formula a critique of the original paradosis (1967, 6n.12), P. Stuhlmacher regards it as consequent development and extension (1975, 133).

[520] Cf. P. Stuhlmacher 1975, 133.

the perspective of faith.[521] This is also the case here; otherwise the insertion would remain mysterious.

Notably, a similar addition to a traditional formula occurs in Gal 3:26: Right after talking about the new era of faith that had come with Christ, Paul asserts that "in Christ Jesus you are all children of God through faith (διὰ τῆς πίστεως)."[522] Two ideas already familiar to us, the keyword πᾶς and the maxim that there is no distinction between Jews and Gentiles (Gal 3:28), prove the apostle's universal structure of thought in this context and anticipate the course of the exegesis of Rom 3:25.

At least three different interpretations found their way into the exegetical discussion: The expression is held to denote either God's covenantal faithfulness, or Jesus' faithfulness, or, traditionally, human faith (in Christ).

(1) The first view[523] seems "attractive"[524] and finds support through contextual arguments and through references to corresponding passages both in the Septuagint and the New Testament. In the immediate context of Rom 3:25, i.e., in 3:22 and 26, πίστις is determined by a genitive; the lack of such a determination in 3:25 might indicate that the syntactical subject – ὁ θεός – is the point of reference of πίστις, as in Rom 3:3. Furthermore, several Septuagintal passages understand πίστις in terms of God's faithfulness,[525] and Deut 32:4 displays a juxtaposition of God's faithfulness and his righteousness in analogy to Rom 3:25.[526] One reason against this solution is the required assumption of different meanings and subjects of πίστις in the context of 3:21-26.[527] More importantly, however, with διὰ [τῆς] πίστεως Paul recurs without doubt to the longer expression διὰ πίστεως Ἰησοῦ Χριστοῦ (3:22) and abbreviates it according to the formula style.[528]

(2) Once the relationship between 3:22 and 3:25 in the present Pauline context is acknowledged,[529] the decisive general question is again which

---

[521] See above pages 241f.

[522] On the secondary character of διὰ τῆς πίστεως, see, e.g., H. Schlier 1965, 171; H.D. Betz 1979, 181; R.B. Hays 1983, 155.

[523] Cf. K. Barth 1922, 86; G. Hebert 1955, 376, and most extensively A. Pluta 1969, 45-56, 105-111.

[524] J.D.G. Dunn 1988, 172; cf. 1997, 266: Possibly, διὰ [τῆς] πίστεως refers to God's faithfulness in analogy to the ἐκ πίστεως of Rom 1:17.

[525] Cf. A. Pluta 1969, 51n.17., who refers to 18 passages in the Septuagint.

[526] Besides, 1John 1:9 contains a similar correlation, even in the framework of the atonement.

[527] Cf. U. Wilckens 1978, 194; W. Kraus 1991, 187 with n.150.

[528] If one insists that διὰ [τῆς] πίστεως belonged to the original formula (thus A. Pluta 1969, 45-56), one has to recognize that the meaning differs between the original (πίστις θεοῦ) and Paul's use (πίστις Χριστοῦ) (cf. U. Wilckens 1978, 194).

[529] Cf., e.g., W. Schenk 1972, 171; G. Eichholz 1972, 191; U. Wilckens 1978, 193.

sense one assigns to the phrase πίστις Χριστοῦ. Obviously, those who had concluded that in 3:22 the phrase denotes the faith(fulness) of Christ, argue even here that God regarded Christ crucified "as a means of expiation due to [his] faith, on account of his blood."[530] In their view, "God's fidelity to the promises made to Abraham" becomes apparent in Jesus' death and resurrection, so that the faithfulness of Jesus Christ unto the cross is "a demonstration of *God's* righteousness" and the fulfillment of the covenantal promises.[531] To be sure, there is some confusion in this language as to whether it is God who acts by putting forward Jesus Christ or Jesus Christ who acts faithfully unto death. Theologically, one might justify the statement that God acts in and through Christ's act, yet the question remains, if it was *Paul's* intention to say so. Rather, both in the original context of the formula and in Paul's reception of the tradition, the story of Christ, the cross, are understood as act of God.[532]

Furthermore, the metaphorical-typological language of sacrifice, which Paul takes over, places a new salvation-historical reality before our eyes: Christ is the ἱλαστήριον, so that the (alleged) way to this new reality, Christ's faithfulness, appears out of place in this context. In Christ's blood, it is already present and established.[533]

(3) The alternative interpretation that had been undisputed over a long period of time argues that through faith (διὰ [τῆς] πίστεως) the atoning,

---

[530] S.K. Williams 1975, 51; cf. 42-51; 1980, 277n.113; S.K. Stowers 1989, 669; B.W. Longenecker 1993; J.L. Martyn 1997, 271 ("Jesus' atoning faithfulness").

[531] R.B. Hays 1983, 160 (italics original); cf. 1997, 284; 2002, xxx. Hays contends that Paul used the expression "the faith of Jesus Christ" by metonymy to indicate the climax of the Jesus-story: the cross. He also refers to G. Howard 1979, 57f., who argues along similar lines. Cf. also A.K. Grieb 2002, 37: "Jesus Christ is both Israel's representative (the Israelite who keeps covenant with God) and God's representative (the righteousness of God enacted through his own faithfulness, his faithful obedience unto death on the cross)... Paul's argument for the righteousness of God in Romans stands or falls precisely here: unless the faithfulness of Jesus Christ is also the righteousness of God as shown in his resurrection from the dead, then as Paul says elsewhere, 'our preaching has been in vain and your faith has been in vain' (1Cor 15:14)."

[532] Cf. F. Büchsel 1938, 321: "Gott ist in diesem ganzem Zusammenhange durchaus als Subjekt ... gedacht." E. Lohse 1963, 150: "Es wird hier ... ausschließlich gesagt, was Gott getan hat." G. Eichholz 1972, 191: "Die Geschichte Jesu Christi ... ist Gottes Handeln." U. Schnelle 2003, 509 ("Theozentrik des Geschehens"). F. Watson 2004, 75: "It is striking that this passage interprets Jesus' death not as the outcome of his own faithfulness but as God's saving action. While this action has its own particular time and place, it is not closed in upon itself but forms the basis of the ongoing divine action in which God justifies the one who responds in faith. Faith, and consequently righteousness, is what is intended in God's action in the death of Jesus."

[533] Thus, L.T. Johnson's contention that "Jesus' faithfulness" and "the shedding of his blood" functions "almost as a hendiadys" (1982, 80), appears strained; the text simply does not talk about the shedding of Jesus' blood.

salvific activity, embodied in the crucified, is experienced and accepted in terms of its relevance *pro me*.[534] This view, however, has to paraphrase and explain with some artistry the instrumental preposition διά: Atonement "comes through faith,"[535] is "to be appropriated by faith,"[536] "grasped through faith,"[537] "effective through faith,"[538] "available through faith,"[539] or simply "for faith."[540] More importantly, as in 3:22 this interpretation that puts human acceptance adjacent to God's salvific action appears to contradict the theocentric *ductus* of the text.[541] Also, the phrase διά [τῆς] πίστεως modifies the verb προτίθεσθαι,[542] just as ἐκ πίστεως refers to ἀποκαλύπτεται (1:17) and διά πίστεως to πεφανέρωται (3:21-22).

Consequently, διά [τῆς] πίστεως describes the means through which God publicly and universally established Christ as the means of atonement. Here, our personal faith is not the primary issue. The insertion of this phrase through Paul makes clear his intention: That God revealed his righteousness through faith is parallel to his manifestation of Christ as ἱλαστήριον to demonstrate his righteousness. Only an entity that correlates to these all-encompassing divine acts can explain Paul's language: Faith is here a phenomenon that transcends human subjectivity, but has the power to bring about righteousness and atonement. The enigmatic term ἔνδειξις therefore also connotes the eschatological manifestation of God's righteousness through faith[543] – rather than taking on a rational, "evidential sense"[544] – and connects to πεφανέρωται (3:21).[545]

When Paul takes up the traditional wording in his own formulation by means of the term ἔνδειξις (3:26), he makes fully clear that the eschatological revelation of righteousness through faith "now" (3:21) is the eschatological manifestation of his righteousness through faith, in Christ's blood, "at the present time" (3:25-26). Notably, faith, righteousness, and Christology belong together for Paul: He included the traditional piece Rom 3:24-26 into the *locus classicus* of his doctrine of justification, 3:21-

---

[534] P. Stuhlmacher 1975, 134f.

[535] W. Kraus 1991, 187.

[536] C.E.B. Cranfield 1975, 201; cf. 210; similarly H. Lietzmann 1928, 48.

[537] E. Käsemann 1980, 85.

[538] The translation of the NRSV.

[539] S. Westerholm 2004, 322.

[540] M. Luther's translation ("für den Glauben"). – Equally unconvincing, the second of the interpretations mentioned (the faithfulness of Christ) translates for instance "due to" (cf. S.K. Williams 1975, 51).

[541] Cf. U. Wilckens 1978, 193f. He, however, wants to distinguish human acceptance from human trust in Christ, which appears to be too subtle a distinction.

[542] Against F. Büchsel 1938, 321.

[543] Cf. P. Stuhlmacher 1966, 89.

[544] Against D.M. Hay 1989, 472. Cf. U. Wilckens 1978, 194.

[545] Cf. W.G. Kümmel 1952, 269.

31,[546] but also inserted the justification-related πίστις into the traditional, christological-soteriological piece itself.

The unique phrase πάρεσις ἁμαρτημάτων with the noun πάρεσις being *hapaxlegomenon* in the Greek Bible, and its use in the present context has received several interpretations. Two basic alternatives can be distinguished: The first regards the term in question to denote "remittance" or "forgiveness" of sins,[547] thus corresponding to ἄφεσις, and the second translates generally with "passing over," either thinking of a "disregarding" of sins[548] or of a "holding back punishment."[549] The cultic character of the context speaks against the second solution with its juridical connotation, while on the other hand the idea of an accumulation of sins until a final punishment or remittance is frequent in Jewish tradition.[550] Possibly, both elements of meaning can be combined: From the perspective of eschatology, which is assumed by Paul since 3:21, the sins of all humanity – not first and foremost "individual" sins – have been accumulated and left "unpunished" until the day of Christ's death on the cross, which is the "new" Day of Atonement at which all previously committed sins are atoned for.[551] Paul will take up the notion of forgiveness in 4:7.[552]

(c) Ὁ ἐκ πίστεως Ἰησοῦ

Paul's own extension of the paradosis in the second half of Rom 3:26 confirms and specifies what has been said on his understanding of "faith" in this context and also on the notion of the "righteousness of God." Again, as in 1:17 (ἐκ πίστεως), 3:22 (διὰ πίστεως), and 3:25 (διὰ [τῆς] πίστεως) not Jesus' own faithfulness is in view,[553] nor God's faithfulness in

---

[546] Cf. W. Mundle 1932, 86. See also the other traditional text Rom 4:24-25.

[547] Cf., e.g., W.G. Kümmel 1952, 262f.; U. Wilckens 1978, 196.

[548] Cf., e.g., E. Preuschen/W. Bauer 1928, 1242.

[549] Cf., e.g., A. Schlatter 1935, 148; O. Michel 1978, 153; S.K. Williams 1975, 19-34; H. Schlier 1977, 112f.; J.D.G. Dunn 1988, 173. See the commentaries for references to the ancient sources. – See most recently R. Penna 2005.

[550] Cf. S.K. Williams 1975, 25-33.

[551] Cf. L. Goppelt 1967, 155: "Der Karfreitag war der eschatologische 'Tag der Sühnung' und als solcher die Erweisung der Gerechtigkeit Gottes" (cf. 1964, 252; O. Michel 1978, 153).

[552] See below pages 352f. These are the only passages, in which Paul speaks of forgiveness (cf. E. Käsemann 1980, 107).

[553] On the basis of the *varia lectio* in Rom 3:26 – D L Ψ 33 614 *et al.*, also Clement of Alexandria read Ἰησοῦν instead of Ἰησοῦ – R.B. Hays claims "that a significant number of interpreters in the church later found no difficulty with the idea that Jesus was justified by faith," but still opts for the common text and translates: "the one who shares the faith of Jesus" (1997, 284; cf. 1983, 160n.144; H.W. Schmidt 1966, 72). A scribal error is most likely (cf. H. Lietzmann 1928, 51; U. Wilckens 1978, 198n.569). At least the proximity to Rom 4:5 (τὸν δικαιοῦντα τὸν ἀσεβῆ) makes Hays's assumption unlikely.

Christ,[554] nor a human attitude, but the new reality that has been instigated
upon his coming and has received a universal dimension through his death.
The causal preposition ἐκ[555] points to the realm where one's existence has
its ground and origin[556]: The one who is ἐκ πίστεως Ἰησοῦ is the one
whose existence grounds in the new salvation-historical sphere of faith and
participates in it.[557] The other, corresponding, but futile basis of one's existence is the law: Those who participate in the sphere of the law are called
οἱ ἐκ νόμου (4:14)[558]; this analogy reinforces the radical contrast between
both ways of salvation from the present eschatological perspective.

Considering the above definition of typology, one could argue for a typological correlation of "those of faith" and "those of the law"; their identity lies in the idea that both express the soil in which one's existence roots
with respect to one's orientation to God. The remarkable singular ὁ ἐκ
πίστεως Ἰησοῦ puts the emphasis on the personal involvement, which results from the fact that God's righteousness is disclosed universally
through the event of faith and has come to and seized the individual believer (cf. 3:22; Phil 3:12).

Though δικαιοσύνη θεοῦ describes God's attribute of being righteous[559]
manifesting itself in a universal-eschatological dimension in Christ's cross
(δίκαιος εἶναι), it becomes real and tangible in the subjective appropriation of the event of salvation when his righteousness is transferred as a gift
to the individual existence (δικαιοῦσθαι).[560] There, elimination of sins and
righteousness correlate. However, while Paul in this paragraph is still occupied primarily with the greater, salvation-historical framework, he will
deal extensively with the aspect of the particularity of the individual existence only in the Abraham-chapter with a similar, but more "personal"
correspondence of justification and forgiveness. Hence, even if the original
Sitz im Leben of the Jewish-Christian paradosis might have been baptism,
the present wideness of Paul's depiction of salvation-history only anticipates and prepares an individual concretization.[561]

---

[554] Cf. again K. Barth 1922, 86, who translates: "…in der Treue, die in Jesus sich bewährt." J.J. O'Rourke 1973, 190f.

[555] Cf. A. Schlatter 1935, 42.

[556] Cf. O. Michel 1978, 154. This is not to be understood though in existential-
philosophical terms.

[557] Cf. Gal 3:7.9 (οἱ ἐκ πίστεως).

[558] See below page 370.

[559] Cf. U. Wilckens 1978, 195, but also C.E.B. Cranfield 1975, 211 (i.e., different
from 1:17; 3:21-22; cf. 98, 202).

[560] Cf. U. Schnelle 2003, 251f.

[561] Cf. A. Schlatter 1935, 157. For Paul ὁ νῦν καιρός means the time after Christ has
come – into the world, not into the life of the individual in baptism.

3. Romans 3:27-31: The Way of Salvation of Faith

In Rom 3:27-31, a "specially difficult" section,[562] Paul returns to the dynamic style of the "diatribe" with its short questions and answers,[563] which was interrupted by his doctrinal-theological expositions of 3:21-26. This section (introduced by οὖν) represents the connecting link between his presentation of the universal-eschatological dimension of God's act in Christ 3:21-26 (νυνί) and the Abraham-chapter (οὖν), where he will explain the materialization of faith in Abraham's life, its circumstances and consequences. Paul is on the way to make clear what ἐκ πίστεως εἰς πίστιν means, how faith concretizes itself in Abraham's life.

One can reasonably argue that this threefold structure corresponds to the development from νόμος (3:21) to ἔργα νόμου (3:28) to ἔργα/ἐργάζειν (4:4-5): The salvation-historical power of the law (3:21) seeks to institute itself as principal condition of life and demands submission through "works of the law" (3:28) – and the individual has to accomplish works (4:4-5).[564] Likewise, the purpose of the power of faith, πίστις Χριστοῦ (3:22.25.26), is to call for participation, to take control over humans, and to show the exclusive way of salvation: πίστις (3:28) – and the individual enters the sphere of faith (ἐπίστευσεν, 4:3).[565] Again, these are Paul's three steps: (1) the fact and effect of the cosmic reality of faith/the law, (2) the condition and foundation of the human existence in that faith/law *sub specie iustificationis*, and finally (3) the historical-concrete manifestation of that faith/law in the individual through participation.

Hence, in 3:27-31 Paul still thinks in salvation-historical categories, but approaches the question how and in whose life faith/the law became a tangible reality, confirming the inefficacy of the law in matters of δικαιοσύνη (3:28; cf. 3:21). The following exegesis seeks to provide evidence for the thesis briefly indicated here.

---

[562] C.E.B. Cranfield 1975, 218.

[563] Cf. S.K. Stowers 1981, 164-167. He extrapolates from Rom 3:27-4:2 a dialogical exchange consisting of five questions of the interlocutor and five answers of Paul.

[564] Cf. R. Bergmeier 2005, 175. – To be sure, the lack of the term νόμος in Rom 4:1-8 is also due to the intention of 4:9-16, i.e., the temporal and material prevalence of πίστις before νόμος (cf. D.-A. Koch 1986, 307n.1).

[565] E. Lohmeyer contended that what Paul calls "from faith to faith" (Rom 1:17) is the counter-expression to "from the law to works" (1929, 119). The two poles "cosmology" and "anthropology" characterize both πίστις and νόμος. Appealing to insights of G. Bornkamm, H. Köster, E. Brandenburger, H.F. Weiß, and M. Hengel, P. Stuhlmacher remarks, "daß die Tora gleichermaßen für das hellenistische und das palästinische Judentum ein kosmisches Prinzip gewesen ist, so daß Hengel ... plastisch von einer 'Toraontologie' zu sprechen wagt, die in der Anthropologie ihre Spitze findet" (1970, 190n.50).

According to M. Neubrand, the structure of 3:27-31 follows the schema ABCB'A'[566]:

A		Exclusion of boasting through νόμος πίστεως (3:27)
	B	Righteousness through πίστις (3:28)
		C	The one God of Jews and Gentiles (3:29)
	B'	Righteousness through πίστις (3:30)
A'		Establishment of the νόμος through πίστις (3:31)

a) Boasting, Law, and Faith

Paul's long and broad exposition of the sinfulness and faithlessness of humankind (1:18-3:20) constitutes the background of 3:27. His generic judgment on the desperate human situation was: "Every mouth may be silenced, and the whole world may be held accountable to God" (3:19) and "All have sinned and fall short of the glory of God" (3:23). Now, where is boasting? Boasting is once and for all excluded, locked out. The keyword καύχησις certainly refers back to the (Jewish) boasting (καυχᾶσθαι) condemned in 2:17 and 2:23.[567] But does it remain limited to the Jewish boasting or does Paul in this context open the horizon of his argument and speak in general-anthropological terms?

An extremely controversial aspect involved in this problem is the relationship between the Jewish understanding of (works of) the law and boasting. Oftentimes, it is argued that righteousness by works belongs intrinsically together with boasting, a view which culminated in the identification of boasting and original sin ("Ursünde") in R. Bultmann's hamartiology[568] and in the antithesis of "faith" and "boasting" in his view of Paul's understanding of faith.[569] Certainly, this perspective, rooted in an existential interpretation of Paul, did not remain without serious opposition, and others suggested a less radical view: The "boasting terminology … is rather neutral; by itself it does not point to a morally perverse 'Selbstruhm'."[570] According to this view, which becomes increasingly

---

[566] Cf. M. Neubrand 1997, 127.

[567] In Rom 2:17.23 the verb καυχᾶσθαι occurs, and in 4:2 Paul will take up this concept with the noun καύχημα. According to J.A. Fitzmyer "there is no real distinction" between καύχημα and καύχησις (1993, 362).

[568] R. Bultmann 1949, 204. "Es gehört also zusammen die Gerechtigkeit aus den Werken und *das Rühmen*," which is nothing else than craving for recognition ("*Geltungsbedürfnis*") (1948, 151; italics original), "die sündig-eigenmächtige Haltung" (1958, 242). Though Bultmann is probably the most eminent representative of this view, he is followed by many others (see below pages 332f.).

[569] Cf. R. Bultmann 1958, 316 and the critique of F. Neugebauer 1961, 165.

[570] J. Lambrecht 1985, 28; cf. J. Lambrecht/R.W. Thompson 1988, 17; see most forcefully E.P. Sanders 1983, 32-36, but also H. Räisänen, 1987, 170f. – With many other

popular in Pauline scholarship, "boasting" rather denotes "Jewish ethnic pride in the Law"[571] or the "racial boast of the Jew."[572] Hence, Paul's critique is directed against *that* boasting that stands for Jewish pride in circumcision and the law, i.e., in Israel's particular election. In his critique of the one-sidedness of this (new) perspective, S.J. Gathercole adds the following, eschatological dimension to this national Jewish boast: Καύχησις also denotes "confidence that God would vindicate Israel on the basis of both election and obedience, and that he would vindicate them both before and over against the gentiles."[573]

These explanations, however, seem to be deficient in some respects, whether or not one adds the eschatological factor to the Jewish racial boast, as they fall short of appreciating the universal-christological outlook of the apostle. For one thing, though the limitation of "boasting" to Jewish ethnic pride is backed by the occurrence of the notion of boasting in 2:17, a wider perspective nevertheless suggests itself on the basis of the eschatological scope implied by the particle νυνί in 3:21 and the general line of thought throughout the section 3:21-31. Furthermore, God is the one (*passivum divinum*) who has accomplished the exclusion of boasting "once for all,"[574] and he has done so as God *of* both Jews and Gentiles (3:29) *for* both Jews and Gentiles. Ultimately, Paul combines both, Jewish boasting and Gentile boasting and thus opposed the stance of πᾶσα σάρξ. Bultmann is not far off when he parallels "works of the law" and "boasting": Whenever Paul uses the generic expression πᾶσα σάρξ he has in mind either of the two categories, works of the law or boasting (Gal 2:16; Rom 3:20; 1Cor 1:29[575]). The difference concerning the way of thought between the Corinthians passage, 1Cor 1:29, and Rom 3:27 is that in Corinthians his primary perspective and starting point is Gentile wisdom, while in Romans

---

exegetes, M. Neubrand points to positive references to boasting in Rom 5:2.3.11 and 15:17 and sees the reason of Paul's critique in 2:17.23 in the discrepancy of a boasting attitude and acts (1997, 129n.13).

[571] R.B. Hays 1996, 153.

[572] N.T. Wright 1997, 129. On the ethnic notion of boasting, see also H. Moxnes 1988, 71; K. Stendahl 1995, 24; M. Cranford 1995, 77.

[573] S.J. Gathercole 2002, 226 (in the original italicized); cf. 9 (taking into account insights of U. Wilckens and P. Stuhlmacher). As for the meaning of καύχησις, Gathercole determines it as "Israel's national boast" (225), though later he seems to widen the perspective of Paul's notion of "boasting" and speaks generically of "anthropological" (232).

[574] C.E.B. Cranfield 1975, 219, with reference to the tense of ἐξεκλείσθη. Cf. O. Michel 1978, 155. – H. Räisänen points to the link between νυνὶ δέ (Rom 3:21) and ἐξεκλείσθη: "Es ist am natürlichsten, daß ἐξεκλείσθη auf 'ein geschichtliches Ereignis' zurückweist" (1979/1980, 110).

[575] The exception is 1Cor 15:39, but its context is a different one.

he predominantly focuses on Jewish works.[576] Nevertheless, on both trains of thought he reaches a universally valid, theologically or rather christologically grounded, conclusion.[577] To what extent, however, Bultmann's anthropological-existential position requires qualifications we will discuss when dealing with Abraham's "boasting" in Rom 4:2.[578] For now, we will put the debate to rest.

For what reasons and on which grounds is boasting so decisively excluded? Again, Paul's answer poses several exegetical problems, with far-reaching implications for his understanding of the law. He says: Not[579] through the νόμος (τῶν) ἔργων, but through the νόμος πίστεως. Basically, there have been three solutions to the meaning of the two occurrences of the enigmatic νόμος in these phrases[580]: Either it denotes metaphorically in both cases "general principle," "order," "criterion," or "norm," as in many instances in ancient literature,[581] or it refers in both cases to the "law,"[582] or – as an intermediate solution – in the first instance the "law" is in view and in the second a principle in a general sense.[583] In a recent study on Rom 3:27, A. Ito demands a methodological distinction between rhetoric and theology, between the meaning(s) acquired by a "casual" reading and a "careful" reading, and thus contends: "It seems that those who take the νόμος πίστεως as referring to the Torah are after the Pauline theology, while those who take it in a general sense are more concerned with the

---

[576] Cf. A. Schlatter 1927, 388.

[577] That Rom 3:27 is meant in a general way is argued by, for instance, K. Barth 1922, 90f.; E. Käsemann 1980, 96f.; E. Gräßer 1998, 17n.78; apparently also C.E.B. Cranfield 1975, 165, 218f.

[578] See below chapter V.B.IV.4.a.(b).

[579] The particle οὐχί suggests that Paul counters an expected answer of his interlocutor, which might have been: Yes, boasting is excluded through the νόμος (τῶν) ἔργων since the required works are wanting (cf. J. Lambrecht 1985, 27). Whether Paul thinks that on the contrary the νόμος (τῶν) ἔργων *provokes* such boasting, is another question.

[580] On an overview of the various positions, see, e.g., H. Räisänen 1979/1980, 95-101; A. Ito 2003, 237f.

[581] Cf., e.g., W.H.P. Hatch 1917, 59n.1; C.K. Barrett 1957, 83; O. Kuss 1963, 175f.; H. Schlier 1977, 116; H. Räisänen 1979/1980; 1983 (with references to Greek literature, 124-141); 1987, 50-52; E. Käsemann 1980, 95f.; E.P. Sanders 1985, 83; D. Zeller 1985, 92f.; S. Westerholm 1988, 122-130; 2004, 322-325; M. Winger 1992, 85; J.A. Fitzmyer 1993, 131; D.J. Moo 1996, 247-250; K. Haacker 1999, 93 with n.56. See further A. Ito 2003, 238n.4 and RSV.

[582] Cf., e.g., G. Friedrich 1954; E. Lohse 1973; 2003, 137; C.E.B. Cranfield 1975, 220; U. Wilckens 1978, 245; C.T. Rhyne 1981, 63-71; J.D.G. Dunn 1988, 185-187; M. Neubrand 1997, 131; T.R. Schreiner 1998, 200-205; R. Bergmeier 2000, 49. See further references in A. Ito 2003, 237f. notes 2 and 3.

[583] H. Lietzmann 1928, 52 ("stilistische[r] Parallelismus"); J. Lambrecht 1985, 27n.1. – It is unlikely, though, that Paul carries out such a distinction and that he assumes his addressees would comprehend it.

Pauline argumentative flow."[584] His own explanation combines the two levels of meaning, presupposing that they have to be complementary and compatible.[585]

Two issues have to be reflected: First, occasionally Paul does speak of νόμος in a figurative sense (e.g., Rom 7:21), but in the majority of passages νόμος denotes the Mosaic law, the Pentateuch, or the Old Testament as a whole.[586] The latter meanings all converge in their orientation towards the revealed divine will for mankind, and this salvation-historical perspective, i.e., the role and function of the law in God's history governs the section 3:27-31. Second, is it conceivable that Paul's audience could or was expected to distinguish *ad hoc* on first hearing or reading different semantic categories and identify them as a complex play on words and in a second step integrate the statements into the whole of Paul's theology?[587] Would they not at first deduce the meaning from the immediate context,[588] where the reference of νόμος is to the salvation-historical dimension of the law[589], which now appears in a completely different light upon the revelation of God in Christ and upon the resultant contrast to the now revealed faith-righteousness?

Probably it is, *inter alia*, again the complex Greek genitive that provokes the confusion. Since God's act in Christ, since the advent of πίστις Χριστοῦ the law is radically re-evaluated: The purpose of the law as παιδαγωγός is to point the way to Christ (Gal 3:24-25), and therefore Christ is also its τέλος (Rom 10:4), insofar as it now lost its function as law for the one who believes.[590] Therefore, Paul's answer to the implicit question "why is boasting excluded?" reads: Not by that (perspective on the[591])

---

[584] A. Ito 2003, 239f. (quote: 240).

[585] Ito concludes that νόμος (τῶν) ἔργων means "the law of works demanded in that part of the Torah concerning (the) works," while νόμος πίστεως refers to "the law of faith described in that part of the Torah concerning Abraham's faith." Thereby, he determines the genitive as "partitive" genitive, but concedes that "the paraphrases overstep the scope of a normal usage of genitives" (2003, 257). In fact, this circumlocution places side by side the controversial solutions and connects them by means of the verbs "demanded" and "described" respectively.

[586] Cf., e.g., P. Stuhlmacher 1997, 261f.

[587] Cf. H. Räisänen 1983, who titles his essay "Sprachliches zum Spiel des Paulus mit νόμος." He concludes that Paul chose the word νόμος for the sake of a polemical-playful reference to the Mosaic law (117).

[588] Cf. U. Schnelle 2003, 353.

[589] By contrast, M. Winger takes the occurrences of νόμος in the immediate context to refer to the Torah (1992, 78-81).

[590] Cf. F. Vouga 1998, 89, on Gal 3:24-25.

[591] This translation is justified by the interrogative pronoun ποῖος, which asks for the quality or property of something. Against K. Haacker 1999, 93; M. Theobald 1999a, 182;

law that regards one's existence grounded in the principal conditions of legal requirements and works (of the law), but by that (perspective on the) law that is characterized by faith, that witnesses to the coming of faith, in which faith comes to light in a proleptic form.[592] Thus, it is not primarily my personal faith that averts the temptation of boasting, but the all-encompassing presence of the phenomenon of faith – then only witnessed to, but now revealed – that excludes boasting "manifestly, primarily and completely."[593]

To be sure, Paul does not propagate two different "kinds" or "parts" of the law, which would contradict each other,[594] but he advocates two different perspectives on the law: The one takes the law as being defined by prescriptions that demand one's submission in order to attain a righteous status, while the other views the law with the perspective of righteousness through faith, which is now, since the Christ-event, present.[595] Hence, this distinction is not without criterion: It is carried out from the standpoint of the question how God justifies, as Paul makes clear in the following verse (3:28, δικαιοῦσθαι).[596] This is why Paul, before expounding on Gen 15:6, makes the statement: "We establish the law," that is, the νόμος πίστεως (Rom 3:31) and further on distinguishes between Abraham's justification by faith and his circumcision as part of fulfilling the law: In the context of 3:27-28, Paul is concerned with nothing else than the questions: How is one justified, and why is boasting excluded? His answer is: through faith, through that perspective on the law that is defined by faith.

U. Schnelle 2003, 353f., who claim that the question διὰ ποίου νόμου presupposes a variety of νόμοι.

[592] Cf. G. Friedrich 1954, 417. See similarly F. Hahn 1976, 47-49; A. Ito 2003, 257.

[593] J. Lambrecht 1985, 30.

[594] Those who propagate a "sociological approach" ultimately have to state two "kinds" of Torah, of which the νόμος πίστεως is authoritative for Jews and non-Jews, while the νόμος (τῶν) ἔργων is the special Torah for Jews only (cf. M. Neubrand 1997, 135, referring to F. Watson 1986, 132-135). Neubrand points to the difference between proselytes and the group of the σεβόμενοι who were both obliged to fulfill the νόμος πίστεως (ethics), while only the first group had to fulfill the νόμος (τῶν) ἔργων (ethnic rites). This view reduces πίστις in an un-Pauline manner to ethics and ἔργα to ethnic distinguishing marks and rites. – G. Friedrich attempts to describe νόμος πίστεως in terms of Rom 4:13 (ἐπαγγελία), but there is the risk of splitting up "geographically" those parts of the Torah that contain assurances from those parts that demand works. For Paul, the perspective on the whole law is decisive, and he attains his perspective through the criterion of πίστις (417).

[595] Therefore, with νόμος (τῶν) ἔργων Paul does not disqualify the Jewish understanding of the law as perverted (against H. Hübner 1982, 97), but argues that since the Christ-event the only possibility to receive justification is by faith.

[596] Cf. in a similar way J. Lambrecht/R.W. Thompson 1988, 26: "Boasting is eliminated because law and works are no longer relevant to the fundamental ground of one's relationship with God."

Paul's own biography is an example how God's act in Christ became reality in his life (Gal 2:12.16) and how this affected his perspective on the law (Phil 3:7-9). But in Romans 4 he appeals to the patriarch because he can deduce from the Abraham figure a general, typological function that possesses validity for both Jews and Gentiles.

A comparable thought occurs in Rom 9:31-32 with regard to Israel: "Israel pursues the Law of righteousness (νόμος δικαιοσύνης),[597] but has not arrived at the Law (νόμος). Why? Because [Israel has pursued it] on the basis of works, not of faith (οὐκ ἐκ πίστεως ἀλλ᾿ ὡς ἐξ ἔργων)." By reason of our findings concerning 3:27, one could paraphrase Paul's implication: If Israel had taken the point of view of faith regarding the law, and not that of works, it would have arrived at the law and taken the perspective of righteousness on that law. Yet Israel seeks to establish its own righteousness (10:3, ἡ ἰδία δικαιοσύνη), just as Paul sought his own righteousness coming from the law (Phil 3:9, ἡ ἐμὴ δικαιοσύνη). Again, neither is Paul arguing against Israel's exclusive-national righteousness (e.g., E.P. Sanders), nor against Israel's legalistic self-righteousness (e.g., R. Bultmann), but against "the *way in which* it had pursued the law."[598] The revelation of God's righteousness in Christ, indeed Christ himself, is the "stumbling stone," over which Israel stumbled (Rom 9:32-33; cf. 3:21).[599] Since Christ, the law is replaced by faith as the way to justification (10:4).

Conversely, this perspective does not *eo ipso* attribute a negative connotation to καύχησις, νόμος (τῶν) ἔργων, or ἔργα νόμου, but poses radically the question of their value and function in the process of justification, now that the righteousness of God has been revealed through faith (3:22). A concrete or potential misunderstanding in the framework of these questions, i.e., the significance of the *sola fide* as foundation of salvation, appears to have triggered the Pauline exposition, which culminates in the general *dictum* 3:28: "For we come to the conclusion that a person is justified through faith (alone), apart from the works of the law."[600] The charac-

---

[597] Of course, even here, some regard νόμος to be metaphorical (cf., e.g., K. Haacker 1999, 199).

[598] C.E.B. Cranfield 1979, 509 (italics original).

[599] It appears that the commentaries do not sufficiently emphasize the new *era* that came about through faith. For instance, Cranfield's further comments (see previous note) imply that Israel could have assumed the perspective of faith even before Christ, in the era of the law. This is an impossibility in Paul's view due to the world's sinfulness apart from Christ (Rom 1:18-3:20).

[600] E. Käsemann calls 3:28 a "Lehrsatz" (1980, 97; cf. J. Lambrecht/R.W. Thompson 1988, 33: "general statement"). See also the study on Gal 2:16 and Rom 3:28 by M. Theobald (1999a). The character of a doctrinal statement does not imply that its content is accepted by all addressees (against M. Neubrand 1997, 137); what is undisputable and

ter of a general verdict derives from the verb λογίζεσθαι, denoting "to come to a judgment in a dispute,"[601] from the generic ἄνθρωπος, including Jews and Gentiles, from the brief, anarthrous style, and from the antithetical opposition of πίστις and ἔργα νόμου.[602] How important this antithesis became for Paul, and how deeply rooted it was in his mind and theology, becomes all the more obvious if one considers again his alterations first of the Psalm quote in 3:20 – Paul added ἔργα νόμου – and second of the traditional Jewish-Christian formula – Paul inserted διὰ [τῆς] πίστεως.

The insight of some early church and medieval, but above all Reformation commentators, is nowadays shared by the majority of theologians: In 3:28 "the emphasis falls on πίστει."[603] Yet in his doctrinal statement Paul is not (yet) concerned with faith concretized in the individual human being, nor with actual works produced, but both, πίστις and ἔργα νόμου, symbolize the criteria for the participation in the salvation-historical spheres of faith or the law, two overarching conditions of human existence.[604] In other words the accent is on faith, but not (yet) in the sense of highlighting the individual believer from the entirety of the new eschatological people of God, but rather in the sense of the universal horizon of the event of salvation: Through faith, and through nothing else, being part of this people is made possible.[605] Faith is the new way of salvation,[606] and

---

valid without further proof for Paul, was indeed a contentious issue for others (cf. E. Lohmeyer 1929a, 66; see Gal 2:16).

[601] Cf. U. Wilckens 1978, 247. See Rom 2:3; 6:11; 8:18. Maybe the term indicates that Paul is already thinking of the key passage Gen 15:6 (cf. R. Bergmeier 2000, 58). – See the parallel expression in 4QMMT B 29.37 (which is also a letter): אנחנו חושבים. Here and there it implies "confidence in one's own exegesis" (O. Betz 1994, 184).

[602] The phrase ἔργα νόμου refers back to Rom 3:20, while the preposition χωρίς recalls 3:21. – It seems unintelligible to neglect a Pauline opposition between the two entities "faith" and "works of the law" and to deny the exclusion of the latter in regard to how God justifies (thus M. Neubrand 1997, 138). Jewish interpretation of Paul seems to acknowledge the Pauline antithesis, but rejects it since faith-righteousness and works-righteousness stand side by side with equal rights (cf. H.-J. Schoeps 1959, 212).

[603] J.A. Fitzmyer 1993, 363. Fitzmyer lists early church and medieval sources (360f.). See among Catholic commentaries also O. Kuss 1963, 177 ("die deutsche Übersetzung 'allein durch den Glauben' ist ganz exakt im Sinne des Paulus"; italics original); B. Byrne 1996, 139. Against that H.-W. Bartsch 1968, 47n.6: "Luther's translation ... is probably mistaken..."

[604] See above page 293. E. Lohmeyer confirms this indirectly by his thesis on "works of the law": "Die Wendung [sc. ἔργα νόμου] weilt nicht im Reiche der vollzogenen Tatsachen, sondern in dem der grundsätzlichen Bedingungen, aus denen jene Tatsachen, d.h. die geschichtliche, an Zeit und Raum und an ein bestimmtes Ich gebundene Erfüllung des Gesetzes erst möglich wird" (1929a, 65). Lohmeyer refers to Gal 3:10 und Rom 2:15 und uses again the term "principle."

[605] Cf. G. Eichholz 1972, 197.

[606] Cf. P. Stuhlmacher 1966, 225.

it is contingent on the Christ-event. Therefore, it is too early to argue that the opposition of πίστις and ἔργα νόμου implicates that both denote "something on the human side of the salvation process."[607] Here, faith is not the individual acceptance of the event of salvation, but part and criterion of the event of salvation, to which there is no alternative: *sola fide*.

Paul's significant antithetical juxtaposition of πίστις [Χριστοῦ] and ἔργα νόμου,[608] but also his use of the term καύχησις leads us into the middle of the debate on the proper understanding of the "works of the law."[609]

b) Works of the Law

The phrase itself, ἔργα νόμου,[610] is a unique formulation, unknown to the Septuagint, the Apostolic Fathers, and the apologetes.[611] Not least because of that, the question of its meaning has received the most different answers in Pauline scholarship and is still greatly disputed. Some basic positions need to be highlighted, since our understanding of πίστις is integrally related to the idea of "works of the law." However, before immersing into the current discussion, we should take note of E. Lohmeyer's suggestion

---

[607] J.D.G. Dunn 1997, 270.

[608] Gal 2:16 clarifies concisely the Pauline antithesis of ἔργα νόμου and πίστις Ἰησοῦ Χριστοῦ. – Paul sometimes uses the abbreviation ἔργα/νόμος or πίστις when he has in mind the full phrase (in Romans: ἔργα: 4:2.6; 9:12; 11:6/νόμος: 10:4-5; cf. E. Lohmeyer 1929a, 64; E. Gräßer 1998, 13; πίστις: 1:17; 3:25.28.30.31; cf. H. Cremer 1900, 316; G. Friedrich 1982, 105).

[609] Generally, the discussion of the phrase ἔργα νόμου starts with Gal 2:16 where it appears three times. Apart from Gal 2:16, it occurs in Rom 3:20.28; Gal 3:2.5.10 (see also the *varia lectio* to Rom 9:32).

[610] Among the vast publications on the theme "works of the law" in Paul, reference could be made to U. Wilckens 1969; J. Blank 1969; D.J. Moo 1983; L. Gaston 1984; H. Hübner 1985; C.E.B. Cranfield 1991; J.D.G. Dunn 1992 etc.; T.R. Schreiner 1991; D. Flusser 1996; H.B.P. Mijoga 1999; J.C.R. de Roo 2000; R.K. Rapa 2001. Mijoga (4-57) and Rapa (15-51) offer an overview of scholarly positions.

[611] This is already stated by E. Lohmeyer, who of course could not know of 4QMMT yet. He calls the phrase "eine Besonderheit paulinischen Sprechens und Denkens" (1929a, 36). According to his own theory only the term מצוה is equivalent. Though this thought has never really been followed up – since מצוה is commonly regarded as equivalent to ἐντολαί –, one should nevertheless take into consideration that the Greek translation of Sir 44,20 has νόμος for מצוה (see above note 131 in chapter III). In light of Paul's frequent use of νόμος as generic term for ἔργα νόμου (cf. Gal 2:21; 3:11; 5:4; Phil 3:6.9; Rom 10:4-5), one could gain a far broader textual basis for the interpretation of the Pauline ἔργα νόμου: Instead of fixating on 4QMMT (and *2Bar* 57,2) as possible background of Paul's phrase, one would have to at least consider occurrences of מצות, presupposing that almost two centuries earlier, the translator of Sirach basically identified them. The inclusion of Old Testament and Qumran texts that combine a form of עשה with תורה would also relieve 4QMMT from its burden of being the only parallel (see above pages 196-198 with note 263).

regarding the linguistic peculiarity of the expression: He argued that the kind of genitive in ἔργα νόμου correlates to its counter expression πίστις Χριστοῦ[612]: The genitive assumes three traits and denotes the origin or affiliation (subjective genitive),[613] the direction or goal (objective genitive), and the quality or characteristic (qualitative genitive).[614] It is correct to maintain that the theological antithesis between ἔργα νόμου and πίστις Χριστοῦ corresponds to a grammatical analogy. The genitive could also be called *genitivus relationis*,[615] as works *per definitionem* only exist in relation to the law, having their source, purpose, and content through the law.

The most radical position is taken by R. Bultmann, who states that in Paul's view we not only *cannot* achieve salvation through works of the law, but also *ought not*: Already the mere attempt to secure salvation through works is *eo ipso* sin,[616] because the meaning of the way of the law lies in its intention to lead to ἰδία δικαιοσύνη (Rom 10:3).[617] The reality of the status of the Jews is not an empirically or phenomenologically verifiable reality, but the exemplary reality of every human being.[618] In Protestant theology and – interestingly – in Catholic theology as well, this understanding enjoyed the status of a "mighty fortress" for a long time.[619] Hence, Paul's pessimism is grounded in his ontology: The power of sin is too forceful and comprehensive so that the will to obedience is unachievable.

Not all agree, however, with this "qualitative" understanding of the law, and the dissent has been increasing in the past decades.[620] According to U.

---

[612] See above page 262.

[613] Note here the idea of L. Gaston to regard ἔργα νόμου generally as subjective genitive in terms of "works which the law does": causing guilt (Rom 3:19), revealing sin (3:20), etc. (1984). Yet it is not only 4QMMT that rules out Gaston's one-sided interpretation (cf. J.C.R. de Roo 2000, 117 with n.5).

[614] Cf. E. Lohmeyer 1929a, 73.

[615] See above pages 263 and 277.

[616] Cf. R. Bultmann 1958, 264f.

[617] Cf. R. Bultmann 1958, 268: Not the transgression of the law makes the way of the law wrong, but the direction of this way itself.

[618] Cf. E. Lohmeyer 1930, 110n.1 (*"sub specie apostoli* Inbegriff des Menschen, wie er ist"); G. Eichholz 1972, 63f.; E. Käsemann 1980, 82 ("der Jude als Typ des homo religiosus"); H.-J. Eckstein 2000, 9.

[619] This is how E. Gräßer puts it (1998, 4; cf. 8f.; Gräßer adopts Bultmann's position and terminology, 15). Among Catholic scholars, he refers to J. Blank 1969; K. Kertelge 1971; H. Schlier 1978 (especially 88f.); J. Gnilka 1994 (especially 70n.67). See further, agreeing with Bultmann, E.D. Burton 1921, 120; F. Hahn 1976, 36; H.D. Betz 1979, 146; E. Käsemann 1980, 83f.; G. Klein 1984.

[620] Cf. again E. Gräßer 1998, 4, who locates the main shift towards the end of the 1970s, though with U. Wilckens (1969) it certainly had an earlier representative. Gräßer also names background and reasons for this shift: a renewed understanding of the history-of-religions data, increasing in intensity in the course of "post-Holocaust" theology. Cf.

Wilckens, who follows A. Schlatter and sets against Bultmann a "quantitative" understanding, it is not the intention or the attempt that Paul criticizes and considers as sin, but the sinful work itself: Paul regards all human beings as sinners, because all have factually sinned, and nobody can fulfill the law perfectly. For Paul, the basic Jewish tenet remains: Whoever *would* obey all the laws would be justified, but one single sinful deed of disobedience places the sinner into the sphere of destruction.[621] Here, Paul's pessimism is grounded in his anthropology: The power of humans is too weak and limited so that the realization of obedience is unachievable.[622]

With respect to Bultmann's exposition, E.P. Sanders contends that "it is wrong by being backwards. It is not the analysis of the nature of sin which determines his view, but his analysis of the way to salvation; not his anthropology, but his Christology and soteriology... The contrast ... is not between self-reliance and reliance on God – two kinds of self-understanding – but between belonging to Christ and not belonging to Christ."[623] "[T]he conclusion that all the world ... equally stands in need of a saviour *springs from* the prior conviction that God had provided such a saviour."[624] For J.D.G. Dunn,[625] ἔργα νόμου have nothing to do with salvific merits achieved through fulfilling the Torah, but they concern primarily food laws and circumcision as "identity markers": "[E]ver since the Maccabean period these two sets of legal requirement had been fundamental to the devout Jew's identity as a Jew, as member of the people whom God had chosen for himself and made covenant with: these two ritual enact-

---

J.D.G. Dunn 1996, 1: "Up until the last fifteen years or so there was no real debate on the subject [*sc.* Paul and the Mosaic Law]."

[621] U. Wilckens 1969, 107 and throughout his commentary. On Rom 2:13, Wilckens states that Paul agrees with the Jewish understanding of law and justification: Who acts as a just person, will be considered righteous by God and receive salvation (1978, 132f.).

[622] A similar view is taken by K. Berger 1966, 63f.; D.J. Moo 1983; C.E.B. Cranfield 1979, 850; 1991; T.R. Schreiner 1991; T. Laato 1995; H. Merklein 1996; J.L. Martyn 1997, 97; L. Thurén 2000, 177: "Theoretically, boasting of human righteousness is possible." S. Westerholm 2004, 391: "[A] law that demands works leaves the door open for human boasting." J. Lambrecht remarks that Wilckens's positions has been called "Catholic" (1986, 243 with n.36), but in fact one has to grant Wilckens that it is more "Jewish" (cf. E. Gräßer 1998, 20n.95). See *2Bar* 54,19 (quoted in O. Hofius 1996, 82n.127), which states – expressed in systematic-theological terms – that all human beings perform themselves the transition from *posse non peccare* to *non posse non peccare*.

[623] E.P. Sanders 1977, 481f.

[624] E.P. Sanders 1977, 443 (italics original), 474: "For Paul, the conviction of a universal solution preceded the conviction of a universal plight." Cf. U. Schnelle 2003, 574 (Pauline hamartiology as "*nachträgliche[.] Rationalisierung* eines bereits feststehenden Argumentationszieles" [italics original]).

[625] Dunn's view (and its development) is extensively discussed in M.W. Yeung 2002, 226-232.

ments had a central role in marking Israel off from the surrounding nations."[626] As such, the antithesis between πίστις and ἔργα νόμου derives
from Paul's agitation against an understanding of the Torah as granting
national-exclusive privileges,[627] i.e., as corroborating a separation from the
Gentiles. With different nuances, this reductionist "new perspective" –
which actually has an old predecessor in Pelagius[628] – has almost become
commonplace in (Anglo-Saxon[629]) exegesis.[630]

Above, some structural analogies have been mentioned between faith,
sin, and the law, which should be taken up again and developed.[631] Just as
faith and sin have the two basic dimensions of being super-individual phenomena, but also existential realities that become historical and tangible in
the individual existence, Paul's idea of the law, too, contains the notion of
these two poles: The law is an salvation-historical entity, manifested by
God, and it carries within itself the call for "works of the law," which all,

---

[626] J.D.G. Dunn 1985, 217.

[627] With regard to the use of מעשי התורה in 4QMMT Dunn contends that "we need simply transpose the attitude expressed in the Qumran use of מעשי התורה from an internal
Jewish dispute regarding particular halakhic rulings to one where the boundary ran between Jew and Gentile to find ourselves with ἔργα νόμου focusing on circumcision in
particular" (1992, 104). Such a transposition is too "simple."

[628] Cf. O. Hofius 1993, 159n.26, with reference to K.H. Schelkle 1956, 105, 113.

[629] See however, e.g., K. Haacker 1999, 83f.

[630] See with regard to Abraham's "works": F. Watson 1986, 137; M. Cranford 1995,
76f. Watson reduces the antithesis "faith – works" to a sociological level, stating that
"faith in Christ is incompatible with works of the law because the church is separate from
the synagogue" (1986, 47). With special reference to 4QMMT, M. Bachmann holds that
the phrase ἔργα νόμου does not concern the actual doing of the law, but the instructions
and prescriptions of the law themselves. "Paulus meint mit dem Ausdruck 'Werke des
Gesetzes' nicht etwas, was auf der durch das Tun gemäß den Regelungen des Gesetzes
markierten Ebene liegt, insbesondere nicht: Gebotserfüllungen, sondern er meint mit dem
Syntagma 'Werke des Gesetzes' die Regelungen des Gesetzes selber" (M. Bachmann
1993, 29). J.D.G. Dunn responds that this interpretation seems to be "driving a wedge
between two meanings ... which is quite unjustified" (2002, 281; cf. 2001, 367n.15; C.
Burchard 1996, 410n.32; see yet again M. Bachmann 2005). Content of the law and conduct in accordance with the law belong together (see already E. Lohmeyer 1929a, 41:
The Pauline concept ἔργα νόμου "faßt den doppelten Gedanken der Norm wie der Nor-
merfüllung in einem Worte zusammen"). – M. Abegg argues on grounds of the parallel
between Paul and Qumran that Paul reacts polemically against the sectarian attitude and
theology of the Essenes (1994), but this interpretation neglects the general character of
his argument against ἔργα νόμου, especially in Romans. Furthermore, one can hardly
assert that the phrase is typically Essenic considering the one single occurrence in all of
Qumran literature. – An extensive discussion of the traditional and new perspective is
provided in S. Westerholm 2004, 3-258 (see especially "A Portrait of the 'Lutheran'
Paul" [88-97] and "The Quotable Anti-'Lutheran' Paul" [249-258]).

[631] See above pages 252f. and 291f.

Jews and Gentiles, have to fulfill.[632] Thus, to follow Lohmeyer, works originate from the law, are directed to the law, and characterize the law.[633] But the law is not a timeless, autonomous norm.[634] God sent Christ (Gal 4:4), the τέλος of the law (Rom 10:4); and together with Christ came faith, the "new" salvation-historical manifestation that contains the claim of faith, that *all* believe.[635] It is indispensable to account for "Paul's assumption that the coming of Christ marked an eschatological division of time. If there was indeed a new ... phase of God's purpose, then the role of the law in relation to Israel belonged to the old phase."[636] On this new time and claim of faith Paul focuses in 3:28.

There, the phrase "works of the law" does not mean (the attempt of) the concrete, historical realization of the requirements of the law, but the wrong way of salvation, a futile ground of existence, the criterion of the participation in the sphere of the law, the τέλος of which is Christ. Yet justification does not happen on grounds of the "works of the law," but only apart from the "works of the law,"[637] i.e., through faith – through faith alone.[638] Paul does not link "works" or "faith" with a personal pronoun, binding both to time and space, but generically with every human being (ἄνθρωπος). Hence, in this verse he is not focusing on contesting the human attempt to secure salvation through the law (R. Bultmann), nor on the failure of fulfilling it (U. Wilckens), nor on certain ritual regulations (J.D.G. Dunn), but on the fundamental incompatibility of "works of the law" with God's will now revealed in and through πίστις Χριστοῦ. Again, the perspective Paul has obtained once and for all is the perspective of faith, which cannot from a neutral standpoint weigh objectively two alternatives, but which identifies the side opposite to faith with hopeless sinfulness (1:18-3:20).

But why and to what extent does Paul link the (works of the) law with sin[639]? Both are "in the world" (Rom 5:13), both are a trans-subjective,

---

[632] As for the Gentiles, cf. Rom 2:14.

[633] Cf. also A. Schlatter 1927, 335.

[634] Cf. E. Lohmeyer 1929a, 70.

[635] Cf. Rom 1:16; 3:22; 4:11; 10:4.11.

[636] J.D.G. Dunn 1998, 145. Cf. E. Käsemann 1980, 178: "Die Angriffsspitze der paulinischen Rechtfertigungslehre liegt darin, daß sie mit Sünde und Tod auch das Gesetz dem alten Äon zurechnet."

[637] The phrase ἔργα νόμου is always connected with either ἐκ (Rom 3:20; Gal 2:16[*ter*]; 3:2.5) or χωρίς (Rom 3:28).

[638] Cf. K. Berger 1966, 66: "Der Glaube ist daher nicht nur als ein anderer Weg als der der Werke, sondern auch der wahre Ausweg aus der dort erreichten Aussichtslosigkeit." See also L. Thurén 2000, 177: "God is said to have chosen another, exclusive way to salvation, in order to prevent such boasting." However, the reason for faith is rather "Aussichtslosigkeit" than the prevention of boasting. See also Gal 2:21.

[639] Cf. Rom 3:20; 5:13.20; 7:7-25; 8:2; 1Cor 15:56; Gal 3:22.

cosmic reality, "under" the power and dominion of which existence takes place.[640] Both drive towards a historical concretization of their power in terms of "works of the law" and "sinful deeds." Both stand in sharp antithesis to faith. But: They themselves are contradictorily antithetical (7:7)! The law is "holy," whereas sin becomes "sinful beyond measure" (7:12-13).

The most precise statement on the relationship between law and sin Paul gives in Rom 5:12-14[641]: Since the coming of the law, sin is counted (ἐλλογεῖσθαι) by God to the sinner, i.e., *a deo ad hominem* (5:13)[642]; also, since the coming of the law, there is knowledge of sin (3:20; cf. 7:7). Yet even before the law, sin has been qualified in negatively eschatological terms[643] – Adam being a "pre-existent" sinner, the forefather of humankind, who received the judgment of condemnation and death "prolepticly" and lost the glory of eternal life intended for him (3:23).[644] In analogy, when Christ came faith came, and from that time onwards, faith is counted (λογίζεσθαι) by God to the believer (4:3), i.e., also *a deo ad hominem*. But even before Christ, faith has had positive, eschatological consequences[645] in a "proleptic" way and Abraham is the "pre-existent" believer, the forefather of all believers, whose acceptance by God led to righteousness and life in eternal glory (5:1-2). This means, both the law and faith – both in terms of their function in God's history with the world – pronounce and

---

[640] Paul knows the expression to be "under sin" (Gal 3:22; Rom 3:9; 7:14), as well as to be "under the law" (Rom 6:14-15; 1Cor 9:20; Gal 3:23; 4:4-5.21; 5:18; cf. Rom 2:12; 3:19; 4:16; Gal 3:25). J.D.G. Dunn's comments on the phrase ὑπὸ νόμον that "the law for Paul was indeed a kind of power" (1998, 141). This interpretation is "generally recognized" (H.-S. Choi 2005, 476n.54).

[641] To R. Bultmann this passage is partly unclear and unintelligible (1958, 252).

[642] On the meaning of ἐλλογεῖσθαι (cf. Phlm 18), see O. Hofius 1996, 92-96. He argues against the interpretation that regards Paul's idea of "counting" as being dependent on the notion of the heavenly books (cf. prominently G. Friedrich 1952, 127f., but also, e.g., H. Schlier 1977, 164f.; U. Wilckens 1978, 319; E. Käsemann 1980, 141; J.D.G. Dunn 1988, 274), both on philological and theological grounds: The verb denotes "to charge a person with something" and not "to put on a person's account" (cf. J.H. Moulton/G. Milligan 1930, 204); God is the implied subject, yet the act of "counting" does not happen in the heavenly world, but the sinner is the addressee, though not explicitly mentioned due to brachylology (cf. Phlm 18: ἐμοί; see also Rom 4:3: αὐτῷ).

[643] Hofius stresses that even *before* the law sin is qualified eschatologically (against E. Jüngel 1972, 158: "Ohne das Gesetz wird die Sünde nicht als Sünde eschatologisch zur Geltung gebracht"; cf. U. Wilckens 1978, 319f.).

[644] Sin prevented this intention from being realized. It is an act of sheer grace, therefore, if sin is *not* counted (cf. Rom 4:8).

[645] Cf. similarly K. Berger 1966, 70.

disclose a previously existing and effective, but undocumented and concealed reality.[646]

The law and consequently the works of the law belong on the side of sin
and death and therefore on the "Adam-side,"[647] while faith belongs on the
side of forgiveness and life and therefore on the "Christ-side."[648] Below, in
the context of Abraham's "ungodliness" and David's "sinfulness," some of
these provocative aspects will be discussed in greater detail.[649]

c) The One God of Jews and Gentiles

The confession to God as the one God of Jews and Gentiles in Rom 3:29
constitutes the undisputed and undisputable center of this section, structurally and theologically. The first commandment remains fully and self-
evidently valid.[650] Since and if indeed (εἴπερ, 3:30) God is one, the creator
and ruler of *all* human beings, of Jews and Gentiles, he will justify circumcision[651] ἐκ πίστεως and uncircumcision διὰ τῆς πίστεως.[652] According to
Paul, this is the outstanding implication of monotheism, "Paul's vision of
God." "God is qualified as the God who justifies through faith..."[653] God's
oneness and singularity corresponds to the universality of justification,
which joins all believers in the unity of πίστις.[654]

As for the relationship between the two phrases ἐκ πίστεως and διὰ τῆς
πίστεως, most commentators nowadays agree with Augustine that there is
no material difference between the two prepositions διά and ἐκ, but that the
variations are of a stylistic or rhetorical kind,[655] i.e., a "paradigmatic varia-

---

[646] Cf. O. Hofius 1996, 94: "Die Torah schafft nicht erst den Sünde-Tod-
Zusammenhang, sondern sie findet ihn bereits vor."

[647] Cf. O. Hofius 1996, 98.

[648] Cf. on this split also A. Schlatter 1927, 359. It can be connected with Paul's theology of baptism: "[I]m 'präbaptismalen Bereich' (in Adam) sind nach Paulus die Menschen Sünder, im 'postbaptismalen Bereich' (in Christus) sind die Getauften Gerechtfertigte" (H. Umbach 1999, 209).

[649] See below pages 353f.

[650] Cf. E. Gräßer 1981; W.H. Schmidt 1987, 55f. with n.54 (with reference to Rom
3:30); J.D.G. Dunn 1988, 189.

[651] The terms περιτομή and ἀκροβυστία are used as metonymies.

[652] Cf. J.D.G. Dunn 1988, 193.

[653] J. Lambrecht 2000, 527. Lambrecht however reconstructs the logic as "conditional
period" with Rom 3:30 being the protasis and 3:29c ("Yes, also of Gentiles") the apodosis. I.e., 3:30b is not a conclusion of 3:30a.

[654] Cf. E. Gräßer 1981, 256f.; U. Schnelle 2003, 354. Some want to see in Rom 3:29-
30 a polemical rhetorical move against Judaism (cf. E. Käsemann 1980, 96f.; U.
Wilckens 1978, 248), but see against that K. Haacker 1999, 95.

[655] Augustine *De Spiritu et Littera* 29,50: "non ad aliquam differentiam, sed ad
varietatem orationis" (referred to in O. Michel 1978, 156n.25). Cf. W. Mundle 1930,
136f.n.2; J.A. Fitzmyer 1993, 365f.

tion."[656] In patristic theology however the varying prepositions were occasionally regarded as reflection of some sort of distinction between Jews and Gentiles,[657] and among recent exegetes it is above all E. Käsemann, who supports this view: He recognizes a fine nuance, contending that possibly with ἐκ Paul has in view the Jewish-Christians who are called from their salvation-historical situation into the righteousness by faith, while διά refers to the Gentile-Christians who through faith receive justification in an unprecedented miraculous way, apart from their previous history.[658] More forcefully, S.K. Stowers contends that there is "a significant distinction in Paul's employment of the two prepositions."[659] According to Stowers, in Rom 3:22.25.31, each time the preposition διά refers to Gentiles,[660] i.e., through the "faith of Christ," the Gentiles are "included," while the correlating expression ἐκ πίστεως can refer to both Jews and Gentiles.[661] However, no distinction between the prepositions may undermine that "there is no distinction" (διαστολή) between Jews and Gentiles as to what is the means of justification (3:22). Furthermore, the analogy between Rom 3:22 and Gal 3:22,[662] as well as the parallelism between Rom 1:17 and 3:21-22,[663] contradict any sophisticated theological utilization of Paul's language in terms of a soteriological separation of Jews and Gentiles. Again, Paul talks about the fundamental conditions of human existence before God, so that both ideas, faith as ground (causality) or as means (instrumentality) of existence, are theologically basically equivalent.

---

[656] D.A. Campbell 1992a, 95. As already noted, if πίστις is understood in a dynamic, salvation-historical sense, the ideas of cause (ἐκ) and means (διά) denote practically the same. Also, the Habakkuk quote in Rom 1:17, which provided Paul with the template for the other ἐκ πίστεως-expressions, has the Hebrew preposition *be*, which *inter alia* has an instrumental meaning.

[657] For instance, by Origen and Theodore of Mopsuestia (see S.K. Stowers 1989, 665f.; also K.H. Schelkle 1956, 119). Origen "concludes that Paul's words show that the Jew is more noble than the Gentile and is thus justified ἐκ πίστεως, whereas being justified διά πίστεως reveals the inferiority of the Gentile" (S.K. Stowers 1989, 666).

[658] E. Käsemann 1980, 97 (considered also in U. Wilckens 1978, 248). See also T. Zahn 1925, 205f.; A. Schlatter 1935, 155f.; H.-W. Bartsch 1968, 49.

[659] S.K. Stowers 1989, 674.

[660] As do *all* διά [τῆς] πίστεως occurrences in Paul, according to Stowers (1989, 672).

[661] Cf. S.K. Stowers 1989, 669. This reading is indeed circular, as he himself concedes (669n.24). See against Stowers's reading, D.A. Campbell 1992a, 93f.n.9; 95f.n.14.

[662] Cf. Rom 3:22: δικαιοσύνη θεοῦ διὰ πίστεως Ἰησοῦ Χριστοῦ εἰς πάντας τοὺς πιστεύοντας with Gal 3:22: ἡ ἐπαγγελία ἐκ πίστεως Ἰησοῦ Χριστοῦ τοῖς πιστεύουσιν.

[663] Cf. Rom 3:22: δικαιοσύνη θεοῦ [πεφανέρωται] διὰ πίστεως with 1:17: δικαιοσύνη θεοῦ ἀποκαλύπτεται ἐκ πίστεως. Also, the prepositions διά and εἰς in 3:22 are parallel to ἐκ and εἰς in 1:17 (cf. A. Schlatter 1935, 140).

Accordingly, it is not "clear beyond dispute" that Paul in Rom 3:30 focuses on πίστις in terms of "human believing."[664] Rather he is concerned to bring out God's decision to justify Jews and Gentiles on the basis of and through the new *Heilsgestalt* of faith, a decision made when he revealed his righteousness through the power of faith. Since the reality of faith already qualifies the present of the believers, the future δικαιώσει not only points to the final judgment, but implicates a present actuality.[665]

Paul's drastic concentration of the universalism of salvation on the entity of "faith," poses the question of the validity of the law (3:31). It is disputed whether this verse concludes what has been said thus far,[666] or it begins a new, separate argumentative entity.[667] The contextual references to both the preceding and the following parts are obvious, so that one could speak of a "smooth transition" from one section to the other.[668] Paul has to answer the question of his interlocutor: Do we annihilate (the salvation-historical function of) the law through this concentrated emphasis of (the salvation-historical reality of) faith[669]? Paul answers sharply: No! Rather, through that global faith-perspective on the law, that also excludes boasting (3:27), we actually establish the law and bring it to its full validity. As a Jew, Paul is deeply convinced that the law is holy (7:12) and God-given[670]; this requires its integration into his theology, and that he accomplishes through his hermeneutics of πίστις, through which he interprets God's history with the world and which he will spell out in the following chapter in more concrete terms.

Paul is using formulations – "invalidate" and "uphold" the law – that have equivalents in rabbinic theological debates on single halakhic regula-

---

[664] Thus J.D.G. Dunn 1997, 270.

[665] It is related to μέλλει λογίζεσθαι in Rom 4:24. J. Lambrecht contends that the "future could be gnomic (pointing to an expected and customary action of God) or perhaps logical (God can be relied on to justify)" (2000, 526).

[666] Cf., e.g., O. Kuss 1963, 179; C.E.B. Cranfield 1975, 223; J. Lambrecht/R.W. Thompson 1988, 45-50.

[667] Cf., e.g., K. Barth 1922, 98-100; H. Lietzmann 1928, 52; J. Jeremias 1970, 51f.; C.T. Rhyne 1981, 25-61; O. Hofius 1997, 53; M. Neubrand 1997, 147; A. Ito 2003, 248. See the different positions in C.T. Rhyne 1981, 26-32.

[668] Cf. E. Käsemann 1980, 98f.; K. Haacker 1999, 95; E. Lohse 2003, 139. Among other things the *inclusio* of Rom 3:21 and 3:31 with their reference to the law, the structure of 3:27-31 (ABCB'A'), and the opening of a new theme by means of a question concerning Abraham in 4:1 suggest to read 3:31 as conclusion of 3:27-31; but the verse is also introducing the new section insofar as law and faith remain a *leitmotif* in the Abraham-chapter.

[669] Cf. H. Binder 1968, 92.

[670] Cf. A. Schlatter 1935, 156: "Einen Juden, der das Gesetz entrechtete, kann es nicht geben."

tions,[671] but Paul elevates this terminology from the common setting of doctrinal disputes[672] and widens the perspective: The law *per se* is at stake,[673] or better: the law as manifestation of the will of God. The law has lost its function as means of salvation,[674] after πίστις Χριστοῦ had come with Christ, but its function to point and witness to[675] the new means of salvation of πίστις Χριστοῦ is only now recognizable from the very perspective of πίστις Χριστοῦ (3:21.31).[676]

Therefore, in the next chapter, Paul takes that verse from the law[677] that says indisputably that righteousness comes from faith; and the person that embodies this truth is Abraham, the figure of identification of the Jews – and now, the father of *all* believers (cf. 4:16).[678]

IV. Romans 4: Individual Participation in Faith: εἰς πίστιν

1. Textual Links between Romans 3:21-31 and Romans 4

It is noteworthy that both the stem πιστ- and the stem δικ- each occur nine times in Rom 3:21-31, i.e., the derivates of these two stems govern and dominate this section. It is thus tightly bound to the thematic statement of 1:17[679] and to the subject matter of the following chapter with its exegesis of Gen 15:6. In chapter 4, the stem πιστ- occurs sixteen times and the stem δικ- ten times. Most commentators therefore recognize and point to explicit textual and terminological links between Romans 4 and 3:21-31.[680]

---

[671] Cf. A. Schlatter 1935, 156; O. Michel 1978, 157; C.E.B. Cranfield 1975, 223.

[672] Against that, e.g., C.E.B. Cranfield 1975, 224: Paul's "teaching of faith is confirmed by the law."

[673] This is why several exegetes dispute the rabbinic background of Rom 3:31. See above all C.T. Rhyne 1981, 73; R.W. Thompson 1987.

[674] Cf. R.K. Rapa 2001, 244.

[675] On the witnessing character of the law, see C.T. Rhyne 1981, 93.

[676] Possibly, "establishing the law" is reminiscent of "establishing the covenant," which appears three times in Genesis 17 (17:7[Abraham] and 17:19.21[Isaac]), the chapter which Paul joins with Genesis 15 in expounding on Abraham's faith. In the covenant language of the Old Testament, the verb ἱστάνειν can assume the idea of "establish" (cf. Gen 6:18; 9:11; 17:7.19.21; Ex 6:4; Lev 26:9; Deut 9:5; Jer 41:18; also Sir 45,7.24), as well as "confirm" (Deut 8:18; 1Chr 16:17; Ezek 17:14; also 1Macc 2,27; Sir 44,20). See also 2Kgs 23:24: "Josiah established the words of the law."

[677] As noted, the idea of the law as a literary entity belongs intrinsically together with the notion of a salvation-historical reality, as both are a manifestation of God's will for mankind.

[678] Against that J. Lambrecht 1979, 5n.9: "Paul n'entend pas prouver avec le chap. 4 qu'il confirme la Loi (cf. 3,31)."

[679] Cf., e.g., J.D.G. Dunn 1988, 163; M. Neubrand 1997, 117.

[680] G. Klein, for instance, says that there cannot be the slightest doubts that both parts, Rom 3:21-31 and 4:1-25 belong together intrinsically on formal grounds (1963, 150).

Some argue more specifically that in his Abraham-chapter Paul illustrates his theses from 3:27-31[681]: Already the diatribe style indicates the close connection between the two sections. 4:1-8 explicates 3:27-28, the connecting key ideas being καύχημα and the justification χωρὶς ἔργων νόμου. 4:9-12 demonstrates that Abraham's justification by faith happened before his circumcision, so that he became the father of all believers, circumcised or uncircumcised – thus 3:29-30 is explained through the temporal relationship between Genesis 15 and 17. Similarly, the topic of the law and its function in the framework of justification, appear both in Rom 3:31 and 4:13-16.

The most obvious links between 3:21-31 and 4:1-25 are laid down in the following table.[682]

	Rom 3:21-31	*Rom 4:1-25*
justification/ righteousness apart from the law	3:21: χωρὶς νόμου δικαιοσύνη θεοῦ 3:28: δικαιοῦσθαι χωρὶς ἔργων νόμου	4:6: δικαιοσύνη χωρὶς ἔργων
justification/ righteousness through faith	3:22: δικαιοσύνη θεοῦ διὰ πίστεως 3:28: δικαιοῦσθαι πίστει 3:30: ἐκ πίστεως/διὰ τῆς πίστεως	4:5: ἡ πίστις εἰς δικαιοσύνην 4:11: δικαιοσύνη τῆς πίστεως
(forgiveness of) sin	3:23: ἁμαρτάνω 3:25: πάρεσις τῶν ἁμαρτημάτων	4:7: ἐπεκαλύπτεσθαι αἱ ἁμαρτίαι (4:25: παραπτώματα)
to the believer(s)	3:22: πάντας τοὺς πιστεύοντας 3:26: τὸν ἐκ πίστεως Ἰησοῦ	4:16: τῷ ἐκ πίστεως Ἀβραάμ
faith and Christ/God	3:22: πίστις Ἰησοῦ Χριστοῦ 3:26: πίστις Ἰησοῦ	4:24: πιστεύειν ἐπὶ τὸν [θεόν]
by grace	3:24: τῇ χάριτι	4:4: κατὰ χάριν 4:16: κατὰ χάριν
exclusion of boasting	3:27: ἡ καύχησις ἐξεκλείσθη	4:2: καύχημα οὐ πρὸς θεόν
circumcision and uncircumcision	3:30: περιτομὴ καὶ ἀκροβυστία	4:9: περιτομὴ ἢ ἀκροβυστία (cf. 4:10-12)

Nevertheless, R.B. Hays (1980) and S.K. Stowers (1981) want to treat only Rom 3:27-4:25 as a unit, ignoring the division between 3:20 and 3:21.

[681] Cf., e.g., U. Wilckens 1964, 61; 1969, 64f.; 1978, 258; E. Käsemann 1980, 100; J.D.G. Dunn 1988, 198; D.J. Moo 1996, 259; T. Otero Lázaro 2001, 18.

[682] Cf. also the table in T.H. Tobin 1995, 442n.12. – Notably, Marcion omitted the entire section Rom 3:22-4:25 (cf. A. von Harnack 1924, 104).

2. The Train of Thought and Structure of Romans 4[683]

The chapter as a whole is an interpretation of Gen 15:6, as can be seen by the framing citations of this verse at the beginning and the end of the chapter (Rom 4:3.22) and the general organizing recurrence of the quote throughout the argumentation, in the literal citation at the outset (4:3), in paraphrasing references (4:9.22), and in the resumption of single terms of the quote which partly serve to extend the implications of Abraham to a wider circle of people (4:5.6.11.16.24).[684] Even the wider context of the verse plays a role in the apostle's Abraham-chapter, as is indicated through the thematic references to "reward," "seed," and "heir."

The function of Gen 15:6 as the basic text of the chapter therefore has to provide the criteria for determining its structure. After introducing the theme (Rom 4:1-2), Paul quotes Gen 15:6 as authoritative argument (Rom 4:3)[685] and offers his exposition of it (4:4-5), seemingly setting aside the Abrahamic context.[686] The dominance of the Genesis quote is retained in the following part that appeals to LXX Ps 31:1-2 as supporting scriptural text, through which Paul positions forgiveness within the wider framework of justification (Rom 4:6-8).[687] Therefore, after presenting Abraham as "justified sinner,"[688] justified through faith apart from works (4:1-8), Paul proceeds by repeating Gen 15:6 and deliberating the situation of Abraham at the time of God's judgment of justification with regard to the issue of circumcision; his conclusion is that Abraham is the father of *all* believers, Jews and Gentiles (4:9-12). In a next step Paul concentrates – retrospectively, as it were – on the content of Abraham's faith, the promise, and asks for its foundation and origin in terms of the divinely established salvation-historical order (4:13-17). Then, he explicates the nature of faith (4:18-21), alluding to and extending the testimony of Gen 15:6a. In the last segment (4:22-25), Paul takes up 4:18-21 by uniting his analysis of the

---

[683] J. Jeremias once stated that "in den Kommentaren zu Röm 4 weithin die Beachtung der Gedankenführung über der Einzelexegese zu kurz kommt" (1970, 51). Fortunately, his analysis can be adjusted, for recent commentators take into consideration Paul's line of thought and argumentative structure to a much greater degree than used to be the case (cf. apart from the commentaries especially M. Neubrand 1997, 149-177). Nevertheless, this issue should be treated in a separate chapter.

[684] Cf. C.D. Stanley 2004, 150: "The quotation is restated in v. 5, echoed in v. 9, expounded in vv. 10-12, abbreviated in v. 13, exemplified in vv. 18-21, requoted in v. 22, and applied in vv. 23-24."

[685] Cf. M. Neubrand 1997, 197. Against the label "authoritative proof" she states rightly that a statement *per se* is not yet a "proof."

[686] Cf. U. Wilckens 1978, 262.

[687] Cf. O. Michel 1978, 165.

[688] A.T. Hanson thus titles his chapter on Abraham (1974, 52-66).

patriarch's faith with God's appraisal of it; i.e., with Gen 15:6b he quotes
the remainder of the central verse of the chapter. By doing so, he enters a
different argumentative level,[689] in which he succinctly formulates the basic principles of his Scripture hermeneutics,[690] which naturally also contain
a christological twist: It is written for us.

I	4:1-8		
		4:1-2	the introduction of the theme
		4:3	the primary and authoritative text: Gen 15:6
		4:4-5	the first exposition[691] of Gen 15:6 with regard to λογίζεσθαι
		4:6-8	an additional, supporting text connected by λογίζεσθαι: LXX Ps 31:1-2
II	4:9-21		
		4:9	repeated reference to Gen 15:6
		4:9-12	πίστις in the antithesis of circumcision and uncircumcision
		4:13-17	the salvation-historical framework of πίστις
		4:18-21	faith and reality – the nature of πίστις
III	4:22-25		
		4:22	concluding reference to Gen 15:6
		4:23-25	the application ("for us")

The way Paul appeals to and draws on scriptural passages (LXX Gen 15:6;
Ps 31:1-2; Gen 15:5; Gen 17:5) has motivated some investigations into the
apostle's approach to Scripture, as well as comparative studies that deliberate the relationship of Paul's interpretation of Scripture with that of the
Rabbis. J. Jeremias pointed out that for the understanding of Rom 4:1-12 it
is important recognize that Paul uses a "conclusion of analogy," a *gezerah
shavah* (גְּזֵרָה שָׁוָה), the second of R. Hillel's seven rules of interpretation,
according to which identical (or synonymous) words that appear in two
different passages of Scripture explain each other.[692] Many have followed

---

[689] Since with διό (Rom 4:22) Paul takes up his description of Abraham's faith (4:18-
21), applying it on a meta-level (cf. M. Neubrand 1997, 285), it is justified to regard
4:22-25 as a separate segment – in contrast to most exegetes who consider 4:22 as conclusion of 4:18-21.

[690] Cf. M. Theobald 2001, 404.

[691] Against H. Boers 1971, 87.

[692] J. Jeremias 1953, 271. Jeremias mentions as an example for the employment of this
rule Hillel's famous decision about the question, whether or not it is allowed to slaughter
the Passover offering at the day of Shabbat, coming to an affirmative answer. Normally
applied for halakhic questions, there are numerous instances in which the rule was used
in haggadic exegesis (1953, 271n.9). According to Jeremias, Paul uses this exegetical
tool in his letter no less than five times (cf. J. Jeremias 1970, 54; also Heb 7:1-3). From
his analysis of Paul's use of this and other Hillelite rules, Jeremias even concluded that

and specified Jeremias's suggestion,[693] arguing that by means of this hermeneutical device Paul carries out an exegesis of Gen 15:6, performing the
different steps of his exegesis through the consultation of another verse
from Scripture. The term λογίζεσθαι connects as a keyword the two passages LXX Gen 15:6 and Ps 31:1-2[694]: From the Genesis quotation, Paul
concludes that righteousness was counted to Abraham not on the basis of a
claim, but of grace (Rom 4:4). That λογίζεσθαι in actuality is about the
counting of righteousness χωρὶς ἔργων (4:6), is affirmed by the Psalm-
verse by means of the *gezerah shavah*. Paul draws on LXX Ps 31:1-2 *via
negationis*, since the Psalmist does not use the respective verb positively,
but negatively: The non-reckoning of sins is the forgiveness of sins.

Thus, apart from the patriarch Abraham, also the king David is appealed
to, and his function might be to comply with another rabbinic rule that requires two witnesses for a debate: David witnesses for God's dealing with
Abraham.[695] Also, it was not uncommon in rabbinic theology to support a
Torah-verse with a quote from the prophets or Ketubim.[696] By bringing
together the two Old Testament passages, "counting of righteousness" and
"non-counting of sins," Paul says in effect: Justification is also forgiveness.[697]

Paul received Hillelite education (1969; cf. the title: "Paulus als Hillelit"). On the label
"Hillelite," see S. Zeitlin 1963 ; J.-N. Aletti 2003, 306.

[693] Cf., e.g., P. Vielhauer 1969, 200n.15; H. Boers 1971, 88; U. Wilckens 1978, 258,
263f.; F. Siegert 1985, 243n.11; D.-A. Koch 1986, 221f.; W. Baird 1988, 376; J. Roloff
1990, 244f.; J.D.G. Dunn 1988, 197; R.B. Hays 1989, 55; L.H. Silberman 1990, 103; J.A.
Fitzmyer 1993, 376; C. Plag 1994, 137f.; D.J. Moo 1996, 266; K. Haacker 1999, 101,
103; J.-N. Aletti 2003, 306-313 (n.4: *gezerah shavah* also in Rom 9:25-26; 9:27-29; 9:32-
33; 1Cor 9:9-10; Gal 3:10-14); E. Lohse 2003, 150. See also, without referring to Jeremias, E. Jacob 1962, 154n.16: "L'apôtre Paul argumente en rabbin, en rapprochant *Genèse* 15 du *Psaume* 32 à cause de la présence du même mot λογίζομαι selon la deuxième
des Règles herméneutiques de Hillel."

[694] The rhetorical device of the *gezerah shavah* makes A.T. Hanson's idiosyncratic
suggestion unlikely that Paul "must have regarded the psalm as uttered originally by
Abraham" (1974, 57). Against Hanson, the "most notable point of contact" between
Abraham's situation and the situation of the psalmist is not their ἀσέβεια (LXX Ps 31:5;
Rom 4:5) (55), but the way how God acts with regard to both situations: λογίζεσθαι.

[695] Cf. E. Käsemann 1969, 142; 1980, 107. Käsemann contends against A. Schlatter
and A. Nygren that David is witness rather than second example. – In a wider sense, one
could refer to the "David-Abraham-typology" in the Old Testament, as elaborated by W.
Dietrich (2000). He contends: "Abraham erscheint als Vorbild und zugleich als Gegen-
bild des nachmaligen Herrschers Israels" (52). Also 4QMMT connected Gen 15:6 with a
reference to David.

[696] Cf. O. Michel 1978, 160, 164; E. Käsemann 1980, 107.

[697] J. Jeremias 1970, 54. Translating δικαιοῦν (Rom 4:5) with "forgive" (E.P. Sanders
1977, 492n.57, following J.A. Ziesler; also A. Nygren) goes too far, since justification
includes, apart from forgiveness, the element of "new creation" (cf. O. Hofius 1987, 85f.)

In the next paragraph, according to Jeremias,[698] Paul conversely explains LXX Ps 31:1-2 from Gen 15:6, raising the question of the beneficiary of the "blessedness (μακαρισμός)": Is it the circumcised or also the uncircumcised (Rom 4:9)? Again, he argues with the help of the "conclusion of analogy," again with the keyword λογίζεσθαι, though in this case the reader/hearer has to complement the logic: Abraham was reckoned righteous as an uncircumcised, i.e., as a Gentile (4:10); therefore – this is what one needs to supplement – even the λογίζεσθαι of the Psalm passage refers to Gentiles as well. As D.-A. Koch points out, this obvious conclusion is reached on the basis Hillel's seventh rule, by "inference from the context."[699] On the basis of the temporal gap between the events of Gen 15:6 and 17:10-11, Paul arrives at his thesis that the consequences of Gen 15:6 and by implication of LXX Ps 31:2 concern both περιτομή and ἀκροβυστία. Hence, Abraham became the father of all believing Gentiles (Rom 4:11) and the father of all believing Jews (4:12).[700]

In result, comparative studies of Paul's use of Scripture and later rabbinic expository rules prove illuminating. If a broad definition of *gezerah shavah* is accepted,[701] Paul indeed appears to be an early witness to the practice of interpretation within a regulated system. It is also true, however, that these rules correspond formally to the contemporary, non-Jewish Hellenistic argumentation and the correlating practice of Greco-Roman rhetoric.[702] This overlap is mirrored in Paul's biography and education: Born in the Diaspora, he received part of his education in Jerusalem[703] in the Hillelite tradition – and thus he both lived in both "worlds" and was

---

and since "'[f]orgiveness' is not quite (what [δικαιοσύνη] in Paul can be) the opposite of 'condemnation'" (S. Westerholm 2004, 277n.39).

[698] J. Jeremias 1953, 272; 1969, 93.

[699] Cf. D.-A. Koch 1986, 222. Koch also maintains that Hillel's seventh rule is equivalent to Cicero's rhetorical device in *De Inventione* 2,40,117, already referred to (see above note 12 in chapter I).

[700] See below page 363 on Rom 4:11-12.

[701] An open description is that of L.H. Silberman, who defines Paul's rhetorical move as "verbal analogy," which "begins with his earlier quotation of Hab 2:4 in Rom 1:17" (1990, 103). On a more restrictive use of the label *gezerah shavah*, see J.-N. Aletti 2003, 307-309. The restrictions concern (1) the exclusive use of the rule in a comparison of two Pentateuchal verses, or even of two laws (in the first form of this restriction, only Gal 3:10.13 [cf. LXX Deut 27:26; 21:23] would be classified as *gezerah shavah*) and (2) the use of the rule in a comparison involving forms that are exactly identical (in this case, no Pauline passage could be found). If, as Aletti argues, such limitations are applied to Paul, other writings would be affected too, such the Old Testament itself, Qumran texts, as well as extra-canonical Greek writings. M. Chernick documents "internal restraints on *Gezerah Shawah*'s application" (1990; see also M. Mielziner 1925, 142-152).

[702] Cf. M. Neubrand 1997, with reference to D. Daube 1949.

[703] Cf. the classic study of W.C. van Unnik 1962.

taught by a teacher whose family seemed to have special interest in the diaspora, Jewish mission, Greek language and culture.[704] Ultimately, "in Paul it is impossible to separate Greek education from Jewish."[705] In sum, for us it is important to note that Paul's application of generally accepted rules of interpretation confers to his argument in Romans 4 effectiveness and force, reaching his entire audience.

It has long been recognized that Paul employs in his argumentation the rhetorical device of question and answer and that this style shows commonalities with the Hellenistic "diatribe." In his dissertation, R. Bultmann compared Paul's missionary, evangelistic activity with Cynic street preachers,[706] while S.K. Stowers locates Paul's use of the diatribe in the school or catechumenical situation and presupposes a Jewish interlocutor.[707] We can leave aside here the controversial issues, whether or not the questions reflect real or fictitious objections and – if the former is the case – whether they are uttered by a positively disposed interlocutor or by an inimical opponent.[708] From a theological and pastoral perspective, for Paul the objections and questions are real and serious and he dedicates great effort and space to prove his point. Paul's concern is to turn a general, intellectual subject-matter into answers for personal-existential life situations.[709] Both dimensions, the general-theological and the subjective-existential, need to be related to each other ("Relationsprinzip").[710] From a rhetorical perspective, therefore, the Abraham-chapter follows on the dialogical exchange as *exemplum*, the exposition of which is interrupted by further questions (4:9.10).[711] This underlying principle of the diatribe contributes a small piece to the confirmation of the thesis that Paul's universal outlook of 3:21-26 finds its specification in 4:1-25. But the formal label *exemplum* may not obscure the wealth of new associations that Paul creates through his appeal to Abraham which take the chapter contextually and

---

[704] Cf. M. Hengel 1979, 71. Hillel himself came as Diaspora Jew from Babylonia to Jerusalem. According to Talmudic tradition, in the house of Gamaliel's grandson 500 children studied the Torah, and another 500 Greek wisdom (*bSota* 49b; *BQam* 83a).

[705] M. Hengel 1991, 3.

[706] Cf. R. Bultmann 1910.

[707] Cf. S.K. Stowers 1981. The interlocutor is defined as "a student" – "a fellow believer, or at least an open-minded fellow Jew," but not an enemy (165). See also M. Theobald 1999, 292 ("Gespräch mit *an Jesus glaubenden Juden*"; italics original).

[708] See the most recent study on the diatribe in Romans by C. Song, whose peculiar thesis is "that the 'body' [*sc.* 1:16-14:23] was originally a real diatribe which was performed before Paul's students; the diatribe was recorded by one of his students; then, the diatribe could be later used to send Paul's message to Rome or other places" (2004, 79).

[709] Cf. T. Schmeller 1987, 222 (referred to in M. Neubrand 1997, 176).

[710] T. Schmeller 1987, 418-423.

[711] Cf. S.K. Stowers 1981, 171-173; M. Theobald 1992, 118.

materially well beyond a merely confirmatory and specifying function.[712] How this function can be described appropriately, is part of the following deliberations.

3. Form and Function of Romans 4

Apart from Romans 4 there is no section in the Pauline writings (except Gal 3:6-14), in which Paul expounds in such breadth on a single passage of Scripture. Two different categories need to be distinguished (though not separated) when analyzing the whole of Romans 4: form and function. Into the first category belong forms such as midrash or homily, while with regard to the second category one has to determine if Paul carried out a proof from Scripture that simply confirms points already made or if he adjoined a more or less self-contained new line of reasoning.

As to the form of Romans 4 we have to ask, if and how far Paul draws on compositional genres, such as midrash or homily, when he offers his extensive exegesis of Gen 15:6. Since the just mentioned rabbinic rules of interpretation appear prominently in the midrashim, some conclude that "Romans 4 is one of the finest examples of Jewish midrash available to us from this era,"[713] that it is "a fine example of the genre."[714] This wholehearted affirmation of the label "midrash" for Paul's Abraham-chapter may appear too uncritical due to the fact that the term is "exceedingly slippery"[715]; midrashim contemporary to Paul are not extant, and some midrashic characteristic elements that appear in later rabbinic literature are missing in Paul. Nevertheless many scholars maintain this general characterization for Romans 4, assuming a fairly broad definition of "midrash."[716]

---

[712] See below pages 318-320.

[713] J.D.G. Dunn 1985, 423; cf. 1988, 197.

[714] L.H. Silberman 1990, 104.

[715] D.J. Moo 1996, 255n.1. Similar cautions are expressed in D.-A. Koch 1986, 224-226. Among the abundant literature, cf., e.g., G.G. Porton 1979.

[716] G.G. Porton defines "midrash" as "a type of literature, oral or written, that stands in direct relationship to a fixed, canonical text, considered to be the authoritative and revealed word of God by the midrashist and his ... audience, and in which this canonical text is explicitly cited or clearly alluded to" (1979, 112; also 2000, 889). Among those who regard Romans 4 as midrash, are, e.g., U. Wilckens 1969, 94; 1978, 181 ("Midraschartig"); H. Schlier 1977, 135; O. Michel 1978, 160f.; L.H. Silberman 1990; J. Roloff 1990, 237; E. Adams 1997, 50; A.T. Lincoln 1992, 163; 2002, 200; E. Lohse 2003, 148n.8 (cautiously). – Following and developing a suggestion of O. Michel (1978, 160: "Vielleicht war dieser Midrasch ursprünglich selbständig."), H.-J. van der Minde even attempted to extrapolate a pre-Pauline non-Jewish-Christian midrash, consisting of 4:3.11-13.16.17a.18c (1976, 68-85). But scholars tend to agree with H. Moxnes who argues for a Pauline origin of the piece, which however adopts traditional working patterns and includes traditional Jewish material (1980, 195-205).

Likewise, the argument for a Jewish-Hellenistic homily stands on thin ice, since the patterns of the originally non-literary homilies have to be hypothetically reconstructed and since "there is little purely Jewish evidence for the homily that is not based on extrapolation from later rabbinic literature."[717]

Therefore, one should refrain from confidently labeling our text as either midrash or homily until firmer criteria are developed. In any case, the *common* characteristic of midrash, homily, and the Abraham-chapter is their starting point from a single scriptural text and their concentration on its exposition,[718] but the heuristic value of this form-critical fact is relatively little.[719]

More fruitful than the discernment of the compositional patterns and structures that Paul presumably relied on is the question of *how* he utilized the passage from Scripture. The *opinio communis* on the function of Romans 4 within the whole of Paul's letter to the Romans states that "from a rhetorical viewpoint" this chapter serves "as an extended scriptural proof for the truth" of the theses of 3:21-31.[720] It is argued that from the establishment of his main thesis in 1:16-17 onwards, Paul attempted to explicate that justification is the divine gift of righteousness by faith; the passage 3:21-4:25 represents the positive explanation of this thesis,[721] whereby the Abraham-chapter clarifies from Gen 15:6 what has been said in Rom 3:21-31. Abraham embodies exemplarily the principle of "justification by faith." Paul himself indicated in 3:21 and 3:31 that he would corroborate his theses through reference to the Scripture.

Those who agree with this insight into the rhetorical-argumentative *modus operandi* of Paul highlight different aspects within Paul's exposition which the proof from Scripture is supposed to verify.[722] However, in essence all start from the assumption that Romans 4 proves the establishment

---

[717] P.H. Davids 2000, 515. See on the topic also H. Thyen 1955 and W.R. Stegner 1988, but also F. Siegert 1980. – P. Borgen studied passages in Philo that could make assume that Jewish-Hellenistic homilies consist of a Torah text around which a short exposition is built (1965, 28-58); however, Paul's use of an additional text taken from a part outside of the Pentateuch is without a point of comparison in Philo. – In an endeavor comparable to that of H.-J. van der Minde, R. Scroggs sought to provide evidence for an exegetical homily in Romans 1-4 and 9-11, in which Paul allegedly presented a reinterpretation of Israel's history (1976). His suggestion, however, found little support due to the lack of criteria.

[718] Cf. D.-A. Koch 1986, 225.

[719] Cf. J. Roloff 1990, 237n.16.

[720] T.H. Tobin 1995, 442; cf. 451. See recently M. Theobald 2001, 401, and the majority of commentaries.

[721] Cf., e.g., U. Wilckens 1974, 150; 1978, 181.

[722] See also the list in M. Neubrand 1997, 74n.186; cf. 74-77.

of righteousness through Christ for faith.[723] Within this agreement, there are various nuances in the description of the precise content and function of the chapter, dependent on the exegetical determination of the theme of 3:21-4:25: In E. Käsemann's view Romans 4 proves that God's will is formulated plainly and finally ("eindeutig und endgültig") in the Old Testament and demands righteousness by faith, which means in a broader framework that the Christ-story is typologically anticipated in the Abraham-story.[724] According to U. Wilckens, the Abraham-chapter serves as testimony and ratification of the divine election history that began with Abraham and is fulfilled in Christ.[725] Against that G. Klein declares that the scriptural proof proclaims the theological lack of difference between Jews and Gentiles.[726] Some concretize the content of the scriptural proof as verification of the doctrinal thesis 3:28, i.e., the antithesis between faith and works,[727] while others point to the connection between the theme of boasting (3:27) and Abraham.[728]

Not all exegetes, however, agree on the function of Romans 4 as scriptural proof[729] and of Abraham as example,[730] because the Abraham-chapter not only looks back and confirms, but also extends and develops what has been said.[731] A. Schlatter speaks of a "sad depletion" of the letter if one determined chapter 4 as proof from Scripture[732]; against such functional-

---

[723] R. Bultmann 1958, 279. See however Bultmann's noteworthy comment on the futility of scriptural proofs, which also sheds a remarkable light on his concept of faith as decision, independent from objective facts and reasoning (1933, 335): "Es steht also nicht nur so, daß faktisch der Schriftbeweis, zumal heute, keinen Menschen überzeugen kann; er *darf* auch keinen überzeugen. Der Glaube, der auf solche Beweise hin glauben würde, ist überhaupt kein echter Glaube, und die Schriftbeweise des NT müssen fallen, nicht erst Grund rationaler historischer Kritik, sondern schon, weil sie den Charakter des Glaubens nur verdunkeln können." See in sharp contrast R. Gyllenberg 1936, 625; also R.L. Brawley counters this view, since it "fails to consider the way intertextuality is in fact a revisionary interplay between a precursor and successor text" (1997, 297).

[724] E. Käsemann 1969, 140, 172; cf. H. Schlier 1977, 121f.; A. Lindemann 1997, 45.

[725] U. Wilckens 1961, 42f. The nullification of all works-righteousness is not an event that breaks in from outside, but is part of the continuity in God's dealing with humanity (43). Similarly H.W. Schmidt 1966, 80.

[726] G. Klein 1963, 151, 163; cf. K. Kertelge 1971, 193.

[727] Cf., e.g., W.H.P. Hatch 1917, 58; K. Kertelge 1971, 191f.; H. Schlier 1977, 120; J. Roloff 1990, 243f.; M. Theobald 2001, 413. See also H.-J. Schoeps 1959, 212.

[728] C.E.B. Cranfield 1975, 224.

[729] For M. Neubrand the label "proof from Scripture" is also insufficient on formal grounds, since Paul recurs to more than one scriptural passage (1997, 76). Materially, Paul's goal goes beyond the proof of the justification of the individual (2, 291f.; cf. approvingly P. Müller 1999, 133).

[730] On Abraham as example, see below chapter VI.A.IV.

[731] Cf. O. Cullmann 1965, 111; K. Berger 1966, 63.

[732] A. Schlatter 1935, 158f. ("traurige Entleerung des Briefs").

"scholastic" classifications, Schlatter holds that the deepest *desideratio* of Paul and the church was to be found as Abraham's children in their faith in Christ. Also emphasizing Abraham's fatherhood, though with a sociological perspective, F. Watson argues: "Rom. 4 becomes much more than a scriptural proof of some aspect or other of 3:21-31. It is a far-reaching reinterpretation of the figure of Abraham with important social implications, and not a purely theoretical argument opposing salvation by one's own achievements with salvation by grace alone."[733] On the other hand, according to F. Hahn, Paul's use of the Abraham figure does not serve as proof for the preceding section, but following on the soteriological statements in Rom 3:21-31, Romans 4 explicates by way of the Abraham figure what faith is.[734]

Above, the two major poles of Paul's expositions in Romans 4, faith and fatherhood, have been pointed out in the presentation of the various scholarly positions. Here they recur as the main elements of what constitutes the *proprium* of Romans 4 compared to 3:21-31. Again, only an integration of both aspects can do justice to the text. In sum, in consideration of some exegetical insights expressed in the course of previous reflections, we can maintain: First, the Abraham-chapter is a scriptural proof of the general points of what precedes, but only insofar as it is acknowledged that it has not only an explicating or confirming purpose: Romans 4 adds the significant aspect how the new eschatological reality of πίστις becomes reality in the individual life and how it is to be appropriated. Second, Abraham is the example for this appropriation, but only insofar as he is also the *typos* of it: Through his faith and God's acceptance of it, Abraham becomes an "ecclesiological" figure, the figure of identification not only for believing Jews but also of believing Gentiles, and therefore the father of all who believe.[735] For Paul, the Scripture is not so much a means to prove the gospel than a witness to the gospel and to the reality created by it.[736]

These two aspects also provide a clue regarding the structure of Romans 4: While in 4:1-17 Paul considers the entity of faith from God's perspective, providing (in a certain sense) a theological definition of faith under the aspect of the new eschatological people of God comprised of all believers, he assumes an anthropological perspective of faith in 4:18-21 with the intention of providing an account of the existence in the presence of the

---

[733] F. Watson 1986, 139.

[734] F. Hahn 1971, 101 (criticized by D. Zeller as too imprecise and vague; 1973, 100). See also W. Baird 1988, 375.

[735] Cf. J. Roloff 1990, 236.

[736] Cf. the programmatic title of D.-A. Koch 1986: *Die Schrift als Zeuge des Evangeliums.*

accomplished salvation.[737] Concluding this theological and anthropological approach, Paul places his elaboration into the light of Christology (4:24-25).

4. Romans 4:1-8

a) Romans 4:1-2: The Introduction of the Theme

(a) Who Found What?

Already the beginning of this passage challenges us with a text-critical *crux*, which led R. Bultmann to the statement that the text is "hopelessly corrupt."[738] Even though numerous attempts have been made to solve the problems that are posed by the text, text-critically, syntactically, or semantically, M. Black's observation is still valid: "[N]o solution hitherto proposed is without serious difficulties."[739] This should not preclude though the search for the most probable solution, since each solution proposed has influence on the overall *scopos* of the chapter. Already here, a preliminary, but vital decision is made whether "faith" or "fatherhood" constitutes the central theme.

The text-critical situation can be schematized as follows: (1) In some manuscripts,[740] the infinitive εὑρηκέναι is missing, while in others εὑρηκέναι is either (2) placed before κατὰ σάρκα or (3) before 'Αβραάμ.[741] The first version is favored primarily in older commentaries that translate: "What shall we say (about) Abraham our forefather according to the flesh,"[742] yet the text-critical basis of this reading is indeed very weak.[743] The second reading, too, is poorly attested[744] so that the best reading is clearly represented by the Egyptian-Western reading, which is also *lectio*

---

[737] Cf. M. Theobald 2001, 411, who also refers to O. Kuss 1963, 191.

[738] R. Bultmann 1938, 649. This was already noticed by Gennadius and Photius, who both say that this "sentence is confused" (see K.H. Schelkle 1956, 123). Against Bultmann's judgment, see, e.g., U. Wilckens 1961, 39n.15; E. Käsemann 1980, 100.

[739] M. Black 1973, 75.

[740] Most significantly the Vaticanus (B), though this reading is also found in Origen and Chrysostom.

[741] For text-critical reasons, conjectures like εἰργάσθαι or εἰρηκέναι are highly unlikely (see J.A. Fitzmyer 1993, 371; O. Michel 1978, 161n.1).

[742] Cf. e.g., W. Sanday/A.C. Headlam 1895, 98f.; E. Kühl 1913, 133; K. Barth 1922, 100; C.H. Dodd 1932, 65; A. Schlatter 1935, 159-161; H. Schlier 1977, 122. See also F. Blass/A. Debrunner/F. Rehkopf 1979, §480n.9 and the translations in RSV and NEB.

[743] As for the style of this reading, the opinions diverge: C.E.B. Cranfield calls it "very odd Greek" (1975, 226), U. Wilckens a torso (1978, 261), but A. Schlatter argues that the formulation would be "vom griechischen Sprachgefühl aus einwandfrei" (1935, 159). However, one would expect the preposition περί (or the like) before "Abraham."

[744] It would support however those interpretations that take κατὰ σάρκα as modifier of εὑρηκέναι (see the following discussion).

difficilior, and hence clearly preferred among contemporary interpreters: Τί οὖν ἐροῦμεν εὑρηκέναι ᾿Αβραὰμ τὸν προπάτορα[745] ἡμῶν κατὰ σάρκα;[746] Yet the correct reading does not solve problems concerning contents, as the following enumeration of different and partly contradicting interpretations shows.

(1) The suggestion of O. Michel[747] that Paul has in the back of his mind the Septuagint expression εὑρίσκειν χάριν has been widely taken over by modern exegetes.[748] "What then shall we say that Abraham, our forefather according to the flesh, has found?" Answer: "Grace" (cf. Rom 4:4.16). However, not all agree on this alleged "echo of Scripture" in Paul[749]: The formulation εὑρίσκειν χάριν would be without parallel in the *Corpus Paulinum*. Furthermore, one has to raise objections against referring κατὰ σάρκα to Abraham, since Paul is concerned throughout the chapter to establish a relationship between Abraham and the believers that is *not* based on the flesh. Paul wants to prove that the criterion "according to the flesh" is insignificant, for faith is the crucial criterion for a connection to Abraham. He "is the father of all of us," not just of those who are of physical descent.[750] To be sure, Paul speaks here as a Jew, to whom Abraham's "physical" fatherhood is something self-evident[751]; but why would Paul, who just advocated the equality of Jews and Gentiles under God (3:29) and

---

[745] Being a well attested *lectio difficilior*, the reading προπάτορα "should no doubt be preferred" over against the alternative πατέρα (C.E.B. Cranfield 1975, 226). However, it is an "insignificant variant" (J.A. Fitzmyer 1993, 371) and neither "feierlicher" (O. Michel 1978, 99n.2; against that G. Klein 1963, 151n.25a) nor "distanzierend[.]" (D.A. Koch 1986, 308n.5).

[746] Cf., e.g., O. Michel 1929, 57; 1978, 161f.; C.K. Barrett 1957, 85n.1; J. Jeremias 1970, 52; B.M. Metzger 1994, 450; R.B. Hays 1985, 77; E. Käsemann 1980, 100; C.E.B. Cranfield 1975, 226f.; U. Wilckens 1978, 260f.; J. Lambrecht 1985, 28; J.A. Fitzmyer 1993, 371; D.J. Moo 1996, 258f.; K. Haacker 1999, 99; E. Lohse 2003, 146f.

[747] Cf. O. Michel 1929, 57.

[748] The expression εὑρίσκειν χάριν is found nine times in Genesis, once with reference to Abraham (Gen 18:3); see also 2Esdr 12,7: *invenire gratiam* (see the longer quote in J. Jeremias 1970, 53) and the New Testament passages Lk 1:30; Acts 7:46; Heb 4:16. In this sense, Rom 4:1 is interpreted for instance by E. Käsemann 1980, 100; K. Berger 1966, 66; J. Jeremias 1970, 52f.; C.E.B. Cranfield 1975, 227; U. Wilckens 1964, 61n.12; 1969, 95; 1978, 261; O. Hofius 1987, 87; J.D.G. Dunn 1988, 198; G.N. Davies 1990, 148; A.T. Lincoln 2002, 185.

[749] Cf. most vigorously R.B. Hays 1985, but also P. Stuhlmacher 1966, 226n.1.

[750] Cf. Rom 4:16 (πατὴρ πάντων ἡμῶν); Rom 9:5-8. See M. Cranford 1995, 74.

[751] Cf. Josephus, *Bell* 5,380. This passage from Josephus gives a terminological and syntactical parallel to Rom 4:1: τί οὖν ταύτης ἀνὴρ ᾿Αβραὰμ προπάτωρ δ᾿ ἡμέτερος. As in Rom 4:1, Abraham is called "forefather," and he is the active subject in the sentence (cf. S.J. Gathercole 2002, 234; he speaks of an "uncanny" similarity; but see the position of R.B. Hays further below).

through faith (3:30), reintroduce the distinction[752]? Does he speak at all of Abraham as a Jew in religio-sociological terms or rather as father of all believers, independent from circumcision[753]?

One should also take note of those commentators who, instead of "grace," add as object to εὑρίσκειν either "righteousness through faith"[754] or "righteousness through works"[755]; the first would be endorsed by Paul, the second refuted.

(2) Recognizing firstly that the problem for Paul is not *what* Abraham found, but *how* he found it, and secondly that the rhetorical formulation τί οὖν ἐροῦμεν otherwise in Paul introduces a new phase of discussion, constituting a complete sentence without further objects,[756] U. Luz breaks down the sentence into two parts: "What then shall we say? Has Abraham, our forefather, found it according to the flesh?" Answer: "No, through faith, not through works." The object of the "finding" is χάριν.[757] For Luz, consequently, κατὰ σάρκα serves as adverbial modifier of the verb. This rendering has against it that one would expect a negative answer like μὴ γένοιτο.[758] Besides, there is at least one instance in Paul in which τί οὖν ἐροῦμεν is used with a different rhetorical purpose as alleged by Luz, namely, Rom 8:31.[759]

(3) With impulses from U. Luz and above all T. Zahn,[760] but primarily motivated by his criticism of the "Western exegetical tradition's characteristic preoccupation with the problem of how Abraham found (and how we might find) justification,"[761] R.B. Hays paraphrases: "Look, do you think that we Jews have considered Abraham our forefather only according to the flesh?"[762] Answer: "No! Abraham is the forefather of more than those who happen to be his physical descendants."[763] Thus, in Hays's view, not Abraham is the subject of εὑρίσκειν, but "we," i.e., the Jews. And the

---

[752] Cf. P. Eisenbaum 2004, 687f.n.54

[753] Cf. K. Berger 1966, 67: "Das einzig maßgebliche Ereignis, die Rechtfertigung Abrahams, liegt vor der Differenzierung in Jude oder Heide." This is not identical with a desacralization or profanization of Abraham (thus, however, G. Klein 1963, 143).

[754] Cf. J. Lambrecht 1985, 28; W. Schmithals 1988, 135.

[755] Cf. D. Zeller 1973, 99.

[756] Cf. Rom 3:6; 6:2; 7:7; 8:31; 9:14.30.

[757] U. Luz 1968, 174 with n.148.

[758] Cf. Rom 3:5; 6:1; 7:7; 9:14; see E. Käsemann 1980, 100.

[759] Cf. J.D.G. Dunn 1988, 199.

[760] Cf. T. Zahn 1925, 212-219. He translates: "Was werden wir nun sagen? ... daß wir Abr[aham] als unseren Ahnherrn nach dem Fleisch erfunden haben?" (215).

[761] R.B. Hays 1985, 81. Hays appeals to the works of K. Stendahl and E.P. Sanders (1985, 78n.9).

[762] R.B. Hays 1985, 87; cf. the title of his essay: "Have we found Abraham to be our forefather according to the flesh?"

[763] R.B. Hays 1985, 88.

theme of Romans 4 is not Abraham's justification by faith, but his father-hood for the believers. Hays gives the following linguistic reasons: The verb εὑρίσκειν would not be a "cryptic allusion" to a Septuagint expression, but an exegetical-theological term, denoting "to find (someone) to be (something)," and "to draw a conclusion on the basis of exegetical evidence."[764] Among others, N.T. Wright,[765] M. Cranford,[766] and M. Neubrand[767] are convinced of the accuracy of Hays's analysis and add some specifications.

Nevertheless, against Hays's viewpoint it is to be said that it fails to provide an adequate connection with the immediately following verses.[768] A γάρ-clause as answer to Paul's question, as Hays puts it, seems unlikely. Furthermore, "the beginning of a sentence with an accusative and infinitive construction where the accusative was unstated would be rather odd"[769] (even though not impossible[770]). Contextually, only the insertion of the particle "only" renders argumentative logic to Hays's proposal; without it, the statement would be affirmed by every Jew.

To summarize, the contentious syntactical issues are first the point of reference of κατὰ σάρκα – either it modifies εὑρίσκειν,[771] ἡμῶν,[772] or προπάτωρ,[773] and second the subject of εὑρίσκειν – either Abraham[774] is

---

[764] R.B. Hays 1985, 81f. The latter aspect is supposed to allude to the rabbinic exegetical idiom 'ב מצינו מה ("What do we find [in Scripture] concerning...?").

[765] According to N.T. Wright, however, Paul asks the questions of his letter to the Galatians, whether (Gentile-)Christians are to be incorporated into Abraham's physical family (1995, 40).

[766] M. Cranford 1995, 73-76.

[767] M. Neubrand (1997, 182-184) follows Hays in almost every detail, with the exception that she does not regard Rom 4:1b as "false inference" (thus R.B. Hays 1985, 79); rather Paul takes recourse on an accepted fact and starts from there with his deliberations. – See further W.J. Dumbrell 1992, 98; P. Eisenbaum 2004, 687f., 701.

[768] Hays has to downgrade Rom 4:2-8 as "preliminary step towards the major thesis of the chapter" (1985, 93).

[769] J.D.G. Dunn 1988, 199.

[770] Cf. M. Neubrand 1997, 183 with n.27.

[771] Cf., apart from Luz, those who read the verse as the question "What did Abraham accomplish by his own natural exertions?," or "What did he find through his circumcision?," – namely: nothing. Among the proponents of this view are Ambrosiaster (cf. O. Michel 1978, 161n.1), J.A. Bengel and J. Wesley (cf. R.B. Hays 1985, 78n.8, 80n.15), but also A. von Dobbeler 1987, 134 with n.114. On a critique, see C.E.B. Cranfield 1975, 227n.2.

[772] C.E.B. Cranfield explains: "[W]hile we (i.e. the Jews) are Abraham's children κατὰ σάρκα, Abraham has other children who are his in a different way" (cf. vv.11,16ff)" (1975, 227).

[773] Thus the great majority of commentators. Most consider the modifier κατὰ σάρκα as something positive (cf. O. Michel 1978, 161n.2; E. Käsemann 1980, 100; U. Wilckens 1978, 261; M. Neubrand 1997, 185f.; differently J.D.G. Dunn 1988, 199).

the subject or "we," whereby "we" is held to refer to Paul,[775] to the Jews,[776] to the alleged Jewish interlocutor,[777] to the Roman Christians,[778] to the Roman Gentile-Christians,[779] or to "all Christians."[780] The syntactical decisions then are interrelated to the determination of the semantic contents of the terms.

(4) What has not yet been considered in the exegesis of Rom 4:1 is an alternate interpunctuation, allowing for the possibility that in Paul's brachyological formulations the modifier κατὰ σάρκα refers back to ἐροῦμεν and denotes "according to human standards."[781] Paraphrased, Rom 4:1-3a would say: "What will we say that Abraham our forefather has found[782]? Will we say according to human standards: 'For if Abraham has been justified by works, he has something to boast.'? But we will not say this (with regard) to God! For what does the Scripture say?"[783]

This reading can explain some of the formal difficulties: First, it accounts for the reiteration of the name "Abraham" in 4:2, i.e., since κατὰ σάρκα refers to the subject "we" of ἐροῦμεν, the repeated mention of Abraham is not redundant. Second, the construction πρὸς θεόν becomes more intelligible; oftentimes it is inaccurately translated with "before" as in

---

[774] Thus most exegetes.

[775] Cf. K. Haacker 1999, 99, who renders εὑρίσκειν with "feststellen" or "klarstellen": "Was behaupten wir damit festgestellt (oder: klargestellt) zu haben im Blick auf die Rolle Abrahams, unseres leiblichen Stammvaters."

[776] Cf. R.B. Hays 1985, 86f.

[777] Cf. S.K. Stowers 1994, 232.

[778] Cf. T. Zahn 1925, 215-218.

[779] Cf. L. Gaston 1987, 124f.

[780] J.A. Bain 1893/1894, 430 (endorsed by R.L. Brawley 1997, 296f.n.36, 301). He refers κατὰ σάρκα to εὑρηκέναι. If referred to προπάτωρ, κατὰ σάρκα would be "an unnecessary appendage." According to that view Paul asks if we have found Abraham to be our forefather by our own works. Against that see J.A. Fitzmyer 1993, 371 ("contrary to Paul's basic attitude").

[781] The expression would be equivalent to Rom 3:5; Gal 3:15: κατὰ ἄνθρωπον λέγειν. That Paul regards κατὰ ἄνθρωπον and κατὰ σάρκα as basically synonymous can be seen by comparing Rom 8:4 and 2Cor 10:2: κατὰ σάρκα περιπατεῖν with 1Cor 3:3: κατὰ ἄνθρωπον περιπατεῖν. Cf. also 2Cor 5:16: οἶδα κατὰ σάρκα and 1Cor 9:8: κατὰ ἄνθρωπον λαλεῖν.

[782] The meaning of εὑρίσκειν advocated here comes close to D.J. Moo's interpretation. Paul "asks his readers to contemplate with him what Abraham *has found to be the case* with respect to the matters he is discussing" (1996, 259n.13; italics added).

[783] A similar juxtaposition of "talking according to human standards" and "the law says" is found in 1Cor 9:8: Μὴ κατὰ ἄνθρωπον ταῦτα λαλῶ ἢ καὶ ὁ νόμος ταῦτα οὐ λέγει; See also Lk 16:15 and its distinction between ἐνώπιον τῶν ἀνθρώπων and ἐνώπιον τοῦ θεοῦ.

2:13[784] or in 1Cor 1:29,[785] even though it more precisely means "with regard to."[786] Notably, the preposition πρός can also take a meaning similar
to κατά,[787] which would corroborate the parallel between κατὰ σάρκα and
πρὸς θεόν: "according to human standards" as opposed to "according to
divine standards." Third, on contextual grounds, this proposal takes account of the structuring function of the verb λέγειν, which is in effect
throughout the chapter.[788] With regard to Gen 15:6, this verb occurs twice,
namely, in Rom 4:3 and 4:9 – this means that in the course of his argument, the apostle will appropriate what "the Scripture says" and claim,
together with his audience: "We say" (4:9). Hence, the crucial point is not
what "we say" κατὰ σάρκα, but what "we say" in line with Scripture:
"Faith was counted to Abraham as righteousness." Fourth, the suggested
reading strengthens the link to the previous section, which dealt in a categorical way with the issue of "boasting," and would concretize and radical-
ize it through the reference to Abraham. Likewise, the general scope of the
Pauline σάρκα takes up the universal, general-anthropological verdict of
3:20. Fifth, one avoids the conclusion that in his introduction of the theme
of the chapter, Paul actually discloses merely half of the truth, i.e., that
Abraham is the father of the Jews, while later (cf. 4:11.16) he will pronounce his proper standpoint on the function of Abraham "in implied contrast,"[789] i.e., that Abraham is the father of all believers. Finally, the
(wrong) position stated first (4:2) correlates to the νόμος ἔργων, while the
second and correct one (4:3), expressed through a word from Scripture,
represents the νόμος πίστεως (cf. 3:27), according to which there is no reason to boast, no human claim on the basis of works. The human, sarkic

---

[784] Many interpreters stress the equivalence of πρός and לִפְנֵי (O. Michel 1978, 162n.3;
cf. C.E.B. Cranfield 1975, 228; H. Schlier 1977, 123; D.J. Moo 1996, 260n.25; E. Lohse
2003, 148n.11). But this suggestion seems problematic, since לִפְנֵי is rather represented by
ἐνώπιον or ἐναντίον (cf. the note after the next).

[785] This passage from the Corinthian correspondence offers an interesting parallel expression: καυχᾶσθαι ἐνώπιον τοῦ θεοῦ; i.e., Paul does *not* write καυχᾶσθαι πρὸς (τὸν)
θεόν, as should be expected with respect to the conventional understanding of Rom 4:1.

[786] The lack of the article before θεόν remains a problem in any case; it is singular in
Paul and appears only six times in the Septuagint (in very different contexts). Possibly
the most suggestive explanation is the parallelism to κατὰ σάρκα.

[787] Cf. R. Kühner/B. Gerth 1898, 520.

[788] Cf. M. Neubrand 1997, 150f. The verb λέγειν occurs in Rom 4:1.3.6.9.18.

[789] J.D.G. Dunn 1998, 65. Many argue along these lines, such as C.E.B. Cranfield
1975, 243; O. Michel 1978, 167; U. Wilckens 1978, 277; F.F. Bruce 1978, 68; J. Lambrecht 1979, 11: "[A]u v. 11 la perspective s'élargit"; E. Lohse 2003, 152, 155. One has
to use qualifying terms to reconcile the tension between Rom 4:1 and the further argumentation (cf. O. Michel: "trotz Röm 4,1"; E. Lohse: "obwohl..."), or one has to suggest
a metaphorical reading (cf. R.L. Brawley 1997, 296: "Not entirely in the literal sense of
genealogy").

(and not only Jewish) thesis is "righteousness by works" and therefore "reason for boasting" (4:2) and "reward" (4:4), while the divine will operates in terms of "righteousness by faith" and "through grace."

In his argumentation, Paul left behind the Jew-Gentile dichotomy in a revolutionary way with his statements on the one God and the one faith (3:29-30), which follows on the universally true *dictum* in 3:28 (ἄνθρωπος). Consequently, he can now mark the position of his (fictitious?) interlocutor with κατὰ σάρκα. While in other instances Paul refutes a wrong inference with the exclamation μὴ γένοιτο,[790] here he uses the correlate ἀλλ' οὐ πρὸς θεόν: With regard to the God, who justifies Jews and Gentiles through faith (3:30), this idea (4:2) is impossible to maintain. Hence, Paul radically destructs the human suggestion: "If Abraham was justified on grounds of works, he has reason to boast"; and he does so by annihilating the very condition: Abraham did not "work," but "believe" – and this brought him justification. With these thoughts, however, we already anticipate the next verse, 4:2, which deals with the issue of Abraham's work and boast.[791]

(b) Abraham's Work and Boast

In Rom 4:2, the reader/hearer recognizes several associations with previous statements: The phrase ἐξ ἔργων refers back to 3:20 and 3:28, and the stem καυχ- to 3:27; moreover, the concept of justification governs the entire preceding section. For Paul, as for all Jews, there is certainly no doubt that Abraham is the one who fulfilled the Torah perfectly[792]; but right now this truth lies at the periphery of his thought: Though "works" always implies "works of the law,"[793] Paul's objective is a theological exploitation of "chronology"[794]: What did Abraham accomplish prior to the law and prior to his justification. What works could Abraham offer[795]? The answer will be: None! No work can contribute to justification; it is all God's grace

---

[790] In connection with τί οὖν ἐροῦμεν the exclamation μὴ γένοιτο appears in Rom 3:6; 6:2; 7:7; 9:14.

[791] On the theme of "boasting" in recent scholarship, see S.J. Gathercole 2002, 2-10.

[792] See above pages 213f. with note 348; also P. Billerbeck 1928, 155-157.

[793] Cf. E. Gräßer 1998, 13, referring to Rom 4:2.6; 9:12; 11:6. Similarly, νόμος functions as an abbreviation of ἔργα νόμου (10:4-5; Gal 2:21; 3:11; 5:4; Phil 3:6.9). See above note 608 and, for instance, the admonition in *TestBen* 5,3 (referred to in E. Lohmeyer 1929a, 40): ἐκλέξασθε ἑαυτοῖς ... ἢ τὸν νόμον κυρίου ἢ τὰ ἔργα τοῦ Βελιάρ.

[794] Cf. even more pronounced in Gal 3:17.

[795] Cf. S. Légasse 2002, 290 (referred to in J.-N. Aletti 2003, 318n.31): "[D]ans ce premier stade d'argumentation (4,1-12) Abraham est allégué non pas spécialement pour montrer l'inanité d'une justification qui s'appuierait sur la pratique des commandements de la Tora, mais plus généralement pour écarter tout efficacité des 'œuvres' humaines en la matière, ce qui vaut autant pour les Gentils que pour les Juifs."

working through faith.[796] The contrast proposed by some exegetes between "faithful Torah obedience" and "good works" is not Pauline, but anti-Reformation.[797]

Certainly, Paul was aware of the tradition that humans in fact potentially build their existence on the soil of the law, unknowingly, but also unwillingly (2:14-15).[798] They might live in accordance with the salvation-historical revelation of the divine will. This idea has been especially vital in relation to Abraham.[799] But here, Paul goes beyond that concept due to his chronological interest, which will be present throughout the chapter.

The structural analogy to Paul's preference of ἔργα instead of ἔργα νόμου is the use of πίστις, which also consistently implies πίστις Χριστοῦ for him. Just as Abraham is for Judaism the "pre-existent" or "primordial" member of the realm of the law, he is for Paul the "pre-existent" or "primordial" member of the realm of faith. Accordingly, he can be *typos* and example for the one ἐκ νόμου[800] and for the one ἐκ πίστεως, even though in the patriarch's times the law had not yet been given and Christ had not yet come.

How then does Paul present Abraham in the context of justification? The main debates concern the question whether Paul intended to state that Abraham did not have *any* grounds for boasting (irrealis) or if he conceded that Abraham indeed had καύχημα *coram hominibus*, but not *coram deo* (realis).[801] In the first case, the idea would be: "For if Abraham (hypothetically) had been justified on grounds of works, he would have had reasons to boast – but before God any boasting is excluded"[802]; the second reading

---

[796] Cf. J. Lambrecht 1986, 126; E. Lohse 2003, 148.

[797] Cf. S.J. Gathercole 2002, 238f. Such a distinction carried out by the New Perspective is evident in J.D.G. Dunn 1988, 200f.; N.T. Wright 1995, 41.

[798] Therefore, Paul can say that "the work of the law (τὸ ἔργον τοῦ νόμου)" is written in their hearts because he wants to express the force itself that drives the existence of the person (cf. E. Lohmeyer 1929a, 65f.).

[799] Cf. CD 3,2-4; Philo, *Abr* 275-276; *mQid* 4,14; see also *2Bar* 57,2. K. Haacker refers to Ovid, *Metamorphoses* 1,89-90, where the "Golden Era" is portrayed as a time where the good was done without a law ("sponte sua, sine lege fidem rectumque colebat") (1999, 65n.47).

[800] Cf. O. Schmitz 1922, 111.

[801] The interpretation as an irrealis would go counter to the classical usage (cf. W. Schmithals 1988, 136), but it is still grammatically possible (cf. G. Klein 1963, 151n.25).

[802] In this solution, both parts of the conditional clause, protasis and apodosis, are thought unreal and rejected, since no boasting is possible before God (cf. Rom 3:27). The expression ἀλλ' οὐ πρὸς θεόν functions as an intensified negation (R. Bultmann 1938, 649n.36). Proponents of this solution are, apart from Bultmann, C.K. Barrett 1957, 87; O. Michel 1978, 162n.3; G. Klein 1963, 151f.; O. Kuss 1963, 180f.; C.E.B. Cranfield 1975, 228; A. von Dobbeler 1987, 134n.114; E. Lohse 2003, 148. For more authors, see M. Neubrand 1997, 189n.45.

would mean: "For if Abraham (really) has been justified on grounds of works, then he has something to boast – but not towards God."[803] A third solution proposes a "'mixed' construction: The protasis stands in the irrealis whereas the apodosis is in the 'realis'."[804] As the following thoughts show, Paul accomplishes an extraordinary rhetorical move: He leaves the reader/hearer, puzzling with the possible meaning of the conditional clause, but then proceeds to disprove the very precondition of this line of thought: Abraham did not "work" after all! So where does Paul lead his audience?

Many commentators maintain that whatever sense the conditional clause assumes (irrealis or realis) Paul is refuting here head-on a Jewish thesis that would attribute to Abraham righteousness and an attitude of boasting, both on grounds of his works.[805] Others however protest against this "mirror-reading" that deduces a Jewish thesis from Paul's opposition to the conditional clause, such as: Ἀβραὰμ ἐξ ἔργων ἐδικαιώθη.[806] In fact, they argue, Judaism does not know any doctrine that assigns to works salvific power.[807] Both groups, it seems, can only sustain their diametrically opposed positions by pushing the evidence in the Jewish writings one way or the other. Neither position can claim to be without weaknesses or explain compellingly those texts that obviously support the respective counter position. This overly polarized debate has long received an ideological varnish. Hence the question: Is Paul arguing against a Jewish position, in line

---

[803] In this case ἀλλ' οὐ πρὸς θεόν denotes Paul's limitation of καύχημα to the human sphere. Cf. W. Sanday/A.C. Headlam 1895, 100; T. Zahn 1925, 218f.; U. Wilckens 1969, 95; 1978, 261f.; H. Schlier 1977, 123; D.J. Moo 1996, 260 with n.23; S.J. Gathercole 2002, 236n.61; against that O. Michel 1978, 162n.3; J. Lambrecht 1985, 29. – G. Klein considers possible a link to Greek oath-formulas such as πρὸς τοῦ Διός or πρὸς τῶν θεῶν (1963, 152n.26; against that U. Wilckens 1978, 261n.824), while R. Bergmeier refers καύχημα to God in the sense: "[D]ieser Ruhm gälte nicht Gott" (2000, 59n.155).

[804] J. Lambrecht 1985, 29; J. Lambrecht/R.W. Thompson 1988, 74-76 (also M. Neubrand 1997, 191f.). Lambrecht himself says: "The line of thought is strained and can hardly be explained unless one accepts a sudden shift in Paul's reasoning" (1987, 367).

[805] Cf. P. Billerbeck 1926, 201, who collects material from Jewish sources that talk of Abraham as one who accomplished works. Such a reading also depends on the interpretation of Rom 3:27 and the way how "works of the law" and "boasting" are interrelated. See also above note 568.

[806] The alleged rabbinic thesis is formulated in P. Billerbeck 1926, 186: "Abraham ist ausschließlich auf Grund seiner Werke für gerecht anerkannt worden" (approvingly referred to in H. Boers 1971, 85f.; E. Lohse 2003, 147f.n.7; see also W.G. Kümmel 1937, 210; J. Jeremias 1954/1955, 368; O. Kuss 1956, 186; A.T. Lincoln 2002, 185). The term "mirror-reading" is used in this context in N. Elliott 1990, 218 (cf. M. Neubrand 1997, 191).

[807] On the problem of the idea of judgment according to deeds in Judaism, see K. Yinger 1999.

with Jewish tradition – or, rather: against the common human stance towards God?

The fact is, in any case, that Paul does not say who represents the point of view he refers to in Rom 4:2. If it is correct that κατὰ σάρκα modifies ἐροῦμεν, the opinion referred to by Paul would be first and foremost a general human one, and not that of a particular religio-sociological group: Anyone who works has reason to boast, or, as Paul will later say: Anyone who works receives a reward (4:4).[808] Hence, the position opposed by Paul is not a specifically or exclusively Jewish one, as if Jews represent the prime example of those who had gone astray by such futile thinking and therefore were the representatives of the "natural human beings." It is only Jewish insofar as Paul argues from his and his interlocutor's Jewish perspective,[809] making Abraham, the father of Jews and Gentiles, the standard for the "process" of justification, and the Scripture the only source that reliably reports about that "process." The Jewish perspective marks the starting point, since Paul's gospel is first for the Jewish believers, then for the Gentile believers (Rom 1:16). The "Jewishness" of Paul's line of reasoning in Romans 4 is first and foremost of argumentative and autobiographical nature, not phenomenological and polemical.[810] Paul knew of course: If his "theology cannot accommodate ... [Abraham], it *must* be false."[811] In other words: Paul's argues *a minore ad maius*, as it were; in responding to the Jewish tradition, he comes to universally true conclusions.[812]

Through his polemics Paul counters the *real* belief that works bring justification and exclaims in a harsh tone "But not with regard to God!," thus making this belief *unreal*. What is real from a human perspective is not realistic from God's perspective as far as justification is concerned.[813] The

---

[808] Cf. Rom 2:6-10: "He will repay according to each one's deeds ... the Jew first and also the Greek." – An investigation on a Greco-Roman idea of "judgment according to deeds" would be illuminating, with regard to both philosophy and folk-belief.

[809] P. Eisenbaum comments that current scholarship largely accepts that "Paul viewed the world through Jewish eyes" (2004, 675). "That Paul thinks and writes as a Jew is clear" (J.D.G. Dunn 1985, 423).

[810] Just as in the beginning of the letter Paul can take Gentile idolaters "as focal instances of something that has gone wrong for all humanity" (R.L. Brawley 1997, 291n.23; against S.K. Stowers 1994, 113), he can do the same with the Jewish "worker."

[811] S.J. Gathercole 2002, 233 (italics original).

[812] Paul made a comparable move in Rom 3:19-20: Israel's disobedience to the Torah leads to Paul's universal conclusion that all world is under God's judgment.

[813] K. Haacker comments similarly: "Die eindeutige Kennzeichnung als Irrealis würde in der Apodosis anstelle des Präsens ἔχει den Indikativ eines Präteritums verlangen" (1999, 99n.9). He refers to analogous verses, "wo die von ihm [*sc.* Paulus] selbst als irreal eingestufte und nachdrücklich bekämpfte Möglichkeit von anderen für real gehal-

divine logic is *totaliter aliter*, compared to the human "common sense" (κατὰ σάρκα). No work can take away Abraham's status of being "ungodly," since works do not play a role in justification, categorically.[814]

Though Paul does not say whose view he is opposing, the Jewish image of Abraham as sinless friend of God, as the perfectly just and faithful, as the one who fulfills the Torah without compromises, is certainly amenable to the idea that his "works" indeed conveyed to him ground for confidence before God; after all, "obedience is meritorious."[815] By his appeal to Abraham, Paul radicalizes his thesis expressed in 3:28 to the greatest possible degree: If someone can aptly present to God his accomplishments, it would be Abraham – he who offered his only son as the unsurpassable ἔργον (or ἔργον νόμου).[816] But all of Abraham's acts and qualities[817] vanish and are without value as reasons for boasting, as soon as they are seen "under the perspective of justification" and judged *de iudicio dei*. Accordingly, P. Melanchthon comments on the particle ἀλλ' οὐ πρὸς θεόν: "Non enim improbat [*sc.* Paulus] iustitiam legis; necesse est enim bona opera facere, necesse est virtutes habere, timorem Dei, dilectionem, patientiam, temperantiam et similes. Sed Paulus de iudicio Dei disputat. Negat has virtutes opponi irae et iudicio Dei, negat homines liberari a morte et ira Dei harum virtutum dignitate. Ideo addit particulam 'coram Deo'."[818]

As a consequence, Paul does not take away Abraham's "great name" (cf. Gen 12:2), nor does he neglect Abraham's "works (of the law)" and his "glory." They do possess significance and value both in the sarkic sphere and from God's perspective, but only as a consequence of God's act

---

ten wird, der Wenn-Satz also sachlich Zitatcharakter hat": 1Cor 15:13.16.29b.32c (99f.). Cf. U. Wilckens 1969, 96. Both however advocate the "Jewishness" of Rom 4:2.

[814] E. Käsemann 1980, 99; H. Schlier 1977, 122f.; E. Gräßer 1998, 17. R. Bultmann even argues: According to Paul's logic, both the "fulfiller" and the "transgressor" of the law needs grace – "ja, der Erfüller erst recht"; the "fulfiller" acts *principally* against God, while the "transgressor" disobeys God's commandments *in each case* (1940, 41). Somewhat ironically, H. Räisänen comments on such statements that "one gets the impression that zeal for the law is more damaging than transgression" (1980, 68).

[815] E.P. Sanders 1977, 190; cf. O. Michel 1978, 162. See especially *Jub* 21,1-3. There, the author put into Abraham's mouth claims to obedience and sinlessness (cf. S.J. Gathercole 2002, 177)

[816] On the sacrifice of Isaac as ἔργον νόμου, see J.D.G. Dunn 1997, 270; M.W. Yeung 2002, 252.

[817] Even though Dunn occasionally uses a more general description of "works of the law" (see previous note), this remains vague, and eventually is overshadowed by "the obligations which marked them [*sc.* the second-temple Jews] off most clearly as the seed of Abraham ... (circumcision, food laws, Sabbath, in particular)" (1988, 201). See also the debate between C.E.B. Cranfield (1991) and Dunn (1992).

[818] P. Melanchthon (quoted in U. Wilckens 1978, 262n.828).

of justification and election, as a fruit of faith.[819] What Paul strictly denies is their taking precedence over faith and their value as contributions on their own to justification. Abraham's "upright status before God comes from divine grace and favor."[820]

Boasting is human "Ursünde" – in Bultmann's terminology – i.e., the opposite of faith and the fundamental separation from God, if it is understood as having the claim to righteousness before God on grounds of works – a claim that ignores the divine revelation of righteousness in Christ.[821] Accordingly, that boasting is "a sin common to *all* people,"[822] is a fundamentally theological rather than psychological verdict. Or, to be more precise, it is a christological statement: The contention that boasting is "the attitude of the natural man, who seeks to establish his position independently from God"[823] has to be specified through an addition such as "... independently from God's eschatological revelation in Christ." Paul's christological-eschatological perspective is of highest importance in this context, both for the notion of "boasting" and of "faith."[824] This is also the *crux* with Bultmann's interpretation: His analysis of the human being according to the existentialist matrix fails to recognize sufficiently the de-

---

[819] Cf. M. Luther 1515/1516, 262: "[O]pera autem sunt ... fructus iustitiae."

[820] J.A. Fitzmyer 1993, 373.

[821] Within these presuppositions, general-anthropological circumlocutions of "boasting" have to be regarded as legitimate. On Rom 3:27, we have already seen R. Bultmann's connection of the concept of "boasting" and hamartiology: "Boasting" is a "sündig-eigenmächtige Haltung" (1958, 242). "Die Worte des Paulus gegen das Sich-rühmen machen ganz deutlich, daß die eigentliche Sünde des Menschen die in diesem Sich-rühmen zutage kommende superbia ist." In a recent study, E. Gräßer defended Bultmann's propositions and calls them the strongest bastion of Bultmann's interpretation of Paul (1998, 10f. with n.41 where he refers to passages in Bultmann). Among those who in some sense adhere to Bultmann's position are, for instance C.K. Barrett 1957, 82; O. Kuss 1963, 175; H. Schlier 1978, 89; O. Michel 1978, 155: "Das jüdische Verständnis des Gesetzes ruft notwendig den Selbstruhm des Menschen hervor"; G. Klein 1963, 152 ("Schlüsselbegriff für die menschliche Verfallenheit"); P. Althaus 1970, 35 ("stolze Selbstbehauptung"); E. Käsemann 1980, 94f.; C.E.B. Cranfield 1975, 165 ("claiming to have put God in one's debt"); H. Hübner 1982, 97 ("Sich-vor-Gott-Behaupten-Müssen"), 118f.; J.A. Fitzmyer 1993, 359, 363; E. Gräßer 1998, 17n.78 ("eingeborene[r] menschliche[r] Stolz überhaupt"), 20 ("Selbstgerechtigkeit," "Selbstglorifizierung").

[822] D.J. Moo 1996, 5 (italics added).

[823] C.K. Barrett 1957, 82.

[824] It appears that the christological dimension of Paul's refutation of boasting is acknowledged only insufficiently in the exegesis of Rom 3:27 and 4:2. But see J. Lambrecht/R.W. Thompson 1988, 21-27; they also distinguish between two kinds of critiques against boasting in Paul: the first is from an inner-Jewish perspective (2:17-3:20) and concerns apparent disobedience, the second is from the uniquely Christian perspective of πίστις.

pendence of Paul's thought on the Christ-event. The Pauline critique of καύχησις is much wider than the Bultmannian "Geltungsbedürfnis."[825] It is less a *gloria sui* or self-boasting, rather than a *gloria sine Christo* or a boasting apart from Christ. It almost goes without saying that a "[l]imitation of the semantics of boasting to refer to possession of the law only, is at odds with this discussion,"[826] but even obedience to it does not make things better[827] – it would still be boasting apart from Christ.

Paul's biography exemplifies such futile ignorance[828]: He considered himself blameless regarding the righteousness possible for those in the law, but his own righteousness (ἡ ἐμὴ δικαιοσύνη) is nullified in light of the righteousness through faith (Phil 3:6.9); also Israel's story is illustrative: Israel sought its own righteousness in the law (ἡ ἰδία δικαιοσύνη), but could not find it (Rom 9:30-33; 10:3). Just like boasting on grounds of works, boasting about wisdom (σοφία) in ignorance of the foolishness of the cross leads to destruction (1Cor 1:18-31). Works and wisdom, apart from faith in what God has done in Christ, cannot influence the divine, eschatological judgment, and boasting about works and wisdom, apart from faith, will not get a positive hearing with the judge.[829]

If our analysis of the theme of Romans 4 can claim to have roughly grasped Paul's intention, his concern is to ask for the conditions that "our father" Abraham found with regard to his position *coram deo*. He has demonstrated the thorough opposition between human and divine standards in answering this problem. Now he can proceed to the question how Abraham found – how a person finds – acceptance with God, or, what notion "under the perspective of justification" implies.

b) Romans 4:3: The Primary and Authoritative Text Genesis 15:6

The only source that provides the authoritative and undisputed information about what "divine standards (πρὸς θεόν)" imply is Scripture.[830] However,

---

[825] R. Bultmann 1948, 151.

[826] L. Thurén 2000, 169. In contrast to the view presented here, Thurén regards the boast in Romans 2 and 3:27 to refer to the possession of the law (170f.), in contrast to the boast in 4:2.

[827] Against L. Thurén 2000, 177.

[828] Among others, A. Schlatter points to the congruence and interdependence of Paul's life with his thinking (1927, 399-404). See also the pointed thesis of J. Jeremias (1971, 20): "Es gibt nur *einen* Schlüssel zur paulinischen Theologie. Er heißt Damaskus" (italics original).

[829] See also Lk 16:15, which talks about the Pharisees' attempt to justify themselves (δικαιοῦν ἑαυτούς); but "what is prized in the sight of human beings (ἐνώπιον τῶν ἀνθρώπων) is an abomination in the sight of God (ἐνώπιον τοῦ θεοῦ)" (cf. 18:9, but also 10:29; 20:20; Mt 23:28).

[830] Γραφή denotes Scripture as a whole (cf., e.g., E. Käsemann 1980, 100).

Paul does not deduce the truth of his thesis from Scripture in a strictly objective, logical and conclusive sense. Rather, the hermeneutical key to his appeal to Gen 15:6 lies in the eschatological revelation of God's righteousness through πίστις (Rom 3:21) and in the revelation of Christ in Paul's life (Gal 1:12),[831] i.e., in that perspective on Scripture that is defined by faith.[832] Not human deliberations, but divine decisions constitute the criteria.[833] Through his hermeneutics of faith, which takes Gen 15:6 (and Hab 2:4) as foundational text(s), he does not factually invalidate the remainder of Scripture,[834] but puts it into perspective.[835]

Paul's theological impetus to appeal to Scripture in this issue of utmost importance connects to a rhetorical-pragmatic reason: "In writing to a Christian community that he himself has neither visited nor founded, he appeals to something that he knows his readers will not only understand but even accept, the testimony of Scripture."[836]

All that follows in the further argumentation is dependent and based on the quote of Gen 15:6. With only two slight variations, Paul takes over the text of Gen 15:6 from the Septuagint,[837] which – as has been already

---

[831] Cf. K. Kertelge 1971, 192. Hence, Paul himself exemplifies the process described above (chapter V.B.I.1): "from faith to faith" (Rom 1:17). On the paradigmatic character of Paul's becoming a believer, see J. Becker 1992, 78f. His personal call and his kerygma may not be plaid against each other (75).

[832] See above pages 296-298 on Rom 3:27 (νόμος πίστεως). The normative character of the "Lehrsatz" 3:28 correlates with the normative character of Scripture (cf. E. Lohmeyer 1929a, 67). See also H. Boers 1971, 76.

[833] Cf. O. Schmitz 1922, 121.

[834] Thus A. Schweitzer 1930, 204.

[835] For instance, Genesis 17 is not "invalidated," but set into a theological relationship with Genesis 15.

[836] J.A. Fitzmyer 1993, 370. Cf. C.D. Stanley 2004, 154: "Paul was aware that arguments from Scripture would exercise this kind of power over the minds of the Christians at Rome."

[837] The particle δέ and the change from Ἀβράμ to Ἀβραάμ are the only differences from the Septuagint. On the use of δέ here, see R. Mosis's theory who attributes the particle both in Paul and in other sources to the peculiar verb form וְהֶאֱמִן of the Masoretic Text (see above note 322 in chapter III). Contrast however D.-A. Koch 1986, 132: "[D]as hinzugefügte δέ [ist] nicht als lediglich stilistische Variante zu dem nicht zitierten καί vor ἐπίστευσεν zu bewerten. Paulus führt Gen 15,6 an, um eine ... entgegengesetzte Interpretation der Abrahamüberlieferung zu widerlegen, daß nämlich Abraham ἐξ ἔργων ἐδικαιώθη (Röm 4,2). Dieser antithetische Rückbezug des Zitats auf Röm 4,2 wird durch die Einfügung von δέ unterstrichen." But why would Paul place the particle before the quote and not before the introduction formula, if he sought to express an antithesis to 4:2? On the other hand, if Paul was using a *Vorlage* containing δέ, one has to explain the omission in Gal 3:6. – J.D.G. Dunn thinks that the use of Ἀβραάμ instead of Ἀβράμ in Paul is a "significant" point, since it reflects the merge of Gen 12, 15, 17, 18, and 22 in Jewish thought (1988, 202). Though this observation might be correct, the replacement of

pointed out – does not render the Masoretic version literally.[838] It seems appropriate to offer in the following a first thetical explanation of the key terms λογίζεσθαι, δικαιοσύνη, and πιστεύειν, and later, in the course of our exegesis, turn to supporting the claims made.

(a) Λογίζεσθαι

As for the term λογίζεσθαι, the context points to a double meaning: first, counting as merit, and second, counting as a sovereign act of the free will of God.[839] Both meanings are valid for Paul,[840] but different contexts require different meanings. He shows that the first use is indeed logical and reasonable, because "[n]o business could survive which simply gave away its stock or paid its employees for not working,"[841] but it is not valid *coram deo*, because God's logic works κατὰ χάριν. In a subtle analysis of this distinction, H.-W. Heidland came to the conclusion that Paul is playing off the Greek commercial-rationalistic meaning against the Hebrew meaning that points to the freedom of the divine will, to a declaratory act, which attributes a certain value to a person's act.[842] Paul's intention would be a polemical attack against the Greek thinking, which notably correlates with the Jewish theology of his time, and its substitution with the correct Hebrew connotation.

For the moment we leave open the question *who* represents the "Greek" opinion and who the "Hebrew," but it is indeed profitable to compare Paul's interpretation of λογίζεσθαι with the verb חשב in the Masoretic Text of Gen 15:6. If one takes into account that in secular Greek λογίζεσθαι is generally used "of numerical calculation ... and of strictly rational thought,"[843] Paul's endorsed meaning is indeed striking. Just as for the narrator of Genesis 15, for Paul God's act of considering Abraham's faith as righteousness is a performative, authoritative-qualitative judgment reached freely and subjectively. It is an act of grace[844] and creation[845] with (es-

---

'Αβραάμ with 'Αβράμ is common in Second Temple Judaism (cf. H.-W. Heidland 1936, 119n.176).

[838] See above chapter IV.C.

[839] Cf. O. Michel 1978, 162f.

[840] Against that, for C.K. Barrett the use of λογίζεσθαι in Rom 4:4 is an improper use, since it is linked with "work" and "debt" (1957, 85).

[841] J.D.G. Dunn 1988, 203.

[842] Cf. H.-W. Heidland 1942, 293-295; cf. 1936, 122: Paul's use of Ps 32:1-2 makes the conclusion irrefutable "daß P[au]l[u]s das λογίζεσθαι in Gen 15,6 nach seiner hebräischen Bedeutung verstanden haben wollte."

[843] C.E.B. Cranfield 1975, 230n.6.

[844] Cf. H.-W. Heidland 1936, 121; G. Schrenk 1935, 210 (also O. Hofius 1987, 87f. with n.45): "Weil das πιστεύειν schlechthin göttliche Gabe und kein verdienstliches ἔργον ist, stellt das ἐλογίσθη den reinen Gnadenakt der göttlichen Schenkung heraus." See also K. Barth 1960, 686f.

chatological-)soteriological implications.[846] This is significant for Paul: The declaration of Abraham as righteous is not descriptive: He accomplished works and is therefore righteous, but creative: He accomplished nothing and is counted righteous. God's judgment does not state what is, but constitute what is not and would never be. Thus, Paul follows the contents of the statement on the patriarch in Gen 15:6,[847] but radicalizes and extends it: Abraham's being is marked by nothingness and requires an act of creation, and God's act of creation is his forgiveness and his justifying judgment, which not only pertains to the earthly situation, but to the final judgment.[848] For Paul, as for the Old Testament, therefore, justification and being correlate and inform each other.[849]

The two extrapolated meanings of λογίζεσθαι could be summarized as follows: "Counting" in the world of business is an act *a homine ad hominem,*[850] whereby counting the wages is an end in itself and concludes the business relationship; it follows economic rules agreed on by both parties. Against that, divine "counting" happens *a deo ad hominem*; it has far-reaching implications and is the beginning of a relationship, but the sovereignty is solely on God's part.[851]

(b) Δικαιοσύνη

In the exegesis of Rom 1:17 and 3:21-22, we saw that just as πίστις (Χριστοῦ) also δικαιοσύνη θεοῦ contains in itself the idea of a global manifestation of divine righteousness in the world, but also the character of a gift to the individual. It is obvious, which dimension is in view here, and it seems also clear that there has not been a significant debate in this concrete instance of Abraham as to what εἰς δικαιοσύνη means: All "parties presumably agreed that to be 'righteous' is to be not so much acceptable

---

[845] Cf. O. Hofius 1987, 88.

[846] Cf. P. Stuhlmacher 1966, 219, 222-236.

[847] See above chapter III.D.I.2. Cf. C. Dietzfelbinger 1961, 16, 26; H. Wildberger 1968, 144; E. Käsemann 1980, 104. In diametrical opposition to this insight, M. Buber says that Paul, influenced by the Greek connotation, distorted the Hebrew idea of divine consideration and ratification into an idea of judicial computation (1950, 683).

[848] On the forensic dimension of λογίζεσθαι, cf., e.g., E. Käsemann 1980, 104; E. Lohse 2003, 148.

[849] Cf. P. Stuhlmacher 1966, 222.

[850] See above pages 305-307 on this terminology in the context of counting sin.

[851] In his commentary on Galatians from 1531, M. Luther reflects on the theological meaning of λογίζεσθαι (see also above page 129 on Gen 15:6): "[Paulus] addit: 'Reputatum ad iustitiam.' Quare addit? Fides est iustitia formalis, sed non esset satis ad iustitiam, quia adhuc reliquium peccati in carne" (quoted in G. Ebeling 1979, 221 with n.148; see also M. Luther 1515/1516, 288). Statements such as "Glaube *ist* Rechtsein" (E. Brandenburger 1988, 195n.99; italics original) disregard this factor. – On the correlation of *iustitia imputativa* and *iustitia efficax* see the following chapter.

by God as accepted by God."[852] Righteousness is the relationship with God instigated through his performative judgment on Abraham's faith: Hence, it is a word-event, as it depends on God's evaluative declaration, it has promissory character, as it anticipates the final realization in the Eschaton, and it has the character of creation and establishes a new being.[853] All this points to the relational nature of the process of justification, in which God not only evaluates or judges, but discloses a dynamic relationship between him as creator and his creature.[854]

Being justified and a new being in justification correlate, i.e., the widespread alternative between *iustitia imputativa* and *iustitia efficax* is not adequate on ontological grounds; the evaluative judgment made with regard to the faith of the believer is intrinsically connected to a new quality.[855] The reason for the inadequacy of a split perspective lies in the fact that participation in the reality of faith and being considered righteous by God determines being and act, just as its diametrical opposite, being under the power of sin, is inadvertedly connected to sinful deeds.[856] The convergence of a "qualitative" and a "quantitative" dimension has also been found pivotal in our analysis of Abraham's "righteousness" in the Hebrew text.[857] But what does the notion of participation in faith encompass and how does it come to pass?

(c) Πιστεύειν

What was noted in our exposition of Rom 1:16-17 and 3:21-31, is confirmed in Romans 4: The idea of faith, in its multifaceted connotations, plays a, probably *the*, main role in the letter to the Romans. The way Paul qualifies λογίζεσθαι through πιστεύειν, i.e., how he discloses the two meanings of λογίζεσθαι by means of the pair of opposition "faith" and "works," makes clear that actually, "it is upon ἐπίστευσεν ... that Paul is fastening."[858] Faith constitutes the foundation of Paul's argument: Since

---

[852] J.D.G. Dunn 1988, 203.

[853] Cf. A. Schlatter 1927, 360 ("kreatorische[r] Akt"); W. Mundle 1930, 135f.; P. Stuhlmacher 1966, 98, 236.

[854] P. Stuhlmacher argues "[daß] Gott in der Rechtfertigung nicht nur (be-)urteilend, sondern ständig schaffend auf den Plan tritt" (1966, 220n.1). "Paul talks about the righteousness of God 'synthetically.' He uses it to designate God's own creative and saving activity ... as well as the grace gift of righteousness in which the believers share" (P. Stuhlmacher/D.A. Hagner 2001, 20).

[855] Cf. E. Jüngel 1962, 46; E. Käsemann 1961, 184; G. Klein 1961, 827; 1967, 234. Against that, for instance, A. Ritschl 1889, 330f.

[856] On the New Testament idea of the unity of a person's being and doing, see also M. Kähler 1896, 94: "Wir können und sollen vom Neuen Testament lernen, Person und Werk zusammenzufassen."

[857] See above chapter III.D.III. Cf. H. Cazelles 1962, 334n.58.

[858] C.E.B. Cranfield 1975, 231.

Abraham believed, and did not work, λογίζεσθαι takes on the intended meaning.[859] Thus, Paul discloses the significance of Abraham's faith from its opposite: works. In analogy to the two meanings of λογίζεσθαι there is a double dimension of "work": No doubt, in the world of commerce, i.e., in earthly matters, works are possible, even indispensable, and they receive retribution *coram hominibus*. However, from the perspective of justification works are an impossibility in terms of their justifying effect and they will receive no retribution *coram deo*. Particularly Paul's presentation of David's desperate situation reveals the factual impossibility of one's own contribution.

One should take note of other Pauline explicit oppositions to "works," which illuminate the character of faith by being parallel expressions: As is clear from 3:24 and 4:4, χάρις is deeply associated with faith[860]: "But if it is by grace, it is no longer on the basis of works" (11:6), and this grace is embodied in God's prevenient call (9:12): God decides and takes the initiative to call humans in his grace (cf. 4:4.16-17).[861] Moving back from faith to the law means being cut off from Christ and falling away from grace (Gal 5:4). Accordingly, the one who stands in faith (1Cor 16:13[862]) is also the one who stands in grace (Rom 5:2[863]). Likewise, justification on grounds of πίστις Χριστοῦ means being justified in Christ (Gal 2:16-17). Accordingly, the one who stands in faith is also the one who stands in the Lord (Phil 4:1; 1Thess 3:8). The ideas "in faith" and "in the Lord/Christ" appear as analogous concepts, both in contrast to "works of the law" and both denoting the same sphere of salvation,[864] established by God in order for humans to participate therein.

On the other hand, apart from "works (of the law)," Paul explicates the other side of faith through the counter expressions ὀφείλημα (Rom 4:4) and ἁμαρτία (14:23) and by doing so manifests implicitly the radical separation of the "Christ-side" (faith and grace) from the "Adam-side" (law and sin).[865]

---

[859] Cf. C.E.B. Cranfield 1975, 231f.: "[W]hile Paul does not start by assuming a special 'Hebrew' sense of λογίζεσθαι, he does, by starting from ἐπίστευσεν, bring out the fact that in Gen 15.6 λογίζεσθαι must be understood in its 'Hebrew' rather than its ordinary Greek sense."

[860] Cf. H. Ridderbos 1970, 127.

[861] Cf. J. Lambrecht 1986, 126.

[862] See also Rom 11:20; 2Cor 1:24; 13:5.

[863] See also Rom 6:14; 11:6; Gal 2:21.

[864] Cf. W.H.P. Hatch 1917, 46; A. Deißmann 1925, 128; H. Lietzmann 1928, 57; E. Lohmeyer 1929, 140; W. Mundle 1932, 150; R. Bultmann 1958, 328f.; H. Binder 1968, 62; and especially F. Neugebauer 1961, 171-174. – See also above chapter II.C, but also the deliberations on πίστις Χριστοῦ as *genitivus relationis* above page 263.

[865] See above page 307.

The impossibility of works is joined by the impossibility, from a human perspective, of the realization of the promise's content given to Abraham. He is radically dependent on God's miraculous, generative power, on God's word, which creates what it says and gives what it offers (cf. Rom 4:21). When in the previous section 3:21-31, Paul had to leave aside the concrete and existential word-character of God's righteousness due to his large-scale outlook, now he takes it up from 1:16-17 all the more forcefully: The access into the sphere of faith happens on grounds of a word, which is given to Abraham through the divinely established "faith-righteousness" (4:13).[866] The power[867] and dynamic[868] of the gospel (εὐαγγέλιον) reveal God's salvation and righteousness to the believer (1:16-17); thus, God accepts Abraham in righteousness as a consequence of his faith, which is marked by his clinging to the promise (ἐπαγγελία)[869] given by the almighty God,[870] abandoning himself in God's hands and knowing that he has nothing to offer to God, nothing to appeal to before God.[871] Abraham accepted the promise of God, against all appearances, against hope; this faith is faith in the one God (3:29), the God who justifies the ungodly (4:5), in the creator who gives life to the dead and calls into existence the things that do not exist (4:17). Unconditional trust in and knowledge of the generative capacity of God, but at the same time acceptance of his sovereignty – this is faith.

---

[866] In Romans 4, the progression of the Abraham narrative differs from Genesis 15: Paul omits the explicit mention of God's self-disclosure through his word, which preceded Abraham's faith (cf. Gen 15:1). Only in Rom 4:13 the promise comes into play: Through the divinely established new order of salvation (δικαιοσύνη πίστεως) the promise came to Abraham – and he believed. Yet despite this rearrangement there is no doubt for Paul and his addressees that Abraham believed upon hearing the word of God. See similarly J. Lambrecht 1979, 18.

[867] Cf. E. Käsemann 1980, 19: "Das Evangelium ist ... die Epiphanie der eschatologischen Gottesmacht schlechthin."

[868] Cf. K. Haacker 1999, 37, citing G. Friedrich: "[Δ]ύναμις 'gehört zur Terminologie der Wunder'." Cf. Rom 1:4 with 4:17, and see 1Cor 6:14; 2Cor 13:4. M. Theobald refers to the possibly traditional connection between λόγος and δύναμις θεοῦ: Isa 55:10-11; Heb 4:12; 1Thess 1:5 (1999, 289 with n.37).

[869] The ἐπαγγελία is the prototype or the *typos* of the εὐαγγέλιον (E. Käsemann [referred to in M. Theobald 1999, 321]; U. Schnelle 2003, 358), upon which faith follows (cf. also Eph 1:13). See also M. Luther 1515/1516, 300 (on this K. Barth 1932, 244-246): "Fides et promissio sunt relativa." 1527-1530, 58, on Isa 7:9: "Sola ergo fides certificat et habet solidum fundamentum. Frustra autem fit promissio, nisi accedat fides." Luther could argue even more forcefully: "[N]ihil maiestatis et divinitatis habet Deus, ubi fides non est" (1531, 360).

[870] Cf. E. Lohse 1977, 158.

[871] Cf. J.-N. Aletti 2003, 321: "[U]ne foi qui s'invoquerait elle-même, s'appuierait en réalité sur elle-même et ne serait plus un total abandon entre les mains de Dieu; elle ne serait plus *foi*." J.A. Fitzmyer 1993, 387.

Hence, faith, in its verbal, individual sense, is rooted in the proclaimed εὐαγγέλιον (Rom 1:17; 1Cor 15:1-2.11.14), in the divine ἐπαγγελία, and becomes real through this word itself (Rom 10:17; Gal 3:2.5[872]). Paul knows that all depends on God's initiative and indicative[873]: Gospel and promise have their power only because they are God's creative word,[874] and personal faith is only possible within the conditions of the new era of salvation, created by God in sending Christ (Rom 3:21-31). What Paul says elsewhere on this fact, elucidates his view of faith: One seizes after being seized (Phil 3:12), knows after being known (Gal 4:9), works since God works (Phil 2:12-13).[875]

As with the term λογίζεσθαι, a fundamental difference between the Hebrew and Greek understanding of faith has been propagated. According to M. Buber,[876] Christian (Pauline) faith is so much influenced by Greek thinking that it is reduced to an a-historical, isolated, rationalistic *credo* – "I believe."[877] However, as noted above, the Septuagint πιστεύειν in fact included the notion of trust into its concept of faith by association with its Hebrew counterpart אמן *hiphil*,[878] even if its language tends toward an un-

---

[872] The phrase ἀκοὴ πίστεως denotes the proclamation that effects faith (cf. O. Hofius 1990, 160: "Glauben wirkende[.] Predigt"; H.-J. Eckstein 2000, 12n.32: "eine[.] die *Wirklichkeit* des Glaubens setzende[.] Macht"; italics original) rather than the proclamation that demands the decision of faith (cf. R. Bultmann 1959, 214: "Predigt, die Glauben fordert," "die die Möglichkeit des Glaubens eröffnet"). R. Gyllenberg argues "daß die paulinische πίστις sehr viel auch von der ἀκοή in sich weiterträgt" (1936, 623).

[873] Cf. F. Neugebauer 1961, 167. – It is noteworthy in this context that Paul never uses the imperative πιστεύετε (contrast Mk 1:15; 5:36; Acts 16:31). The spatial notion of πίστις is however reflected in the imperative στήκετε ἐν τῇ πίστει (1Cor 16:13).

[874] Cf. O. Hofius 1990, 158. On the tradition history of the idea of the divine word of creation, see Hofius's exposition in 163-165; see also below pages 376f. on Rom 4:17.

[875] Cf. A. Schlatter 1910, 336; R. Bultmann 1958, 323; 1959, 225; G. Friedrich 1982, 111.

[876] On Buber's concept of faith in general, see L. Wachinger 1970; also M. Fishbane 1997. See also above chapter II.G.II (on E. Lohse's discussion with Buber).

[877] Cf. M. Buber 1950, 683, 723, 780f. – From a different starting point, namely F. Watson's sociological reading of Paul (see above page 232), D. Rokéah comes to comparable results. He wants to clarify "the relationship between conditions in the Jerusalem church and Paul's position and actions." In order to consolidate his position in the community's leadership, Paul had to establish many Gentile churches and therefore waived the ritual laws of the Torah. He responded to Jerusalem's opposition by collecting money for its poor (1991, 300). As for Paul's concept of faith Rokéah examines whether Paul's antithesis between faith and works is philologically at all possible. He notes (without verifying this claim on a textual basis) that the "theological meaning" of faith "does not exist at all in the Hebrew Bible" (302), nor in Classical and Hellenistic Greek (see against this view D.R. Lindsay [see above chapter II.G.VII]). Therefore, Paul's two main proof-texts (Gen 15:6; Hab 2:4) "cannot support the meaning with which he proposes to endow the term, faith" (304).

[878] Cf. D.R. Lindsay 1993, 114.

derstanding in terms of *credere deo*. Despite this linguistically verifiable shift of the theological peak in the translation of the Septuagint, Paul averts any rationalistic element through his description of Abraham's situation, which leaves no other possibility for him than to fasten himself trustfully to God.[879] Hence, *credere deo* and *credere in deum* are mutually dependent for Paul.[880] Faith takes place in the sphere of an "I-Thou relationship."[881]

Then again, while on the one hand the Hebrew points to Abraham's continuous believing attitude, and on the other hand the Septuagint regards his faith as onetime, outstanding act in the past, Paul seems to be primarily interested in Abraham's transition into the sphere of faith. This is certainly not to argue that Paul omits the durative connotation of faith, which has figured as the predominant aspect in the Masoretic Text of Gen 15:6. Abraham remained in faith and showed his perseverance despite the desperate situation he found himself in (Rom 4:19-21). Overall, Paul overcomes an a-historical view of faith by this dynamic salvation-historical perspective,[882] through which he talks of faith as a phenomenon greater than an individualized acceptance and a psychological approval of a certain truth, and views Abraham as ("pre-existent") part of this reality of faith.

It is evident from these statements that for Paul faith is "naked trust in God's promise"[883] that awaits everything from God and knows about the impossibility of one's own contribution and the impossibility of the contents of the promise. Abraham's standing before God empty-handed is in sharp contrast to the "well-established theme of Jewish theology at that time, which tied the covenant promise made to Abraham to Abraham's faithfulness under testing, and which regarded Abraham's offering of Isaac as the key to understanding Gen 15:6."[884] Paul fundamentally reinterprets and qualifies the *relectures* of the Abraham narratives undertaken by his predecessors and contemporaries.[885]

Hence, there is no textual evidence in Paul's Abraham-chapter allowing for an interpretation that regards "Jesus' and Abraham's faithfulness" as

---

[879] This is the basic meaning of אמן *hiphil* (see above chapter III.D.IV.2).

[880] A dichotomy of both aspects is not in place, but a distinction is necessary (cf. R. Holst 1997, 319).

[881] J. de Zwaan 1936, 138 ("Sphäre der Ich-Du-Bezogenheit").

[882] Cf. J.-N. Aletti 1989, 248 (against M. Buber's critique of Paul's allegedly a-historical concept of faith).

[883] J.D.G. Dunn 1997, 265.

[884] J.D.G. Dunn 1988, 201.

[885] See below chapter VI.B. This is overlooked, e.g., in D.A. Campbell 2005, 185-187.

"sources for the righteousness of others,"[886] thus having "vicarious sote-riological consequences" for those who know Jesus as Lord and those who know Abraham as father.[887] It would be "damaging to Paul's argument"[888] against the traditional Jewish view of Abraham's faithfulness, if he portrayed Abraham's faithfulness as prototype of Christ's faithfulness. Abraham's faith in the promise – not his faithfulness in offering Isaac – is central to Paul, and no parallelism can be established to Christ's faithfulness to death on these grounds. If his intention had been different, i.e., if he were to follow the Jewish tradition and create a parallel between Jesus and Abraham, one would expect a much clearer indication of this intention, which would at least include the reference to the Aqedah.[889] Paul's one allusion to the Aqedah in Rom 8:32, however, highlights *God* as the one who did not spare his son rather than Jesus' faithfulness to the cross.[890]

In correlation to the brief reference to the relationship of *iustitia imputativa* and *iustitia efficax*, one needs to point to the fact that for Paul existence in faith affects the person in its totality.[891] Just as Paul has an wholly pessimistic view on the one who lives in the sphere of ungodliness and sinfulness, he thinks of the one in faith in wholly positive terms (cf. Rom 6:14). In the dominion of sin, sin governs, and there are no meritorious works, no works at all – *sub specie iustificationis*. But, according to Paul's

---

[886] S.K. Stowers 1989, 672. – Or, even, to regard both Abraham and Jesus as heroes of faithfulness (674).

[887] R.B. Hays 1985, 97f. This interpretation will have difficulties to answer the question "Why Jesus?" If Abraham's faith(fulness) has soteriological consequences and paradigmatic purpose, what is the role of Jesus? Hays somewhat unsatisfactorily asserts that "with the hindsight of narrative logic" "the Christ-story is understood ... as the fit sequel to the Abraham story" (1983, 197). See also D.M. Hay 1989, 474n.45.

[888] A.T. Hanson 1974, 83.

[889] Cf. A.T. Hanson 1974, 83: "Paul gives us no hint of the *'Aqedah* in Rom 4." O. Michel assumes that Paul does not mention the sacrifice of Isaac, "vielleicht eben deshalb, um den Glauben auch nicht mit dem Schein eines Verdienstes zu belasten" (1929, 146; cf. also J. Roloff 1990, 242n.25). In view of Heb 11:19, others see Genesis 22 reflected in Rom 4:17 (cf. C.K. Barrett 1957, 96f.; C.E.B. Cranfield 1975, 244; J.D.G. Dunn 1985, 423).

[890] Cf. J.D.G. Dunn 1997, 265, 270f.; 1998, 225. See also above chapter V.B.III.1.c. This is criticized by R.B. Hays as an anachronistic semantic distinction between faith and faithfulness (1997, 295); however, both, the context of Paul's thesis of righteousness through faith apart from the law, and the comparison of Paul's view of Gen 15:6 with Jewish tradition, leaves no other choice than to apply this distinction here. – This is why even in Gal 3:9 it is adequate to translate "the believing Abraham" for πιστὸς Ἀβραάμ, coming from Gal 3:6 (cf. A. Schlatter 1927, 603: "Als ὁ πιστεύσας ist er πιστός."). See in a similar context, e.g., Philo, *Leg* 3,228, where he parallels Abraham's and Moses' faith, quoting Gen 15:6 and Num 12:7 (ἐν ὅλῳ τῷ οἴκῳ μου πιστός ἐστιν); "Philo takes πιστός actively, 'believing'" (F.H. Colson 1929, 457).

[891] Cf. M. Theobald 2001, 412.

holistic anthropology, in the sphere of faith, faith governs our existence, and works ensue. This is why in Paul we find several unrestrictedly positive references to the "law,"[892] to "work(s),"[893] even to "boasting."[894] Paul talks of ὑπακοὴ πίστεως (Rom 1:5[; 16:26]), νόμος πίστεως (3:27) and ἔργον (τῆς) πίστεως (1Thess 1:3; 2Thess 1:11),[895] and while ethical commands are missing in Rom 1:18-3:20 due to the inescapability of the power of sin, the imperative does belong to the doctrine of baptism (Romans 6), the Spirit (Romans 8), and to the paraenesis (Romans 12).[896] An existence determined by faith is marked by active obedience and perseverance, as Paul will show in his further elaboration on Abraham; the state ἐν πίστει is "at the same time utterly giving and utterly demanding."[897]

c) Romans 4:4-5: The First Exposition of Genesis 15:6

In Rom 4:4-5 Paul reflects in a general way on the relationship between faith and righteousness. The case of Abraham has only seemingly "slipped into the background"[898] – rather, Abraham is *the* paradigm for the justification χωρὶς ἔργων νόμου[899] and from his case Paul deduces a general pattern, which remains intrinsically connected to the patriarch's situation. Formally, the term λογίζεσθαι underlies his deliberations, with which Paul enters the realm of business and commerce.[900] To this effect, he construes two "parallel" clauses that serve to contrast the two keywords χάρις and ὀφείλημα. The first remains fully within the world of thought of business: "To one who works, wages (μισθός) are not counted as a gift (χάρις) but as

---

[892] Cf., e.g., Rom 3:27; 8:2 (νόμος τοῦ πνεύματος); 9:4; 1Cor 9:21; Gal 6:2 (νόμος τοῦ Χριστοῦ).

[893] Cf., e.g., Rom 2:6-7; 15:18; 1Cor 3:13-15; 15:58; 16:10 (ἔργον κυρίου); 2Cor 9:8; Gal 6:4; 1Thess 1:3; 2Thess 1:11.

[894] Cf., e.g., Rom 5:11; 15:17; 1Cor 1:31; 9:15-16; 2Cor 1:14; 9:3; 10:17; Gal 6:4; Phil 1:26; 2:16; 3:3.

[895] Cf. E. Peterson 1997, 94 (quoted in E. Lohse 2003, 138: "Werke [als] Lebensäußerung des Glaubens"); G. Klein 1961, 827 ("...zu einem verantwortlichen Gehorsam befreit"); O. Michel 1978, 154. – The holistic nature of faith cannot be without the confession of the heart (10:9); faith drives towards the public (cf. G. Friedrich 1982, 113; also Rom 1:8; 2Cor 4:13; 1Thess 1:8). See also below chapter VI.A.VI.

[896] Cf. O. Michel 1978, 95. Rom 1:18-3:20 also lacks the terms ὑπακοή and ὑπακούειν (cf. W. Schenk 1972, 165).

[897] This is the formulation of W. Brueggemann (1997, 419) with regard to God's covenant with the people of Israel. (There, he accuses Paul of a "false distinction" between the unconditional gospel connected to Abraham and conditional law connected to Moses.)

[898] Against J. Knox 1959, 440.

[899] Cf. E. Gräßer 1998, 12, 15.

[900] Possibly, Paul was aware that "the gospel in Rome came about through the presence of Christians in the discharge of their ordinary duties or business" (C.E.B. Cranfield 1975, 17).

something due (ὀφείλημα)" (4:4). Paul is not concerned with the question *who* will receive repayment,[901] but with the measurability of the repayment in terms of its being immanent in the works.[902] The term μισθός links Paul's comparison again to the narrative of Genesis 15,[903] possibly also to Num 18:31,[904] while χάρις takes up Rom 3:24 and anticipates 4:16.

Instead of a proper antithetical-parallel continuation of the commercial metaphor, he interrupts his comparison for contextual reasons[905] and inter-weaves the *tertium comparationis* into the following sentence[906]: "But to the one who does not work, but believes in the one who justifies the un-godly,[907] his faith is counted as righteousness" (4:5).

Again, the question of a possible "mirror-reading" poses itself: Is Paul polemizing frontally against a Jewish notion of soteriology in terms of re-payment[908] or does his metaphor rather point to a "fundamental agreement" between his and the Jewish position[909]? Yet again, it seems rather that Paul accomplishes a "mirror-reading" of the general human stance towards God, taking his own and his interlocutor's Jewish tradition as *Ausgangspunkt* and impulse. His primary target is a false motivation to secure one's own righteousness through "works," and his primary intention is a sharp, mutu-ally exclusive distinction of "works" and "faith" from the perspective of justification.[910] From these presuppositions, he rejects the traditional Jew-ish Abraham image both implicitly and explicitly. The "worker" that Paul talks about has not yet realized the "ugly ditch" that separates him from God. He still thinks he can accomplish or uphold a right relationship with God through his own power. As a consequence, he also has not realized

---

[901] Against M. Neubrand 1997, 206.

[902] Cf. E. Gräßer 1998, 18.

[903] Cf. U. Wilckens 1969, 95; M. Neubrand 1997, 198, 207.

[904] Cf. J.-N. Aletti 2003, 312. Num 18:31 is in the context of two passages on the "priestly counting" (18:27.30), which has proven decisive for G. von Rad's exegesis of Gen 15:6 (see above chapter III.C.I).

[905] Cf. U. Wilckens 1978, 262. Rom 4:5 is formed according to the Genesis quote.

[906] The logical continuation of Paul's image would have to say: "Who does not work, will not receive repayment, except as a gift κατὰ χάριν." Cf., e.g., H.-W. Heidland 1936, 120; H. Boers 1971, 87; H. Schlier 1977, 124; S. Westerholm 2004, 280n.45.

[907] On later rabbinic interpretations of this idea, see A.B. Kolenkow 1967.

[908] Cf. K. Kertelge 1971, 185-195; S.J. Gathercole 2002, 244, with reference to *PsSol* 2,34; 9,1-5; *TestJob* 4,6-7; *SibOr* 2,304; *L.A.B.* 3,10; *2En* 2,2; 45,1-2: "*[T]he interlocutor of Romans 2:1-3:20 and the 'worker' of Romans 4:4 are one and the same person*" (245; italics original). Both O. Michel (1978, 163) and P. Stuhlmacher (1966, 226) see in Rom 4:5 an antithetical "Kampfformel."

[909] J.D.G. Dunn 1998, 367; cf. 1988, 204, 228f.

[910] Cf. A. Schlatter 1927, 338.

that God justifies the ungodly.[911] He still thinks that the logic of God's "commutative justice" goes according to the scheme *do ut des*.[912] Only through faith that opens itself to the divine promise it is possible to overcome both the separation from God and the imprisonment in the retributionary thought system.

Nowhere does Scripture call Abraham (anything like) "ungodly," yet it is impossible *not* to deduce from the apostle's line of thought that he *de facto* does so. Though Abraham is not mentioned explicitly in 4:4-5, he is the case in point and example *par excellence* for what takes place.[913] Oftentimes, exegetes take the edge of Paul's statement by neglecting or obscuring the identification of the "ungodly one" with Abraham or by ignoring the problem altogether.[914] And indeed, this equation sounds disconcerting at first, to say the least, rather shocking and repugnant, not just for those Christians with Jewish heritage,[915] but also for Gentile-Christians.[916]

---

[911] The worker is the εὐσεβής who claims the right of reward to be measured in accordance to his works (A. Schlatter 1935, 161).

[912] Cf. S.J. Gathercole 2002, 245.

[913] Cf. F. Hahn 1971, 102; A.T. Hanson 1974, 60.

[914] Against U. Wilckens (1978, 263), K. Berger is keen to emphasize that Romans 4 does not talk yet of the *iustificatio impii* (1966, 66n.32, 72n.50; cf. M. Neubrand 1997, 205n.31), since this would not be possible apart from Christ. Also W. Sanday and A.C. Headlam argue that 4:5 is "not meant as a description of Abraham" (1895, 101), and J.A. Fitzmyer thinks that it does not mean "that Abraham was himself *asebēs*" (1993, 375). Some contend that the point of contact between Abraham's individual situation (4:3) and the general "theological" situation of every person (4:4-5) is not the common ungodliness, but rather "righteousness by faith" (A. Nygren 1951, 129), the state of the believer (D. Zeller 1985, 100; endorsed by M. Neubrand 1997, 210), or the state of the person "who cannot advance a plea for being justified on the ground of what he has done" (J. Knox 1954, 440). K. Barth also somewhat weakens the radicalism of Paul's statement by using the translation "ehrfurchtslos" (1922, 99; cf. O. Michel 1978, 163n.7; against Michel, see E. Käsemann 1980, 106). All these positions, however, "undermine[.] the logic of Paul's argument in Rom. 4" (E. Adams 1997, 52n.17), but also neglect the fundamentally christological outlook of the apostle even in Romans 4 (cf. A. von Dobbeler 1987, 134).

[915] Cf. A.T. Hanson 1974, 60; O. Michel 1978, 163 ("Kampfformel"); J. Lambrecht 1979, 23.

[916] Cf. G. Bornkamm 1969, 152 ("nicht nur für jüdische Ohren geradezu blasphemisch"). – As G. Mayer points out, Abraham was a crucial figure in Jewish missions, as his life demonstrates God's free election independent from the boundaries of the empiric people of Israel. This strategy must have resulted in an extraordinarily positive image of the patriarch, which was in turn countered by a derogatory propaganda of both the leading philosophical schools and political propagandists (1972, 119f.). Mayer concludes: "Gift und Galle, welche die antiken Antisemiten spucken, lassen sich begreifen als Reaktion auf den Erfolg [der jüdischen Mission], den man dem Rivalen neidet" (127). On Abraham as "Greek philosopher," see L.H. Feldmann 1968.

But how is Abraham's and in consequence everybody's ungodliness defined[917]? What is the theological peak of this extraordinary thought?

Is it Paul's intention in 4:5 to argue that the "ungodly" is the member of the covenant who factually did not accomplish the works of the law and therefore became guilty before God, not able to regain the status of righteousness? The primary difference from Jewish tradition would be the idea that Abraham – already being in a relationship with God – factually sinned and was justified as one who trespassed the law.[918] Or does Paul mean to present Abraham as the first convert who turned away from paganism and idolatry to the true God? Paul's departure from traditional Jewish thought would lie in the thought that Abraham's leaving behind idolatry happened not through his own efforts or obedience,[919] but through faith and justification, both taking place apart from and prior to works. This interpretation would tie Gen 15:6 with 12:1-4 – but on which grounds[920]?

In each case, Paul's interpretation and conclusions would be entirely new and radically different compared to Jewish thought.[921] Acknowledging the specific communicative and argumentative situation of his letter, in which persuasion and conviction are more called for than rejection and conflict,[922] one has to identify more accurately Paul's distinctive perspective and look for events in Abraham's life that might explain the label "ungodly," i.e., situations in which he was or became ἀσεβής in moral and/or religious terms[923]: Was it his behavior towards Sarah (Gen 12:10-20; 20:1-18), Hagar and Ishmael (Gen 21:8-21), his questioning objections with

---

[917] On the problem of Rom 4:5 in relation to biblical-Jewish tradition, see especially S. Kreuzer 2002; also E. Adams 1997, 55-65.

[918] Cf. U. Wilckens 1978, 210, 263; H. Merklein 1996, 125f.

[919] See, for instance, the passages referred to in K. Berger 1972, 373; also below note 936)

[920] Cf., e.g., D. Zeller 1985, 100; J.D.G. Dunn 1988, 205; A.T. Lincoln 1992, 173; E. Adams 1997; S.J. Gathercole 2002, 243; M. Cranford 1995, 82n.45: "The term 'ungodly' must refer ... to his [*sc.* Abraham's] status as an uncircumcised Gentile."

[921] P. Stuhlmacher (1989, 68) however illuminates Paul's argumentation from the perspective of biblical theology, pointing to a development reaching from the "Book of the Covenant" to Second Temple Judaism texts: While Ex 23:7 states categorically that God does not justify the ungodly (ἀσεβής; cf. G. Schrenk 1935, 219; S. Westerholm 2004, 264f.n.7), Ezekiel stresses that God does not have any pleasure in the death of the wicked (ἄνομος, Ezek 18:23); moreover, it is the ungodly and wicked who plead for mercy in God's judgment (cf. Psalm 51; Dan 9:18-27; 2Esdr 8,35-36; 1QS 11,11-12). With a similar intention, O. Hofius finds the "Sache" of the *iustificatio impii* anticipated in Hosea, Jeremiah and Deutero-Isaiah (1987, 91-100), but also in the Yahwist (Gen 12:1-3) (100-103). See also S.J. Gathercole 2004, 166. – Paul's application of this idea to Abraham, however, remains revolutionary.

[922] Cf. with regard to Romans 4, S. Kreuzer 2002, 208, 210, 211. See also above chapter V.A.II.

[923] Cf. also the summary in K. Haacker 1999, 102.

regard to God's promise (Gen 15:2-3.8), or his laughing (Gen 17:17) – possibly also his lack of *pietas* when he broke with his religious family traditions, left his kindred, and got estranged from his paternal land (Gen 12:1.4-5)[924]? Or did Paul equate "ungodly" with "uncircumcised," in which case Abraham would be described as Gentile before his justification?

Obviously, a consideration of the pragmatics and logic of text and context is essential for understanding Paul's intention. Only the wider framework of Paul's argument, the horizon of the eschatological division of time through πίστις Χριστοῦ (Rom 3:21-22), is able to illuminate the background and foundation of his depiction of the patriarch: Abraham remained in the sphere of ungodliness (1:18-3:20), as long as faith did not govern his life, as long as he had not lived under the domain of faith; consequently, he is still outside the realm of God's righteousness through faith.[925] Paul even stretches his thought back to the beginning of his letter: There, Gentiles are accused of "ungodliness," which equals unrighteousness (ἀδικία), suppressing the truth of God's faithfulness (1:18), ignorance towards God the creator and his power (1:20), and the rejection to give glory to God (1:21). We have already reflected on "Jacob's ungodliness" (cf. 11:26),[926] consisting in disputing the truth of God's words (ἀπιστία) and standing iniquitously before God (ἀδικία) (3:1-8).[927] Hence, all have sinned and are apart from faith, Gentiles and Jews, and their sinfulness and ungodliness is not merely a passive being apart from God, but an active neglect of his godliness. In and through faith, the "happy exchange" happens: The believer receives a righteous standing before God through his word of creation[928] (4:5) and hears and believes the truth of God's promissional and creative word in order to give glory (δόξα) to him (4:20). The situation of faith then is not only a passive being on the side of God, but an active involvement for his purpose. God returns the glorious mode of being (δόξα) that Adam

---

[924] Cf. K. Haacker 1999, 102, with reference to some texts (Philo, *Her* 25-26; *GenR* 39,7) which show awareness of this ethical problem. Since Abraham's exodus took place on God's command, it is however hardly conceivable that this act would justify the label "ungodly."

[925] Later, we will deal with the question of the "Christology" of Abraham's faith. See below chapter VI.A.VI.

[926] See above chapter V.B.II.2. The noun ἀσέβεια occurs twice in Paul: Rom 1:18 and 11:26, once denoting Gentile ungodliness, once Israel's ungodliness.

[927] While E. Adams concentrates on the "structural pattern of contrast between Abraham and the rebellious Gentiles" (1997, 54), one has to take into account the contrast between the rebellious Jews and Abraham as well.

[928] Cf. E. Käsemann 1980, 106.

had in paradise (3:23) and that was lost through sin[929] to the one who believe and so realizes what he had envisioned from creation.[930]

Consequently, ungodliness needs to be conceived of as anthropological-ontological term, denoting one's existence and being apart from God's righteousness. Here, the question: "Did Abraham really commit sins?" is not as much in view as his being in the general, "natural-human" state of weakness, ungodliness, and sinfulness (cf. 5:6.8).[931] When Paul quotes Gen 15:6a, "and Abraham believed," he thinks of ἐπίστευσεν (aorist) as the act of coming to faith, as the transition from the sphere of unbelief (ἀπιστία, cf. Rom 3:3) and ungodliness (ἀσέβεια) into the sphere of faith, as portrayed in 3:21-26, the first encounter with the reality of faith.[932] Therefore, the aorist is understood as inchoative or ingressive.[933]

Elsewhere, Paul explains *vice versa* that God's new reality defined by faith entered the sphere of ungodliness, for Christ died for us ungodly, when we still were weak and sinners (5:6.8[934]), but from Abraham's perspective (which Paul assumes here) faith is his step into this new reality.

While the state of ungodliness characterizes universally all apart from faith, we can ask: Where is such a "change of spheres" located specifically in Abraham's biography? According to the order of Genesis, Abraham's "transitus" is his exit from paganism, taking place upon God's call to leave his home country (Genesis 12); hence, according to the context of the narrative, as it presents itself to us, in Genesis 15 he is not justified as ungodly, but rather as one who had proved his trust and obedience on several occasions.[935] However, as pointed out above, there is not only a wide-

---

[929] Cf. P. Stuhlmacher 1975, 134.

[930] Cf. O. Hofius 1996, 81. With the eschatological resurrection of the dead this δόξα will be given to those justified through faith (cf. Rom 5:1-2; see also Rom 8:17-18; 1Cor 2:7; 15:43; 2Cor 3:18; Phil 3:20-21; 1Thess 2:12).

[931] Cf. F. Hahn 1971, 102n.51 (Abraham as prototype of all human beings having no access to God by nature).

[932] Cf. H. Binder 1968, 64.

[933] K. Haacker enumerates occurrences of the inchoative/ingressive aorist in Acts (2:44[*v.l.*]; 4:4.32; 8:12.13; 9:42; 11:17.21; 13:12.48; 14:1; 15:7; 16:31; 17:12.34; 18:8; 19:2.4) and in the letters (Rom 10:14; 13:11; 1Cor 3:5; 15:2.11; Gal 2:16; Eph 1:13; 2Thess 1:10; Heb 4:3; 11:16; 1John 3:23).

[934] As believers we confess that Christ has died for us in the state of our being ἀσεβεῖς, while we were still weak (Rom 5:6), i.e., while we were still sinners (5:8). See also E. Lohse 2003, 149.

[935] See the references to H. Gunkel (1910, 180) and R.W.L. Moberly (1990, 118f.) and the discussion of this issue above pages 139f. That Abraham's acts of obedience, according to the order in Genesis, partly precede the first mention of faith is oftentimes neglected in the interpretation of our passage. Cf. F.F. Bruce 1963, 110: "Abraham's good works, his obedience to the divine commandments, were the fruit of his unquestioning

spread Jewish tradition of Abraham turning from paganism to the true God,[936] but also the idea that the events reported in Genesis 15 happened chronologically before Abraham's migration from Haran, inspired by the differences of the time spans in Gen 15:13 (400 years) and Ex 12:40 (430 years).[937] Paul seems to have been aware of such Jewish numerical calculations and in particular of the combination of Gen 15:13 and Ex 12:40[938]: In Gal 3:17[939] he relates the 430 years to the time span between promise and law, i.e., between Abraham and Moses, an inference which cannot be deduced from Ex 12:40 alone.

As a consequence, Paul has in mind Abraham's initial contact with and step into the realm of faith, as Gentile and insofar as "ungodly." To be sure, it is God who entered the world of ungodliness by giving his promise and opening up the possibility of faith for Abraham without requiring any preconditions. Paul is concerned with the *activitas dei*, God's turning to humankind, in a global, eschatological sense (δικαιοσύνη θεοῦ πεφανέρωται, Rom 3:21), as well as in an existential and individual sense (ὁ δικαιῶν τὸν ἀσεβῆ, 4:5). The appropriate reaction of Abraham – "and he came to faith" – marks his departure from ungodliness into faith and his new existence outside of his former milieu.[940] In 4:5 Paul uses the unusual construction πιστεύειν ἐπί (with accusative),[941] whose meaning correlates to the inchoative connotation of the aorist ἐπίστευσεν (4:3),[942] but also gives the contents and direction of faith[943]: God, who is confessed as the

---

faith in God; had he not first believed the promises of God he would never have conducted his life from then on in the light of what he knew of God's will."

[936] E. Adams gathers passages from Jewish texts which interpret Gen 11:27-12:9 as Abraham's rejection of idolatry and turning to the creator God (*Jub* 11,16-17; 12,1-21; Philo, *Virt* 211-216; *Abr* 68-72; *Her* 97-99; Josephus, *Ant* 1,155-156; *ApcAbr* 7,10-12) (1997, 55-59), but remains vague as for Paul's connecting this Genesis passage with Gen 15:6: "Paul sees a deep inner resonance between these two episodes" (60f.n.40; "Abraham's response to God's call to leave Mesopotamia ... as a nascent expression of the faith which God would subsequently account to the patriarch as righteousness"). See also S.J.D. Cohen 1999, 151.

[937] See above chapter III.E.I.

[938] Cf. S. Kreuzer 2002, 218f.

[939] Cf. on this verse D. Lührmann 1988.

[940] Cf. S. Kreuzer 2002, 219.

[941] Cf. Wis 12,2 (cf. C.A. Keller 1970, 15). The only other Pauline occurrence is in Rom 4:24 (cf. also Acts 22:19). With an indirect object, πιστεύειν ἐπί occurs for instance in Isa 28:16, which Paul quotes in Rom 9:33; 10:11.

[942] Cf. J. Jeremias 1970, 53 ("Bekehrung"; "Glaubensentschluss"); A. von Dobbeler 1987, 134.

[943] Cf. E. Lohse 2003, 149.

God who justifies the ungodly,[944] and whose promissory and creative word is true.

In sum, now, it is clear what Paul intended through the conditional clause in the introduction to the chapter: Abraham cannot have had works, he cannot have been justified on the grounds of works, and he has no reason of boasting by virtue of justification by works. He reduces the whole system of thought to absurdity by deconstructing the sense of the very precondition.

d) Romans 4:6-8: An Additional, Supporting Text LXX Psalm 31:1-2

Above we found Paul using the exegetical device of the *gezerah shavah* (λογίζεσθαι) when he introduced LXX Ps 31:1-2 into his explication as supporting passage from Scripture.[945] The quote follows literally the text of the Septuagint. One has to ask now if this move is – to use J. Jeremias's words – great and with conquering simplicity[946] or if it is forced and unconvincing, as for instance G. Klein thinks.[947] Coming from his foundational authoritative text, Gen 15:6, an adequate parallel had to fulfill the following criteria: (1) Of course, the keyword connection has to be expressive and meaningful; (2) also, there has to be a particular syntax: God is the (implied) subject, a person's act or attitude is "counted," and the person is existentially affected by the declarative, creative act of "counting"[948]; (3) finally, human works cannot be the decisive factor of God's act.

As the term in question occurs around 120 times in the Septuagint, Paul theoretically had at his disposal a vast number of verses; but already the

---

[944] Cf. E. Käsemann 1980, 106. – According to R. Bultmann the expression follows the ἐλπίζειν ἐπί (1959, 212n.273).

[945] On the use and meaning of חשב in the Masoretic Text of Ps 32:2, see above pages 123f. – The mention of these Psalm-verses in Rom 4:6-8 receives surprisingly little attention, both in commentaries as well as in monographs dealing *inter alia* with Romans 4. U. Wilckens's monumental commentary, for instance, dedicates a mere nine lines to the exegesis of this passage (1978, 263), while K. Kertelge does not even make explicit mention of the Psalm-verse (1971).

[946] J. Jeremias 1970, 53 ("der grossartige Analogieschluss"; "mit bezwingender Schlichtheit"). But taking Phil 1:13-17; 2Tim 1:17; 4:16 as a clue, Jeremias also concludes that despite its brilliance, the Pauline argument in Romans 4 could not convince the Roman Jewish-Christians and ultimately remained unsuccessful (58).

[947] Cf. G. Klein 1963, 152 ("Gewaltsamkeit"). Also J.-N. Aletti asks the question of the adequacy of the citation and adds the following three observations: (1) There are around 120 occurrences of the verb λογίζεσθαι in the Septuagint, i.e., why would Paul chose LXX Ps 31:2; (2) the tense does not match; (3) in Gen 15:6, the verb is used positively, in LXX Ps 31:2 negatively (2003, 310). See however Aletti's positive evaluation of Paul's *gezerah shavah* (325).

[948] I.e., God counts something to someone.

second criterion reduces the potential parallels greatly to eight or six re-spectively in number.[949] The implementation of the third restriction leaves Paul with but one adequate, unique parallel,[950] namely, LXX Ps 31:2.[951] Apart from Gen 15:6, only here, it is *not* human works, or rather negative human works (sins),[952] that lie at the basis of God's judgment.[953] If works were decisive, this would lead to fatal consequences and torments (cf. LXX Ps 31:10).

Nevertheless, the text that suggests itself to Paul as only unique and adequate parallel does not in fact speak of "justification apart from works" in a direct sense. But it is precisely these notions that Paul seeks to extract from his quote, as his introductory statement shows (Rom 4:6). The paral-lelism between 4:6 (Paul's introduction) and 4:8 (LXX Ps 31:2) proves this: To Paul χωρὶς ἔργων is equivalent to ἁμαρτία and λογίζεσθαι δι-καιοσύνην correlates to μὴ λογίζεσθαι ἁμαρτίαν.

Obviously, no text in the Old Testament would match completely Paul's argumentative goal and thus he had to take recourse to an indirect proof for his thesis of "justification without works." But even though the Old Tes-tament nowhere strictly equates forgiveness with justification, there are several hints towards the correlation of these concepts,[954] not to mention the obvious association between the removal of the fatal distance to God (forgiveness of sin) and the establishment of a right relationship with him (justification).[955]

---

[949] Cf. J.-N. Aletti 2003, 311f. and the table presented above page 119: LXX Lev 7:18; 17:4; Num 18:27.30; Ps 31:2; 105:31; Job 31:28; 1Macc 2,52. LXX Ps 105:31 and 1Macc 2,52 can be left aside, since they are dependent on Gen 15:6; Job 31:28 is some-what unusual as it does not have the Hebrew חשׁב in its *Vorlage*, but rather פלל.

[950] Cf. J.-N. Aletti 2003, 312 ("[un] rapport unique ... entre deux passages des Écritu-res"). Hence, Paul's rhetorical move is grounded on sound syntactical and semantic con-siderations (no "anarchie sémantique"). "Bref, nonobstant les différences, les caractéris-tiques formelles de l'exégèse faite par Paul en Rm 4,1-8 appartiennent bien à celles des G[ezerah]S[hawah]" (313).

[951] Another striking λογίζεσθαι-occurrence, 2Sam 19:20, also contains the notion of forgiveness and grace, but it reports about human affairs (see above pages 122f.).

[952] Cf. LXX Ps 31:1.2.5 (ἁμαρτία); 31:10 (ἁμαρτωλός). The Psalm obviously refers to David's committing adultery with Bathsheba and the murder of her husband Uriah, the Hittite (cf. 2Samuel 11) (cf. T.R. Schreiner 1998, 219).

[953] Presupposing Gen 15:6 and the opposition of ἐργάζειν and μὴ ἐργάζειν (Rom 4:5) as matrix, Paul will not interpret LXX Ps 31:2 in conformity with related passages such as Lev 7:18; 17:4; Num 18:27.30, as those take human works as a basis for God's act of counting.

[954] Cf. Ex 34:7: καὶ δικαιοσύνην διατηρῶν καὶ ποιῶν ἔλεος εἰς χιλιάδας ἀφαιρῶν ἀνομίας καὶ ἀδικίας καὶ ἁμαρτίας (cf. Ezek 3:20; 18:24; 33:14-16).

[955] In Rom 5:21; 6:13.16.18.20; 8:10; 1Cor 5:21 Paul contrasts righteousness and sin (cf. Rom 3:20; 6:7; Gal 2:17), while in Rom 14:23; 1Cor 15:17; Gal 3:22 he states an opposition of faith and sin. See however K. Stendahl's thoughts on the theme "justifica-

David, the author of the Psalm, considers his personal experiences as a lawless and ungodly man,[956] who however upon confession of his sins was forgiven,[957] as typical and turns them into a general phrase (31:1-2). Therefore, Paul can use David as type for those who are under the reality of the law, who are in the covenant, but who are in fact without works (χωρὶς ἔργων) and find themselves cut off from the law and from God.[958] Yet even they will be forgiven through their trusting and throwing themselves unto God's mercy, since God's steadfast love is unconditional; it surrounds those who trust him.[959] But now, even though David clearly represents primarily those under the law, the general conclusion about God's merciful dealing comprises also non-Jews: Characteristically, they are labeled "lawless,"[960] "ungodly,"[961] and "sinners,"[962] which are precisely the terms that David attributes to himself. Hence, there is no distinction between Jews and Gentiles (cf. Rom 3:22-23; 10:12); they all have sinned, and God shows no partiality, whether they have sinned apart from the law or under the law (cf. 2:11-12).[963]

One might wonder why Paul considered it necessary to quote LXX Ps 31:1, even though 31:2 could have sufficed to establish the *gezerah shavah*

---

tion rather than forgiveness" which builds on the general "spectacular" absence of the notion of forgiveness in Paul (1976, 23). – On the relationship between faith and forgiveness in Jesus' teaching, see Mk 2:5par (cf. Acts 26:18); Jesus also linked closely faith and salvation (see especially in Luke's gospel, Lk 7:50; 8:48; 17:19; 18:42: ἡ πίστις σου σέσωκέν σε), which resonates in Paul's programmatic statement Rom 1:16 (cf. especially M.W. Yeung 2002). Thus, faith, forgiveness, salvation, and justification all belong to the same complex of ideas.

[956] Cf. LXX Ps 31:1.5 (ἀνομία); 31:5 (ἀσέβεια).

[957] O. Michel rightly states that for Paul all depends on the event of forgiveness, not on the act of confession as in the Psalm itself (1978, 165n.11). – In discussion with J. Jeremias on Rom 4:5, J. Cambier makes a similar point: "c'est l'impie, – et pas en tant que priant, – que Dieu justifie" (1970, 63).

[958] Cf. the *a-privativum* in both ἀνομία and ἀσέβεια.

[959] Cf. LXX Ps 31:10: "Steadfast love surrounds those who trust in Yahweh." For "to trust in Yahweh" the Greek reads ἐλπίζειν ἐπὶ κύριον, which is a translation of the Hebrew בֹטֵחַ בַּיהוָה (cf. A. Weiser's considerations on the relationship between בטח and אמן, 1959, 191-193). As mentioned, R. Bultmann sees a parallel between ἐλπίζειν ἐπί and πιστεύειν ἐπί (Rom 4:5) (1959, 212n.273).

[960] Cf. LXX Ps 13:4; 58:6; Ezek 44:7; 1Macc 3,20 (referred to in J.-N. Aletti 2003, 315n.24, 320f.n.37).

[961] Cf. Deut 9:4-5. In *Ant* 20,45 Josephus calls the state of "not-being-circumcised" ἀσέβεια.

[962] Cf. Ps 9:18; Sir 16,8-9; 1Macc 1,34; 2,44.48; 2Macc 6,14; Gal 2:15 (see J.D.G. Dunn 1988, 206; J.-N. Aletti 2003, 320f.n.37).

[963] Cf. the generic ἄνθρωπος (Rom 4:6) and ἀνήρ (4:8).

and to prove his point. Several answers are conceivable[964]: The explicit notion of "forgiveness" was so crucial for him in this context that he could not leave the verse unmentioned. Possibly, in case already at the time of Paul Ps 32:1 was associated with the Day of Atonement,[965] he wanted to introduce the idea of atonement and establish a close connection to Rom 3:25.[966] On that day, atonement was effected and all sin extinguished; for post-exilic Judaism the importance of this day can hardly be overrated.[967] Furthermore, the significant christological conclusion of the Abraham-chapter (4:24-25) also incorporates the terminology of justification and (annihilation of) transgressions.[968]

It is worth mentioning that the word for "sin," ἁμαρτία, appears in the plural in LXX Ps 31:1 and in the singular in 31:2. Paul decided to include the traditional plural use of the term, even though in his own formulations he consistently chooses the singular.[969] As mentioned before, through the singular Paul expresses the character of sin as power, which predetermines both a person's being and doing, whereby its power is both evident in and manifested by sinful deeds. In other words, this trans-subjective reality transfers its power to the individual human being both in "qualitative" and "quantitative" terms. As noted, this distinction is strongly reminiscent of the two aspects of "faith," which described faith as both salvation-historical force and individual participation in it.[970] Both concepts, πίστις and ἁμαρτία, connote on the one hand a reality that transcends the perception of subjectivity and evades human influence, and on the other hand a conscious, active, and existential appropriation of that reality.

For Paul, who through such differentiations shaped a new conception of these entities compared to contemporary Jewish theology,[971] "sin" is therefore the radically other side of "faith"; sin is related to the revelation of God's wrath (Rom 1:18-3:20) as faith is related to the revelation of God's righteousness (3:21-4:25); sin is the sphere in which the sinner is impris-

---

[964] In any case it is wrong to think that "poor Paul ... had to quote Psalm 32:1" and hence to introduce the concept of forgiveness (against K. Stendahl 1976, 23). Neither the first Psalm-verse nor the *gezerah shavah* are indispensable for his argument.

[965] Cf. O. Michel 1978, 165n.11, referring to *Yoma* 86b and *PesiqRab* 45 (185b, 186a). Also C.E.B. Cranfield 1975, 234f.n.4.

[966] The idea of forgiveness binds Rom 4:7-8 to 3:25 (cf. M. Neubrand 1997, 214).

[967] Cf. P. Stuhlmacher 1975, 124n.37.

[968] There, Paul uses the term παραπτώματα.

[969] Many interpreters stress the "non-Pauline" language in this context (cf., e.g., E. Käsemann 1980, 107; E. Lohse 2003, 150), but fail to give an explanation for this uncommon use of ἁμαρτία in the plural, except that it is traditional usage.

[970] Cf. again E. Lohmeyer's distinction of faith as force and deed and the like distinction regarding sin (1929, 138f.). See above chapter V.B.II.1 and pages 304f.

[971] Cf. H. Conzelmann 1967, 217, with regard to ἁμαρτία.

oned and forced to do sin as faith is the sphere into which the believer is released and freed to believe. Coming back to the distinction between a "qualitative" and a "quantitative" understanding of sin,[972] one can conclude that both poles are integrated into one conception governed by a certain ontology: There, both are true: We do what we are,[973] and we are what we do.[974] Our sinful being correlates to our doing sins, even to the acutely sinful effort of achieving own righteousness, while on the other hand our factual sinful works are innately linked to our status as sinful human beings.[975]

Yet this specific ontology is grounded in Paul's Christology: Above all, it is not our being that determines our acts, nor our acts that determine our being, but God's act in Christ determines the reality in which our being and doing takes place. For Paul, the fact of the coming of Christ (Gal 4:4), the coming of faith (3:23) itself is decisive; a new order of the world and a new lordship has been established through πίστις Χριστοῦ (Rom 3:21-22). Outside of this new reality, sin rules, determining both the quality of humans and their factual conduct (1:18-3:20). On the other hand, being embraced by faith creates new qualitative preconditions and a factual living in faith. Both concepts imply an inescapable force and responsible acts.

Is it not plausible that Paul had both of these aspects of "sin(s)" in view when he was quoting LXX Ps 31:1-2? Blessed is the one, whose sinful, unlawful deeds have been done away with; blessed is the one to whom God does not count the fact that his being and doing belonged to the sphere of sin.[976] Hence, God saves and forgives by setting free the person from the power exercised by sin.[977]

In sum, Paul accomplishes an ingenious and brilliant, but at the same time highly provocative move through his *gezerah shavah*: The connection of LXX Gen 15:6 and Ps 31:1-2 is by no means an arbitrary or forced harmonization of distant ideas, but a unique and powerful support of his ar-

---

[972] Cf. again J. Lambrecht 1986, 243f.

[973] Cf. G. Klein 1984, 71; see also H. Conzelmann 1967, 217; O. Hofius 1987, 80f.

[974] Cf. H. Merklein 1996, 147.

[975] The correlation of "act" and "being" is also pointed out by O. Hofius 1993, 156: "Seit Adam und von Adam her sind ausnahmslos *alle* Menschen, Juden wie Heiden, unentrinnbar der Sünde verfallen, und zwar nicht bloß in ihrem bösen *Tun*, sondern ganz umfassend in ihrem gottfernen und gottfeindlichen *Sein*. Sie sind ἀσεβεῖς – 'Gottlose'." To be sure, Hofius considers the sinful *being* as the more comprehensive and profound expression of the human dilemma. Similarly, H. Weder 1985, 331.

[976] This conclusion is reached by taking into account Paul's overall view of sin, while the immediate and original context suggests regarding ἁμαρτία as deed (O. Hofius 1996, 69n.31), referring back to the plural ἁμαρτίαι, which is parallel to ἀνομίαι (*parallelismus membrorum*) and denotes transgressions of the law (90).

[977] Cf. R. Bultmann 1958, 287; E. Käsemann 1980, 107.

gumentation based on formal and contextual criteria: (1) As we have seen, out of the wide range of λογίζεσθαι-occurrences in the Septuagint, only LXX Ps 31:2 concurs meaningfully with Paul's argumentative intentions. Also, the two quotations describe what God *does* count and what God *does not* count, and hence embrace descriptively God's action from both ends. (2) Another intriguing feature of Paul's *gezerah shavah* is that it features both, Abraham, the first patriarch and Israel's figure of identification, and David, the Messianic king and image for Israel's strength and unity.[978] Thereby, Paul makes use of a typically Jewish "remembrance" motif, which we also encountered in Sirach 44, 4QMMT, and 1Maccabees 2.[979] At the same time, appealing to Abraham and David enables Paul to draw on authoritative verses representing the Scripture as a whole[980]: Both Torah and Ketubim have their say. (3) Paul accomplishes to incorporate yet another characteristic of a *gezerah shavah*, namely to apply one principle to two different situations[981]: Abraham is first and foremost the representative of the uncircumcised, who are not (yet) under the law, while David's situation is primarily that of the circumcised who are under the law. But Paul levels out these categorical differences, first by generalizing the Genesis quote on Abraham in Rom 4:4-5, then by applying the situation of David to all humans in 4:6. For Paul – and this is indeed revolutionary – God's dealing with humankind is no longer a matter of Jew or non-Jew.

Paul shows that neither Abraham nor David have anything to present to God but are totally dependent on God's activity: Their existence takes place outside of any relationship with God (ἀσέβεια), apart from the law (ἀνομία) and from works (χωρὶς ἔργων), and is marked by the dominion of sin (ἀμαρτία). From God's perspective this means damnation, non-existence, death (5:12-21). The provocation of this view lies in its contrast to Jewish interpretation according to which Abraham fulfilled the (still unwritten) Torah perfectly and David likewise accomplished deeds of righteousness.[982] Nevertheless, for Paul both are equally *typoi* for all humans prior to and apart from faith; all are separated from God, ungodly sinners. This "spatial" distance to God can only be bridged by God himself, who elects prior to any deeds[983] and discloses, in a salvation-historical

---

[978] David functions more as a witness to God's dealing with Abraham rather than as an autonomous part of the argumentation (cf. E. Käsemann 1980, 107).

[979] Cf. S.J. Gathercole 2002, 233. See above page 214.

[980] Cf. E. Käsemann 1980, 100.

[981] Cf. J.-N. Aletti 2003, 313.

[982] Cf. 4QMMT C 24-25; Sir 49,4.

[983] Cf. Rom 9:11: Isaac's election happened prior to any deeds, even before his birth; even he has been chosen "apart from the law," just as Abraham and David (cf. C.E.B. Cranfield 1991, 97). – On the notion of election and its reference to God's creative call from non-existence into existence, see below pages 376f. on Rom 4:17.

sense, the possibility for faith, enabling an individual appropriation of it. In and through faith the fatal distance to God is removed (forgiveness of sin) and a salvific relationship with God established (justification).

5. Romans 4:9-21

a) Romans 4:9-12: Πίστις in the Antithesis of Circumcision and Uncircumcision

(a) Circumcision as Seal of Faith-Righteousness

In evaluating Paul's *gezerah shavah* we had to anticipate parts of his further argumentation, to which we turn now. In order for his logic to be intelligible, the apostle has to further prove that God's acceptance of the ungodly Abraham is principally equivalent to his having mercy with the sinner David.[984] Therefore, after illuminating the basic quote Gen 15:6 by means of the Psalm-verses, he reverses the argumentative line of thought and applies Ps 32:1-2 to the story of Abraham: On whom is the blessedness pronounced? These verses prove remarkable, for Paul has to refute the necessity of circumcision for salvation, even though he cannot refute that Abraham received and followed the command of circumcision.[985]

To what extent then are David's and Abraham's situations compatible? According to Jewish conviction, not being circumcised is equivalent to being a sinner, which connects the uncircumcised Abraham with the sinner David on an outward level. Both, Abraham and David also find themselves in total dependence on God, for none is able to contribute anything to his right standing before God, but is dependent on God's act of justification and forgiveness. Hence, their respective predicament and its solution correspond in the fundamental points.[986]

By his exegetical conclusions, Paul accomplishes his deep concern of showing that the way Abraham received righteousness not only pertains to the situation of Jewish believers, but also of Gentile believers.[987] Paul even steers towards the indeed striking inference that the situation of the patriarch, the figure of identification of the Jews, relates to Gentile-Christians in the first place, since it is his faith in the state of uncircumcision that was

---

[984] Cf. A.T. Hanson 1974, 52-66, on "Abraham the justified sinner."

[985] Cf. K. Haacker 1999, 103. Contrast, however, Galatians 3, where Paul omits any reference to Abraham's circumcision, "in order to underline the sole criterion of faith" (J.M.G. Barclay 1988, 87).

[986] Hence the conclusion of J.-N. Aletti (2003, 322): "Les situations décrites respectivement en Gn 15,6 et Ps 31[32],1-2 sont donc bien semblables ... La G[ezerah]S[hawah] a donc bien fait son travail."

[987] See P. Billerbeck 1926, 203, for a rabbinic passage that refers Ps 32:1 exclusively to Israel, to the circumcised.

counted to him as righteousness.[988] Hence, Paul asks: What was Abraham's situation when faith was counted to him as righteousness? All have to agree: He was still uncircumcised, for the simple and obvious fact that Genesis 15 precedes Genesis 17; in line with the biblical presuppositions, therefore, one can deduce that faith comes before circumcision.[989] Throughout the chapter, Paul will keep in mind and maintain this temporal interval, which is indispensable for his case of the material priority of faith and the ensuing interpretation of circumcision.[990]

Now, in Rom 4:11, the function of Abraham shifts from being a theme and means of a proof to being a historical subject. As for Paul's talk of how Abraham received circumcision, it is significant that he avoids the reference to the covenant, when he names the sign (σημεῖον) of circumcision[991] the "seal of faith-righteousness (σφραγὶς τῆς δικαιοσύνης τῆς πίστεως)"[992]; for Gen 17:11 reads that circumcision is the sign of the covenant (σημεῖον διαθήκης).[993] Hence, Paul retains the sign-character of circumcision, but intentionally omits the reference to the covenant. This is no meaningless omission, and claims such as: In Romans 4 "Paul concentrates on the covenant as God's *modus operandi*,"[994] require at least some speci-

---

[988] Cf. E. Adams 1997, 63; E. Lohse 2003, 151; J.-N. Aletti 2003, 323f.: "Gn 15,6 reste ainsi le modèle de l'expérience proposée aux ethnico-chrétiens." Paul's goal is not to "establish a principle of precedence of the uncircumcized," but to establish a principle of precedence of faith, i.e., the equality of Jewish and Gentile believers (H. Boers 1971, 88f.).

[989] According to rabbinic interpretation the temporal gap between the covenants of Genesis 15 and 17 consists of several decades (cf. P. Billerbeck 1926, 203).

[990] Cf. U. Luz 1968, 182.

[991] The genitive σημεῖον περιτομῆς should be understood as "genitive of ... identity: the sign consists in circumcision" (C.E.B. Cranfield 1975, 236; cf. J. Lambrecht 1979, 9n.22; M. Neubrand 1997, 221n.16).

[992] On the depiction of the circumcision as σφραγίς, see K. Haacker 1999, 104, who also refers to the (partly pre-Pauline) parallels given in D. Flusser/S. Safrai 1979. Also C.E.B. Cranfield (1975, 236) and O. Michel (1978, 166n.6) think that this usage predates Paul, while others prefer a later date (cf., e.g., D.J. Moo 1996, 268f.). – Whether the use of σφραγίς in Rom 4:11 implies in a proleptic sense Christian baptism, as for instance U. Wilckens suggests (1978, 266f.; cf. G. Klein 1963, 154f.; O. Cullmann 1965, 237f. with n.1; J. Roloff 1990, 245n.32) with reference to mid-second century texts (especially *Hermas*), can be left undiscussed here (cf. the careful weighing of the data in E. Käsemann 1980, 108f.; against a baptismal allusion, see, e.g., E. Lohse 2003, 152).

[993] The terms ἀκροβυστία, περιτομή, and σημεῖον all derive from Genesis 17.

[994] R. Holst 1997, 325; cf. W.J. Dumbrell 1992, 101n.23. The omission of the covenant in Rom 4:11, but also, more generally, "its peripheral character in his [*sc.* Paul's] epistles" (S. Westerholm 2004, 287n.60) weakens the foundations of those interpreters who consider the covenant-motif as *the* central motif in Paul's theology as a whole.

fication.[995] Among those who deal with this issue one finds a large spectrum of solutions suggested: Some argue radically that since the old covenant is in discontinuity with the Christ-event, Paul had to eliminate forcefully and thoroughly the notion of the covenant in this context.[996] Or, less
strongly, Paul might have "identified the covenant too much with the law
and insinuates that God's true covenant was made with people of faith."[997]
The least theology-laden answer thinks that from a rhetorical-
argumentative reasoning the covenant was simply not in view for Paul, as
his objective has been circumcision.[998]

However, rather than wrestling with the absence of the notion of the
covenant, it appears more constructive to ask positively for Paul's actual
statements and for their material weight and their consequences. In any
case, "Paul's decision to connect the signatory value of circumcision with
'the righteousness of faith' ... is emphatic."[999] What does Paul mean with
the phrase δικαιοσύνη (τῆς) πίστεως (cf. 4:13)? Since the term "seal" in
the figurative sense is connected to the idea of "a visible mark of ownership,"[1000] which confirms and authenticates the affiliation to or being in a
certain (divinely instituted) power or authority,[1001] one has to probe, how
far a one-sided "personalized" or "individualized" understanding of faith-
righteousness is appropriate. Commonly, translations and commentaries
either speak of *his* faith[1002] or of *his* righteousness that he had by faith,[1003]

---

[995] The term διαθήκη appears numerous times in the two Genesis-chapters relevant in
this context: Gen 15:18; Gen 17:2.4.7.9.10.11.13.14.19.21 – but not in the whole chapter
Romans 4 (cf. K. Berger 1966, 67).

[996] G. Klein 1963, 154: "Das ist eine sehr gewaltsame, völlig analogielose Usurpation
des vorgegebenen alttestamentlichen Textes." Less polemically E. Käsemann 1980, 108:
The notion of the covenant is not useful in the present context.

[997] J.A. Fitzmyer 1993, 381.

[998] U. Wilckens 1964, 62n.13 (in reaction to G. Klein). Cf. M. Neubrand 1997, 222:
Paul's argumentative goal is the election from the peoples *not* to be integrated into the
covenant with Israel (Neubrand provides no positive explanation why "covenant" is replaced by "faith-righteousness"). However, Paul rather steers towards a redefinition of
the covenant in terms of faith, towards a redefinition of the people of Israel. See further
D. Zeller 1985, 101; M. Theobald 1999, 321.

[999] D.J. Moo 1996, 268.

[1000] J.D.G. Dunn 1998, 330.

[1001] In 1Cor 9:2, the only other occurrence of σφραγίς in Paul's letters, the Corinthians
are said to be the seal of Paul's apostleship, i.e., they confirm the authority and power of
his apostleship, which he has received from "our Lord Jesus Christ" (Rom 1:4-5). In Eph
1:13 the idea of "being marked with a seal" signifies the believers' being in the domain
of the Holy Spirit (cf. also 2Cor 1:21-22).

[1002] Cf. the translation of M. Luther: "... den Glauben, den er hatte."

[1003] Cf. NRSV: "... a seal of the righteousness that he had by faith while he was still
uncircumcised."

before he was circumcised[1004] – though modifiers such as personal pronouns are absent. Clearly, Abraham's circumcision functions as "a pointer to the reality of that which it signifies,"[1005] but does it signify a concrete-existential or a salvation-historical reality? The context makes one assume that the expression in question oscillates between the two poles: On the one hand, the divinely instituted entity of "faith-righteousness" is documented and verified through the ritual of circumcision, while on the other hand one thinks of the transference and appropriation of this reality with regard to Abraham who receives the outward sign of circumcision to confirm his righteous status. The patriarch belongs fully to faith-righteousness, and faith-righteousness belongs fully to Abraham. And Paul's point is that this is true *prior* to circumcision, as the order of Genesis 15 and 17 duly demonstrates. In the subsequent argumentation, in Rom 4:13, the expression δικαιοσύνη (τῆς) πίστεως will recur, but there it primarily takes the more comprehensive meaning of a manifestation within the framework of God's plan of salvation.

For Paul, also "circumcision" and "uncircumcision" in their association with faith imply more than merely a physical procedure or circumstance: Just as Abraham's entrance and transition into faith-righteousness happened prior to his circumcision, faith-righteousness itself has its salvation-historical place in the realm of uncircumcision, i.e., χωρὶς νόμου.[1006] Hence, circumcision – in a certain sense *typos* of the law[1007] – confirms, documents, and authenticates faith-righteousness as a valuable,[1008] visible sign, but does not constitute or create faith-righteousness by obtaining an independent or autonomous value.[1009] Rather, the relationship of circumcision to faith-righteousness is that of total dependence; circumcision is temporally and materially secondary, and it has a relative character.[1010]

[1004] The prepositional expression ἐν τῇ ἀκροβυστίᾳ is either understood to refer to "righteousness" (thus, e.g., C.E.B. Cranfield 1975, 236n.3) or to "faith" (thus, e.g., M. Neubrand 1997, 225). But in any case the two elements constitute the one unit "faith-righteousness."

[1005] C.E.B. Cranfield 1975, 236.

[1006] Obedience to the Torah is no longer "a *sine qua non* of faith and righteousness" (R.W.L. Moberly 1990, 129).

[1007] Cf. C. Dietzfelbinger 1961, 12.

[1008] Cf. J. Lambrecht 1979, 10n.23; J.D.G. Dunn 1988, 232: "Paul does not disparage circumcision here."

[1009] Cf. again 1Cor 9:2: Though *confirming* his apostleship, the Corinthians do not *constitute* it. – The idea of the seal, therefore, fits Paul's argumentative purpose, as a seal confirms after the event.

[1010] Cf. K. Berger 1966, 67; J. Lambrecht 1979, 10n.23: "La circoncision est encore considérée de manière positive; mais en même temps, en insistant clairement sur le fait que, survenue plus tard, elle ne peut en aucun cas être la cause de la justification, Paul lui enlève une grande part de son importance." Since the effect or authority of that which is

Coming back to the question why Paul chose to modify his *Vorlage* from Gen 17:11, excluding the concept of the covenant,[1011] one could think that the eminence of the concept of righteousness has resulted in its gradual displacement.[1012] On the other hand there is good reason to believe that when Paul claims to establish the law through his acquired faith-perspective (Rom 3:27.31) he regards the law no longer in its function as means of salvation, but in its character as testimony, witnessing to the "new covenant," which is established by God as the only way accepted by him: faith. For Paul, πίστις in its salvation-historical and participatory dimensions figures as God's new covenant,[1013] as the factor that both redefines and characterizes the people of God. "Getting in," "staying in" and communal existence in the sphere of faith happens through and in faith.

Since faith-righteousness belongs to uncircumcision and has priority-character, there can be no doubt about the divine will: Abraham is the father of all those who believe in uncircumcision. As consequence and according to God's purpose, righteousness is counted to the believers on grounds of their faith.[1014]

(b) Abraham as Father of Circumcised and Uncircumcised

According to the *opinio communis* on Rom 4:11, Paul thinks of Gentile-Christians and apparently goes so far as to claim that God's aim has been realized at first with the uncircumcised, i.e., the Gentile-Christians, and that Abraham has become first the father of the uncircumcised,[1015] for faith is the only and sufficient criterion to be part of both God's salvation plan

---

sealed remains independent from the seal itself, the priority and sufficiency of faith remains untouched. This is how opposing arguments like: "But Abraham was subsequently circumcised; ... that is what we are proposing for ourselves" can be rejected (F.F. Bruce 1978, 69).

[1011] Notably, Philo's treatment of the covenant theme is very meager (cf. M. Böhm 2004, 380).

[1012] Cf. K. Haacker 1999, 104. Similarly U. Wilckens 1978, 265.

[1013] Cf. H. Binder 1968, 48.

[1014] Most commentators regard the first of two infinitive clauses εἰς τὸ εἶναι... and εἰς τὸ λογισθῆναι... as expressing the divine purpose (final; differently R. Bultmann 1959, 207: content; M.J. Lagrange 1950, 90: consecutive) and the second as presenting the consequence of the believers' faith (consecutive). Cf., e.g., R. Holst 1997, 322n.13; C.E.B. Cranfield 1975, 236f.; E. Käsemann 1980, 109; U. Wilckens 1978, 265 with nn.842 and 845; E. Lohse 2003, 152. As for the second clause, it seems best to integrate both consecutive and final meaning (cf. O. Michel 1978, 167; M. Neubrand 1997, 226: final), since according to God's will, the consequence of faith is being counted righteous.

[1015] Cf. C.K. Barrett 1957, 90; K. Berger 1966, 68; O. Michel 1978, 167; E. Lohse 2003, 152.

and Abraham's seed.[1016] In 4:12, according to this interpretation, Paul continues to argue that Abraham's circumcision made him the father also of those who belong to circumcision, i.e., the Jews,[1017] – in case they are not only circumcised, but are in agreement with "the way of our father Abraham, who believed while still uncircumcised."[1018] Hence, in an inversion of 1:16, "the Gentiles are not added on to Israel," but "Israel is added to the Gentiles."[1019]

However, in 4:12, we are confronted with a stylistic and syntactical *crux interpretationis*: The two dative expressions in the clause τοῖς οὐκ ἐκ περιτομῆς μόνον ἀλλὰ καὶ τοῖς στοιχοῦσιν has left most exegetes with some perplexity. For this enigmatic construction poses the question whether Paul in this verse wants to denote two characteristics of the *same* group of people, the Jewish-Christians – this is the contention of most exegetes[1020] –, or two *different* sociological groups – this is actually implied by grammar and syntax of the text.[1021] We have to deal briefly with this problem, presenting the various explanations and offering a tentative suggestion of our own.

The first, most widespread solution has to reckon with an error by Paul or an early scribe, or with a stylistic imprecision or a mistake.[1022] Against such hypotheses, L. Cerfaux and J. Swetnam suggested that Paul speaks of

---

[1016] Very strongly G. Klein 1963, 156; E. Käsemann 1980, 109: "Faktisch werden dem Judentum sowohl Abraham wie die Beschneidung entrissen."

[1017] Ἐκ implies origin and affiliation.

[1018] Cf. U. Wilckens 1978, 265.

[1019] R.L. Brawley 1997, 301.

[1020] Cf., e.g., T. Zahn 1925, 226; G. Klein 1963, 155f.; K. Berger 1966, 68f.; O. Michel 1978, 167; C.E.B. Cranfield 1975, 237; U. Wilckens 1978, 265f.; J. Lambrecht 1979, 10n.26; D.J. Moo 1996, 270f.; E. Lohse 2003, 152.

[1021] See the arguments gathered in M. Neubrand 1997, 234-236; also T.H. Tobin 1995, 447n.21. Neubrand contends that without exception in the Pauline language an ἀλλὰ καί, following on οὐ μόνον, represents a further, equivalent addition, whereby this addition never qualifies or restricts the first element, given by οὐ μόνον. – The main syntactical objection against the "two-groups-thesis" concerns the position of the particle οὐ, which regularly appears before the article: οὐ τοῖς instead of τοῖς οὐκ (cf. J.D.G. Dunn 1988, 210f.). This point is countered by reference to Rom 4:4 and 4:23, which likewise display unexpected positions of the negative particle. However, they in turn can be explained by considering the emphasis Paul attempted to make: "To the worker reward is *not* reckoned according to grace…" "It is *not* written, however, for his sake only…"

[1022] Cf. O. Michel 1978, 167n.6. He also notes possible conjectures, of which the first takes καὶ τοῖς as old scribal error for the abbreviation κ. αυτοις, while others want to eliminate καί or τοῖς. Cf. H. Lietzmann 1928, 54; C.E.B. Cranfield 1975, 237 ("a simple mistake, whether of Paul himself or of Tertius or of a very early copyist"); see also those mentioned in M. Neubrand 1997, 234n.52, and F. Blass/A. Debrunner/F. Rehkopf 1979, §276n.2 (καὶ τοῖς equivalent to καὶ αὐτοῖς).

two groups, Jewish-Christians and Gentile-Christians,[1023] assuming that
περιτομή has acquired two different meanings in this verse, the first referring to spiritual circumcision, the other to physical circumcision. Also E.
Käsemann proposes a metaphorical understanding of the first occurrence
of περιτομή and understands the entire verse as an antithesis, in which Paul
confronts the group of the Jews with the group of the Jewish-Christians,
implying that only the Christian is the true Jew and that the keyword περιτομή is solely fitting for Christians. As he has elaborated in 2:25-29, all is
dependent on the reality of a life in obedience.[1024]

Against a questionable Christian appropriation of the text, M. Neubrand
contends that the faith, which according to God's plan is counted as righteousness, may not be understood exclusively as Christian faith. For Paul,
God does indeed accept Jewish believers not accepting the message of
Christ.[1025] Paul's only concern is to refer Abraham's fatherhood to non-
Jews as well, i.e., to put forward a separate, equivalent election of the peoples, without denying or qualifying the biblical-Jewish tradition of Abraham's fatherhood of the Jewish people. According to Neubrand, therefore,
in 4:12, Paul has in mind two Jewish groups, one being comprised of To-
rah-observant Jews and Jewish-Christians, the other of Jewish-Christians,
who left the confines of the Jewish law for the sake of the gospel.[1026]

Against that, it would be counter to Paul's self-understanding and theology if he left his christological perspective in this context; even in his
exposition of an Old Testament text of faith, i.e., in contexts that do not
name explicitly Χριστός as the one to whom faith relates, he has in mind a
christologically determined faith. His basic agenda in 4:11-12 and also in
1:16-17[1027] is not fundamentally different to that in 3:21-31, as far as his
view of πίστις is concerned[1028]: This conclusion suggests itself *inter alia*
on grounds of the phrase πάντων τῶν πιστευόντων. Abraham was intended
by God to become the father of *all* believers. A proper understanding of
this key phrase is pivotal, and its occurrence in fundamental, strategic
places in Romans provides clues as to its implications. In 1:16, 3:22, 10:4,
and 10:11 it first refers to and involves the Christ-event as contents of faith
and second has inclusive character and speaks of *all* believers, Jews and

---

[1023] L. Cerfaux 1945; J. Swetnam 1980; also J.A. Fitzmyer 381f.

[1024] E. Käsemann 1980, 109f., 115; cf. also C.K. Barrett 1991, 91f.; U. Luz 1968, 175.

[1025] An explaining reference by Neubrand to passages such as Rom 10:1-13 would
prove illuminating, as there one would have to comment on the Christology of the Israel
chapters.

[1026] M. Neubrand 1997, 237-244. See also T.H. Tobin 1995, 446f.

[1027] In Rom 1:16-17, Χριστός is not mentioned, but implied (see above pages 247f.).

[1028] On the essential christological determination of faith, see again F. Neugebauer
1961, 163 and also below chapter VI.A.VI.

Gentiles.[1029] Hence, there is reason to believe that 4:11 fulfills both criteria as well: christological content and universal character of faith.[1030] One should note already here that in 4:16 this most significant keyword πᾶς will recur.

The divine purpose of Abraham's universal fatherhood has been realized in his uncircumcised status (δι' ἀκροβυστίας) and not after his circumcision. According to God's plan, therefore, he became the father of Jews and Gentiles *before* their differentiation into "circumcised" and "uncircumcised."[1031]

The terminological and material association of the theme of the letter 1:16 with our passage in question calls for an attempt of a synopsis in order to detect related ideas contained in both passages:

Rom 1:16	Rom 4:11-12
εὐαγγέλιον παντὶ τῷ πιστεύοντι	πατὴρ πάντων τῶν πιστευόντων
	καὶ πατὴρ περιτομῆς
Ἰουδαίῳ τε πρῶτον	τοῖς οὐκ ἐκ περιτομῆς μόνον
καὶ Ἕλληνι.	ἀλλὰ καὶ τοῖς στοιχοῦσιν τοῖς ἴχνεσιν τῆς
	ἐν ἀκροβυστίᾳ πίστεως τοῦ πατρὸς ἡμῶν
	Ἀβραάμ.

According to this scheme, the two puzzling dative constructions signify two groups: First, Jewish believers, and second Gentile believers. A difficulty presents itself to us with the first occurrence of the term περιτομή, which in line with the exegetes mentioned above has to be explained in a figurative sense. Clearly, 2:25-29 demonstrates that a metaphorical understanding is no impossibility for Paul, but rather in place, if the subject matter is connected with human alignment with God's purpose and will. Just as faith is counted (λογίζεσθαι) as righteousness, obedience in uncircumcision will be counted (λογίζεσθαι) as "circumcision" (2:26), i.e., as membership in God's people, in the seed of Abraham. Thus, Paul has gained a

---

[1029] Cf. Rom 1:16: Ἰουδαίῳ τε πρῶτον καὶ Ἕλληνι; 3:22: οὐ γάρ ἐστιν διαστολή; 10:12: οὐ γάρ ἐστιν διαστολὴ Ἰουδαίου τε καὶ Ἕλληνος. Hence, Paul's faith-formula πᾶς ὁ πιστεύων *always* includes Jews and Gentiles and stresses the equality of both in God's plan of salvation.

[1030] Without referring to the parallels of Rom 4:12 within the letter (1:16; 3:22; 10:4.11), K. Berger also argues that πάντων τῶν πιστευόντων denotes all believers, Jewish and Gentile (1966, 68f.).

[1031] The prepositional expression δι' ἀκροβυστίας qualifies the entire infinitive clause and therefore belongs to the depiction of God's goal. The preposition διά designates the mode or the attendant circumstances, in which God's purpose finds its realization. – Against that K. Berger thinks that δι' ἀκροβυστίας signifies not the actual circumcision, but the kind of faith in its relationship to Abraham (1966, 68f. with n.38; against this suggestion U. Wilckens 1978, 265n.844).

double meaning of περιτομή, one – to use G. Klein's terminology – "soteriological," the other "ethnological,"[1032] i.e., the one denoting existence in faith, the other affiliation to the ethnic group of the Jews through circumcision.

Consequently, the introducing καί of 4:12 is epexegetical, specifying the fatherhood of Abraham: He was intended to become the father of all believers in uncircumcision, and thus he is the father of "circumcision," because belonging to the new covenant of faith implies having true circumcision, having Abraham as father. This is true for (physically) circumcised Jewish believers – for those at first (πρῶτον) –, as well as for those Gentile believers who follow the steps of Abraham by having faith without circumcision.[1033]

b) Romans 4:13-17: The Salvation-Historical Framework of πίστις

(a) The Promise to Abraham and His Seed through Faith-Righteousness

In the important middle piece of the chapter, Rom 4:13-17,[1034] Paul employs a dense, non-verbal and non-adjectival, prepositional style, consisting of nominal clauses and logical conclusions[1035]; also, Paul appeals to traditional formulations (4:17). Notably, therefore, in some regards the style resembles that of 3:21-26.[1036] Is this also true regarding contents? With the term ἐπαγγελία Paul introduces a concept into the discussion, which had obtained a prominent position already in Galatians 3, but has been left unmentioned in our letter up until this point.[1037] Here, it is greatly

---

[1032] G. Klein 1963, 155. Against that H. Boers 1971, 89f. Klein, however, draws different consequences compared to those reached here. He clearly goes beyond the text when he contends that Paul reserved the soteriological notion of περιτομή exclusively for Abraham.

[1033] In this proposed interpretation, faith takes absolute precedence (Rom 4:11), both concerning the progression of thought and materially. This follows the order in Abraham's biography, even though it is also true that in contrast to Abraham, Jewish-Christians believe after their circumcision (cf. K. Berger 1966, 68; J. Lambrecht 1979, 11). The interpretation also accounts for the πρῶτον of 1:16, so important for Paul. – K. Haacker points out that here Paul attributes faith *and* circumcision to Jews, whereas in Galatians it appears that circumcision is almost ruled out (1999, 104).

[1034] Cf. O. Michel 1978, 168.

[1035] Cf. M. Theobald 2001, 404n.23.

[1036] Also in Rom 3:21-26 adjectives and verbs recede, prepositions and loaded theological terms play a significant role, being arranged without verbal connections, but enabling logical conclusions (cf. O. Michel 1978, 146); Paul also incorporates a traditional text-piece.

[1037] Most ἐπαγγελία-occurrences are found in direct reference to Paul's view of Abraham: Rom 4:13.14.16.20; 9:8.9; Gal 3:14.16.17.18(*bis*).22.29; 4:23.28.

emphasized, signifying a new sub-topic[1038] and one of *the* eminent themes of the chapter,[1039] which will dominate the further logic.[1040] One would have expected that Paul referred to the promise and to God's self-disclosure through his word before his quotation of Gen 15:6 in order to denote God's word as the ground and impetus for Abraham's faith (cf. Gen 15:1). Yet in contrast to the order of Genesis 15, Paul arranges the event of justification through faith at the outset of the chapter (Rom 4:3) and places the foundation of faith, God's promise, into the center, since his considerations started from the opposition faith – works and led from there to the relationship of faith and the promise and their independence from the law.

Thereby, circumcision which figured in the previous section as dominant topic is understood as the law *in nuce*, or as *typos* of the law.[1041] By contrast, the new theme of the divine promise (ἐπαγγελία)[1042] functions as the gospel *in nuce*, or as *typos* of the gospel.[1043] Three dimensions of the divine promise are equally significant for Paul: fact, circumstances, and content[1044]: The event of God's assurance (fact) builds on the foundation of the unnomistic faith-righteousness (circumstances), and it comprises a universalistic extension of God's promise of land-inheritance and descendants, both derived from Genesis 15 (content).

It has already become clear that Paul does not base his argument on a single, isolated Old Testament verse, but like a thorough exegete he takes into account the context of Genesis 15; this chapter constitutes and remains the basis of his argumentation throughout, while other facets and elements of the Abraham cycle have a secondary, supporting purpose. He incorporates both the theme of descendants through the keyword σπέρμα[1045] as well as the question of the inheritance of the land through the term κληρονόμος.[1046] As for the land-promise, it is true that Paul uses words that

---

[1038] Cf. M. Neubrand 1997, 246.

[1039] Cf. J. Jeremias 1970, 54.

[1040] Cf. Rom 4:13.14.16.20, but also 4:21 (ἐπαγγέλλεσθαι). Some interpreters take 4:13-22 as a unity due to the theme of "promise" throughout this section (cf., e.g., H. Moxnes 1980, 113; D.J. Moo 1996, 272).

[1041] Cf. again C. Dietzfelbinger 1961, 12.

[1042] On the term ἐπαγγελία, see, e.g., C. Dietzfelbinger 1961, 7-13; U. Luz 1968, 66-72; D.-A. Koch 1986, 309-312; M. Neubrand 1997, 247-250.

[1043] Cf. U. Schnelle 2003, 358. E. Käsemann specifies: "Das Evangelium ist ... die eschatologisch sich realisierende Verheißung" (1980, 112).

[1044] Against that C. Dietzfelbinger argues that Paul has no interest in the details of the promise (1961, 8). This objection neglects that Paul starts his deliberations from the concrete promises of Genesis 15. See also S.K. Williams 1980, 279.

[1045] See the occurrence of σπέρμα in Gen 15:3.5.13.18 and Rom 4:13.16.

[1046] See the occurrence of κληρονομεῖν and κληρονόμος in Gen 15:3.4(*bis*).7.8 and Rom 4:13.14. Generally, in Jewish theology, the term κληρονόμος ist mostly used in connection with the land (cf. J.D.G. Dunn 1988, 213). K.E. Bailey (1994) discusses the land-

do not match any Abrahamic land-promise, but it is likewise improbable that he has in view a conglomerate or summation of the various versions of the land-promises given to Abraham[1047]; for, after his careful distinction of the "faith-chapter" (Genesis 15) and the "circumcision-chapter" (Genesis 17) in the preceding section (Rom 4:9-12), one can assume that his further argumentation starts from Genesis 15 and from the faith-perspective which has occupied him since the initial quote of Gen 15:6 in Rom 4:3.[1048]

But clearly, the land-promise experiences an amplification, which occurs in none of the Old Testament Abrahamic promises: Abraham will be inheritor of the whole world (κόσμος). Paul does not specify, however, whether he thinks of Abraham as inheritor of this world[1049] or the future world[1050] – he is concerned with the righteousness of faith as foundation of the universalistic promise.[1051] Not because of his faithfulness, but through

---

promise in Rom 4:13 in comparison with passages from *Jubilees*, Sirach, *Enoch*, and the *Psalms of Solomon*. He concludes that Paul "borrows language already available but gives it his own unique meaning," possibly being influenced by Jesus (cf. Mt 5:5). "The promise *had to expand*, because the very 'people of God' had expanded! Gentiles across the known world *had become a part of 'the people of God'*" (68; italics original). – One could ask whether the promises given before faith (Gen 15:3-5) should be distinguished from those given "after" faith (Gen 15:7-21) (cf. K. Berger 1966, 69), but since the two elements of "seed" and "land" on which Paul concentrates appear on both sides, there seems no need of a separation. Both dimensions of the promise are included in the word ἐπαγγελία (singular!), and so the "faith-chapter" Genesis 15 is conceived as one entity.

[1047] See the table above page 141 (cf. Gen 12:1.7; 13:15.17; 15:7.18; 17:8; 18:18; 22:17; also 26:3.4).

[1048] Against that most interpreters presuppose a combination of the various land-promises (cf., e.g., K.E. Bailey 1994, 59f.: Gen 12:7 and 17:8; E. Lohse 2003, 153: Gen 22:18). J. Lambrecht regards Genesis 17 as background of Rom 4:13-21: "Les vv. 13-16 comportent des allusions suffisamment claires à Gn 17,[1-]8; les vv. 18-21 paraphrasent Gn 17-21" (1979, 11; but see 7 on the centrality of Gen 15:6).

[1049] Cf. Sir 44,21; *Jub* 17,3; 19,21; 22,14; 32,19. Especially the last passage, *Jub* 32,19, testifies to a universalizing of the land promise comparable to that of Paul (cf. K.E. Bailey 1994, 60f., 68). Rom 4:13 is interpreted in this sense in, e.g., H. Moxnes 1980, 247-249; D.J. Moo 1996, 274.

[1050] Cf. *1En* 40,9; *MekEx* 14,31; see also Gal 5:21. See in this futuric sense, e.g., C.E.B. Cranfield 1975, 239f.; U. Wilckens 1978, 269; E. Käsemann 1980, 113; R. Holst 1997, 323. – While *1En* 40,9 does not mention Abraham explicitly, the rabbinic passage *MekEx* 14,31 is significant, as it also appeals to Gen 15:6 and represents, even according to E.P. Sanders, one of the "very few instances in which the world to come is specified as the reward of merit" (1977, 189): "And so you find that Abraham, our father, inherited this world and the world to come, only through the merit of his faith (בזכות אמנה), as it is written... (Gen 15:6)." Symptomatically, Sanders refers to this passage only in passing. See also H.-W. Heidland 1936, 101.

[1051] Such an "imperialistic" tone might have been surprising to the Romans, even open to misunderstandings (cf. K. Haacker 1999, 106), but Paul, the apostle to the Gentiles

faith-righteousness, the promise was given.[1052] Thus, Paul's *relecture* of Genesis 15 also mirrors the fundamental structural and theological correlation of Gen 15:6 and 15:18, Abraham's faith as foundation for the covenantal assurance of the land,[1053] even if Paul both redefines the notion of "covenant" (cf. Rom 4:11) and widens the scope of "faith," perceiving it in the light of God's "Heilssetzung."[1054] Also Paul takes up the promise of the seed[1055] without citing or clearly alluding to a specific Genesis passage,[1056] but his thoughts again proceed from the context of Genesis 15, whose horizon he extends to a universal, global measure.[1057] In the later discussion (Rom 4:16-22), the descendant-promise receives central meaning and is reflected from different perspectives.

In evaluation of Paul's dealing with the contents of the Abrahamic promises, we conclude that he neither shows indifference towards the single elements,[1058] nor carries out a reduction[1059] but extracts and extends the basic ideas of the assurance of Genesis 15: The land refers to the *whole* world, and the seed to *all* believers. This represents the ultimate perceivable amplification and development of both land- and descendant-promise[1060]; furthermore, it connects to the present situation of the congre-

---

"understood, perhaps better than most" that God's "parish was the world" (R. Holst 1997, 323).

[1052] A different perspective is that of Sir 44,21 and later rabbinic interpreters: Abraham's faithfulness to the law resulted in the promise. See the exegesis above chapter IV.D; also P. Billerbeck 1926, 204-206. For instance, S.K. Stowers's exegesis of this verse is in line with Ben Sira rather than with Paul (1989, 670).

[1053] See above pages 93f.

[1054] U. Wilckens 1978, 270; cf. C.K. Barrett 1957, 94; E. Käsemann 1980, 113 (δι-καιοσύνη πίστεως as "Machtbereich, in welchem Verheißung möglich wird"). – But see against this A. von Dobbeler 1987, 138 (δικαιοσύνη πίστεως as "einzig gangbare Möglichkeit, Erbe der Verheißung zu werden"); L. Gaston 1980, 57; M.D. Hooker 1989, 173 (God's/Christ's faithfulness as the grounds of the promise).

[1055] In contrast to the parallel passage in Galatians 3, Paul attributes no obvious christological meaning to σπέρμα (cf. Gal 3:16.19).

[1056] See the table above page 141 (cf. Gen 12:2; 13:16; 15:5; 17:2.6; 18:18; 22:17; also 26:3.4).

[1057] The universalism of the son-promise is also in view in Gen 12:3; 18:18; 22:18 (see also 26:4), but there in terms of the universal blessing in Abraham (and using the word γῆ). Notably, both the term and notion of blessing are absent in Romans 4 (contrast Gal 3:8-9), since Paul is interested in the concept of faith; already Rom 4:11 with the coinage σφραγὶς τῆς δικαιοσύνης τῆς πίστεως attests this interest by omitting the term διαθήκη (contrast Gal 3:15.17).

[1058] Against C. Dietzfelbinger 1961, 8f.

[1059] Against D.-A. Koch 1986, 310.

[1060] The insistence that Paul's starting point is Genesis 15 may not be interpreted as a denial that his overall perspective comprised the whole of the Abrahamic promises and even the lines of tradition of post-Old Testament Jewish theology (cf. J. Lambrecht 1979,

gation in Rome, the "center of the world," whose members belong to Abraham's seed through their faith apart from the law and who are therefore bound into the current process of the promise's confirmation, even receive the status of equivalent recipients of God's assurance.[1061] Paul uses this "eschatological motif to introduce his argument that both Jews and non-Jews are children of Abraham."[1062]

The consideration that Paul preserves the chronological and material distinction between Genesis 15 and 17 and bases his reflections concerning ἐπαγγελία essentially on the occurrences of σπέρμα and κληρονομεῖν from Genesis 15 rests on a certain succession and progression of events to be reconstructed from the *ductus* of the chapter: God's salvation-historical manifestation of faith-righteousness opens up the sphere in and through which the promise is uttered; and Abraham's faith, i.e., his entrance and being in faith happens upon his hearing the promise. Circumcision functions as the seal of faith-righteousness, hence playing a confirmative, but not determinative role in this process pertaining to salvation.

This order extracted from the Abraham-chapter functions as correlate to parts of the first three chapters of Romans: The entity of faith-righteousness corresponds to ἐκ πίστεως (Rom 1:17), which in turn is explicated by 3:21-26(.27-31); and in the εὐαγγέλιον, which stands in a terminological, contextual, and typological relationship to ἐπαγγελία,[1063] a personal access and existence in faith has its foundation (εἰς πίστιν) (1:17). Though the concept of ἐπαγγελία is filled through the concrete divine assurances of seed and land and has therefore word-character,[1064] it equally has for Paul the quality of divine power,[1065] which is suggested *inter alia* by its prevalent use in the singular and in the absolute,[1066] its opposition to σάρξ[1067] and to νόμος,[1068] the mentioned association to "faith-righteousness" in 4:13, and the notion of "strength" in 4:16.

12n.29; on the tradition history of κληρονόμος κόσμου, see K. Berger 1966, 69 with n.41). On the one hand, his argumentative line of thought is developed from Genesis 15 ("causal exposition"), while on the other hand his retrospective point of view knows about the broader tradition and regards the promises as confirmed in a comprehensive sense.

[1061] The conjunction ἤ takes the meaning "and ... respectively" (cf. F. Blass/A. Debrunner/F. Rehkopf 1979, §446,1b) and therefore includes the present descendants of Abraham.

[1062] H. Moxnes 1980, 249.

[1063] Cf. K. Haacker 1999, 106; U. Schnelle 2003, 358.

[1064] Cf. D.-A. Koch 1986, 311.

[1065] Cf. again Rom 1:17 (δύναμις θεοῦ).

[1066] Cf. again the analogy with εὐαγγέλιον, which from the imperial language is primarily known in the plural.

[1067] Cf. Rom 9:8; Gal 4:23.

[1068] Cf. Gal 3:18; similarly Rom 4:13.

In correspondence to this wider scope, Paul is no longer concerned with the human attitude of faith and works (as in 4:4-8),[1069] but with the divine salvation purpose, which sets in the place of the law[1070] the righteousness of faith. The precise relationship between the law and faith-righteousness depends on the verb to be supplied in our verse,[1071] but possible additions such as "to be mediated" or "to remain"[1072] convey the same principal idea. The law makes known sin (3:20), produces wrath (4:15) and can therefore not be the realm in which the promise has its place,[1073] i.e., in which the promise is mediated to and remains for Abraham and his descendants. Only in the sphere of faith, which is diametrically opposed to the dominion of sin and entails both freedom from ungodliness (4:5) and forgiveness (4:6-8), is the promise mediated and confirmed.[1074]

By taking the phrase δικαιοσύνη πίστεως in terms of the divine "Heilssetzung" and sphere of power, a noteworthy analogy with the "righteousness through Christ-faith" (3:21-22) opens up. God's act (in Christ), the divine manifestation of faith-righteousness, inaugurates and enables human faith, thus being a category of transfer and participation.[1075]

In sum, Paul dissolved the causal relationship of νόμος and ἐπαγγελία, which has been fundamental for his Jewish contemporaries,[1076] placing them in antithetical contrast[1077] and identifying faith-righteousness as the medium in which God's promise is made possible.

[1069] Against that, commonly, the phrase δικαιοσύνη πίστεως is conceived of as Abraham's "personal" righteousness which he gained through his faith (e.g., K. Berger 1966, 69), and the law as one's individual works (e.g., J. Lambrecht 1979, 11; G.N. Davies 1990, 140).

[1070] The entity of the law is strongly accentuated: Rom 4:13.14.15(*bis*).16. – The lack of the article in 4:13 can be compared to 3:25 (διὰ [τῆς] πίστεως) and might be due to the preposition (see N. Turner 1963, 179).

[1071] Cf. J. Lambrecht 1979, 12n.30: "C'est de ce verbe que dépend la nuance exacte à attribuer au complément introduit par διὰ + génitif."

[1072] Cf. M. Neubrand 1997, 251.

[1073] Cf. C.K. Barrett 1957, 96 ("domain of law"); U. Wilckens 1978, 270.

[1074] Thus, the antithesis of νόμος and δικαιοσύνη πίστεως speak in favor of a salvation-historical, rather than individual understanding. Moreover, the promise came *through* "faith-righteousness," i.e., as part and consequence of the salvation-historical realization of the divine will, while at the same time it is presupposed as the content and condition of Abraham's faith. Hence, the implied logic is "faith-righteousness" – promise – faith, even if Paul does not place the promise before the statement on Abraham's faith – as does Gen 15:1-5.

[1075] On the term "Transfer- und Partizipialkategorie," see U. Schnelle 2003, 352.

[1076] According to C. Dietzfelbinger this separation is one of Paul's most powerful theological achievements, which however runs counter to the sense of the Old Testament texts (1961, 10).

[1077] Cf. E. Käsemann 1980, 113.

(b) Abraham's Heirs, Abraham's Children

Paul confirms (γάρ) the fundamental opposition of faith-righteousness and the law *a negativo*, i.e., by the theoretical, but wrong assumption that the promise belongs to those of the law. The style of Rom 4:14-15 is extremely dense,[1078] which could point to the character of a generally valid doctrinal statement,[1079] but the immediate "reference to Gen 15:6 is clear" as well.[1080] As little as Abraham's and all believers' justification is dependent on works (Rom 4:4-5), so little the promise given to him and his descendants is dependent on the law.[1081] Neither for Abraham, nor for anybody, does the law become a determinative element. With οἱ ἐκ νόμου Paul designates those, who base their existence (solely[1082]) on the law, who are part of the domain of the law and hence members of the "other" side of faith. The causal preposition ἐκ verifies the typological relationship to the parallel expressions ὁ ἐκ πίστεως Ἰησοῦ (3:26) in that it designates the cause and origin of one's existence in view of one's standing before God.[1083]

Paul therefore by no means refers to Jews *per se* in order to exclude and eliminate them from the seed of Abraham,[1084] but to those Jews, living in the present eschatological time brought about through Christ, who are not believers in the God "who raised Christ from the dead" (4:25). Logically, if those were to inherit what is promised, the power of faith would lose its meaning in the divine plan of salvation and become powerless; faith would have come in vain (κενοῦσθαι).[1085] And the *kenosis* of faith would concur with the decay and nullification of the promise (καταργεῖσθαι), since the

---

[1078] Cf. J. Lambrecht 1979, 12.

[1079] Cf. R. Bultmann 1959, 214; E. Käsemann 1980, 114.

[1080] J.D.G. Dunn 1988, 214.

[1081] Cf. J. Jeremias 1970, 43.

[1082] D.J. Moo also adds "only" in analogy to Rom 3:28 (1996, 275).

[1083] See above chapter V.B.III.2.b.(c). It is misleading however to reduce the confrontation of νόμος and πίστις to the confrontation of two opposing principles of salvation in the sense of two possibilities of *Dasein* (thus R. Bultmann 1959, 214). – On the antithetical relationship between ἐκ πίστεως and ἐκ νόμου/ἐξ ἔργων νόμου/ἐξ ἔργων, cf. D.A. Campbell 1992a, 98f. *et passim* (also commenting on prepositional constructions with διά/δι'). That Paul's evaluation of νόμος has its content only from its contrast to πίστις, i.e., that "Paul's νόμος paradigm" does not derive its meaning "from any internal logic or content of its own" (102) cannot be verified though.

[1084] Against G. Klein 1963, 158. Certainly, "Paul is not specifically anti-Jewish, or against the Law as such," but he knows – not least from own experience (cf. Phil 3:4-11) – that "existence under the Law cannot continue in an existence in faith" (H. Boers 1971, 94).

[1085] 1Cor 15:14 has πίστις ἡμῶν and does therefore not denote the universal meaning of πίστις (against D.J. Moo 1996, 275n.30).

promise is mediated in and belongs essentially to the sphere of faith.[1086]
The apostle's conclusion is true for Abraham's situation, but in an even
more pertinent and profound way also in the present, now, that the eschatological time has set in.[1087]

There is a notable material parallelism to 4:2, insofar as Paul constructs
a conditional clause, which refutes itself due to an impossible precondition[1088]: Just as Abraham did not work with respect to his justification
(4:2), those of the law are not heirs. In effect, therefore, Paul destroys the
exclusivist idea of election and of the status of heirs, insofar as this idea
seeks its legitimation in the law. "Israel" is not defined through genealogical descent or the succession of generations, but through a continual divine
act of election, through which God in absolute freedom entertains the right
to choose the members of his chosen people.[1089] According to God's will,
the legitimate seed of Abraham are not those of the law, but those of faith
(cf. Gal 3:7).[1090]

Ultimately, therefore, Romans 4 offers in a quite revolutionary manner
the foundation of a new definition of the people of God[1091] and a foundation of Paul's ecclesiology. Just as God in his sovereignty directed the
promise to the patriarch and called him into his plan of salvation, his present act of election through the gospel calls people to faith, into the es-

---

[1086] Against that U. Wilckens attempts to refer the verbs to the validity of Scripture
(1978, 270).

[1087] The permanent validity of this truth explains adequately the use of the perfect
tense κεκένωται and κατήργηται.

[1088] Cf., on Rom 4:14, C.E.B. Cranfield 1975, 240: "The condition is unfulfilled according to the author's thought."

[1089] See, however, G. Mayer 1972, 122f., who refers to writers who attempt to prove
Abraham's universal fatherhood genealogically (e.g., Cleodemos, quoted in Josephus,
Ant 1,239-241). But Mayer also mentions authors for whom genealogical descent is not
equivalent with membership in God's people (119f.; see also on the impact of this view
on missions).

[1090] Cf. D.-A. Koch 1986, 311; W. Kraus 1996, 299; J.-N. Aletti 2003, 324. The problematic theme of the "seed of Abraham" is well-known in Judaism and occurs in the New
Testament (Mt 3:9; Lk 3:8; Jn 8:39) and throughout Jewish apocalyptic and Hellenistic
writings (cf. the numerous passages listed in K. Berger 1972, 377f.). But while these
texts restrict the group of Abraham's children according to paraenetical-ethical criteria
and with polemical varnish, Paul extends it to non-Jews, to those who believe (cf. K.
Haacker 1999, 104).

[1091] Cf. W. Kraus 1996, 276, 282f.: "Paulus ... [begründet] die Identität Israels selbst
anders als üblich...: nämlich in der Verheißung an Abraham und der Glaubensgerechtigkeit und nicht in der Beschneidung oder im Bundesschluß am Sinai." M. Theobald 2001,
402n.19.

chatological people of believers from Jews and Gentiles.[1092] God's call creates a new identity, the identity of being Abraham's seed, his heirs.[1093]

In a next step Paul reiterates his basic conviction concerning the purpose and predicament of the law, by making a division of two domains, the one characterized by the law, the other apart from the law. The logic and structure of the elliptical clauses necessitate the following additions: Each half-verse in effect consists of three elements:

4:15a: νόμος [– παράβασις] – ὀργή

4:15b[1094]: οὐ νόμος – οὐ παράβασις [– οὐδὲ ὀργή][1095]

In the realm *extra fide* God's wrath is revealed, since it is the realm of sinfulness and transgression. And the law is the factor that makes known sin (3:20) and the entity by which, since its coming, sin is counted (5:13); "it was added because of transgressions" (Gal 3:19).[1096] Belonging to the domain of the law is thus essentially connected to entanglement in sinfulness. Paul therefore formulates in very strong words that the law effectively produces wrath (κατεργάζεσθαι) – it belongs on the "Adam-side," the large "parenthesis" of Rom 1:18-3:20.[1097] Its radical opposite, the side of faith is not defined by the law, by transgression, by God's wrath, since the one justified by faith apart from the law is also the forgiven one, so that there is no παράβασις (cf. 4:6-8).[1098] Without doubt, the promise cannot exist on the side of God's wrath, and consequently the allotment of the inheritance happens apart from the criterion of the law.

As a result (4:16, διὰ τοῦτο),[1099] those whose existence roots in the soil of faith (ἐκ πίστεως) and who have been transferred into the reality of faith

---

[1092] On God's free, independent election, see also Rom 9:6-13.

[1093] Cf. M. Neubrand 1997, 254f.

[1094] The different text traditions disagree with respect to the conjunction: Is it γάρ (confirmatory) or δέ (adversative). The second reading has stronger attestation (cf. H. Lietzmann 1928, 55; against T. Zahn 1925, 228n.64) and is to be preferred on grounds of the context, as it signifies the fundamental opposition of the two realms of the law (Rom 4:15a) and apart from the law (4:15b) (cf. K. Haacker 1999, 105n.1).

[1095] Cf. O. Hofius 1996, 90n.179, but already M. Luther 1515/1516, 302.

[1096] See above pages 305f.

[1097] Paul argues on grounds of a profoundly theological concept of the law, not in terms of a profane, Greco-Roman understanding (against K. Haacker 1999, 107, who considers Rom 4:15b to be the first literary evidence of the juridical maxim "nulla poena sine lege").

[1098] The side of faith is either the time *ante legem*, as in Abraham's case, or the realm *sine lege* (cf. Rom 3:21), as in the Christians' case. Therefore, 4:15b can serve only indirectly as explanation of 5:13 and 7:8 (cf. U. Wilckens 1978, 318n.1059), since this half-verse refers to the situation of the justified one (but see, e.g., O. Michel 1978, 169 with n.7; E. Lohse 2003, 154f.).

[1099] Against that D.J. Moo 1996, 277, who argues that διὰ τοῦτο "looks ahead."

are the ones who are the true seed of Abraham.[1100] Since, however, the entrance and existence in faith only happens upon God's free call, it is a matter of grace, *sola gratia* – just as the outcome of faith, justification, has the character of a gift of grace (3:24) and is counted according to grace independent from any achievement (4:4). In fact grace and faith are so close to each other that in Paul's discussion with the law they become almost interchangeable entities,[1101] and occasionally assume a "spatial" connotation: Being on the "Christ-side," i.e., standing in Christ (Phil 4:1; 1Thess 3:8) equals standing in grace (Rom 5:2) and standing in faith (11:20; 1Cor 16:13).[1102] The reasoning proceeds as follows: "Therefore, the heirs are those of faith, so that the realization of the promise comes about solely according to grace."

As both consequence and purpose of this divine logic of faith and grace,[1103] the promise remains in full power and does not fall apart (cf. Rom 4:14). The beneficiaries of this universal validity of the promise – and this is the primary goal of this verse[1104] and the entire section 4:13-17 – are the totality of Abraham's seed. Indeed, Paul's expression οὐ τῷ ἐκ τοῦ νόμου μόνον ἀλλὰ καὶ τῷ ἐκ πίστεως 'Αβραάμ is somewhat imprecise.[1105] Does the first phrase (τὸ ἐκ τοῦ νόμου [σπέρμα]) signify Jewish-Christians[1106] or Jews *and* Jewish-Christians, i.e., members of the Jewish people in general,[1107] or even exclusively Jews not believing in Christ[1108]?

[1100] The elliptic verse Rom 4:16 should be supplemented by κληρονόμοι from 4:14 due to the parallelism of ἐκ νόμου and ἐκ πίστεως. Others suggest for a supplement ἐπαγγελία (cf. O. Kuss 1963, 189; E. Lohse 2003, 155) or God's salvation plan (W. Sanday/A.C. Headlam 1895, 112; C.K. Barrett 1957, 95f.; C.E.B. Cranfield 1975, 242) or even a general "Heilsprinzip" (H. Schlier 1977, 131).

[1101] Cf. H. Ridderbos 1970, 127; G. Friedrich 1982, 111.

[1102] See above chapter V.B.IV.4.b.(c).

[1103] Some prefer a final meaning of the infinitive clause, co-ordinate with ἵνα κατὰ χάριν (cf., e.g., C.E.B. Cranfield 1975, 242; R. Holst 1997, 322n.13), while others consider it consecutive (U. Wilckens 1978, 271n.878; E. Käsemann 1980, 114).

[1104] Cf. E. Käsemann 1980, 114. Against that C.E.B. Cranfield thinks that the main emphasis falls on βεβαίαν (1975, 242).

[1105] Cf. E. Käsemann 1980, 115.

[1106] Cf., e.g., C.E.B. Cranfield 1975, 242; U. Wilckens 1978, 272 (according to Wilckens, Gentile-Christians are only in view in the final part of the verse, i.e., τὸ ἐκ πίστεως 'Αβραάμ also refers to Jewish-Christians); E. Käsemann 1980, 113-115; J. Roloff 1990, 247 with n.36; D.J. Moo 1996, 279; K. Haacker 1999, 107; A.T. Lincoln 2002, 186; E. Lohse 2003, 155. See additional references in M. Neubrand 1997, 270n.19.

[1107] Cf., e.g., K. Berger 1966, 70; O. Michel 1978, 170; J.D.G. Dunn 1988, 216; M. Neubrand 1997, 271f.

[1108] Cf. F. Mußner 1980, 161f.; L. Gaston 1980, 58.

And the second phrase: Does it refer to Gentile-Christians[1109] or to believers in general[1110]? Again, one has to bear in mind that the Abraham-chapter firstly is addressed to a Christian audience and secondly cannot be read in isolation from Paul's account of the universal revelation of righteousness through πίστις Χριστοῦ to *all* who believe (3:21-22), of the truth that only through faith are we justified (3:28). Possibly, as with 4:11-12, a schematic comparison with the theme of the letter from 1:16 might indicate the apostle's intention and line of thought:

Rom 1:16	Rom 4:16
τὸ εὐαγγέλιον	ἐπαγγελία
δύναμις θεοῦ	βεβαία
παντὶ τῷ πιστεύοντι	παντὶ τῷ σπέρματι
Ἰουδαίῳ τε πρῶτον	οὐ τῷ ἐκ τοῦ νόμου μόνον
καὶ Ἕλληνι.	ἀλλὰ καὶ τῷ ἐκ πίστεως Ἀβραάμ.

The consequence and purpose of the *typos* of the gospel – the promise – is to become powerful for all those who believe, i.e., the entire true and legitimate seed of Abraham (Gal 3:7).[1111] There is no doubt in Paul of the Jews' salvation-historical advantage (πρῶτον),[1112] and so they remain the first addressees of the promise, but the force of God's word is effective (for salvation) only for those who believe.[1113] When Paul formulates ἐκ πίστεως Ἀβραάμ,[1114] not merely ἐκ πίστεως (as in the beginning of the

---

[1109] Cf. the majority of exegetes, e.g., T. Zahn 1925, 230-232; O. Michel 1978, 170; C.E.B. Cranfield 1975, 242f.; J. Roloff 1990, 247; D.J. Moo 1996, 279; K. Haacker 1999, 107; A.T. Lincoln 2002, 186; E. Lohse 2003, 155.

[1110] Cf., e.g., G. Klein 1963, 160f.; K. Berger 1966, 70n.44; F. Mußner 1980, 162.

[1111] Cf. D.J. Moo 1996, 278. The dative is *dativus commodi*.

[1112] Cf. H. Boers 1971, 89f., 92; O. Michel 1978, 88; J.C. Beker 1986. K. Barth distinguishes "Vorsprung" from "Vorrang" – and only the first is given to the Jews (1922, 16); yet since Abraham's faith stands for faith *before* circumcision, one could question the term "Vorsprung." One has to note the "ironic reversal" (R.L. Brawley 1997, 300) of the πρῶτον in Rom 2:9.

[1113] Cf. M. Neubrand 1997, 273, with reference to Rom 9:4; 15:8.

[1114] The expression ἐκ πίστεως Ἀβραάμ is anomalous from a grammatical point of view, as it lacks the article (cf. J.D.G. Dunn 1997, 254). With regard to the meaning of the subjective genitive R.B. Hays has claimed forcefully that the "parallelism between 3:26 and 4:16 is a fatal embarrassment for all interpreters who seek to treat Ἰησοῦ [in 3:26] as an objective genitive" (1997, 284; cf. M.D. Hooker 1989, 169; S.K. Stowers 1994, 201). Such a judgment misses the complex and multivalent character of the Greek genitive, which has been dealt with in regard to the πίστις Χριστοῦ-question: There, it has been argued that the meaning of the genitive oscillates between a subjective and an objective connotation and says that Christ brings, fills, and requires faith. Another occurrence of πίστις + genitive is 3:3, which means that "God is trustworthy because he is true to his promises," while in our present context the "faith of Abraham" "does not mean that

verse), his intention is to point to the specific circumstances of Abraham's believing, namely faith apart from the law, apart from being circumcised (Rom 4:11); this characterizes the faith of Gentiles. If according to this scheme, Ἰουδαῖος equals τὸ ἐκ τοῦ νόμου (σπέρμα), denoting the Jews *per se*, then this is immediately qualified insofar as the power and validity of gospel and promise are only effective in those who believe and are therefore true descendants of Abraham.[1115] In sum, therefore, both the gospel as the power of God and the promise in its unconditional validity benefit all those Jews and Gentiles who believe – and only them.

Notwithstanding the particular election of the Jewish people, Abraham's faith in uncircumcision warrants his typological function for Gentile believers. The sole criterion of faith for being among the descendants of the patriarch identifies the situation of Abraham more immediately with that of the Gentile believers than with that of the Jewish believers – from the perspective of the universal era of faith brought about by Christ. The person of Abraham prefigures both the advantage of the Jews in that he marks the beginning of Israel's "election history"[1116] and the position of Gentile believers, who like Abraham believe in uncircumcision.

With a solemn statement,[1117] Paul confirms that Abraham is the father of us all, of all Jewish and Gentile believers, and therefore specifies – not modifies[1118] – the formulation of the chapter's theme "Abraham our forefather" (4:1) in terms of "Abraham the father of all of us," of all his seed, of all who believe. Thereby, the inclusive πᾶς in 4:16 clearly reflects the πᾶς in 1:16 and 3:22, which refers to the believers.[1119]

Now that Paul has made unmistakably clear from his exegesis of Genesis 15 that the promise, faith, righteousness, and grace derive from the law-free sphere, he can open the exegetical horizon without the risk of misunderstandings and refer to a passage from that chapter in Genesis, which he had continuously considered in distinction to the "faith-chapter" (Genesis 15), namely from Genesis 17.[1120] By means of the quote from Gen 17:5

Abraham was trustworthy, but that he trusted God, relying totally on him who was able to do what he had promised" (S.K. Williams 1980, 275). Each context requires a fresh determination of the meaning, and analogous syntactical phenomena do not *a priori* require a parallelism concerning semantics.

[1115] Accordingly, the group designated with οἱ ἐκ νόμου (Rom 4:14) is different to τὸ ἐκ τοῦ νόμου (σπέρμα) (4:16) (cf. G.N. Davies 1990, 169n.2).

[1116] Cf. U. Wilckens 1961, 45; see Neh 9:7; also Deut 4:37; 10:15.

[1117] Cf. the introduction ὅς ἐστιν; O. Michel 1978, 170.

[1118] See the interpretation of Rom 4:1 given above pages 325-327.

[1119] Cf. J.D.G. Dunn 1988, 216.

[1120] Though it is true that the quote derives from the divine promise to Abraham given in Gen 17:4-8 and not to the command of circumcision (17:9-14), it is likely that just as Paul considers Genesis 15 as one entity, he obtains a like stance regarding Genesis 17,

Paul reaffirms Abraham's fatherhood of innumerable peoples,[1121] and affirms that in the sight of God (κατέναντι)[1122] this promise had become reality, just when Abraham entered the sphere of faith (ἐπίστευσεν).[1123] Abraham's call into faith through the promise, which itself has its place in faith (Rom 4:13-14), coincides with the realization of the promise, whose content had been part of God's plan from the beginning of his relationship with Abraham.[1124]

The greatness of the promise and the impossibility of its realization in the sight of Abraham pose the question: Who is the God in whom Abraham believed? We have to draw together previous statements to attain the whole picture: He is the one God, who justifies Jews and Gentiles on grounds of and through faith (3:30), i.e., who justifies the ungodly (4:5), who[1125] "gives life to the dead and calls into existence the things that do not exist" (4:17).[1126] Through these characteristics, Paul assembles four fundamental pillars of his vision of God, which uphold, in their innate relationship, the structure and contents of Christian faith: monotheism, *iustificatio impii*, *resurrectio mortuorum* and *creatio ex nihilo*.[1127] Since "God is one," creator and ruler of all things, he is able to transcend and transform obvious realities and their consequences: Through his miraculous

---

which reports events taking place a full 29 years later, according to rabbinic theology (cf. P. Billerbeck 1926, 203).

[1121] Cf. J. Jeremias 1970, 55: "Πολλοί ist includierend."

[1122] On this translation see C.E.B. Cranfield 1975, 243. For Abraham, the visible fulfillment of the promise remains an object of his hope (cf. Rom 4:18 and the expression παρ' ἐλπίδα ἐπ' ἐλπίδι; see below pages 379f.).

[1123] Cf. E. Lohse 2003, 155. – On the attraction of the relative clause see F. Blass/A. Debrunner/F. Rehkopf 1979, §294.

[1124] The perfect form τέθεικα or יתתנ from Gen 17:5 parallels the ותחנ from Gen 15:18 (but see Septuagint: δώσω) and is performative perfect (cf. C. Brockelmann 1956, §41d), in which the speech act itself concurs with the realization of the promise.

[1125] On the participle-style, see G. Delling 1963, 31f.

[1126] The phrase ὡς ὄντα is somewhat problematic due to the particle ὡς, which regularly points to a comparison ("... as if they existed"); cf. the different possibilities of translation in W. Sanday/A.C. Headlam 1895, 113, to which C.E.B. Cranfield points (1975, 244). He himself argues that the particle might as well be consecutive and that the infinitive (or indicative) has been replaced by the participle "to express vividly the immediacy of the result." See similarly E. Käsemann 1980, 117; J.D.G. Dunn 1988, 218; T.H. Tobin 1995, 450n.26.

[1127] That Paul thinks of a *creatio ex nihilo* is obvious on grounds of the context. Cf. O. Hofius 1971/1972; C.E.B. Cranfield 1975, 244. See, however, against that D.J. Moo 1996, 281f.

power,[1128] ungodliness, death, nothingness become justification, life, creation.[1129]

In his statement Paul incorporates two liturgically shaped divine predicates, which have several counterparts in Jewish writings[1130] and which constitute together with the confession to monotheism basic tenets of the belief of Paul's Jewish contemporaries. But amidst this agreed-upon foundation he places his revolutionary teaching of the justification of the ungodly, which both interprets and is interpreted by the traditional fundamentals: God's generative capacity, which creates *ex nihilo* through the word of creation and gives life to the dead, is an expression of and is effective in his value-judgment on Abraham's faith.

The portrayal of God's character in 4:17 creates multiple links to other parts of the chapter, but also reaches beyond its boundaries. With the first predication of God Paul has already in mind the miracle of the revivification of the dead bodies of Abraham and Sarah (4:19), and in the climax of the chapter he will point to the salvation-historical meaning of this predication, which lies in the resurrection of Jesus from the dead.[1131] The language of new creation is connected to the Day of Atonement,[1132] which establishes links to 3:24-26, 4:7-8, and 4:25, while the καλεῖν-terminology implicates God's word of creation and election, which belongs fundamentally to the language of justification.[1133]

[1128] Cf. Rom 1:4 with 4:17 (δύναμις). See also R. Bultmann 1959, 207.

[1129] S.J. Gathercole contends: "What has not been sufficiently recognized is how Paul's God-language comes in the context of faith. It is an essential pre-requisite of faith that it is faith in such a God" (2004, 165).

[1130] O. Hofius provides parallels from early Jewish sources (1971/1972): The sentence ὁ ζῳοποιῶν τοὺς νεκρούς is found literally in the Jewish-Hellenistic writing *Joseph and Aseneth* (*JosAs* 20,7), and a Hebrew parallel appears in the second benediction of the *Shemoneh Esreh* (cf. 4Q521 7 + 5 ii 6; *bKetub* 8b; but also 2Cor 1:9). Concerning the second phrase ὁ καλῶν τὰ μὴ ὄντα ὡς ὄντα, which speaks of a *creatio ex nihilo*, Hofius refers to *2Bar* 21,4; 48,8; *JosAs* 12,1-2. Comparable passages in Philo (e.g., *Spec* 4,187) are improper parallels due to the Platonic influence on the Alexandrinian theologian, according to which the world was an "unformed mass (ἄμορφος ὕλη)" before creation (O. Hofius 1971/1972, 60n.10). While the juxtaposition of both predicates in Joseph and Asenath (20,7; 12,2) lacks the eschatological dimension of the resurrection of the dead, another parallel is closer to Paul: 2Macc 7,28-29 (cf. 7,23). There, eschatological resurrection is seen as expression and work of the generative power of God. See also H. Moxnes 1980, 241-247.

[1131] Cf. C.E.B. Cranfield 1975, 244.

[1132] Cf. P. Stuhlmacher 1975, 134.

[1133] See Rom 8:30(*bis*); 9:7.12.24.25.26. Cf. P. Stuhlmacher 1966, 233; M. Neubrand 1997, 280. – According to L. Gaston, Paul refers to God's calling into being a church that includes Gentiles (1980, 57, with reference to D. Zeller 1973, 105).

c) Romans 4:18-21: Faith and Reality – the Nature of πίστις[1134]

After elaborating the foundational salvation-historical framework in which he sees the place of faith, Paul explores and analyzes Abraham's *modus fidei* from its beginning as response to God's promise (ἐπίστευσεν; Gen 15:6), but also reaching into the desolation of its non-fulfillment.[1135] The motifs of his presentation, Paul extracts and selects from the Old Testament story.[1136] Throughout this part, Abraham figures as subject and all verbal elements appear in the narrative tense of the aorist. The result is not an a-historical, abstract definition of faith, but a description of faith according to Abraham's biography.[1137] Notably, these verses are notoriously neglected in those exegetes who exclusively concentrate on Abraham's fatherhood as undergirding theme of Romans 4.[1138]

The oxymoron[1139] παρ' ἐλπίδα ἐπ' ἐλπίδι,[1140] which in a remarkable way expresses the two extremes of the whole spectrum of Abraham's mode of faith, has been said to prefigure at the same time the structure of the ensuing verses.[1141] On the one hand Abraham knows and feels the despair in view of his and his wife's dead bodies (νέκρωσις) (4:19) – therefore, he

---

[1134] On this section see especially M. Theobald 2001.

[1135] Cf. E. Kühl 1913, 152 ("Art des Glaubens Abrahams"); F. Hahn 1971, 103 ("Wesen des Glaubens Abrahams"); C.E.B. Cranfield 1975, 225 ("the essential character of Abraham's faith"); O. Michel 1978, 173 (*"Analyse des Glaubensvorgangs"*; italics original); J. Roloff 1990, 247 ("Wesensbeschreibung des Glaubens Abrahams"); J.D.G. Dunn 1998, 377 (Rom 4:13-22: "clearest and most powerful exposition of what he [*sc.* Paul] understood by *pistis*"); S.J. Gathercole 2004, 162 (Rom 4:[18]19-21: "most revealing depiction of faith"; "definition of the nature of faith").

[1136] Such "selective and dramatic retelling of biblical stories was quite common in Jewish of this period" (T.H. Tobin 1995, 449, listing passages from *Jubilees*, Philo, or Josephus – some of which have already figured in our previous discussion).

[1137] Cf. J. Jeremias 1970, 55.

[1138] Cf. R.B. Hays 1985, 90f.; M. Cranford 1995, 86f. M. Neubrand's elaborate exegesis does not take into consideration the description of Abraham's faith as "hope against hope" at all (cf. 1997, 280f.), and the section 4:19(!)-22 is assigned a mere four pages (282-285).

[1139] Cf. J. Jeremias 1970, 55; M. Theobald 2001, 406, with reference to relevant literature.

[1140] The construction παρ' ἐλπίδα could denote either "beyond hope" or "against hope," but because of the "sheer impossibility (according to human calculations) of the promise ... we should ... understand πάρα to mean 'against'" (C.E.B. Cranfield 1975, 245; cf. Vulgate: "contra spem"; also Rom 11:24). The expression ἐπ' ἐλπίδι is either "on the basis of hope," i.e., of God's promise (thus most commentators), or "formelhaft" Abraham's state of mind when he began to believe (cf. O. Michel 1978, 172); the promise from Gen 15:5 quoted by Paul in this verse makes the first solution most likely, while the psychologizing tendency of the latter appears to miss Paul's intention.

[1141] Cf. E. Kühl 1913, 152; J. Jeremias 1970, 55; O. Michel 1978, 173; M. Theobald 2001, 406; E. Lohse 2003, 160f.

believed against hope. On the other hand Abraham knows about and was filled with the certainty that God is able to fulfill what he has promised (4:20-21) – therefore, he believed on the basis of hope.

Attractive as this exegesis is, an alternate solution suggests itself on grounds of the following considerations: Paul's entire argumentation and his conclusion that Abraham is the father of all believers depend to a great degree on the chronological distance of Genesis 15 and 17; a nullification of this principle seems awkward. Above, we saw that for Paul Abraham's response to God's initial promise (Gen 15:6) marks the entrance into his relationship with God, his access into faith.[1142] Already there the tension of the extremes of faith materialize in Abraham's hopelessness of not having a son to inherit his land (Gen 15:2-3) and the hope based upon the word of God (Gen 15:5; cf. Rom 4:18), reaching the patriarch amidst the crisis.[1143] Only subsequent to this stage in Abraham's life, years later, in the growing despair about the still unfulfilled assurance of an heir, Abraham's (and Sarah's) age (Gen 17:1.17; cf. Rom 4:19) and the motif of Abraham's and Sarah's barrenness come into play (Gen 17:17; 18:12-13; cf. Rom 4:19). In all that, Abraham knew that what God has promised he is able to do (Gen 18:14; cf. Rom 4:21). Consequently, the temporal gap between Genesis 15 and 17-18 is reflected in Rom 4:18 and 4:19-21,[1144] but at the same time bridged by the continuance of Abraham's faith.

This suggestion by no means advocates that the section 4:19-21 stands for a psychological analysis of a development of faith in various steps[1145]; rather it analyzes the challenges and trials of faith, which already determine the beginning of faith (4:18), but extend to the existence in and through faith as well (4:19-21).[1146] What is regarded by Paul as Abraham's "faith" comprises both his entering and his being in the sphere of faith as one continuous mode.

Once Paul's temporal differentiation between two perspectives on Abraham's faith is acknowledged, the direction of meaning of the infini-

---

[1142] See the inchoative character of ἐπίστευσεν. Thus, Rom 4:18 paraphrases Gen 15:6 (cf. O. Michel 1978, 172), not the entire faith-history of Abraham.

[1143] Some particularly apt interpretations of the expression παρ᾽ ἐλπίδα ἐπ᾽ ἐλπίδι may be mentioned: Chrysostom, *Homiliae in epistulam ad Romanos* 8 (quoted in C.E.B. Cranfield 1975, 245): Παρ᾽ ἐλπίδα τὴν ἀνθρωπίνην, ἐπ᾽ ἐλπίδι τῇ τοῦ Θεοῦ. M. Luther 1515/1516, 308: "Primum 'spem' significat rem speratam naturaliter... Secundum vero significat rem supernaturaliter speratam." J.A. Bengel 1773, 561: "*Praeter spem* rationis, *in spe* promissionis *credidit*" (italics original). A. Jülicher (quoted in H. Lietzmann 1928, 55): "Er hat, wo nichts zu hoffen war, glaubensvoll zu hoffen gewagt."

[1144] Against M. Theobald 2001, 409: "Paulus projeziert Gen 15 und 17 ineinander."

[1145] See also K. Barth 1922, 111.

[1146] Cf. O. Michel 1978, 173; M. Theobald 2001, 407. Against M.J. Lagrange, who detects in Rom 4:19-21 "trois degrés dans l'état d'âme d'Abraham" (1950, 96).

tive clause (εἰς τὸ γενέσθαι...) is easier to determine[1147]: It does not transfer Gen 17:5 into the content of the initial impulse of Abraham's faith,
merging this promise with Gen 15:5,[1148] but provides its prospect – either
in terms of its consequence,[1149] or in terms of its divinely instituted purpose.[1150] Abraham found access in the salvation-historical reality of faith,
so that he would become the father of many people; this purpose has already been encapsulated in the initial promise: "So numerous shall your
descendants be" (Gen 15:5).[1151]

In Rom 4:19 we become witnesses of the struggles and sufferings of a
believer's existence who desperately awaits the fulfillment and realization
of what God has promised.[1152] Perseverance belongs essentially to faith
and combines the punctual reaction to the promise and the coming to faith
with a permanent, enduring disposition.[1153] But despite his despair, Abraham had not become weak in faith, but rather the consideration of his
physical νέκρωσις emerges from the faith, in which he stands: "And[1154]
since he did not weaken in faith," or: "And by not weakening in faith,[1155]

[1147] On a brief summary of possible explanations of the infinitive clause, see R. Holst
1997, 322n.13.

[1148] The following exegetes, for instance, regard the infinitive clause as portraying the
content of Abraham's faith: E. Kühl 1913, 151f.; R. Bultmann 1959, 207 (with caution);
O. Kuss 1963, 192; O. Michel 1972, 172 (as one option); M. Theobald 2001, 405, 409.
Such a designation of faith would be singular in Paul (cf. E. Lohse 2003, 160).

[1149] On the consecutive meaning, see M. Luther 1515/1516, 304; C.E.B. Cranfield
1975, 246; H. Schlier 1977, 133; D.J. Moo 1996, 283; E. Lohse 2003, 160.

[1150] On the final meaning, see J. Murray 1959, 148; N. Turner 1963, 143; K. Berger
1966, 72n.52; J.D.G. Dunn 1988, 219.

[1151] In his quote of Gen 15:5, Paul follows the Septuagint word by word.

[1152] Especially D. Lührmann pointed out that in biblical tradition faith has its place in
situations of crises and function as mediation of confession and experience (cf. 1976,
34f.; 47, 51, 53, 59, 86f.).

[1153] Cf., e.g., K. Haacker 1984, 298; 1993, 135f. Paul expresses the durative character
of faith also through the present participle of πιστεύειν (Rom 1:16; 3:22; 4:11.24;
10:4.11; Gal 3:22). These elements of perseverance and constancy agree with the result
of our analysis of וְהֶאֱמִן in Gen 15:6 (see above chapter III.D.IV.2).

[1154] The καί is not καί-*explicativum* (thus M. Theobald 2001, 407 with n.33), but it introduces a next argumentative step.

[1155] Hence, the regular grammatical relationship between participle and finite verb is
retained (cf. on this syntax M. Zerwick 1994, 263, 376; most exegetes follow this rule);
yet an alternate syntactical solution has been considered on grounds of the fact that occasionally, the finite verb of a clause subordinates to the participle, which in turn assumes
the main emphasis (cf. M. Zerwick 1994, 130, who suggests this solution for Rom 4:19;
see also D.J. Moo 1996, 283).

he looked at his body as a body that was irrevocably dead[1156] ... and at the death[1157] of the womb of Sarah."

To justify this reading, brief note should be made of a most interesting textual issue[1158]: Did Abraham consider his and his wife's unpromising physical circumstances (κατενόησεν) or did he refuse to take into account this reality, trusting blindly in God's promise (οὐ κατενόησεν)[1159]? Here, a text-critical issue symbolizes two kinds of attitudes of faith with two contrary perspectives on reality.[1160] Clearly, both from a text-critical and theological perspective the first reading is to be preferred: Being in faith means not overlooking the human condition, means believing against hope and "set[ing] at defiance all known canons of probability"[1161]; being empowered through the power of faith allows for a rational (νοῦς) and critical

---

[1156] The perfect tense of the participle νενεκρωμένον, used predicatively, expresses definiteness. The translation "as good as dead" (NRSV; also, e.g., F.F. Bruce 1978, 70; W. Baird 1988, 377; J.A. Fitzmyer 1993, 387; T.H. Tobin 1995, 450) is clearly too weak. Apart from Rom 4:19, the verb νεκροῦν occurs only in Col 3:5 and Heb 11:12; the close convergence of the vocabulary in Paul and the author of Hebrews might point to the existence of a pre-formed Abraham tradition. Heb 11:11-12 reads: "Through faith (πίστει) he received power (δύναμιν) of procreation, even though Sarah herself was barren, because he considered him faithful (πιστόν) who had promised (ἐπαγγειλάμενον). Therefore from one person, and this one as dead (νενεκρωμένου), descendants were born, as many as the stars of heaven" (cf. J. Jeremias 1970, 56 with n.22; H. Moxnes 1980, 195-203. Jeremias refers to M. Black's suggestion [1964] that the phrase καὶ αὐτὴ Σάρρα στεῖρα represents a semitizing element pointing to the condition of Sarah, while Abraham remains the syntactical subject. He receives the power of a seminal emission [καταβολή] and becomes the father of many; cf., e.g., G. Schunack 2002, 172-175). See also Heb 11:19: "He considered the fact that God is able (δυνατὸς ὁ θεός) even to raise someone from the dead (ἐκ νεκρῶν ἐγείρειν)..."

[1157] Apart from Rom 4:19, the term νέκρωσις appears only in 2Cor 4:10, there referring to the death of Jesus. See below note 1169.

[1158] See B.M. Metzger 1994, 451, on the manuscripts representing the two readings.

[1159] Only with the publication of "modern" text-critical editions, the original reading could slowly get the upper hand (cf. C. von Tischendorf [1865]; B.F. Westcott/F.J.A. Hort; H. von Soden; E. Nestle). The secondary version, which most likely goes back to a scribal emendation, adding the particle οὐ according to a certain understanding of faith, was widespread among commentators in the first centuries, in the middle ages, until the 20th century; cf., e.g., Origen, Jerome, Augustine, Pelagius, Abaelard, Thomas Aquinas, M. Luther, and J. Calvin. The ancient commentaries are partly listed in K.H. Schelkle 1956, 139f. – See on these data especially M. Theobald 2001, 400f.

[1160] D.J. Moo denies a "significant meaning in difference" – assuming different (verifiable?) connotations of κατανοεῖν – but opts for the nowadays preferred reading without οὐ (1996, 271f.n.2); however, in his explanation he approvingly quotes J. Calvin, who calls Christian to close their eyes in view of themselves – just like Abraham closed his eyes (284). F. Hahn, too, considers the variant theologically insignificant (1971, 104f.n.60; cf. B.M. Metzger 1994, 451).

[1161] F.F. Bruce 1978, 70.

dealing with the actual conditions, averting the danger of falling prey to illusions.[1162] In Paul's wording, the strength received in faith is even pre-supposed as the proper background of Abraham's critical considera-tions.[1163] Abraham represents the "paradox of being"[1164] that actively ac-cepts the dilemma of human incapability and helplessness and believes despite or rather because of this[1165]; it is a disposition that even deals with the fact of death with open eyes![1166]

But for Paul's Abraham the paradox is broken, not through human strength, but through the one who fills the sphere of faith with power, the one to whom individual faith is directed, to God who "gives life to the dead (τοὺς νεκρούς)" (4:17) and who "raised Jesus, our Lord, from the dead (ἐκ νεκρῶν)" (4:24).[1167] Upon realizing one's own utter powerless-ness, one is left with a radical abandonment in the hands of God, who cre-ates new future and life – and who therefore receives glory (4:20). The godless Abraham (4:5) and the hopeless Abraham, the Abraham *ante fidem* and the Abraham *in fide* finds himself in total dependence on God and his promise.

With these thoughts on Abraham's desperate situation, but also his well-founded hope, Paul anticipates the theme of the following chapter (5:1-11): The one who is justified through faith can expect with certainty the future glory of God (5:2) and salvation from his wrath (5:9), since faith is di-rected to the God who raised Jesus from the dead for our justification (4:24-25), and in his life we are saved (5:10).[1168] In this well-founded and exultant hope, we can boast (5:2), since hope never puts us to shame (5:5); but at the same time hope is inevitably connected with existential border-

---

[1162] Cf. A. Schlatter 1935, 170; E. Käsemann 1969, 162: The believer is not character-ized by the *credo quia absurdum*, but by the *credo absurdum*. H. Schlier 1977, 134: "Ge-rade in der Nüchternheit, die die menschlichen Fakten nicht übersieht, bewährt sich die Hoffnung, die gegen alle Hoffnung ist."

[1163] Cf. the participle construction μὴ ἀσθενήσας: "As he did not weaken in faith..."

[1164] S. Kierkegaard (quoted in O. Schmitz 1922, 123).

[1165] Cf. A. Schlatter 1935, 170: "Nicht trotz seines Unvermögens, sondern wegen des-selben glaubt er."

[1166] Cf. E. Fuchs 1958, 243: "Der Glaube spekuliert nicht; Paulus idealisiert nicht."

[1167] Notably, this important aspect is the main critique of A. Schlatter against K. Barth's adaptation of S. Kierkegaard's "paradox" in his commentary on Romans (cf., e.g., K. Barth 1922, 6, 80f.): "[B]ei Barth [bleibt] der Glaube 'ein Sprung ins Leere' [K. Barth 1922, 81], und damit öffnet sich zwischen der Auslegung und dem Römerbrief eine tiefe Kluft. Paulus sprang nicht in das Leere, sondern schloß sich Jesus an" (A. Schlatter 1922, 146).

[1168] Some argue therefore that the following three chapters (Rom 5:1-8:39) are created as an advocacy and encouragement for the Christian hope (cf., e.g., U. Schnelle 2002, 137: Romans 5-8 as "Ringkomposition"); yet there is great scholarly dissent regarding the place and function of Romans 5 in the structure of the letter.

line experiences, which are likewise accepted in the reality of life – "we also boast in our sufferings."[1169] This profound and paradox ambivalence – παρ' ἐλπίδα ἐπ' ἐλπίδι – is solved through the love of God, exhibited in Jesus Christ, poured into our hearts and therefore moulding our existence as believers (5:5). God's love is the power that infuses logic into the chain-conclusion of 5:2-5.

But after this brief outlook into Paul's further argumentation, we have to ask how does Paul understand πίστις here, in 4:19? At first one might note the agreement of 3:28 and 4:19 regarding the grammatical case[1170]: Neither there nor here does Paul put the majority of weight on the human side of the relationship with God, or even on the act of faith produced in the soul, but rather on the larger picture of faith and on the horizon of the event of salvation, consisting in God's giving and realizing his promise. After coming to faith, Abraham's existence *coram deo* happens in and is determined by this reality. In 4:19, therefore, Paul is *not* focusing on Abraham's "strong faith,"[1171] but on his becoming strong in the sphere of faith,[1172] whereby faith again takes on a "spatial" meaning.[1173] Abraham's "strength" describes the manner how the dynamics of faith affects his existence, how the "measure of faith" (12:3) becomes operative in his life.[1174]

A compilation of analogous Pauline expressions, using πίστις in the dative, affirms this point: In his retrospective on 3:21-4:25, Paul says: "In and through faith (τῇ πίστει)[1175] we have obtained access to this grace in which we stand" (5:2), i.e., in the faith that comes through Christ and in which we participate, we also participate and stand in grace. Therefore, the

---

[1169] In this context, M. Theobald (2001, 415f.) refers to the remarkable passages in 2Corinthians where Paul deals in an open, realistic way with his own weaknesses, limitations, failures, sufferings and illness, "always carrying in the body the death (νέκρωσις) of Jesus, so that the life of Jesus may also be made visible in our body" (2Cor 4:10).

[1170] Cf. Rom 3:28: πίστει with 4:19: τῇ πίστει. The lack of the article in 3:28 is explained by the doctrinal style (cf. E. Lohse 2003, 138).

[1171] Against D.J. Moo 1996, 283. This plus a consecutive understanding of the infinitive clause in Rom 4:18 comes close to the pattern work – reward, so ardently refuted by Paul. Cf. again Sir 44,21. Paul does not talk about "his faith" (ἡ πίστις αὐτοῦ) (against, e.g., S.J. Gathercole 2002, 239).

[1172] Paul is also not concerned with a parallelism between sinful flesh (Rom 3:20; σάρξ) and Abraham's dead body (4:19; σῶμα) (against S.J. Gathercole 2002, 239).

[1173] Even though many exegetes determine the dative in Rom 4:19 as *dativus relationis* (cf. E. Lohse 2003, 160n.3), it does have a local, spatial connotation. – The (clearly secondary) *varia lectio* ἐν τῇ πίστει also brings to expression this feature (thus the manuscripts D* F G).

[1174] Starting from Paul's personal faith, J. de Zwaan stresses "daß die Initiative, die Kraft, usw. ganz von der andern Seite kommen" (1936, 134; cf. 122).

[1175] On the text-critical problem of τῇ πίστει in Rom 5:2, see, e.g., H. Lietzmann 1928, 58.

believer stands in faith[1176] and lives in faith.[1177] When Paul knows of Abraham that he did not become weak in faith, he also knows of some Roman Christians who are indeed "weak in faith."[1178] Nevertheless, Paul never retreats from his basic conviction that we are justified in and through faith (3:28); in whatever conditions participation in the realm of faith happens (weakness or strength), faith remains *fides iustificans*.

In notable contrast to Gen 15:2-3.8 and Gen 17:17, Paul removes all traces of protest, weakness or doubt from Abraham's state of faith and hence adheres to an idealized image of Abraham common in his time.[1179] He does not exhibit disbelieving doubts against the promise,[1180] and therefore does not stand on the side of distrust and disbelief,[1181] which, as we have seen,[1182] means not accepting that God is God,[1183] that he is the judge who decrees, the creator, "who calls into existence things that do not exist" (Rom 4:17).[1184] Doubt, therefore, may not be limited to the realm of the psyche in terms of a struggle in the inner life generated by the contrariety of reality, but doubt essentially incorporates the notion of arguing against

---

[1176] Cf. Rom 11:20: τῇ πίστει ἑστάναι; 1Cor 16:13: ἑστάναι ἐν τῇ πίστει; 2Cor 1:24: τῇ πίστει ἑστάναι; 13:5: εἶναι ἐν τῇ πίστει.

[1177] Cf. Gal 2:20: ἐν πίστει ζῶν.

[1178] Cf. Rom 14:1: ἀσθενεῖν τῇ πίστει. On the basis of this and several other keyword connections between Romans 4 and 14, A.T. Lincoln argues – "and this has been virtually totally neglected" (1992, 166; but see, e.g., A. von Dobbeler 1987, 236) – that "Paul signals clearly ahead of time where he stands theologically in the debate in Rome. Abraham does not merely exemplify the Pauline gospel as one who is righteous by faith, but he also joins the debate in Rome on the side of the strong in faith" (172; approvingly cited in N. Calvert-Koyzis 2005, 137f.).

[1179] Cf., e.g., W. Baird 1988, 377. See, however, L.M. Barth 1992, 258-262, on rabbinic texts that problematize Abraham's reaction to God's promise. He refers to *bNed* 32a: "He [*sc.* Abraham] went too far in testing the promises of the Lord." *TgPs-J* Gen 15:13: God accuses Abraham that "you did not believe." *ExR* 5,22 (cf. R. Davidson 1983, 44). On the other hand, there are numerous, partly elaborate, arguments from most different contexts that Abraham believed without wavering (cf. Philo, *Mut* 175-217; CD 3,2-4; *Pirqe Rabbi Eliezer*, 26-31). – On the interpretation according to which Gen 15:2-3.8 do not express doubt, see above page 97.

[1180] It seems that "doubts in unbelief" is stronger than merely "doubts," for the notion of unbelief expresses the separation from God, which is not true for "doubts" *per se*.

[1181] Τῇ ἀπιστίᾳ includes a causal sense (see F. Blass/A. Debrunner/F. Rehkopf 1979, §196,1 and n.1), but is also "dative of 'sphere'" (D.J. Moo 1996, 284n.79). See above note 1173 on τῇ πίστει.

[1182] See above page 255 on Rom 3:3.

[1183] Cf. E. Käsemann 1980, 141 (sin as denial that God is God, i.e., as offense against the first commandment).

[1184] Cf. again P. Stuhlmacher 1966, 227.

the sovereign God and his decrees – here, against his promise.[1185] Like-wise, unbelief is not merely lack of trust in God's miraculous power,[1186] but it is for Paul the basic sin marked by sarkic reasoning which correlates with an existence apart from God, even active hostility to God (8:7). Moving away from faith toward unbelief would implicate Abraham's return to that stage in his life, which he has left behind through his coming to faith upon God's promise (4:3), i.e., his return into this negative sphere that Paul described in 1:18-3:20, marked by ἀσέβεια and ἀδικία (1:18; cf. 4:3-5).

Yet Paul assures us that Abraham became strong in and through the reality that determined his existence as believer since his exit from paganism, from ungodliness. In contrast to M. Buber's view on the Pauline faith, therefore, faith is not restricted to an inner-human, psychological act,[1187] through which one places oneself as individual being at God's side, maintaining an emotionally nourished relationship with God. Faith is not merely in the inside, but surrounds the believer, who is part of the community of believers in a divinely established salvation-historical, salvation-giving reality.[1188] The divine passive[1189] ἐνεδυναμώθη spells out that God (is not only the originator of this phenomenon of faith, but also) gave him the power to remain and grow in this faith and to believe in the promise against all appearances. It also expresses Abraham's utter dependence on God and his inability to contribute anything to the fulfillment of the promise.[1190] Abraham's faith is not primarily characterized by his heroic "Dennoch!,"[1191] through which he himself offers resistance against the trials and sufferings attacking his very faith, but by his knowledge that everything is possible to God and that his word can accomplish miracles,[1192] even physi-

---

[1185] Cf. M. Barth 1970a, 59f., who supports his view by etymological and lexicographical considerations. The term διακρίνεσθαι is not known from pre-New Testament times, but appears as opposite of faith in Rom 14:23; Mk 11:23; Jas 1:6.

[1186] Against R. Bultmann 1959, 207.

[1187] Cf. M. Buber 1953, 683. Against that, e.g., L. Gaston 1980, 57 (no "existential abstraction").

[1188] Therefore, as in Rom 4:19, the dative τῇ πίστει in 4:20 again incorporates a local connotation and is not merely "dative of respect" (C.E.B. Cranfield 1975, 248).

[1189] Against that D.J. Moo wants to read a "genuine passive" (1996, 285n.83).

[1190] Thus, there is a profound association between the two phrases ἐνδυναμοῦσθαι τῇ πίστει (Rom 4:20) and δικαιοῦσθαι πίστει (3:28).

[1191] See, however, K. Barth 1922, 80: "Glaube an Jesus ist das radikale Trotzdem." A. Deißmann 1925, 127f.; J. Jeremias 1970, 56, 58. See against this view M. Barth 1970a, 59f., but also above note 1167.

[1192] On the significance and complexity of the phenomenon of "miracle faith" in Hellenistic religiosity, see G. Schunack 1999, 312, 322-326 (see above chapter II.G.VIII).

cal miracles (4:21; cf. Gen 18:14).[1193] Therefore, even though the meaning
of ἐνεδυναμώθη has a distinctive spiritual component,[1194] in Paul's view the
physical miracle is included, and Abraham *regained* his sexual virility[1195] –
though not in a sense that God *retained* it, for this understanding would
stand in contradiction to the perfect form νενεκρωμένον.[1196] In any case,
however, for Paul, the mode of realization of the promise is rather insignificant, for he is interested in the fact that Abraham and Sarah overcame
their infertility in faith, knowing that God's omnipotence is bound to and
realizes what he has promised.

God's making strong Abraham in and through faith receives an explication by means of two aorist participles that elucidate what preceded his
being strengthened: Through clinging to God's promise and through his
recognition that he stands empty-handed before God with respect to the
promise's fulfillment, he gave glory to God, hence taking a position opposite to "the ungrateful pagan of 1:21, 23"[1197] and opposite to the one who
trusts in his own achievement before God (cf. 4:2). He was fully convinced[1198] that solely God has the power to fulfill what he has promised.

[1193] Paul's use of δυνατός (and ἐνεδυναμώθη) recalls the keyword δύναμις from his
propositio in Rom 1:17. Both terms belong to the miracle-terminology. – In this context
Jesus' word to the father of the epileptic boy are noteworthy: ὁ δὲ Ἰησοῦς εἶπεν αὐτῷ·
τὸ εἰ δύνῃ, πάντα δυνατὰ τῷ πιστεύοντι (Mk 9:23). "Die Macht des Glaubens ist
geradezu gekennzeichnet als die Macht Gottes" (G. Ebeling 1958, 96; it is not likely that
Jesus is perceived as the subject of faith, as propagated, for instance, in M. Buber 1953,
661; E. Fuchs 1958, 254). One could assume here an overestimation of the possibilities
of human faith that concentrates on the individual realization of the divine power in the
subjective existence. But see the careful exegetical and theological treatment of this passage by O. Hofius (2004), which responds to such concerns: The goal is to point to the
power of God.

[1194] O. Michel regards this as primary meaning (1978, 173f.n.8).

[1195] Especially M. Barth stresses the sexual or biological component; even the second
divine passive πληροφορηθείς denotes "fruchtbaren Sexualverkehr" (1970a, 60f.; quote:
61); cf. T. Zahn 1925, 239; M.-E. Boismard 1955, 71; J. Jeremias 1970, 56, who points to
the parallel passage Heb 11:11, where the physical component is clearly present.

[1196] Against O. Kuss 1963, 192. – M. Theobald refers to passages in Philo (*Cher* 40-
52), which could indicate the idea in Judaism of a virginal conception, i.e., God as the
actual father of Isaac (2001, 410).

[1197] J.A. Fitzmyer 1993, 388. The "contrast between Abraham's faith and the Gentiles'
failure" (E. Adams 1997, 47) has been noted by many exegetes (see, e.g., C.E.B. Cranfield 1975, 249; U. Wilckens 1978, 276n.895; J.D.G. Dunn 1988, 22; M.D. Hooker 1989,
170; and additional literature referred to in E. Adams 1997, 47n.1). In addition to the
correlation between Rom 1:21 and 4:20, Adams points to verbal and thematic links between 1:18 and 4:5 (ἀσέβεια/ἀδικία and δικαιοῦν/ἀσεβής), 1:20.25 and 4:17b (God as
creator); 1:20 and 4:21 (δύναμις and δυνατός) (1997, 51-55).

[1198] The καί before the second participle is probably epexegetical (cf. J. Jeremias
1970, 57), hence not – as most argue – coordinating the two participles.

Paul's concept of faith is essentially shaped by its orientation to the almighty God, whose promise calls for, creates, and at the same time sustains faith, and who calls the individual into the reality of faith, in which
the promise roots, and who strengthens the believer's existence therein.
God's act and his glory constitute origin and goal of human faith,[1199] while
the claim of own meritorious acts and the failure to give glory to God are
human "Ursünde," "the core sin."[1200]

6. Romans 4:22-25: The Application of Abraham's Faith ("For Us")

With another appeal to Gen 15:6 in Rom 4:22 Paul reaches the christological climax of his interpretation of Abraham.[1201] Paul omits the first part of
the Genesis-verse, but the logic of his line of thought makes plain what his
incomplete quotation rests on: 4:18 is introduced by ὃς ἐπίστευσεν and the
entire previous segment (4:18-21) dealt comprehensively with Abraham's
justifying faith. This means that the conjunction διό takes up this explication of Gen 15:6a, but also applies it on a meta-level[1202]: Here, in Rom
4:22-25, Paul actualizes his interpretation of the Old Testament text and
pronounces the relevance of Gen 15:6 for the present believers, for the
sake of whom the text has been written down. Just as the exilic community
has taken the Abraham narrative to give meaning to its current situation,
and just as the various *relectures* of Genesis 15 pointed out the significance of the text for the present self-understanding, Paul appeals to his
addressees: *Tua res agitur.*[1203]

That the meaning of events and stories narrated in the Old Testament is
not limited to the past, but pertains to the present situation of believers, is
not singular in Paul[1204]: A similar idea occurs in Rom 15:4: What is written

---

[1199] J. Jeremias therefore considers the phrase δοὺς δόξαν τῷ θεῷ as key-statement of
Paul's understanding of faith (1970, 57). – This goes back to M. Luther, for whom the
purpose and goal of faith is "dare gloriam deo" (cf. 1531, 360: "Et illam gloriam posse
tribuere Deo est sapientia sapientiarum, iustitia iustitiarum, religio religionum et sacrifi-
cium sacrificiorum"; also 1515/1516, 310).

[1200] E. Adams 1997, 48.

[1201] See L. Goppelt 1964, 248n.44; F. Hahn 1971, 105 (4:23-25: "Angelpunkt für den
Gesamtzusammenhang"); A. von Dobbeler 1987, 140 ("Schlüssel"); J. Roloff 1990, 248.

[1202] Cf. M. Neubrand 1997, 285.

[1203] Cf. E. Käsemann 1969, 164. The *tua res agitur* does not function in terms of a
common anthropological maxim, but aims at the *Christian* existence (cf. K. Haacker
1999, 110, demarcating Paul's actualization of the text from R. Bultmann's existential-
ism or E. Drewermann's depth psychology).

[1204] Cf. T.H. Tobin 1995, 451. – Notably, Paul says "written" for our sake, not "happened." It is a misrepresentation of Paul's hermeneutics, if one tries to read into the text
that "Paul is explicating his doctrine of justification in terms analogous to the Jewish idea
of 'the merits of the fathers'" (R.B. Hays 1985, 95); Paul does not have in view here the
"vicarious soteriological consequences" of Abraham's faith-righteousness (98) or the

in former days is written for our instruction (εἰς τὴν ἡμετέραν δι-δασκαλίαν), in 1Cor 9:10: What Moses says in the law, he says for our sake (δι' ἡμᾶς), and in 1Cor 10:11: Events in Israel's history were written down for our instruction (πρὸς νουθεσίαν ἡμῶν). As much as Paul's account of Abraham's faith has full value and validity for Paul concerning its historicity and theological meaning (οὐ μόνον), it at the same time witnesses to, anticipates, and prefigures in a typological sense the eschatological realization of πίστις through Christ (ἀλλὰ καί). And now, in the present time (Rom 3:21.26), those who believe appropriate this eschatological reality and will receive the acquittal of the merciful God in the final judgment, whereby the divine verdict already qualifies their present.[1205]

Here, Paul steers his Abraham-chapter to a christological peak, in which he identifies the God "who justifies the ungodly" (4:5) and "who gives life to the dead and who calls into being the things that do not exist" (4:17) with the God "who raised from the dead Jesus our Lord."[1206] Since faith knows and trusts in the life-giving power of God, its character as hope receives an incontestable foundation in the resurrection of Jesus and hence distinguishes itself from any vague expectation and vain illusion. Even the readers/hearers themselves embody another proof of the validity of these divine predicates and of his promise, which creates and yields future: As believers, as part of those who take part in this reality of faith, they are Abraham's seed and can call him their father.[1207]

With the christological verse concluding the chapter (4:25)[1208] Paul probably appeals to a Jewish-Christian, liturgical formula of confes-

---

idea that Abraham's "destiny 'contains' the destiny of others" (90; cf. 92; see Hays's own comments on Rom 4:23-25: "It is important ... to pay close attention to exactly what he [*sc.* Paul] does and does *not* [!] say here" [93; italics original]). See similarly to Hays, L. Gaston 1980, 58f.; G. Howard 1990, 55: "The idea is that the Gentiles are blessed not simply like Abraham but because of Abraham." "The figure of Abraham" is used "as the representative forefather who brings righteousness to all those related to him by their faith, whether Jew or Greek" (88). See against this view already A. Schlatter 1927, 396n.2, but also J.M.G. Barclay 1988, 87; U. Heckel 2002, 125 with nn.84f., on the formulation σὺν τῷ πιστῷ 'Αβραάμ in Gal 3:9: "Abraham [ist] nicht Urheber, sondern Empfänger des Segens ... (vgl. das Passivum divinum εὐλογοῦνται)" (125n.85).

[1205] Both poles are expressed through the verb μέλλει (cf. E. Lohse 2003, 161), but they are also logical consequence of the fact that the believers participate *now* in the *eschatological* manifestation of πίστις. See also above page 309 on Rom 3:30.

[1206] As in Rom 4:5, πιστεύειν ἐπί denotes both the beginning of faith (cf. J. Jeremias 1970, 57) and its direction and contents (cf. E. Lohse 2003, 149)

[1207] It is true however that Paul does not speak explicitly of a present fulfillment of past promises (D.-A. Koch 1986, 309).

[1208] See on this verse most recently M. Bird 2003; B.A. Lowe 2006.

sion,[1209] as he did in 3:24-26.[1210] By using traditional imagery and formulations he seeks to connect his findings and theses with the consensus of the early church. Both traditional formulas, 3:24-26 and 4:25, are also linked through their use of atonement terminology (cf. also 4:7-8.17) and their making God the (implied) subject of the act of atonement.[1211] Their purpose is however not limited to the pragmatic intention of the apostle to build his argument on a commonly agreed foundation in order to prevent controversies, but there is also a theological reason, as the formula points to God's disclosing the salvation-historical possibility of faith, which is at the same time the core content of our faith: Christ's death and resurrection.[1212]

The likewise pre-Pauline formula 1Thess 4:14 – possibly one of the oldest formulas of faith in the New Testament[1213] – impressively shows that since "the time of its foundation," the church adhered to the creed that

---

[1209] Cf. E. Lohse 1963, 133; E. Käsemann 1969, 164; J. Jeremias 1970, 58; see also the discussion and bibliographical data in H.-J. van der Minde 1976, 89-102. The formula-style indicates itself in the relative clause (ὅς; cf. Phil 2:6; 1Tim 3:16), the structure of the clause as exact synthetic parallelism (divine passive + διά + noun + personal pronoun; cf. C.H. Dodd 1932, 70), but also the position of the verbs being placed in front. The pre-Pauline character of the formula is suggested by the terminology employed: παράπτωμα (in the plural) and δικαίωσις (otherwise only in 5:18); and a Palestinian Jewish-Christian origin of the confessional formula, whose first part clearly appeals to Isaiah 53, has been given great probability after the discovery of the Isaiah scroll in Qumran (cf. 1QIsa[a.b] on Isa 53:12; cf. P. Stuhlmacher 2001a, 58) with its textual closeness to the Septuagint version, which in turn resembles closely the *Isaiah Targum* on Isa 53:12 (cf. apart from the commentaries H. Patsch 1969). – The strictly parallel clauses have to be regarded in their mutual association, i.e., Christ's death refers equally to our justification, just as his resurrection qualifies the forgiveness of our sins. As a consequence of this syntactical unity, the preposition διά assumes the same meaning in both clauses (cf. A. Charbel 1975; 1976; E. Käsemann 1980, 150; J.A. Fitzmyer 1993, 389), not, as is oftentimes argued, a causal and a final meaning (thus, e.g., U. Wilckens 1978, 278; O. Michel 1978, 175; C.E.B. Cranfield 1978, 252). A. Schlatter, for instance, takes both as causal (1935, 173), while J. Jeremias opts for the final meaning (1970, 58; cf. D. Zeller 1985, 104; E. Lohse 2003, 159). – D.M. Stanley lists and evaluates the various interpretations that 4:25 received in the Greek and Latin church tradition (1951).

[1210] Among those who defend Pauline authorship of this verse are, e.g., U. Wilckens 1978, 279f.

[1211] Cf. the occurrences of παραδιδόναι in the passion formulas 1Cor 11:23; Rom 8:32; Gal 2:20; Eph 5:2 (cf. O. Michel 1978, 175).

[1212] Rom 4:25 represents another compelling piece of evidence for the intrinsic Pauline correlation between justification and Christology, which is often neglected (cf. P. Stuhlmacher 2001, 355; against N.T. Wright and J.D.G. Dunn); this neglect has led some to "rehabilitate" the union of justification and Christology by means of the subjective reading of the πίστις Χριστοῦ-formula (cf. N.T. Wright 1997, 128; R.B. Hays 2002, xxix; see also above page 74).

[1213] Cf. G. Friedrich 1982, 103.

"Jesus died and rose again."[1214] Christ's death and resurrection are the essential components of Christian faith (Rom 10:9; 1Cor 15:1-17): "If Christ has not been raised, your faith is in vain and you are still in your sins" (1Cor 15:17). Accordingly, in the christological conclusion of the pivotal section Rom 3:21-4:25, Paul substantiates on the basis of tradition that faith, justification, and forgiveness of sins are united as expressions of the revelation of God's righteousness through πίστις Χριστοῦ, i.e., through that faith which came with the Christ-event, with cross and resurrection, and which enables human appropriation and participation.

[1214] G.L. Green 2002, 220. 1Thess 4:14 reads: πιστεύομεν ὅτι Ἰησοῦς ἀπέθανεν καὶ ἀνέστη. In contrast to Rom 4:25, Jesus is subject (cf. W. Kramer 1963, 25, 28).

Chapter VI

Results and Prospect

We will present the results of this study first by summarizing the exegesis of the pertinent Romans passages dealing with πίστις (cf. chapter V) and reviewing the issues raised in connection with our presentation of the exegetical perspectives on the Pauline concept of faith (cf. chapter II) and on Romans 4 (cf. chapter V.A.I), second by comparing Paul's *relecture* of the Abraham narrative with that in Jewish tradition (cf. chapter IV), and finally by posing the question of his use of Scripture (cf. chapter III).

The following six questions will structure the first part: (1) Does Paul use the Abraham figure primarily in justification-theological terms: faith is the means to receive justification, or in sociological terms: circumcision is not the decisive criterion to be included in the people of God? (2) Does Paul conceive of πίστις in an existential-individual way or as trans-subjective entity within God's history with humankind? (3) Is there an underlying substructure in terms of a salvation history or "story" in Paul's argument? (4) Does Paul present Abraham as example, model, paradigm of faith or as *typos* of faith? (5) What is the significance and place of the notion of trust in Paul's concept of faith? (6) Is faith for Paul theocentric or christocentric, or: How does Paul see the relationship between Abraham's faith and our faith?

A. Faith and Romans 4

I. Faith and Fatherhood

Just as the isolation of the individual's faith is an oversimplification of Paul's concern in Romans 4, the exclusive focus on Abraham's fatherhood is a one-sided polarization as well. Faith and fatherhood, justification and inclusion collaborate in Paul's Abraham-chapter for the same end. From the *propositio* of the letter's theme in 1:16-17 it is evident that πίστις constitutes the subject-matter, with which Paul's gospel stands or falls. In 3:22 the concept of faith receives its fundamental christological content and determination, which – from a rhetorical perspective – has already been in view in 1:16-17 and will remain constitutive throughout. The expression πᾶς ὁ πιστεύων receives a crucial function: Whenever it occurs (1:16;

3:22; 10:4.11) it is connected to salvation and/or righteousness and speaks to and of both Jews and Gentiles.[1] "There is no distinction (διαστολή) between Jew and Greek" (cf. 3:22; 10:12).[2] Accordingly, there is no reason to believe that Paul empties faith of its christological disposition in any occurrence of πίστις/πιστεύειν and with regard to any religio-sociological group. This categorical statement is not to neglect the complexity and difficulty of the relationship between Jews and Gentiles in Paul, which for him (and for us) is not merely an intellectual challenge, but a deep theological and existential struggle. Without denying the particular Jewish election he leads the reader/hearer to the insights that first the foundation of Abraham's universal fatherhood was laid *before* the differentiation into "uncircumcised" and "circumcised"[3] and that second Christ's universal lordship laid the foundation for a theological indifference of Jews and Gentiles.[4]

Paul's soteriology is exclusive,[5] for faith has its source, contents, direction, and strength in Christ.[6] Faith (*sola fide*) brings about access to the (new) people of God, characterizes and governs it, for with the coming of Christ, the new era of faith and faith-righteousness has been set off; hence, it is an anthropological (*subjective*),[7] an ecclesiological (*intersubjective*)

---

[1] On the phrase πᾶς ὁ πιστεύων, see also M. Neubrand 1997, 101; L. Gaston 1987, 116-123. They come to opposing conclusions however.

[2] Many have noted the eminent place of πᾶς in the letter to the Romans. It occurs also Rom 2:9-10, where Paul affirms the equality of Jews and Gentiles and the impartiality of God (προσωπολημψία παρὰ τῷ θεῷ, 2:11; cf. 3:9.19-20; see on the concept of God's impartiality J.M. Bassler 1982).

[3] Cf. K. Berger 1966, 67.

[4] Cf. G. Klein 1963, 163. This does not imply that Paul fused Jews and Gentiles into "one category of *homo universalis*" (cf. J.C. Beker, quoted in P. Eisenbaum 2004, 696n.83), for the πρῶτον of the Jews remains valid (cf. Rom 1:16; 2:10, but also 2:9). – The issue is complex indeed, and it has generated rather diverse views on Paul's stance towards the Gentiles. Two books, both written in 1997, testify to this complexity: According to T.L. Donaldson, the pattern of Paul's "convictional world" regarding the Gentiles did not change essentially after his conversion (1997, 151-161): Gentiles can escape God's wrath only by becoming proselytes; but since Paul's conversion replaced the law with Christ, entrance into the elect people only happens through faith in Christ rather than through works of the law. By contrast, for D.J.-S. Chae "the apostle is on the gentiles' side" (1997, 286). Overall, the pro-Gentile Paul is concerned to demonstrate the salvation of the Gentiles rather than the priority of the Jews.

[5] Cf. expressly H.-J. Eckstein 1996, 118.

[6] Cf. A. Schlatter 1927, 587; E. Lohmeyer 1929a, 74; G. Ebeling 1958, 64f.; U. Schnelle 2003, 605. Particularly J. de Zwaan highlights that Christ is the power which seizes and fills the believer (1936, 122, 125, 133, 134).

[7] E. Käsemann stresses this aspect (1980, 103) against F. Neugebauer (1961, 167), who places in front the ecclesiological connotation. Also for A. von Dobbeler, faith is not a new self-understanding, but a new community-understanding (1987, 276).

and a salvation-historical (*trans-subjective*) concept. All three dimensions figure in Paul's argumentation 3:21-4:25. "Abraham serves as a model of faith.[8] But the purpose of this faith is so that he may become the 'father of many nations' (Rom 4:18)."[9] Justification through faith and fatherhood of all believers constitute an indissoluble unity[10]; and so Abraham's situation is typologically related to the situation of the Christian believer, but he is also an ecclesiological "father-figure," the *typos* of the new people of God.[11]

When Paul makes Abraham and David two pillars of his reasoning he demonstrates at the same time that he is not concerned with any boundary markers that separate Jews from Gentiles, but rather the non-existence of works is a boundary marker that separates every person from God.[12] This borderline can only be crossed through faith, through entering the realm of faith in compliance with the divine establishing of πίστις Χριστοῦ. Notably, three quarters of Paul's explicit quotations of Scripture in Romans are concentrated on three passages: 4:1-25; 9:6-11:36; 15:1-12 – and they all "center on one common theme: the plan of God to create a chosen people that would include both Jews and Gentiles."[13] And faith is the only and sufficient criterion of membership.

II. Faith in Universal and Individual Terms

Apart from the phrase πᾶς ὁ πιστεύων, another expression found in the letter's *propositio* operates as structuring element: We have seen that with ἐκ πίστεως εἰς πίστιν (Rom 1:17) Paul anticipates contents and arrangement of 3:21-31 and 4:1-25. We followed the two essential steps of Paul's route on which he walked from a description of faith as objective, divine event to a concretization and individualization through his portrayal of the patriarch's faith. To be sure, the different categories of meaning are not separated schematically, for in the Abraham-chapter Paul continually con-

---

[8] On this terminology, see below chapter VI.A.IV.

[9] T.H. Tobin 1995, 450.

[10] Cf. A. Schlatter 1935, 160 ("die Rechtfertigung aus dem Glauben und die Vaterschaft für alle Glaubenden").

[11] On the latter aspect, cf. F. Neugebauer 1961, 168; E. Käsemann 1969, 141; H. Binder 1968, 42f. – The ideas of type and father supplement and explain each other (against L. Gaston 1980, 57).

[12] As for David, T. Schreiner states: "Scholars who detect a reference to boundary markers separating Jews from gentiles in the term ἔργα have not appreciated the testimony of David sufficiently" (1998, 219). Cf. succinctly S.J. Gathercole 2002, 247: "*David although circumcised, sabbatarian, and kosher, is described as without works because of his disobedience*" (italics original). See, for instance, 1Macc 2,49-60, where boundary issues (e.g., Phinehas) and non-national good works (Abraham; David) are all subsumed under ἔργα.

[13] C.D. Stanley 2004, 143.

siders the salvation-historical place of faith both in relation to the law and
the promise. *Vice versa* the individual notion of faith occurs expressly in
3:22 in the verb πιστεύειν.

(1) In 3:21-26, Paul first presents the objective-universal, salvation-
historical fact, reality and purpose of πίστις, the place of faith in God's
history. Through faith God has now (νυνί), in the present eschatological
time, revealed his righteousness (3:21),[14] put forward Christ as ἱλαστήριον
(3:25), and disclosed a ground and possibility of existence (3:26)[15] –
though not in existential-philosophical, but in salvation-historical terms.[16]
In the Christ-event, faith has its origin, content, and goal. Paul's argumentative, doctrinal style corresponds fittingly with the trans-subjective objectivity of the subject-matter, with which he deals in this section.[17]

This new reality of faith that came with Christ is understood as a category whose purpose is to transfer its salvific power to human beings (3:27-
31). In other words, it calls for participation in its salvation-bringing
realm, in which God works justification. As Paul maintains in his doctrinal
statement in 3:28, the sole means of entering and being in that realm is
πίστις itself. In and through this exclusive way of salvation, a human being
(ἄνθρωπος) receives the gift of salvation, justification, and an entirely new
standing and condition before God. The salvation-historical possibility of
faith discloses faith as the right ground of existence *coram deo* (3:30).[18]
These insights Paul formulates in the dialogic style of the diatribe, marked
by astonishing and challenging theses.

Accordingly, depending on the perspective, different descriptions of the
universal, christologically determined πίστις are conceivable: If the perspective is spatial, πίστις is salvific sphere,[19] if it is dynamic-temporal,
πίστις is the new salvation-historical age, if it is existential, πίστις is a
new ground, reality, or possibility of life. Neither of the descriptions is to
be set absolute, for only in their combination the different aspects constitute the unity of πίστις. In a comparable way, the formula ἐν Χριστῷ has

---

[14] H. Binder 1968, 76n.90 ("der Glaube die von Gott 'objektiv' gesetzte Vorbedingung des Geschehens der *dikaiosyne*").

[15] M.D. Hooker comes on a rather different route to similar conclusions: "[F]aith [is]
made possible in and through Christ" (1989, 174). "[Π]ίστις Χριστοῦ *[is] the ground of
the believer's existence*" (180; italics original; cf. 183). See also H. Schlier 1965, 128
(πίστις as "Lebensprinzip").

[16] See also above pages 278-280 (on Gal 3:23.25).

[17] Cf. J. Moltmann 1999, 15.

[18] Cf. H. Ridderbos 1970, 163: "Der Glaube als neue Existenzweise hat heilsgeschichtliche Bedeutung."

[19] Cf. H. Binder 1968, 56-59 (πίστις as "oikologische Größe").

spatial,[20] dynamic-temporal-historical[21] and existential-individual meaning.[22]

(2) But through his appeal to Abraham (4:1-25), Paul also presents the condition of the individual prior to faith, which in its essence is ungodliness and sinfulness, existence apart from God. Solely faith can overcome this distance. In faith, Abraham grasped the promise, fully trusting in the God who justifies the ungodly, because actually, he himself had been grasped by the sphere of power of faith-righteousness (δικαιοσύνη πίστεως), in which the promise had been given.[23] In this context, the law has no positive salvation-historical function. Since for Paul, as for his predecessors and contemporaries, Abraham is not merely an individual, but also corporate and "ecclesiological" figure, the argument is put into a wider scope: Abraham is the father of all believers, figure of identification and authority, and most prominent part of God's history with humanity. Accordingly, the single believer is always part of something larger, namely, the (true) seed of Abraham and the (new) eschatological people of God. Hence, the Abraham-chapter expounds on the individual-historical concretion of faith, on the place of faith in the individual existence, which however is never isolated from God's history. The life-historical subjectivity of Romans 4 is associated with the predominantly "midrashic"-narrative style,[24] which however serves the argumentative goal to present God's dealing with Abraham as typical for all believers.

Not only "faith," but also "gospel" and "law," "righteousness" and "wrath," "grace" and "sin," "Spirit" and "flesh," "love" and "peace," even Christ[25] figure as universal concepts, as powerful forces, which at the same time include the category of participation and appropriation. In Paul's world of thought, therefore, objectivity and subjectivity do not represent two mutually exclusive perspectives on the divinely instituted reality, in which (religious) existence takes place, but both are combined in mutual influence.[26] In his concept of faith, the poles of objectivity and subjectivity, passivity and activity, super-individual event and existential involvement belong to God's dealing with humanity. Thereby it is the work of the Holy Spirit to mediate the individual appropriation, which articulates itself

---

[20] Cf., e.g., A. Deißmann 1892; 1925, 111.

[21] Cf., e.g., F. Neugebauer 1961, 41.

[22] Cf., e.g., J.D.G. Dunn 1998, 401.

[23] Cf. E. Käsemann 1980, 113.

[24] Cf. again J. Moltmann 1999, 15.

[25] Cf. the enumeration in E. Käsemann 1969a, 137n.27, but also 1980, 26.

[26] K. Barth's position has oftentimes received the label "objectivism" and R. Bultmann's position "subjectivism" (cf. H. Binder 1968, 22n.58). The category of participation, as presented here, could be a means to integrate both positions.

in the confession of the Lord Christ[27] and in the call "Abba! Father!" (Gal 4:6).[28]

One question arises in this context: Did Abraham, in Paul's view, have the opportunity or ability to make a choice between faith and unbelief[29]? For many interpreters, faith is clearly a indispensable and necessary condition on the human side,[30] part of a successful communicative process,[31] the acceptance of the Christian kerygma,[32] a choice,[33] a willful act of obedience,[34] even an achievement[35] or own human activity.[36] Yet the *ductus* of his argumentation, starting with the fundamental entanglement of humankind in the dilemma of sin, which God counters by means of the cosmic-universal revelation of his righteousness through faith, with the intention that all might believe – this *ductus* puts all emphasis on the *activitas dei*. God has taken the initiative, and he makes the decisions. Therefore, for Paul faith is not the subjective condition for the event of salvation.[37] "From

---

[27] Cf. 1Cor 12:3 with Rom 10:9.

[28] Cf. R. Slenczka 1984, 357; O. Hofius 1990, 167-169, with reference to 1Cor 2:4-5.6-16; U. Schnelle 2003, 599; also K. Barth 1960, 835. R. Bultmann, on the other hand, denies that πίστις is to be attributed to the Holy Spirit (1958, 331; 1959, 221, with reference to Gal 3:2.5.14; cf. M.-E. Boismard 1955, 83: "[L]e don de l'Esprit serait logiquement postérieur au don de la justification"). Notably, there is a certain ambiguity in the Augsburg Confession concerning the relationship of faith and the Holy Spirit: "[P]er verbum et sacramenta ... donatur spiritus sanctus, qui fidem efficit" (CA 5). "[P]er fidem accipitur spiritus sanctus" (CA 20). See the "solution" in O. Hofius 1990, 168n.143: "Zwischen beidem [*sc.* Glaube und Geistempfang] besteht ... Koinzidenz." H. Binder 1968, 75 ("Koinzidenz").

[29] See on the following also G. Friedrich 1982, 108 with nn.59-64.

[30] Cf. B. Weiß 1899, 70; P. Feine 1919, 291.

[31] Cf. A. von Dobbeler 1987, 20.

[32] Cf. F.C. Baur 1867, 161; W. Wrede 1907, 67; H.J. Holtzmann 1911, 132; E. Wißmann 1926, 38; R. Bultmann 1958, 91, 318; 1959, 209; E. Käsemann 1980, 12, 101.

[33] Cf. J.-N. Aletti 1989, 249.

[34] Cf. with partly widely divergent theological intentions, e.g., O. Pfleiderer 1902, 246; A. Jülicher 1917, 232; W.H.P. Hatch 1917, 35, 47f.; T. Zahn 1925, 79, 85; E. Wißmann 1926, 32; A. Schlatter 1927, 336, 346f., 362, 379; W. Mundle 1932, 101, 108, 137; O. Kuss 1956, 197; C.F.D. Moule 1956/1957, 157; R. Bultmann 1958, 315, 317; 1959, 221; C.E.B. Cranfield 1975, 66f.

[35] Cf., e.g., E. Kühl 1913, 13; H.-J. Schoeps 1959, 216; O. Kuss 1956, 197.

[36] Cf. W. Mundle 1932, 101 ("menschliche[.] Selbsttätigkeit").

[37] Developing and refining considerations of A. Deißmann, W. Michaelis seeks to disprove that πίστις is the condition or prerequisite of justification, since faith itself is an act of divine grace (1927, 122). In line with Deißmann he finds a strong mystical connotation in the term πίστις so that faith is the experience of justification rather than its precondition (cf. A. Deißmann 1925, 132; but see also the critique in W. Mundle 1932, 1f. and R. Bultmann 1958, 317). – A thought similar to that of Michaelis and Deißmann is expressed by D.E.H. Whiteley: "Faith is not the reason why God justifies some and not

faith to faith" means that our faith is the consequence of God's act of salvation,[38] the mode of participation therein.[39] The radical opposition of faith and works in Paul, which roots in a categorical-qualitative, not merely quantitative, distinction of the two entities, renders inadequate all attempts that seek to retain the deed-character of faith.

The divine act in Christ and our inclusion in it transcend the classical dogmatic issue whether or not God's grace is a *gratia irrestibilis*,[40] or – as we have to put it – if the faith brought by Christ is a *fides irrestibilis*. One has to take seriously the global salvation-historical dimension of faith as "Machtsphäre," but also the character of the gospel as δύναμις θεοῦ, which calls human beings into this sphere.[41] According to K. Barth humans are not facing the alternative of taking or letting go – "à prendre ou à laisser" – for in the Christ-event faith has become the objective, real, and ontological necessity for all humans.[42] E. Jüngel describes the effect of God's act by means of the following metaphor: Faith is that kind of "yes" of the entire human being, with which the one who has been awakened up from his slumber, affirms that he has been woken up and from now on may and shall realize himself as an awake human being, as a human being of the light and of the day and no longer of the night and of the darkness (1Thess 5:5; cf. 2Cor 4:3-6).[43]

These thoughts could be further illuminated by one of the most debated Pauline phrases containing the word πίστις: ὑπακοὴ πίστεως (Rom 1:5[; 16:26]). C.E.B. Cranfield offers a comprehensive list with basically seven grammatical and semantic possibilities, which he divides up into four genitive categories[44]: As an objective genitive, the phrase could denote (1) obedience to the faith in terms of *fides quae creditur*, (2) obedience to (the authority of) faith, or (3) obedience to God's faithfulness attested in the gospel; assuming a subjective genitive, one could think of (4) the obedi-

---

others, but the 'response' of those who are justified" (1966, 165, referred to in R.B. Hays 1983, 150).

[38] Cf. G. Friedrich 1982, 109f.

[39] Cf. O. Hofius 1990, 172f.

[40] In opposition to R. Bultmann, G. Bornkamm, O. Kuss, and G. Friedrich, O. Hofius answers this question in the affirmative (1990, 171n.162; 1996, 87f.).

[41] Cf. O. Hofius 1990, 158.

[42] K. Barth 1960, 835.

[43] E. Jüngel 1999, 205. Cf. K. Barth 1960, 836: "Glaube ist das Wunderbarste und das Einfachste zugleich: es geschieht in ihm, daß der Mensch die Augen aufschlägt, *sieht*, wie Alles – objektiv, real, ontologisch – ist, und nun eben Alles *nimmt*, wie es ist. Glaube ist die simple Entdeckung des Kindes, daß es sich im Hause seines Vaters oder auf dem Schoß seiner Mutter befindet" (emphasis original). See also D. Lührmann 1981, 71.

[44] C.E.B. Cranfield 1975, 66.

ence which faith works[45] or (5) the obedience required by faith; (6) an adjectival genitive would require the translation "believing obedience"[46] and (7) an epexegetical genitive the translation "the obedience which consists in faith," whereby the genitive can indicate identity or have descriptive function. Obviously, whatever solution one decides to follow, this has a critical impact on one's understanding of the Pauline concept of faith and touches upon one's inherent epistemological, ethical, and theological presuppositions and starting points.

Several of the exegetes we have already encountered in the history of scholarship on πίστις in Paul opt for the last possibility, for a qualitative equivalence of "faith" and "obedience" according to which both terms explicate themselves reciprocally: A. Ritschl,[47] A. Schlatter,[48] E. Lohmeyer,[49] R. Gyllenberg,[50] R. Bultmann,[51] and R.B. Hays.[52] While many other commentators agree on this issue,[53] there is an ongoing debate on the meaning

---

[45] Cf., e.g., H.-W. Bartsch 1965; 1968. According to Bartsch's distinctive hypothesis, the situation of the Roman Christians, the tensions between Jewish and Gentile Christians, provides the immediate background of the "provocative connection" ὑπακοὴ πίστεως (1968, 48). Hence, Romans is not a "compendium of Pauline theology," but serves to "solve a vital problem of their own" (42). Gentile-Christians, who despised the Jewish-Christian minority as weak in faith (Rom 14:1), claimed "faith" as their "watchword" (46), while Jewish-Christians made "obedience" their "watchword." In sum, "Paul endeavors to unite the two antagonizing groups by uniting the two concepts to one 'obedience of faith'" (47). Eventually, Gentiles have to obey the law (46, 50, 52f.) and Jews have to rediscover faith as unnomistic, *geschichtlich* reliance on God's grace (47, 52). Against a "dogmatic" interpretation, Bartsch holds, "daß der Gehorsam aus dem Glauben erwächst. Der Gehorsam wird nur recht vom Glauben her geübt, und der Glaube wird nur im Gehorsam Wirklichkeit" (1965, 290). Not only the phrase following on ὑπακοὴ πίστεως: "among all the Gentiles," but also the largely hypothetical character of Bartsch's proposal renders almost impossible a satisfactory verification.

[46] Cf., e.g., F. Neugebauer 1961, 158f.n.13 ("der gläubige Gehorsam").

[47] A. Ritschl 1889, 325.

[48] A. Schlatter 1935, 23 ("Glaube, der Gehorsam, und Gehorsam, der Glaube ist").

[49] E. Lohmeyer 1929, 127.

[50] R. Gyllenberg 1936, 628.

[51] R. Bultmann 1958, 315 (especially due to the parallelism of Rom 1:8 and 16:19); 1959, 206: "Ihm [*sc.* Paulus] ist πίστις geradezu gleich ὑπακοή."

[52] R.B. Hays 1983, 152; 1997, 278 ("epexegetical construction virtually equating the two nouns"), 286.

[53] Cf., e.g., J.A. Bengel 1773, 539 ("*obedientia[.]* in ipsa *fide* consisten[s]"; italics original); R.A. Lipsius (referred to in H. Lietzmann 1928, 26); T. Zahn 1910, 45; O. Kuss 1956, 197; C.E.B. Cranfield 1975, 66; H. Schlier 1977, 66; U. Wilckens 1978, 67; O. Michel 1978, 76 (see however below note 58); L.T. Johnson 1982, 86: "[T]he functional equivalence of faith and obedience is virtually complete." M.D. Hooker 1989, 182; O. Hofius 1990, 156n.64; E. Lohse 2003, 67f.; D.A. Campbell 2005, 187. See also K. Barth 1960, 847-851: "[Glaube] ist eigentlich und ursprünglich ein Anerkennen, die freie Tat

of ὑπακοή: The different camps disagree over the question whether ὑπακοή has first and foremost an ethical implication in terms of a *nova oboedientia*[54] or an ecclesiological-missionary[55] or an eschatological dimension.[56]

Possibly, the proposed redefinition of the Pauline πίστις as eschatological event provides the hermeneutical means to explain the genitive construction and to reconcile the ethical, ecclesiological and eschatological solutions. If πίστις is powerful sphere, it also has an authority and a claim to include and involve people; if it is part of God's purpose and plan it does not remain ineffective. For that reason, one should understand ὑπακοὴ πίστεως as human obedience towards the authority exercised by the reality of faith, which God has created and put under the lordship of Jesus Christ. This understanding is to be preferred over others: obedience towards the authority of God's faithfulness[57] or obedience towards the authority of the message of faith.[58]

Accordingly, in these first few lines of his letter to the Romans, Paul describes the goal of his apostolic mission as bringing about the obedience towards the reality of faith among all Gentiles. Through the gospel which

---

eines Gehorsams (848). Evidently, the agreement concerning the grammatical category does not preclude far-reaching theological differences.

[54] Cf. A. Schlatter 1935, 22: "Die Annahme des Worts und den Entschluß zum Gehorsam hat Paulus nicht voneinander getrennt; beides ist eine und dieselbe Bewegung des Willens." C.E.B. Cranfield 1975, 67. In his comprehensive treatment of Paul's expression ὑπακοὴ πίστεως, D.B. Garlington classifies the genitive as adjectival genitive, "believing obedience," which denotes both "the obedience which consists in faith, and the obedience which is the product of faith," even "brought into connection with the harmony of the church" (1994, 30f.; cf. 1991; 1994, 10-31). Similarly, A.B. du Toit determines obedience both as "part of the faith-event" (1991, 68) and as "Christian behaviour or life-style" (70, with reference to Rom 5:19; 6:12.16.17; 2Cor 7:15; 10:6; Phil 2:12; Phlm 21; 2Thess 3:14); both aspects are not consecutive, but simultaneous (against K. Kertelge 1971, 271). – Against that W. Schenk 1972, 165. Schenk does not consider as "ethical" the occurrences of ὑπακοή and ὑπακούειν in Paul and refers to the following passages: Rom 5:19; Phil 2:8 (Jesus' obedience); Phil 2:12 (obedience towards the apostle; also 2Cor 2:9; 2Thess 3:14; Phlm 21; 2Cor 7:15); Rom 10:16; 2Thess 1:8 (obedience towards the gospel); Rom 6:16 (obedience towards righteousness); 2Cor 10:5 (obedience towards Christ); ethical ὑπακούειν appears only in post-Pauline writings (Col 3:20.22; Eph 6:1-5); see also O. Hofius 1990, 156; K. Haacker 1999, 28.

[55] Cf. W. Schenk 1972, 165, following W. Wiefel 1968, 143 ("Annehmen und Festhalten der christlichen Botschaft").

[56] Cf. E. Käsemann 1980, 12.

[57] Against K. Barth 1922, 3.

[58] Cf., e.g., H. Lietzmann 1928, 26; O. Kuss 1963, 10; W. Schenk 1972, 165; G. Friedrich 1981; 1982, 108; C.H. Cosgrove 1988, 57f. See also O. Michel 1978, 76: "Glaube ist für Paulus zunächst Gehorsam gegenüber dem Wort." But see Michel's further thoughts: "Der neue Gehorsam wird also durch den Glauben, der als eschatologisches Ereignis in die Welt kam (Gl 3,25), bestimmt."

he proclaims and which reveals God's righteousness ἐκ πίστεως εἰς πίστιν (1:1.16-17),[59] God's powerful call reaches human beings and compels them to obey this call, enter and live in realm of πίστις and submit to the Lord of this realm, Jesus Christ. Obeying the divine call, however, does not imply some kind of free acceptance or refusal of God's invitation, but it is the obedience of the creature towards the creator whose word calls into being the non-existing,[60] whose salvation-historical manifestation of πίστις remains "irresistible." That Paul's framework of thought has primarily eschatological nature appears evident on grounds of his eschatological notion of δικαιοσύνη and πίστις, the universality of his messianic idea, his mission, and the whole world's submission to Christ, but also his use of the Habakkuk-quote in 1:17, where πίστις does not mean faithfulness or obedience, but describes the foundation upon which eschatological existence (ζήσεται) and salvation (σωτηρία, 1:16) is based.[61]

The character of πίστις as *fides irrestibilis* makes the believers realize that they have been raised from the death of unbelief and called to the life of faith,[62] that they are now children of the day through grace,[63] that they have entered a history,[64] indeed, the whole reality without any subtraction,[65] that they are "being involved in that which God is doing,"[66] taken into the event of salvation in Christ,[67] and bound up with an overarching "Ereigniszusammenhang,"[68] that they are conformed to the new divine re-

---

[59] See above chapter V.B.I.1.

[60] Cf. O. Hofius 1990, 156n.66, 164f., with reference to *2Bar* 21,4 (see above note 1130 in chapter V).

[61] See above chapter V.B.I.2.

[62] Cf. K. Barth 1960, 836.

[63] Cf. again E. Jüngel 1999, 205.

[64] Cf. J.-N. Aletti 1989, 248: "L'acte de foi ... fait entrer dans une histoire."

[65] Cf. M. Buber 1952, 505: "'Glaube' ist nicht Gefühl in der Seele des Menschen ..., sondern sein Eintritt in die Wirklichkeit, in die *ganze* Wirklichkeit, ohne Abstrich und Verkürzung" (italics original). For Christian faith, this whole reality can be "*nur eine Wirklichkeit*, und das ist die in Christus offenbargewordene Gotteswirklichkeit in der Weltwirklichkeit" (D. Bonhoeffer 1940, 43): "*In Jesus Christus ist die Wirklichkeit Gottes in die Wirklichkeit dieser Welt eingegangen*" (39; italics original).

[66] H.-W. Bartsch 1968, 50; cf. R. Gyllenberg 1936, 626f: "Der Mensch wird eingeordnet" "in die neue Gottesgemeinschaft." R. Schnackenburg 1962, 37 ("von der Wirklichkeit und Kraft des Glaubens erfaßt sein").

[67] Cf. W.G. Kümmel 1937, 221: "[D]er Glaube [bedeutet] den Eintritt in das Heilsgeschehen." G. Delling 1965, 118 (quoted in H. Binder 1968, 68n.60): "Und auch das Glauben des Gerechtfertigten, gerade auch das Zum-Glauben-Kommen, ist letzlich ein Hineingenommenwerden in das Heilsgeschehen in Christus."

[68] O. Cullmann 1965, vi. Cullmann "möchte ... zeigen, daß es falsch ist, christliche Existenz und Heilsgeschichte einander als Gegensätze gegenüberzustellen. Jene heute beliebte Sicht des Urchristentums, derzufolge die Heilsgeschichte einen Abfall vom existentialen Verständnis des ursprünglichen 'Kerygmas' darstelle, scheint mir auf einer

ality of πίστις[69] and apprehend the generative power of God, that they are even granted to participate in God's omnipotence[70] – or, as Paul puts it austerely, but affectingly: that Jesus Christ has seized them (Phil 3:12). Hence, neutrality or indifference towards God's act and call is not an option for Paul,[71] for faith will reach its goal.[72]

To be sure, those who obey to πίστις, pronounced in the gospel, become part of the community and belong to those who are called (Rom 1:16: κλητοί), so that "the obedience to faith" brings forth an ecclesiological dimension. Also, an ethical implication is insofar present, as – in E. Käsemann's words – Christian "ethics" is lived out eschatology.[73] Eschatological existence in "the obedience to faith" is an existence which is characterized and governed by love.[74]

In sum, Pauline theology is not primarily characterized as anthropology, i.e., first, the human being before the revelation of πίστις, and second the human being under πίστις,[75] but rather in broader, salvation-historical terms: first, humankind before and apart from πίστις, and second, the reality of and participation in the divinely established πίστις.

III. Faith and Salvation History – Narrative Dynamics

The question whether Paul advocates salvation-historical continuity by means of his appeal to Abraham cannot be answered without acknowledging the substantial argumentative unity of Rom 3:21-4:25. From there one can conclude that the identity and oneness of God (3:28) establishes and

---

falschen Alternative zu beruhen. Gewiß enthält das ganze Neue Testament den Anruf zur Glaubensentscheidung und impliziert ein neues Existenzverständnis. Aber beruht dieses nicht gerade auf dem Glauben, daß sich eine göttliche Geschichte ereignet hat, ereignet und weiter ereignen wird, die zwar diesen Glauben visiert, aber zunächst unabhängig von ihm und mir fremd ist? Und heißt dann Glauben nicht gerade, *meine Existenz in diesen Ereigniszusammenhang hic et nunc einzureihen?*" (italics original).

[69] Cf. P. Stuhlmacher 1966, 81 ("Sich-Schicken").

[70] Cf. G. Ebeling 1958, 106: "Der Glaube ist das Partizipieren an der Allmacht Gottes." Ebeling makes this statement on grounds of the correspondence between Mk 10:27 (πάντα γὰρ δυνατὰ παρὰ τῷ θεῷ) and 9:23 (πάντα δυνατὰ τῷ πιστεύοντι).

[71] Cf. W. Mundle 1932, 43.

[72] Cf. E. Fuchs 1958, 242.

[73] Cf. E. Käsemann 1980, 177 (on Rom 6:22): "Gerechtigkeit bei P[au]l[u]s [darf] nicht auf das Rechtfertigungsurteil und nicht einmal auf die Gabe der Glaubensgerechtigkeit beschränkt werden... Regnum Dei im Zeichen der Gnade ist ihre Sachmitte, Rechtfertigung die Partizipation daran, in der man in das Regnum Christi ... und in die nova oboedientia gestellt wird."

[74] On the idea and implication of the believer's "eschatological existence," see R. Bultmann 1954, 102; 1959, 222. – Several times, Paul juxtaposes faith and love: 1Cor 13:2.13; Gal 5:6; 1Thess 1:3; 3:6; 5:8; 2Thess 1:3; Phlm 5; also Eph 1:15; 3:17; 6:23; Col 1:4. See also below chapter VI.A.V.

[75] Thus R. Bultmann 1958, 574.

constitutes the unity of his dealing with humankind, both *before* the revelation of righteousness through πίστις Χριστοῦ, and *in* the present eschatological time.[76] However, Paul does not appear as proponent of a continuous *Heilsgeschichte*, whether "historical-real" or "factual-historical,"[77] but God's acting and his person *per se* warrant the continuity between old and new.[78] Hence, Paul himself does not give the answer to the question of the presence of God's righteousness before Christ, and he does not offer a coherent theology of history.[79] In fact, in the argument of Romans 4 – in contrast to Rom 3:1-8 and Romans 9-11 – he does not seem interested in the period between Abraham and Christ (Abraham-law, law-Christ), but asks back from the present eschatological situation of the σωτηρία and δικαιοσύνη for all believers (1:16; 3:21-22): Where in Scripture does God act in an analogous and at the same time anticipatory manner?

The figure of the patriarch serves as demonstration of the identity of God's acting then and now: Just as the one God has justified the believing Abraham on grounds of his grace upon calling him through the promise, thus he will justify those who believe upon being called into the people of God through the gospel.[80] Yet Abraham's function is not only to prove analogy, but also to point in an anticipatory mode to the present community of believers consisting of Jews and Gentiles; they call Abraham their father and understand themselves as his legitimate seed, since the ground of their being believers God has prepared in Abraham.[81] For Paul, Abraham's call is *in nuce* the call of Jewish and Gentile believers, which has been fully realized through the salvation-bringing act in Christ. The sovereignty and freedom of God's dealing with humanity secures that both the idea of an "automatism" and the exclusive claim of God's help are ruled out in the relationship between God and humans.

While the claim of an underlying idea of an uninterrupted history of salvation is question-begging, the other extreme of a radical discontinuity[82] and a-historical, isolated interpretation of Abraham[83] is likewise doubtful.[84] One has to acknowledge that his obvious indifference concerning

---

[76] Cf. P. Vielhauer 1969, 54: "[D]ie Identität Gottes ist es, was die Einheit der Schrift mit der Heilsoffenbarung in Christus konstituiert" (approvingly cited in E. Lohse 2003, 149); D. Zeller 1973, 96f.

[77] On this terminology, see U. Wilckens 1961, 45; 1978, 266. See also J.C. Beker 1980, 99: "Romans 4 allows for the continuity of salvation-history…"

[78] Cf. U. Schnelle 2003, 359.

[79] Cf. L. Goppelt 1966/1967, 230; D. Sänger 1994, 109.

[80] The basis of this continuity is God's faithfulness. Cf. T. Otero Lázaro 2001, 32.

[81] Cf. U. Luz 1968, 181-185; D.-A. Koch 1986, 311, 314.

[82] Especially G. Klein. See above pages 223f.

[83] Thus, e.g., U. Luz 1968, 182; E. Gräßer 1981, 190n.4.

[84] Similarly K. Berger 1966, 74f.; D. Sänger 1994, 111, 117.

salvation-historical, speculative elements results from his particular intention and standpoint: He speaks from the present eschatological era to those
who believe and who are therefore part of this present sphere of salvation
of πίστις Χριστοῦ. And in light of these circumstances the story of the
patriarch can figure as supreme witness. But the pragmatic indifference (as
much as one has to acknowledge it in the present context) may not be confused with a general theological indifference[85]: Deliberations on Israel's
history receive a large portion in his letter (especially Romans 9-11), and
in this he conforms to tradition.[86] More importantly, God's dealing with
David (4:6-8) – even if he has a merely confirmatory function for the situation of Abraham – provides evidence for a kind of continuity rooting in the
identity and freedom of God himself.[87]

In sum, Paul does not present a closely knit salvation-historical progress
since Abraham or an a-historical isolation of the patriarch, but rather talks
about the historically mediated unity of God's salvation work – then in an
anticipatory manner with Abraham, now in the universal fulfillment
through Christ.

As for the idea of a coherent underlying narrative in Paul – an idea,
which is closely linked to the notion of a continuous salvation history[88] – a
similar conclusion suggests itself: Paul's framework of thought and logic
is not governed by a unified narrative (sub)structure like the "story of Jesus Christ,"[89] but he builds an argument and "comment[s] on the story and
its implications for his readers."[90] "The trouble" with some of the various
narrative theories in Paul "is that neither Galatians nor Romans is a narrative but an argument"[91] and, furthermore, his ideas of the gospel, of faith,
of Christ encompass more than the concept of story. Keeping that in mind,
one can observe that "[i]n his typological pattern of thinking," Paul "brings
together the stories of Abraham and of Christian believers" and transfers
Abraham's situation before God to the situation of all believers in the present eschatological time.[92] This is Paul's argumentative goal (4:23).[93]

---

[85] Even within Romans 4 the chronological progression of faith and circumcision
points to Paul's historical concern (cf. P. Müller 1997, 138).

[86] Cf. only Sirach 44.

[87] Cf. E. Jacob 1962, 154n.16: Gen 15:6 and Ps 32:2 show "le thème de la permanence
de l'élection gratuite de Dieu."

[88] Cf. again J.D.G. Dunn 1998, 20n.62.

[89] Against R.B. Hays 1983, 6f.

[90] I.H. Marshall 2004, 423; cf. J.D.G. Dunn 1998, 18 ("complex interactions"); A.T.
Lincoln 2002, 189 ("intricate interplay"), 199.

[91] J.D.G. Dunn 1997, 270; cf. I.H. Marshall 2002, 206.

[92] A.T. Lincoln 2002, 189. Hence, "[t]he narrative itself is not enough; it needs interpretation" (200).

[93] Cf. L. Goppelt 1964, 248n.44.

IV. (The Faith of) Abraham as Typos or Example/Model/Paradigm?

Apart from L. Goppelt and E. Käsemann,[94] many others accept the view that Abraham functions as *typos* and that the classification "typology" is an adequate description of Paul's argument in Romans 4.[95] On the other hand, however, some deem that essential aspects of "typology" are missing: (1) Paul does not assign to Abraham an explicit antitype superseding him[96]; (2) the doctrine of the two eons is missing[97]; (3) there is no notion of cyclic repetition.[98] Those who reject the notion of "typology" prefer to speak of Abraham's function in Romans 4 as exemplary, paradigmatic or analogous.[99] But to reduce Paul's appeal to Abraham to the mere presentation of an "example" fails to appreciate the full theological implication of the Genesis quotation and of the allusions to the Abraham tradition and might fall prey to a too narrow definition of "typology" dictated by an unreflected acceptance of history-of-religions insights.[100]

First of all it is true that no τύπος-terminology occurs in Romans 4; but nevertheless the subject-matter of typology is present.[101] Answering the objections against the classification "typology" one has to see that (1) an antithetical correlation type-antitype is not indispensable, for the aspect of

---

[94] See above chapter V.A.I.1.b, but also the *excursus* chapter V.B.III.2.a.

[95] Cf. H. Lietzmann 1928, 52-57 ("Abraham als Typus des Gläubigen"); J. Jeremias 1953, 272; 1970, 57; E.E. Ellis 1957, 130; F. Neugebauer 1961, 168; C. Dietzfelbinger 1961; H. Boers 1971, 95, 96; A.T. Hanson 1974, 62; O. Michel 1978, 161; H. Moxnes 1980, 275f.; F.E. Wieser 1987, 66; D.M. Hay 1989, 472; R.A. Harrisville 1992, 87; J.A. Fitzmyer 1993, 388; S.J. Gathercole 2004, 163. See in addition those mentioned in U. Luz 1968, 180n.174 (there, Luz lists reasons against the description of Abraham as *typos*). Also R.B. Hays argues that Paul's appeal to Abraham happens in terms of a typological interpretation, which sees Abraham "not as a 'historical' figure but as a metaphorical figure in Paul's symbolic world." "Abraham typologically prefigures Christian believers" (1997, 286; cf. 1985, 90). Apart from the fact that the dimension of "history" does not get lost in the typological perspective (see below note 103), one should note that the category of typology counters Hays's contention that Abraham's faith prefigures both Jesus' faith and the believers' faith, since Jesus is thought to have faith that is typologically related to Abraham's faith, even though his death on the cross only *inaugurates* the new eon (see also M.A. Seifrid 2000, 142f.). – U. Wilckens contends that the typological relevance of Abraham is entirely in the shade of the election-historical continuum (1961, 49n.27).

[96] Cf. D.-A. Koch 1986, 219.

[97] Cf. U. Luz 1968, 180n.174.

[98] Cf. R. Bultmann 1950, 377.

[99] Cf. C.H. Dodd 1932, 83; R. Bultmann 1950, 377; H. Conzelmann 1967, 190f.; U. Luz 1968, 180.

[100] Cf. U. Wilckens 1961, 44; E. Käsemann 1969, 168; D.-A. Koch 1986, 308.

[101] Cf. R. Bultmann 1950, 369, and K.-H. Ostmeyer 2000, 112f., on the fact that the typological perspective is not bound to the terminology of τύπος.

"anticipation" represents an adequate criterion of typology[102]; (2) Abraham represents the *Urzeit* and anticipates the reality of the eschatological time inaugurated by Christ's coming[103]; (3) it is not the idea of a cosmic cycle that connects the "then" and "now," but solely God's salvation plan.[104] Positively speaking, typology signifies the relationship of aspects between two entities, which are identical in essence. This fundamental premise we have already encountered above in the discussion of 3:25.

Here, in Romans 4, the typological perspective operates on different levels, comprising the following aspects: Just as Abraham received and heard the ἐπαγγελία, the Christian believers receive and hear the εὐαγγέλιον as sovereign divine act of election and as performative word-event; they believe upon obtaining the word, leaving their status of ungodliness and entering the reality of faith (ἐπίστευσεν), whereby circumcision and the law remain without salvation-historical function[105]; they are counted righteous (λογίζεσθαι), again through a free divine decision.[106] Abraham is presented as ("pre-existent") participant in the reality of faith, in the eschatological people of God, and what his faith anticipated in a typical, but singular, way has received a global, eschatological dimension through Christ's way and work.[107] The continuity between Abraham and the present believers is constituted and conserved by God himself, for he is and remains one and the same, the one God, who justifies the ungodly, who creates and gives life.

Hence, "typology" is Paul's "method" of scriptural interpretation, which he employs to relate God's judgment on faith, as witnessed in the Scriptures, to his present eschatological acting.[108] The typological relevance of Abraham's faith therefore does not lie primarily in the constancy of human existential experience, but has its theological place within the framework of the typological relevance of God's acting, in which a believing relationship to God is both made possible and counted as righteousness.[109] The

---

[102] Cf. E. Käsemann 1969, 172f.

[103] J. Roloff deems it significant that Paul in Romans 4 (as in Galatians 3) starts with the *exegesis* of a text and in the course of his argument emphasizes the dimension of *history*, when Abraham comes into play as a figure of the past; in this distance between past and presence the method of typology is located (1990, 242f.).

[104] Cf. L. Goppelt 1964, 252.

[105] As noted before (see above page 365) ἐπαγγελία and εὐαγγέλιον as well as περὶ τομή and νόμος are related typologically.

[106] Cf. similarly J. Jeremias 1970, 57: Abraham is both the *typos* of the Christian (πιστεύειν) and the *typos* of what is promised to faith (λογίζεσθαι).

[107] Cf. U. Schnelle 2003, 359: "[D]ie Gestalt Abrahams [ist] für ihn [*sc.* Paulus] eine Vorabdarstellung dessen, was nun im Christusgeschehen zum Ziel gelangt."

[108] J. Roloff 1990, 252f.

[109] Cf. F. Neugebauer 1961, 168; R.B. Hays 1985, 96: "Even more important than Abraham's faith is *God's* faithfulness" (italics original). J. Roloff 1990, 252: "Was Pau-

concept of πίστις in its universal and individual dimension accomplishes to incorporate the aspect of God's action and human faith, for it is God who has established the eschatological reality of faith, which is transferred to us.

In addition to his function as *typos* of the believer and the justified, who proves the identity of God's act in past and present, Abraham also comes into view as "our forefather," who is symbol and figure of identification for the people of God. In this respect, he is certainly also "the paradigm *par excellence* for God's people,"[110] the paradigmatic prolepsis, and an especially qualified, anticipatory example[111] of the criterion (faith) and consequence (justification) of one's becoming member in the eschatological covenant people.[112] The extraordinary quality of the Abraham-example receives its force from various directions: He is the first patriarch and thus the father of Israel, figure of identification for Judaism, biblical chief witness[113]; he is the first who is reported to have believed, and thus he is the primordial "beginning" of faith,[114] father of all who believe, and as father he is to be imitated; if he, who has been generally regarded as exemplarily pious and righteous man, is justified as an *impius*, then all people are dependent on *sola gratia* and *sola fide*[115]; he has been justified in uncircumcision and can therefore be appealed to not merely as "corporate personality" for Jews, but for all believers, Jews and Gentiles, alike. For Paul's argumentative goal and from his christological hermeneutical presuppositions, Abraham is the perfect example. *Vice versa*, when Paul calls Abra-

---

lus interessiert, ist *nicht die Konstanz menschlicher Existenzerfahrungen, sondern die Identität des Handelns Gottes*" (italics original). K. Haacker 1999, 110.

[110] S.J. Gathercole 2002, 233. "[A]s 'our forefather' he is *the* example."

[111] K. Berger 1966, 66.

[112] There is general agreement on Abraham's function as example, though the term "example" can imply different features. See only M. Luther 1515/1516, 254; J.A. Bengel 1773, 560; R. Bultmann 1950, 377; M.-E. Boismard 1955, 70, 72 ("exemple"; "modèle"); H.-J. Schoeps 1959, 214 ("Vorbild"); U. Wilckens 1961, 44, 47; G. Klein 1963, 153, 162; H. Ridderbos 1970, 127 ("Vorbild des Glaubens"); J. Lambrecht 1979, 5, 19 ("le croyant par excellence"); D.-A. Koch 1986, 307 ("Modell des πιστεύων"); A. von Dobbeler 1987, 140 ("Vorbild rechten Glaubens"); W. Baird 1988, 378 ("model of Christian faith"); J.-N. Aletti 1989, 245 ("exemple"); D.M. Hay 1989, 472; M.D. Hooker 1989, 169, 174; M.A. Seifrid 1992, 223 ("example"); J.A. Fitzmyer 1993, 388 ("pattern for Christian faith"); T.H. Tobin 1995, 450 ("model for faith"); E. Adams 1997, 49, 51 ("example"; "model"; "prototype"); J.D.G. Dunn 1997, 265 ("model of faith = trust"); K. Haacker 1999, 105 ("Beispiel"); E. Lohse 2003, 151 ("Exempel"); S. Westerholm 2004, 280, 392 ("example").

[113] Cf. M. Theobald 2001, 402.

[114] Cf. H. Gese 1991, 29: "Für altes Denken, und eben auch biblisches Denken, ist der Anfang das principium, die ἀρχή, re'šît, Urbild oder doch Vorbild des Ganzen."

[115] Cf. E. Gräßer 1998, 12, 15; R. Bergmeier 2000, 60; E. Lohse 2003, 149f.

ham "the father of all who believe," his intention is not to show real-historical continuity: Abraham *is* the father mediated through (salvation) history,[116] *nor* individual-historical continuity: Abraham *becomes* the father through one's individual faith,[117] *nor* "christologically" defined continuity, in which the "positions" of figures like Abraham and others appear in the light of Christ.[118] For Paul, Abraham's status in the Jewish consciousness and his situation before God are decisive.

Yet one may not neglect that one decisive reason for Paul's appeal to the patriarch "is undoubtedly polemical."[119] Paul's opponents in Galatia had claimed Abraham for their purpose,[120] arguing that only the one who answers God's call by circumcision and Torah obedience and who thus proves to have faith can be full member of God's eschatological people.[121] In the "notoriously passionate and convoluted"[122] letter to the Galatians Paul rebutted harshly and directly these claims, while in our letter he deals with them in a more didactic,[123] distanced, nuanced, and perhaps "much richer"[124] manner, though not without polemical accents.[125]

To these reasons for Paul's appeal to the example of Abraham – positive and negative – one has to add the observation that in the compositional arrangement of the diatribe the Abraham-chapter serves as *exemplum*,

---

[116] Thus U. Wilckens.

[117] Thus G. Klein.

[118] Cf. K. Barth 1922, 100f. Abraham appears in a row with Jeremiah, Socrates, M. Grünewald, M. Luther, S. Kierkegaard, and F. Dostoevski. – See on this H. Boers 1971, 100, who parallels Barth with the author of Hebrews (cf. Heb 11:1-12:1), but see also Justin, *Apologia* 1,46, who calls those "Christians" who lived according to the Logos: Greeks such as Socrates and Heraclitus and non-Greeks such as Abraham, Ananias, Azarias, Misael, and Elias.

[119] D.J. Moo 1996, 256; cf. J. Roloff 1990, 243.

[120] Cf. O. Schmitz 1922, 120.

[121] Cf. P. Stuhlmacher 1989, 67.

[122] D.A. Campbell 1992, 101n.30.

[123] Cf. M.-E. Boismard 1955, 79.

[124] L. Gaston 1980, 56.

[125] On the relationship between the interpretations of Abraham found in Galatians and Romans, see, e.g., J. Lambrecht 1979, 21-23; T.H. Tobin 1995, 438, 451 *et passim*; T. Otero Lázaro 2001; on the relationship of the two letters in general, see, e.g., M. Theobald 1982, 27: "Signalisiert der Römerbrief eine 'Tendenzwende' im theologischen Denken des Paulus? Hat der Apostel mit seinem Brief an die Römer den an die Galater überholt? Kein Jota seines Kampfbriefes hat er im Römerbrief zurückgenommen, und in einer ähnlichen Situation, so darf man gewiss sein, wäre seine Reaktion wieder ähnlich ausgefallen... Aber vielleicht hat Paulus durch den Widerstand, den er von judaistischer Seite erfahren hat, sowie in Distanz zur galatischen Krise die *perspektivische Begrenztheit* seines im Galaterbrief vertretenen Standpunktes selbst durchschaut... Ist der Galaterbrief in prophetischem Zorn geschrieben, so spricht der Römerbrief die überlegene Ruhe des Theologen Paulus" (italics original).

which relates the general-theological with the subjective-existential dimension.[126]

V. Πίστις and "Trust" – The Nature of Faith

The aspect of the relationship between πίστις and "trust" requires particular consideration with regard to the positions of two persons: R. Bultmann and M. Buber. As we have seen, Bultmann concedes the element of trust in Paul's concept of πίστις/πιστεύειν, but affirms immediately thereafter that "trust" in the traditional Old Testament-Jewish sense does not occur in Paul[127] – with the exception of Gal 3:6 and Rom 4:3, i.e., the quotation from Gen 15:6.[128] On grounds of rather different presuppositions and with a different intention, Buber comes to comparable results: Paul's idea of faith is nourished by Greek thinking that aims at the acceptance of a certain event or fact, and hence stands in contrast to the Hebrew trust.[129] As has been argued, Buber's claims can be largely defused on linguistic-historical grounds, for the connotation of πίστις as the totality of the human relationship to God is by no means missing in the Greek conception of πίστις, and it is even more present in the Septuagint.[130] Against Bultmann's subtracting the motif of "trust" from the Pauline faith, one has to reiterate Paul's methodology and rhetoric: Abraham functions both as *typos* and example of faith, which necessarily implies that the portrayal of his faith describes comprehensively the basic features of what it means to have and to stand in πίστις.[131]

In Paul's exposition of πίστις, Rom 3:21-4:25, we find as a unity what later dogmatics distinguished and separated both terminologically and theologically: on the one hand, the objective reality of salvation manifested by God through πίστις and the individual appropriation of this reality, by believing in the God who has acted in Christ (4:24, πιστεύειν ἐπί); on the other hand the content of faith, which incorporates the facts of the salvation event in the form of doctrinal statements (*fides quae*), and the act of faith, which assents to these facts, trusts and desires that they take shape in the individual existence (*fides qua*).[132] Since the believer's existence takes

---

[126] Cf. the authors mentioned above pages 316f. (S.K. Stowers and T. Schmeller); also M. Theobald 1992, 118.

[127] R. Bultmann 1959, 219. See above page 42.

[128] R. Bultmann 1958, 323f. – E. Wißmann's dissertation (1926) (see above chapter II.C.II) sought to radically limit Paul's concept of πίστις to the intellectual-dogmatic realm in terms of "assent."

[129] M. Buber 1950, 653-657, 682-686, 723, 779-782; cf. D. Rokéah 1991, 302f.

[130] Cf. again D.R. Lindsay 1993, 114; G. Schunack 1999, 296f.

[131] Cf., e.g., E. Lohse 1977, 158; 2003, 149. Interestingly, R. Bultmann himself calls Abraham "Ur- und Vorbild der Glaubenden" (1950, 377).

[132] Cf. B.S. Childs 1992, 606. See also above note 391 in chapter V.

place under entirely new criteria and conditions, faith is a holistic concept, comprising the notion of a personal relationship of trust, submission, assent of certain contents, knowledge, confession, perseverance, but also the idea that faith is only possible in the community of believers. In 3:21-31 Paul elaborates on these new salvation-historical facts and conditions, and in his portrayal of Abraham's faith in chapter 4 he shows how Abraham directed his faith trustfully to God, assenting to and knowing the facts about who God is and what he does,[133] and showing a *perseverantia* which holds on to faith in spite of and also because of the contrarieties of life; the community-aspect is essential as well, for the figure of Abraham functions as "corporate personality" for the community of faith: He is the father of all believers. As an indispensable component and consequence of faith, thinking, willing and doing of the believer are determined by being in the domain of faith.[134] The meaning of faith for Paul "includes not just 'belief' or 'trust' in a narrow sense, but the acceptance of a new way of life, with all the beliefs, ethical norms and social reorientation which this entails."[135]

R. Bultmann is probably right when he argues that the phrases πίστις Χριστοῦ, πιστεύειν εἰς Χριστόν (Rom 10:14; Gal 2:16; Phil 1:29), and πιστεύειν with a ὅτι-clause containing the events of salvation (Rom 10:9; 1Thess 4:14; cf. Rom 4:24) denote at first faith in what God has done in Christ.[136] But since participation in the realm of faith affects and requires the existence of the believer in its totality[137] and binds the person fully to the Lord of this realm, faith also comprises the personal-relational dimen-

---

[133] Thereby, the divine predications in the participle-style (Rom 4:5.17.25) signify both, the direction of faith (to God) and its contents. – W. Mundle argues that Paul does not separate faith, trust, considering true, and knowledge (1932, 16-18, 29, 35, 38f.; "trust" though is not the decisive element of πίστις, 36); see also K. Barth's emphasis on the believer's "Erkennen" (K. Barth 1960, 851-867) and his reference to J. Calvin's famous statement: "Non in ignoratione/ignoriantia, sed in cognitione sita est fides" (quoted in K. Barth 1932, 241; 1960, 851). – On the contents of faith, see for instance Rom 6:8; 10:9; 1Cor 15:14; 1Thess 4:14; on the knowledge of faith see Rom 6:9; 1Cor 3:16; 6:2-19; 2Cor 4:4; 5:1; Gal 2:16.

[134] Cf. A. Schlatter 1927, 371; O. Michel 1978, 154; W.H.P. Hatch 1917, 35: "[F]aith is from the beginning much more than belief or conviction, for it involves the feelings and the will as well as the intellect."

[135] F. Watson 1986, 78. Cf. E. Lohse 1977, 152, 156; P. Stuhlmacher 1989, 72 ("ganzheitlicher Lebensakt"); D.M. Hay 1989, 471: Πίστις is "affirmation that the Christian kerygma is valid and determinative for the experience, outlook, and decisions of the individual believer."

[136] R. Bultmann 1958, 91-93; 1959, 203f. Cf. E. Wißmann 1926, 75; F. Neugebauer 1961, 168; E. Brandenburger 1988, 197f.

[137] Cf. A. Schlatter 1927, 361.

sion as trustful πίστις πρὸς τὸν κύριον Ἰησοῦν (Phlm 5).[138] Christ is the one to be proclaimed,[139] heard, believed, confessed, and called upon (Rom 10:10-14).[140] The complex question of the interdependence between Jesus' talk of faith, the editorial work of the Synoptics,[141] and Paul's faith terminology[142] would bring to light further aspects with respect to the Christology of faith and to the believer's personal relationship to Christ.

VI. Abraham's Faith and Christian Faith – The Christology of Faith

"Paul both emphasized the depth of Abraham's faith and homologized his faith to that of believers in Christ."[143] The renewed appeal to the Genesis quote in Rom 4:22 and the subsequent application to the present situation of Christian believers, but also the father-terminology and the faith-typology throughout the chapter implies a direct association between the patriarch's and our faith.[144] It is not true therefore that Paul makes "no im-

---

[138] Cf. U. Schnelle 2003, 601. The personal dimension of πίστις is present in both Jewish and Greek linguistic usage (cf. G. Schunack 1999, 298) and is also found in Paul (cf. K. Haacker 1984, 297; E. Schnabel 1991; H.-J. Eckstein 2000, 12f.). According to his presuppositions, R. Bultmann has to label Phlm 5 singular and exceptional (1958, 93).

[139] On the material correspondence of the contents of faith and of the proclaimed gospel, see G. Friedrich 1982, 102-106; O. Hofius 1990, 154-157. This correspondence becomes visible most notably first in 1Cor 15:11.14, second in the ὅτι-clauses 1Thess 4:14; Rom 10:9 and 1Cor 15:12.15, and finally in Rom 10:9 and 2Cor 4:5.

[140] Cf. F. Hahn 1971, 106.

[141] See the important essay of G. Ebeling (1958, especially 86-110; on the difference between Ebeling and Bultmann, cf. R. Slenczka 1984, 357); also E. Fuchs 1958. Ebeling maintains that the majority of the occurrences of πίστις and πιστεύειν are found in logia attributed to Jesus and in contexts derived from them. He considers *inter alia* the words on the disciples' little faith (Mt 6:30; 8:26; 14:31; 16:8; 17:20; Lk 12:28) and on the power of faith (Mt 17:20; 21:21; Mk 11:23; Lk 17:6 and Mt 21:22; Mk 11:24 and Mt 9:28; Mk 9:23), as well as the phrase ἡ πίστις σου σέσωκέν σε (Mk 5:34; 10:52; Mt 9:22; Lk 7:50; 8:48; 17:19; 18:42) to be *viva vox Iesu*.

[142] See M.W. Yeung 2002 and her conclusions: "Just as Jesus 'pronounces' ... membership of the Kingdom of God to the nonelect on the basis of their faith in his own person [*sc.* through his words ἡ πίστις σου σέσωκέν σε], Paul asserts that sinners are 'reckoned' righteous on the basis of their faith in Jesus Christ's atoning sacrifice. The correspondence between the two cannot be accidental but speaks for Paul's dependence on Jesus" (291). See also the influence of Mt 17:20 on 1Cor 13:2 (considered as possible in R. Bultmann 1929a, 191) and the notable thesis of J. Jeremias: "Paul's doctrine of justification is ... simply a development of our Lord's own preaching" (1954/1955, 369f.).

[143] T.H. Tobin 1995, 449.

[144] Paul's appeal to Abraham only makes sense if Abraham's faith somehow anticipated the Christian faith (E. Käsemann 1969, 140). In Galatians 3, however, Paul's is not concerned with showing "any clear correspondence between Abrahamic and Christian faith" (J.M.G. Barclay 1988, 87n.31).

plicit appeal to the reader to imitate Abraham's example."[145] But how does this homologizing express itself?

The theocentrism of Romans 4 – in notable distinction to the christocentrism of Galatians 3[146] – calls for an explanation as to the direction and content of Abraham's faith. Already W. Sanday and A.C. Headlam noted: "It is rather a departure from St. Paul's more usual practice to make the object of faith God the Father rather than God the Son."[147] Some have taken this anomaly to strengthen their point that πίστις Χριστοῦ means the "faith of Jesus Christ."[148] Since this view has insurmountable weaknesses, other solutions are called for; the following are imaginable: (1) Either Paul did not at all pose this question of the relationship of Abraham's faith to Christ, or – granted he had this aspect in mind – his concern is (2) merely the equality of the structure of faith, not the identical content or even (3) the idea that Abraham himself believed in Christ and has therefore been, as it were, an *anima naturaliter christiana* or an "anonymous Christian."[149]

In any case, God's justification of the ungodly cannot be separated from the revelation of his righteousness through πίστις Χριστοῦ[150]; this is evident on grounds of the close relationship between Rom 3:21-31 and chapter 4[151]: "[P]arallels between 3:21-31 and chap. 4 induce readers to view Abraham's story through messianist lenses."[152] Generally, Paul's idea of faith is saturated with christological connotations, and it is strictly and unconditionally related to the Christ-event.[153] Only because of Christ faith is what it is,[154] for faith came with Christ.[155] Furthermore, in 5:6 Paul says

---

[145] Thus R.B. Hays 1985, 91f.; cf. G. Howard 1990, 88: "Abraham is not offered as a model of our faith." S.K. Stowers 1994, 247: Paul does not recommend "Abraham as a model of Christian faith."

[146] Cf., e.g., H. Boers 1971, 91; 1994, 110; R.B. Hays 1983, 156.

[147] W. Sanday/A.C. Headlam 1895, 101. J.D.G. Dunn speaks of a "tension between the christocentric faith for which Paul's Gospel calls and the fact that he is able to document, define and justify that faith from OT precedents and texts" (1997b, 111). This observation has been criticized by F. Watson and S.J. Gathercole (cf. 2004, 163f.).

[148] Cf. already G. Kittel 1906.

[149] The latter expression was coined by K. Rahner (1965).

[150] Against E. Wißmann 1926, 90, who criticizes Paul of contradicting himself.

[151] Cf. W. Mundle 1932, 96.

[152] R.L. Brawley 1997, 299. Cf. U. Wilckens 1969, 97n.43; 1978, 281; J. Roloff 1990, 248 (latent christological perspective throughout Rom 4:1-22); A. Behrens 1997, 336; U. Heckel 2002, 113 with n.10; S.J. Gathercole 2004, 165, 167. With reference to Gal 3:6, J. Lambrecht concludes: "Abraham's faith too was not without 'christological' content" (1991, 287). See also the table above page 311, which shows the wealth of mutual associations between Rom 3:21-31 and chapter 4.

[153] Cf. F. Neugebauer 1961, 163. See also A. Jülicher 1917, 26f.; G. Ebeling 1958, 67; G. Friedrich 1982, 102-106; D. Lührmann 1985, 102: "Paul met constamment en relation πίστις/πιστεύειν avec le titre christologique (ὁ χριστός." M. Theobald 1999, 292n.50.

[154] Cf. J. Becker 1992, 439: "Der Glaube ist, was er ist, weil es Christus gibt"

that "Christ died for the ungodly," referring back to 4:5 through the key-word ἀσεβής and implying that God has presented himself even to Abraham as the God who justifies the ungodly, namely, through Christ (cf. 4:25).[156] All this means that only a one-sided, isolated exegesis of Romans 4 can assert that the πίστις-concept in this chapter is without christological implication.[157] Even within his Abraham-chapter Paul leaves no doubt that he never deserts his Christ-centered standpoint: Abraham believed in the God who gives life to the dead and calls into being the non-existing, and this God is the God who has raised Jesus from the dead and who justifies the ungodly.[158] His "justifying faith was already belief in the God of the gospel."[159] The divine predications (4:5.17.24; cf. 3:30) acquire their full force only if heard from the perspective of God's act in Christ.

That Paul was indeed capable of actualizing the message of the Old Testament in light of the Christ-event shines through some of his formulations: According to 1Cor 10:4, the rock in the desert from which Israel drank the spiritual drink was Christ (cf. Ex 17:6)[160]; this means that for Paul Christ and the sacraments have been present – though in a concealed way – in the desert generation. 1Cor 8:6 explicates Paul's logic behind such statements: All of the divine creative work is mediated through Christ (δι' οὗ τὰ πάντα). If therefore those events that reveal God to the Old Testament people are mediated through Christ,[161] then God's self-disclosure and promise to Abraham, who symbolizes Israel, did not happen apart

---

[155] Cf. A. Schlatter 1910, 336: "Der Glaube kam damit, dass der Christus kam." G. Ebeling 1958, 67: "Das Kommen Christi [ist] das Kommen des Glaubens." H.W. Schmidt 1966, 66: "[Der Glaube] kommt in Christus." M. Barth 1970, 204: "[W]hen Christ came faith came." J.L. Martyn 1997, 23: In Galatians Paul "is constructing an announcement designed to wake the Galatians up to the real cosmos, made what it is by the fact that faith has now arrived with the advent of Christ."

[156] Cf. P. Stuhlmacher 1989, 68.

[157] Against that M. Neubrand 1997, 274 *et passim*. Cf. also R.A. Harrisville 1992, 279n.94; H. Boers 1971, 98: "[F]aith is here understood un-Christologically." 102: "[I]n Rom. 4 he did not impose the Christian concept of faith on Abraham," and this is "a level of thought that was not caught up within the framework of … his 'system'," i.e., "his ghetto" (104). See also Boers's somewhat modified view in 1994, 110: "[N]otwithstanding the remarkably non-christological discussion of the faith of Abraham in Romans compared with Galatians, Romans 4 is no less christological than Galatians."

[158] Cf. D. Lührmann 1976, 46f., 53. U. Wilckens points out that the part in which Paul deals with the essence of Abraham's faith (Rom 4:17-22) leads to the resurrection of the crucified Christ (4:23-25), i.e., even the structure of the chapter points to the christological dimension of faith (1969, 97n.43).

[159] A.T. Lincoln 2002, 187, with reference to Rom 8:11; 1Cor 1:28; 15:22.

[160] Cf. D.-A. Koch 1986, 306, who stresses the past tense: ἡ πέτρα δὲ ἦν ὁ Χριστός.

[161] Cf. A. Schlatter 1934, 290.

from Christ (cf. Gal 3:16).[162] Moreover, Abraham has become an anticipatory part of the eschatological domain of faith, which now, in the time after Christ's death and resurrection, has been unfolded fully and universally as a work of God mediated through Christ. Both, the question of logical inconsistency and the claim for a sound analysis of faith in terms of its theocentrism or christocentrism are only problematic to the modern interpreter, while for Paul's mind and line of reasoning these aspects are without difficulty.[163] He does not think historical-critically in modern terms, but reasons out the present by a retrospective appeal to the Scripture,[164] in order to point out analogous or typological correspondences between past and present. Paul reads his Bible *from* the present *for* the present.[165]

Accordingly, his perspective and concern is our right standing before God, which consists in faith apart from works. Just as Paul does not specify "works" as "works of the law" in Rom 4:1-12, he does not specify "faith" as "Christ-faith." Yet his logic is not: Abraham could not accomplish works of the law, since the law had not come yet, but: Abraham works had no effect towards his justification. With regard to faith, his logic is not: Abraham could not believe in Christ, since Christ had not come yet, but: Faith is the way to justification. Nevertheless, "works" in the Pauline sense are always related to the law and "faith" is always related to Christ, so that Abraham could become type and paradigm for the one ἐκ νόμου and for the one ἐκ πίστεως. "Justification," on the other hand is mediated "christologically," through faith, not "nomistically," through works.

As has been seen, in Romans 4 Paul employs the hermeneutical method of "typology," through which he seeks to establish a relationship between "then" and "now" under certain aspects: Abraham's faith as response to God's word, and God's acceptance of faith. Within this premise it is misleading to say that the "Christian has faith in a much deeper sense than Abraham had it"[166] or that "[r]etrospective Christian faith is fuller than the prospective faith of Abraham,"[167] for Paul is not concerned with distinguishing a "shallower" Old Testament-Abrahamic faith from a "deeper" or "fuller" New Testament-Christian faith. Yet it is likewise problematic to

---

[162] H. Boers, though, argues that "Rom. 4:17-22 contradicts the reasoning of Gal. 3:16" (1971, 101; see however 1994, 159f.).

[163] Cf. W. Mundle 1932, 97; O. Kuss 1956, 203. Against that, D.A. Campbell perceives "a temporal problem" in this interpretation (2005, 194; cf. 229), even though he admits, for instance, "that creation was through Christ for Paul" (106n.27).

[164] Cf. A. Jülicher 1917, 26f.; D.-A. Koch 1986, 307. Paul shows the Christian believers their place in the divine faith-righteousness, but does not "nostrify" Abraham in Christian terms (cf. U. Wilckens 1978, 283f.).

[165] Cf. D.-A. Koch 1986, 327 ("prinzipielle[.] Gegenwartsbezogenheit der Schrift").

[166] Against W.H.P. Hatch 1917, 58.

[167] Against R. Holst 1997, 326.

argue with reference to Abraham and Habakkuk that for Paul "[f]aith is surely not new."[168] For, "[b]efore Christ's coming, faith existed only exceptionally [better: prolepticly] in Abraham and in Scripture as a promise,"[169] or, as in Habakkuk, as prophecy – and thus faith is indeed "new." Only now, in the present time, faith has been revealed in its fullness, as πίστις Χριστοῦ, and insofar it is a new salvation-historical entity with all its consequences for the individual and humanity in general. And only from this new time of salvation, the proper meaning of Abraham's faith as pointing to and anticipating the Christian faith is fully disclosed in terms of a *sensus plenior*. The factor that distinguishes Abraham's faith from Christian faith is not associated with faith *per se*, but with the unfolding of God's salvation plan, when through Christ anticipation and promise became full realization.[170]

Above we posed the question: "Did Abraham then, according to Paul, believe in Christ?" Some would answer: "Very nearly, if not exactly. There is no difference between the character of his faith and that of Christians."[171] Yet this thought is beyond the scope of Paul's intention and interest: Even if Paul might have allowed for the idea that the pre-existent Christ worked as mediator of God's self-disclosure to Abraham and of the justification of the ungodly Abraham, here his primary hermeneutical concern is to look at the present through Scripture to find analogies or typologies to the human situation and God's dealing with humankind. Abraham's faith and Christian faith are the same, insofar as Abraham believed in God who gives descendants to a man whose body has died, and Christians believe in God who gave life to the one who died on the cross.[172] There exists a structural analogy, a qualitative equivalence, and an essential identity,[173]

---

[168] Against G.N. Davies 1990, 43. Cf. C. Dietzfelbinger 1961, 23.

[169] H.D. Betz 1979, 176. Cf. E. Fuchs 1960, 387: „Auch der Glaube ist an seine Zeit „in Christus" gebunden, so daß Abraham nur der *Vorläufer* des Glaubens war. Aber nachdem das Evangelium gekommen war, ist mit dem Evangelium für jedermann genau die Zeit zum Glauben gekommen"

[170] Cf. similarly K. Kertelge 1971, 193.

[171] A.T. Hanson 1974, 66; cf. S.J. Gathercole 2004, 164. John in fact transposes the "christological" perspective into the Abraham narratives themselves (Jn 8:56). But "[i]t is not appropriate to read into Paul the Johannine idea" (R.B. Hays 1983, 150), even if "Augustine, Luther, Calvin, and Wesley believed that the promise of the coming Christ was the object of the faith ... of the Old Testament saints" (S. Westerholm 2004, 279f.n.44).

[172] Cf. L. Goppelt 1964, 251.

[173] Cf., e.g., O. Schmitz 1922, 121 ("innere Gleichartigkeit"); A. Deißmann 1925, 127f. ("inhaltlich identisch"); A. Schlatter 1927, 396n.2 ("analoges Verhältnis"); H. Lietzmann 1928, 55; M.-E. Boismard 1955, 72 ("le même effet"; "le même [objet]"); L. Goppelt 1966/1967, 231; E. Käsemann 1969, 140 ("letztlich sogar identisch"); H. Boers 1971, 83f.; E. Lohse 1977, 158; O. Michel 1978, 175 ("*Gleichartigkeit* des Glaubens

since both Abraham's and Christian faith are directed to the one life-giving God and dominated by the "mystery" of death and resurrection.[174] It is the same faith in the same God,[175] but the present is characterized as the new salvation-historical age of faith, eschatologically qualified through the cross.[176] Faith is disclosed universally, to all, Jews and Gentiles. What Abraham anticipated has been fully realized through Christ.

A specification of the second question hinted at above calls for a brief comment: Granted that for Paul faith is not conceivable apart from Christology, one has to ask whether or not Paul's concept of faith included the thought of a personal relationship to Christ. In the course of scholarship, both extremes of a radical elimination and a thorough endorsement of the element of a bond with Christ have found supporters among those who analyzed the Pauline πίστις.[177] In our discussion of the genitive in the πίστις Χριστοῦ-formula in Rom 3:22, the designation *genitivus relationis* appeared to convey fairly accurately the relationship between faith, Christ, and the believer: Faith only exists in relation to Christ, and it establishes a relation to Christ. Christ was found to be origin, content, and goal of faith (cf. also 10:1-13) – though not so much in terms of a "person opposite," with whom one may (or may not) entertain a personal relationship, but rather in terms of the Lord and savior sent by God whose death and resurrection inaugurated the new era of faith,[178] a sphere of salvation as *regnum Christi*, which draws human beings into its sphere of influence. God's act and Christ's work cannot be separated, and therefore, "faith directed to God" and "faith directed to Christ" illuminate themselves mutually and are not conceivable independently and isolated from each other.[179] In the pre-

---

Abrahams und der christlichen Gemeinde," italics original); U. Wilckens 1978, 258 ("ein und derselbe Glaube"); J.-N. Aletti 1989, 247 ("le même acte de croire"), 249; J. Roloff 1990, 248 ("wesenhafte Gleichheit"); R.A. Harrisville 1992, 27, 158; J.A. Fitzmyer 1993, 388 ("exact correspondence"); R. Holst 1997, 326 ("essentially the same"); E. Gräßer 1998, 22.

[174] Cf. M.-E. Boismard 1955, 71.

[175] Cf. W. Sanday/A.C. Headlam 1895, 115; H. Lietzmann 1928, 55; H. Boers 1971, 84 (with further references in n.1); C.K. Barrett 1957, 99; J.A. Fitzmyer 1993, 388.

[176] Cf. U. Wilckens 1978, 277.

[177] Cf. on the one hand for instance E. Wißmann (1926), and on the other J. de Zwaan (1936).

[178] Cf. D. Lührmann 1976, 48f.: Χριστός constantly occurs in statements on the salvific importance of Christ's death and resurrection.

[179] Cf. O. Michel 1978, 154: "Der Glaube an Jesus ist die durch Kreuz und Auferstehung gegebene Form des Glaubens an Gott." See similarly F. Hahn 1971, 105; E. Lohse 2003, 149.

sent eschatological age, God meets us in Christ, only in Christ[180] – the crucified one is the only authentic image of the living God.[181]

B. Abraham's Faith in Tradition and Paul

Having presented elements of the Jewish interpretation of Gen 15:6 up until the first century A.D. and Paul's *relecture* of the Abraham narrative, we must filter out the theological agreements, but also the aspects where Paul departs from the Judaism of his time. Undoubtedly, according to his own subjective perspective, the revelation and implication of the Christ-event lead to an "Umwertung aller Werte,"[182] concerning both, one's individual life and the course of God's salvation history.[183] The encounter with Christ in his own biography caused him to view as loss (Phil 3:7-8) the things so dear to him in his life as a Pharisee. But what changes occurred? Despite Paul's clear words, some interpreters argue that the discrepancy between Paul and the exegetical tradition of his time can be reduced to a minimum: L. Gaston, for instance, states that "it is possible to interpret Paul in continuity with the tradition before him," and he asks: "Why should we assume 'opponents,' against whom Paul's words must be understood as 'polemic,' where none is indicated?" Paul writes "in conformity with the exegetical tradition."[184] Exegetes at the other extreme of the spectrum call Paul's interpretation of the Abraham figure almost blasphemous not only for Jewish ears,[185] assigning to Paul the boldness of presenting a

---

[180] R. Bultmann 1959, 218.

[181] D. Lührmann 1985, 103. See also the deliberations in O. Pfleiderer 1890, 168-172. – The devotion to Christ, the Lord and God, arose already in the pre-Pauline communities, which is evident for instance in prayers, doxologies, and confessional formulas such as Rom 4:24. L.W. Hurtado points to this remarkable fact "that at an … early point in the emergent Christian movement we find what I have described as a 'binitarian pattern' of devotion and worship, in which Christ is treated as recipient of devotion with God and in ways that can be likened only to the worship of a deity" (2003, 135). A sense of incompatibility or competition between Jesus and God is absent in this "binitarian pattern."

[182] M. Hengel uses this Nietzsche quote in relation to Paul (1991, 290).

[183] The individual and universal dimension can be illustrated by two occurrences of ἀποκαλύπτεσθαι in Gal 1:16 (individual) and Rom 1:17 (universal).

[184] L. Gaston 1980, 59, 54; cf. 53. Gaston therefore calls for a "fresh interpretation" of Paul (1980, 59; cf. R. Mosis 1989, 93). See the more differentiated and comprehensive attempt of H. Gese to illustrate the unity of biblical theology in terms of a tradition-historical approach (1970). – In our exegesis of Rom 4:23-24, we pointed to one instance, in which a Jewish idea is read into Paul without any textual basis: the idea that the vicarious power of Abraham's faith ensures the blessing for Gentiles (cf. G. Howard 1990, 55). See above note 1204 in chapter V.

[185] Cf. G. Bornkamm 1969, 152.

totally new picture of the Abraham-story,[186] "directly contrary to contemporary ... tradition."[187]

Neither the suggestion of an uninterrupted continuity nor the claim of a rupture of all ties with the Jewish tradition is fully adequate. The identity of God, the creator and giver of life, presents itself to Paul as unshakable truth; God, the father of Jesus Christ, is the God who called Abraham, gave and fulfilled the promise given to him. Also, both to Paul and his Jewish contemporaries, Abraham is figure of identification, father of the people of God,[188] inheritor of the world[189]; and by calling Abraham "father," he draws on the Jewish motifs of remembrance.[190] Paul's method of argumentation is fully congruent with rabbinic exegesis[191]; the same is true for his use of Scripture: Scriptural passages are applied to the present situation with a specific interest of reception.[192]

But on the other hand, his appeal to Abraham in Romans 4 cannot be adequately understood without specifying those elements that exhibit his distinct *theological* "Anti-Ἰουδαϊσμός."[193] Many proposals have emerged to pinpoint the most consequential point of departure and the most revolutionary novelty in his Abraham image. Generally, one identifies two con-

---

[186] Cf. J. Jeremias 1970, 52.

[187] A.T. Hanson 1974, 60. Cf. C.E.B. Cranfield 1975, 228-230; J. Lambrecht 1979, 17 ("une véritable révolution"); A. von Dobbeler 1987, 133f.; W. Baird 1988, 375 ("radical revision of the exegetical tradition"); M. Cranford 1995, 71: "Paul turns the common Jewish conception of Abraham on its head." B. Ego 1996, 26: "[D]ie Vorstellung des gesetzesfrommen Abraham ... [steht] den paulinischen Ausführungen in Röm 4 mit ihrer Betonung des Glaubens des Patriarchen diametral entgegen[.]" J.D.G. Dunn 1985, 424; 1997, 265: "[Paul] was in effect attacking the traditional Jewish understanding of Abraham."

[188] Cf. J. Roloff 1990, 253.

[189] Cf. J. Lambrecht 1979, 17.

[190] Cf. S.J. Gathercole 2002, 233, with n.48, with reference to passages also relevant in our discussion of the reception history of Gen 15:6, namely, Sirach 44; 1Macc 2,51; 4QMMT C 23-25; in addition, Tob 4,12; Jdt 8,26; 1Macc 4,9; Sir 2,10; Heb 11; 12:1-3; 2Tim 2:8.

[191] Cf., e.g., C. Dietzfelbinger 1961, 32-36; F. Hahn 1971, 107; D.-A. Koch 1986, 327. See *inter alia* the *gezerah shavah*.

[192] As has been seen, this method has been effective even within the Old Testament (cf. Ps 106:31; Neh 9:8). See A.T. Lincoln 1992, 176: "[I]n the meeting between the world of the text and Paul's world the semantic potential of the text can be exploited for his strategy of pastoral persuasion" (1992, 176). A. Behrens 1997, 335n.48.

[193] E. Gräßer states that a Christian-theological "Antijudaism" cannot be separated from Paul's identity (1998, 7). The horrible abuse of this concept in political, societal, and ecclesiastical matters is clearly to be named as "abuse," but clarity in this difficult subject only comes by naming and defining the content of Paul's opposition against certain features of his contemporary Judaism, not by avoiding it and pushing it away as nonexistent.

cepts, which belong essentially together in Jewish theology, but have been broken apart by Paul, such as promise and law,[194] grace and law,[195] grace and works,[196] faith and law,[197] Christ and law,[198] faith-righteousness and works-righteousness,[199] above all faith and works.[200] Overall, therefore, Paul fights against wrong syntheses and futile "middle courses."[201] In critique of the allegedly "un-Pauline" individualistic perspective inherent in these antagonistic pairs of concepts, other commentators suggested alternatively that the break is "not over belief and obedience as competing soteriological paradigms, but over Jewish ethnicity and faith as competing boundary markers of God's people."[202]

The heuristically most precise approach is the one that directs the attention to a comparison between Paul and Jewish theology in terms of the situation of Abraham prior to his justification and how this "unjustified" state is overcome. Throughout Jewish tradition, Abraham's *entire* life conduct was considered as evidence for his obedience to God's will and for works that suit anybody paying attention to God's commandments. He was the friend of God, perfectly just, righteous, and obedient. And his faith was an integral part of this piety.[203] Accordingly, God's act of justification was considered as an approving response to the patriarch's faithfulness, as his vindication subsequent to trials and to being found faithful.[204] "It is faithful obedience that is counted for righteousness by God." This means that at the time of justification, he was faithful already, "and thus the divine declaration is a *descriptive* judgment."[205] *Per definitionem*, descriptive statements have the character of a legitimation and confirmation of a present status.

---

[194] Cf. C. Dietzfelbinger 1961, 10.

[195] Cf. E. Gräßer 1998, 15.

[196] H. Conzelmann 1973, 379; E. Käsemann 1980, 100f.

[197] Cf. J. Roloff 1990, 252.

[198] Cf. J. Roloff 1990, 251; T.L. Donaldson 1997, 116.

[199] Cf. H.-J. Schoeps 1959, 212.

[200] Cf. O. Schmitz 1922, 120; F. Hahn 1971, 99; C.E.B. Cranfield 1975, 229; O. Michel 1978, 162; H.D. Betz 1979, 141; D.-A. Koch 1986, 221; P. Stuhlmacher 1989, 68; B.S. Childs 1992, 607. C. Burchard asks for the "Vor- und Nebengeschichte" (1996, 405) of the *Grundsatz* "not by the works of the law but through faith in Jesus Christ."

[201] E.P. Sanders believes "that it is safe to say that the notion that God's grace is in any way contradictory to human endeavour is totally foreign to Palestinian Judaism" (1977, 297; cf. 543).

[202] M. Cranford 1995, 73.

[203] Cf. E. Lohse 2003, 147.

[204] J.-N. Aletti 2003, 319: "[L]a foi du patriarche fut une longue démarche de confiance et d'obéissance à Dieu, qui apprécia cette attitude constante et la compta comme justice parce qu'il s'agissait d'une foi opérante."

[205] S.J. Gathercole 2002, 237f.

In contrast to this interpretative matrix, Paul affirms that Abraham entered the sphere of salvation and righteousness *not* through obedience, but through his faith "prior and apart from works."[206] Unlike several of the analyzed Jewish *relectures* of Gen 15:6, Paul exploits the temporal and material primacy of the "faith-chapter" Genesis 15 compared to the "circumcision-chapter" Genesis 17,[207] while in contrast to the multiply attested Jewish practice he in a remarkable way leaves entirely aside the Aqedah (Genesis 22).[208] Paul's silence on the covenant of circumcision and his omission of the Aqedah in Romans 4 are in themselves most eloquent reactions to contemporary theologizing, given the eminence of these themes in

---

[206] J.D.G. Dunn 1988, 205. But see the different perspective in J.D.G. Dunn 2001, 366: "[T]he new perspective enables us to see not only the grace in Second Temple soteriology, but also the judgment in Paul's soteriology. Both start from election/grace; both demand obedience (Torah obedience, the obedience of faith); both embrace what can fairly be called a two-stage soteriology" (cf. 368). With similar intention, K.L. Yinger argues that traditional scholarship failed to demonstrate that "the grace-works axis in Judaism is any more synergistic or meritorious than in Paul" (K.L. Yinger 1999, 4).

[207] Cf. M. Oeming 1998, 89.

[208] In marked difference to Paul, other New Testament authors follow the Jewish tradition: Jas 2:21-24 and Heb 11:17-19; see also *1Clem* 10,6. "Jc 2,14-26 ... est ... représentatif de l'interprétation que le judaïsme inter- et paratestamentaire fait de ce passage" (J.-N. Aletti 2003, 319n.33). This is not the place to discuss and survey the mass of the secondary literature on the relationship between Paul and James. It suffices to name the different suggestions (see for a brief appraisal F. Avemarie 2001, 282-284 [undocumented references can be found there]).
(1) James offers a well thought-out critique of Paul and is "stracks widder Sanct Paulon" (M. Luther). See also M. Dibelius; A. Lindemann; J.D.G. Dunn 1985, 425; F. Avemarie 2001; others contrast James with Paul by aligning James with the author of Ps 106:31 (F. Delitzsch 1887, 276) or Philo (J.D. Levenson 1987, 59).
(2) James misunderstood Paul or used the keywords in a rather different sense or merely attacked a Pseudo-Paulinism (see classically J. Jeremias 1954/1955: "There can be no doubt that Ja 2:24 presupposes Paul" (368). But James, for instance, has "a popular conception of faith" in terms of "the intellectual acceptance of monotheism." On the other hand, "πίστις with Paul means the faith of salvation, the confidence that Christ died for my sins and that God has raised Him for my justification." "Έργα with Paul means the keeping of the Commandments of the law ... Έργα with James means Christian love" (370). Justification is for Paul "justification at baptism," for James it is "the last judgment" (371). In the end, "James has his full right to stand after Paul. His message can be understood only after Paul has been understood" (371). On this type of interpretation, see also F. Vouga, A. Chester, E. Lohse, K. Haacker, D. Lührmann, R. Schnackenburg; in addition R.N. Longenecker 1977; D.J. Moo 1985, 108f.
(3) James did not know Paul and his theology. Within this interpretation James is mostly considered post-Pauline (see R. Heiligenthal, H. Frankemölle, D. Verseput, E. Baasland, K. Berger), but occasionally also before or next to Paul (see J.B. Lightfoot 1896, 164, 201; see also above chapter IV.K.II on the idiomatic character of Gen 15:6).
(4) James and Paul can be harmonized without using logical and exegetical "tricks" (see A. Schlatter 1927, 460: "ohne alle logische Taschenspielerei").

Jewish piety and in the Jewish Abraham image. On the other hand, he
seems to follow a familiar numerical calculation, which connects the beginning of Abraham's relationship with God to Genesis 15, prior to his
exodus from Haran (Genesis 12). At the time of his justification, therefore,
Abraham's existence took place in the sphere of sinfulness, paganism, and
ungodliness, apart from works, obedience, and God. "Paul's reestablish-
ment of the correct sequence shows the condition of Abraham at the point
of his justification: he was ungodly rather than faithful, and God's declaration of justification is emphatically *not* descriptive."[209] God's judgment
does not state, but constitute Abraham's righteous status, or, differently
put, it is not rational-informative, but creative-performative. It changes
authoritatively and independently (χωρὶς ἔργων) the standing of Abraham
before God from ungodliness and death to acceptance with God and life.
To Jewish minds this is an impossible or at least paradoxical thought,
when Paul proclaims the *iustificatio impii* – rather than the *iustificatio pii* –
with regard to the patriarch, *the* paradigm of piety.[210] In consequence, in
duplicating how God justified and how Abraham entered the sphere of salvation, Paul concludes that πίστις was not part of his ἔργα, but preceded
them.[211] No work contributed to Abraham's justification. But Paul's intention is not to diminish or denigrate Abraham's works, but to highlight faith
as the only criterion of and way to salvation, as the only "boundary
marker" that permits the access into the eschatological people of God.

By revisiting the meaning and significance of faith in its subjective-
individual and intersubjective-ecclesiological dimensions, Paul arrives at a
redefinition of God's people; "those who believe in Christ are the true
children of Abraham."[212] And insofar as faith universally defines the mark
of the members of the people of salvation, it also transcends their individu-
ality and subjectivity, assuming the aspect of a trans-subjective salvation-
historical phenomenon, through which God established a new time and
sphere, having power-character. In contrast to Jewish theology, but in

---

[209] S.J. Gathercole 2002, 237; cf. 243. See also P. Stuhlmacher 1966, 220n.1.

[210] Cf. M. Dibelius/H. Greeven 1984, 210.

[211] This can arguably be deemed one of the most decisive differences between Paul's
and the Jewish concept of faith (cf. E. Lohse 1977, 156). To be sure, as pointed out on
different occasions, the *sequence* faith – works is significant, and not any *separation* of
works from faith (cf. A. Schlatter 1927, 374f., 381). Paul certainly cannot imagine an
isolation of faith from its concrete expressions in the believer's existence (see also F.
Watson 1986, 78).

[212] H. Boers 1971, 74. As for Galatians 3 and Paul's redefinition of the "Abrahamic
family" in this chapter, see J.M.G. Barclay 1988, 86-96. Both passages, Galatians 3 and
Romans 4, seek to persuade Paul's addressees that "their identity as children of Abraham
is secure on the basis of their faith in Christ" (92).

analogy to Paul's own extension of the concept of sin,[213] Paul also accomplished a redefinition of faith in terms of its double orientation as both existential-individual category and super-individual phenomenon. According to the eschatological character of the new era of faith, being a part in this era is also qualified eschatologically, and by this conception, Paul takes up the "eschatologizing" tendency in the Jewish interpretation of Gen 15:6.

Having stated Paul's principal points of departure from Jewish theology, we have to briefly review those texts referred to in the context of the Jewish *relecture* of Gen 15:6 and the Abraham narratives in order to concretize and corroborate our theses.

(1) The terminologically closest parallel to Gen 15:6, Ps 106:31, being part of the inner-biblical reception history of the Genesis-verse, attributes righteousness to Phinehas who through an act of violence defended the boundaries that demarcated Israel from other peoples. Ps 106:31 "provides a perfect proof text against Paul's teaching"[214] and he "could not have appealed to Psalm 106:31 in this connection without violating his whole argument,"[215] for to the psalmist "faith" is an act of national-religious zeal. According to Psalm 106, Phinehas's zeal led to an eternal, exclusive priesthood, while for Paul, Abraham's faith opens up his universal fatherhood to all, Jewish and Gentile, believers. Both, Phinehas and Abraham enjoy as "patriarchs" highest reputation in Jewish theology and are named in one breath, but Paul's concentration on faith apart from works has to result in a reduction of father-figures and in an elevation of Abraham.[216]

(2) Also the other Old Testament text appealing to Gen 15:6, the penitential prayer Nehemiah 9, is concerned with the "works of the law" (9:34: עֲשׂה תוֹרָה/ποιεῖν τὸν νόμον), with obedience, which leads to life (9:29: ζήσεται), and with Abraham's faithfulness (9:8: נֶאֱמָן/πιστός), which God confirmed, recognized (15:6b), and answered by the covenant. For Paul, Abraham's faith is decisive, for it is faith that is counted by God as righteousness and that leads to life (Rom 1:17: ζήσεται), not "works of the law."[217] The author of the prayer – subtly, but unmistakably – characterizes Abraham's "faith" as his faithful obedience, which is in line with God's work of grace in his people and therefore fitting for the repenting congregation. However, in contrast to, for instance, Ben Sira, the passages on

---

[213] See above pages 252f.

[214] W.R. Farmer 1952, 29.

[215] J. Murray 1959, 131; cf. T. Otero Lázaro 2001, 31n.68.

[216] For the Greek translator of Ps 106:30, Phinehas's act has some kind of redemptive implication (ἐξιλάσκεσθαι; cf. Num 25:13), which Paul does *not* state with respect to Abraham's faith, but only with respect to Christ's death (cf. Rom 3:25: Christ as ἱλαστήριον).

[217] To be sure, both, the author of the prayer and Paul, agree on the life-giving power of the creator God (cf. Neh 9:6; Rom 4:17: ζωοποιεῖν)

Abraham in both Romans 4 and Nehemiah 9 place a significant emphasis on God's action, so that overall the *ductus* is theocentric.

(3) How Paul adopts the Septuagint version of Gen 15:6 has been addressed above.[218] In sum, the translation defines Abraham's faith as a one-time reaction to God's promise, as single act,[219] which Paul specifies as Abraham's step into the realm of faith, in which the promise is mediated and remains for Abraham and his seed (Rom 4:13).

(4) In contrast to Paul's exposition in Romans 4 (and in line with the author of Hebrews), Ben Sira is interested in a prehistory of faith(fulness) before Abraham and hence considers him as *one* – not the first – outstanding believer.[220] Furthermore, pairs such as Abraham-Isaac "create a sense of sequence and succession,"[221] emphasizing real historical continuity. God saw in Abraham a man who obeyed his law fully and displayed utmost faithfulness (Sir 44,20),[222] while Paul assigns to Abraham the serious attribute "ungodly," one who is without faithful works – a deplorable standing, according to Sir 41,8, and surely not applicable to Abraham: "Woe to you, the ungodly (ἀσεβεῖς)!" The sequence of the "stages" in Abraham's life and their logical conditions and consequences are likewise illuminating: According to Sir 44,20-21, Abraham observed the law, entered the covenant of circumcision, proved his faithfulness, and received therefore (διὰ τοῦτο) the divine promise. For Paul, God's "Heilssetzung" of faith-righteousness provides the foundation of the promise to Abraham, upon which his faith and justification followed[223]; and circumcision functions as seal. According to Sirach 44, Abraham's "faith" is ethical norm and paradigm for subsequent generations, part of a relationship with God, which will be rewarded by him. For Paul, Abraham is *typos*, father, and example of faith, and his situation points to the unconditional divine affection to humankind, to the justification of the impious.

(5) In the book of *Jubilees*, Abraham figures as a hero of faithfulness, who already in his early years was full of zeal against any kind of idolatry. None of the tests he has to endure can inhibit his full obedience and inner steadfastness, through which he permanently holds on to God and from which his righteous deeds follow. The writer of *Jubilees* perceives Abraham's inner strength as basis and condition of his "faith" and of his flawlessness with respect to God's will. Paul's Abraham, too, shows his perse-

---

[218] See above chapter V.B.IV.4.b.

[219] Cf. M. Oeming 1998, 90.

[220] Cf. C. Dietzfelbinger 1961, 15; U. Luz 1968, 181n.177.

[221] B.L. Mack 1985, 45.

[222] David too did not abandon the νόμος τοῦ ὑψίστου (Sir 49,4).

[223] Cf. J.D.G. Dunn 1985, 424. Dunn remarks that "Paul could well have had this passage [*sc.* Sir 44,19-21] in mind, since it associates so many of the same themes."

verance in that he becomes strong in the power of faith and holds on to the reliability of God (Rom 4:20-21); but he is not a hero of faith(fulness) and "saint" for the sons of Jacob,[224] but father of all believers and "pre-existent" participant in πίστις[225]; he is not the perfect obedient one (cf. *Jub* 23,10), who can duly expect spiritual resurrection, but the justified un-godly one.

(6) 4QPseudo-Jubilees is focused on the testing of Abraham's unwaver-ing fidelity in the face of the attacks of Mastemah (Genesis 22),[226] but also on God's faithfulness to his promise. Abraham's faith, described as one-time act and later confirmed as veritable in testing, determines the circum-stances, in which the promise can come to its fulfillment. It leads to the annihilation of the powers of darkness. Certain analogies to Paul are in-deed present here,[227] though according to Paul, Abraham's faith did not take place in a neutral sphere of free decision, but God's promise and indi-vidual faith are embraced by the cosmic force of faith, which God himself has set against the power of sin and which became universally effective through the cross. Against that, the Joban setting of 4QPseudo-Jubilees interprets Abraham's "faith" in terms of his faithfulness, which he proves in his decision at the crossroads not to abandon God due to the trials, but to commit unconditionally to him. In the world of thought of 4QPseudo-Jubilees, such an act has cosmological consequences, while for Paul only the Christ-event, Christ's righteousness (δικαίωμα) can terminate the do-minion of sin (Rom 5:18.21).

(7) The second non-Abrahamic text apart from Ps 106:31 representing a significant item in the reception history of Gen 15:6 is 4QMMT. The read-ers are reminded that David was a man of righteous deeds, whom God for-gave as a consequence (C 25). In notable contrast to this conception, Paul makes clear that David's forgiveness happened apart from works (Rom 4:6). Even more striking is the manner, in which the Genesis-verse is quoted and altered: What is counted as righteousness is not faith *per se*, but "faith" as the "works of the Torah," for doing what is righteous and good in God's eyes will be rewarded with personal and communal welfare (C 31). Both the Teacher of Righteousness and Paul know about human entanglement in evil and sinfulness (C 29; Rom 3:23), but they differ about the way out: The first teaches that righteous "works of the law" are the

---

[224] Cf. O. Schmitz 1922, 105 ("die große Heiligengestalt des exklusiven Judentums").

[225] M. Müller notes the following analogy between *Jubilees* and Paul: "Beide Male dient die Gestalt [*sc.* des Abraham] zur Legitimation der jeweiligen Auffassung, wer der wahren Gottesgemeinde angehört" (1996, 256).

[226] Cf. F. García Martínez 2002, 47, 49; B. Ego/A. Lange 2003, 179.

[227] B. Ego and A. Lange point to the similarity between 4QPseudo-Jubilees and Paul consisting in the emphasis on trust in God and the overcoming of darkness/sin (2003, 180 with n.42).

criterion of getting into the community of those who will rejoice at the end of time, while Paul contends that only in and through faith can we become member of the people of salvation, of the seed of Abraham. "Believing" is not a theme in the Qumran letter, but a most prominent one in Paul's.

(8) The author of 1Maccabees realized the most explicit and expressive amalgamation of Genesis 15 with 22. "Here it is no longer a question of Abraham's faith, but rather of his faithfulness to God who tested him."[228] His proven faithfulness in testing is verified and confirmed by God through the declaration of his righteousness (1Macc 2,52). Through remembrance and imitation of the "deeds (ἔργα) of the ancestors," one will "achieve great honor and an everlasting name" (2,51), just like Abraham did. Hence, remarkably different to Paul[229] but similar to Ps 106:31, "faith" is equated with a war-hero's national-religious enthusiasm[230] and readiness for martyrdom. The Maccabean zealot strives for personal honor (δόξα) through faithfulness (1Macc 2,51; cf. Sir 44,19), while the believer, according to Paul, seeks to give glory (δόξα) to God, gaining strength through faith (Rom 4:20).

(9) The frequency of the stem πιστ- in Philo and the fact that he appeals to Abraham when talking about faith[231] places him formally alongside Paul. But concerning the relationship of contents and meaning of faith in Philo and Paul, diametrically opposing opinions have been espoused in scholarship. Some predominately older interpreters propagate the virtual identity of the Pauline and Philonic πίστις in major areas: "Saepissime Philo sensu paene Paulino πίστει loquitur."[232] Current exegesis tends to insist that "we have two types of interpretation of Gen 15:6, a Pauline type ... and a Philonic type."[233] Despite some parallel ideas, the points of contact between Paul and Philo are rare, because "Philo's exegesis is determined by his own apologetic religious and philosophic concerns"[234] and

---

[228] J.A. Fitzmyer 2003, 259.

[229] Cf. R.A. Harrisville 1992, 128 ("directly opposite").

[230] Cf. O. Schmitz 1922, 100.

[231] Cf. D.M. Hay 1989, 464n.11.

[232] M. Schneckenburger (quoted and criticized in A. Schlatter 1927, 75). Cf., with various qualifications, P. Billerbeck 1926, 188; M. Buber 1953, 683; H.-J. Schoeps 1959, 212; E. Bammel 1984, 305.

[233] J.D. Levenson 1987, 59. Yet the distinguishing characteristics that Levenson names are hardly convincing, given our interpretation of Paul's use of the quote. He argues that Paul "takes the verse in isolation and insists on the autonomy of faith," while Philo combines "faith and the observance of commandments ... on the basis of texts in Genesis." Against that, Paul's interpretation does take into account the context and intends not an isolating separation of faith, but a proper theological classification of faith and a proper sequence of faith and works.

[234] J.D.G. Dunn 1988, 202; cf. G. Ebeling 1958, 85; E. Käsemann 1980, 101; G.W. Hansen 1989, 191; R.A. Harrisville 1992, 84.

because it shows little interest in Abraham's fatherhood of all believers[235] due to Philo's rather "static" conception of reality.[236] Accordingly, one should adopt a "skeptical view of Philo's value for understanding Paul's view of faith and justification."[237]

In any case, a comparison of Paul's and Philo's statements about Abraham and his faith has to be alert to the respective perception of Scripture, the socio-cultural and philosophical background, and the argumentative intention of the use of the Abraham figure.[238] For Philo, the Abraham narratives reported in the Scripture were "not a history, but an allegory; or, if a history as well, it was as such of infinitely little importance."[239] Abraham's migration from Haran represents allegorically his transition from unbelief to faith (*Migr* 32-33).[240] He is portrayed as striving for the life of a noble Alexandrinian Jew,[241] having high societal, intellectual and moral aspirations. Consequently, "faith" is characterized as a great and "olympian" work of understanding and a "work of righteousness" (*Her* 93), and the place of faith is his inner life; it is a διάθεσις of the soul,[242] leading to a firm character. Philo's intellectualism[243] and individualism[244] his notion of achievement,[245] the reduction to the psyche, and the placing of faith at the *end* of one's relationship with God[246] mark the most profound divergences between the two theologians.[247]

---

[235] Cf. J.B. Lightfoot 1896, 163: "Abraham's *seed* was almost meaningless to him" (italics original).

[236] Cf. R. Gyllenberg 1936, 624.

[237] S.J. Gathercole 2002, 29; cf. F. Neugebauer 1961, 162.

[238] Cf. M. Böhm 2004, 378f.

[239] J.B. Lightfoot 1896, 160.

[240] Paul's interpretation of ἐπίστευσεν as Abraham's coming to faith (inchoative) is somewhat related to Philo's making Abraham the prototype of Gentiles who turn to the true faith in the one God (cf. E. Brandenburger 1988, 178).

[241] Cf. M. Böhm 2004, 380f.

[242] Cf. R. Bultmann 1958, 317; E. Käsemann 1980, 101; see also O. Schmitz 1922, 113; O. Michel 1978, 93.

[243] Cf. S. Sandmel 1971, 139.

[244] Cf. R. Gyllenberg 1936, 624.

[245] The description of faith as virtue or "work of righteousness" ultimately makes dispensable God's act of counting faith as righteousness, since faith *per se* contains God's approval. Accordingly, in contrast to Paul, Philo's attention is generally directed to Gen 15:6a (cf. A. Schlatter 1927, 66).

[246] Cf. A. Schlatter 1927, 67 ("Ziel der auf Gott gerichteten Lebensbewegung"), 74; similarly E.R. Goodenough (referred to in R.A. Harrisville 1992, 84f.).

[247] One interesting passage should be noted in addition: Philo counters the claim of an interlocutor arguing that even the most unjust and impious (ἀδικώτατος καὶ ἀσεβέστατος) would believe God's word and declares that faith is the most perfect of all virtues (*Her* 90-91). Reversing this thought, Paul depicts Abraham precisely as one who was in the

Above we mentioned the observation by D.M. Hay that Philo uses πίστις frequently in the sense of "evidence" or "objective ground for subjective faith."[248] In fact, there is an interesting relationship to Paul's salvation-historical notion of πίστις, which in a like manner elucidates the association between divine and human, between objective and subjective.[249] However, Paul decisively expands the Philonic idea of "objective ground" in that he views πίστις as the new epoch in God's history with humankind, as the eschatological revelation of faith-righteousness.

C. Faith in Romans 4 and Genesis 15:6: Paul's Dealing with Scripture

Undoubtedly, "it was not the Hebrew text [of Gen 15:6] but a Greek translation that was ... the medium of understanding" in the Roman congregation.[250] The Septuagint was *the* Scripture.[251] Above we dealt with the variations between the Hebrew text of Gen 15:6 and the Septuagintal version used by Paul. Supposedly, Paul was familiar with both language traditions and had both texts before his mind's eye, which enabled him to minimize the problems inherent in a translation.

In this paragraph, however, we are only concerned with the following aspects of Paul's hermeneutics: In which sense does Paul employ Gen 15:6 for his argumentation? Can he said to be doing justice to the nature of the text?

The two poles in this discussion are, for instance, represented by B. Jacob, a Jewish exegete, and H.-W. Heidland, a Protestant scholar, who formulated their opinions in the same theological atmosphere of the 1930s: The former contends categorically that neither is the verb האמין of Gen 15:6 Paul's notion of "believing," nor the noun צדקה "righteousness" in the Pauline sense.[252] Against that the latter states: In Paul the original Old Tes-

---

realm of ἀσέβεια and ἀδικία (Rom 1:18; 4:5) and who escaped through faith – not through virtuous faith, but through faith in the God who justifies the ungodly.

[248] D.M. Hay 1989, 461, 465. See above chapter II.G.VI.

[249] Cf. D.M. Hay 1989, 475.

[250] L.H. Silberman 1990, 100. He also states: "It may well be that the scriptural lessons were read in Hebrew in Rome as elsewhere and that there were some or even many who understood it." – Most would also argue that the Christian history of interpretation of Gen 15:6 is to a greater degree dependent on the Septuagint than on the Masoretic Text (cf., e.g., K. Haacker 1984, 283).

[251] Cf. A. Lindemann 1997, 50. See also his reflections on the relationship between the *veritas Hebraica* and the *veritas Graeca*.

[252] B. Jacob 1934, 394. M. Buber finds an "Einengung" und "Verkargung" in Paul's use of Gen 15:6 compared to the original Old Testament meaning (1953, 683). See also

tament meaning found its fulfillment and restoration, both as regards form and contents.[253] Whether or not these statements can be attributed to some kind of apologetics – either for the demarcation of Jewish exegesis from the Christian or for the legitimacy of Paul's interpretation and the Protestant view of it – they at least point to the fact that Gen 15:6 is a "classic case-study for the wider question of the use of the Hebrew Bible as scripture."[254]

In the current exegetical discussion, which increasingly seeks to integrate the ideological-critical insights of reception history, such categorical labels of "right" or "wrong" are replaced by the categories of reception, reflection, and dialogue.[255] One understands inner-biblical and post-biblical history of interpretation as dynamic discourse rather than the process of uncovering a definite truth. However, taking seriously various interpretive positions and stages makes it all the more relevant, not to level out the differences, but to articulate them by an accurate analysis of the facts, the hermeneutical methods and presuppositions, and the argumentative intentions of reception, and their power of persuasion.

When Paul was reading his Scriptures he found Abraham to be the first who believed upon receiving the promises and the first to whom righteousness was accredited. The passage testifying to these events, Gen 15:6, represents the core of chapter 15, which itself functions as central and foundational text within the Abraham cycle and the Old Testament as a whole. Containing and unfolding the promises of a son, of descendants and of land, it deals with the basic themes of the Abraham narratives and the patriarchal narratives in general. Paul himself lived in the atmosphere of a Jewish consciousness of identity, in which Abraham figured as forefather and representative of the people of God; he also was aware of the use of

---

M. Oeming 1983, 196; D. Rokéaḥ 1991, 304; D.U. Rottzoll, 1994, 22, 27. According to P. Vielhauer, Paul has a tendency to modify his *Vorlage* radically and to do violence to the Hebrew meaning (1969, 198).

[253] H.-W. Heidland 1936, 103. On πιστεύειν, see also A. Weiser 1959, 197: "LXX und NT haben sachlich das Richtige gesehen, wenn sie ihren Glaubensbegriff (πιστεύειν) an den a[lt]t[estament]lichen Stamm אמן angeschlossen haben; denn an ihm kommt das Besondere und auch das Tiefste zur Geltung, was das AT zum Glauben zu sagen hat." On λογίζεσθαι, see H. Wildberger 1968, 144: "Paulus [ist] mit seiner Deutung, es handle sich um ein λογίζεσθαι κατὰ χάριν durchaus im Recht." On δικαιοσύνη, see H. Cazelles 1962, 334n.58: "Quant à cette 'justice' de Dieu conférée à l'homme [Gen 15:6], elle implique toute l'économie de grâce et de salut que développera saint Paul."

[254] R.W.L. Moberly 1990, 129f. – On the debate over Gen 15:6 in early Christianity, see D. Sutherland 1991.

[255] See for example the shift in M. Oeming's judgment on Paul's use of Gen 15:6: In 1983, he formulated that Paul's exegesis is "schlicht falsch" (196), while in 1998, he denies the possibility of coming to any of such definite evaluations (90; cf. 81f.). Cf. also the deliberations in A. Behrens 1997, 339-341. – See most recently J.L. Roura 2006.

Gen 15:6 in Jewish theology. Thus, if he accomplishes to integrate the figure of Abraham and the Genesis-verse meaningfully into his theology, he
strengthens its credibility and plausibility to a great degree.[256] Paul's interpretation of Gen 15:6 can only be understood against the background of
Jewish exegesis and his struggle with it; and therefore Paul, in discussion
with Jewish views (that were once his own), brings forth new aspects of
this verse in a pointed manner – and thus he actualizes and creates a new
meaning.[257]

"A comparison of Rom 4 with Gen 15" would show the reader/hearer
"that Paul had adhered fairly closely to the biblical storyline."[258] His *relecture* of Gen 15:6 with its emphasis on the fundamental terms πιστεύειν,
λογίζεσθαι, and δικαιοσύνη shows that Paul has in mind not only an isolated, context-less *dictum*, but is aware and makes use of its wider background.[259] This is indicated by the additional quote of Gen 15:5 in Rom
4:18 and the occurrence of the terms μισθός,[260] σπέρμα,[261] and
κληρονομεῖν/κληρονόμος.[262] Furthermore, Paul considers the chronology
and the wider context of the "faith-chapter" – especially Genesis 17, implying that with God's initial promise, upon which Abraham believed, his
universal fatherhood had been given already.[263] Romans 4 also displays
Paul's interest to assign the proper theological place to the thematic of circumcision. Hence, his quotations and allusions to the details of the Abraham narrative shows that "throughout the chapter he assumes that the Romans know the story of Abraham,"[264] but also that he is interested in a
thorough, convincing exegesis.

---

[256] Cf. S.J. Gathercole 2002, 233. See also J. Roloff 1990, 249: Since for Paul Abraham belongs on the side of the believers according to the Scripture, he is the case in point
for the Christian community's claim of the Scripture.

[257] C. Dietzfelbinger 1961, 16.

[258] C.D. Stanley 2004, 151. Stanley analyzes Paul's use of Scripture according to
communication-theoretical criteria: If Paul's audience was an "informed audience," his
close adherence to the story line lends credibility to his argument; it can be verified. But
somewhat problematic is his stance regarding works, the covenant, and the Torah. To a
"competent audience," Paul appears to be an expert exegete due to his multiple references to the text, while even a "minimal audience" finds enough – possibly overwhelm-
ingly many – clues to understand his point (151-155).

[259] Cf. M. Neubrand 1997, 198.

[260] Gen 15:1/Rom 4:4.

[261] Gen 15:3.5.13.18/Rom 4:13.16.

[262] Gen 15:3.4(*bis*).7.8/Rom 4:13.14.

[263] Gen 17:5 = Rom 4:17.

[264] C.D. Stanley 2004, 150. That *all* Romans are thought to be able to fill in the gaps
is true even if one assumes with S.K. Stowers and others that Paul actually talks to a
Jewish interlocutor (150n.34). Already in the context of Rom 3:24-26 we have seen that

It is true that Paul did not acquire the results of his exegesis on grounds of a scholarly-neutral, philological study of Scripture, but rather through the powerful event at the outset of his mission, which presented to him Christ as the end of the law (10:4)[265] and πίστις Χριστοῦ as the hermeneutical key of Scripture, opening up an entirely new perspective on its testimony. Is it correct to say, therefore, that his "contention that Gen 15:6 proves his understanding of 'justification by faith' as opposed to 'by works of the Torah' can convince only those who share his theological and methodological presuppositions"[266]? Obviously, Paul himself considered his strategy, his artful rhetoric and consequent argumentation to possess the potential to convince those who take this verse as authoritative text. In his self-understanding as a missionary and letter writer he was aware of the power of his message, and thus of his scriptural interpretation and sought to plant into the people's hearts his theological presuppositions, symbolized as πίστις Χριστοῦ.[267]

No one can claim neutrality as an interpreter, but still there are criteria to evaluate one's specific interpretation despite unavoidable presuppositions and subjectivity. Within the pluralism of readings, there are "limits of interpretation,"[268] which demarcate a "misreading" from valid readings. The question is whether or not the interpreter uncovers something about the nature of the text.[269] Our thetical exposition of the key terms πιστεύειν, λογίζεσθαι, and δικαιοσύνη above was intended to show that Paul's carefully attained understanding of Gen 15:6 by no means misses the nature of the text, but "is genuinely sensitive to the OT text"[270] – though it accomplishes a remarkable development: In sum, Paul carries out a radicalization, universalization, and eschatologization of this verse so significant to his theology.

(1) God's judgment on Abraham's faith has a creative, qualitative-authoritative character already in Gen 15:6; it builds on Abraham's existing relationship with God, but transforms and essentially determines his and his descendants' existence. For Paul now God's judgment encounters Abraham in a state of a fundamental antithesis to God, of ungodliness (4:5)

Paul credits his audience with considerable biblical knowledge (cf. also K. Haacker 1999, 105n.2).

[265] Cf. J. Roloff 1990, 251.

[266] H.D. Betz 1979, 141; affirmed by C.D. Stanley 2004, 123.

[267] Nevertheless, his efforts were ultimately not crowned by success (cf. E. Fuchs 1958, 247; J. Jeremias 1970, 58).

[268] Thus the title of U. Eco 1990.

[269] U. Eco 1990, 57.

[270] R.W.L. Moberly 1990, 129. F. Hahn speaks of the openness of the Old Testament text to the specific Pauline interpretation (1971, 107). See also R.A. Harrisville 1992, 178 *et passim*.

and nothingness, symbolized through the notion of "death" (4:17). Para-
doxically, God creates and establishes Abraham's righteous relationship to
him *ex nihilo*, through faith.[271] (2) This radicalization in matters of justification is associated with the universal scope of the message of justification, for there is equivalence and continuity in God's dealing with Abraham and with all of humankind, warranted through the identity of God itself. If he justified Abraham as ungodly *sola fide*, without any preconditions, he will justify without any religious, moral or ethnic prerequisites all
those who believe, Jews and Gentiles, and who therefore call Abraham
their father. (3) In a third basic extension of the testimony of Gen 15:6
Paul assigns to faith and justification an eschatological-soteriological dimension, hence widening the horizon of his proof text, which lacked an
eschatological connotation.

The way Paul interacts with this Old Testament verse illustrates that the
horizon of his hermeneutics is eschatology,[272] his hermeneutical method
typology, and his hermeneutical key the salvation-historical reality πίστις
Χριστοῦ.

---

[271] This radicalization of the Old Testament testimony is seconded by a concentration
on πίστις (cf. C. Dietzfelbinger 1961, 18: "Paulus [bezieht] das Gesamte der Abrahams-
geschichten auf die πίστις Abrahams und ihre Folgen.").

[272] Cf., e.g., E. Käsemann 1962, 130 *et passim*; F. Hahn 1971, 106. P. Stuhlmacher
pleads: "*Wenn wir Paulus wirklich Paulus sein lassen wollten, sollten wir versuchen, uns
die endzeitlichen Perspektiven, in denen der Apostel missionarisch dachte und wirkte,
klarzumachen und seine Aussagen über Rechtfertigung und Mission in den eschatologischen Rahmen einzuordnen, der sich dabei ergibt. Auf diese Weise könnte aus der 'New
Perspective on Paul' die 'True Perspective of Paul' werden, deren Rezeption wir noch
weitgehend vor uns haben*" (2001, 361; italics original; see also P. Stuhlmacher/D.A.
Hagner 2001).

Bibliography

A. Bible

Biblia Hebraica Stuttgartensia. (K. Elliger & W. Rudolph, eds.) 2nd ed. Stuttgart: Deutsche Bibelgesellschaft, 1984.

Biblia Hebraica. (R. Kittel et al., eds.) Stuttgart: Württembergische Bibelanstalt, 1937.

Biblia Sacra iuxta vulgatam versionem. Vol. 1: *Genesis – Psalmi.* (R. Weber, ed.) Stuttgart: Württembergische Bibelanstalt, 1969.

Buber, M. & F. Rosenzweig. *Die fünf Bücher der Weisung.* Berlin: Schneider, 1930 (= Stuttgart: Deutsche Bibelgesellschaft, 1992).

Die Bibel nach der Übersetzung Martin Luthers. Mit Apokryphen. Stuttgart: Deutsche Bibelgesellschaft, 1984.

Holy Bible with the Apocryphal/Deuterocanonical Books. New Revised Standard Version. New York: American Bible Society, 1989.

Novum Testamentum Graece. 27th ed. (B. Aland, K. Aland, J. Karavidopoulos, C.M. Martini & B.M. Metzger, eds.) Stuttgart: Deutsche Bibelgesellschaft, 1993.

Septuaginta. Id est Vetus Testamentum graece iuxta LXX interpretes. (A. Rahlfs, ed.) Stuttgart: Deutsche Bibelgesellschaft, 1935.

Septuaginta. Vetus Testamentum Graecum. Vol. 1: *Genesis.* (J.W. Wevers, ed.) Göttingen: Vandenhoeck & Ruprecht, 1974.

Septuaginta. Vetus Testamentum Graecum. Vol. 12/2: *Sapientia Jesu Filii Sirach.* (J. Ziegler, ed.) Göttingen: Vandenhoeck & Ruprecht, 1965.

The Holy Bible. Revised Standard Version. New York: Nelson, 1952.

The New English Bible with the Apocrypha. (C.H. Dodd, ed.) Oxford: Oxford University Press, 1970.

The Old Testament in Syriac According to the Peshitta Version. (The Peshitta Institute Leiden, ed.) Vol. 1/1: *Preface, Genesis – Exodus.* Leiden: Brill, 1977.

Vetus Latina. Die Reste der altlateinischen Bibel. Vol. 2: *Genesis.* (B. Fischer, ed.) Freiburg: Herder, 1951-1954.

B. Ancient Sources, Versions, and Translations

Allegro, J. *Qumran Cave 4.* Vol. 1: *4Q158-4Q186.* Discoveries in the Judean Desert 5. Oxford: Clarendon, 1968.

Avigad, N. & Y. Yadin. *A Genesis Apocryphon. A Scroll from the Wilderness of Judaea.* Jerusalem: Magnes, 1956.

Beentjes, P.C. *The Book of Ben Sira in Hebrew. A Text Edition of all Extant Hebrew Manuscripts and a Synopsis of all Parallel Hebrew Ben Sira Texts.* Vetus Testamentum Supplements 68. Leiden: Brill, 1997.

Berger, K. *Das Buch der Jubiläen.* Jüdische Schriften aus hellenistisch-römischer Zeit 2/3. Gütersloh: Mohn, 1981.

Charles, R.H. (rev. C. Rabin) "Jubilees," in: H.F.D. Sparks (ed.). *The Apocryphal Old Testament.* Oxford: Clarendon, 1984.

Charles, R.H. *The Book of Jubilees or the Little Genesis.* London: Black, 1902.

Chavel, C.B. *Commentary on the Torah. Ramban (Nachmanides).* New York: Shilo Publishing House, 1971.

Clarke, E.G. *Targum Pseudo-Jonathan of the Pentateuch. Text and Concordance.* Hoboken: KTAV, 1984.

Cohn, L. & P. Wendland. *Philonis Alexandrini Opera quae supersunt omnia.* Vols. 1-7. Berlin: Reimer, 1896-1930 (= 1962-1963).

Colson, F.H. & G.H. Whitaker. *Philo. With an English Translation.* Loeb Classical Library 3, 4, 5. Cambridge: Harvard University Press, 1930, 1930, 1932 (= 2001, 1996, 1988).

Colson, F.H. *Philo. With an English Translation.* Loeb Classical Library 1, 6, 8. Cambridge: Harvard University Press, 1929, 1935, 1939 (= 1991, 2002, 1999).

Dièz Macho, A. *Neophyti 1. Targum palestinense MS de la Bibliotheca Vaticana. Tomo I Génesis.* Madrid: Consejo Superior de Investigaciones Científicas, 1968.

Earp, J.W. *Philo. Indices to Volumes I-X.* Loeb Classical Library 10. Cambridge: Harvard University Press, 1962 (= 2004).

García Martínez, F. & E.J.C. Tigchelaar. *The Dead Sea Scrolls Study Edition.* Vols. 1-2. Leiden: Brill, 1997, 1998.

Grossfeld, B. *The Targum Onqelos to Genesis. Translated, with a Critical Introduction, Apparatus, and Notes.* The Aramaic Bible 6. Wilmington: M. Glazier, 1988.

Jacobson, H. *A Commentary on Pseudo-Philo's* Liber Antiquitatum Biblicarum. *With Latin Text and English Translation.* Arbeiten zur Geschichte des antiken Judentums und Urchristentums 31. Leiden: Brill, 1996.

Littmann, E. "Das Buch der Jubiläen," in: E. Kautzsch (ed.). *Die Apokryphen und Pseudepigraphen des Alten Testaments.* Vol. 2: *Die Pseudepigraphen des Alten Testaments.* Tübingen: Mohr (Siebeck), 1900, 31-119.

Lohse, E. *Die Texte aus Qumran. Hebräisch und Deutsch.* 2nd ed. Darmstadt: Wissenschaftliche Buchgesellschaft, 1971 (= 4th ed. 1986)

Maher, M. *Targum Pseudo-Jonathan, Genesis. Translated, with Introduction and Notes.* The Aramaic Bible 1B. Collegeville: Liturgical Press, 1992.

Maier, J. *Die Qumran-Essener. Die Texte vom Toten Meer.* Vol. 2: *Die Texte der Höhle 4.* UTB 1863. München: Reinhardt, 1995.

Marcus, R. *Philo. Supplement.* Vol. 1: *Questions and Answers on Genesis.* Cambridge: Harvard University Press, 1953.

McNamara, M.J. *Targum Neofiti 1, Genesis. Translated, with Apparatus and Notes.* The Aramaic Bible 1A. Collegeville: Liturgical Press, 1992.

Milik, J.T. "Le roulau de cuivre provenant de la grotte 3 Q (3 Q 15)," in: Baillet, M. et al. (eds.) *Les 'Petites Grottes' de Qumrân.* Discoveries in the Judean Desert 3. Oxford: Clarendon, 1962, 199-317.

Parpola, S. *Assyrian Prophecies.* State Archives of Assyria 9. Helsinki: Helsinki University Press, 1997.

Qimron, E. & J. Strugnell in consultation with Y. Sussmann and with contributions by Y. Sussmann and A. Yardeni. *Qumran Cave 4.* Vol. 5: *Miqṣat maʿaśe ha-Torah.* Discoveries in the Judean Desert 10. Oxford: Clarendon, 1994.

Qimron, E. & J. Strugnell. "An Unpublished Halakhic Letter from Qumran," in: J. Amitai (ed.). *Biblical Archaeology Today. Proceedings of the International Congress on Biblical Archaeology, Jerusalem, April 1984.* Jerusalem: Israel Exploration Society, 1985, 400-407.

Rottzoll, D.U. *Rabbinischer Kommentar zum Buch Genesis.* Studia Judaica 14. Berlin: de Gruyter, 1994a.

Sauer, G. *Jesus Sirach (Ben Sira)*. Jüdische Schriften aus hellenistisch-römischer Zeit 3/5. Gütersloh: Mohn, 1981.

Schunck, K.-D. *1. Makkabäerbuch*. Jüdische Schriften aus hellenistisch-römischer Zeit 1/4. Gütersloh: Mohn, 1980.

Sperber, A. *The Bible in Aramaic*. Vol. 1. Leiden: Brill, 1959.

Tanzer, S. "424. 4QInstruction-like Composition B," in: S.J. Pfann et al. (eds.) *Qumran Cave 4*. Vol 26: *Cryptic Texts and Miscellania, Part 1*. Discoveries in the Judean Desert 36. Oxford: Clarendon, 2000, 333-346

Thackeray, H.S.J. *Josephus*. Loeb Classical Library. Cambridge: Harvard University Press, 1926.

Tov, E., in collaboration with S.J. Pfann. *The Dead Sea Scrolls on Microfiche. A Comprehensive Facsimile Edition of the Texts from the Judean Dessert*. Leiden, 1993.

Uhlemann, F.G. *Institutiones linguae Samaritanae*. Vol. 2: *Chrestomathia Samaritana*. Leipzig: Tauchnitius, 1837.

VanderKam, J.C. & J.T. Milik. "225. 4QPseudo-Jubilees[a]," "226. 4QPseudo-Jubilees[b]," "227. 4QPseudo-Jubilees[c]," in: H. Attridge et al. (eds.) *Qumran Cave 4*. Vol 8: *Parabiblical Texts Part 1*. Discoveries in the Judean Desert 13. Oxford: Clarendon, 1994, 141-155, 157-169, 171-175.

VanderKam, J.C. *The Book of Jubilees*. Corpus scriptorum christianorum orientalium 511. Scriptores Aethiopici 88. Leuven: Peeters, 1989.

Wacholder, B.Z. & M.G. Abegg. *A Preliminary Edition of the Unpublished Dead Sea Scrolls. The Hebrew and Aramaic Texts from Cave 4*. Fascicle 2. Washington: Dead Sea Scroll Research Council/Biblical Archaeology Society, 1992.

C. Dictionaries and Grammars

Aland, K. (ed.) in collaboration with H. Bachmann and W.A. Slaby. *Vollständige Konkordanz zum griechischen Neuen Testament. Unter Zugrundelegung aller modernen kritischen Textausgaben und des Textus receptus*. Vol. 2: *Spezialübersichten*. Berlin: de Gruyter, 1978.

Bauer, W., K. Aland, B. Aland, W.F. Arndt, F.W. Gingrich & F.W. Danker. *A Greek-English Lexicon of the New Testament and Other Early Christian Literature*. 3rd ed. Chicago: University of Chicago Press, 2000.

Blass, F., A. Debrunner & F. Rehkopf. *Grammatik des neutestamentlichen Griechisch*. 17th ed. Göttingen: Vandenhoeck & Ruprecht, 1990.

Brockelmann, C. *Hebräische Syntax*. Neukirchen-Vluyn: Verlag der Buchhandlung des Erziehungsvereins Neukirchen, 1956.

Charlesworth, J.H. *Graphic Concordance to the Dead Sea Scrolls*. Tübingen: Mohr (Siebeck), 1991.

Clines, D.J.A. (ed.) *The Dictionary of Classical Hebrew*. Vol. 1: א. Sheffield: Sheffield Academic Press, 1993.

Driver, S.R. *A Treatise on the Use of the Tenses in Hebrew and Some Other Syntactical Questions*. 3rd ed. Oxford: Oxford University Press, 1892 (= 4th ed. with an introduction by W.R. Garr. Grand Rapids: Eerdmanns, 1998).

Gesenius, W. & F. Buhl. *Hebräisches und Aramäisches Handwörterbuch über das Alte Testament*. 17th ed. Berlin: Springer, 1915 (= 1962).

Gesenius, W. & E. Kautzsch. *Hebräische Grammatik*. 28th ed. Leipzig: Vogel, 1909 (= 1962).

Johnson, B. *Hebräisches Perfekt und Imperfekt mit vorangehendem w^e.* Coniectanea biblica: Old Testament Series 13. Stockholm: Almqvist & Wiksell International, 1979.

Joüon, P. & T. Muraoka. *A Grammar of Biblical Hebrew.* Vol. 1: *Orthography and Phonetics. Morphology.* Vol. 2: *Syntax.* Subsidia Biblica 14/1 and 2. Rome: Pontifical Biblical Institute, 1991.

Köhler, L. & W. Baumgartner. *Hebräisches und Aramäisches Lexikon zum Alten Testament.* Vol. 1. 3rd ed. Leiden: Brill, 1967.

König, E. *Historisch-kritisches Lehrgebäude der hebräischen Sprache.* Vol. 3/2/2: *Historisch-comparative Syntax der hebräischen Sprache.* Leipzig: Hinrichs, 1897 (= Hildesheim: Olms, 1979).

König, E. *Hebräisches und aramäisches Wörterbuch zum Alten Testament.* 6th and 7th ed. Leipzig: Hinrichs, 1936.

Kühner, R. & B. Gerth. *Ausführliche Grammatik der griechischen Sprache.* Vol. 1: *Satzlehre.* 3rd ed. Hannover: Hahn, 1898 (= Darmstadt: Wissenschaftliche Buchgesellschaft, 1966).

Liddell, H.G., R. Scott & H.S. Jones. *A Greek-English Lexicon.* 9th ed. with revised supplement. Oxford: Clarendon, 1996.

Muraoka, T. *Hebrew/Aramaic Index to the Septuagint. Keyed to the Hatch-Redpath Concordance.* Grand Rapids: Baker, 1998.

Mayer, G. *Index Philoneus.* Berlin: de Gruyter, 1974.

Michel, D. *Grundlegung einer hebräischen Syntax.* Vol. 1: *Sprachwissenschaftliche Methodik, Genus und Numerus des Nomens.* Neukirchen-Vluyn: Neukirchener Verlag, 1977 (= 2004).

Morgenthaler, R. *Statistik des neutestamentlichen Wortschatzes.* Zürich: Gotthelf, 1958.

Moulton, J.H. *A Grammar of the New Testament Greek.* Vol. 1: *Prolegomena.* Edinburgh: T. & T. Clark, 1908.

Moulton, J.H. & G. Milligan. *The Vocabulary of the Greek Testament Illustrated from the Papyri and Other Nonliterary Sources.* London: Hodder and Stoughton, 1930 (= Peabody: Hendrickson, 1997).

Preuschen, E. & W. Bauer. *Griechisch-deutsches Wörterbuch zu den Schriften des Neuen Testaments und der übrigen urchristlichen Literatur.* 2nd ed. Gießen: Töpelmann, 1928.

Schmidt, J.H.H. *Handbuch der Lateinischen und Griechischen Synonymik.* Leipzig: Teubner, 1889.

Turner, N. *A Grammar of New Testament Greek.* Vol. 3: *Syntax.* Edinburgh: T. & T. Clark, 1963.

Wallace, D.B. *Greek Grammar Beyond the Basics. Exegetical Syntax of the New Testament.* Grand Rapids: Zondervan, 1996.

Waltke, B.K. & M. O'Connor. *An Introduction to Biblical Hebrew Syntax.* Winona Lake: Eisenbrauns, 1990.

Zerwick, M. *Biblical Greek. Illustrated by Examples.* Scripta Pontificii Instituti Biblici 114. 4th ed. Rome: Pontifical Biblical Institute, 1963 (= 1990).

D. Commentaries, Monographs, Essays, and Selected Dictionary Entries

Abegg, M.G. "4QMMT C 27, 31 and 'Works Righteousness'." *Dead Sea Discoveries* 6 (1999) 139-147.

Abegg, M.G. Art. "Miqsat Ma'aśey Ha-Torah (4QMMT)." *Dictionary of New Testament Background* 2000, 709-711.

Abegg, M.G. "Paul, 'Works of the Law,' and MMT." *Biblical Archeology Review* 20 (1994) 52-55.82.

Abel, F.M. *Histoire de la Palestine depuis la conquête d'Alexandre jusqu'a l'invasion arabe*. Vol. 1: *De la conquête d'Alexandre jusqu'à la guerre juive*. Paris: Gabalda, 1952.

Abela, A. "Genesis 15: A Non-Genetic Approach." *Melita theologica* 37 (1986) 9-40.

Adams, E. "Abraham's Faith and Gentile Disobedience: Textual Links between Romans 1 and 4." *Journal for the Study of the New Testament* 65 (1997) 47-66.

Albright, W.F. *Yahweh and the Gods of Canaan. A Historical Analysis of Two Contrasting Faiths*. 1968.

Aletti, J.-N. "L'acte de croire pour l'apôtre Paul." *Recherche de science religieuse* 77 (1989) 233-250.

Aletti, J.-N. "La Justice de Dieu en Rom (1:16f.)." *Biblica* 73 (1992) 359-375.

Aletti, J.-N. "Rm 1,18-3,20. Incohérence ou cohérence de l'argumentation paulinienne?" *Biblica* 69 (1988) 47-62.

Aletti, J.-N. "Romains 4 et Genèse 17. Quelle énigme et quelle solution?" *Biblica* 84 (2003) 305-325.

Allen, L.C. *Psalms 101-150*. Word Biblical Commentary. Waco: Word, 1983.

Alt, A. *Der Gott der Väter. Ein Beitrag zur Vorgeschichte der israelitischen Religion*. Beiträge zur Wissenschaft vom Alten und Neuen Testament 48. Stuttgart: Kohlhammer, 1929.

Althaus, P. *Der Brief an die Römer*. Das Neue Testament Deutsch 6. 11th ed. Göttingen: Vandenhoeck & Ruprecht, 1970.

Anbar, M. "Genesis 15: A Conflation of Two Deuteronomic Narratives." *Journal of Biblical Literature* 101 (1982) 39-55.

Auffret, P. "La justice pour Abram. Etude structurelle de Gen 15." *Zeitschrift für die alttestamentliche Wissenschaft* 114 (2002) 342-354.

Avemarie, F. "Die Werke des Gesetzes im Spiegel des Jakobusbriefs. A Very Old Perspective on Paul." *Zeitschrift für Theologie und Kirche* 98 (2001) 282-309.

Avemarie, F. *Tora und Leben. Untersuchungen zur Heilsbedeutung der Tora in der frühen rabbinischen Literatur*. Texte und Studien zum antiken Judentum 55. Tübingen: Mohr (Siebeck), 1996.

Bach, L. *Der Glaube nach der Anschauung des Alten Testaments. Eine Untersuchung über die Bedeutung von* הֶאֱמִין *im alttestamentlichen Sprachgebrauch*. Beiträge zur Förderung christlicher Theologie 6/6. Gütersloh: Bertelsmann, 1900.

Bachmann, M. "4QMMT und Galaterbrief, מעשי התורה und ΕΡΓΑ ΝΟΜΟΥ." *Zeitschrift für die neutestamentliche Wissenschaft* 89 (1998) 91-113 = in: *Antijudaismus im Galaterbrief. Exegetische Studien zu einem polemischen Schreiben und zur Theologie des Apostels Paulus*. Novum Testamentum et Orbus Antiquus 40. Göttingen: Vandenhoeck & Ruprecht, 1999, 33-56.

Bachmann, M. "Keil oder Mikroskop? Zur jüngeren Diskussion um den Ausdruck 'Werke' des Gesetzes," in: M. Bachmann (ed.) *Lutherische und Neue Paulusperspektive. Beiträge zu einem Schlüsselproblem der gegenwärtigen exegetischen Diskussion*. Tübingen: Mohr (Siebeck) 2005, 69-134.

Bachmann, M. "Rechtfertigung und Gesetzeswerke bei Paulus." *Theologische Zeitschrift* 49 (1993) 1-33 = in: *Antijudaismus im Galaterbrief. Exegetische Studien zu einem polemischen Schreiben und zur Theologie des Apostels Paulus*. Novum Testamentum et Orbus Antiquus 40. Göttingen: Vandenhoeck & Ruprecht, 1999, 1-31.

Bailey, D.P. "Jesus as the Mercy Seat. The Semantics and Theology of Paul's Use of Hilasterion in Romans 3:25." Ph.D. Dissertation. Cambridge, 1999.

Bailey, K.E. "St. Paul's Understanding of the Territorial Promise of God to Abraham. Romans 4:13 in Its Historical and Theological Context." *Near East School of Theology Theological Review* 15 (1994) 59-69.

Bain, J.A. "Romans iv. 1." *Expository Times* 5 (1893-1894) 430.

Baird, W. "Abraham in the New Testament: Tradition and the New Identity." *Interpretation* 42 (1988) 367-379.

Bammel, E. Art. "Glaube III. Zwischentestamentliche Zeit und rabbinisches Judentum." *Theologische Realenzyklopädie* 13, 1984, 304-305.

Barclay, J.M.G. *Obeying the Truth. A Study of Paul's Ethics in Galatians.* Edinburgh: T. & T. Clark, 1988.

Barr, J. *The Semantics of Biblical Language.* London: Oxford University Press, 1961.

Barrett, C.K. *A Commentary on the Epistle to the Romans.* Black's New Testament Commentaries. London: Black, 1957.

Barth, G. "Pistis in hellenistischer Religiosität." *Zeitschrift für die neutestamentliche Wissenschaft* 73 (1982) 110-126.

Barth, G. Art. "πίστις κτλ." *Exegetisches Wörterbuch zum Neuen Testament* 2. 2nd ed., 1992, 216-233.

Barth, K. "Der Christ in der Gesellschaft. Eine Tambacher Rede." Würzburg: Patmos-Verlag, 1920 = in: *Gesammelte Vorträge.* Vol. 1: *Das Wort Gottes und die Theologie.* München: Kaiser, 1924, 33-69 = in: J. Moltmann (ed.). *Anfänge der dialektischen Theologie.* Part 1: *Karl Barth, Heinrich Barth, Emil Brunner.* Theologische Bücherei 17. 2nd ed. München: Kaiser, 1966, 3-37.

Barth, K. *Der Römerbrief.* 2nd ed. Zürich: Theologischer Verlag, 1922 (= 16th ed. 1999).

Barth, K. *Die kirchliche Dogmatik.* Vol. 1/1: *Die Lehre vom Wort Gottes. Prolegomena zur kirchlichen Dogmatik.* München: Kaiser, 1932

Barth, K. *Die kirchliche Dogmatik.* Vol. 4/1: *Die Lehre von der Versöhnung.* Zürich: EVZ-Verlag, 1960.

Barth, L.M. "Genesis 15 and the Problem of Abraham's Seventh Trial." *Maarav* 8 (1992) 245-263.

Barth, M. 1970a: see J. Jeremias 1970.

Barth, M. *Ephesians. Introduction, Translation and Commentary on Chapters 1-3.* Anchor Bible. Garden City: Doubleday, 1981.

Barth, M. "Rechtfertigung. Versuch einer Auslegung paulinischer Texte im Rahmen des Alten und Neuen Testamentes," in: *Foi et Salut selon S. Paul. Épître aux Romains 1,16.* Analecta Biblica 42. Rome: Pontifical Biblical Institute, 1970, 137-197, and discussion with J. Cambier, E. Schweizer, S. Lyonnet, C. Butler, C.K. Barrett, 197-209.

Barth, M. "The Faith of the Messiah." *Heythrop Journal* 10 (1969) 363-370.

Barthélemy, D. "L'enchevêtrement de l'histoire textuelle et de l'histoire littéraire dans les relations entre la Septante et le Texte Massorétique – Modifications dans la manière de concevoir les relations existants entre la LXX et le TM, depuis J. Morin jusqu'à E. Tov," in: A. Pietersma & C. Cox (eds.). *De Septuaginta.* FS J.W. Wevers. Massasauga: Benben, 1984, 21-40.

Bartsch, H.-W. "Der Begriff 'Glaube' im Römerbrief," in: F. Theunis (ed.). *Kerygma und Mythos.* Vol. 6/4: *Hermeneutik, Mythos und Glaube.* Theologische Forschung 44. Hamburg: Reich, 1960, 119-127.

Bartsch, H.-W. "Die historische Situation des Römerbriefes." *Communio Viatorum* 8 (1965) 199-208 = in: F.M. Cross (ed.). *Studia Evangelica.* Vol. 4. Texte und Untersuchungen zur Geschichte der Altchristlichen Literatur 102. Berlin: Akademie-Verlag, 1968, 281-291.

Bartsch, H.-W. "The Concept of Faith in Paul's Letter to the Romans." *Biblical Research* 13 (1968) 41-53.

Bassler, J.M. *Divine Impartiality. Paul and a Theological Axiom.* Society of Biblical Literature Dissertation Series 59. Chico: Scholars Press, 1982.

Baur, F.C. *Paulus, der Apostel Jesu Christi. Sein Leben und Wirken, seine Briefe und seine Lehre.* Vols. 1-2. 2nd ed. (E. Zeller, ed.) Leipzig: Fuess, 1866, 1867.

Baur, F.C. "Über Zweck und Veranlassung des Römerbriefes und die damit zusammen-hängenden Verhältnisse der römischen Gemeinde." *Tübinger Zeitschrift für Theologie* 3 (1836) 59-178 = in: K. Scholder (ed.). *Ausgewählte Werke in Einzelausgaben.* Vol. 1: *Historisch-kritische Untersuchungen zum Neuen Testament.* Stuttgart/Bad Cannstatt: Frommann, 1963, 147-266.

Baur, F.C. *Vorlesungen über Neutestamentliche Theologie.* Leipzig: Fues, 1864 (= Darmstadt: Wissenschaftliche Buchgesellschaft, 1973, with an introduction by W.G. Kümmel).

Beasley-Murray, G.R. *Baptism in the New Testament.* Grand Rapids: Eerdmans, 1973.

Beasley-Murray, G.R. "Faith in New Testament Perspective." *American Baptist Quarterly* 1-2 (1982) 137-143.

Becker, Joachim. *Esra/Nehemia.* Neue Echter Bibel 25. Würzburg: Echter, 1990.

Becker, Jürgen. *Paulus, der Apostel der Völker.* 2nd ed. Tübingen: Mohr (Siebeck), 1992 (= 3rd ed. 1998).

Begrich, J. "Das priesterliche Heilsorakel." *Zeitschrift für die alttestamentliche Wissenschaft* 52 (1934) 81-92 = in: *Gesammelte Studien zum Alten Testament.* Theologische Bücherei 21. München: Kaiser, 1964, 217-231.

Behrens, A. "Gen 15,6 und das Vorverständnis des Paulus." *Zeitschrift für die alttestamentliche Wissenschaft* 109 (1997) 327-341.

Beker, J.C. *Paul the Apostle. The Triumph of God in Life and Thought.* Philadelphia: Fortress, 1980.

Beker, J.C. "The Faithfulness of God and the Priority of Israel in Paul's Letter to the Romans," in: G.W.E. Nickelsburg & G.W. MacRae (eds.). *Christians Among Jew and Gentiles.* Philadelphia: Fortress, 1986, 10-16 = in: K.P. Donfried (ed.). *The Romans Debate. Revised and Expanded Edition.* Peabody: Hendrickson, 1991, 327-332.

Bell, R.H. *No One Seeks for God. Exegetical and Theological Study of Romans 1.18-3.20.* Wissenschaftliche Untersuchungen zum Neuen Testament 106. Tübingen: Mohr (Siebeck), 1998.

Bengel, J.A. *Gnomon Novi Testamenti.* 3rd ed. Stuttgart: Steinkopf, 1773 (8th ed. edited by P. Steudel, 1887).

Berger, K. Art. "Abraham. II. Im Frühjudentum und Neuen Testament." *Theologische Realenzyklopädie* 1, 1972, 372-382.

Berger, K. "Abraham in den paulinischen Hauptbriefen." *Münchener Theologische Zeitschrift* 17 (1966) 47-89.

Berger, K. Art. "Jubiläenbuch." *Realenzyklopädie für Antike und Christentum* 19, 1998, 31-38.

Bergmeier, R. *Das Gesetz im Römerbrief und andere Studien zum Neuen Testament.* Wissenschaftliche Untersuchungen zum Neuen Testament 121. Tübingen: Mohr (Siebeck), 2000.

Bergmeier, R. "Vom Tun der Tora," in: M. Bachmann (ed.) *Lutherische und Neue Paulusperspektive. Beiträge zu einem Schlüsselproblem der gegenwärtigen exegetischen Diskussion.* Tübingen: Mohr (Siebeck) 2005, 161-181.

Betz, H.D. *Galatians. A Commentary on Paul's Letter to the Churches in Galatia.* Hermeneia. Philadelphia: Fortress, 1979.

Betz, O. "Rechtfertigung in Qumran," in: J. Friedrich et al. (eds.) *Rechtfertigung*. FS E. Käsemann. Tübingen: Mohr (Siebeck), 1976, 17-36.

Betz, O. "The Qumran Halakhah Text Miqṣat Maʿasê Ha-Tôrāh (4QMMT) and Sadducean, Essene, and Early Pharisaic Tradition," in: D.R.G. Beattie & M.J. McNamarna. *The Aramaic Bible. Targums in Their Historical Context*. Journal for the Study of the Old Testament: Supplement Series 166. Sheffield: Sheffield Academic Press, 1994, 176-202.

Betz, O. *Was wissen wir von Jesus?* 2nd ed. Wuppertal: Brockhaus, 1991.

Billerbeck, P. (/Strack, H.) *Kommentar zum Neuen Testament aus Talmud und Midrasch*. Vol. 3: *Die Briefe des Neuen Testaments und die Offenbarung Johannis*. München: Beck, 1926.

Billerbeck, P. (/Strack, H.) *Kommentar zum Neuen Testament aus Talmud und Midrasch*. Vol. 4/1: *Exkurse zu einzelnen Stellen des Neuen Testaments*. München: Beck, 1928.

Binder, H. *Der Glaube bei Paulus*. Berlin: Evangelische Verlagsanstalt, 1968.

Bird, M. "'Raised for Our Justification.' A Fresh Look at Romans 4:25." *Colloquium* 35 (2003) 31-46.

Black, M. "Critical and Exegetical Notes on Three New Testament Texts Hebrews XI.11, Jude 5, James I.27," in: *Apophoreta*. FS E. Haenchen. Beihefte zur Zeitschrift für die neutestamentliche Wissenschaft 30. Berlin: de Gruyter, 1964, 39-44 = in: *An Aramaic Approach to the Gospels and Acts*. 3rd ed. Oxford: Clarendon, 1967, 83-89.

Black, M. *Romans*. New Century Bible. London: Oliphants, 1973.

Blank, J. "Warum sagt Paulus: 'Aus Werken des Gesetzes wird niemand gerecht'?," in: *EKK Vorarbeiten*. Vol. 1. Neukirchen-Vluyn: Neukirchener Verlag, 1969, 79-95 = in: *Paulus. Von Jesus zum Christentum*. München, 1982, 42-68.

Blenkinsopp, J. *The Pentateuch. An Introduction to the First Five Books of the Bible*. Anchor Bible Reference Library. New York: Doubleday, 1992.

Bligh, J. "Did Jesus Live by Faith?" *Heythrop Journal* 9 (1968) 414-419.

Blum, E. *Die Komposition der Vätergeschichte*. Wissenschaftliche Monographien zum Alten und Neuen Testament 57. Neukirchen-Vluyn: Neukirchener Verlag, 1984.

Boda, M.J. *Praying the Tradition. The Origin and Use of Tradition in Nehemiah 9*. Beihefte zur Zeitschrift für die alttestamentliche Wissenschaft 277. Berlin: de Gruyter, 1999.

Bodendorfer, G. "'Der Gerechte wird aus dem Glauben leben' – Hab 2,4b und eine kanonisch-dialogische Bibeltheologie im jüdisch-christlichen Gespräch," in: G. Bodendorfer & M. Millard (eds.). *Bibel und Midrasch. Zur Bedeutung der rabbinischen Exegese für die Bibelwissenschaft*. Forschungen zum Alten Testament 22. Tübingen: Mohr (Siebeck), 1998, 13-41.

Boehm, O. "The Binding of Isaac: An Inner-Biblical Polemic on the Question of 'Disobeying' a Manifestly Illegal Order." *Vetus Testamentum* 52 (2002) 1-12.

Boers, H. *The Justification of the Gentiles. Paul's Letter to the Galatians and Romans*. Peabody: Hendrickson, 1994.

Boers, H. *Theology out of the Ghetto. A New Testament Exegetical Study concerning Religious Exclusiveness*. Leiden: Brill, 1971.

Böhm, M. "Abraham und die Erzväter bei Philo. Überlegungen zur Exegese und Hermeneutik im frühen Judentum," in: R. Deines & K.-W. Niebuhr (eds.). *Philo und das Neue Testament. Wechselseitige Wahrnehmungen*. Wissenschaftliche Untersuchungen zum Neuen Testament 172. Tübingen: Mohr (Siebeck), 2004, 377-395.

Boismard, M.-E. "La foi selon saint Paul." *Lumière et Vie* 22 (1955) 65-90.

Bonhoeffer, D. "Christus, die Wirklichkeit und das Gute. Christus, Kirche, Welt" (1940), in: E. Bethge et al. (eds.) *Ethik. Manuskripte in rekonstruierter Entstehungsfolge*. Dietrich Bonhoeffer Werke 6. München Kaiser, 1992.

Bonnard, P. *L'Épître de Saint Paul aux Galates*. Commentaire du Nouveau Testament. 2nd ed. Neuchâtel: Delachaux et Niestlé, 1972.

Borgen, P. *Bread from Heaven. An Exegetical Study of the Concept of Manna in the Gospel of John and the Writings of Philo*. Novum Testamentum Supplements 10. Leiden: Brill, 1965.

Bornkamm, G. "Die Offenbarung des Zornes Gottes." *Zeitschrift für die neutestamentliche Wissenschaft* 34 (1935) 239-262 = in: *Das Ende des Gesetzes. Paulusstudien. Gesammelte Aufsätze*. Vol. 1. Beiträge zur Evangelischen Theologie 16. 2nd ed. München: Kaiser, 1958, 9-33.

Bornkamm, G. *Paulus*. Urban-Bücher 119. Stuttgart: Kohlhammer, 1969.

Bornkamm, G. "The Letter to the Romans as Paul's Last Will and Testament." *Australian Biblical Review* 11 (1963) 2-14 = in: K.P. Donfried (ed.). *The Romans Debate. Revised and Expanded Edition*. Peabody: Hendrickson, 1991, 16-28.

Botha, J.E. "The meanings of pisteúō in the greek New Testament: A semantic-lexicographical study." *Neotestamentica* 21 (1987) 225-240.

Bousset, W. & H. Greßmann. *Die Religion des Judentums im späthellenistischen Zeitalter*. Handbuch zum Neuen Testament 21. 4th ed. Tübingen: Mohr (Siebeck), 1966.

Bousset, W. *Jesus der Herr. Nachträge und Auseinandersetzungen zu Kyrios Christos*. Forschungen zur Religion und Literatur des Alten und Neuen Testaments 25 NF 8. Göttingen: Vandenhoeck & Ruprecht, 1916.

Bousset, W. *Kyrios Christos*. Forschungen zur Religion und Literatur des Alten und Neuen Testaments 21 NF 4. 3rd ed. Göttingen: Vandenhoeck & Ruprecht, 1926.

Bousset, W. Review of A. Deißmann, *Paulus. Eine kultur- und religionsgeschichtliche Skizze. Theologische Literaturzeitung* 25 (1911) 778-782.

Brandenburger, E. "Pistis und Soteria. Zum Verstehenshorizont von 'Glaube' im Urchristentum." *Zeitschrift für Theologie und Kirche* 85 (1988), 165-198 (quoted thereafter) = in: *Studien zur Geschichte und Theologie des Urchristentums*. Stuttgart: Katholisches Bibelwerk, 1993, 251-288

Brandscheidt, R. "Das Opfer des Abraham (Genesis 22,1-19)." *Trierer Theologische Zeitschrift* 110 (2001) 1-19.

Brauch, M.T. "Perspectives on 'God's Righteousness' in Recent German Discussion'," appendix in: E.P. Sanders. *Paul and Palestinian Judaism. A Comparison of Patterns of Religion*. London: SCM Press, 1977, 523-542.

Brawley, R.L. "Multivocality in Romans 4," in: *Society of Biblical Literature Seminar Papers 1997*. Atlanta: Scholars Press, 1997, 285-305.

Bréhier, E. *Les Idées Philosophiques et religieuses de Philon d'Alexandrie*. Etudes de philosophie médiévale 8. Paris: Vrin, 1925 (= 1950).

Brin, G. "Studies in 4Q424 1-2." *Revue de Qumran* 18 (1997) 21-42.

Brown, R.E. *An Introduction to the New Testament*. Anchor Bible Reference Library. New York: Doubleday, 1998.

Bruce, F.F. *Commentary on Galatians*. New International Greek Testament Commentary. Grand Rapids: Eerdmans, 1982.

Bruce, F.F. *The Epistle of Paul to the Romans. An Introduction and Commentary*. Tyndale New Testament Commentaries. Grand Rapids: Eerdmans 1963.

Bruce, F.F. *The Time Is Fulfilled. Five Aspects of the Fulfilment of the Old Testament in the New*. Exeter: Paternoster, 1978.

Brueggemann, W. *Theology of the Old Testament. Testimony, Dispute, Advocacy.* Minneapolis: Fortress, 1997.

Buber, M. *Eclipse of God. Studies in the Relation between Religion and Philosophie.* New York: Harper, 1952 = *Gottesfinsternis. Betrachtungen zur Beziehung zwischen Religion und Philosophie.* Zürich: Manesse, 1953 = in: *Werke.* Vol. 1: *Schriften zur Philosophie.* München: Kösel, 1962, 503-603.

Buber, M. *Zwei Glaubensweisen.* Zürich: Manesse, 1950 = in: *Werke.* Vol. 1: *Schriften zur Philosophie.* München: Kösel, 1962, 651-782.

Büchsel, F. Art. "ἱλαστήριον." *Theologisches Wörterbuch zum Neuen Testament* 3, 1938, 320-324.

Bultmann, R. "Anknüpfung und Widerspruch." *Theologische Zeitschrift* 2 (1946) 401-418 = in: *Glauben und Verstehen.* Vol. 2. 5th ed. Tübingen: Mohr (Siebeck), 1968, 117-132.

Bultmann, R. "Christus des Gesetzes Ende," *Beiträge zur Evangelischen Theologie* 1 (1940) 3-27 = in: *Glauben und Verstehen.* Vol. 2. 5th ed. Tübingen: Mohr (Siebeck), 1968, 32-58.

Bultmann, R. "Das Verhältnis der urchristlichen Christusbotschaft zum historischen Jesus." *Sitzungsberichte der Heidelberger Akademie der Wissenschaften. Philologisch-historische Klasse.* Heidelberg: Winter, 1960.

Bultmann, R. *Das Urchristentum im Rahmen der antiken Religionen.* Erasmus Bibliothek. Zürich: Artemis, 1949 (= 3rd ed. 1963).

Bultmann, R. *Der Stil der paulinischen Predigt und die kynisch-stoische Diatribe.* Forschungen zur Religion und Literatur des Alten und Neuen Testaments 13. Göttingen: Vandenhoeck & Ruprecht, 1910.

Bultmann, R. "Die Bedeutung des Alten Testaments für den christlichen Glauben" (1933), in: *Glauben und Verstehen.* Vol. 1. 3rd ed. Tübingen: Mohr (Siebeck), 1958, 313-336.

Bultmann, R. "Die Bedeutung des geschichtlichen Jesus für die Theologie des Paulus." *Theologische Blätter* 8 (1929a) 137-151 = in: *Glauben und Verstehen.* Vol. 1. 3rd ed. Tübingen: Mohr (Siebeck), 1958, 188-213.

Bultmann, R. "ΔΙΚΑΙΟΣΥΝΗ ΘΕΟΥ." *Journal of Biblical Literature* 83 (1964) 12-16 = in: *Exegetica. Aufsätze zur Erforschung des Neuen Testaments.* (E. Dinkler, ed.) Tübingen: Mohr (Siebeck), 1967, 470-475.

Bultmann, R. "Geschichte und Eschatologie im Neuen Testament" *New Testament Studies* 1 (1954) 5-16 = in: *Glauben und Verstehen.* Vol. 3. 4th ed. Tübingen: Mohr (Siebeck), 1993, 91-106.

Bultmann, R. "Gnade und Freiheit," in: *Glaube und Geschichte.* FS F. Gogarten. Giessen: Schmitz, 1948, 7-20 = in: *Glauben und Verstehen.* Vol. 2. 5th ed. Tübingen: Mohr (Siebeck), 1968, 149-161.

Bultmann, R. Art. "καυχάομαι κτλ." *Theologisches Wörterbuch zum Neuen Testament* 3, 1938, 646-654.

Bultmann, R. Art. "πιστεύω κτλ." *Theologisches Wörterbuch zum Neuen Testament* 6, 1959, 174-182, 197-230.

Bultmann, R. Review of A. Schlatter, *Der Glaube im Neuen Testament. Theologische Literaturzeitung* 54 (1929) 195-196.

Bultmann, R. *Theologie des Neuen Testaments.* 3rd ed. Tübingen: Mohr (Siebeck), 1958 (9th ed. revised and supplemented by O. Merk, 1984).

Bultmann, R. "Ursprung und Sinn der Typologie als hermeneutischer Methode." *Pro Regno Pro Sanctuario*. FS G. van der Leeuw. Nijkerk: Gallenbach, 1950, 89-100 = *Theologische Literaturzeitung* 75 (1950) 205-212 = in: *Exegetica. Aufsätze zur Erforschung des Neuen Testaments*. (E. Dinkler, ed.) Tübingen: Mohr (Siebeck), 1967, 369-380.

Bultmann, R. "Zur Frage der Christologie." *Zwischen den Zeiten* 5 (1927a) 41-69 = in: *Glauben und Verstehen*. Vol 1. 3rd ed. Tübingen: Mohr (Siebeck), 1958, 85-113.

Burton, E.D. *A Critical and Exegetical Commentary on the Epistle to the Galatians*. International Critical Commentary. Edinburgh: T. & T. Clark, 1921.

Byrne, B. *Romans*. Sacra Pagina. Collegeville: Liturgical Press, 1996.

Calhoun, R.M. "John Chrysostom on ΕΚ ΠΙΣΤΕΩΣ ΕΙΣ ΠΙΣΤΙΝ in Rom. 1:17. A Reply to Charles L. Quarles." *Novum Testamentum* 48 (2006) 131-146.

Calvert-Koyzis, N. *Paul, Monotheism and the People of God: The Significance of Abraham Traditions for Early Judaism and Christianity*. Journal for the Study of the New Testament: Supplement Series 273. London: T. & T. Clark, 2005

Calvin, J. *Auslegung der Genesis* (1554) (W. Goeters, ed.). Neukirchen-Vluyn: Verlag der Buchhandlung des Erziehungsvereins, 1956.

Cambier, J. 1970: see J. Jeremias 1970.

Campbell, D.A. "False Presuppositions in the ΠΙΣΤΙΣ ΧΡΙΣΤΟΥ Debate. A Response to Brian Dodd." *Journal of Biblical Literature* 166 (1997) 713-719.

Campbell, D.A. "Romans 1:17 – A *Crux Interpretum* for ΠΙΣΤΙΣ ΧΡΙΣΤΟΥ Debate." *Journal of Biblical Literature* 113 (1994) 265-285.

Campbell, D.A. "The Meaning of ΠΙΣΤΙΣ and ΝΟΜΟΣ in Paul. A Linguistic and Structural Perspective." *Journal of Biblical Literature* 111 (1992a) 91-103.

Campbell, D.A. *The Quest for Paul's Gospel. A Suggested Strategy*. Journal for the Study of the New Testament: Supplement Series 274. T. & T. Clark, 2005.

Campbell, D.A. *The Rhetoric of Righteousness in Romans 3.21-26*. Journal for the Study of the New Testament: Supplement Series 65. Sheffield: JSOT Press, 1992.

Caquot, A. "L'alliance avec Abram (Genèse 15)." *Semitica* 12 (1962) 51-66.

Carr, D.M. "Genesis in Relation to the Moses Story. Diachronic and Synchronic Perspectives," in: A. Wénin (ed.). *Studies in the Book of Genesis. Literature, Redaction and History*. Bibliotheca ephemeridum theologicarum lovaniensium 155. Leuven: Leuven University Press, 2001, 273-295.

Carr, D.M. Review of J. Ha, *Genesis 15. A Theological Compendium of Pentateuchal History*. *Journal of Biblical Literature* 110 (1991) 505-507.

Castelli, E.A. *Imitating Paul. A Discourse of Power*. Literary Currents in Biblical Interpretation. Louisville: Westminster/John Knox, 1991.

Cavallin, H.C.C. "'The Righteous Shall Live by Faith.' A Decisive Argument for the Traditional Interpretation." *Studia theologica* 32 (1978) 33-43.

Cazelles, H. "Connexions et structure de Gen., XV." *Revue biblique* 69 (1962) 321-349.

Cerfaux, L. "Abraham 'père en circoncision' des Gentils (*Rom.*, IV,12)," in: *Études de sciences religieuses*. FS E. Podechard. Lyons: Facultés Catholiques, 1945, 57-62.

Chae, D.J.-S. *Paul as Apostle to the Gentiles. His Apostolic Self-Awareness and its Influence on the Soteriological Argument in Romans*. Paternoster Biblical and Theological Monographs. Carlisle: Paternoster, 1997.

Charbel, A. "Ancora su Rom 4,25: construzione semiticia?" *Bibliotheca orientalis* 18 (1976) 28.

Charbel, A. "Nota a Rom 4,25: construzione semiticia?" *Bibliotheca orientalis* 17 (1975) 194.

Chernick, M. "Internal Restraints on *Gezerah Shawah*'s Application." *Jewish Quarterly Review* 80 (1990) 253-282.

Childs, B.S. *Biblical Theology of the Old and New Testament. Theological Reflection on the Christian Bible.* Minneapolis: Fortress, 1992.

Childs, B.S. "Critique of Recent Intertextual Canonical Interpretation." *Zeitschrift für die alttestamentliche Wissenschaft* 115 (2003) 173-184.

Childs, B.S. *Exodus. A Commentary.* The Old Testament library. Philadelphia: Westminster, 1974.

Choi, H.-S. "ΠΙΣΤΙΣ in Galatians 5:5-6. Neglected Evidence for the Faithfulness of Christ." *Journal of Biblical Literature* 124 (2005) 467-490.

Clements, R.E. *Abraham and David. Genesis 15 and Its Meaning for Israelite Tradition.* Studies in Biblical Theology 2/5. London: SCM Press, 1967.

Coats, G.W. "Abraham's Sacrifice of Faith. A Form-Critical Study of Genesis 22." *Interpretation* 27 (1973) 389-400.

Coats, G.W. *Genesis, with an Introduction to Narrative Literature.* Forms of the Old Testament Literature. Grand Rapids: Eerdmanns, 1983.

Cohen, S.J.D. *The Beginnings of Jewishness. Boundaries, Varieties, Uncertainties.* Hellenistic Culture and Society 31. Berkeley: University of California Press, 1999.

Collins, J.J. *Apocalypticism in the Dead Sea Scrolls.* London: Routledge, 1997.

Collins, J.J. Art. "Apocalyptic Literature." *Dictionary of New Testament Background* 2000, 40-45.

Collins, J.J. Art. "Eschatologies of Late Antiquity." *Dictionary of New Testament Background* 2000a, 330-337.

Collins, J.J. "Faith Without Works. Biblical Ethics and the Sacrifice of Isaac," in: S. Beyerle (ed.). *Recht und Ethos im Alten Testament – Gestalt und Wirkung.* FS H. Seebass. Neukirchen-Vluyn: Neukirchener Verlag, 1999, 115-131.

Conzelmann, H. *Grundriss der Theologie des Neuen Testamentes.* München: Kaiser, 1967.

Conzelmann, H. "Heutige Probleme der Paulusforschung." *Der evangelische Erzieher* 18 (1966) 241-252.

Conzelmann, H. Art. "χάρις κτλ." *Theologisches Wörterbuch zum Neuen Testament* 9, 1973, 377-405.

Corsani, B. "*ek pisteōs* in the Letters of Paul," in: W.C. Weinrich (ed.). *The Testament Age.* FS B. Reicke. Vol 1. Macon: Mercer University Press, 1984, 87-105.

Cosgrove, C.H. *The Cross and the Spirit. A Study in the Argument and Theology of Galatians.* Macon: Mercer University Press, 1988.

Cousar, C.B. *A Theology of the Cross. The Death of Jesus in the Pauline Letters.* Minneapolis: Fortress, 1990.

Cranfield, C.E.B. *A Critical and Exegetical Commentary on the Epistle to the Romans.* Vols. 1-2. International Critical Commentary. Edinburgh: T. & T. Clark, 1975, 1979.

Cranfield, C.E.B. "On the Πίστις Χριστοῦ Question," in: *On Romans and Other New Testament Essays.* Edinburgh: T. & T. Clark, 1998, 81-97.

Cranfield, C.E.B. "'The Works of the Law' in the Epistle to the Romans." *Journal for the Study of the New Testament* 43 (1991) 89-101 = in: *On Romans and Other New Testament Essays.* Edinburgh: T. & T. Clark, 1998, 1-14.

Cranford, M. "Abraham in Romans 4. The Father of All Who Believe." *New Testament Studies* 41 (1995) 71-88.

Cremer, H. *Die paulinische Rechtfertigungslehre im Zusammenhang ihrer geschichtlichen Voraussetzungen.* 2nd ed. Gütersloh: Bertelsmann, 1900.

Cross, F.M. "Palaeography and the Dead Sea Scrolls," in: P.W. Flint & J.C. VanderKam (eds.). *The Dead Sea Scrolls After Fifty Years. A Comprehensive Assessment I.* Leiden: Brill, 1998, 379-402.

Cross, F.M. "The Development of the Jewish Scripts," in: G.E. Wright (ed.). *The Bible and the Ancient Near East.* FS W.F. Albright. Garden City: Doubleday, 1961, 133-202.

Crüsemann, F. "Jahwes Gerechtigkeit (צְדָקָה/צֶדֶק) im Alten Testament." *Evangelische Theologie* 36 (1976) 427-450.

Cullmann, O. *Heil als Geschichte. Heilsgeschichtliche Existenz im Neuen Testament.* Tübingen: Mohr (Siebeck), 1965.

Dabourne, W. *Purpose and Cause in Pauline Exegesis. Romans 1.16-4.25 and a New Approach to the Letter.* Society for New Testament Studies Monograph Series 104. Cambridge: Cambridge University Press, 1999.

Dassmann, E. "'Bindung' und 'Opferung' Isaaks in jüdischer und patristischer Auslegung," in: M. Hutter, W. Klein & U. Vollmer (eds.). *Hairesis.* FS K. Hoheisel. Jahrbuch für Antike und Christentum Ergänzungsheft 34. Münster: Aschendorff, 2002, 1-18.

Daube, D. "Rabbinic Methods of Interpretation and Hellenistic Rhetoric." *Hebrew Union College Annual* 22 (1949) 239-265.

Davenport, G. *The Eschatology of the Book of Jubilees.* Studia post-biblica 20. Leiden: Brill, 1971.

Davids, P.H. Art. "Homily, Ancient." *Dictionary of New Testament Background* 2000, 515-518.

Davidson, R. *Genesis 12-50.* The Cambridge Bible Commentary. Cambridge: Cambridge University Press, 1979.

Davidson, R. *The Courage to Doubt.* London: SCM Press, 1983.

Davies, G.N. *Faith and Obedience in Romans. A Study in Romans 1-4.* Journal for the Study of the New Testament: Supplement Series 39. Sheffield: JSOT Press, 1990.

Davies, P.R. & B.D. Chilton. "The Aqedah: A Revised Tradition History." *Catholic Biblical Quarterly* 40 (1978) 514-546.

De Boer, W.P. *The Imitation of Paul. An Exegetical Study.* Kampen: Kok, 1962.

Deißmann, A. "Adolf Deißmann," in: E. Stange (ed.). *Die Religionswissenschaft der Gegenwart in Selbstdarstellungen.* Leipzig: Meiner, 1925, 43-78.

Deißmann, A. *Die neutestamentliche Formel "in Christo Jesu."* Marburg: Elwert, 1892.

Deißmann, A. "Der Krieg und die Religion," in: Zentralstelle für Volkswohlfahrt und dem Verein für volkstümliche Kurse von Berliner Hochschullehrern (ed.). *Deutsche Reden in schwerer Zeit.* Berlin: Heymann, 1915, 281–305.

Deißmann, A. "ΙΛΑΣΤΗΡΙΟΣ und ΙΛΑΣΤΗΡΙΟΝ – eine lexikalische Studie." *Zeitschrift für die neutestamentliche Wissenschaft* 4 (1903) 193-212.

Deißmann, A. *Paulus. Eine kultur- und religionsgeschichtliche Skizze.* 2nd ed. Tübingen: Mohr (Siebeck), 1925.

Delitzsch, F. *Commentar über die Genesis.* 3rd ed. Leipzig: Dörffling und Franke, 1860.

Delitzsch, F. *Neuer Commentar über die Genesis.* Leipzig: Dörffling und Franke, 1887.

Delling, G. *Die Botschaft des Paulus.* Berlin: Evangelische Verlagsanstalt, 1965.

Delling, G. "Partizipiale Gottesprädikationen in den Briefen des Neuen Testaments." *Studia Theologica* 17 (1963) 1-59.

Di Lella, A.A. "Conservative and Progressive Theology. Sirach and Wisdom." *Catholic Biblical Quarterly* 28 (1966) 139-154.

Dibelius, M. *An die Thessalonicher I, II. An die Philipper.* Handbuch zum Neuen Testament. 3rd ed. Tübingen: Mohr (Siebeck), 1937.

Dibelius, M. (rev. H. Greeven). *Der Brief des Jakobus.* Kritisch-exegetischer Kommentar über das Neue Testament. 6th ed. Göttingen: Vandenhoeck & Ruprecht, 1984.

Dibelius, M. "Glaube und Mystik bei Paulus." *Neue Jahrbücher für Wissenschaft und Jugendbildung* 7 (1931) 683-699.

Dibelius, M. *Paulus und die Mystik.* München: Reinhardt, 1941.

Dietrich, W. "Die David-Abraham-Typologie im Alten Testament," in: *Verbindungslinien.* FS W.H. Schmidt. Neukirchen-Vluyn: Neukirchener Verlag, 2000, 41-55.

Dietzfelbinger, C. *Paulus und das Alte Testament. Die Hermeneutik des Paulus, untersucht an seiner Deutung der Gestalt des Abraham.* Theologische Existenz heute 95. München: Kaiser, 1961.

Dillmann, A. *Die Genesis.* Kurzgefasstes exegetisches Handbuch zum Alten Testament. 6th ed. Leipzig: Hirzel, 1892.

Dimant, D. "Mikra in the Apocrypha and Pseudepigrapha," in: M.J. Mulder (ed.). *Mikra. Text, Translation, Reading and Interpretation of the Hebrew Bible in Ancient Judaism and Early Christianity.* Compendia rerum iudaicarum ad Novum Testamentum 2/1. Assen: van Gorcum, 1988, 379-419.

Dion, H.M. "The Patriarchal Traditions and the Literary Form of the 'Oracle of Salvation'." *Catholic Biblical Quarterly* 29 (1967) 198-206.

Dobbeler, A. von. *Glaube als Teilhabe. Historische und semantische Grundlagen der paulinischen Theologie und Ekklesiologie des Glaubens.* Wissenschaftliche Untersuchungen zum Neuen Testament 2/22. Tübingen: Mohr (Siebeck), 1987.

Dobbeler, A. von. "Metaphernkonflikt und Missionsstrategie. Beobachtungen zur personifizierenden Rede vom Glauben in Gal 3,23-25." *Theologische Zeitschrift* 54 (1998) 14-35.

Dodd, B. "Romans 1:17 – A *Crux Interpretum* for the ΠΙΣΤΙΣ ΧΡΙΣΤΟΥ Debate?" *Journal of Biblical Literature* 114 (1995) 470-473.

Dodd, C.H. *The Epistle of Paul to the Romans.* Moffatt New Testament Commentary. New York: Harper, 1932.

Donaldson, T.L. *Paul and the Gentiles. Remapping the Apostle's Convictional World.* Minneapolis: Fortress, 1997.

Donfried, K.P. "Introduction 1991," in: K.P. Donfried (ed.). *The Romans Debate. Revised and Expanded Edition.* Peabody: Hendrickson, 1991, xlix-lxxii.

Donfried, K.P. (ed.) *The Romans Debate. Revised and Expanded Edition.* Peabody: Hendrickson, 1991.

Dozeman, T.B. & K. Schmid (eds.). *A Farewell to the Yahwist? The Composition of the Pentateuch in Recent European Interpretation.* Society of Biblical Literature Symposium Series. Atlanta: Society of Biblical Literature, 2006.

Dumbrell, W.J. "Justification in Paul: A Covenantal Perspective." *Reformed Theological Review* 51 (1992) 91-101.

Dunn, J.D.G. "4QMMT and Galatians." *New Testament Studies* 43 (1997a) 147-153.

Dunn, J.D.G. "A Response to Peter Stuhlmacher," in: F. Avemarie & H. Lichtenberger (eds.). *Auferstehung – Resurrection.* Wissenschaftliche Untersuchungen zum Neuen Testament 135. Tübingen: Mohr (Siebeck), 2001, 363-368.

Dunn, J.D.G. "In Quest of Paul's Theology. Retrospect and Prospect," in: E.E. Johnson & D.M. Hay (eds.). *Pauline Theology.* Vol. 4: *Looking Back, Pressing On.* Society of Biblical Literature Symposium Series. Atlanta: Scholars Press, 1997b, 95-115.

Dunn, J.D.G. "In Search of Common Ground," in: J.D.G. Dunn (ed.). *Paul and the Mosaic Law.* Tübingen: Mohr (Siebeck) 1996, 309-334.

Dunn, J.D.G. "Introduction," in: J.D.G. Dunn (ed.). *Paul and the Mosaic Law.* Tübingen: Mohr (Siebeck) 1996a, 1-5.

Dunn, J.D.G. "Once More, ΠΙΣΤΙΣ ΧΡΙΣΤΟΥ," in: E.E. Johnson & D.M. Hay (eds.). *Pauline Theology.* Vol. 4: *Looking Back, Pressing On.* Society of Biblical Literature Symposium Series. Atlanta: Scholars Press, 1997, 61-81 = in: R.B. Hays. *The Faith of Jesus Christ. The Narrative Substructure of Galatians 3:1-4:11.* 2nd ed. Grand Rapids: Eerdmans, 2002, 249-271.

Dunn, J.D.G. "Paul's Epistle to the Romans: An Analysis of Structure and Argument." *Aufstieg und Niedergang der Römischen Welt* 2,25,4, 1987, 2842-2890.

Dunn, J.D.G. *Romans.* Word Biblical Commentary. Dallas: Word, 1988.

Dunn, J.D.G. "Some Ecumenical Reflections on Romans 4," in: G.D. Dragas (ed.). *Aksum Thyateira.* FS Archbishop Methodios. London: Thyateira House, 1985.

Dunn, J.D.G. "The New Perspective on Paul." *Bulletin of the John Rylands University Library of Manchester* 65 (1983) 95-122 = in: *Jesus, Paul and the Law. Studies in Mark and Galatians.* Louisville, 1990, 183-214.

Dunn, J.D.G. *The Theology of Paul the Apostle.* Grand Rapids: Eerdmans, 1998.

Dunn, J.D.G. "Whatever Happened to the Works of the Law," in: Jan Kerkovský (ed.). *Epitoauto.* FS P. Pokorný. Prague: Mlýn, 1998a.

Dunn, J.D.G. "Works of the Law and the Curse of the Law (Galatians 3.10-14)." *New Testament Studies* 32 (1985) 522-542 = in: *Jesus, Paul and the Law. Studies in Mark and Galatians.* Louisville, 1990, 215-236 (with additional note 237-241).

Dunn, J.D.G. "Works of the Law," in: I. Dunderberg, C. Tuckett & Kari Syreeni (eds.). *Fair Play. Diversity and Conflicts in Early Christianity.* FS H. Räisänen. Leiden: Brill, 2002, 273-290.

Dunn, J.D.G. "Yet Once More – 'The Works of the Law': A Response." *Journal for the Study of the New Testament* 46 (1992) 99-117.

Ebeling, G. *Das Wesen des christlichen Glaubens.* Tübingen: Mohr (Siebeck), 1959 (= 3rd ed. München: Siebenstern Taschenbuch Verlag, 1967).

Ebeling, G. "Fides occidit rationem. Ein Aspekt der theologia crucis in Luthers Auslegung von Gal 3,6," in: C. Andresen & G. Klein (eds.). *Theologia crucis – Signum Crucis.* FS E. Dinkler. Tübingen: Mohr (Siebeck), 1979, 97-135 = in: *Lutherstudien.* Vol. 3: *Begriffsuntersuchungen – Textinterpretationen, Wirkungsgeschichtliches.* Tübingen: Mohr (Siebeck), 181-222.

Ebeling, G. "Jesus und Glaube." *Zeitschrift für Theologie und Kirche* 55 (1958) 64-110 (quoted thereafter) = in: *Wort und Glaube.* Vol. 1. Tübingen: Mohr (Siebeck), 1960, 203-254.

Ebeling, G. "Zwei Glaubensweisen?," in: H.J. Schultz (ed.). *Juden, Christen, Deutsche.* Stuttgart: Kreuz-Verlag, 1961, 159-168 = in: *Wort und Glaube.* Vol. 3: *Beiträge zur Fundamentaltheologie, Soteriologie und Ekklesiologie.* Tübingen: Mohr (Siebeck), 1975, 236-245.

Eckstein, H.-J. "Das Wesen des christlichen Glaubens. Nachdenken über das Glaubensverständnis bei Paulus," in: W. Härle, H. Schmidt & M. Welker (eds.) *Das ist christlich. Nachdenken über das Wesen des Christentums.* Gütersloh: Gütersloher Verlagshaus 2000, 105-117 = in: *Der aus Glauben Gerechte wird leben. Beiträge zur Theologie des NT.* Beiträge zum Verstehen der Bibel 5. Münster: Lit, 2003, 3-18.

Eckstein, H.-J. "'Denn Gottes Zorn wird vom Himmel her offenbar werden.' Exegetische Erwägungen zu Röm 1,18." *Zeitschrift für die neutestamentliche Wissenschaft* 78 (1987) = (revised) in: *Der aus Glauben Gerechte wird leben. Beiträge zur Theologie des NT.* Beiträge zum Verstehen der Bibel 5. Münster: Lit, 2003, 18-35.

Eckstein, H.-J. *Verheißung und Gesetz. Eine exegetische Untersuchung zu Gal 2,15-4,7.* Wissenschaftliche Untersuchungen zum Neuen Testament 86. Tübingen: Mohr (Siebeck) 1996.

Eco, U. *The Limits of Interpretation.* Advances in Semiotics. Bloomington: Indiana University Press, 1990.

Egger, P. *Verdienste vor Gott? Der Begriff z^{e}khut im rabbinischen Genesiskommentar Bereshit Rabba.* Novum Testamentum et Orbus Antiquus 43. Göttingen: Vandenhoeck & Ruprecht, 2000.

Ego, B. & A. Lange. "'Und es ward ihm zur Gerechtigkeit angerechnet' (4QpsJub^a 2 I 8)," in: U. Mittmann-Richert, F. Avemarie & G.S. Oegema (eds.). *Der Mensch vor Gott. Forschungen zum antiken Menschenbild in Bibel, antikem Judentum und Koran.* FS H. Lichtenberger. Neukirchen-Vluyn: Neukirchener, 2003, 171-192.

Ego, B. "Abraham als Urbild der Toratreue Israels," in: F. Avemarie & H. Lichtenberger (eds.). *Bund und Tora. Zur theologischen Begriffsgeschichte in alttestamentlicher, frühjüdischer und urchristlicher Tradition.* Wissenschaftliche Untersuchungen zum Neuen Testament 92. Tübingen: Mohr (Siebeck), 1996, 25-40.

Ehrlich, A.B. *Randglossen zur hebräischen Bibel. Textkritisches, Sprachliches und Sachliches.* Vol. 1. Leipzig: J.C. Hinrichs, 1908.

Eichholz, G. *Die Theologie des Paulus im Umriß.* Neukirchen-Vluyn: Neukirchener Verlag, 1972 (= 7th ed., 1991).

Eichrodt, W. *Theologie des Alten Testaments.* Vol. 2/3: *Gott und Welt und Gott und Mensch.* Stuttgart: Klotz, 1961.

Eisenbaum, P. "A Remedy for Having Been Born of Woman: Jesus, Gentiles, and Genealogy in Romans." *Journal of Biblical Literature* 123 (2004) 671-702.

Eißfeldt, O. *Einleitung in das Alte Testament unter Einschluß der Apokryphen und Pseudepigraphen sowie der apokryphen- und pseudepigraphenartigen Qumranschriften. Entstehungsgeschichte des Alten Testaments.* Neue theologische Grundrisse. 3rd ed. Tübingen: Mohr (Siebeck), 1964.

Elliott, N. *The Rhetoric of Romans. Argumentative Constraint and Strategy and Paul's Dialogue with Judaism.* Journal for the Study of the New Testament: Supplement Series 45. Sheffield: JSOT Press, 1990.

Ellis, E.E. *Paul's Use of the Old Testament.* Edinburgh: Oliver & Boyd, 1957.

Emerton, J.A. "The Origin of the Promises to the Patriarchs in the Older Sources of the Book of Genesis." *Vetus Testamentum* 32 (1982) 14-32.

Emerton, J.A. "The Textual and Linguistic Problems of Habakkuk ii.4-5." *Journal of Theological Studies* 28 (1977) 1-18.

Eskola, T. *Theodicy and Predestination in Pauline Soteriology.* Wissenschaftliche Untersuchungen zum Neuen Testament 2/100. Mohr (Siebeck), 1998.

Evans, C.A. Art. "Abraham." *Encyclopedia of the Dead Sea Scrolls* 1, 2000, 2-4.

Farmer, W.R. "The Patriarch Phineas. A Note on 'It was Reckoned to Him as Righteousness'." *Anglican Theological Review* 34 (1952) 26-30.

Feine, P. *Theologie des Neuen Testaments.* 3rd ed. Leipzig: Hinrichs, 1919.

Feldmann, L.H. "Abraham the Greek Philosopher in Josephus." *Transactions and Proceedings of the American Philological Association* 99 (1968) 143-156.

Feuillet, A. "La citation d'Habakuk II,4 et les huit premiers chapitres aux Romains." *New Testament Studies* 6 (1959/1960) 52-80.

Fischer, G. "Die Josefsgeschichte als Modell für Versöhnung," in: A. Wénin (ed.). *Studies in the Book of Genesis. Literature, Redaction and History.* Bibliotheca ephemeridum theologicarum lovaniensium 155. Leuven: Leuven University Press, 2001, 243-271.

Fishbane, M. "Justification through Living. Martin Buber's Third Alternative," in: W.G. Dever & J.E. Wright (eds.). *Echoes of Many Texts. Reflections on Jewish and Christian Traditions.* FS L.H. Silberman. Brown Judaic Studies 313. Atlanta: Scholars Press, 1997, 219-230.

Fitzmyer, J.A. "Der semitische Hintergrund des neutestamentlichen Kyriostitels," in: G. Strecker (ed.). *Jesus Christus in Historie und Theologie.* FS H. Conzelmann. Tübingen: Mohr (Siebeck) 1975, 267-298 = "The Semitic Background of the New Testament *Kyrios*-Title," in: *A Wandering Aramean. Collected Aramaic Essays.* Society of Biblical Literature Monograph Series 25. Missoula: Scholars Press, 1979, 115-142 = in: *The Semitic Background of the New Testament.* Grand Rapids: Eerdmans, 1997, 115-142.

Fitzmyer, J.A. "Habakkuk 2:3-4 and the New Testament," in: M. Carez (ed.). *De la Tôrah au Messie. Études d'exégèse et d'herméneutique bibliques.* FS H. Cazelles. Paris: Desclée, 1981, 447-455 = in: *To Advance the Gospel. New Testament Studies.* New York: Crossroads, 1981, 236-246.

Fitzmyer, J.A. *Romans. A New Translation with Introduction and Commentary.* Anchor Bible. New York: Doubleday, 1993.

Fitzmyer, J.A. "The Interpretation of Genesis 15:6. Abraham's Faith and Righteousness in a Qumran Text," in: S.M. Paul et al. (eds.) *Emanuel. Studies in Hebrew Bible, Septuagint, and Dead Sea Scrolls.* FS E. Tov. Vetus Testamentum Supplements 94. Leiden: Brill, 2003, 257-268.

Fitzmyer, J.A. "The Sacrifice of Isaac in Qumran Literature." *Biblica* 83 (2002) 211-229.

Flusser, D. & S. Safrai. "'Der den Geliebten geheiligt hat von Mutterleib an.' Betrachtungen zum Ursprung der Beschneidung." *Immanuel* 8 (1979) 2-6.

Flusser, D. "Die Gesetzeswerke in Qumran und bei Paulus," in: H. Cancik, H. Lichtenberger & P. Schäfer (eds.). *Geschichte-Tradition-Reflexion.* FS M. Hengel. Vol. 3: *Frühes Christentum.* Tübingen: Mohr (Siebeck), 1996, 395-403.

Fridrichsen, A. "Aus Glauben zu Glauben: Röm 1,17." *Coniectanea neotestamentica* 12 (1948) 54.

Friedman, R.E. "Some Recent Non-Arguments Concerning the Documentary Hypothesis," in: M.V. Fox et al. (eds.) *Texts, Temples, and Traditions.* FS M. Haran. Winona Lake: Eisenbrauns, 1996, 92-101.

Friedrich, G. "'Ἁμαρτία οὐκ ἐλλογεῖται Röm 5,13." *Theologische Literaturzeitung* 77 (1952) 523-528 = in: *Auf das Wort kommt es an. Gesammelte Aufsätze* (J.H. Friedrich, ed.). Göttingen: Vandenhoeck & Ruprecht, 1978, 123-131.

Friedrich, G. "Das Gesetz des Glaubens, Röm 3,27." *TZ* 10 (1954) 401-417 = in: *Auf das Wort kommt es an. Gesammelte Aufsätze* (J.H. Friedrich, ed.). Göttingen: Vandenhoeck & Ruprecht, 1978, 107-122.

Friedrich, G. "Glaube und Verkündigung bei Paulus," in: F. Hahn & H. Klein (eds.). *Der Glaube im Neuen Testament.* FS H. Binder. Neukirchen-Vluyn: Neukirchener Verlag, 1982, 93-113.

Friedrich, G. "Muß ὑπακοὴ πίστεως Röm 1,5 mit 'Glaubensgehorsam' übersetzt werden?" *Zeitschrift für die neutestamentliche Wissenschaft* 72 (1981) 118-123.

Fuchs, E. "Aus der Marburger Zeit" (1977), in: *Wagnis des Glaubens.* Neukirchen-Vluyn: Neukirchener Verlag, 1979, 73-75.

Fuchs, E. "Die Theologie des Neuen Testaments und der historische Jesus," in: *Gesammelte Aufsätze.* Vol. 2: *Zur Frage nach dem historischen Jesus.* Tübingen: Mohr (Siebeck), 1960, 377-404

Fuchs, E. "Jesus und der Glaube." *Zeitschrift für Theologie und Kirche* 55 (1958) 170-185 = in: *Gesammelte Aufsätze*. Vol. 2: *Zur Frage nach dem historischen Jesus*. Tübingen: Mohr (Siebeck), 1960, 238-257.

Gager, J.G. *The Origins of Anti-Semitism. Attitudes Toward Judaism in Pagan and Christian Antiquity*. Oxford: Oxford University Press, 1975.

García Martínez, F. "4QMMT in a Qumran Context," in: J. Kampen & M.J. Bernstein (eds.). *Reading 4QMMT. New Perspectives on Qumran Law and History*. Society of Biblical Literature Symposium Series. Atlanta: Scholars Press, 1996, 15-28.

García Martínez, F. "The Heavenly Tablets in the Book of Jubilees," in: M. Albani, J. Frey & A. Lange (eds.). *Studies in the Book of Jubilees*. Texte und Studien zum antiken Judentum 65. Tübingen: Mohr (Siebeck), 1997, 243-260.

García Martínez, F. "The Sacrifice of Isaac in 4Q225," in: E. Noort & E.J.C. Tigchelaar (eds.). *The Sacrifice of Isaac. The Aqedah (Genesis 22) and Its Interpretations*. Themes in Biblical Narrative 4. Leiden: Brill, 2002, 44-57.

Garlington, D.B. *Faith, Obedience, and Perseverance. Aspects of Paul's Letter to the Romans*. Wissenschaftliche Untersuchungen zum Neuen Testament 79. Tübingen: Mohr (Siebeck), 1994.

Garlington, D.B. *'The Obedience of Faith'. A Pauline Phrase in Historical Context*. Wissenschaftliche Untersuchungen zum Neuen Testament 2/38. Tübingen: Mohr (Siebeck), 1991.

Gaston, L. "Abraham and the Righteousness of God." *Horizons in Biblical Theology* 2 (1980) 39-68 = in: *Paul and the Torah*. Vancouver: University of British Columbia Press, 1987, 45-63.

Gaston, L. "For *All* the Believers: The Inclusion of Gentiles as the Ultimate Goal of Torah in Romans," in: *Paul and the Torah*. Vancouver: University of British Columbia Press, 1987, 116-134.

Gaston, L. "Paul and the Law in Galatians 2 and 3," in: P. Richardson (ed.). *Anti-Judaism in Early Christianity*. Vol. 1: *Paul and the Gospels*. Waterloo: Wilfrid Laurier University Press, 1986, 37-57 = (with appendix) in: *Paul and the Torah*. Vancouver: University of British Columbia Press, 1987, 64-79.

Gaston, L. "Paul and the Torah," in: A.T. Davies (ed.). *Antisemitism and the Foundations of Christianity*. New York: Paulist Press, 1979, 48-71 = in: *Paul and the Torah*. Vancouver: University of British Columbia Press, 1987, 15-34.

Gaston, L. "'Works of the Law' as a Subjective Genitive." *Studies in Religion* 13 (1984) 39-46 = in: *Paul and the Torah*. Vancouver: University of British Columbia Press, 1987, 100-106.

Gathercole, S.J. "Justified by Faith, Justified by his Blood. The Evidence of Romans 3:21-4:25," in: D.A. Carson, P.T. O'Brien & M.A. Seifrid (eds.). *Justification and Variegated Nomism: A Fresh Appraisal of Paul and Second Temple Judaism*. Vol. 2: *The Paradoxes of Paul*. Tübingen: Mohr (Siebeck), 2004, 147-184.

Gathercole, S.J. "Torah, Life and Salvation. Leviticus 18.5 in Early Judaism and the New Testament," in: C.A. Evans & J.A. Sanders (eds.). *From Prophecy to Testament. The Function of the Old Testament in the New*. Peabody: Hendrickson, 2004, 131-150.

Gathercole, S.J. *Where Is Boasting? Early Jewish Soteriology and Paul's Response in Romans 1–5*. Grand Rapids: Eerdmans, 2002.

Georgi, D. *Theocracy in Paul's Praxis and Theology* (D.E. Green, tr.). Minneapolis: Fortress, 1991.

Gertz, J.C., et al. (eds.) *Abschied vom Jahwisten*. Beihefte zur Zeitschrift für die alttestamentliche Wissenschaft 315. Berlin: de Gruyter, 2002.

Gertz, J.C. "Abraham, Mose und der Exodus. Beobachtungen zur Redaktionsgeschichte von Gen 15," in: J.C. Gertz et al. (eds.) *Abschied vom Jahwisten*. Beihefte zur Zeitschrift für die alttestamentliche Wissenschaft 315. Berlin: de Gruyter, 2002, 63-81.

Gese, H. "Die Komposition der Abrahamerzählung," in: *Alttestamentliche Studien*. Tübingen: Mohr (Siebeck), 1991, 29-51.

Gese, H. "Erwägungen zur Einheit der biblischen Theologie." *Zeitschrift für Theologie und Kirche* 67 (1970) 417-436.

Gilbert, M. "La prière de Néhémie 9," in: M. Carez (ed.). *De la Tôrah au Messie. Études d'exégèse et d'herméneutique bibliques*. FS H. Cazelles. Paris 1981, 307-316.

Gnilka, J. *Theologie des Neuen Testaments*. Herders theologischer Kommentar zum Neuen Testament Supplement 5. Freiburg: Herder, 1994.

Goldingay, J. *Old Testament Theology*. Vol. 1: *Israel's Gospel*. Downers Grove: Inter-Varsity Press, 2003.

Goldstein, J. *I Maccabees*. Anchor Bible. Doubleday: New York, 1976.

Goodenough, E.R. "Paul and the Hellenization of Christianity," in: J. Neusner (ed.). *Religions in Antiquity*. Leiden: Brill, 1968, 23-70.

Goppelt, L. "Apokalyptik und Typologie bei Paulus." *Theologische Literaturzeitung* 89 (1964) 321-344 = in: *Christologie und Ethik. Aufsätze zum Neuen Testament*." Göttingen: Vandenhoeck & Ruprecht, 1968, 234-267.

Goppelt, L. "Paulus und die Heilsgeschichte. Schlußfolgerungen aus Röm. 4 und 1. Kor. 10,1-13." *New Testament Studies* 13 (1966/1967) 31-42 = in: *Christologie und Ethik. Aufsätze zum Neuen Testament*." Göttingen: Vandenhoeck & Ruprecht, 1968, 220-233.

Goppelt, L. *Theologie des Neuen Testaments*. 3rd ed. Göttingen: Vandenhoeck & Ruprecht, 1991.

Goppelt, L. *Typos. Die typologische Deutung des Alten Testaments im Neuen*. Beiträge zur Förderung christlicher Theologie 2/43. Gütersloh: Bertelsmann, 1939 (= Darmstadt: Wissenschaftliche Buchgesellschaft, 1966).

Goppelt, L. "Versöhnung durch Christus." *Lutherische Monatshefte* 6 (1967) 263-269 = in: *Christologie und Ethik. Aufsätze zum Neuen Testament*." Göttingen: Vandenhoeck & Ruprecht, 1968, 147-164.

Grafe, E. Review of A. Schlatter, *Der Glaube im Neuen Testament*. *Theologische Literaturzeitung* 16 (1886) 367-374.

Gräßer, E. *Der Glaube im Hebräerbrief*. Marburger Theologische Studien 2. Marburg: Elwert, 1965.

Gräßer, E. "Der ruhmlose Abraham (Röm 4,2). Nachdenkliches zu Gesetz und Sünde bei Paulus," in: M. Trowitzsch (ed.). *Paulus, Apostel Jesu Christi*. FS G. Klein. Tübingen: Mohr (Siebeck), 1998, 3-22.

Gräßer, E. "'Ein einziger ist Gott' (Röm 3,30). Zum christologischen Gottesverständnis bei Paulus," in: *"Ich will euer Gott werden". Beispiele biblischen Redens von Gott*. Stuttgarter Bibelstudien 100. Stuttgart, 1981, 179-205 = in: *Der Alte Bund im Neuen*. Wissenschaftliche Untersuchungen zum Neuen Testament 35. Tübingen: Mohr (Siebeck), 1985, 231-258.

Graupner, A. *Der Elohist. Gegenwart und Wirksamkeit des transzendenten Gottes in der Geschichte*. Wissenschaftliche Monographien zum Alten und Neuen Testament 97. Neukirchen-Vluyn: Neukirchener Verlag, 2002.

Green, G.L. *The Letters to the Thessalonians*. Pillar New Testament Commentary. Grand Rapids: Eerdmans, 2002.

Grieb, A.K. *Romans. The Story of God's Righteousness*. Louisville: Westminster/John Knox, 2002.

Groß, H. "Der Glaube an Mose nach Exodus (4.14.19)," in: H.J. Stoebe (ed.). *Wort – Gebot – Glaube. Beiträge zur Theologie des Alten Testaments.* FS W. Eichrodt. Abhandlungen zur Theologie des Alten und Neuen Testaments 59. Zürich: Zwingli Verlag, 1970, 57-65.

Groß, H. "Glaube und Bund. Theologische Bemerkungen zu Genesis 15," in: G. Braulik (ed.). *Studien zum Pentateuch.* FS W. Kornfeld. Wien: Herder, 1977, 25-35.

Groß, H. "'Rechtfertigung' nach dem Alten Testament. Bibeltheologische Bemerkungen," in: H.-P. Müller & W. Stenger (eds.). *Kontinuität und Einheit.* FS F. Mußner. Freiburg: Herder, 1981, 17-29.

Gunkel, H. *Die Psalmen.* Göttingen: Vandenhoeck & Ruprecht, 1926.

Gunkel, H. *Genesis übersetzt und erklärt.* Handkommentar zum Alten Testament. 3rd ed. Göttingen: Vandenhoeck & Ruprecht, 1910 (= 9th ed. 1977).

Gunneweg, A.H.J. *Biblische Theologie des Alten Testaments. Eine Religionsgeschichte Israels in biblisch-theologischer Sicht.* Stuttgart: Kohlhammer, 1993.

Gunneweg, A.H.J. *Nehemia.* Kommentar zum Alten Testament. Gütersloh: Mohn, 1987.

Gyllenberg, R. "Die Paulinische Rechtfertigungslehre und das Alte Testament." *Studia theologica* 1 (1935) 35-52.

Gyllenberg, R. "Glaube bei Paulus." *Zeitschrift für systematische Theologie* 13 (1936) 613-630.

Gyllenberg, R. "Glaube und Gehorsam." *Zeitschrift für systematische Theologie* 14 (1937) 547-566.

Ha, J. *Genesis 15. A Theological Compendium of Pentateuchal History.* Beihefte zur Zeitschrift für die alttestamentliche Wissenschaft 181. Berlin: de Gruyter, 1989.

Haacker, K. *Der Brief des Paulus an die Römer.* Theologischer Handkommentar zum Neuen Testament. Leipzig: Evangelische Verlagsanstalt, 1999.

Haacker, K. "Der Römerbrief als Friedensmemorandum." *New Testament Studies* 36 (1990) 25-41.

Haacker, K. Art. "Glaube II. Altes und Neues Testament." *Theologische Realenzyklopädie* 13, 1984, 277-304.

Haacker, K. "Glaube im Neuen Testament," in: *Biblische Theologie als engagierte Exegese.* Wuppertal: Brockhaus, 1993, 122-138.

Haacker, K. "Was meint die Bibel mit dem Glauben." *Theologische Beiträge* 1 (1970) 133-152 = in: *Biblische Theologie als engagierte Exegese.* Wuppertal: Brockhaus, 1993, 102-121.

Hagelia, H. *Numbering the Stars. A Phraseological Analysis of Genesis 15.* Coniectanea biblica: Old Testament Series 39. Stockholm: Almqvist & Wiksell International, 1994.

Hahn, F. & H. Klein. "Vorwort," in: F. Hahn & H. Klein (eds.). *Der Glaube im Neuen Testament.* FS H. Binder. Neukirchen-Vluyn: Neukirchener Verlag, 1982, 5-7.

Hahn, F. "Das Gesetzesverständnis im Römer- und Galaterbrief." *Zeitschrift für die neutestamentliche Wissenschaft* 67 (1976) 29-63.

Hahn, F. "Gen 15,6 im Neuen Testament," in: H.W. Wolff (ed.). *Probleme Biblischer Theologie.* FS Gerhard von Rad. München: Kaiser, 1971, 90-107.

Hahn, F. "Gibt es eine Entwicklung in den Aussagen über die Rechtfertigung bei Paulus?" *Evangelische Theologie* 53 (1993) 342-366

Hamilton, V.P. *The Book of Genesis 1-17.* New International Commentary on the Old Testament. Grand Rapids: Eerdmanns, 1990.

Hamm, D. "Faith in Hebrews." *Catholic Biblical Quarterly* 52 (1990) 270-291.

Hansen, G.W. *Abraham in Galatians. Epistolary and Rhetorical Contexts.* Journal for the Study of the New Testament: Supplement Series 29. Sheffield: JSOT Press, 1989.

Hanson, A.T. *Studies in Paul's Technique and Theology*. Grand Rapids: Eerdmans, 1974.

Harnack, A. von. *Marcion. das Evangelium vom fremden Gott. Eine Monographie zur Geschichte der Grundlegung der katholischen Kirche. Neue Studien zu Marcion.* Texte und Untersuchungen zur Geschichte der altchristlichen Literatur 45. 2nd ed. Leipzig: Hinrichs, 1924 (= Darmstadt: Wissenschaftliche Buchgesellschaft, 1985).

Harrisville, R.A. III. "ΠΙΣΤΙΣ ΧΡΙΣΤΟΥ. Witness of the Fathers." *Novum Testamentum* 36 (1994) 233-241.

Harrisville, R.A. III. *The Figure of Abraham in the Epistles of St. Paul. In the Footsteps of Abraham.* San Francisco: Mellen Research University Press, 1992.

Hatch, W.H.P. *The Idea of Faith in Christian Literature from the Death of St. Paul to the Close of the Second Century*. Strasbourg: Imprimerie Alsacienne, 1925.

Hatch, W.H.P. *The Pauline Idea of Faith in Its Relation to Jewish and Hellenistic Religion*. Harvard Theological Studies 2. Cambridge: Harvard University Press, 1917 (= New York: Kraus, 1969).

Haußleiter, J. "Der Glaube Jesu Christi und der christliche Glaube. Ein Beitrag zur Erklärung des Römerbriefs." *Neue kirchliche Zeitschrift* 2 (1891) 109-145, 205-230.

Haußleiter, J. "Was versteht Paulus unter christlichem Glauben?" *Greifswalder Studien* (1895) = FS H. Cremer, 159-182.

Hawthorne, G.F. & R.P. Martin. *Philippians*. Revised. Word Biblical Commentary. [Nashville:] Nelson, 2004.

Hay, D.M. "Pistis as 'Ground for Faith' in Hellenized Judaism and Paul." *Journal of Biblical Literature* 108 (1989) 461-476.

Hays, R.B. *Echoes of Scripture in the Letters of Paul*. New Haven: Yale University Press, 1989.

Hays, R.B. "Have we Found Abraham to be our Forefather according to the Flesh? A Reconsideration of Romans 4:1." *Novum Testamentum* 27 (1985) 76-98.

Hays, R.B. "Πίστις and Pauline Christology: What Is at Stake?," in: E.E. Johnson & D.M. Hay (eds.). *Pauline Theology*. Vol. 4. *Looking Back, Pressing On*. Society of Biblical Literature Symposium Series. Atlanta: Scholars Press, 1997, 35-60 = in: *The Faith of Jesus Christ. The Narrative Substructure of Galatians 3:1-4:11*. 2nd ed. The Biblical Resource Series. Grand Rapids: Eerdmans, 2002, 272-297.

Hays, R.B. "Psalm 143 and the Logic of Romans 3." *Journal of Biblical Literature* 99 (1980) 107-115.

Hays, R.B. *The Faith of Jesus Christ. The Narrative Substructure of Galatians 3:1-4:11.* Society of Biblical Literature Dissertation Series 56. Chico: Scholars Press, 1983 (2nd ed. with a new introduction. The Biblical Resource Series. Grand Rapids: Eerdmans, 2002).

Hays, R.B. *The Moral Vision of the New Testament. A Contemporary Introduction to New Testament Ethics.* San Francisco: HarperCollins, 1996.

Hays, R.B. "Three Dramatic Roles. The Law in Romans 3-4," in: J.D.G. Dunn (ed.). *Paul and the Mosaic Law*. Tübingen: Mohr (Siebeck) 1996, 151-164.

Hayward, C.T.R. "The Present State of Research into the Targumic Account of the Sacrifice of Isaac." *Journal of Jewish Studies* 32 (1981) 127-150.

Hebert, A.G. "'Faithfulness' and 'Faith'." *Theologica* 58 (1955) 373-379.

Heckel, U. *Der Segen im Neuen Testament. Begriff, Formeln, Gesten. Mit einem praktisch-theologischen Ausblick.* Wissenschaftliche Untersuchungen zum Neuen Testament 150. Tübingen: Mohr (Siebeck), 2002.

Heen, E.M. Review of M.W. Yeung. *Faith in Jesus and Paul. A Comparison with Special Reference to 'Faith that can remove Mountains' and 'Your Faith has healed/saved you.'* *Journal of Biblical Literature* 122 (2003) 175-179.

Heidegger, M. *Sein und Zeit = Jahrbuch für Philosophie und phänomenologische Forschung* 8. Tübingen: Niemeyer, 1927 (= 18th ed. 2001).

Heidland, H.-W. *Die Anrechnung des Glaubens zur Gerechtigkeit. Untersuchungen zur Begriffsbestimmung von חשׁב und λογίζεσθαι.* Beiträge zur Wissenschaft vom Alten und Neuen Testament 4/18. Stuttgart: Kohlhammer, 1936.

Heidland, H.-W. Art. "λογίζομαι κτλ." *Theologisches Wörterbuch zum Neuen Testament* 4, 1942, 287-298.

Heinisch, P. *Das Buch Genesis.* Die Heilige Schrift des Alten Testaments. Bonn: Hansstein, 1930.

Heitmüller, W. "Die Bekehrung des Paulus." *Zeitschrift für Theologie und Kirche* 27 (1917) 136-153.

Hengel, M. & R. Deines. "E. P. Sander's 'Common Judaism.' Jesus and the Pharisees." *Journal of Theological Studies* 46 (1995) 1-70.

Hengel, M. (in collaboration with R. Deines). *The Pre-Christian Paul.* London: SCM Press, 1991.

Hengel, M. "Der vorchristliche Paulus," in: M. Hengel & U. Heckel (eds.). *Paulus und das antike Judentum.* Wissenschaftliche Untersuchungen zum Neuen Testament 58. Tübingen: Mohr (Siebeck), 1996, 177-293.

Hengel, M. *Die Zeloten. Untersuchungen zur jüdischen Freiheitsbewegung in der Zeit von Herodes I. bis 70 n.Chr.* 2nd ed. Leiden: E.J. Brill, 1976.

Hengel, M. *Judentum und Hellenismus. Studien zu ihrer Begegnung unter ihrer besonderen Berücksichtigung Palästinas bis zur Mitte des 2. Jh. v. Chr.* Wissenschaftliche Untersuchungen zum Neuen Testament 10. 3nd ed. Tübingen: Mohr (Siebeck), 1988.

Hengel, M. "The Scriptures and Their Interpretation in Second Temple Judaism," in: D.R.G. Beattie & M.J. McNamarna (eds.). *The Aramaic Bible. Targums in Their Historical Context.* Journal for the Study of the Old Testament: Supplement Series 166. Sheffield: Sheffield Academic Press, 1994, 158-175.

Hengel, M. *Zur urchristlichen Geschichtsschreibung.* Calwer Paperback. Stuttgart: Calwer Verlag, 1979.

Henten, J.W. van. "The Tradition-Historical Background of Romans 3,25. A Search for Pagan and Jewish Parallels," in: M. de Boer (ed.). *From Jesus to John.* FS M. de Jonge. Journal for the Study of the New Testament: Supplement Series 87. Sheffield: JSOT Press, 1993, 101-128.

Henten, J.W. van. Art. "Mastemah משׁטמה." *Dictionary of Deities and Demons in the Bible.* 2nd ed., 1999, 1033-1035.

Hermisson, H.-J. "Glauben im Alten Testament," in: H.-J. Hermisson, & E. Lohse. *Glauben.* Stuttgart: Kohlhammer, 1978, 9-78.

Hermisson, H.-J. *Sprache und Ritus im alttestamentlichen Kult.* Wissenschaftliche Monographien zum Alten und Neuen Testament 19. Neukirchen-Vluyn: Neukirchener Verlag, 1965.

Hertel, W. *Existentieller Glaube. Eine Studie über den Glaubensbegriff von Karl Jaspers und Paul Tillich.* Monographien zur philosophischen Forschung 74. Meisenheim: Hain, 1971.

Hill, D. *Greek Words and Hebrew Meanings. Studies in the Semantics of Soteriological Terms.* Society for New Testament Studies Monograph Series 5. Cambridge: Cambridge University Press, 1967.

Hofius, O. "Das Gesetz des Mose und das Gesetz Christi." *Zeitschrift für Theologie und Kirche* 80 (1983) 262-286 = in: *Paulusstudien.* Wissenschaftliche Untersuchungen zum Neuen Testament 51. Tübingen: Mohr (Siebeck), 1989, 50-74.

Hofius, O. "Der Psalter als Zeuge des Evangeliums. Die Verwendung der Septuaginta-Psalmen in den ersten beiden Hauptteilen des Römerbriefes," in: H. Graf Reventlow (ed.). *Theologische Probleme der Septuaginta und der hellenistischen Hermeneutik.* VWGTh 11. Gütersloh: Mohn, 1997, 72-90 = in: *Paulusstudien II.* Wissenschaftliche Untersuchungen zum Neuen Testament 143. Tübingen: Mohr (Siebeck), 2002, 38-57.

Hofius, O. "Die Adam-Christus-Antithese und das Gesetz. Erwägungen zu Röm 5,12-21," in: J.D.G. Dunn (ed.). *Paul and the Mosaic Law.* Tübingen: Mohr (Siebeck), 1996, 165-206 = in: *Paulusstudien II.* Wissenschaftliche Untersuchungen zum Neuen Testament 143. Tübingen: Mohr (Siebeck), 2002, 62-103.

Hofius, O. "Die Allmacht des Sohnes Gottes und das Gebet des Glaubens. Erwägungen zu Thema und Aussage der Wundererzählung Mk 9,14-29." *Zeitschrift für Theologie und Kirche* 101 (2004) 117-137.

Hofius, O. "Eine altjüdische Parallele zu Röm IV.17b." *New Testament Studies* 18 (1971/1972) 93-94 = (revised as: "Die Gottesprädikation Röm 4,17b") in: *Paulusstudien II.* Wissenschaftliche Untersuchungen zum Neuen Testament 143. Tübingen: Mohr (Siebeck), 2002, 58-61.

Hofius, O. "Glaube und Taufe nach dem Zeugnis des NT." *Zeitschrift für Theologie und Kirche* 91 (1994) 134-156.

Hofius, O. "'Rechtfertigung des Gottlosen' als Thema biblischer Theologie," in: I. Baldermann et al. (eds.) *Der eine Gott der beiden Testamente.* Jahrbuch für Biblische Theologie 2. Neukirchen-Vluyn: Neukirchener Verlag, 1987, 79-105 (quoted thereafter) = in: *Paulusstudien.* Wissenschaftliche Untersuchungen zum Neuen Testament 51. Tübingen: Mohr (Siebeck), 1989, 121-147.

Hofius, O. "Wort Gottes und Glaube bei Paulus" = in: *Paulusstudien.* Wissenschaftliche Untersuchungen zum Neuen Testament 51. Tübingen: Mohr (Siebeck), 1990, 148-174.

Hofius, O. "Zur Auslegung von Römer 9,30-33," in: J. Mertin, D. Neuhaus & M. Weinrich (eds.). *'Mit unsrer Macht ist nichts getan...'* FS D. Schellong. Arnoldshainer Texte 80. Frankfurt: Haag und Herchen, 1993, 163-174 = in: *Paulusstudien II.* Wissenschaftliche Untersuchungen zum Neuen Testament 143. Tübingen: Mohr (Siebeck), 2002, 155-166.

Hoftijzer, J. *Die Verheißungen an die drei Erzväter.* Leiden: Brill, 1956.

Hölscher, G. *Geschichtsschreibung in Israel. Untersuchungen zum Jahwisten und Elohisten.* Lund: Gleerup, 1952.

Holst, R. "The Meaning of 'Abraham Believed God' in Romans 4:3." *Westminster Theological Journal* 59 (1997) 319-326.

Holtzmann, H.J. *Lehrbuch der neutestamentlichen Theologie.* Vol. 2. Sammlung theologischer Lehrbücher. 2nd ed. (A. Jülicher & W. Bauer, eds.). Tübingen: Mohr (Siebeck), 1911.

Holzinger, H. *Das erste Buch Mose oder die Genesis.* Die Heilige Schrift des Alten Testaments (E. Kautzsch, ed.). Tübingen: Mohr (Siebeck), 1922.

Holzinger, H. *Genesis erklärt.* Kurzer Hand-Commentar zum Alten Testament. Freiburg: Mohr (Siebeck), 1898.

Hooker, M.D. Art. "Glaube." *Religion in Geschichte und Gegenwart* 3, 4th ed., 2000, 947-953.

Hooker, M.D. "Interchange in Christ," *Journal of Theological Studies* 22 (1971) 349-361 = in: *From Adam to Christ. Essays on Paul.* Cambridge: Cambridge University Press, 1990, 13-25.

Hooker, M.D. *Paul. A Short Introduction.* Oxford: Oneworld, 2003.

Hooker, M.D. "Πίστις Χριστοῦ." *New Testament Studies* 35 (1989) 321-342 = in: *From Adam to Christ. Essays on Paul*. Cambridge: Cambridge University Press, 1990, 165-186.

Howard, G. "Faith of Christ." *Anchor Bible Dictionary* 2, 1990a, 758-760.

Howard, G. "On the 'Faith of Christ'." *Harvard Theological Review* 60 (1967) 459-465.

Howard, G. *Paul: Crisis in Galatia. A Study in Early Christian Theology*. Society for New Testament Studies Monograph Series 35. 2nd ed. Cambridge: Cambridge University Press, 1990.

Howard, G. "Romans 3:21-31 and the Inclusion of the Gentiles." *Harvard Theological Review* 63 (1970) 223-233.

Howard, G. "The Faith of Christ." *Expository Times* 85 (1974) 212-215.

Hübner, H. *Das Gesetz bei Paulus. Ein Beitrag zum Werden der paulinischen Theologie*. Forschungen zur Religion und Literatur des Alten und Neuen Testaments 119. 3nd ed. Göttingen: Vandenhoeck & Ruprecht, 1982.

Hübner, H. "Was heißt bei Paulus 'Werke des Gesetzes'?," in: E. Gräßer & O. Merk (eds.). *Glaube und Eschatologie*. FS W.G. Kümmel. Tübingen: Mohr (Siebeck), 1985, 123-133 = in: *Biblische Theologie als Hermeneutik. Gesammelte Aufsätze* (A. & M. Labahn, eds.). Göttingen: Vandenhoeck & Ruprecht, 1995, 166-174.

Huesman, J. "The Infinitive Absolute and the Waw Perfect Problem." *Biblica* 37 (1956) 410-434.

Huizenga, L.A. "Akedah in Jubilees." *Journal for the Study of the Pseudepigrapha* 13 (2002) 33-59.

Hultgren, A.J. "The *Pistis Christou* Formulation in Paul." *Novum Testamentum* 22 (1980) 248-263.

Hurtado, L.W. *Lord Jesus Christ. Devotion to Jesus in Earliest Christianity*. Grand Rapids: Eerdmans, 2003.

Ishida, T. "The Structure and Historical Implications of the List of Pre-Israelite Nations." *Biblica* 60 (1979) 461-490.

Ito, A. "ΝΟΜΟΣ (ΤΩΝ) ἘΡΓΩΝ and ΝΟΜΟΣ ΠΙΣΤΕΩΣ. The Pauline Rhetoric and Theology of ΝΟΜΟΣ." *Novum Testamentum* 45 (2003) 237-259.

Jacob, B. *Das erste Buch der Torah – Genesis. Übersetzt und erklärt*. Berlin: Schocken, 1934 (= Stuttgart: Calwer Verlag, 2000).

Jacob, E. "Abraham et sa signification pour la foi chrétienne." *Revue de l'histoire et de philosophie religieuse* 42 (1962) 148-156.

Janowski, B. "Psalm CVI 28-31 und die Interzession des Pinchas." *Vetus Testamentum* 33 (1983) 237-248.

Janzen, J.G. "Coleridge and *Pistis Christou*." *Expository Times* 107 (1996) 265-268.

Jastrow, M. *Die Religion Babyloniens und Assyriens*. Vol. 2. Giessen: Töpelmann, 1912.

Jepsen, A. Art. "אָמַן etc." *Theologisches Wörterbuch zum Alten Testament* 1, 1973, 313-348.

Jepsen, A. "צדק und צדקה im Alten Testament," in: H. Graf Reventlow (ed.). *Gottes Wort und Gottes Land*. FS H.-W. Hertzberg. Göttingen: Vandenhoeck & Ruprecht, 1965, 78-89 (quoted thereafter) = in: *Der Herr ist Gott. Aufsätze zur Wissenschaft zum Alten Testament*. Berlin: Evangelische Verlagsanstalt, 1978, 221-229.

Jepsen, A. "Zur Überlieferungsgeschichte der Vätergestalten." *Wissenschaftliche Zeitschrift der Karl-Marx-Universität Leipzig* 3 (1953/1954) = FS A. Alt, 139-155.

Jeremias, J. *Der Schlüssel zur Theologie des Apostels Paulus*. Calwer Hefte 115. Stuttgart: Calwer Verlag, 1971.

Jeremias, J. "Die Gedankenführung in Röm 4. Zum paulinischen Glaubensverständnis," in: *Foi et Salut selon S. Paul. Épître aux Romains 1,16*. Analecta Biblica 42. Rome: Pontifical Biblical Institute, 1970, 51-58, and discussion with E. Schweizer, M. Barth, R. Pesch, J. Cambier, S. Lyonnet, W.C. van Unnik, 59-65.

Jeremias, J. "Paul and James." *Expository Times* 66 (1954/1955) 368-371.

Jeremias, J. "Paulus als Hillelit," in: E.E. Ellis & M. Wilcox (eds.). *Neotestamentica et Semitica*. FS M. Black. Edinburgh: T. & T. Clark, 1969, 88-94.

Jeremias, J. "Zur Gedankenführung in den paulinischen Briefen," in: J.N. Sevenster & W.C. van Unnik (eds.). *Studia Paulina*. FS J. de Zwaan. Haarlem: Bohn, 1953, 146-153 = *Abba. Studien zur neutestamentlichen Theologie und Zeitgeschichte*. Göttingen: Vandenhoeck & Ruprecht, 1966, 269-276.

Jervell, J. "Der Brief nach Jerusalem. Über Veranlassung und Adresse des Römerbriefs." *Studia Theologica* 25 (1971) 61-73.

Johnson, B. "Who Reckoned Righteousness to Whom?" *Svensk Exegetisk Årsbok* 51/52 (1986/1987) 108-115.

Johnson, B. Art. "צדק etc." *Theologisches Wörterbuch zum Alten Testament* 6, 1989, 898-924.

Johnson, L.T. "Foreword," in: R.B. Hays. *The Faith of Jesus Christ. The Narrative Substructure of Galatians 3:1-4:11*. 2nd ed. with a new introduction. The Biblical Resource Series. Grand Rapids: Eerdmans, 2002, xi-xv.

Johnson, L.T. "Romans 3:21-26 and the Faith of Jesus." *Catholic Biblical Quarterly* 44 (1982) 77-90.

Jüngel, E. *Das Evangelium von der Rechtfertigung des Gottlosen als Zentrum des christlichen Glaubens. Eine theologische Studie in ökumenischer Absicht*. 3rd ed. Tübingen: Mohr (Siebeck), 1999.

Jüngel, E. "Das Gesetz zwischen Adam und Christus. Eine theologische Studie zu Röm 5,12-21," in: *Unterwegs zur Sache. Theologische Bemerkungen*. Beiträge zur Evangelischen Theologie 61. München: Kaiser, 1972, 145-172.

Jüngel, E. *Jesus und Paulus. Eine Untersuchung zur Präzisierung der Frage nach dem Ursprung der Christologie*. Hermeneutische Untersuchungen zur Theologie 2. Tübingen: Mohr (Siebeck), 1962.

Kähler, M. *Der sogenannte historische Jesus und der geschichtliche, biblische Christus*. 2nd ed. Leipzig: Deichert, 1896.

Kaiser, O. "Die Bindung Isaaks. Untersuchungen zur Eigenart und Bedeutung von Genesis 22," in: *Zwischen Athen und Jerusalem*. Beihefte zur Zeitschrift für die alttestamentliche Wissenschaft 320. Berlin: de Gruyter, 2003, 199-224.

Kaiser, O. "Traditionsgeschichtliche Untersuchung von Genesis 15." *Zeitschrift für die alttestamentliche Wissenschaft* 70 (1958) 107-126.

Käsemann, E. *An die Römer*. Handbuch zum Neuen Testament. 4th ed. Tübingen: Mohr (Siebeck), 1980.

Käsemann, E. "Der Glaube Abrahams in Röm 4," in: *Paulinische Perspektiven*. Tübingen: Mohr (Siebeck), 1969, 140-177.

Käsemann, E. "Gottesgerechtigkeit bei Paulus." *Zeitschrift für Theologie und Kirche* 58 (1961) 367-378 = in: *Exegetische Versuche und Besinnungen*. Vol. 2. Göttingen: Vandenhoeck & Ruprecht, 1964, 181-193.

Käsemann, E. "Rechtfertigung und Heilsgeschichte im Römerbrief," in: *Paulinische Perspektiven*. Tübingen: Mohr (Siebeck), 1969a, 108-139.

Käsemann, E. "Zum Thema der urchristlichen Apokalyptik." *Zeitschrift für Theologie und Kirche* 59 (1962) 257-284 = in: *Exegetische Versuche und Besinnungen*. Vol. 2. Göttingen: Vandenhoeck & Ruprecht, 1964, 105-131.

Käsemann, E. "Zum Verständnis von Römer 3,24-26." *Zeitschrift für die neutestamentliche Wissenschaft* 43 (1950/1951) 150-154 = in: *Exegetische Versuche und Besinnungen*. Vol. 1. 4th ed. Göttingen: Vandenhoeck & Ruprecht, 1965.

Kautzsch, E. *Über die Derivate des Stammes צדק im alttestamentlichen Sprachgebrauch.* Tübingen: Fues, 1888.

Keck, L.E. "'Jesus' in Romans." *Journal of Biblical Literature* 108 (1989) 443-460.

Keck, L.E. *Romans.* Abingdon New Testament Commentaries. Nashville: Abingdon, 2005.

Keller, C.A. "Glaube in der 'Weisheit Salomos'," in: H.J. Stoebe (ed.). *Wort – Gebot – Glaube. Beiträge zur Theologie des Alten Testaments.* FS W. Eichrodt. Abhandlungen zur Theologie des Alten und Neuen Testaments 59. Zürich: Zwingli Verlag, 1970, 11-20.

Kerényi, K. *Die Antike Religion.* 2nd ed. Düsseldorf: Diederichs, 1952.

Kertelge, K. *"Rechtfertigung" bei Paulus. Studien zur Struktur und zum Bedeutungsgehalt des paulinischen Rechtfertigungsbegriffs.* 2nd ed. Münster: Aschendorff, 1971.

Kettunen, M. *Der Abfassungszweck des Römerbriefes.* AASF Dissertationes Humanarum Litterarum 18. Helsinki: Suomalainen Tiedeakatemia, 1979.

Kilian, R. "Der heilsgeschichtliche Aspekt in der elohistischen Geschichtstradition." *Theologie und Glaube* 56 (1966a) 369-384.

Kilian, R. *Die vorpriesterlichen Abrahamstraditionen literarkritisch und traditiongeschichtlich untersucht.* Bonner biblische Beiträge 24. Bonn: Hanstein 1966.

Kilian, R. *Isaaks Opferung. Zur Überlieferungsgeschichte von Gen 22.* Stuttgarter Bibelstudien 44. Stuttgart: Katholisches Bibelwerk, 1970.

Kinneavy, J.L. *Greek Rhetorical Origins of Christian Faith. An Inquiry.* New York: Oxford University Press, 1987.

Kittel, G. "Πίστις Ἰησοῦ Χριστοῦ bei Paulus." *Theologische Studien und Kritiken* 79 (1906) 419-436.

Klauck, H.J. *Hausgemeinde und Hauskirche im frühen Christentum.* Stuttgarter Bibelstudien 103. Stuttgart: Katholisches Bibelwerk, 1981.

Klein, G. "Der Abfassungszweck des Römerbriefes," in: *Rekonstruktion und Interpretation. Gesammelte Aufsätze zum Neuen Testament.* Beiträge zur Evangelischen Theologie 50. München: Kaiser, 1969, 129-144.

Klein, G. "Exegetische Probleme in Röm 3,21-4,25. Antwort an Ulrich Wilckens." *Evangelische Theologie* 24 (1964) 676-683 = in: *Rekonstruktion und Interpretation. Gesammelte Aufsätze zum Neuen Testament.* Beiträge zur Evangelischen Theologie 50. München: Kaiser, 1969, 170-177 (with "Nachtrag": 177-179).

Klein, G. Art. "Gesetz. III. Neues Testament." *Theologische Realenzyklopädie* 13, 1984, 58-75.

Klein, G. "Gottes Gerechtigkeit als Thema der neuesten Paulus-Forschung." *Verkündigung und Forschung* 12 (1967) 1-11 = in: *Rekonstruktion und Interpretation. Gesammelte Aufsätze zum Neuen Testament.* München: Kaiser, 1969, 225-236.

Klein, G. "Heil und Geschichte nach Römer iv." *New Testament Studies* 13 (1966/1967) 43-47.

Klein, G. "Individualgeschichte und Weltgeschichte. Eine Interpretation ihres Verhältnisses im Galaterbrief." *Evangelische Theologie* 24 (1964) 126-165 = in: *Rekonstruktion und Interpretation. Gesammelte Aufsätze zum Neuen Testament.* Beiträge zur Evangelischen Theologie 50. München: Kaiser, 1969, 180-221 (with "Nachtrag," 221-224).

Klein, G. Art. "Rechtfertigung. I. Im NT." *Religion in Geschichte und Gegenwart* 5, 3rd ed., 1961, 825-828.

Klein, G. "Römer 4 und die Idee der Heilsgeschichte." *Evangelische Theologie* 23 (1963) 424-447 = in: *Rekonstruktion und Interpretation. Gesammelte Aufsätze zum Neuen Testament*. Beiträge zur Evangelischen Theologie 50. München: Kaiser, 1969, 145-169.

Klein, R. "Ezra and Nehemiah in Recent Studies," in: *Magnalia Dei. The Mighty Acts of God*. Garden City: Doubleday, 1976, 361-376.

Knoke, F. *Der christliche Glaube nach Paulus*. Osnabrück: Rockhorst, 1922.

Knox, J. "The Epistle to the Romans. Introduction and Exegesis," in: G.A. Buttrick (ed.). *The Interpreter's Bible*. Vol. 9. New York: Abingdon, 1954.

Koch, D.-A. "Der Text von Hab 2,4b in der Septuaginta und im Neuen Testament." *Zeitschrift für die neutestamentliche Wissenschaft* 76 (1985) 68-85.

Koch, D.-A. *Die Schrift als Zeuge des Evangeliums. Untersuchungen zur Verwendung und zum Verständnis der Schrift bei Paulus*. Beiträge zur historischen Theologie 69. Tübingen: Mohr (Siebeck), 1986.

Koch, K. "Gibt es Hebräisches Denken?," in: *Spuren hebräischen Denkens. Beiträge zur alttestamentlichen Theologie. Gesammelte Aufsätze*. Vol. 1. Neukirchen-Vluyn: Neukirchener Verlag, 1991, 3-24.

Koch, K. Art. "צדק etc." *Theologisches Handwörterbuch zum Alten Testament* 2, 1971, 507-530.

Köckert, M. *Vätergott und Väterverheißungen. Eine Auseinandersetzung mit Albrecht Alt und seinen Erben*. Forschungen zur Religion und Literatur des Alten und Neuen Testaments 142. Göttingen: Vandenhoeck & Ruprecht, 1988.

Kolenkow, A.B. "The Ascription of Romans 4:5." *Harvard Theological Review* 60 (1967) 228-230.

König, E. *Die Genesis. Eingeleitet, übersetzt und erklärt*. Gütersloh: Bertelsmann, 1919.

Koperski, V. "The Meaning of *Pistis Christou* Philippians 3:9." *Louvain Studies* 18 (1993) 198-216.

Körner, J. "Das Wesen des Glaubens nach dem Alten Testament." *Theologische Literaturzeitung* 104 (1979) 713-720.

Kornfeld, W. Art. "Satan (et démons)." *Dictionnaire de la Bible: Supplément* 66. Paris, 1992, 1-21.

Korthaus, M. *"Was uns unbedingt angeht". Der Glaubensbegriff in der Theologie Paul Tillichs*. Forum Systematik 1. Stuttgart: Kohlhammer, 1999.

Kramer, W. *Christos Kyrios Gottessohn. Untersuchungen zu Gebrauch und Bedeutung der christologischen Bezeichnungen bei Paulus und den vorpaulinischen Gemeinden*. Abhandlungen zur Theologie des Alten und Neuen Testaments 44. Zürich: Zwingli, 1963.

Kraus, H.-J. *Psalmen*. Biblischer Kommentar, Altes Testament. 5th ed. Neukirchen-Vluyn: Neukirchener Verlag, 1978.

Kraus, W. *Das Volk Gottes. Zur Grundlegung einer Ekklesiologie bei Paulus*. Wissenschaftliche Untersuchungen zum Neuen Testament 85. Tübingen: Mohr (Siebeck), 1996.

Kraus, W. *Der Tod Jesu als Heiligtumsweihe. Eine Untersuchung zum Umfeld der Sühnevorstellung in Römer 3,25-26a*. Wissenschaftliche Monographien zum Alten und Neuen Testament 66. Neukirchen-Vluyn: Neukirchener Verlag, 1991.

Kraus, W. "Der Tod Jesu als Sühnetod bei Paulus." *Zeitschrift für Neues Testament* 3 (1999) 20-30.

Kreuzer, S. "430 Jahre, 400 Jahre oder 4 Generationen. Zu den Zeitangaben über den Ägyptenaufenthalt der 'Israeliten'." *Zeitschrift für die alttestamentliche Wissenschaft* 98 (1986) 199-210.

Kreuzer, S. "'Der den Gottlosen rechtfertigt' (Römer 4,5). Die frühjüdische Einordnung von Gen 15 als Hintergrund für das Abrahambild und die Rechtfertigungslehre des Paulus." *Theologische Beiträge* 33 (2002) 208-219.

Kugler, R.A. & J.C. VanderKam. "A Note on 4Q225 (4QPseudo-Jubilees)." *Revue de Qumran* 20 (2001) 109-116.

Kühl, E. *Der Brief des Paulus an die Römer*. Leipzig: Quelle & Meyer, 1913.

Kümmel, W.G. "Der Glaube im Neuen Testament, seine katholische und reformatorische Deutung." *Theologische Blätter* 16 (1937) 209-221 (quoted thereafter) = *Heilsgeschehen und Geschichte*. Vol. 1: *Gesammelte Aufsätze 1933-1964*. (E. Gräßer, O. Merk & A. Fritz, eds.) Marburger Theologische Studien 3. Marburg: Elwert, 1965, 67-80.

Kümmel, W.G. "Πάρεσις und ἔνδειξις. Ein Beitrag zum Verständnis der paulinischen Rechtfertigungslehre." *Zeitschrift für Theologie und Kirche* 49 (1952) 154-164 = in: *Heilsgeschehen und Geschichte*. Vol. 1: *Gesammelte Aufsätze 1933-1964* (E. Gräßer, O. Merk & A Fritz, eds.). Marburger Theologische Studien 3. Marburg: Elwert, 1965, 260-270.

Kundert, L. *Die Opferung/Bindung Isaaks*. Vol. 1: *Gen 22,1-19 im Alten Testament, im Frühjudentum und im Neuen Testament*. Vol. 2: *Gen 22,1-19 in frühen rabbinischen Texten*. Wissenschaftliche Monographien zum Alten und Neuen Testament 78. Neukirchen-Vluyn: Neukirchener Verlag, 1998.

Kuss, O. "Der Glaube nach den paulinischen Hauptbriefen." *Theologie und Glaube* 46 (1956) 1-26 = in: *Auslegung und Verkündigung*. Vol. 1: *Aufsätze zur Exegese des Neuen Testaments*. Regensburg: Pustet, 1963, 187-212.

Kuss, O. *Der Römerbrief*. First installment. 2nd ed. Regensburg: Pustet, 1963.

Laato, T. *Paul and Judaism. An Anthropological Approach*. Atlanta: Scholars Press, 1995.

Lagrange, M.J. *Saint Paul. Epître aux Romains*. Etudes Bibliques. 6th ed. Paris: Gabalda, 1950.

Lambrecht, J. & R.W. Thompson. *Justification by Faith. The Implications of Romans 3:27-31*. Zacchaeus studies: New Testament. Wilmington: Michael Glazier, 1988.

Lambrecht, J. "'Abraham, notre Père à tous'. La figure d'Abraham dans les écrits pauliniens." *Publications de l'Institutum Judaicum* 2 (1979) 118-158 = in: *Pauline Studies. Collected Essays*. Bibliotheca ephemeridum theologicarum lovaniensium 115. Leuven: Peeters, 1994, 3-25.

Lambrecht, J. "Curse and Blessing. A Study of Galatians 3,10-14." *Collationes* 21 (1991) 133-157 = in: *Pauline Studies. Collected Essays*. Bibliotheca ephemeridum theologicarum lovaniensium 115. Leuven: Peeters, 1994, 271-298.

Lambrecht, J. "Gesetzesverständnis bei Paulus," in: K. Kertelge (ed.). *Das Gesetz im Neuen Testament*. Quaestiones disputatae 108. Freiburg: Herder, 1986, 88-127 = in: *Pauline Studies. Collected Essays*. Bibliotheca ephemeridum theologicarum lovaniensium 115. Leuven: Peeters, 1994, 231-270.

Lambrecht, J. "Paul's Logic in Romans 3:29-30." *Journal of Biblical Literature* 119 (2000) 526-528.

Lambrecht, J. "Unreal Conditions in the Letters of Paul. A Clarification." *Ephemerides theologicae lovanienses* 63 (1987) 153-156 = in: *Pauline Studies. Collected Essays*. Bibliotheca ephemeridum theologicarum lovaniensium 115. Leuven: Peeters, 1994, 365-368.

Lambrecht, J. "Why is boasting excluded? A Note on Rom 3:27 and 4:2." *Ephemerides theologicae lovanienses* 61 (1985) 365-369 = (with additional note) in: *Pauline Studies. Collected Essays*. Bibliotheca ephemeridum theologicarum lovaniensium 115. Leuven: Peeters, 1994, 27-31.

Lampe, P. *Die stadtrömischen Christen in den beiden ersten Jahrhunderten.* Wissenschaftliche Untersuchungen zum Neuen Testament 2/18. 2nd ed. Tübingen: Mohr (Siebeck), 1989.

Lange, A. "Kriterien essenischer Texte," in: J. Frey & H. Stegemann (eds.). *Qumran kontrovers: Beiträge zu den Textfunden vom Toten Meer.* Einblicke 6. Paderborn: Bonifatius, 2003, 59-70.

Lange, A. "Qumran. 1. Die Textfunde von Qumran." *Theologische Realenzyklopädie* 28, 1997, 45-65.

Larsson, E. *Christus als Vorbild. Eine Untersuchung zu den paulinischen Tauf- und Eikontexten.* Acta seminarii neotestamentici upsaliensis 23. Uppsala: Almquist & Wiksells, 1962.

Le Déaut, R. *La Nuit Pascale.* Analecta Biblica 22. Rome: Pontifical Biblical Institute, 1963.

Légasse, S. *L'épître de Paul aux Romains.* Lectio divina: Commentaires. Paris: Cerf, 2002.

Lerch, D. *Isaaks Opferung christlich gedeutet. Eine auslegungsgeschichtliche Untersuchung.* Beiträge zur historischen Theologie 12. Tübingen: Mohr (Siebeck), 1950.

Levenson, J.D. *The Death and Resurrection of the Beloved Son.* New Haven: Yale University Press, 1993.

Levenson, J.D. "Why Jews Are Not Interested in Biblical Theology," in: J. Neusner et al. (eds.) *Judaic Perspectives on Ancient Israel.* Philadelphia: Fortress, 1987, 281-307 = in: *The Hebrew Bible, the Old Testament, and Historical Criticism. Jews and Christians in Biblical Studies.* Louisville: Westminster/John Knox, 1993, 33-61, 165-170.

Levin, C. "Abschied vom Jahwisten?" *Theologische Rundschau* 69 (2004) 329-344.

Licht, J. *Storytelling in the Bible.* Jerusalem: Magnes Press, 1978.

Lichtenberger, H. "Das Tora-Verständnis im Judentum zur Zeit des Paulus. Eine Skizze," in: J.D.G. Dunn (ed.). *Paul and the Mosaic Law.* Tübingen: Mohr (Siebeck), 1996, 7-23.

Lietzmann, H. *An die Galater.* Handbuch zum Neuen Testament. 3rd ed. Tübingen: Mohr (Siebeck), 1933.

Lietzmann, H. *An die Römer.* Handbuch zum Neuen Testament. 3rd ed. Tübingen: Mohr (Siebeck), 1928 (= 5th ed. 1971).

Lightfoot, J.B. *Saint Paul's Epistle to the Galatians.* New York: Macmillan, 1896.

Lincoln, A.T. "Abraham goes to Rome. Paul's Treatment of Abraham in Romans 4," in: M.J. Wilkins & T. Paige (eds.). *Worship, Theology and Ministry in the Early Church.* FS R.P. Martin. Journal for the Study of the New Testament: Supplement Series 87. Sheffield: JSOT Press, 1992, 163-179.

Lincoln, A.T. "The Stories of Predecessors and Inheritors in Galatians and Romans," in: B.W. Longenecker (ed.). *Narrative Dynamics in Paul. A Critical Assessment.* Louisville: Westminster/John Knox, 2002, 172-203.

Lindemann, A. "'Es steht geschrieben.' Überlegungen zur christlichen Hermeneutik der jüdischen Bibel." *Theologie und Glaube* 87 (1997) 39-54.

Lindsay, D.R. *Josephus and Faith.* πίστις and πιστεύειν *as Faith Terminology in the Writings of Flavius Josephus and in the New Testament.* Arbeiten zur Geschichte des antiken Judentums und Urchristentums 19. Leiden: Brill, 1993a.

Lindsay, D.R. "The Roots and Developments of the πιστ- Word Group as Faith Terminology." *Journal for the Study of the New Testament* 49 (1993) 103-118.

Lipsius, R.A. "Briefe an die Galater, Römer, Philipper," in: H.J. Holtzmann et al. (eds.) *Hand-Commentar zum Neuen Testament.* Vol. 2/2. 2nd ed. Freiburg: Mohr (Siebeck), 1892.

Ljungman, H. *Pistis. A Study of Its Presuppositions and Its Meaning in Pauline Use.* Lund: Gleerup, 1964.

Lohfink, N. *Die Landverheißung als Eid. Eine Studie zu Gn 15.* Stuttgarter Bibelstudien 28. Stuttgart: Katholisches Bibelwerk, 1967.

Lohmeyer, E. "Die Idee des Martyriums in Judentum und Urchristentum." *Zeitschrift für systematische Theologie* 5 (1927) 232-249.

Lohmeyer, E. *Grundlagen paulinischer Theologie.* Beiträge zur historischen Theologie 1. Tübingen: Mohr (Siebeck) 1929 (= Nendeln, Liechtenstein: Kraus Reprint, 1966).

Lohmeyer, E. "Probleme paulinischer Theologie. II. Gesetzeswerke." *Zeitschrift für die neutestamentliche Wissenschaft* 28 (1929a) 177-207 = "'Gesetzeswerke'," in: *Probleme paulinischer Theologie.* Darmstadt: Wissenschaftliche Buchgemeinschaft, 1954, 31-74.

Lohmeyer, E. "Probleme paulinischer Theologie. III. Sünde, Fleisch und Tod." *Zeitschrift für die neutestamentliche Wissenschaft* 29 (1930) 1–59 = in: *Probleme paulinischer Theologie.* Darmstadt: Wissenschaftliche Buchgemeinschaft, 1954, 75-156.

Lohse, E. "Das Präskript des Römerbriefes als theologisches Programm," in: M. Trowitzsch (ed.). *Paulus, Apostel Jesu Christi.* FS G. Klein. Tübingen: Mohr (Siebeck), 1998, 65-78.

Lohse, E. *Der Brief an die Römer.* Kritisch-exegetischer Kommentar über das Neue Testament. Göttingen: Vandenhoeck & Ruprecht, 2003.

Lohse, E. "Emuna und Pistis. Jüdisches und urchristliches Verständnis des Glaubens" *Zeitschrift für die neutestamentliche Wissenschaft* 68 (1977) 147-163.

Lohse, E. "Glauben im Neuen Testament," in: H.-J. Hermisson, & E. Lohse. *Glauben.* Stuttgart: Kohlhammer, 1978, 79-132.

Lohse, E. *Märtyrer und Gottesknecht.* Forschungen zur Religion und Literatur des Alten und Neuen Testaments 64. 2nd ed. Göttingen: Vandenhoeck & Ruprecht, 1963.

Lohse, E. "ὁ νόμος τοῦ πνεύματος τῆς ζωῆς. Exegetische Anmerkungen zu Röm 8,2," in: H.D. Betz & L. Schottroff (eds.). *Neues Testament und christliche Existenz.* FS H. Braun. Tübingen: Mohr (Siebeck), 1973, 279-287.

Lohse, E. "Summa Evangelii – zu Veranlassung und Thematik des Römerbriefes," in: *Nachrichten der Akademie der Wissenschaften in Göttingen. Philologisch-historische Klasse.* Göttingen, 1993, 89-119.

Longenecker, B.W. "Defining the Faithful Character of the Covenant Community. Galatians 2.15-21 and Beyond," in: J.D.G. Dunn (ed.). *Paul and the Mosaic Law.* Tübingen: Mohr (Siebeck) 1996, 75-97.

Longenecker, B.W. "ΠΙΣΤΙΣ in Romans 3.25: Neglected Evidence for the 'Faithfulness of Christ'." *New Testament Studies* 39 (1993) 478-480.

Longenecker, R.N. *Paul, Apostle of Liberty.* New York: Harper & Row, 1964.

Longenecker, R.N. "The 'Faith of Abraham' in Paul, James and Hebrews. A Study in the Circumstantial Nature of New Testament Teaching." *Journal of the Evangelical Theological Society* 20 (1977) 203-212.

Longenecker, R.N. "The Obedience of Christ in the Theology of the Early Church," in: R. Banks (ed.). *Reconciliation and Hope. New Testament Essays on Atonement and Eschatology.* FS L.L. Morris. Grand Rapids: Eerdmans, 1974, 142-152.

Lowe, B.A. "Oh διά! How is Romans 4:25 to be Understood?" *Journal of Theological Studies* 57 (2006) 149-157

Lüdemann, G. *Paulus, der Heidenapostel.* Vol. 1: *Studien zur Chronologie.* Forschungen zur Religion und Literatur des Alten und Neuen Testaments 123. Göttingen: Vandenhoeck & Ruprecht, 1980.

Lüdemann, H. *Die Anthropologie des Apostels Paulus und ihre Stellung innerhalb seiner Heilslehre. Nach den vier Hauptbriefen.* Kiel: Universitäts-Buchhandlung, 1872.

Lührmann, D. "Confesser sa foi à l'époque apostolique." *Revue de théologie et de philosophie* 117 (1985) 93-110.

Lührmann, D. *Das Offenbarungsverständnis bei Paulus und in den paulinischen Gemeinden.* Wissenschaftliche Monographien zum Alten und Neuen Testament 16. Neukirchen-Vluyn: Neukirchener Verlag, 1965.

Lührmann, D. "Die 430 Jahre zwischen den Verheißungen und dem Gesetz (Gal 3,17)." *Zeitschrift für die alttestamentliche Wissenschaft* 100 (1988) 420-423.

Lührmann, D. Art. "Faith. New Testament." *Anchor Bible Dictionary* 2, 1990, 749-758.

Lührmann, D. Art. "Glaube." *Realenzyklopädie für Antike und Christentum* 11, 1981, 48-122.

Lührmann, D. "Glaube, Bekenntnis, Erfahrung," in: W. Härle & R. Preul (eds.). *Glaube.* Marburger Jahrbuch für Theologie 4. Marburg: Elwert, 1992, 13-36.

Lührmann, D. *Glaube im frühen Christentum.* Gütersloh: Gütersloher Verlag, 1976.

Lührmann, D. "Pistis im Judentum." *Zeitschrift für die neutestamentliche Wissenschaft* 64 (1973) 19-38.

Lührmann, D. "Rechtfertigung und Versöhnung. Zur Geschichte der paulinischen Tradition." *Zeitschrift für Theologie und Kirche* 67 (1970) 437-452.

Luther, M. *In epistolam S. Pauli ad Galatas Commentarius* (1531). WA 40/1. Weimar: Hermann Böhlaus Nachfolger, 1911.

Luther, M. *Vorlesung über den Römerbrief von 1515/1516. Lateinisch-Deutsche Ausgabe.* Vols. 1-2. Darmstadt: Wissenschaftliche Buchgesellschaft, 1960.

Luther, M. *Vorlesung über Jesaias* (1527-1530). WA 31/2. Weimar: Hermann Böhlaus Nachfolger, 1914, 1-585.

Luz, U. *Das Geschichtsverständnis des Paulus.* Beiträge zur Evangelischen Theologie 49. München: Kaiser, 1968.

Luz, U. "Kann die Bibel heute noch Grundlage für die Kirche sein? Über die Aufgabe der Exegese in einer religiös-pluralistischen Gesellschaft." *New Testament Studies* 44 (1998) 317-339.

Luz, U. "Zum Aufbau von Röm 1-8." *Theologische Zeitschrift* 25 (1969) 161-181.

Lyonnet, S. "De notione expiationis." *Verbum domini* 37 (1959) 336-352.

Lyonnet, S. "Note sur le plan de l'Épître aux Romains." *Recherches de science religieuse* 39 (1951) 301-316.

Macholz, C. "Das 'Passivum Divinum', seine Anfänge im Alten Testament und der 'Hofstil'." *Zeitschrift für die neutestamentliche Wissenschaft* 81 (1990) 247-253.

Mack, B.L. *Wisdom and the Hebrew Epic. Ben Sira's Hymn in Praise of the Fathers.* Chicago: University of Chicago Press, 1985.

Maertens, T. *L'Eloge des Pères. Ecclésiastique XLIV-L.* Bruges: Abbaye de Saint-André, 1956.

Manson, T.W. "ΙΛΑΣΤΗΡΙΟΝ." *Journal of Theological Studies* 46 (1945) 1-10.

Marböck, J. "Das Gebet um die Rettung Zions in Sir 36,1-22 (G: 33,1-13a; 36,16b-22) im Zusammenhang der Geschichtsschau Ben Siras," in: J.B. Bauer & J. Marböck (eds.). *Memoria Jerusalem.* FS F. Sauer. Graz: Akademische Druck- und Verlagsanstalt, 1977, 93-115 = in: *Gottes Weisheit unter uns. Zur Theologie des Buches Sirach* (I. Fischer, ed.). Herders biblische Studien 6. Freiburg: Herder, 1995, 149-166.

Marböck, J. "Die 'Geschichte Israels' als 'Bundesgeschichte' nach dem Sirachbuch," in: E. Zenger (ed.). *Der Neue Bund im Alten. Studien zur Bundestheologie der beiden Testamente.* Quaestiones disputatae 146. Freiburg: Herder, 1993, 177-197 = in: *Gottes Weisheit unter uns. Zur Theologie des Buches Sirach* (I. Fischer, ed.). Herders biblische Studien 6. Freiburg: Herder, 1995, 103-123.

Marcus, J. "Mark – Interpreter of Paul." *New Testament Studies* 46 (2000) 473-487.

Marshall, I.H. *New Testament Theology. Many Witnesses, One Gospel.* Downers Grove: InterVarsity Press, 2004.

Marshall, I.H. "Response to A.T. Lincoln: 'The Stories of Predecessors and Inheritors in Galatians and Romans'," in: B.W. Longenecker (ed.). *Narrative Dynamics in Paul. A Critical Assessment.* Louisville: Westminster/John Knox, 2002, 204-214.

Martyn, J.L. *Galatians.* Anchor Bible. New York: Doubleday, 1997.

Martyn, J.L. "Paul's Understanding of the Textual Contradiction between Habakkuk 2:4 and Leviticus 18:5," in: C.A. Evans & S. Talmon (eds.). *The Quest for Context and Meaning. Studies in Biblical Intertextuality.* FS J.A. Sanders. Biblical Interpretation Series 28. Leiden: Brill, 1997a, 465-473.

Matlock, R.B. "'Even the Demons Believe': Paul and πίστις Χριστοῦ." *Catholic Biblical Quarterly* 64 (2002) 300-318.

Matlock, R.B. "Detheologizing the ΠΙΣΤΙΣ ΧΡΙΣΤΟΥ Debate: Cautionary Remarks from a Lexical Semantic Perspective." *Novum Testamentum* 42 (2000) 1-23.

Matlock, R.B. "Πίστις in Galatians 3.26: Neglected Evidence for 'Faith in Christ'?" *New Testament Studies* 49 (2003) 433-39.

Mayer, E.W. *Das christliche Gottvertrauen und der Glaube an Christus. Eine dogmatische Untersuchung auf biblisch-theologischer Grundlage und unter Berücksichtigung der symbolischen Litteratur.* Göttingen: Vandenhoeck & Ruprecht, 1899.

Mayer, G. "Aspekte des Abrahambildes in der hellenistisch-jüdischen Literatur." *Evangelische Theologie* 32 (1972) 118-127.

McLay, R.T. *The Use of the Septuagint in New Testament Research.* Grand Rapids: Eerdmans, 2003.

Merk, A. "Iustus ex fide vivit." *Verbum domini* 3 (1922) 193-198.

Merk, O. "Vorwort zur Neuausgabe," in: W. Mundle. *Der Glaubensbegriff des Paulus. Eine Untersuchung zur Dogmengeschichte des ältesten Christentums.* Darmstadt: Wissenschaftliche Buchgesellschaft, 1977, ix-xi.

Merklein, H. "Paulus und die Sünde," in: H. Frankemölle (ed.). *Sünde und Erlösung im Neuen Testament.* Quaestiones disputatae 161. Freiburg: Herder, 1996, 123-163 (quoted thereafter) = in: *Studien zu Jesus und Paulus.* Vol. 2. Wissenschaftliche Untersuchungen zum Neuen Testament 105. Tübingen: Mohr (Siebeck), 1998, 316-356.

Metzger, B.M. *A Textual Commentary on the Greek New Testament.* 2nd ed. London: United Bible Societies, 1994.

Meyer, B.F. "The Pre-Pauline Formula in Rom 3:25-26a." *New Testament Studies* 29 (1983) 198-208.

Michaelis, W. "Rechtfertigung aus Glauben bei Paulus," in: FS A. Deißmann. Tübingen: Mohr (Siebeck) 1927, 116-138.

Michel, D. "Begriffsuntersuchung über sädäq-sᵉdaqa und 'ᵃmät-'ᵃmuna." *Habilitationsschrift.* Heidelberg, 1964.

Michel, D. "Das Ansehen des Glaubens als Gerechtigkeitstat: Gen 15,6. Ein Gespräch mit Horst Seebass," in: S. Beyerle (ed.). *Recht und Ethos im Alten Testament – Gestalt und Wirkung.* FS H. Seebass. Neukirchen-Vluyn: Neukirchener Verlag, 1999, 103-113.

Michel, O. *Der Brief an die Römer*. Kritisch-exegetischer Kommentar über das Neue Testament 4. 5th ed. Göttingen: Vandenhoeck & Ruprecht, 1978.

Michel, O. *Paulus und seine Bibel*. Beiträge zur Förderung christlicher Theologie 2/18. Gütersloh: Bertelsmann, 1929.

Mielziner, M. *Introduction to the Talmud*. 3rd ed. New York: Bloch, 1925.

Mijoga, H.B.P. *The Pauline Notion of Deeds of the Law*. San Francisco: International Scholars Publications, 1999.

Milgrom, J. *Leviticus 17-22. A New Translation with Introduction and Commentary*. Anchor Bible. New York: Doubleday, 2000.

Minde, H.-J. van der. *Schrift und Tradition bei Paulus. Ihre Bedeutung und Funktion im Römerbrief*. München: Schöningh, 1976.

Moberly, R.W.L. "Abraham's Righteousness (Genesis xv 6)," in: J.A. Emerton (ed.). *Studies in the Pentateuch*. Vetus Testamentum Supplements 41. Leiden: Brill, 1990, 103-130 (quoted thereafter) = in: *From Eden to Golgotha. Essays in Biblical Theology*. South Florida Studies in the History of Judaism 52. Atlanta: Scholars Press, 1992, 29-54.

Moberly, R.W.L. "The Earliest Commentary on the Akedah." *Vetus Testamentum* 38 (1988) 302-323 = in: *From Eden to Golgotha. Essays in Biblical Theology*. South Florida Studies in the History of Judaism 52. Atlanta: Scholars Press, 1992, 55-73.

Moberly, R.W.L. *The Old Testament of the Old Testament. Patriarchal Narratives and Mosaic Yahwism*. Overtures to Biblical Theology. Minneapolis: Fortress, 1992.

Mölle, H. *Genesis 15. Eine Erzählung von den Anfängen Israels*. Forschung zur Bibel 62. Würzburg: Echter, 1988 [preface from 1989].

Moltmann, J. *Erfahrungen theologischen Denkens. Wege und Formen christlicher Theologie*. Gütersloh: Kaiser, Gütersloher Verlagshaus, 1999.

Montefiore, C.G. *Judaism and St. Paul. Two Essays*. London: Goschen, 1914.

Moo, D.J. *A Commentary on the Epistle to the Romans*. New International Commentary on the New Testament. Grand Rapids: Eerdmans, 1996.

Moo, D.J. "'Law,' 'Works of the Law,' and Legalism in Paul." *Westminster Theological Journal* 45 (1983) 73-100.

Moo, D.J. *The Letter of James. An Introduction and Commentary*. The Tyndale New Testament Commentaries. Grand Rapids: Eerdmans, 1985.

Moody, R.M. "The Habakkuk Quotation in Romans 1:17." *Expository Times* 92 (1981) 205-208.

Moore, G.F. *Judaism in the First Centuries of the Christian Era. The Age of the Tannaim*. Vols. 1-3. Cambridge 1927, 1927, 1930.

Mosis R. "Gen 15,6 in Qumran und in der Septuaginta," in: *Gesammelte Aufsätze zum Alten Testament*. Forschung zur Bibel 93. Würzburg: Echter, 1999, 95-118.

Mosis, R. "'Glauben' und 'Gerechtigkeit' – zu Gen 15,6," in: M. Görg (ed.). *Die Väter Israels. Beiträge zur Theologie der Patriarchenüberlieferungen im Alten Testament*. FS J. Scharbert. Stuttgart: Katholisches Bibelwerk, 1989, 225-257 = in: *Gesammelte Aufsätze zum Alten Testament*. Forschung zur Bibel 93. Würzburg: Echter, 1999, 55-93.

Moule, C.F.D. "The Biblical Conception of 'Faith'." *Expository Times* 68 (1956/1957) 157, 222.

Mowinckel, S. *Erwägungen zur Pentateuch Quellenfrage*. Oslo: Universitetsforlaget, 1964.

Moxnes, H. "Honour and Righteousness in Romans." *Journal for the Study of the New Testament* 32 (1988) 62-77.

Moxnes, H. *Theology in Conflict. Studies in Paul's Understanding of God in Romans.* Novum Testamentum Supplements 53. Leiden: Brill, 1980.

Müller, C. *Gottes Gerechtigkeit und Gottes Volk. Eine Untersuchung zu Römer 9-11.* Forschungen zur Religion und Literatur des Alten und Neuen Testaments 86. Göttingen: Vandenhoeck & Ruprecht, 1964.

Müller, M. "Die Abraham-Gestalt im Jubiläenbuch. Versuch einer Interpretation." *Scandinavian Journal of the Old Testament* 10 (1996) 238-257.

Müller, P. "Unser Vater Abraham. Die Abrahamrezeption im Neuen Testament – im Spiegel der neueren Literatur." *Berliner Theologische Zeitschrift* 16 (1999) 132-143.

Mundle, W. *Das religöse Leben des Apostels Paulus.* Leipzig: Hinrichs, 1923.

Mundle, W. *Der Glaubensbegriff des Paulus. Eine Untersuchung zur Dogmengeschichte des ältesten Christentums.* Leipzig: M. Heinsius Nachfolger, 1932 (= Darmstadt: Wissenschaftliche Buchgesellschaft, 1977).

Mundle, W. *Glaube, Hoffnung, Liebe. Nach dem Zeugnis des NT.* Metzingen: Brunnquell, 1949.

Murray, J. *The Epistle to the Romans.* New International Commentary on the New Testament. Grand Rapids: Eerdmans, 1959.

Mußner, F. *Der Galaterbrief.* Herders theologischer Kommentar zum Neuen Testament. Freiburg: Herder, 1981a.

Mußner, F. "'Ganz Israel wird gerettet werden' (Röm 11,26)." *Kairos* 18 (1976) 241-255.

Mußner, F. "Heil für alle. Der Grundgedanke des Römerbriefs." *Kairos* 23 (1981) 207-214 = in: *Dieses Geschlecht wird nicht vergehen. Judentum und Kirche.* Freiburg: Herder, 1991, 29-38.

Mußner, F. "Wer ist 'der ganze Samen' in Röm 4,16?," in: J. Zmijewski & E. Nellessen (eds.). *Begegnung mit dem Wort.* FS H. Zimmermann. Bonner biblische Beiträge 53. Bonn: Hanstein, 1980, 213-217 = in: *Die Kraft der Wurzel. Judentum – Jesus – Kirche.* 2nd ed. Freiburg: Herder, 1989, 160-163.

Myers, J.M. *Ezra-Nehemiah.* Anchor Bible. Garden City: Doubleday, 1965.

Neef, H.-D. *Die Prüfung Abrahams. Eine exegetisch-theologische Studie zu Gen 22,1-19.* Stuttgart, 1998.

Neubrand, M. *Abraham – Vater von Juden und Nichtjuden. Eine exegetische Studie zu Röm 4.* Forschung zur Bibel 85. Würzburg: Echter, 1997.

Neuer, W. *Adolf Schlatter. Ein Leben für Theologie und Kirche.* Stuttgart: Calwer Verlag, 1996.

Neugebauer, F. *In Christus = En Christoi. Eine Untersuchung zum paulinischen Glaubenverständnis.* Göttingen: Vandenhoeck & Ruprecht, 1961.

Newman, J.H. *Praying by the Book. The Scripturalization of Prayer in Second Temple Judaism.* Society of Biblical Literature Early Judaism and Its Literature 14. Atlanta: Scholars Press, 1999.

Nickelsburg, G.W.E. *Jewish Literature Between the Bible and the Mishnah.* Philadelphia: Fortress, 1981.

Noegel, S.B. "A Crux and a Taunt: Night-Time then Sunset in Genesis 15," in: P.R. Davies & D.J.A Clines (eds.). *The World of Genesis. Persons, Places, Perspectives.* Journal for the Study of the Old Testament: Supplement Series 257. Sheffield: Sheffield Academic Press, 1998, 128-135.

Noort, E. "'Land' in the Deuteronomistic Tradition. Genesis 15: The Historical and Theological Necessity of a Diachronic Approach," in: J.C. de Moor (ed.). *Synchronic or Diachronic? A Debate on Method in Old Testament Exegesis.* Old Testament Studies 34. Leiden: Brill, 1995, 129-144.

Noth, M. *Überlieferungsgeschichte des Pentateuch.* 2nd ed. Stuttgart: Kohlhammer, 1948.

Nygren, A. *Der Römerbrief.* Göttingen: Vandenhoeck & Ruprecht, 1951.

O'Rourke, J.J. "Pistis in Romans." *Catholic Biblical Quarterly* 35 (1973) 188-194.

Oegema, G.S. *Für Israel und die Völker. Studien zum alttestamentlich-jüdischen Hintergrund der paulinischen Theologie.* Novum Testamentum Supplements 95. Leiden: Brill, 1999.

Oeming, M. *Das wahre Israel. Die genealogische Vorhalle 1Chronik 1-9.* Beiträge zur Wissenschaft vom Alten und Neuen Testament 128. Stuttgart: Kohlhammer, 1990.

Oeming, M. "Der Glaube Abrahams. Zur Rezeptionsgeschichte von Gen 15,6 zur Zeit des zweiten Tempels." *Zeitschrift für die alttestamentliche Wissenschaft* 110 (1998) 16-33 = in: *Verstehen und Glauben. Exegetische Bausteine zu einer Theologie des Alten Testaments.* Bonner biblische Beiträge 142. Berlin: Philo, 2003, 77-91.

Oeming, M. "Ist Genesis 15,6 ein Beleg für die Anrechnung des Glaubens zur Gerechtigkeit?" *Zeitschrift für die alttestamentliche Wissenschaft* 95 (1983) 182-197 = in: *Verstehen und Glauben. Exegetische Bausteine zu einer Theologie des Alten Testaments.* Bonner biblische Beiträge 142. Berlin: Philo, 2003, 63-75.

Oh, S.-J. "'Der Gerechte wird aus Glauben leben': eine exegetische und traditionsgeschichtliche Untersuchung zum Zitat Hab 2,4b bei Paulus als ein Beitrag zum Verständnis des Ursprungs des neutestamentlichen Glaubensbegriffes in biblisch-theologischer Betrachtung." Ph.D. Dissertation. Tübingen, 1992.

Ostmeyer, K.-H. "Typologie und Typos. Analyse eines schwierigen Verhältnisses." *New Testament Studies* 46 (2000) 112-131.

Ota, S. "Absolute Use of ΠΙΣΤΙΣ and ΠΙΣΤΙΣ ΧΡΙΣΤΟΥ in Paul." *Annual of the Japanese Biblical Institute* 23 (1997) 64-82.

Otero Lazáro, T. "Abraham justificación par la fe (Gal 3; Rom 4)." *Burgense* 42 (2001) 5-32.

Patsch, H. "Zum alttestamentlichen Hintergrund von Römer 4,25 und I Petrus 2,24." *Zeitschrift für die neutestamentliche Wissenschaft* 60 (1969) 273-279.

Pederson, J. *Israel, Its Life and Culture.* Part 1. London: Oxford University Press, 1926 (quoted therafter) (= as South Florida Studies in the History of Judaism 28, with an introduction by J. Strange. Atlanta: Scholars Press, 1991).

Penna, R. "The Meaning of πάρεσις in Romans 3:25c and the Pauline Thought of Divine Acquittal," in: M. Bachmann (ed.) *Lutherische und Neue Paulusperspektive. Beiträge zu einem Schlüsselproblem der gegenwärtigen exegetischen Diskussion.* Tübingen: Mohr (Siebeck) 2005, 251-274.

Perlitt, L. *Bundestheologie im Alten Testament.* Wissenschaftliche Monographien zum Alten und Neuen Testament 36. Neukirchen-Vluyn: Neukirchener Verlag, 1969.

Peterson, E. *Ausgewählte Schriften.* Vol. 6: *Der Brief an die Römer* (B. Nichtweiß & F. Hahn, eds.). Würzburg: Echter, 1997.

Pfeiffer, E. "Glaube im Alten Testament. Eine grammatisch-lexikalische Nachprüfung gegenwärtiger Theorien." *Zeitschrift für die alttestamentliche Wissenschaft* 71 (1959) 151-164.

Pfleiderer, O. *Das Urchristentum. Seine Schriften und Lehren, in geschichtlichem Zusammenhang.* Vol. 1: *Vorwort. Einleitung. Der Apostel Paulus. Geschichtsbücher.* 2nd ed. Berlin: Reimer, 1902.

Pfleiderer, O. *Der Paulinismus. Ein Beitrag zur Geschichte der urchristlichen Theologie.* 2nd ed. Leipzig: Reisland, 1890.

Philonenko, M. "L'Apocalyptique Qumrânienne," in: D. Hellholm (ed.). *Apocalypticism in the Mediterranean World and the Near East*. Tübingen: Mohr (Siebeck), 1983, 211-218.

Plag, C. "Paulus und die *Gezera schawa*: Zur Übernahme rabbinischer Auslegungskunst." *Judaica* 50 (1994) 135-140.

Pluta, A. *Gottes Bundestreue. Ein Schlüsselbegriff in Röm 3,25a*. Stuttgarter Bibelstudien 34. Stuttgart: Katholisches Bibelwerk, 1969.

Portnoy, S.L. & D.L. Petersen."Genesis, Wellhausen and the Computer: A Response." *Zeitschrift für die alttestamentliche Wissenschaft* 96 (1984) 421-425.

Porton, G.G. "Midrash: Palestinian Jews and the Hebrew Bible in the Greco-Roman Period." *Aufstieg und Niedergang der Römischen Welt* 2,19,2, 1979, 103-138.

Porton, G.G. Art. "Rabbinic Literature: Midrashim." *Dictionary of New Testament Background* 2000, 889-893.

Preisker, M. *Der Glaubensbegriff bei Philon*. Breslau: Gärtner, 1936.

Preuß, H.D. *Theologie des Alten Testaments*. Vol 2: *Israels Weg mit JHWH*. Stuttgart: Kohlhammer, 1992.

Procksch, O. *Die Genesis übersetzt und erklärt*. Kommentar zum Alten Testament. 2nd and 3rd ed. Leipzig: Deichert, 1924.

Procksch, O. *Theologie des Alten Testaments*. Gütersloh: Bertelsmann, 1950.

Quarles, C.L. "From Faith to Faith. A Fresh Examination of the Prepositional Series in Romans 1:17." *Novum Testamentum* 45 (2003) 1-21.

Rad, G. von. *Das Erste Buch Mose. Genesis*. Das Alte Testament Deutsch. Göttingen: Vandenhoeck & Ruprecht, 8th ed. 1967, 9th 1972 (= 12th ed. 1987).

Rad, G. von. *Das Opfer des Abraham. Mit Texten von Luther, Kierkegaard, Kolakowski und Bildern von Rembrandt*. Kaiser Traktate 6. München: Kaiser, 1971.

Rad, G. von. *Der Heilige Krieg im alten Israel*. Zürich: Zwingli, 1951a.

Rad, G. von. "Die Anrechnung des Glaubens zur Gerechtigkeit." *Theologische Literaturzeitung* 76 (1951) 129-132 = in: *Gesammelte Studien zum Alten Testament*. Theologische Bücherei 8. München: Kaiser, 1965, 130-135.

Rad, G. von. *Theologie des Alten Testaments*. Vol. 1: *Die Theologie der geschichtlichen Überlieferungen Israels*. München: Kaiser, 1957, 4th ed. 1962 (= 9th ed. 1987). Vol. 2: *Die Theologie der prophetischen Überlieferungen Israels*. München: Kaiser, 1960, 4th ed. 1965 (= 8th ed. 1984).

Radday, Y.T., H. Shore, M.A. Pollatschek & D. Wickmann. "Genesis, Wellhausen and the Computer." *Zeitschrift für die alttestamentliche Wissenschaft* 94 (1982) 467-481.

Rahner, K. "Die anonymen Christen," in: *Schriften zur Theologie*. Vol. 6: *Neuere Schriften*. Einsiedeln: Benziger, 545-554.

Räisänen, H. "Das 'Gesetz des Glaubens' (Röm. 3.27) und das 'Gesetz des Geistes' (Röm. 8.2)." *New Testament Studies* 26 (1979/1980) 101-117 = in: *The Torah and Christ. Essays in German and English on the Problem of the Law in Early Christianity*. Publications of the Finnish Exegetical Society 45. Helsinki: Finnish Exegetical Society, 1986, 95-118.

Räisänen, H. "Die Wirkungsgeschichte der Bibel. Eine Herausforderung an die exegetische Forschung." *Evangelische Theologie* 52 (1992) 337-347.

Räisänen, H. "Legalism and Salvation by the Law. Paul's Portrayal of the Jewish Religion as a Historical and Theological Problem," in: S. Pederson (ed.). *Die paulinische Literatur und Theologie*. Göttingen: Vandenhoeck & Ruprecht, 1980, 63-83 = in: *The Torah and Christ. Essays in German and English on the Problem of the Law in Early Christianity*. Publications of the Finnish Exegetical Society 45. Helsinki: Finnish Exegetical Society, 1986, 25-54.

Räisänen, H. "Sprachliches zum Spiel des Paulus mit νόμος," in: J. Kiilunen et al. (eds.) *Glaube und Gerechtigkeit. In memoriam R. Gyllenberg.* Helsinki: Finnish Exegetical Society, 1983, 131-154 = in: *The Torah and Christ. Essays in German and English on the Problem of the Law in Early Christianity.* Publications of the Finnish Exegetical Society 45. Helsinki: Finnish Exegetical Society, 1986, 119-147.

Rapa, R.K. *The Meaning of "Works of the Law" in Galatians and Romans.* Studies in Biblical Literature 31. New York: P. Lang, 2001.

Reichert, A. *Der Römerbrief als Gratwanderung. Eine Untersuchung zur Abfassungsproblematik.* Forschungen zur Religion und Literatur des Alten und Neuen Testaments 194. Göttingen: Vandenhoeck & Ruprecht, 2001.

Reitzenstein, R. *Die hellenistischen Mysterienreligionen. Nach ihren Grundgedanken und Wirkungen.* 3rd. ed. Leipzig: Teubner, 1927 (= Darmstadt: Wissenschaftliche Buchgesellschaft, 1980).

Rendtorff, R. *Das überlieferungsgeschichtliche Problem des Pentateuch.* Beihefte zur Zeitschrift für die alttestamentliche Wissenschaft 147. Berlin: de Gruyter, 1977.

Rendtorff, R. *Die Gesetze in der Priesterschrift. Eine gattungesgeschichtliche Untersuchung.* Forschungen zur Religion und Literatur des Alten und Neuen Testaments 44. Göttingen: Vandenhoeck & Ruprecht, 1954.

Rendtorff, R. "Genesis 15 im Rahmen der theologischen Bearbeitung der Vätergeschichten," in: R. Albertz et al. (eds.) *Werden und Wirken des Alten Testaments.* FS C. Westermann. Göttingen: Vandenhoeck & Ruprecht, 1980, 74-81.

Rendtorff, R. *Theologie des Alten Testaments. Ein kanonischer Entwurf.* Vol. 1: *Kanonische Grundlegung.* Neukirchen-Vluyn: Neukirchener Verlag, 1999.

Reventlow, H. Graf. *Opfere deinen Sohn. Eine Auslegung von Genesis 22.* Biblische Studien 53. Neukirchen-Vluyn: Neukirchener Verlag, 1968.

Rhee, V. *Faith in Hebrews. Analysis within the Context of Christology, Eschatology, and Ethics.* Studies in Biblical Literature 19. Frankfurt: Lang, 2001.

Rhyne, C.T. *Faith Establishes the Law.* Society of Biblical Literature Dissertation Series 55. Chico: Scholars Press, 1981.

Richter, W. *Die Bearbeitungen des "Retterbuches" in der deuteronomischen Epoche.* Bonner biblische Beiträge 21. Bonn: Hanstein, 1964.

Ricœur, R. "Stellung und Funktion der Metapher in der biblischen Sprache," in: P. Ricœur & E. Jüngel. *Metapher. Zur Hermeneutik religiöser Sprache.* Evangelische Theologie Sonderheft. München: Kaiser, 1974, 24-45.

Ridderbos, H. *Paulus. Ein Entwurf seiner Theologie.* Wuppertal: Brockhaus, 1970.

Rieger, H.-M. "Eine Religion der Gnade. Zur 'Bundesnomismus'-Theorie von E. P. Sanders," in: F. Avemarie & H. Lichtenberger (eds.). *Bund und Tora. Zur theologischen Begriffsgeschichte in alttestamentlicher, frühjüdischer und urchristlicher Tradition.* Wissenschaftliche Untersuchungen zum Neuen Testament 92. Tübingen: Mohr (Siebeck), 1996, 129-161.

Ritschl, A. *Die christliche Lehre von der Rechtfertigung und Versöhnung.* Vol. 2: *Der biblische Stoff der Lehre.* 3rd. ed., Vol. 3: *Die positive Entwickelung der Lehre.* 3rd ed. Bonn: Marcus, 1889, 1888.

Robinson, D.W.B. "'Faith of Jesus Christ' – A New Testament Debate." *Reformed Theological Review* 29 (1970) 71-81.

Robinson, J.A.T. *The Body. A Study in Pauline Theology.* London: SCM Press, 1952.

Röhser, G. *Metaphorik und Personfikation der Sünde.* Wissenschaftliche Untersuchungen zum Neuen Testament 2/25. Tübingen: Mohr (Siebeck), 1987.

Rokéah, D. "A Note on the Philological Aspect of Paul's Theory of Faith." *Theologische Zeitschrift* 47 (1991) 299-306.

Roloff, J. "Abraham im Neuen Testament. Beobachtungen zu einem Aspekt Biblischer Theologie," in: *Exegetische Verantwortung in der Kirche. Aufsätze* (M. Karrer, ed.). Göttingen: Vandenhoeck & Ruprecht, 1990, 231-254.

Römer, T.C. "Gen 15 und Gen 17. Beobachtungen und Anfragen zu einem Dogma der 'neueren' und 'neuesten' Pentateuchkritik." *Dielheimer Blätter zum Alten Testament* 26 (1990) 32-47.

Römer, T.C. "Recherches actuelles sur le cycle d'Abraham," in: A. Wénin (ed.). *Studies in the Book of Genesis. Literature, Redaction and History*. Bibliotheca ephemeridum theologicarum lovaniensium 155. Leuven: Leuven University Press, 2001, 179-211.

Roo, J.C.R. de. "The Concept of 'Works of the Law' in Jewish and Christian Literature," in: S.E. Porter & B.W.R. Pearson (eds.). *Christian-Jewish Relations through the Centuries*. Journal for the Study of the New Testament: Supplement Series 192. Sheffield: Sheffield Academic Press, 2000, 116-147.

Rose, C. *Die Wolke der Zeugen. Eine exegetisch-traditionsgeschichtliche Untersuchung zu Hebräer 10,32-12,3*. Wissenschaftliche Untersuchungen zum Neuen Testament 2/60. Tübingen: Mohr (Siebeck), 1994.

Rottzoll, D.U. "Gen 15,6 – Ein Beleg für den Glauben als Werkgerechtigkeit." *Zeitschrift für die alttestamentliche Wissenschaft* 106 (1994) 21-27.

Roura, J.L. "Paul: Exégète et théologien dans Romains 4,1-12." *Revue des sciences religieuses* 80 (2006) 83-97.

Rudolph, W. *Esra und Nehemia*. Handbuch zum Alten Testament. Tübingen: Mohr (Siebeck), 1949.

Rüger, H.-P. "Le Siracide: un livre à la frontière du canon," in: J.-D. Kaestli & O. Wermelinger (eds.). *Le Canon de l'Ancien Testament. Sa formation et son histoire*. Geneva: Labor et Fides, 1984, 47-69.

Ruppert, L. "Abraham als Stammvater und Vorbild Israels," in: C. Niemand (ed.). *Forschungen zum Neuen Testament und seiner Umwelt*. FS A. Fuchs. Linzer Philosophisch-Theologische Beiträge 7. Frankfurt: Lang, 2002, 15-29.

Ruppert, L. "Überlegungen zur Überlieferungs-, Kompositions- und Redaktionsgeschichte von Genesis 15," in: A. Graupner (ed.). *Verbindungslinien*. FS W.H. Schmidt. Neukirchen-Vluyn: Neukirchener Verlag, 2000, 295-309.

Sanday, W. & A.C. Headlam. *A Critical and Exegetical Commentary on the Epistle to the Romans*. International Critical Commentary. New York: Charles Scribner's Sons, 1895.

Sanders, E.P. *Paul and Palestinian Judaism. A Comparison of Patterns of Religion*. London: SCM Press, 1977.

Sanders, E.P. *Paul, the Law, and the Jewish People*. Philadelphia: Fortress, 1983.

Sanders, J.A. "Habakkuk in Qumran, Paul and the Old Testament." *Journal of Religion* 39 (1959) 232-244.

Sandmel, S. *Philo's Place in Judaism. A Study of Conceptions of Abraham in Jewish Literature*. New York: KTAV, 1971.

Sänger, D. *Die Verkündigung des Gekreuzigten und Israel. Studien zum Verhältnis von Kirche und Israel bei Paulus und im frühen Christentum*. Wissenschaftliche Untersuchungen zum Neuen Testament 75. Tübingen: Mohr (Siebeck), 1994.

Sauer, G. "Die Abrahamgestalt im 'Lob der Väter.' Auswahl und Intention." *Wiener Jahrbuch für Theologie* 1 (1996) 387-412.

Sauer, G. *Jesus Sirach/Ben Sira*. Das Alte Testament Deutsch, Apokryphen. Göttingen: Vandenhoeck & Ruprecht, 2000.

Schelkle, K.H. *Paulus der Lehrer der Väter. Die altkirchliche Auslegung von Römer 1-11*. Düsseldorf: Patmos, 1956.

Schenk, W. "Die Gerechtigkeit Gottes und der Glaube Christi." *Theologische Literatur-zeitung* 97 (1972) 161-174.

Schenk, W. "Glaube im lukanischen Doppelwerk," F. Hahn & H. Klein (eds.). *Der Glaube im Neuen Testament.* FS H. Binder. Neukirchen-Vluyn: Neukirchener Verlag, 1982, 69-92.

Schiffmann, L.H. "Origin and Early History of the Qumran Sect." *Biblical Archeologist* 58 (1995) 37-48.

Schiffmann, L.H. "The New Halakhic Letter (4QMMT) and the Origins of the Dead Sea Sect." *Biblical Archeologist* 53 (1990) 64-73.

Schiffmann, L.H. "The Sadducean Origins of the Dead Sea Scrolls Sect," in: H. Shanks (ed.). *Understanding the Dead Sea Scrolls.* New York, 1992, 35-49.

Schlatter, A. *Der Glaube im Neuen Testament.* 4th ed. Stuttgart: Calwer Verlag, 1927 (= 6th ed. with an introduction by P. Stuhlmacher, 1982).

Schlatter, A. *Die Theologie des Neuen Testaments.* Vol. 2: *Die Lehre der Apostel.* Calw: Verlag der Vereinsbuchhandlung, 1910.

Schlatter, A. *Gottes Gerechtigkeit. Ein Kommentar zum Römerbrief.* Stuttgart: Calwer Verlag, 1935 (= 5th ed. 1975).

Schlatter, A. "Karl Barth's 'Römerbrief'." *Die Furche* 12 (1922) 228-232 = in: J. Moltmann (ed.). *Anfänge der dialektischen Theologie.* Part 1: *Karl Barth, Heinrich Barth, Emil Brunner.* Theologische Bücherei 17. 2nd ed. München: Kaiser, 1966, 142-147.

Schlatter, A. *Paulus der Bote Jesu. Eine Deutung seiner Briefe an die Korinther.* Stuttgart: Calwer Vereinsbuchhandlung, 1934.

Schlatter, A. *Rückblick auf meine Lebensarbeit.* 2nd ed. Stuttgart: Calwer Verlag, 1977.

Schlatter, W. *Glaube und Gehorsam.* Beiträge zur Förderung christlicher Theologie 5/6. Gütersloh: Bertelsmann, 1901, 31-48.

Schlier, H. *Der Brief an die Galater.* Kritisch-exegetischer Kommentar über das Neue Testament. 4th ed. Göttingen: Vandenhoeck & Ruprecht, 1965.

Schlier, H. *Der Römerbrief.* Herders theologischer Kommentar zum Neuen Testament. Freiburg: Herder, 1977.

Schlier, H. *Grundzüge einer paulinischen Theologie.* Freiburg: Herder, 1978.

Schmeller, T. *Paulus und die 'Diabtribe.' Eine vergleichende Stilinterpretation.* Neutestamentliche Abhandlungen 19. Münster: Aschendorff, 1987.

Schmid, H.H. "Gerechtigkeit und Glaube. Genesis 15,1-6 und sein biblisch-theologischer Kontext." *Evangelische Theologie* 40 (1980) 396-420.

Schmid, H.H. "Rechtfertigung als Schöpfungsgeschehen. Notizen zur alttestamentlichen Vorgeschichte neutestamentlicher Themen," in: J. Friedrich et al. (eds.) *Rechtfertigung.* FS E. Käsemann. Tübingen: Mohr (Siebeck), 1976a, 403-414.

Schmid, H.H. *Der sogenannte Jahwist. Beobachtungen und Fragen zur Pentateuchforschung.* Zürich: Theologischer Verlag, 1976.

Schmid, H.H. *Gerechtigkeit als Weltordnung.* Beiträge zur historischen Theologie 40. Tübingen: Mohr (Siebeck), 1968.

Schmid, K. *Erzväter und Exodus. Untersuchungen zur doppelten Begründung der Ursprünge Israels innerhalb der Geschichtsbücher des Alten Testaments.* Wissenschaftliche Monographien zum Alten und Neuen Testament 81. Neukirchen-Vluyn: Neukirchener Verlag, 1999.

Schmidt, H.W. *Der Brief des Paulus an die Römer.* Theologischer Handkommentar zum Neuen Testament. 2nd ed. Berlin: Evangelische Verlagsanstalt, 1966.

Schmidt, L. "Weisheit und Geschichte beim Elohisten," in: A.A. Diestel et al. (eds.) *'Jedes Ding hat seine Zeit...' Studien zur israelitischen und altorientalischen Weisheit.* FS D. Michel. Beihefte zur Zeitschrift für die alttestamentliche Wissenschaft 241. Berlin: de Gruyter, 1996, 209-225.

Schmidt, W.H. "Die Frage nach der Einheit des Alten Testaments – im Spannungsfeld von Religionsgeschichte und Theologie," in: I. Baldermann et al. (eds.) *Der eine Gott der beiden Testamente.* Jahrbuch für Biblische Theologie 2. Neukirchen-Vluyn: Neukirchener Verlag, 1987, 33-57.

Schmithals, W. *Der Römerbrief als historisches Problem.* Studien zum Neuen Testament 9. Gütersloh: Mohn, 1975.

Schmithals, W. *Der Römerbrief. Ein Kommentar.* Gütersloh: Mohn, 1988.

Schmitt, H.-C. "Redaktion des Pentateuch im Geiste der Prophetie. Beobachtungen zur Bedeutung der 'Glaubens'-Thematik innerhalb der Theologie des Pentateuch." *Vetus Testamentum* 32 (1982) 170-189.

Schmitt, R. *Gottesgerechtigkeit – Heilsgeschichte – Israel in der Theologie des Paulus.* Europäische Hochschulschriften 23/240. Frankfurt: Lang, 1984.

Schmitz, O. "Abraham im Spätjudentum und im Urchristentum," in: *Aus Schrift und Geschichte.* FS A. Schlatter. Stuttgart: Calwer Vereinsbuchhandlung, 1922, 99-123.

Schmitz, O. *Das Lebensgefühl des Paulus.* München: Beck, 1922.

Schmitz, O. *Die Christusgemeinschaft des Paulus im Lichte seines Genetivgebrauchs.* Neutestamentliche Forschungen 1/2. Gütersloh: Bertelsmann, 1924.

Schnabel, E. "Glauben als unbedingtes Vertrauen im NT," in: *Jahrbuch für evangelikale Theologie.* Wuppertal: Brockhaus, 1991, 63-86.

Schnackenburg, R. "Glauben im Verständnis der Bibel," in: J.M. Reuss (ed.). *Glauben heute. Überlegungen für den Dienst am Glauben.* Mainz: Matthias-Grünewald-Verlag, 1962, 13-35 = in: *Aufsätze und Studien zum Neuen Testament.* Leipzig: St. Benno, 1973, 61-85.

Schnelle, U. *Einleitung in das Neue Testament.* 4th ed. Göttingen: Vandenhoeck & Ruprecht, 2002.

Schnelle, U. *Gerechtigkeit und Christusgegenwart. Vorpaulinische und paulinische Tauftheologie.* Göttinger theologische Arbeiten 24. 2nd ed. Göttingen: Vandenhoeck & Ruprecht, 1986.

Schnelle, U. *Paulus. Leben und Denken.* Berlin: de Gruyter, 2003.

Schoeps, H.-J. *Paulus. Die Theologie des Apostels im Lichte der jüdischen Religionsgeschichte.* Tübingen: Mohr (Siebeck), 1959 (= Darmstadt: Wissenschaftliche Buchgesellschaft, 1972).

Schoeps, H.-J. "The Sacrifice of Isaac in Paul's Theology." *Journal of Biblical Literature* 65 (1946) 385-392.

Schottroff, W. Art. "חשב." *Theologisches Handwörterbuch zum Alten Testament* 1, 1971, 641-646.

Schrage, W. *Ethik des Neuen Testaments.* Grundrisse zum Neuen Testament. Das Neue Testament Deutsch. Ergänzungsreihe 4. 2nd ed. Göttingen: Vandenhoeck & Ruprecht, 1989.

Schreiner, T.R. *Paul, Apostle of God's Glory in Christ. A Pauline Theology.* Downers Grove: InterVarsity Press, 2001.

Schreiner, T.R. *Romans.* Baker exegetical commentary on the New Testament. Grand Rapids: Baker, 1998.

Schreiner, T.R. "'Works of Law' in Paul." *Novum Testamentum* 33 (1991) 217-244.

Schrenk, G. Art. "δικη κτλ." *Theologisches Wörterbuch zum Neuen Testament* 2, 1935, 180-229.

Schunack, G. *Der Hebräerbrief.* Zürcher Bibelkommentare. Zürich: Theologischer Verlag, 2002.

Schunack, G. "Exegetische Beobachtungen zum Verständnis des Glaubens im Hebr.," in: S. Maser & E. Schlarb (eds.). *Text und Geschichte.* FS D. Lührmann. Marburger Theologische Studien 50. Marburg: Elwert, 1999, 208-232.

Schunack, G. "Glaube in griechischer Religiosität," in: B. Kollmann, W. Reinbold & A. Steudel (eds.). *Antikes Judentum und frühes Christentum.* FS H. Stegemann. Beihefte zur Zeitschrift für die neutestamentliche Wissenschaft 97. Berlin: de Gruyter, 1999.

Schürmann, H. "'Das Gesetz des Christus' (Gal. 6.2). Jesu Verhalten und Wort als letztgültige sittliche Norm nach Paulus," in: J. Gnilka (ed.). *Neues Testament und Kirche.* FS R. Schnackenburg. Freiburg: Herder, 1974, 282-300 = in: *Studien zur neutestamentlichen Ethik* (ed. T. Söding). Stuttgarter biblische Aufsatzbände 7. Stuttgart: Katholisches Bibelwerk, 1990, 53-77.

Schweitzer, A. *Geschichte der paulinischen Forschung von der Reformation bis auf die Gegenwart.* Tübingen: Mohr (Siebeck), 1911.

Schweitzer, A. *Mystik des Apostels Paulus.* Tübingen: Mohr (Siebeck), 1930 (= 1981 as UTB 1091 with an introduction by W.G. Kümmel).

Scott, J.M. "A New Approach to Habakkuk II 4-5a." *Vetus Testamentum* 35 (1985) 330-340.

Scroggs, R. "Paul as Rhetorician. Two Homilies in Romans 1-11," in: R. Hamerton-Kelly & R. Scroggs (eds.). *Jews, Greeks and Christians. Religious Cultures in Late Antiquity.* FS W.D. Davies. Studies in Judaism in Late Antiquity 21. Leiden: Brill, 1976, 271-298.

Seebass, H. "Gehörten Verheißungen zum ältesten Bestand der Väter-Erzählungen?" *Biblica* 64 (1983) 189-210.

Seebass, H. *Genesis.* Vol. 2/1: *Vätergeschichte I (11,27-22,24).* Neukirchen-Vluyn: Neukirchener Verlag, 1997.

Seebass, H. "Zu Gen 15." *Wort und Dienst* 7 (1963) 132-149.

Seeberg, A. *Der Katechismus der Urchristenheit.* Leipzig: Deichert, 1903 (= as Theologische Bücherei 26, with an introduction by F. Hahn. München: Kaiser, 1966).

Segal, A.F. "'He who did not spare his own son...': Jesus, Paul, and Akedah," in: P. Richardson & J.C. Hurd (eds.). *From Jesus to Paul.* FS F.W. Beare. Waterloo: Wilfried Laurier University Press, 1984, 169-184.

Segal, A.F. "The Akedah. Some Reconsiderations," in: H. Cancik, H. Lichtenberger & P. Schäfer (eds.). *Geschichte-Tradition-Reflexion.* FS M. Hengel. Vol. 1. Tübingen: Mohr (Siebeck), 1996, 99-116.

Seifrid, M.A. & R.K.J. Tan. *The Pauline Writings. An Annotated Bibliography.* IBR Bibliographies 9. Grand Rapids: Baker, 2002.

Seifrid, M.A. *Christ, Our Righteousness. Paul's Theology of Justification.* Leicester: Apollos, 2000.

Seifrid, M.A. *Justification By Faith. The Origin and Development of a Central Pauline Theme.* NovTSup 68. Leiden: Brill, 1992.

Seifrid, M.A. "Paul's Use of Righteousness Language Against Its Hellenistic Background," in: Carson, D.A., P.T. O'Brien & M.A. Seifrid (eds.). *Justification and Variegated Nomism:* Vol. 2: *The Paradoxes of Paul.* Tübingen: Mohr (Siebeck), 2004, 39-74.

Seils, M. *Glaube.* Handbuch Systematischer Theologie 13. Gütersloh: Gütersloher Verlagshaus, 1996.

Sellin, E. & L. Rost. *Einleitung in das Alte Testament.* 8th ed. Heidelberg: Quelle & Meyer, 1949.

Seybold, K. *Die Psalmen.* Handbuch zum Alten Testament. Tübingen: Mohr (Siebeck), 1996.

Seybold, K. Art. "חשׁב." *Theologisches Wörterbuch zum Alten Testament* 3, 1982, 243-261.

Siegert, F. *Argumentation bei Paulus, gezeigt an Röm 9-11.* Wissenschaftliche Untersuchungen zum Neuen Testament 34. Tübingen: Mohr (Siebeck), 1985.

Siegert, F. *Drei hellenistisch-jüdische Predigten. Ps.-Philon, "Über Jona," "Über Simson" und "Über die Gottesbezeichnung 'wohltätig verzehrendes Feuer'."* Wissenschaftliche Untersuchungen zum Neuen Testament 20. Tübingen: Mohr (Siebeck), 1980.

Siker, J.S. *Disinheriting the Jews. Abraham in Early Christian Controversy.* Louisville: Westminster/John Knox, 1991.

Silberman, L.H. "Paul's Midrash: Reflections on Romans 4," in: J.T. Carroll, C.H. Cosgrove & E.E. Johnson (eds.). *Faith and History.* FS P.W. Meyer. Atlanta: Scholars Press, 1990, 99-104.

Simpson, C.A. *The Early Traditions of Israel. A Critical Analysis of the Predeuteronomic Narrative of the Hexateuch.* Oxford: Blackwell, 1948.

Ska, J.L. "Essai sur la nature et la signification du cycle d'Abraham," in: A. Wénin (ed.). *Studies in the Book of Genesis. Literature, Redaction and History.* Bibliotheca ephemeridum theologicarum lovaniensium 155. Leuven: Leuven University Press, 2001, 153-177.

Skinner, J. *Genesis.* International Critical Commentary. 2nd ed. Edinburgh: T. & T. Clark, 1930 (= 1969).

Slenczka, R. "Glaube VI. Reformation/Neuzeit/Systematisch-Theologisch." *Theologische Realenzyklopädie* 13, 1984, 318-365.

Smend, R. (sen.) *Die Erzählung des Hexateuch auf ihre Quellen untersucht.* Berlin: Reimer, 1912.

Smend, R. (sen.) *Die Weisheit des Jesus Sirach.* Berlin: Reimer, 1906.

Smend, R. "Zur Geschichte von הֶאֱמִין," in: *Hebräische Wortforschung.* FS W. Baumgartner. Vetus Testamentum Supplements 16. Leiden: Brill, 1967.

Smith, D.M. "O DE DIKAIOS EK PISTEWS ZHSETAI," in: B.L. Daniels & M.J. Suggs (eds.). *Studies in the History and Text of the New Testament.* FS K.W. Clark. Salt Lake City: University of Utah, 1967, 13-25.

Snijders, L.A. "Genesis xv. The Covenant with Abram," in: B. Gemser & J. Hoftijzer (eds.). *Studies on the Book of Genesis.* Old Testament Studies 12. Leiden: Brill, 1958, 261-279.

Soggin, J.A. *Das Buch Genesis. Kommentar* (T. Frauenlob et al., trs.). Darmstadt: Wissenschaftliche Buchgesellschaft, 1997.

Soggin, J.A. "'Fede' e 'giustizia' in Abramo, Genesi Cap. 15," in: M. Weippert & S. Timm (eds.). *Meilenstein.* FS H. Donner. Ägypten und Altes Testament 30. Wiesbaden: Harrassowitz, 1995, 259-265.

Sommerlath, E. *Der Ursprung des neuen Lebens nach Paulus.* Leipzig: Dörffling & Franke, 1923.

Song, C. *Reading Romans as a Diatribe.* Studies in Biblical Literature 59. Frankfurt: Lang, 2004.

Speiser, E.A. *Genesis.* Anchor Bible. Garden City, 1964.

Staerk, W. "Zur alttestamentlichen Literarkritik." *Zeitschrift für die alttestamentliche Wissenschaft* 42 (1924) 34-74.

Stanley, C.D. *Arguing with Scripture. The Rhetoric of Quotations in the Letters of Paul.* London: T. & T. Clark, 2004.

Stanley, D.M. "Ad historiam Exegeseos Rom 4,25." *Verbum domini* 29 (1951) 257-274.

Stegner, W.R. "The Ancient Jewish Synagogue Homily," in: D.E. Aune (ed.). *Greco-Roman Literature and the New Testament. Selected Forms and Genres*. Society of Biblical Literature Sources for Biblical Study 21. Atlanta: Scholars Press, 1988, 51-69.

Steins, G. *Die 'Bindung Isaaks' im Kanon (Gen 22). Grundlagen und Programm einer kanonisch-intertextuellen Lektüre. Mit einer Spezialbibliographie zu Gen 22*. Herders biblische Studien 20. Freiburg: Herder, 1999.

Steins, G. "Die Versuchung Abrahams (Gen 22,1-19). Ein neuer Versuch," in: A. Wénin (ed.). *Studies in the Book of Genesis. Literature, Redaction and History*. Bibliotheca ephemeridum theologicarum lovaniensium 155. Leuven: Leuven University Press, 2001, 509-519.

Stemberger, G. "Die Stephanusrede (Apg 7) und die jüdische Tradition." *Studien zum Neuen Testament und seiner Umwelt* 1 (1976) 154-174 = in: *Studien zum rabbinischen Judentum*. Stuttgarter Biblische Aufsatzbände 10. Stuttgart: Katholisches Bibelwerk, 1990, 229-250.

Stendahl, K. *Final Account*. Minneapolis: Fortress, 1995.

Stendahl, K. "Paul Among Jews and Gentiles," in: *Paul among Jews and Gentiles, and Other Essays*. Philadelphia: Fortress, 1976, 1-77.

Stendahl, K. "Paul and the Introspective Conscience of the West." *Harvard Theological Review* 56 (1963) 199-215 = in: *Paul among Jews and Gentiles, and Other Essays*. Philadelphia: Fortress, 1976, 78-96.

Sterling, G.E. Art. "Philo." *Dictionary of New Testament Background* 2000, 789-793.

Steudel, A. *Die Midrasch zur Eschatologie aus der Qumrangemeinde (4QMidr Eschat^{a.b}). Materielle Rekonstruktion, Textbestand, Gattung und traditionsgeschichtliche Einordnung des durch 4Q 174 ("Florilegium") und 4Q 177 ("Catena A") repräsentierten Werkes aus den Qumranfunden*. Studies on the texts of the desert of Judah 13. Leiden: Brill, 1994.

Stowers, S.K. *A Rereading of Romans. Justice, Jews, and Gentiles*. New Haven: Yale University Press, 1994.

Stowers, S.K. "ΕΚ ΠΙΣΤΕΩΣ and ΔΙΑ ΤΗΣ ΠΙΣΤΕΩΣ in Romans 3:30." *Journal of Biblical Literature* 108 (1989) 665-674.

Stowers, S.K. "Paul's Dialogue with a Fellow Jew in Romans 3:1-9." *Catholic Biblical Quarterly* 46 (1984) 707-722.

Stowers, S.K. Review of R.H. Bell, *No One Seeks for God. Exegetical and Theological Study of Romans 1.18-3.20. Journal of Biblical Literature* 119 (2000) 370-373.

Stowers, S.K. *The Diatribe and Paul's Letter to the Romans*. Society of Biblical Literature Dissertation Series 58. Chico: Scholars Press, 1981.

Strack, H.L. *Die Genesis übersetzt und ausgelegt. Kurzgefaßter Kommentar zu den heiligen Schriften Alten und Neuen Testamentes*. Vol. A 1/1. 2nd ed. München: Beck, 1905.

Strecker, G. *Theologie des Neuen Testaments* (ed. F.W. Horn). De Gruyter Lehrbuch. Berlin: de Gruyter, 1996.

Strobel, A. *Untersuchungen zum eschatologischen Verzögerungsproblem. Auf Grund der spätjüdisch-urchristlichen Geschichte von Habakuk 2,2ff*. Novum Testamentum Supplements 2. Leiden: Brill, 1961.

Stuhlmacher, P. & D.A. Hagner. *Revisiting Paul's Doctrine of Justification. A Challenge to the New Perspective*. Downers Grove: InterVarsity Press, 2001.

Stuhlmacher, P. *Biblische Theologie des Neuen Testaments*. Vol. 1: *Grundlegung. Von Jesus zu Paulus*. 2nd ed. Göttingen: Vandenhoeck & Ruprecht, 1997.

Stuhlmacher, P. "'Christus ist hier, der gestorben ist, ja vielmehr, der auch auferweckt ist, der zur Rechten Gottes ist und uns vertritt'," in: F. Avemarie & H. Lichtenberger (eds.). *Auferstehung – Resurrection.* Wissenschaftliche Untersuchungen zum Neuen Testament 135. Tübingen: Mohr (Siebeck), 2001, 351-361.

Stuhlmacher, P. "Das Ende des Gesetzes. Über Ursprung und Ansatz der paulinischen Theologie." *Zeitschrift für Theologie und Kirche* 67 (1970) 14-39 = in: *Versöhnung, Gesetz und Gerechtigkeit. Aufsätze zur biblischen Theologie.* Göttingen: Vandenhoeck & Ruprecht, 1981, 166-191.

Stuhlmacher, P. *Der Brief an die Römer.* Das Neue Testament Deutsch. Göttingen: Vandenhoeck & Ruprecht, 1989.

Stuhlmacher, P. "Die Gerechtigkeitsanschauung des Apostels Paulus," in: *Versöhnung, Gesetz und Gerechtigkeit. Aufsätze zur biblischen Theologie.* Göttingen: Vandenhoeck & Ruprecht, 1981, 87-116.

Stuhlmacher, P. *Gerechtigkeit Gottes bei Paulus.* Forschungen zur Religion und Literatur des Alten und Neuen Testaments 87. 2nd ed. Göttingen: Vandenhoeck & Ruprecht, 1966.

Stuhlmacher, P. "Jesustradition im Römerbrief?" *Theologische Beiträge* 14 (1983) 240-250.

Stuhlmacher, P. "Paul's Understanding of the Law in the Letter to the Romans." *Svensk Exegetisk Årsbok* 51/52 (1986/1987) 87-104.

Stuhlmacher, P. "Zum Neudruck von Adolf Schlatters 'Der Glaube im Neuen Testament'," in: A. Schlatter. *Der Glaube im Neuen Testament.* 6th ed. Stuttgart: Calwer Verlag, 1982, v-xxiii.

Stuhlmacher, P. "Zur neueren Exegese von Röm 3,24-26," in: E.E. Ellis & E. Gräßer (eds.). *Jesus und Paulus.* FS W.G. Kümmel. 1975, 315-333 = in: *Versöhnung, Gesetz und Gerechtigkeit. Aufsätze zur biblischen Theologie.* Göttingen: Vandenhoeck & Ruprecht, 1981, 117-135.

Sutherland, D. "Gen. 15.6 and Early Christian Struggles over Election." *Scottisch Journal of Theology* 44 (1991) 443-456.

Sweeney, M.A. "Form Criticism," in: S.L. McKenzie & S.R. Haynes (eds.). *To Each Its Own Meaning. An Introduction to Biblical Criticisms and Their Application.* 2nd ed. Louisville: Westminster/John Knox, 1999, 58-89.

Swete, H.B. (rev. R.S. Ottley) *An Introduction to the Old Testament in Greek.* Cambridge: Cambridge University Press, 1914.

Swetnam, J. "The Curious Crux at Romans 4,12." *Biblica* 61 (1980) 110-115.

Taglia, A. *Il concetto di pistis in Platone.* Storia della filosofia e del pensiero scientifico 6. Firenze: Le lettere, 1998.

Talbert, C.H. "A Non-Pauline Fragment at Romans 3:24-26." *Journal of Biblical Literature* 85 (1966) 287-296.

Talmon, S. "'400 Jahre' oder 'vier Generationen' (Gen 15,13-15). Geschichtliche Zeitangaben oder literarische Motive?," in: E. Blum et al. (eds.) *Die Hebräische Bibel und ihre zweifache Nachgeschichte.* FS R. Rendtorff. Neukirchen-Vluyn: Neukirchener Verlag, 1990, 13-25.

Taylor, G.M. "The Function of ΠΙΣΤΙΣ ΧΡΙΣΤΟΥ in Galatians." *Journal of Biblical Literature* 85 (1966) 58-76.

Theobald, M. "'Abrahams sah hin…'. Realitätssinn als Gütesiegel des Glaubens (Röm 4,18-22)," in: J. Frühwald-König, F.R. Prostmeier, & R. Zwick (eds.). *"Steht nicht geschrieben?" Studien zur Bibel und ihrer Wirkungsgeschichte.* FS G. Schmuttermayr. Regensburg: Pustet, 2001, 283-301 = in: *Studien zum Römerbrief.* Tübingen: Mohr (Siebeck) 2001, 398-416.

Theobald, M. "Der Kanon von der Rechtfertigung (Gal. 2,16; Rom. 3,28)," in: T. Söding (ed.). *Worum geht es in der Rechtfertigungslehre?* Quaestiones disputatae 180. Freiburg: Herder, 1999a = in: *Studien zum Römerbrief*. Tübingen: Mohr (Siebeck) 2001, 164-225.

Theobald, M. *Der Römerbrief*. Erträge der Forschung 294. Darmstadt: Wissenschaftliche Buchgesellschaft, 2000.

Theobald, M. "Der 'strittige Punkt' (Rhet. a. Her. I,26) im Diskurs des Römerbriefs. Die propositio 1,16f und das Mysterium der Errettung ganz Israels," in: R. Kampling (ed.). *'Nun steht aber diese Sache im Evangelium...'*. *Zur Frage nach den Anfängen des christlichen Antijudaismus*. Paderborn 1999, 183-228 = in: *Studien zum Römerbrief*. Tübingen: Mohr (Siebeck) 2001, 278-323.

Theobald, M. "Rechtfertigung und Ekklesiologie nach Paulus. Anmerkungen zur 'Gemeinsamen Erklärung zur Rechtfertigungslehre'." *Zeitschrift für Theologie und Kirche* 95 (1998) 103-117 = in: *Studien zum Römerbrief*. Tübingen: Mohr (Siebeck) 2001, 226-240.

Theobald, M. *Römerbrief*. Vols. 1-2. Stuttgarter Kleiner Kommentar, Neues Testament. Stuttgart: Katholisches Bibelwerk, 1992, 1993.

Theobald, M. "Verantwortung vor der Vergangenheit. Die Bedeutung der Traditionen Israels für den Römerbrief." *BiLi* 37 (1982) 13-20 = (revised) in: *Studien zum Römerbrief*. Tübingen: Mohr (Siebeck) 2001, 15-28.

Theobald, M. "Warum schrieb Paulus den Römerbrief." *Bibel und Liturgie* 56 (1983) 150-158 = (revised) in: *Studien zum Römerbrief*. Tübingen: Mohr (Siebeck) 2001, 2-14.

Theobald, M. "Zorn Gottes. Ein nicht zu vernachlässigender Aspekt der Theologie des Römerbriefs," in: *Studien zum Römerbrief*. Tübingen: Mohr (Siebeck) 2001a, 68-100.

Thielicke, H. "Zum Geleit," in: A. Schlatter. *Die philosophische Arbeit seit Descartes. Ihr religiöser und ethischer Ertrag*. 4th ed. Stuttgart: Calwer Verlag, 1959, 7-21.

Thielmann, F.S. *From Plight to Solution. A Jewish Framework for Understanding Paul's View of the Law in Galatians and Romans*. Leiden: Brill, 1989.

Thiselton, A.C. *The Two Horizons. New Testament Hermeneutics and Philosophical Description with Special Reference to Heidegger, Bultmann, Gadamer, and Wittgenstein*. Grand Rapids: Eerdmans, 1980.

Thompson, R.W. "The Alleged Rabbinic Background of Rom 3,31." *Ephemerides theologicae lovanienses* 63 (1987) 136-148.

Thon, J. *Pinhas ben Eleasar – Der levitische Priester am Ende der Tora. Traditions- und literargeschichtliche Untersuchung unter Einbeziehung historisch-geographischer Fragen*. Arbeiten zur Bibel und ihrer Geschichte 20. Leipzig: Evangelische Verlagsanstalt, 2006.

Thyen, H. *Der Stil der Jüdisch-Hellenistischen Homilie*. Forschungen zur Religion und Literatur des Alten und Neuen Testaments 47. Göttingen: Vandenhoeck & Ruprecht, 1955.

Tillich, P. *Wesen und Wandel des Glaubens*. Frankfurt: Ullstein, 1961.

Tobin, T.H. "What Shall We Say that Abraham Found? The Controversy behind Romans 4." *Harvard Theological Review* 88 (1995) 437-452.

Toit, B.A. du. "Faith and Obedience in Paul." *Neotestamentica* 25 (1991) 65-74.

Torrance, T.F. "One Aspect of the Biblical Conception of Faith." *Expository Times* 68 (1956/1957) 111-114.

Torrance, T.F. "The Biblical Conception of 'Faith'." *Expository Times* 68 (1956/1957a) 221-222

Tov, E. "The Nature of the Large-Scale Differences between the LXX and MT S T V, Compared with Similar Evidence in Other Sources," in: A. Schenker (ed.). *The Earliest Text of the Hebrew Bible. The Relationship between the Masoretic Text and the Hebrew Base of the Septuagint Reconsidered.* Society of Biblical Literature Septuagint and Cognate Studies 52. Atlanta: Society of Biblical Literature, 2003, 121-144.

Trobisch, D. *Die Entstehung der Paulusbriefsammlung. Studien zu den Anfängen christlicher Publizistik.* Novum Testamentum et Orbus Antiquus 10. Göttingen: Vandenhoeck & Ruprecht, 1989.

Umbach, H. *In Christus getauft – von der Sünde befreit. Die Gemeinde als sünden-freier Raum bei Paulus.* Forschungen zur Religion und Literatur des Alten und Neuen Testaments 181. Göttingen: Vandenhoeck & Ruprecht, 1999.

Unnik, W.C. van. *Tarsus or Jerusalem. The City of Paul's Youth* (G. Ogg, tr.). London: Epworth Press, 1962 (originally published in Dutch, 1952) = in: *Sparsa Collecta.* Vol. 1: *Evangelia, Paulina, Acta.* Novum Testamentum Supplements 29. Leiden: Brill, 1973, 259-320.

Vallotton, P. *Le Christ et la Foi. Étude de Théologie Biblique* Geneva: Labor et Fides, 1960.

Van Seters, J. *Abraham in History and Tradition.* New Haven: Yale University Press, 1975.

VanderKam, J.C. *Textual and Historical Studies in the Book of Jubilees.* Harvard Semitic Monographs 14. Missoula: Scholars Press, 1977.

VanderKam, J.C. "The *Aqedah, Jubilees,* and Pseudojubilees," in: C.A. Evans & S. Talmon (eds.). *The Quest for Context and Meaning. Studies in Biblical Intertextuality.* FS J.A. Sanders. Biblical Interpretation Series 28. Leiden: Brill, 1997, 241-261.

VanderKam, J.C. "The Origins and Purposes of the Book of Jubilees," in: M. Albani, J. Frey & A. Lange (eds.). *Studies in the Book of Jubilees.* Texte und Studien zum antiken Judentum 65. Tübingen: Mohr (Siebeck), 1997a, 3-24.

Vanhoye, A. "Πίστις Χριστοῦ. Fede in Cristo o affidabilità di Cristo." *Biblica* 80 (1999) 1-21.

Vawter, B. *On Genesis. A New Reading.* Garden City: Doubleday, 1977.

Veijola, T. "Das Opfer des Abraham – Paradigma des Glaubens aus dem nachexilischen Zeitalter." *Zeitschrift für Theologie und Kirche* 85 (1988) 129-164.

Vermès, G. "New Light on the Sacrifice of Isaac from 4Q225." *Journal of Jewish Studies* 47 (1996) 140-146.

Vermès, G. *Scripture and Tradition in Judaism. Haggadic Studies.* Studia post-biblica 4. Leiden: Brill, 1961.

Vielhauer, P. "Paulus und das Alte Testament," in: L. Abramowski & J.F.G. Goeters. *Studien zur Geschichte und Theologie der Reformation.* FS E. Bizer. Neukirchen-Vluyn: Neukirchener Verlag, 1969, 33-62 = in: *Oikodome. Aufsätze zum Neuen Testament.* Vol. 2. München: Kaiser, 1979, 196-228.

Volz, P. & W. Rudolph. *Der Elohist als Erzähler – ein Irrweg der Pentateuchkritik.* Beihefte zur Zeitschrift für die alttestamentliche Wissenschaft 63. Berlin: de Gruyter, 1933.

Vorster, J.N. "Strategies of Persuasion in Romans 1.16-17," in: S.E. Porter & T.H. Olbricht (eds.). *Rhetoric and the New Testament.* Journal for the Study of the New Testament: Supplement Series 90. Sheffield: JSOT Press, 1993, 152-170.

Vouga, F. *An die Galater.* Handbuch zum Neuen Testament 10. Tübingen: Mohr (Siebeck), 1998.

Wachinger, L. *Der Glaubensbegriff Martin Bubers.* Beiträge zur ökumenischen Theologie 4. München: Hueber, 1970.

Walker, W.O. "Romans 1.18-2.29. A Non-Pauline Interpolation?" *New Testament Studies* 45 (1999) 533-552.

Wallis, I.G. *The Faith of Jesus Christ in Early Christian Traditions.* Society for New Testament Studies Monograph Series 84. Cambridge: Cambridge University Press, 1995.

Wallis, W.B. "The Translation of Romans 1.17 – a Basic Motif in Paulinism." *Journal of the Evangelical Theological Society* 16 (1973) 17-23.

Watson, F. *Paul and the Hermeneutics of Faith.* London: T. & T. Clark, 2004.

Watson, F. *Paul, Judaism and the Gentiles. A Sociological Approach.* Society for New Testament Studies Monograph Series 56. Cambridge: Cambridge University Press, 1986.

Watts, R.E. "'For I Am Not Ashamed of the Gospel.' Romans 1:16-17 and Habakkuk 2:4," in: S.K. Soderlund & N.T. Wright. *Romans and the People of God.* FS G.D. Fee. Grand Rapids: Eerdmans, 1999, 3-25.

Wedderburn, A.J.M. *The Reason for Romans.* Studies of the New Testament and Its World. Edinburgh: T. & T. Clark, 1988.

Weder, H. "Gesetz und Sünde. Gedanken zu einem qualitativen Sprung im Denken des Paulus." *New Testament Studies* 31 (1985) 357-376 = in: *Einblicke ins Evangelium. Exegetische Beiträge zur neutestamentlichen Hermeneutik.* Göttingen: Vandenhoeck & Ruprecht, 1992, 323-346.

Weimar, P. "Genesis 15. Ein redaktionskritischer Versuch," in: M. Görg (ed.). *Die Väter Israels. Beiträge zur Theologie der Patriarchenüberlieferungen im Alten Testament.* FS J. Scharbert. Stuttgart: Katholisches Bibelwerk, 1989, 305-325.

Weinberg, J. "Job versus Abraham: The Quest for the Perfect God-Fearer in Rabbinic Tradition," in: W.M.A. Beuken (ed.). *The Book of Job.* Bibliotheca ephemeridum theologicarum lovaniensium 114. Leuven: Leuven University Press, 1994, 281-296.

Weiser, A. *Die Psalmen.* Das Alte Testament deutsch. 4th ed. Göttingen: Vandenhoeck & Ruprecht, 1955.

Weiser, A. "Glauben im Alten Testament," in: A. Alt et al. (eds.) FS G. Beer. Stuttgart: Kohlhammer, 1935, 88-99.

Weiser, A. Art. "πιστεύω κτλ." *Theologisches Wörterbuch zum Neuen Testament* 6, 1959, 182-197.

Weiß, B. *Der Brief an die Römer.* Kritisch-exegetischer Kommentar über das Neue Testament. 9th ed. Göttingen: Vandenhoeck & Ruprecht, 1899.

Wellhausen, J. *Die Composition des Hexateuchs und der historischen Bücher des Alten Testaments.* 3rd ed. Berlin: Reimer, 1898 (= 4th ed. Berlin: de Gruyter, 1963).

Wellhausen, J. *Israelitische und jüdische Geschichte.* 9th ed. Berlin: de Gruyter, 1958 (= 1981).

Wengst, K. *Christologische Formeln und Lieder des Urchristentums.* Studien zum Neuen Testament 7. Gütersloh: Mohn, 1972.

Wenham, G.J. *Genesis 1-15.* Word Biblical Commentary. Waco: Word, 1988.

Wenham, G.J. "The Symbolism of the Animal Rite in Genesis 15: A Response to G.F. Hasel, *JSOT* 19 (1981)." *Journal for the Study of the Old Testament* 22 (1982) 134-137.

Werline, R.A. *Penitential Prayer in Second Temple Judaism. The Development of a Religious Institution.* Society of Biblical Literature Early Judaism and Its Literature 13. Atlanta: Scholars Press, 1998.

Wernecke, H.H. *Faith in the New Testament.* Grand Rapids: Zondervan, 1934.

Westerholm, S. *Israel's Law and the Church's Faith. Paul and his Recent Interpreters.* Grand Rapids: Eerdmans, 1988.

Westerholm, S. *Perspectives Old and New on Paul. The "Lutheran" Paul and His Critics.* Grand Rapids: Eerdmans, 2004.

Westermann, C. "Arten der Erzählung in der Genesis," in: *Forschung am Alten Testament. Gesammelte Studien.* Theologische Bücherei 24. München 1964, 9-91.

Westermann, C. *Die Verheißungen an die Väter. Studien zur Vätergeschichte.* Göttingen: Vandenhoeck & Ruprecht, 1976.

Westermann, C. *Genesis.* Vol. 2: *Genesis 12-36.* Biblischer Kommentar, Altes Testament 1/2. Neukirchen-Vluyn: Neukirchener Verlag, 1981.

Wetter, G.P. *"Der Sohn Gottes". Eine Untersuchung über den Charakter und die Tendenz des Johannes Evangeliums; zugleich ein Beitrag zur Kenntnis der Heilandsgestalten der Antike.* Forschungen zur Religion und Literatur des Alten und Neuen Testaments 26. Göttingen: Vandenhoeck & Ruprecht, 1916.

Whiteley, D.E.H. *The Theology of St. Paul.* Philadelphia: Fortress, 1966.

Wiefel, W. "Glaubensgehorsam? Erwägungen zu Röm 1,5," in: *Wort und Gemeinde.* FS E. Schott. Aufsätze und Vorträge zur Theologie und Religionswissenschaft 42. Berlin: Evangelische Verlagsanstalt, 1968, 137-144.

Wiencke, G. *Paulus über Jesu Tod. Die Deutung des Todes Jesu bei Paulus und ihre Herkunft.* Beiträge zur Förderung christlicher Theologie 2/42. Gütersloh: Bertelsmann, 1939.

Wieser, F.E. *Die Abrahamvorstellungen im Neuen Testament.* Europäische Hochschulschriften 23/317. Frankfurt: Lang, 1987.

Wilckens, U. *Der Brief an die Römer.* Vols. 1-3. Evangelisch-Katholischer Kommentar 6/1-3. Neukirchen-Vluyn: Neukirchener Verlag, 1978, 1980, 1982.

Wilckens, U. "Die Rechtfertigung Abrahams nach Römer 4," in: R. Rendtorff & K. Koch (eds.). *Studien zur Theologie der alttestamentlichen Überlieferungen.* FS G. von Rad. Neukirchen-Vluyn: Neukirchener Verlag, 1961, 111-127 = in: *Rechtfertigung als Freiheit. Paulusstudien.* Neukirchen-Vluyn: Neukirchener Verlag, 1974, 33-49.

Wilckens, U. "Über Abfassungszweck und Aufbau des Römerbriefes," in: *Rechtfertigung als Freiheit. Paulusstudien.* Neukirchen-Vluyn: Neukirchener Verlag, 1974, 110-170.

Wilckens, U. "Vorwort" (1974a), in: *Rechtfertigung als Freiheit. Paulusstudien.* Neukirchen-Vluyn: Neukirchener Verlag, 1974, 7-10.

Wilckens, U. "Was heißt bei Paulus: 'Aus Werken des Gesetzes wird kein Mensch gerecht'?," in: *EKK Vorarbeiten.* Vol. 1. Neukirchen-Vluyn: Neukirchener Verlag, 1969, 51-77 = in: *Rechtfertigung als Freiheit. Paulusstudien.* Neukirchen-Vluyn: Neukirchener Verlag, 1974, 77-109.

Wilckens, U. "Zu Römer 3,21-4,25. Antwort an G. Klein." *Evangelische Theologie* 11 (1964) 586-610 = in: *Rechtfertigung als Freiheit. Paulusstudien.* Neukirchen-Vluyn: Neukirchener Verlag, 1974, 50-76.

Wildberger, H. Art. "אמן etc." *Theologisches Handwörterbuch zum Alten Testament* 1, 5th ed., 1994, 177-211.

Wildberger, H. "'Glauben', Erwägungen zu הֶאֱמִין," in: *Hebräische Wortforschung.* FS W. Baumgartner. Vetus Testamentum Supplements 16. Leiden: Brill, 1967, 372-386.

Wildberger, H. "'Glauben' im Alten Testament." *Zeitschrift für Theologie und Kirche* 65 (1968) 129-159.

Williams, S.K. "Again *Pistis Christou.*" *Catholic Biblical Quarterly* 49 (1987) 431-447.

Williams, S.K. *Jesus' Death as Saving Event. The Background and Origin of a Concept.* Harvard Dissertations in Religion 2. Missoula: Scholars Press, 1975.

Williams, S.K. "The 'Righteousness of God' in Romans." *Journal of Biblical Literature* 99 (1980) 241-290.

Williamson, H.G.M. *Ezra, Nehemiah.* Word Biblical Commentary. Waco: Word, 1985.

Williamson, P.R. *Abraham, Israel and the Nations. The Patriarchal Promise and its Covenantal Development in Genesis.* Journal for the Study of the Old Testament: Supplement Series 315. Sheffield: Sheffield Academic Press, 2000.

Willi-Plein, I. "Zu A. Behrens, Gen 15,6 und das Vorverständnis des Paulus, ZAW 109 (1997), 327-341." *Zeitschrift für die alttestamentliche Wissenschaft* 112 (2000) 396-397.

Winger, M. *By What Law? The Meaning of Νόμος in the Letters of Paul.* Society of Biblical Literature Dissertation Series 128. Atlanta: Scholars Press, 1992.

Winger, M. "The Law of Christ." *New Testament Studies* 46 (2000) 537-546

Wise, M.O. "4QFlorilegium and the Temple of Adam." *Revue de Qumran* 15 (1991) 103-132.

Wißmann, E. *Das Verhältnis von ΠΙΣΤΙΣ und Christusfrömmigkeit bei Paulus.* Forschungen zur Religion und Literatur des Alten und Neuen Testaments 23. Göttingen: Vandenhoeck & Ruprecht, 1926.

Witherington, B. III. *Grace in Galatia A Commentary on St Paul's Letter to the Galatians.* Edinburgh: T. & T. Clark, 1998.

Wolff, H.W. *Dodekapropheton 1. Hosea.* Biblischer Kommentar, Altes Testament 14/1. Neukirchen-Vluyn: Neukirchener Verlag, 1961.

Woyke, J. "'Einst' und 'Jetzt' in Röm 1-3. Zur Bedeutung von νυνὶ δέ Röm 3,21." *Zeitschrift für die neutestamentliche Wissenschaft* 92 (2001) 195-206.

Wrede, W. *Paulus.* Religionsgeschichtliche Volksbücher für die deutsche christliche Gegenwart 1/5,6. 2nd ed. Tübingen: Mohr (Siebeck), 1907.

Wright, B.G. III & C.V. Camp. "'Who Has Been Tested by Gold and Found Perfect?' Ben Siras's Discourse of Riches and Poverty." *Henoch* 23 (2001) 153-174.

Wright, N.T. "Romans and the Theology of Paul," in: D.M. Hay & E.E. Johnson (eds.). *Pauline Theology.* Vol. 3: *Romans.* Minneapolis: Fortress, 1995, 30-67.

Wright, N.T. *The Climax of the Covenant. Christ and the Law in Pauline Theology.* Edinburgh: T. & T. Clark, 1991.

Wright, N.T. "The Letter to the Romans. Introduction, Commentary, and Reflections," in: L. Keck (ed.) *The New Interpreter's Bible.* Vol. 10. Nashville: Abingdon, 2002.

Wright, N.T. "The Paul of History and the Apostle of Faith." *Tyndale Bulletin* 29 (1978) 61-88.

Wright, N.T. *What Saint Paul Really Said.* Oxford: Lion, 1997.

Yeung, M.W. *Faith in Jesus and Paul. A Comparison with Special Reference to 'Faith that can remove Mountains' and 'Your Faith has healed/saved you.'* Wissenschaftliche Untersuchungen zum Neuen Testament 2/147. Tübingen: Mohr (Siebeck), 2002.

Yinger, K.L. *Paul, Judaism, Judgment According to Deeds.* Society for New Testament Studies Monograph Series 105. Cambridge: Cambridge University Press, 1999.

Zahn, T. *Der Brief des Paulus an die Römer.* Kommentar zum Neuen Testament. 3rd ed. Leipzig: Deichert, 1925.

Zakovitch, Y. "The Pattern of the Numerical Sequence Three-Four in the Bible" (Hebrew). Ph.D. Dissertation. Jerusalem, 1977.

Zeitlin, S. "Hillel and the Hermeneutic Rules." *Jewish Quarterly Review* 53 (1963) 161-173.

Zeller, D. *Der Brief an die Römer.* Regensburger Neues Testament. Regensburg: Pustet, 1985.

Zeller, D. *Juden und Heiden in der Mission des Paulus. Studien zum Römerbrief.* Stuttgart: Katholisches Bibelwerk, 1973.

Zenger, E. et al. *Einleitung in das Alte Testament.* Studienbücher Theologie 1/1. 3rd ed. Stuttgart: Kohlhammer, 1995.

Zimmerli, W. *1. Mose 12-25. Abraham.* Zürcher Biblischer Kommentar, Altes Testament 1/2. Zürich: Theologischer Verlag, 1976.

Zimmerli, W. "Ich bin Jahwe," in: W.F. Albright et al. (eds.) *Geschichte und Altes Testament.* Beiträge zur historischen Theologie 16. FS A. Alt. Tübingen: Mohr (Siebeck), 1953, 179-209 = *Gottes Offenbarung. Gesammelte Aufsätze.* Theologische Bücherei 19. München: Kaiser, 1963, 11-40.

Zwaan, J. de. "Persönlicher Glaube bei Paulus." *Zeitschrift für systematische Theologie* 13 (1936) 114-149.

Index of References

A. Old Testament

B. New Testament

12:3	396	10:6	399
11:25	236, 283, 287	10:15	244, 276
13:2	401, 410	10:17	343
13:13	401	13:4	339
14:30	267	13:5	338, 384
15:1-2	340		
15:2	348	*Galatians*	
15:3	253	1:4	253
15:1-17	390	1:12	334
15:11	265, 340, 348, 410	1:16	267, 416
15:12	410	2:12	299
15:13.16.		2:15	252
29b.32c	331	2:15-16	265
15:14	276, 289, 340, 409f.	2:16	248, 256f., 259f., 265,
15:15	410		268, 274, 295, 299-
15:17	253, 276, 351, 390		301, 305, 348, 409
15:22	412	2:16-17	338
15:34	253	2:17	351
15:39	295	2:19	268
15:43	348	2:20	259, 263, 384, 389
15:56	253, 305	2:21	268, 301, 305, 327, 338
15:58	343	3	219, 356, 364, 367,
16:10	343		405, 410f., 420
16:13	338, 340, 373, 384	3:1-4:11	73
		3:2.5	301, 305, 340, 396
2Corinthians		3:6	101, 164, 334, 342,
1:9	377		408, 411
1:14	343	3:6-14	317
1:21-22	358	3:7	292, 371, 374
1:24	276, 338, 384	3:8	248
2:9	399	3:8-9	367
2:16	244	3:9	292, 342, 388
3:18	244, 271, 348	3:10	300f., 315
4:3-4	255	3:10-14	314
4:3-6	397	3:11	250, 301, 327
4:4	409	3:13	314
4:5	410	3:14	266, 364, 396
4:10	381, 383	3:15	325, 367
4:10-12	271	3:16	268, 364, 367, 413
4:13	343	3:17	327, 349, 364, 367
5:1	409	3:18	364, 368
5:16	271, 325	3:19	279, 372, 367
5:19	287	3:19-26	254
5:21	272	3:22	246, 248, 253, 259,
7:15	399		273, 278f., 305f., 308,
9:3	343		351, 364, 380
9:8	343	3:23	266f., 278f., 306, 394
10:2	325	3:23-25	279
10:5	399	3:23-26	266, 278

C. Old Testament Apocrypha

D. Old Testament Pseudepigrapha

E. Dead Sea Scrolls

G. Josephus

H. Rabbinic Literature

I. Targums

J. Early and Medieval Christian Literature

K. Greco-Roman Literature

Index of Modern Authors

Index of Subjects and Names

Bockmuehl, Markus N.A.: Revelation and Mystery in Ancient Judaism and Pauline Christianity. 1990. *Vol. II/36.*

Bøe, Sverre: Gog and Magog. 2001. *Vol. II/135.*

Böhlig, Alexander: Gnosis und Synkretismus. Vol. 1 1989. *Vol. 47* – Vol. 2 1989. *Vol. 48.*

Böhm, Martina: Samarien und die Samaritai bei Lukas. 1999. *Vol. II/111.*

Böttrich, Christfried: Weltweisheit – Menschheitsethik – Urkult. 1992. *Vol. II/50.*

Bolyki, János: Jesu Tischgemeinschaften. 1997. *Vol. II/96.*

Bosman, Philip: Conscience in Philo and Paul. 2003. *Vol. II/166.*

Bovon, François: Studies in Early Christianity. 2003. *Vol. 161.*

Brändl, Martin: Der Agon bei Paulus. 2006. *Vol. II/222.*

Brocke, Christoph vom: Thessaloniki – Stadt des Kassander und Gemeinde des Paulus. 2001. *Vol. II/125.*

Brunson, Andrew: Psalm 118 in the Gospel of John. 2003. *Vol. II/158.*

Büchli, Jörg: Der Poimandres – ein paganisiertes Evangelium. 1987. *Vol. II/27.*

Bühner, Jan A.: Der Gesandte und sein Weg im 4. Evangelium. 1977. *Vol. II/2.*

Burchard, Christoph: Untersuchungen zu Joseph und Asenath. 1965. *Vol. 8.*

– Studien zur Theologie, Sprache und Umwelt des Neuen Testaments. Ed. by D. Sänger. 1998. *Vol. 107.*

Burnett, Richard: Karl Barth's Theological Exegesis. 2001. *Vol. II/145.*

Byron, John: Slavery Metaphors in Early Judaism and Pauline Christianity. 2003. *Vol. II/162.*

Byrskog, Samuel: Story as History – History as Story. 2000. *Vol. 123.*

Cancik, Hubert (Ed.): Markus-Philologie. 1984. *Vol. 33.*

Capes, David B.: Old Testament Yaweh Texts in Paul's Christology. 1992. *Vol. II/47.*

Caragounis, Chrys C.: The Development of Greek and the New Testament. 2004. *Vol. 167.*

– The Son of Man. 1986. *Vol. 38.*

– see *Fridrichsen, Anton.*

Carleton Paget, James: The Epistle of Barnabas. 1994. *Vol. II/64.*

Carson, D.A., O'Brien, Peter T. and *Mark Seifrid* (Ed.): Justification and Variegated Nomism.
Vol. 1: The Complexities of Second Temple Judaism. 2001. *Vol. II/140.*
Vol. 2: The Paradoxes of Paul. 2004. *Vol. II/181.*

Chae, Young Sam: Jesus as the Eschatological Davidic Shepherd. 2006. *Vol. II/216.*

Ciampa, Roy E.: The Presence and Function of Scripture in Galatians 1 and 2. 1998. *Vol. II/102.*

Classen, Carl Joachim: Rhetorical Criticsm of the New Testament. 2000. *Vol. 128.*

Colpe, Carsten: Iranier – Aramäer – Hebräer – Hellenen. 2003. *Vol. 154.*

Crump, David: Jesus the Intercessor. 1992. *Vol. II/49.*

Dahl, Nils Alstrup: Studies in Ephesians. 2000. *Vol. 131.*

Deines, Roland: Die Gerechtigkeit der Tora im Reich des Messias. 2004. *Vol. 177.*

– Jüdische Steingefäße und pharisäische Frömmigkeit. 1993. *Vol. II/52.*

– Die Pharisäer. 1997. *Vol. 101.*

Deines, Roland and *Karl-Wilhelm Niebuhr* (Ed.): Philo und das Neue Testament. 2004. *Vol. 172.*

Dennis, John A.: Jesus' Death and the Gathering of True Israel. 2006. *Vol. 217.*

Dettwiler, Andreas and *Jean Zumstein* (Ed.): Kreuzestheologie im Neuen Testament. 2002. *Vol. 151.*

Dickson, John P.: Mission-Commitment in Ancient Judaism and in the Pauline Communities. 2003. *Vol. II/159.*

Dietzfelbinger, Christian: Der Abschied des Kommenden. 1997. *Vol. 95.*

Dimitrov, Ivan Z., James D.G. Dunn, Ulrich Luz and *Karl-Wilhelm Niebuhr* (Ed.): Das Alte Testament als christliche Bibel in orthodoxer und westlicher Sicht. 2004. *Vol. 174.*

Dobbeler, Axel von: Glaube als Teilhabe. 1987. *Vol. II/22.*

Dryden, J. de Waal: Theology and Ethics in 1 Peter. 2006. *Vol. II/209.*

Du Toit, David S.: Theios Anthropos. 1997. *Vol. II/91.*

Dübbers, Michael: Christologie und Existenz im Kolosserbrief. 2005. *Vol. II/191.*

Dunn, James D.G.: The New Perspective on Paul. 2005. *Vol. 185.*

Dunn, James D.G. (Ed.): Jews and Christians. 1992. *Vol. 66.*

– Paul and the Mosaic Law. 1996. *Vol. 89.*

– see *Dimitrov, Ivan Z.*

–, *Hans Klein, Ulrich Luz* and *Vasile Mihoc* (Ed.): Auslegung der Bibel in orthodoxer und westlicher Perspektive. 2000. *Vol. 130.*

Ebel, Eva: Die Attraktivität früher christlicher Gemeinden. 2004. *Vol. II/178.*

Ebertz, Michael N.: Das Charisma des Gekreuzigten. 1987. *Vol. 45.*

Eckstein, Hans-Joachim: Der Begriff Syneidesis bei Paulus. 1983. *Vol. II/10.*
- Verheißung und Gesetz. 1996. *Vol. 86.*
Ego, Beate: Im Himmel wie auf Erden. 1989. *Vol. II/34.*
Ego, Beate, Armin Lange and *Peter Pilhofer (Ed.):* Gemeinde ohne Tempel – Community without Temple. 1999. *Vol. 118.*
- and *Helmut Merkel* (Ed.): Religiöses Lernen in der biblischen, frühjüdischen und frühchristlichen Überlieferung. 2005. *Vol. 180.*
Eisen, Ute E.: see *Paulsen, Henning.*
Elledge, C.D.: Life after Death in Early Judaism. 2006. *Vol. II/208.*
Ellis, E. Earle: Prophecy and Hermeneutic in Early Christianity. 1978. *Vol. 18.*
- The Old Testament in Early Christianity. 1991. *Vol. 54.*
Endo, Masanobu: Creation and Christology. 2002. *Vol. 149.*
Ennulat, Andreas: Die 'Minor Agreements'. 1994. *Vol. II/62.*
Ensor, Peter W.: Jesus and His 'Works'. 1996. *Vol. II/85.*
Eskola, Timo: Messiah and the Throne. 2001. *Vol. II/142.*
- Theodicy and Predestination in Pauline Soteriology. 1998. *Vol. II/100.*
Fatehi, Mehrdad: The Spirit's Relation to the Risen Lord in Paul. 2000. *Vol. II/128.*
Feldmeier, Reinhard: Die Krisis des Gottessohnes. 1987. *Vol. II/21.*
- Die Christen als Fremde. 1992. *Vol. 64.*
Feldmeier, Reinhard and *Ulrich Heckel* (Ed.): Die Heiden. 1994. *Vol. 70.*
Fletcher-Louis, Crispin H.T.: Luke-Acts: Angels, Christology and Soteriology. 1997. *Vol. II/94.*
Förster, Niclas: Marcus Magus. 1999. *Vol. 114.*
Forbes, Christopher Brian: Prophecy and Inspired Speech in Early Christianity and its Hellenistic Environment. 1995. *Vol. II/75.*
Fornberg, Tord: see *Fridrichsen, Anton.*
Fossum, Jarl E.: The Name of God and the Angel of the Lord. 1985. *Vol. 36.*
Foster, Paul: Community, Law and Mission in Matthew's Gospel. *Vol. II/177.*
Fotopoulos, John: Food Offered to Idols in Roman Corinth. 2003. *Vol. II/151.*
Frenschkowski, Marco: Offenbarung und Epiphanie. Vol. 1 1995. *Vol. II/79 –* Vol. 2 1997. *Vol. II/80.*
Frey, Jörg: Eugen Drewermann und die biblische Exegese. 1995. *Vol. II/71.*

- Die johanneische Eschatologie. Vol. I. 1997. *Vol. 96.* – Vol. II. 1998. *Vol. 110.* – Vol. III. 2000. *Vol. 117.*
Frey, Jörg and *Udo Schnelle (Ed.):* Kontexte des Johannesevangeliums. 2004. *Vol. 175.*
- and *Jens Schröter* (Ed.): Deutungen des Todes Jesu im Neuen Testament. 2005. *Vol. 181.*
-, *Jan G. van der Watt,* and *Ruben Zimmermann* (Ed.): Imagery in the Gospel of John. 2006. *Vol. 200.*
Freyne, Sean: Galilee and Gospel. 2000. *Vol. 125.*
Fridrichsen, Anton: Exegetical Writings. Edited by C.C. Caragounis and T. Fornberg. 1994. *Vol. 76.*
Gäbel, Georg: Die Kulttheologie des Hebräerbriefes. 2006. *Vol. II/212.*
Gäckle, Volker: Die Starken und die Schwachen in Korinth und in Rom. 2005. *Vol. 200.*
Garlington, Don B.: 'The Obedience of Faith'. 1991. *Vol. II/38.*
- Faith, Obedience, and Perseverance. 1994. *Vol. 79.*
Garnet, Paul: Salvation and Atonement in the Qumran Scrolls. 1977. *Vol. II/3.*
Gemünden, Petra von (Ed.): see *Weissenrieder, Annette.*
Gese, Michael: Das Vermächtnis des Apostels. 1997. *Vol. II/99.*
Gheorghita, Radu: The Role of the Septuagint in Hebrews. 2003. *Vol. II/160.*
Gordley, Matthew E.: The Colossian Hymn in Context. 2007. *Vol. II/228.*
Gräbe, Petrus J.: The Power of God in Paul's Letters. 2000. *Vol. II/123.*
Gräßer, Erich: Der Alte Bund im Neuen. 1985. *Vol. 35.*
- Forschungen zur Apostelgeschichte. 2001. *Vol. 137.*
Green, Joel B.: The Death of Jesus. 1988. *Vol. II/33.*
Gregg, Brian Han: The Historical Jesus and the Final Judgment Sayings in Q. 2005. *Vol. II/207.*
Gregory, Andrew: The Reception of Luke and Acts in the Period before Irenaeus. 2003. *Vol. II/169.*
Grindheim, Sigurd: The Crux of Election. 2005. *Vol. II/202.*
Gundry, Robert H.: The Old is Better. 2005. *Vol. 178.*
Gundry Volf, Judith M.: Paul and Perseverance. 1990. *Vol. II/37.*
Häußer, Detlef: Christusbekenntnis und Jesusüberlieferung bei Paulus. 2006. *Vol. 210.*
Hafemann, Scott J.: Suffering and the Spirit. 1986. *Vol. II/19.*

- Paul, Moses, and the History of Israel. 1995. *Vol. 81.*
Hahn, Ferdinand: Studien zum Neuen Testament.
  Vol. I: Grundsatzfragen, Jesusforschung, Evangelien. 2006. *Vol. 191.*
  Vol. II: Bekenntnisbildung und Theologie in urchristlicher Zeit. 2006. *Vol. 192.*
Hahn, Johannes (Ed.): Zerstörungen des Jerusalemer Tempels. 2002. *Vol. 147.*
Hamid-Khani, Saeed: Relevation and Concealment of Christ. 2000. *Vol. II/120.*
Hannah, Darrel D.: Michael and Christ. 1999. *Vol. II/109.*
Harrison; James R.: Paul's Language of Grace in Its Graeco-Roman Context. 2003. *Vol. II/172.*
Hartman, Lars: Text-Centered New Testament Studies. Ed. von D. Hellholm. 1997. *Vol. 102.*
Hartog, Paul: Polycarp and the New Testament. 2001. *Vol. II/134.*
Heckel, Theo K.: Der Innere Mensch. 1993. *Vol. II/53.*
- Vom Evangelium des Markus zum viergestaltigen Evangelium. 1999. *Vol. 120.*
Heckel, Ulrich: Kraft in Schwachheit. 1993. *Vol. II/56.*
- Der Segen im Neuen Testament. 2002. *Vol. 150.*
- see *Feldmeier, Reinhard.*
- see *Hengel, Martin.*
Heiligenthal, Roman: Werke als Zeichen. 1983. *Vol. II/9.*
Hellholm, D.: see *Hartman, Lars.*
Hemer, Colin J.: The Book of Acts in the Setting of Hellenistic History. 1989. *Vol. 49.*
Hengel, Martin: Judentum und Hellenismus. 1969, ³1988. *Vol. 10.*
- Die johanneische Frage. 1993. *Vol. 67.*
- Judaica et Hellenistica. Kleine Schriften I. 1996. *Vol. 90.*
- Judaica, Hellenistica et Christiana. Kleine Schriften II. 1999. *Vol. 109.*
- Paulus und Jakobus. Kleine Schriften III. 2002. *Vol. 141.*
- Studien zur Christologie. Kleine Schriften IV. 2006. *Vol. 201.*
- and *Anna Maria Schwemer:* Paulus zwischen Damaskus und Antiochien. 1998. *Vol. 108.*
- Der messianische Anspruch Jesu und die Anfänge der Christologie. 2001. *Vol. 138.*
Hengel, Martin and *Ulrich Heckel* (Ed.): Paulus und das antike Judentum. 1991. *Vol. 58.*

- and *Hermut Löhr* (Ed.): Schriftauslegung im antiken Judentum und im Urchristentum. 1994. *Vol. 73.*
- and *Anna Maria Schwemer* (Ed.): Königsherrschaft Gottes und himmlischer Kult. 1991. *Vol. 55.*
- Die Septuaginta. 1994. *Vol. 72.*
-, *Siegfried Mittmann* and *Anna Maria Schwemer* (Ed.): La Cité de Dieu / Die Stadt Gottes. 2000. *Vol. 129.*
Hentschel, Anni: Diakonia im Neuen Testament. 2007. *Vol. 226.*
Hernández Jr., Juan: Scribal Habits and Theological Influence in the Apocalypse. 2006. *Vol. II/218.*
Herrenbrück, Fritz: Jesus und die Zöllner. 1990. *Vol. II/41.*
Herzer, Jens: Paulus oder Petrus? 1998. *Vol. 103.*
Hill, Charles E.: From the Lost Teaching of Polycarp. 2005. *Vol. 186.*
Hoegen-Rohls, Christina: Der nachösterliche Johannes. 1996. *Vol. II/84.*
Hoffmann, Matthias Reinhard: The Destroyer and the Lamb. 2005. *Vol. II/203.*
Hofius, Otfried: Katapausis. 1970. *Vol. 11.*
- Der Vorhang vor dem Thron Gottes. 1972. *Vol. 14.*
- Der Christushymnus Philipper 2,6-11. 1976, ²1991. *Vol. 17.*
- Paulusstudien. 1989, ²1994. *Vol. 51.*
- Neutestamentliche Studien. 2000. *Vol. 132.*
- Paulusstudien II. 2002. *Vol. 143.*
- and *Hans-Christian Kammler:* Johannesstudien. 1996. *Vol. 88.*
Holtz, Traugott: Geschichte und Theologie des Urchristentums. 1991. *Vol. 57.*
Hommel, Hildebrecht: Sebasmata.
  Vol. 1 1983. *Vol. 31.*
  Vol. 2 1984. *Vol. 32.*
Horbury, William: Herodian Judaism and New Testament Study. 2006. *Vol. 193.*
Horst, Pieter W. van der: Jews and Christians in Their Graeco-Roman Context. 2006. *Vol. 196.*
Hvalvik, Reidar: The Struggle for Scripture and Covenant. 1996. *Vol. II/82.*
Jauhiainen, Marko: The Use of Zechariah in Revelation. 2005. *Vol. II/199.*
Jensen, Morten H.: Herod Antipas in Galilee. 2006. *Vol. II/215.*
Johns, Loren L.: The Lamb Christology of the Apocalypse of John. 2003. *Vol. II/167.*
Jossa, Giorgio: Jews or Christians? 2006. *Vol. 202.*
Joubert, Stephan: Paul as Benefactor. 2000. *Vol. II/124.*

Jungbauer, Harry: „Ehre Vater und Mutter". 2002. *Vol. II/146.*

Kähler, Christoph: Jesu Gleichnisse als Poesie und Therapie. 1995. *Vol. 78.*

Kamlah, Ehrhard: Die Form der katalogischen Paränese im Neuen Testament. 1964. *Vol. 7.*

Kammler, Hans-Christian: Christologie und Eschatologie. 2000. *Vol. 126.*

– Kreuz und Weisheit. 2003. *Vol. 159.*

– see *Hofius, Otfried.*

Kelhoffer, James A.: The Diet of John the Baptist. 2005. *Vol. 176.*

– Miracle and Mission. 1999. *Vol. II/112.*

Kelley, Nicole: Knowledge and Religious Authority in the Pseudo-Clementines. 2006. *Vol. II/213.*

Kieffer, René and *Jan Bergman (Ed.):* La Main de Dieu / Die Hand Gottes. 1997. *Vol. 94.*

Kierspel, Lars: The Jews and the World in the Fourth Gospel. 2006. *Vol. 220.*

Kim, Seyoon: The Origin of Paul's Gospel. 1981, ²1984. *Vol. II/4.*

– Paul and the New Perspective. 2002. *Vol. 140.*

– "The 'Son of Man'" as the Son of God. 1983. *Vol. 30.*

Klauck, Hans-Josef: Religion und Gesellschaft im frühen Christentum. 2003. *Vol. 152.*

Klein, Hans: see *Dunn, James D.G.*

Kleinknecht, Karl Th.: Der leidende Gerechtfertigte. 1984, ²1988. *Vol. II/13.*

Klinghardt, Matthias: Gesetz und Volk Gottes. 1988. *Vol. II/32.*

Kloppenborg, John S.: The Tenants in the Vineyard. 2006. *Vol. 195.*

Koch, Michael: Drachenkampf und Sonnenfrau. 2004. *Vol. II/184.*

Koch, Stefan: Rechtliche Regelung von Konflikten im frühen Christentum. 2004. *Vol. II/174.*

Köhler, Wolf-Dietrich: Rezeption des Matthäusevangeliums in der Zeit vor Irenäus. 1987. *Vol. II/24.*

Köhn, Andreas: Der Neutestamentler Ernst Lohmeyer. 2004. *Vol. II/180.*

Kooten, George H. van: Cosmic Christology in Paul and the Pauline School. 2003. *Vol. II/171.*

Korn, Manfred: Die Geschichte Jesu in veränderter Zeit. 1993. *Vol. II/51.*

Koskenniemi, Erkki: Apollonios von Tyana in der neutestamentlichen Exegese. 1994. *Vol. II/61.*

– The Old Testament Miracle-Workers in Early Judaism. 2005. *Vol. II/206.*

Kraus, Thomas J.: Sprache, Stil und historischer Ort des zweiten Petrusbriefes. 2001. *Vol. II/136.*

Kraus, Wolfgang: Das Volk Gottes. 1996. *Vol. 85.*

Kraus, Wolfgang and *Karl-Wilhelm Niebuhr* (Ed.): Frühjudentum und Neues Testament im Horizont Biblischer Theologie. 2003. *Vol. 162.*

– see *Walter, Nikolaus.*

Kreplin, Matthias: Das Selbstverständnis Jesu. 2001. *Vol. II/141.*

Kuhn, Karl G.: Achtzehngebet und Vaterunser und der Reim. 1950. *Vol. 1.*

Kvalbein, Hans: see *Ådna, Jostein.*

Kwon, Yon-Gyong: Eschatology in Galatians. 2004. *Vol. II/183.*

Laansma, Jon: I Will Give You Rest. 1997. *Vol. II/98.*

Labahn, Michael: Offenbarung in Zeichen und Wort. 2000. *Vol. II/117.*

Lambers-Petry, Doris: see *Tomson, Peter J.*

Lange, Armin: see *Ego, Beate.*

Lampe, Peter: Die stadtrömischen Christen in den ersten beiden Jahrhunderten. 1987, ²1989. *Vol. II/18.*

Landmesser, Christof: Wahrheit als Grundbegriff neutestamentlicher Wissenschaft. 1999. *Vol. 113.*

– Jüngerberufung und Zuwendung zu Gott. 2000. *Vol. 133.*

Lau, Andrew: Manifest in Flesh. 1996. *Vol. II/86.*

Lawrence, Louise: An Ethnography of the Gospel of Matthew. 2003. *Vol. II/165.*

Lee, Aquila H.I.: From Messiah to Preexistent Son. 2005. *Vol. II/192.*

Lee, Pilchan: The New Jerusalem in the Book of Relevation. 2000. *Vol. II/129.*

Lichtenberger, Hermann: Das Ich Adams und das Ich der Menschheit. 2004. *Vol. 164.*

– see *Avemarie, Friedrich.*

Lierman, John: The New Testament Moses. 2004. *Vol. II/173.*

– (Ed.): Challenging Perspectives on the Gospel of John. 2006. *Vol. II/219.*

Lieu, Samuel N.C.: Manichaeism in the Later Roman Empire and Medieval China. ²1992. *Vol. 63.*

Lindgård, Fredrik: Paul's Line of Thought in 2 Corinthians 4:16-5:10. 2004. *Vol. II/189.*

Loader, William R.G.: Jesus' Attitude Towards the Law. 1997. *Vol. II/97.*

Löhr, Gebhard: Verherrlichung Gottes durch Philosophie. 1997. *Vol. 97.*

Löhr, Hermut: Studien zum frühchristlichen und frühjüdischen Gebet. 2003. *Vol. 160.*

– see *Hengel, Martin.*

Löhr, Winrich Alfried: Basilides und seine Schule. 1995. *Vol. 83.*

Luomanen, Petri: Entering the Kingdom of Heaven. 1998. *Vol. II/101.*

Luz, Ulrich: see *Dunn, James D.G.*

Mackay, Ian D.: John's Raltionship with Mark. 2004. *Vol. II/182.*

Mackie, Scott D.: Eschatology and Exhortation in the Epistle to the Hebrews. 2006. *Vol. II/223.*

Maier, Gerhard: Mensch und freier Wille. 1971. *Vol. 12.*

– Die Johannesoffenbarung und die Kirche. 1981. *Vol. 25.*

Markschies, Christoph: Valentinus Gnosticus? 1992. *Vol. 65.*

Marshall, Peter: Enmity in Corinth: Social Conventions in Paul's Relations with the Corinthians. 1987. *Vol. II/23.*

Mayer, Annemarie: Sprache der Einheit im Epheserbrief und in der Ökumene. 2002. *Vol. II/150.*

Mayordomo, Moisés: Argumentiert Paulus logisch? 2005. *Vol. 188.*

McDonough, Sean M.: YHWH at Patmos: Rev. 1:4 in its Hellenistic and Early Jewish Setting. 1999. *Vol. II/107.*

McDowell, Markus: Prayers of Jewish Women. 2006. *Vol. II/211.*

McGlynn, Moyna: Divine Judgement and Divine Benevolence in the Book of Wisdom. 2001. *Vol. II/139.*

Meade, David G.: Pseudonymity and Canon. 1986. *Vol. 39.*

Meadors, Edward P.: Jesus the Messianic Herald of Salvation. 1995. *Vol. II/72.*

Meißner, Stefan: Die Heimholung des Ketzers. 1996. *Vol. II/87.*

Mell, Ulrich: Die „anderen" Winzer. 1994. *Vol. 77.*

– see *Sänger, Dieter.*

Mengel, Berthold: Studien zum Philipperbrief. 1982. *Vol. II/8.*

Merkel, Helmut: Die Widersprüche zwischen den Evangelien. 1971. *Vol. 13.*

– see *Ego, Beate.*

Merklein, Helmut: Studien zu Jesus und Paulus. Vol. 1 1987. *Vol. 43.* – Vol. 2 1998. *Vol. 105.*

Metzdorf, Christina: Die Tempelaktion Jesu. 2003. *Vol. II/168.*

Metzler, Karin: Der griechische Begriff des Verzeihens. 1991. *Vol. II/44.*

Metzner, Rainer: Die Rezeption des Matthäusevangeliums im 1. Petrusbrief. 1995. *Vol. II/74.*

– Das Verständnis der Sünde im Johannesevangelium. 2000. *Vol. 122.*

Mihoc, Vasile: see *Dunn, James D.G.*

Mineshige, Kiyoshi: Besitzverzicht und Almosen bei Lukas. 2003. *Vol. II/163.*

Mittmann, Siegfried: see *Hengel, Martin.*

Mittmann-Richert, Ulrike: Magnifikat und Benediktus. 1996. *Vol. II/90.*

Mournet, Terence C.: Oral Tradition and Literary Dependency. 2005. *Vol. II/195.*

Mußner, Franz: Jesus von Nazareth im Umfeld Israels und der Urkirche. Ed. von M. Theobald. 1998. *Vol. 111.*

Mutschler, Bernhard: Das Corpus Johanneum bei Irenäus von Lyon. 2005. *Vol. 189.*

Niebuhr, Karl-Wilhelm: Gesetz und Paränese. 1987. *Vol. II/28.*

– Heidenapostel aus Israel. 1992. *Vol. 62.*

– see *Deines, Roland*

– see *Dimitrov, Ivan Z.*

– see *Kraus, Wolfgang*

Nielsen, Anders E.: "Until it is Fullfilled". 2000. *Vol. II/126.*

Nissen, Andreas: Gott und der Nächste im antiken Judentum. 1974. *Vol. 15.*

Noack, Christian: Gottesbewußtsein. 2000. *Vol. II/116.*

Noormann, Rolf: Irenäus als Paulusinterpret. 1994. *Vol. II/66.*

Novakovic, Lidija: Messiah, the Healer of the Sick. 2003. *Vol. II/170.*

Obermann, Andreas: Die christologische Erfüllung der Schrift im Johannesevangelium. 1996. *Vol. II/83.*

Öhler, Markus: Barnabas. 2003. *Vol. 156.*

– see *Becker, Michael*

Okure, Teresa: The Johannine Approach to Mission. 1988. *Vol. II/31.*

Onuki, Takashi: Heil und Erlösung. 2004. *Vol. 165.*

Oropeza, B. J.: Paul and Apostasy. 2000. *Vol. II/115.*

Ostmeyer, Karl-Heinrich: Kommunikation mit Gott und Christus. 2006. *Vol. 197.*

– Taufe und Typos. 2000. *Vol. II/118.*

Paulsen, Henning: Studien zur Literatur und Geschichte des frühen Christentums. Ed. von Ute E. Eisen. 1997. *Vol. 99.*

Pao, David W.: Acts and the Isaianic New Exodus. 2000. *Vol. II/130.*

Park, Eung Chun: The Mission Discourse in Matthew's Interpretation. 1995. *Vol. II/81.*

Park, Joseph S.: Conceptions of Afterlife in Jewish Insriptions. 2000. *Vol. II/121.*

Pate, C. Marvin: The Reverse of the Curse. 2000. *Vol. II/114.*

Peres, Imre: Griechische Grabinschriften und neutestamentliche Eschatologie. 2003. *Vol. 157.*

Philip, Finny: The Origins of Pauline Pneumatology. 2005. *Vol. II/194.*

Philonenko, Marc (Ed.): Le Trône de Dieu. 1993. *Vol. 69.*

Pilhofer, Peter: Presbyteron Kreitton. 1990. *Vol. II/39.*

– Philippi. Vol. 1 1995. *Vol. 87.* – Vol. 2 2000. *Vol. 119.*

– Die frühen Christen und ihre Welt. 2002. *Vol. 145.*

– see *Becker, Eve-Marie.*

– see *Ego, Beate.*

Pitre, Brant: Jesus, the Tribulation, and the End of the Exile. 2005. *Vol. II/204.*

Plümacher, Eckhard: Geschichte und Geschichten. 2004. *Vol. 170.*

Pöhlmann, Wolfgang: Der Verlorene Sohn und das Haus. 1993. *Vol. 68.*

Pokorný, Petr and *Josef B. Souèek:* Bibelauslegung als Theologie. 1997. *Vol. 100.*

Pokorný, Petr and *Jan Roskovec* (Ed.): Philosophical Hermeneutics and Biblical Exegesis. 2002. *Vol. 153.*

Popkes, Enno Edzard: Die Theologie der Liebe Gottes in den johanneischen Schriften. 2005. *Vol. II/197.*

Porter, Stanley E.: The Paul of Acts. 1999. *Vol. 115.*

Prieur, Alexander: Die Verkündigung der Gottesherrschaft. 1996. *Vol. II/89.*

Probst, Hermann: Paulus und der Brief. 1991. *Vol. II/45.*

Räisänen, Heikki: Paul and the Law. 1983, ²1987. *Vol. 29.*

Rehkopf, Friedrich: Die lukanische Sonderquelle. 1959. *Vol. 5.*

Rein, Matthias: Die Heilung des Blindgeborenen (Joh 9). 1995. *Vol. II/73.*

Reinmuth, Eckart: Pseudo-Philo und Lukas. 1994. *Vol. 74.*

Reiser, Marius: Syntax und Stil des Markusevangeliums. 1984. *Vol. II/11.*

Rhodes, James N.: The Epistle of Barnabas and the Deuteronomic Tradition. 2004. *Vol. II/188.*

Richards, E. Randolph: The Secretary in the Letters of Paul. 1991. *Vol. II/42.*

Riesner, Rainer: Jesus als Lehrer. 1981, ³1988. *Vol. II/7.*

– Die Frühzeit des Apostels Paulus. 1994. *Vol. 71.*

Rissi, Mathias: Die Theologie des Hebräerbriefs. 1987. *Vol. 41.*

Roskovec, Jan: see *Pokorný, Petr.*

Röhser, Günter: Metaphorik und Personifikation der Sünde. 1987. *Vol. II/25.*

Rose, Christian: Die Wolke der Zeugen. 1994. *Vol. II/60.*

Rothschild, Clare K.: Baptist Traditions and Q. 2005. *Vol. 190.*

– Luke Acts and the Rhetoric of History. 2004. *Vol. II/175.*

Rüegger, Hans-Ulrich: Verstehen, was Markus erzählt. 2002. *Vol. II/155.*

Rüger, Hans Peter: Die Weisheitsschrift aus der Kairoer Geniza. 1991. *Vol. 53.*

Sänger, Dieter: Antikes Judentum und die Mysterien. 1980. *Vol. II/5.*

– Die Verkündigung des Gekreuzigten und Israel. 1994. *Vol. 75.*

– see *Burchard, Christoph*

– and *Ulrich Mell* (Hrsg.): Paulus und Johannes. 2006. *Vol. 198.*

Salier, Willis Hedley: The Rhetorical Impact of the Semeia in the Gospel of John. 2004. *Vol. II/186.*

Salzmann, Jorg Christian: Lehren und Ermahnen. 1994. *Vol. II/59.*

Sandnes, Karl Olav: Paul – One of the Prophets? 1991. *Vol. II/43.*

Sato, Migaku: Q und Prophetie. 1988. *Vol. II/29.*

Schäfer, Ruth: Paulus bis zum Apostelkonzil. 2004. *Vol. II/179.*

Schaper, Joachim: Eschatology in the Greek Psalter. 1995. *Vol. II/76.*

Schimanowski, Gottfried: Die himmlische Liturgie in der Apokalypse des Johannes. 2002. *Vol. II/154.*

– Weisheit und Messias. 1985. *Vol. II/17.*

Schlichting, Günter: Ein jüdisches Leben Jesu. 1982. *Vol. 24.*

Schließer, Benjamin: Abraham's Faith in Romans 4. 2007. *Vol. II/224.*

Schnabel, Eckhard J.: Law and Wisdom from Ben Sira to Paul. 1985. *Vol. II/16.*

Schnelle, Udo: see *Frey, Jörg.*

Schröter, Jens: see *Frey, Jörg.*

Schutter, William L.: Hermeneutic and Composition in I Peter. 1989. *Vol. II/30.*

Schwartz, Daniel R.: Studies in the Jewish Background of Christianity. 1992. *Vol. 60.*

Schwemer, Anna Maria: see *Hengel, Martin*

Scott, Ian W.: Implicit Epistemology in the Letters of Paul. 2005. *Vol. II/205.*

Scott, James M.: Adoption as Sons of God. 1992. *Vol. II/48.*

– Paul and the Nations. 1995. *Vol. 84.*

Shum, Shiu-Lun: Paul's Use of Isaiah in Romans. 2002. *Vol. II/156.*

Siegert, Folker: Drei hellenistisch-jüdische Predigten. Teil I 1980. *Vol. 20* – Teil II 1992. *Vol. 61.*
- Nag-Hammadi-Register. 1982. *Vol. 26.*
- Argumentation bei Paulus. 1985. *Vol. 34.*
- Philon von Alexandrien. 1988. *Vol. 46.*
Simon, Marcel: Le christianisme antique et son contexte religieux I/II. 1981. *Vol. 23.*
Snodgrass, Klyne: The Parable of the Wicked Tenants. 1983. *Vol. 27.*
Söding, Thomas: Das Wort vom Kreuz. 1997. *Vol. 93.*
- see *Thüsing, Wilhelm.*
Sommer, Urs: Die Passionsgeschichte des Markusevangeliums. 1993. *Vol. II/58.*
Souèek, Josef B.: see *Pokorný, Petr.*
Spangenberg, Volker: Herrlichkeit des Neuen Bundes. 1993. *Vol. II/55.*
Spanje, T.E. van: Inconsistency in Paul? 1999. *Vol. II/110.*
Speyer, Wolfgang: Frühes Christentum im antiken Strahlungsfeld. Vol. I: 1989. *Vol. 50.*
- Vol. II: 1999. *Vol. 116.*
Stadelmann, Helge: Ben Sira als Schriftgelehrter. 1980. *Vol. II/6.*
Stenschke, Christoph W.: Luke's Portrait of Gentiles Prior to Their Coming to Faith. *Vol. II/108.*
Sterck-Degueldre, Jean-Pierre: Eine Frau namens Lydia. 2004. *Vol. II/176.*
Stettler, Christian: Der Kolosserhymnus. 2000. *Vol. II/131.*
Stettler, Hanna: Die Christologie der Pastoralbriefe. 1998. *Vol. II/105.*
Stökl Ben Ezra, Daniel: The Impact of Yom Kippur on Early Christianity. 2003. *Vol. 163.*
Strobel, August: Die Stunde der Wahrheit. 1980. *Vol. 21.*
Stroumsa, Guy G.: Barbarian Philosophy. 1999. *Vol. 112.*
Stuckenbruck, Loren T.: Angel Veneration and Christology. 1995. *Vol. II/70.*
Stuhlmacher, Peter (Ed.): Das Evangelium und die Evangelien. 1983. *Vol. 28.*
- Biblische Theologie und Evangelium. 2002. *Vol. 146.*
Sung, Chong-Hyon: Vergebung der Sünden. 1993. *Vol. II/57.*
Tajra, Harry W.: The Trial of St. Paul. 1989. *Vol. II/35.*
- The Martyrdom of St.Paul. 1994. *Vol. II/67.*
Theißen, Gerd: Studien zur Soziologie des Urchristentums. 1979, ³1989. *Vol. 19.*
Theobald, Michael: Studien zum Römerbrief. 2001. *Vol. 136.*

Theobald, Michael: see *Mußner, Franz.*
Thornton, Claus-Jürgen: Der Zeuge des Zeugen. 1991. *Vol. 56.*
Thüsing, Wilhelm: Studien zur neutestamentlichen Theologie. Ed. von Thomas Söding. 1995. *Vol. 82.*
Thurén, Lauri: Derhethorizing Paul. 2000. *Vol. 124.*
Tolmie, D. Francois: Persuading the Galatians. 2005. *Vol. II/190.*
Tomson, Peter J. and *Doris Lambers-Petry* (Ed.): The Image of the Judaeo-Christians in Ancient Jewish and Christian Literature. 2003. *Vol. 158.*
Trebilco, Paul: The Early Christians in Ephesus from Paul to Ignatius. 2004. *Vol. 166.*
Treloar, Geoffrey R.: Lightfoot the Historian. 1998. *Vol. II/103.*
Tsuji, Manabu: Glaube zwischen Vollkommenheit und Verweltlichung. 1997. *Vol. II/93.*
Twelftree, Graham H.: Jesus the Exorcist. 1993. *Vol. II/54.*
Ulrichs, Karl Friedrich: Christusglaube. 2007. *Vol. II/227.*
Urban, Christina: Das Menschenbild nach dem Johannesevangelium. 2001. *Vol. II/137.*
Visotzky, Burton L.: Fathers of the World. 1995. *Vol. 80.*
Vollenweider, Samuel: Horizonte neutestamentlicher Christologie. 2002. *Vol. 144.*
Vos, Johan S.: Die Kunst der Argumentation bei Paulus. 2002. *Vol. 149.*
Wagener, Ulrike: Die Ordnung des „Hauses Gottes". 1994. *Vol. II/65.*
Wahlen, Clinton: Jesus and the Impurity of Spirits in the Synoptic Gospels. 2004. *Vol. II/185.*
Walker, Donald D.: Paul's Offer of Leniency (2 Cor 10:1). 2002. *Vol. II/152.*
Walter, Nikolaus: Praeparatio Evangelica. Ed. von Wolfgang Kraus und Florian Wilk. 1997. *Vol. 98.*
Wander, Bernd: Gottesfürchtige und Sympathisanten. 1998. *Vol. 104.*
Waters, Guy: The End of Deuteronomy in the Epistles of Paul. 2006. *Vol. 221.*
Watt, Jan G. van der: see *Frey, Jörg*
Watts, Rikki: Isaiah's New Exodus and Mark. 1997. *Vol. II/88.*
Wedderburn, A.J.M.: Baptism and Resurrection. 1987. *Vol. 44.*
Wegner, Uwe: Der Hauptmann von Kafarnaum. 1985. *Vol. II/14.*
Weissenrieder, Annette: Images of Illness in the Gospel of Luke. 2003. Vol. II/164.

–, *Friederike Wendt* and *Petra von Gemünden* (Ed.): Picturing the New Testament. 2005. *Vol. II/193.*

Welck, Christian: Erzählte ‚Zeichen'. 1994. *Vol. II/69.*

Wendt, Friederike (Ed.): see *Weissenrieder, Annette.*

Wiarda, Timothy: Peter in the Gospels. 2000. *Vol. II/127.*

Wifstrand, Albert: Epochs and Styles. 2005. *Vol. 179.*

Wilk, Florian: see *Walter, Nikolaus.*

Williams, Catrin H.: I am He. 2000. *Vol. II/113.*

Wilson, Todd A.: The Curse of the Law and the Crisis in Galatia. 2007. *Vol. II/225.*

Wilson, Walter T.: Love without Pretense. 1991. *Vol. II/46.*

Wischmeyer, Oda: Von Ben Sira zu Paulus. 2004. *Vol. 173.*

Wisdom, Jeffrey: Blessing for the Nations and the Curse of the Law. 2001. *Vol. II/133.*

Wold, Benjamin G.: Women, Men, and Angels. 2005. *Vol. II/2001.*

Wright, Archie T.: The Origin of Evil Spirits. 2005. *Vol. II/198.*

Wucherpfennig, Ansgar: Heracleon Philologus. 2002. *Vol. 142.*

Yeung, Maureen: Faith in Jesus and Paul. 2002. *Vol. II/147.*

Zimmermann, Alfred E.: Die urchristlichen Lehrer. 1984, ²1988. *Vol. II/12.*

Zimmermann, Johannes: Messianische Texte aus Qumran. 1998. *Vol. II/104.*

Zimmermann, Ruben: Christologie der Bilder im Johannesevangelium. 2004. *Vol. 171.*

– Geschlechtermetaphorik und Gottesverhältnis. 2001. *Vol. II/122.*

– see *Frey, Jörg*

Zumstein, Jean: see *Dettwiler, Andreas*

Zwiep, Arie W.: Judas and the Choice of Matthias. 2004. *Vol. II/187.*

For a complete catalogue please write to the publisher
Mohr Siebeck • P.O. Box 2030 • D–72010 Tübingen/Germany
Up-to-date information on the internet at www.mohr.de